THIS BOOK
BELONGS TO

DATE

BIBLE
DICTIONARY
& CONCORDANCE

BIBLE
DICTIONARY
& CONCORDANCE

CASTLE BOOKS

This edition published in 2009 by
CASTLE BOOKS®
an imprint of Book Sales
a division of Quarto Publishing Group USA Inc.
276 Fifth Avenue Suite 206
New York, New York 10001

Published by arrangement with:
Ottenheimer Publishers, LLC
1314 Bedford Avenue, Suite 113
Baltimore, MD 21208

BI-063A

ISBN-13: 978-0-7858-2526-5
ISBN-10: 0-7858-2526-6

Printed in the United States of America

ABBREVIATIONS FOR THE NAMES OF THE BOOKS OF THE BIBLE

OLD TESTAMENT

Genesis	Gen.
Exodus	Exod.
Leviticus	Lev.
Numbers	Num.
Deuteronomy	Deut.
Joshua	Josh.
Judges	Judg.
Ruth	Ruth
1 Samuel	1 Sam.
2 Samuel	2 Sam.
1 Kings	1 Kings
2 Kings	2 Kings
1 Chronicles	1 Chron.
2 Chronicles	2 Chron.
Ezra	Ezra
Nehemiah	Neh.
Esther	Esther
Job	Job
Psalms	Ps. (*pl.* Pss.)
Proverbs	Prov.
Ecclesiastes	Eccles.
Song of Solomon	Song of Sol.
Isaiah	Isa.
Jeremiah	Jer.
Lamentations	Lam.
Ezekiel	Ezek.
Daniel	Dan.
Hosea	Hos.
Joel	Joel
Amos	Amos
Obadiah	Obad.
Jonah	Jon.

Micah	Mic.
Nahum	Nah.
Habakkuk	Hab.
Zephaniah	Zeph.
Haggai	Hag.
Zechariah	Zech.
Malachi	Mal

New Testament

Matthew	Matt.
Mark	Mark
Luke	Luke
John	John
Acts of the Apostles	Acts
Romans	Rom.
1 Corinthians	1 Cor.
2 Corinthians	2 Cor.
Galatians	Gal.
Ephesians	Eph.
Philippians	Phil.
Colossians	Col.
1 Thessalonians	1 Thess.
2 Thessalonians	2 Thess.
1 Timothy	1 Tim.
2 Timothy	2 Tim.
Titus	Titus
Philemon	Philem.
Hebrews	Heb.
James	James
1 Peter	1 Pet.
2 Peter	2 Pet.
1 John	1 John
2 John	2 John
3 John	3 John
Jude	Jude
Revelation	Rev.

A

A and **O**, or **Al′pha** and **O′mega**, or **Omeg′a**, first and last letters of Greek alphabet, used of Jehovah, Isa. 41:4; 44:6, and of Christ, Rev. 1:8, 11; 21:6; 22:13, to denote the idea of the beginning and the end, or of eternity. Often used in connection with the cross as the symbol of Christ.

Aaron, ar′on (*enlightened*), the first high-priest of the Israelites, was born B. C. about 1570. He was the elder brother and the spokesman of Moses, and aided him in the deliverance of the Israelites from bondage in Egypt. As high-priest he was an eminent type or emblem of Christ. He was about 120 years old when he died on Mount Hor, now called the "Mountain of Aaron." His son Eleazar succeeded him as high-priest. See ELEAZAR, HOR, PRIEST.

Exod. 4:14, 27-30; 5:1, 4, 20; 6:13, 20, 23, 25-27; 7:1, 2, 6-10, 12, 19, 20; 8:5, 6, 8, 12, 16, 17, 25; 9:8, 27; 10:3, 8, 16; 11:10; 12:1, 28, 31, 43, 50; 15:20; 16:2, 6, 9, 10, 33, 34; 17:10, 12; 18:12; 19:24; 24:1, 9, 14; 27:21; 28:1-4, 12, 29, 30, 35, 38, 40, 41, 43; 29:4, 5, 9, 10, 15, 19-21, 24, 26-29, 32, 35, 44; 30:7, 8, 10, 19, 30; 31:10; 32:1-3, 5, 21, 22, 25, 35; 34:30, 31; 35:19; 38:21; 39:1, 27, 41; 40:12, 13, 31.

Lev. 1:5, 7, 8, 11; 2:2, 3; 3:2, 5, 8, 13; 6:9, 14, 16, 18, 20, 25; 7:10, 31, 33-35; 8:2, 6, 12-14, 18, 22-24, 27, 30, 31, 36; 9:1, 2, 7-9, 12, 18, 21-23; 10:1, 3, 4, 6, 8, 12, 16, 19; 11:1; 13:1, 2; 14:33; 15:1; 16:1-3, 6, 8, 9, 11, 21, 23; 17:2; 21:1, 17, 21, 24; 22:2, 4, 18; 24:3, 9.

Num. 1:3, 17, 44; 2:1; 3:1-4, 6, 9, 10, 32, 38, 39, 48, 51; 4:1, 5, 15-17, 19, 27, 28, 33, 34, 37, 41, 45, 45; 6:23; 7:8; 8:2, 3, 11, 13, 19-22; 9:6; 10:8; 12:1, 4, 5, 10, 11, 13:26; 14:2, 5, 26; 15 33; 16:3, 11, 16-18, 20, 37, 40-43, 46, 47, 50; 17:3, 6, 8, 10; 18:1, 8, 20, 28; 19:1; 20:2, 6, 8, 10, 12, 23-26, 28, 29; 25:7, 11; 26:1, 9, 59, 60, 64; 27:13, 33:1, 38, 39.

Deut 9:20; 10:6; 32:50.

Josh. 21:4, 10, 13, 19; 24:5, 33.

Judg 20:28.

1 Sam. 12:6, 8.

1 Chron. 6:3, 49, 50, 54, 57; 15:4; 23:13, 28, 32; 24:1, 19, 31.

2 Chron. 13:9, 10; 26:18; 29:21; 31:19; 35:14.

Ezra 7 5.

Neh. 10:38; 12:47

Pss. 77:20; 99:6; 105 26; 106:16; 115:10, 12; 118:3; 133:2; 135:19.

Mic. 6:4.

Luke 1:5.

Acts 7:40.

Heb. 5:4; 7:11; 9:4.

Aaronites, ar′on-ites, descendants of Aaron the high-priest. 1 Chron. 12:27; 27:17.

Aar′on's Rod The staff of Aaron which was preserved in the ark as a symbol of priesthood, ever blossoming and yielding fruit. Heb. 9:4. See ALMOND TREE, and ARK.

Ab (*father*). [1] A part of many compound Hebrew names, such as Abner, Absalom. [2] The fifth month of the Jewish sacred year and the eleventh month of their civil year. It corresponded nearly with our August. See MONTH.

Abad′don (*destroyer*) is a Hebrew word having the same meaning as the Greek APOLL′YON. It is applied to the angel of the bottomless pit. Rev. 9:11.

Abag′tha (*prosperous*), a chamberlain of Ahasuerus, king of Persia. Esther 1:10.

Ab´ana (*permanent*), a river of Damascus, 2 Kings 5:12, generally supposed to be the modern BARADA. See AMANA.

Ab´arim (*passages*), a range of mountains in the land of Moab, on the east side of the river Jordan, opposite Jericho, having summits three thousand feet above the level of the ocean and over four thousand feet above that of the Dead Sea. Mount Neba or Nebbeh, the highest summit, is supposed to be Mount Nebo, from which Moses viewed the Land of Promise. Num. 27:12; 33:47.

Ab´ba (*father*), a Chaldee word corresponding to the Hebrew *ab, father*; applied to God. Mark 14:36; Rom. 8:15; Gal. 4:6.

Ab´da (*servant*) [1] Father of Adoniram, the officer whom Solomon set over the tribute. 1 Kings 4:6. [2] The name of a chief man among the Levites, who dwelt in Jerusalem after the captivity. Neh. 11:17. Called OBADIAH in 1 Chron. 9:16.

Abdeel, ab´de el (*servant of God*), father of Shelemiah. Jer. 36:26.

Ab´di (*servant of Jehovah*). [1] A descendant of Merari, the son of Levi. 1 Chron. 6:44; 2 Chron. 29:12. [2] A descendant of one of the two Elams. Ezra 10:26.

Abdiel, ab´di-el, an ancestor of one of the families of Gad. 1 Chron. 5:15.

Ab´don (*service*). [1] A city of Asher which was afterwards assigned to the Levites. Josh. 21:30; 1 Chron. 6:74. [2] A man of Ephraim who was one of the judges of Israel. Judg. 12:13, 15. [3] A descendant of Benjamin. 1 Chron. 8:23. [4] The eldest son of the father of Gibeon. 1 Chron. 8:30; 9:36. [5] The name apparently of one of the priests in the time of Josiah, king of Judah, whom the king sent to enquire of the Lord when the book of the law had been found. 2 Chron. 34:20.

Abed´nego (*servant of Nego*), a name given by the prince of the king of Babylon's eunuchs to Azariah, one of the young Jewish princes who were carried to Babylon by Nebuchadnezzar. Dan. 1:7; 2:49; 3:12, 20.

A´bel (*transitoriness*, or, when applied to a town, *grassy place* or *meadow*). [1] The second son of Adam. He was a shepherd; offered to God a sacrifice from his flocks, and was killed by his brother Cain because Abel's sacrifice was received, and not Cain's. Gen. 4. Abel was the first martyr of faith, who, "being dead, yet speaketh." Matt. 23:35; Heb. 11:4. See SACRIFICE. [2] The name of a place in the north-west part of Judah, where the ark rested when it was sent back by the Philistines. 1 Sam. 6:18. [3] The name of a place near Beth-maachah, sometimes called Abel of Beth-maachah, and sometimes Abel. 2 Sam. 20:14, 15, 18. [4] Abel is also the beginning of the names of several towns.

Abel-Beth-maachah, a´bel-beth-ma´-a-kah (*meadow of the house of Maachah*), a city (otherwise called Beth-maachah, or simply Abel) in the northern part of the territory of Manasseh, beyond Jordan, near the foot of Mount Hermon. 1 Kings 15:20; 2 Kings 15:29.

Abel-maim, a´bel-ma´im (*meadow of the waters*), a town in the northern part of the territory of Manasseh, east of the Jordan, 2 Chron. 16:4, supposed to be the same with Abel-Beth-maachah and with Abel.

Abel-meholah, a´bel-me-ho´lah (*meadow of the dance*), a city in Issachar at the north of the Jordan valley. It was the birthplace of Elisha the prophet. Judg. 7:22; 1 Kings 19:16.

Abel-mizraim, a´bel-miz´ra-im (*meadow* or *mourning of the Egyptians*), a place at the threshing-floor at Atad, "beyond Jordan." It was named from the seven days' lamentation of Joseph and his company when they brought up the body of Jacob from Egypt to be buried. Gen. 50:11.

A´bel-shit´tim (*meadow of the acacias*) was situated east of the Jordan in the plains of Moab, Num. 33; 49, and near Mount Peor. It was the last encampment of the Israelites before crossing the Jordan into Canaan, B. C. 1450. Also called SHITTIM.

A´bez (*whiteness*), a city of Issachar. Josh. 19:20.

A´bi (*Jehovah is father*), the wife of Ahaz and mother of Hezekiah, kings of Judah. 2 Kings 18:2. She is called ABIJAH in 2 Chron. 29:1.

Abi´a or Abi´ah (*Jehovah is father*). See ABIJAH. [1] Samuel's second son. He and his brother did wickedly, so that Israel desired and obtained a king. 1 Sam 8:2; 1 Chron. 6:28. [2] The wife of Hezron, the grandson of Judah by Pharez. 1 Chron. 2:24. [3] The name given in Chronicles to the son of Rehoboam who succeeded his father as king of Judah, 1 Chron. 3:10; Matt. 1:7, and who is called Abijam in 1 Kings 15. [4] One of the sons of Becher, the son of Benjamin. 1 Chron. 7:8. [5] A priest in the time of David, set over a particular course of service in the tabernacle. Luke 1:5. See ABIJAH.

Abi-albon, a´bi-al´bon (*father of strength*), one of David's mighty men from Arabah. 2 Sam. 23:31. He is called ABIEL in 1 Chron. 11:32.

Abi-asaph, a-by´a-saf (*father of gathering*), a son of Korah. Exod. 6:24. See EBIASAPH.

Abiathar, a-by´a-thar (*father of superfluity*), the son of Abimelech the priest, who escaped when his father was slain by order of Saul, and who became highpriest after the death of Saul. He was expelled from office by Solomon.
1 Sam. 22:20-22; 23:6, 9; 30:7.
2 Sam. 8:17; 15:24, 27, 29, 35, 36; 17:15; 19:11; 20:25.
1 Kings 1:7, 19, 25, 42; 2:22, 26, 27, 35; 4:4.
1 Chron. 15:11; 18 16; 24:6; 27:34.
Mark 2:26.

A´bib (*sprouting*), the first month of the Hebrew sacred year and the seventh month of the civil year. It was so called because grain, especially barley, was then in ear. After the Babylonian captivity it was called Nisan. It corresponded nearly with our April. See MONTH.
Exod. 13:4; 23:15; 34:18.
Deut. 16:1.

Abi´da or Abi´dah (*father of knowledge*). A son of Midian, the son of Abraham by Keturah. Gen. 25:4; 1 Chron. 1:33.

Ab´idan (*father of judgment*), the captain of the tribe of Benjamin, who was appointed with Moses and a chief man from every tribe to number the people. Num. 1 11; 2:22.

Abi´el (*father of might*). [1] An Israelite of the tribe of Benjamin, who was the grandfather of Saul, the first king of Israel. 1 Sam. 9:1; 14:51. [2] One of David's valiant men. 1 Chron. 11:32. He is called ABI-ALBON in 2 Sam. 23:31.

Abiezer, ab-i-e´zer (*father of help*). [1] Head of a family descended from Manasseh, probably same as Jeezer, the son of Gilead (Num. 26:30). Josh. 17:2; 1 Chron. 7:18. [2] A district in Manasseh inhabited by the Abiezrites. Judg. 6:34; 8:2 [3] One of David's valiant men, an inhabitant of Anathoth, in the tribe of Benjamin. 2 Sam. 23:27; 1 Chron. 11:28.

Abiezrite, ab-i-ez´rite (*belonging to*

Abiezer), a descendant of Abiezer, Judg. 6:11, 24; 8:32.

Ab´igail (*cause of delight*). [1] The wife of Nabal of Carmel, and afterward of David. [2] A sister or a niece of Zeruiah and mother of Amasa.
1 Sam. 25:3, 14, 18, 23, 32, 36, 39, 40, 42; 27:3; 30:5.
2 Sam. 2:2; 3:3; 17:25.
1 Chron. 2:16, 17; 3:1.

Abi-gibeon, ab´i-gib´e-on (*father of Gibeon*), a descendant of Benjamin who dwelt at Gibeon. 1 Chron. 8:29.

Abihail, ab-i-ha´il (*father of might*). [1] A Levite of the family of Merari, who was the father of Zuriel, the chief of the Merarites in the time of Moses. Num. 3:35. [2] The wife of Abishur, a descendant of Hezron, of the tribe of Judah. 1 Chron. 2:29. [3] Head of a family in the tribe of Gad. 1 Chron. 5:14. [4] A daughter of Eliab, David's brother, who became wife of Rehoboam, the son of Solomon. 2 Chron. 11:18. [5] The father of Esther the Jewess, whom Ahasuerus, king of Persia, made queen instead of Vashti. Esther 2:15; 9:29.

Abi´hu (*he is my father*), a son of Aaron who was slain by fire from the Lord for offering strange fire.
Exod. 6:23; 24:1, 9; 28:1.
Lev. 10:1.
Num. 3:2, 4; 26:60, 61.
1 Chron. 6:3; 24:1, 2.

Abi´hud (*father of honor*), a son of Bela, the son of Benjamin. 1 Chron. 8:3.

Abi´jah (*my father is Jehovah*). See ABIAH. [1] A son of Jeroboam who died young. 1 Kings 14:1. [2] A priest in the time of David who was at the head of eighth course in the temple service. 1 Chron. 24:10. [3] A Levite appointed in the time of David over the treasures of the sanctuary.

1 Chron. 26:20. [4] One of the sons of Rehoboam, the son of Solomon, by Maachah, the daughter of Absalom. [5] The mother of Hezekiah, king of Judah. 2 Chron. 29:1. [6] A priest that sealed the covenant made by Nehemiah and the people to serve the LORD. Neh. 10:7. [7] A priest that went up from Babylon with Zerubbabel. Neh. 12:4, 17. May be same as No. 6.
Also see 2 Chron. 11:20, 22; 12:16; 13:1-4; 15, 17, 19, 20-22; 14:1.

Abi´jam (*father of light*), the name of Rehoboam's son who succeeded his father as king of Judah. 1 Kings 14:31; 15:1. In 2 Chron. 12:16 he is called ABIJAH.

Abilene, ab-i-le´ne (*region of Abila*), a district on the eastern slope of Anti-Lebanon in the region watered by the Abana River. It was governed by a tetrarch under Lysanias in the fifteenth year of Tiberius. Luke 3:1.

Abim´ael (*my father is God*), a son of Joktan. Gen. 10:28; 1 Chron. 1:22.

Abimelech, a-bim´e-lek (*father of the king*). [1] A king of Gerar of the Philistines who made a league with Abraham. [2] Another king of Gerar contemporary with Isaac. He made a league with Isaac at Beersheba. Gen. 26. [3] A son of Gideon by a concubine in Shechem. He made himself king after the death of his father and slew his father's seventy sons, leaving only Jotham, the youngest. Abimelech was disgracefully killed in attacking Thebez. [4] Abimelech, the son of Abiathar, who was high-priest in David's time. 1 Chron. 18:16. [5] The name given in one place apparently to Achish, the king of Gath to whom David fled (1 Sam. 21:10). Ps. 34, title.
Also see Gen. 20: 2-4, 8-10, 14, 15, 17, 18; 21:22, 25-27, 29, 32. Judg. 8:31;

9:1, 3, 4, 6, 16, 18-25, 27-29, 31, 34, 35, 38-42, 44, 45, 47-50, 52, 53, 55, 56; 10:1.
2 Sam. 11:21.
Ps. 34.

Abin´adab (*source of liberality*). [1] An Israelite who lived near Kirjath-jearim and in whose house the ark of God was kept after it had been returned by the Philistines. 1 Sam. 7:1; 2 Sam. 6:3, 4. [2] The second son of Jesse, the father of David. 1 Sam. 16:8; 1 Chron. 2:13. [3] A son of King Saul, slain at Gilboa by the Philistines with his brother Jonathan. 1 Sam. 31:2; 1 Chron. 8:33. [4] Father of one of Solomon's officers, set over Dor in territory of Issachar. 1 Kings 4:11.

Ab´iner, 1 Sam. 14:50, in the marginal notes, same as ABNER.

Abinoam a-bin´o-am (*father of pleasantness*), father of Barak. Judg. 4:6, 12; 5:1, 12.

Abi´ram (*father of elevation*). [1] A son of Eliab a Reubenite, who with Korah and others undertook to overthrow the authority of Moses and Aaron in the wilderness. See KORAH. [2] Son of Hiel the Bethelite, who attempted to rebuild Jericho. 1 Kings 16:34.
Also see Num. 16:1, 12, 24, 25, 27; 26:9.
Deut. 11:6.
1 Kings 16:34.
Ps. 106:17.

Ab´ishag (*cause of wandering*), a beautiful virgin of Shunem in Issachar. She was chosen as a member of the household of David to cherish him in his old age.
1 Kings 1:3, 15; 2:17, 21, 22.

Abishai, a-bish´a-i (*source of wealth*), one of the bravest of David's "mighty men," was the eldest son of David's sister Zeruiah. He was generally a personal

attendant of David, and was victorious in many battles.
1 Sam. 26:6-9.
2 Sam. 2:18, 24; 3:30; 10:10, 14; 16:9, 11; 18:2, 5, 12; 19:21; 20:6, 10; 21:17; 23:18.
1 Chron. 2:16; 11:20; 18:12; 19:11, 15.

Abish´alom (*father of peace*), father of Maachah. 1 Kings 15:2, 10.

Abish´ua (*father of safety*). [1] Son of Phinehas, grandson of Aaron. 1 Chron. 6:4, 5, 50; Ezra 7:5. [2] A son of Bela, the son of Benjamin. 1 Chron. 8:4.

Ab´ishur (*father of oxen*), son of Shammai. 1 Chron. 2:28, 29.

Ab´ital (*source of dew*), wife of David. 2 Sam. 3:4; 1 Chron. 3:3.

Ab´itub (*source of good*), son of Shaharaim. 1 Chron. 8:11.

Abi´ud (*father of honor*) son of Zerubbabel. Matt. 1:13.

Ab´jects, in Ps. 35:15, means outcasts; despised persons.

Ab´ner (*father of light*) 1 Sam. 14:50, the son of Ner, was either uncle or cousin of Saul, the first king of Israel, and became his general. He supported King Ishbosheth seven years after Saul's death, and endeavored afterward to unite the whole kingdom under David, then king of Judah, but was treacherously slain by Joab. See JOAB.
Also see 1 Sam. 14:50, 51; 17:55, 57; 20:25; 26:5, 7, 14, 15.
2 Sam. 2:8, 12, 14, 17, 19-25, 29-31; 3:6-9; 11, 12, 16, 17, 19-28, 30-33, 37; 4:1, 12.
1 Kings 2:5, 32.
1 Chron. 26:28; 27:21.

Abomina´tion, in Scripture, means an object of abhorrence. Idols and the worship of them were so called. Deut. 7:25, 26; 12:31. The same term was applied to the Hebrews in Egypt. Exod. 8:26; Gen. 46:34.

Also see Gen. 43:32.

Lev. 7:18; 11:10-13, 20, 23, 41, 42; 18:22, 26, 27, 29; 20:13.

Deut. 13:14, 17:1, 4; 18:9, 12; 20:18; 22:5; 23:18; 24:4; 25:16; 27:15; 29:17; 32:16.

1 Sam. 13:4.

1 Kings 11:5, 7; 14:24.

2 Kings 16:3; 21:2, 11; 23:13, 24.

2 Chron. 28:3; 33:2; 34:33; 36:8, 14.

Ezra 9:1, 11, 14.

Ps. 88:8.

Prov. 3:32; 6:16; 8:7; 11:1, 20; 12:22; 13:19; 15:8, 9, 26; 16:5, 12; 17:15; 20:10, 23; 21:27; 24:9; 26:25; 28:9; 29:27.

Isa. 1:13; 41:24; 44:19; 66:3, 17.

Jer. 2:7; 4:1; 6:15; 7:10, 30; 8:12; 13:27; 32:34, 35; 44:22.

Ezek. 5:9, 11: 6:9, 11; 7:3, 4, 8, 9, 20; 8:6, 9, 13, 15, 17; 9:4; 11:18, 21; 12:16; 14:6; 16:2, 22, 36, 43, 47, 50, 51, 58; 18:12, 13, 24; 20:4, 7, 8, 30; 22:2, 11; 23:36; 33:26, 29; 36:31; 43:8; 44:6, 7, 13.

Dan. 9:27; 11:31; 12:11.

Hos. 9:10.

Zech. 9:7.

Mal. 2:11.

Matt. 24:15.

Mark 13:14.

Luke 16:15.

Rev. 17:4, 5; 21:27.

A´braham (*father of a multitude*), Gen. 17:4, 5, formerly ABRAM, a Hebrew patriarch, was called the "Father of the faithful." He was born at Ur in Chaldea. The year of his birth is doubtful, and is given by Ussher as B. C. 1996, and by Hales as B. C. 2153. According to Bunsen he lived B. C. about 2850. At the call of God, Gen. 12:1, Abram (afterward called Abraham) left his idolatrous kindred and migrated to Canaan. He lived a wandering life in tents, and was greatly distinguished for his piety and wisdom. In the Bible he is repeatedly called "the friend of God." He was chiefly remarkable for his simple and unwavering faith, and died at the age of 175 years. See Genesis, chapters 11–25; Acts 7; Rom. 4:1-6, 9-22; Heb. 11:8-17. See ISAAC, and MACHPELAH.

Also see Gen. 26:1, 3, 5, 15, 18, 24; 28:4, 9, 13; 31:42, 53; 32:9; 35:12, 27; 48:15, 16; 49:30, 31; 50:13, 24.

Exod. 2:24, 3:6, 15, 16; 4:5; 6:3, 8; 32:13; 33:1.

Lev. 26:42.

Num. 32:11.

Deut. 1:8; 6:10; 9:5, 27; 29:13; 30:20; 34:4.

Josh. 24:2, 3.

1 Kings 18:36.

2 Kings 13:23.

1 Chron. 1:27, 28, 32, 34; 16:16; 29:18.

2 Chron. 20:7; 30:6.

Neh. 9:7.

Pss. 47:9; 105:6, 9, 42.

Isa. 29:22; 41:8; 51:2; 63:16.

Jer. 33:26.

Ezek. 33:24.

Mic. 7:20.

Matt. 1:1, 2, 17; 3:9; 8:11; 22:32.

Mark 12:26.

Luke 1:55, 73; 3:8, 34; 13:16, 28; 16:22-25, 29, 30; 19:9; 20:37.

John 8:33, 37, 39, 40, 52, 53, 56-58.

Acts 3:13, 25; 13:26.

Rom. 9:7; 11:1.

2 Cor. 11:22.

Gal. 3:6-9, 14, 16, 18, 29; 4:22.

Heb. 2:16; 6:13; 7:1, 2, 4-6, 9.

James 2:21, 23.

1 Pet. 3:6.

A´braham's Bosom, in Luke 16:22, means the bliss that Lazarus was enjoying in paradise, or paradise itself, Luke 16:23. *Leaning on one's bosom*, John 13 23, refers to the Oriental manner of reclining at table.

A´bram (*father of height*), afterward Abraham, was the son of Terah. He was the founder of the Jewish nation.

Ab´salom (*father of peace*), the third son of King David, born B. C. about 1033. His mother was a Syrian princess named Maacah. Absalom was remarkable for beauty of person. After gaining the favor of the people he rebelled against his father and raised a large army, which was defeated by that of David. While he was retreating from battle Absalom was killed by Joab, although David had ordered that his life should be spared. 2 Sam. 13–19. See JOAB and DAVID.

Ab´stinence. See FASTING.

Acacia, a-ka´shur (*a thorn*), a tree or bush. A species of Acacia resembling the Shillah tree is now found at Sinai, and may possibly be the same kind as was the Burning Bush mentioned in Exod. 3:2.

Accad, ak´kad (*fortress*), one of the four cities built by Nimrod in the plain of Shinar. Gen. 10:10.

Ac´caron, the same as EK´RON.

Accept´ed, in Luke 4:24; Eph. 1:6, means received with favor.

Accho, ak´ko (*compressed*), Judg. 1:31, a seaport of the tribe of Asher. It is called Ptolemais in the New Testament. Acts 21:7. It is situated on the Mediterranean Sea, at the foot of Mount Carmel. Its ancient inhabitants were Phoenicians. It is the same as ACRE, AKKA, or ST. JEAN D'ACRE, a city and seaport of Syria.

Accur´sed, devoted to destruction. See ANATHEMA.

Accusa´tion, a written statement of the crime for which a person was executed.

Accu´ser. [1] An enemy or adversary, particularly in a court of law. Matt. 5:25. [2] In Job 1:6; Zech. 3:1; Rev. 12:10, Satan is the public accuser of the people of God.

Aceldama, a-sel´da-mah (*field of blood*), Acts 1:19, a small field south of Jerusalem, purchased by the chief priests with the thirty pieces of silver which Judas received as the price of our Saviour's blood. Aceldama was the "potter's field," and was used for the burial-place of strangers. In Acts 1:18 *Judas* is said to have purchased the field, because it was bought with his money. See JUDAS.

Achaia, a-ka´yah (*land of Achaicus*), signifies, in the Old Testament, the whole region of Greece south of Macedonia, including the Peloponnesus or Morea; also some territory north of the Gulf of Corinth. In Paul's time it was a Roman province governed by a pro-consul called "deputy" in Acts 18:12. Achaia proper embraced only the north-west part of Peloponnesus.

Achaicus, a-kay´i-kus (*belonging to Achaia*), a Corinthian convert who visited Paul. 1 Cor. 16:17.

Achan, a´kan (*trouble*), son of Carmi of the tribe of Judah, disobeyed the command of the Lord by taking some of the spoils of Jericho which were to be destroyed. This action brought a curse and defeat upon the people. He was discovered by lot and stoned to death with all his family in the valley of Achor. Josh. 6:18; 7:18. He is also called ACHAR in 1 Chron. 2:7. See ACHOR.

Achar, a´kar. See ACHAN.

Achaz, a´kaz (*he holds*), Matt. 1:9, Greek form of Ahaz. See AHAZ.

Achbor, ak´bor (*a mouse*). [1] The

father of the seventh Edomite king. Gen. 36:38, 39; 1 Chron. 1:49. [2] A messenger of Josiah sent to inquire concerning the denunciation of wrath against the national sins as recorded in the book of the law found by Hilkiah in the temple. 2 Kings 22:12, 14. In 2 Chron. 34:20 ABDON is used in place of ACHBOR. [3] A Jew whose son was sent by Jehoiakim to bring back Urijah the prophet. Jer. 26:22; 36:12.

Achim, a´kim (*woes*), an ancestor of Joseph, husband of Mary, mother of Jesus. Matt. 1:14.

Achish, a´kish (*serpent-charmer*). [1] A king of Gath to whom David fled. [2] A king of Gath who reigned in the time of Solomon. 1 Kings 2:39, 40.

Also see 1 Sam. 21:10-12, 14; 27:2, 3, 5, 6, 9, 10, 12; 28:1, 2; 29:2, 3, 6, 8, 9.

Achmetha, ak-me´thah (*a place of horses*), a city of Media, perhaps the same as ECBATANA, the modern HAMADAN. Ezra 6:2.

Achor, a´kor (*trouble*), a valley leading up from Ai to Jericho, and thence to Jerusalem. In this valley Achan was stoned to death and buried with his property. See ACHAN. This valley was regarded as the key of the land. Josh. 7:24, 26; Isa. 65:10.

Achsah, ak´sah. or **Achsa** (*serpent-charmer*), daughter of Caleb, was given with a large dowry in marriage to Othniel for taking the city of Debir, formerly called Kirjath-sepher. Josh. 15:16, 17; Judg. 1:12, 13; 1 Chron. 2:49. See OTHNIEL.

Achshaph, ak´shaf (*dedicated*), a royal city of the Canaanites. It was conquered by Joshua and assigned to the tribe of Asher. Josh. 11:1; 12:20.

Achzib, ak´zib (*a lie*). [1] A town in west of Judah. Josh. 15:44; Mic. 1:14. Perhaps same as CHEZIB in Gen. 38:5. [2] A

city of Asher, now called Ezzib, on the Mediterranean, 9 miles N. of Acre. Josh. 19:29; Judg. 1:31.

A´cra, one of the hills on which Jerusalem is built.

Acrab´bim. Josh. 15:3, in the marginal notes. See MAALEH-ACRABBIM.

A´cre. The Jews had no such system as our "square measure," which enables us to name an area by its size. In the original the word signifies *a yoke*, and the meaning intended was apparently the extent of ground that could be plowed by a yoke of oxen in a day. Isa. 5:10. In 1 Sam. 14:14 the Hebrew expression used means literally *half a furrow of a yoke*.

A´cre, a city and seaport of Syria. See ACCHO.

Acts of the Apos´tles, the fifth book of the New Testament. It was written by Luke, probably about A. D. 63 or 64, and forms the sequel to his Gospel. It contains the history of the progress of Christianity from Jerusalem, the capital of Judaism, to Rome, the capital of heathenism. It embraces the period from 30–63. Although this part of the Scriptures is called the Acts of the Apostles, it mentions only the acts of Peter, Paul, and James. Only Paul's acts are given fully and connectedly in this book. It gives an account of those great events in the history of the apostles which would naturally most interest the Christian Church. Prominent among them are the ascension of our Lord, the outpouring of the Holy Spirit at Pentecost, the martyrdom of Stephen, the conversion of Paul (then called Saul), and his principal missionary journeys and labors till his arrival and first imprisonment in Rome, which lasted two years (61–63). The Acts is an inspiring book of spiritual conquests. It illustrates the EPISTLES, as these illustrate and confirm the ACTS.

Ad´adah (*bordering*), a town in the south of Judah. Josh. 15:22.

A´dah (*pleasure*). [1] One of the wives of Lamech. Gen. 4:19, 20, 23. [2] One of the wives of Esau. Gen. 36:2, 4, 10, 12, 16. Called BASHEMATH in Gen. 26:34.

Adaiah, ad-a-i´ah (*pleasing to Jehovah*). [1] Maternal grandfather of King Josiah. 2 Kings 22:1. [2] A Levite descended from Gershom. 1 Chron. 6:41. [3] A son of Shimhi the Benjamite. 1 Chron. 8:21. [4] A Levite of the family of Aaron. 1 Chron. 9:12. [5] The father of a captain that aided Jehoiada to put Joash on the throne of Judah. 2 Chron. 23:1. [6] One of the family of Bani, who took a foreign wife in the exile. Ezra 10:29. [7] Another, of a different family, who had also taken a foreign wife. Ezra 10:39. [8] A descendant of Judah by Pharez. Neh. 11:5. [9] A Levite of the family of Aaron, probably same as No. 4. Neh. 11:12.

Adalia, ad-a-li´a (*honor of Ized*), one of the sons of Haman, the enemy of the Jews. Esther 9:8.

Ad´am (*red,* or *earth-born*). [1] The first man. He was created, according to Hebrew chronology, B. C. 4004, and, according to the Septuagint or Greek chronology, B. C. 5411. Adam was made in "the likeness of God." Gen. 5:1. He was the last and greatest work of the creation, and received dominion over all the earth. He was made pure and holy, yet liable to fall by the abuse of free will, and placed in EDEN on probation. He broke the express command of God, and brought a curse upon himself and his descendants. He was banished from Eden, and died at the age of 930 years. It is generally believed that he is the first among the saved as he was the first among sinners. See CREATION, EDEN, ABEL, CAIN. [2] The REDEEMER is called

"the last Adam," 1 Cor. 15:45, who is the author of righteousness and life, as the first Adam was the author of sin and death. Rom. 5:12-21. [3] A town on the east of the Jordan, some distance above the place where the Israelites, under Joshua, crossed it. Josh. 3:16. [4] The word is found in the original in many passages, where it is translated MAN. Also see Gen. 2:19-21, 23; 3:8, 9, 17, 20, 21; 4:1, 25; 5:2-5.

Deut. 32:8.
1 Chron. 1:1.
Job 31:33.
Luke 3:38.
Rom. 5:14.
1 Cor. 15:22.
1 Tim. 2:13, 14.
Jude :14.

Ad´amah (*fortress*), a fenced city in Naphtali. Josh. 19:36. Probably *Dâmieh*, west of Sea of Galilee.

Ad´amant (*that cannot be subdued or broken*), an ancient name used figuratively in Ezek. 3:9 for the diamond; also indicates any substance of extreme hardness. It is an old English name for diamond, the hardest of minerals. The diamond seems to have been unknown to the ancients as a precious stone. In the Bible it means the corundum known to us in a ground state as emery-powder. Adamant is once (Exod. 28:18) translated "diamond," and was used for engraving upon stone.

Ad´ami (*fortified*), a town of Naphtali. Josh. 19:33. Probably the modern *Khurbet Admah*.

A´dar (*fire-god*), the sixth month in the civil year of the Jews. It included part of February and March. The celebrated feast of Purim occurred on the fourteenth and fifteenth of this month. Adar was the twelfth month of the sacred year of the Jews. It was doubled every second year to make the lunar year agree with the solar year. Ezra 6:15; Esther 3:7. See MONTH.

A´dar or **Ad´dar** (*height*). **[1]** A city, called also Hazar-Addar, in the S. of Judah near Edom. Josh. 15:3. **[2]** Son of Bela and grandson of Benjamin. 1 Chron. 8:3.

Ad´asa or **Had´ashah**. See HAD-ASHAH.

Adbeel, ad´be-el (*languishing for God*), son of Ishmael and grandson of Abraham. Gen. 25:13; 1 Chron. 1:29.

Ad´dan (*strong*), a place from which some of the inhabitants came with Zerubbabel to Jerusalem; others suppose it to be the name of a man unable to show his genealogy to be of Israel. Ezra 2:59. Called also ADDON. Neh. 7:61.

Ad´der, a common name given to the viper, is a species of serpent. Adder is used in the Bible as a translation of four Hebrew words. In the Authorized Version it signifies four different serpents—namely, the cobra, Pss. 58:4; 91:13 (see ASP); the horned snake or cerastes, Gen. 49:17; the viper, Ps. 140:3; and in Prov. 23:32 a snake elsewhere called the "cockatrice," and may represent indefinitely different species of vipers. The horned snake or cerastes, Gen. 49:17, is about a foot long, and has black spots and two horns. It lies hidden in the sand, which is like it in color, and darts upon the unsuspecting traveller. It has a very deadly bite, and is often found in the wilderness of Judea. See ASP.

Ad´di, an ancestor of Joseph, the husband of Mary, mother of Jesus. Luke 3:28.

Ad´don (*strong*). Neh. 7:61. Called ADDAN in Ezra 2:59.

A´der (*a flock*), a son of Berah, a Benjamite. 1 Chron. 8:15.

A´diel (*ornament of God*). **[1]** A descendant of Simeon. 1 Chron. 4:36. **[2]** A descendant of Aaron. 1 Chron. 9:12. **[3]** Father of

Azmaveth, who was David's treasurer (same as No. 2). 1 Chron. 27:25.

A´din (*ornament*). **[1]** An Israelite whose descendants returned from Babylon with Zerubbabel. Ezra 2:15; Neh. 7:20. **[2]** One whose posterity came up with Ezra. Ezra 8:6. **[3]** Probably same as No. 1. The name of a family who, with Nehemiah and the people, sealed the covenant. Neh. 10:16.

Ad´ina (*ornament*), a Reubenite captain of David. 1 Chron. 11:42.

Ad´ino (*ornament*), one of David's thirty valiant men. 2 Sam. 23:8. See JASHOBEAM.

Adithaim, ad-i-tha´im (*two passages*), a city in the plain of Judah. Josh. 15:36.

Adjure´, Josh. 6:26, to bind under a curse or put under oath. See OATH.

Adlai, ad´la-i (*weary*), father of Shaphat, who was an overseer of David's herds. 1 Chron. 27:29.

Ad´mah (*earthwork*), one of the cities in the vale of Siddim, near the Dead Sea, destroyed with Sodom. Gen. 10:19; Hos. 11:8.

Ad´matha (*God-given*), one of the seven princes of Persia and Media in the time of Ahasuerus. Esther 1:14.

Admira´tion, in Rev. 17:6, means wonder; astonishment.

Ad´na (*pleasure*). **[1]** One of the family of Pahath-moab, who had taken a foreign wife during or after the captivity. Ezra 10:30. **[2]** A priest in the time of Joiakim. Neh. 12:15.

Ad´nah (*pleasure*). **[1]** A captain of Manasseh. 1 Chron. 12:20. **[2]** The chief captain of Jehoshaphat. 2 Chron. 17:14.

Ado, a-doo´, in Mark 5:39, means stir; tumult; commotion.

Adonibezek, a-don-i-be´zek (*lord of lightning*), a Canaanite king of Bezek captured by men of Judah and Simeon and taken to Jerusalem. Judg. 1:5, 6, 7.

Adonijah, ad-o-ni´jah (*Jehovah is my lord*). [1] Fourth son of David. He was put to death by Solomon for aspiring to the throne. [2] One of the Levites sent by Jehoshaphat to teach the law. 2 Chron. 17:8. [3] A chief of the people that with Nehemiah sealed the covenant. Neh. 10:16.

Also see 2 Sam. 3:4.

1 Kings 1:5, 7-9, 11, 13, 18, 24, 25, 41-43, 49-51; 2:13, 19, 21-24, 28.

1 Chron. 3:2.

Adon´ikam (*my lord is risen*). [1] An Israelite whose descendants returned from Babylon after the exile. Ezra 2:13; Neh. 7:18. [2] An Israelite, some of whose posterity returned from Babylon with Ezra. Ezra 8:13. Probably the same as No. 1.

Adoniram, ad-o-ni´ram (*my lord is high*), a tribute officer of David and Solomon. He superintended the thirty thousand men sent by Solomon to cut timber for building the temple. 1 Kings 4:6; 5:14. See ADORAM.

Adonizedek, a-don-i-ze´dek (*lord of justice*), a king of the Canaanites, or of the Amorites. He dwelt at Jerusalem, and made an alliance with four other kings against Joshua. A great battle was fought at Gibeon (see GIBEON), where Israel was aided by the Lord by a terrible hail-storm, and by miraculously prolonging the day. The five kings were utterly routed, and were put to death by Joshua. Josh. 10:1, 3. See JOSHUA.

Adop´tion (*placing as a son*) is used for many kinds of admission to a more intimate relation, and is nearly equivalent to *reception*. [1] The taking and treating of another as one's own child. Mordecai adopted Esther as a daughter. Esther 2:7.

The daughter of Pharaoh adopted Moses, and he became her son. Exod. 2:10. [2] In the New Testament adoption means the act of God's free grace by which, being justified through faith in Christ, we are received into God's family and made heirs of the inheritance of heaven. Gal. 4:4, 5; Rom. 8:14-17.

Adoraim, ad-o-ra´im (*double honor*), a city in south-west Judah, built and fortified by Rehoboam, the son of Solomon. 2 Chron. 11:9. It is supposed to be the modern *Dura*.

Ado´ram (*high honor*). [1] An officer of David who was set over the tribute. 2 Sam. 20:24. [2] An officer of Rehoboam. 1 Kings 12:18. Supposed to be same as ADONIRAM.

Adora´tion. See WORSHIP.

Adrammelech, a-dram´e-lek (*honor of the king*). [1] An idol of the people of Sepharvaim whom Shalmaneser brought to Samaria after he had carried away the inhabitants into captivity. 2 Kings 17:31. [2] Son of Sennacherib, king of Assyria, who, along with his brother Sharezer, killed their father in the temple of Nisroch, an idol of the Assyrians. 2 Kings 19:37; Isa. 37:38.

Adramyttium, ad-ra-mit´ti-um, now called *Adramyti*, a large seaport of Mysia in Asia Minor, opposite to the island of Lesbos. Acts 27:2-5.

A´dria is the Adriatic Sea between Italy and Greece, and reaching on the south from Crete to Sicily. It includes Malta or Melita. Acts 27:27.

A´driel (*honor of God*), an Israelite of the tribe of Issachar, to whom, instead of David, Merab (Saul's eldest daughter) was given to wife. 1 Sam. 18:19; 2 Sam. 21:8. His five sons were delivered to the Gibeonites to be put to death before the Lord, in order to avenge the cruelty of

Saul against the Gibeonites. 2 Sam. 21:9.

Adul´lam (*resting-place*). [1] An ancient royal city south-west of Jerusalem, situated in the "plain of Judah." Joshua slew its king. It was rebuilt by Rehoboam and fortified, and was again occupied by the Jews after the captivity. Josh. 12:15; 2 Chron. 11:7. [2] A large cave near the city of Adullam. David escaped to this cave. 1 Sam. 22:1; 2 Sam. 23:13; 1 Chron. 11:15.

Adul´lamite, a native of Adullam. Gen. 38:1, 12, 20.

Adul´tery, a crime forbidden in the seventh commandment. The unlawful intercourse of a man with a married or betrothed woman, not his own, is adultery as defined by Jewish law. Our Saviour makes adultery the only sufficient ground for divorce. Matt. 5:32.
Also see Exod. 20:14.
Lev. 20:10.
Deut. 5:18.
Prov. 6:32.
Jer. 3:8, 9; 5:7; 7:9; 13:27; 23:14; 29:23.
Ezek. 16:32; 23:37, 43.
Hos. 2:2; 4:2, 13, 14.
Matt. 5:27, 28; 15:19; 19:9, 18.
Mark 7:21; 10:11, 12, 19.
Luke 16:18; 18:20.
John 8:3, 4.
Rom. 2:22; 13:9.
Gal. 5:19.
James 2:11.
2 Pet. 2:14.
Rev. 2:22.

Adum´mim (*red places*), a ridge of hills between Benjamin and Judah, near Jericho, on the road to Jerusalem. This ascent in a desolate and rocky region was a famous hiding-place for robbers, and was the scene of the parable of the Good Samaritan. It is still infested by robbers.

Josh. 15:7; 18:17.

Ad´versary. See ACCUSER.

Ad´vertise, in Num. 24:14; Ruth 4:4, means to give notice; to inform.

Advise´ment, in 1 Chron. 12:19, means counsel.

Ad´vocate, or **Par´aclete**, one that pleads the cause of another. The office was unknown to the Jews in a technical sense until their subjection to the Romans. The word is used to signify Christ as our Intercessor. 1 John 2:1. It is also applied, John 14:16; 15:26, to the Holy Spirit as our Teacher and Comforter.

Æneas, e-ne´as. See ENEAS.

Æ´non. See ENON.

Affect´, in Gal. 4:17, means to desire earnestly; to pay court to.

Affin´ity, in 1 Kings 3:1, means relationship by marriage. In ancient times good men looked for wives among their relations who worshipped the true God. Chap. 18 of Lev. gives the degrees within which relatives were not allowed to intermarry.

Afore´, in Ps. 129:6, means before.

Af´rica (*a colony*), one of the continents of the globe, is bounded on the north by the Mediterranean Sea, and was known as LIBYA by the ancients. The name LIBYA was generally applied by them only to the northern part of Africa. See LIBYA.

Ag´abus. [1] A disciple who went from Jerusalem to Antioch while Paul was there, and foretold a famine about to come. Acts 11:28. [2] (Perhaps same as No. 1.) A disciple who came from Judea to Ptolemais and foretold the imprisonment of Paul. Acts 21:10.

A´gag (*warlike*), a common name of the Amalekite kings. Num. 24:7. Samuel "hewed in pieces" before the Lord in Gilgal the last one mentioned in the Bible. 1 Sam. 15:8, 33.

Ag´agite (*belonging to Agag*), indicates the nation to which Haman belonged. Josephus states that Agagite means Amalekite. Esther 3:1, 10; 8:5. See AMALEKITES, and HAMAN.

A´gar (*stranger*), Greek name of Sarah's handmaid HAGAR (which see). Gal. 4:24, 25.

Ag´ate, Exod. 28:19; 39:12, one of the precious stones mentioned in the Bible, is supposed to be named from the river Achates in Sicily, where it was found in abundance. It is a semi-transparent variety of quartz, often beautifully clouded or veined. In Isa. 54:12 it is spoken of as a material for windows. The agate of Isa. 54:12 and Ezek. 27:16 is thought by some to be the ruby.

Age. In ancient times the aged were venerated for their wisdom, and, as in Job 5:26, old age was considered a token of God's favor. The law, Lev.19:32, required the young to honor old people.

Agee, aj´e-e (*fugitive*), father of Shammah. 2 Sam. 23:11.

A-gone´, in 1 Sam. 30:13, means ago.

Ag´riculture, the science of cultivating the ground. In very ancient times the Jews and their ancestors were extensively employed in the care of sheep and cattle. The change to an agricultural life took place among the Jews when they entered Canaan, where each family received an inalienable inheritance. Lev. 25:8-16, 23-35. See PLOWING, THRESHING, RAIN, and SABBATICAL YEAR.

A-grip´pa. See HEROD AGRIPPA.

A´gue, Lev. 26:16, "burning ague," an intermittent fever, with alternate cold and hot fits.

A´gur (*gatherer*), son of Jakeh. It has been claimed that Prov. 30 was written by him. Prov. 30:1.

A´hab (*uncle*). [1] Seventh king of Israel, who reigned B. C. 919–896. He lived at Jezreel, which he ornamented with beautiful buildings. Through the influence of Jezebel his wife, a passionate and ambitious idolatress, the worship of Baal and Ashtoreth was introduced in Israel, and the prophets of God were persecuted and slain. Ahab continued in sin, and God sent Elijah to denounce judgments upon him and his descendants. He was slain in battle. 1 Kings 22:34. See BAAL, and ASHTORETH. [2] A false prophet who corrupted the Israelites at Babylon, was denounced by Jeremiah, and burned by Nebuchadnezzar. Jer 29:21, 22.

Also see 1 Kings 16:28-30, 33; 17:1; 18:1-3, 5, 6, 9, 12, 16, 17, 20, 41, 42, 44-45; 19:1; 20:2, 13, 14, 34; 21:1-4, 8, 15, 16, 18, 20, 21, 24, 25, 27, 29; 22:20, 39-41, 49, 51.

2 Kings 1:1; 3:1, 5; 8:16, 18, 25, 27-29; 9:7-9, 25, 29; 10:1, 10, 11, 17, 18, 30; 21:3, 13.

2 Chron. 18:1-3, 19; 21:6, 13; 22:3-8.

Mic. 6:16.

Ahar´ah (*after a brother*), third son of Benjamin. 1 Chron. 8:1.

Ahar´hel (*after might*), son of Harum. 1 Chron. 4:8.

Ahasai, a-has´a-i (*protector*), a priest of the family of Immer. Neh. 11:13. He is called Jahzerah in 1 Chron. 9:12.

Ahasbai, a-has´ba-i (*shining*), father of one of David's valiant men. 2 Sam. 23:24.

Ahashve´rosh, Ezra 4:6, in the marginal notes, Hebrew form of AHASUERUS.

Ahasuerus, a-has-u-e´rus (*king*). [1] A king of Persia, B. C. 529–521, who succeeded Cyrus and preceded Darius, in whose time the rebuilding of the temple at Jerusalem was interrupted. Ezra 4:6. He was probably the Cambyses of profane history. [2] A king of the Medes, B. C. 594; was the one called Astyages in profane history. Dan. 9:1. [3] A king of Persia, B. C. 485, who seems to have been subsequent to Darius, and is undoubtedly the Xerxes of profane history. Esther 1:1; 8:1, 7. He was the husband of ESTHER (which see).

Aha´va (*stream*), a district near Babylon; also a stream on the banks of which Ezra collected the exiled Jews when they were about to return to Jerusalem, and proclaimed a fast. Ezra 8:15, 21, 31.

A´haz (*he holds*). [1] Eleventh king of Judah, B. C. 740–724. He was attacked by Rezin, king of Damascus, and Pekah, king of Israel; also by the Edomites and Philistines. He allied himself with Tiglath-Pileser, king of Assyria, who conquered Judah's enemies, but made Ahaz his vassal and carried away rich treasures from the temple of Jerusalem and its palaces. [2] An Israelite of the tribe of Benjamin and family of Saul. 1 Chron. 8:35, 36; 9:42.

Also see 2 Kings 15:38; 16:1, 2, 5, 7, 8, 10, 11, 15-17, 19, 20; 17:1; 18:1; 20:11; 23:12.

1 Chron. 3:13; 9:41.

2 Chron. 27:9; 28:1, 16, 19, 21, 22, 24, 27; 29:19.

Isa. 1:1; 7:1, 3, 10, 12; 14:28; 38:8.

Hos. 1:1.

Mic. 1:1.

Ahazi´ah (*Jehovah possesses*). [1] The son and successor of Ahab; was the eighth king of Israel. He reigned two years, including the time in which he was associated with his father, which commenced B. C. 896. He was idolatrous like his father. Elijah the prophet foretold his speedy death. [2] Azariah or Jehoahaz, fifth king of Judah, son of Jehoram and Athaliah. He succeeded his father B. C. 885, and reigned

only one year. He was idolatrous, and was killed by Jehu.

He is called JEHOAHAZ in 2 Chron. 21:17.

Also see 1 Kings 22:40, 49, 51.

2 Kings 1:2, 18; 8:24-26, 29; 9:16, 21, 23, 27, 29; 10:13; 11:1, 2; 12:18; 13:1; 14:13.

1 Chron. 3:11.

2 Chron. 20:35, 37; 22:1, 2, 7-11.

Ah´ban (*brother of intelligence*), son of Abishur. 1 Chron. 2:29.

A´her (*one that is behind*), a descendant of Benjamin. 1 Chron. 7:12. Perhaps same as AHIRAM in Num. 26:38.

A´hi (*my brother*). [1] Head of a family in Gad. 1 Chron. 5:15. [2] An Israelite of Asher. 1 Chron. 7:34.

Ahi´ah (*Jehovah is a brother*). [1] Grandson of Phinehas, the son of Eli. 1 Sam. 14:3, 18. [2] One of Solomon's secretaries. 1 Kings 4:3. [3] A descendant of Benjamin. 1 Chron. 8:7. Ahiah in the English version is often given AHIJAH.

Ahi´am or **Ahi´ham** (*a mother's brother*), one of David's valiant men. 2 Sam. 23:33; 1 Chron. 11:35.

Ahi´an (*brother of day*), son of Shemidah. 1 Chron. 7:19.

Ahie´zer (*helping brother*). [1] A prince of Dan. Num. 1:12; 10:25. [2] A Danite chief who joined David in Ziklag. 1 Chron. 12:3.

Ahi´hud (*brother of honor*), a prince of Asher appointed to divide the land west of Jordan among the tribes of Israel. Num. 34:27.

Ahi´hud (*brother of mystery*), a Benjamite. 1 Chron. 8:7.

Ahi´jah (*Jehovah is brother*). [1] The name of a prophet who foretold to Jeroboam the revolt of the ten tribes from Rehoboam. [2] An Israelite whose son,

Baasha, conspired against Nadab, the son of Jeroboam, and reigned in his stead. 1 Kings 15:27; 2 Kings 9:9. [3] Son of Jerahmeel. 1 Chron. 2:25. [4] One of David's mighty men. 1 Chron. 11:36. [5] A Levite set over the treasures of God's house in David's time. 1 Chron. 26:20. [6] A Levite who, in the time of Nehemiah, sealed a covenant to serve the Lord. Neh. 10:26.

Also see 1 Kings 11:29, 30; 12:15; 14:2, 4-6, 18; 15:29, 33; 21:22.

2 Chron. 9:29; 10:15.

Ahi´kam (*my brother has risen*) was sent by Josiah to the prophetess Huldah when the book of the law was found in the temple. He and his son were friends of Jeremiah the prophet. Jer. 26:24 and 39:14.

Also see 2 Kings 22:12, 14; 25:22.

2 Chron. 34:20.

Jer. 40:5-7, 9, 11, 14, 16; 41:1, 2, 6, 10, 16, 18; 43:6.

Ahi´lud (*a brother born*), father of Jehoshaphat the recorder. 2 Sam. 8:16; 1 Chron. 18:15.

Ahimaaz, a-him´a-az (*powerful brother*). [1] Father of Ahinoam, wife of King Saul. 1 Sam. 14:50. [2] The son and successor of Zadok; probably became high-priest in Solomon's reign. In the reign of David Ahimaaz made known to him the counsels of Absalom and his advisers in rebellion, and carried to David the news of Absalom's defeat. [3] An officer of Solomon. 1 Kings 4:15.

Also see 2 Sam. 15:27, 36; 17:17, 20; 18:19, 22, 23, 27-29.

1 Chron. 6:8, 9, 53.

Ahi´man (*brother of man*). [1] A son of Anak. Num. 13:22; Judg. 1:10. [2] One of the porters in Solomon's temple. 1 Chron. 9:17.

Ahimelech, a-him´e-lek (*brother of the king*). [1] The son of Ahitub and brother of Ahiah. He succeeded the latter as high-priest, and received David at the tabernacle in Nob when fleeing from Saul, and gave him the show-bread and Goliath's sword. Saul caused Ahimelech to be put to death for this act. [2] A Hittite, an officer of David's army when pursued by Saul. 1 Sam. 26:6.

Also see 1 Sam 21:1, 2, 8; 22:9, 11, 14, 16, 20; 23:6; 30:7.

2 Sam. 8:17.

1 Chron. 24:3, 6, 31.

Ps. 52.

Ahi´moth (*brother of death*), son of Elkanah. 1 Chron. 6:25.

Ahin´adab (*brother of liberality*), an officer of Solomon. 1 Kings 4:14.

Ahinoam, a-hin´o-am (*pleasant brother*). [1] The wife of Saul. 1 Sam. 14:50. [2] A woman of Jezreel. She was the wife of David and the mother of Amnon. 1 Sam. 25:43; 2 Sam. 2:2; 3:2; 1 Chron. 3:1.

Ahi´o (*his brother*). [1] A son of Abinadab. He went before the ark of God when it was carried from his father's house to Jerusalem. 2 Sam. 6:3, 4. 1 Chron. 13:7. See UZZAH. [2] One of the tribe of Benjamin. 1 Chron. 8:14. [3] A Benjamite of the family of Gibeon, from which Saul descended. 1 Chron. 8:31. 9:37.

Ahi´ra (*brother of evil*), a captain of Naphtali. Num. 1:15; 10:27.

Ahi´ram (*exalted brother*), a descendant of Benjamin. Num. 26:38. Supposed by some to be same as Aher in 1 Chron. 7:12.

Ahi´ramites, descendants of Ahiram. Num. 26:38.

Ahisamach, a-his´a-mak (*supporting brother*), father of Aholiab. Exod. 31:6; 35:34.

Ahish´ahar (*brother of the dawn*), son of Bilhan. 1 Chron. 7:10.

Ahi´shar (*brother of song*), a household officer of Solomon. 1 Kings 4:6.

Ahithophel, a-hith´o-fel (*foolish brother*), one of David's intimate friends and counsellors. He afterward joined Absalom in his rebellion and became a bitter enemy of David. Foreseeing the result of the rebellion, he hanged himself.
2 Sam 15:12, 31, 34; 16:15, 20, 21, 23; 17:1, 6, 7, 14, 15, 21, 23; 23:34.
1 Chron. 27:33, 34.

Ahi´tub (*a good brother*). [1] A grandson of Eli and son of Phinehas. He succeeded Eli as high-priest, Phinehas having been killed in battle. 1 Sam. 14:3; 22:11. [2] Father of Zadok, who was high-priest in David's time. Sometimes supposed to be the same as No. 1. [3] Another priest, who lived in seventh generation after No. 2. 1 Chron. 6:11, 12. [4] Perhaps same as No. 3. He was a priest and the ruler of God's house in Nehemiah's time. 1 Chron. 9:11; Neh. 11:11.
Also see 1 Sam. 2:29, 12, 20.
2 Sam. 8:17.
1 Chron. 6:7, 8, 52; 18:16.
Ezra. 7:2.

Ah´lab (*fruitful place*), a town in the land of Asher. Judg. 1:31.

Ah´lai (*Jehovah is staying*). [1] A daughter of Shehan. 1 Chron. 2:31. [2] Father of one of David's valiant men. 1 Chron. 11:41.

Aho´ah (*a brother's reed*), son of Bela. 1 Chron. 8:4.

Aho´hite. [1] A descendant of Ahoah. 2 Sam. 23:28; 1 Chron. 11:12. [2] This word is in the English version of 2 Sam. 23:9, but in the original it means the son of Ahohi, and seems to be a proper name. 1 Chron. 11:12, 29.

Aho´lah (*her own tent*) and **Ahol´ibah**

(*my tent in her*) are symbolical names used by Ezekiel to represent the kingdoms of Samaria and Judah. They are spoken of as sisters of Egyptian descent in an allegory which is a history of the Jewish church.
Ezek. 23:4, 5, 11, 22, 36, 44.

Aho´liab (*a father's tent*), a skilled worker employed in the construction of the Tabernacle. Exod. 31:6; 35:34.

Ahol´ibah. See AHOLAH.

Aholibamah, a-ho-lib´a-mah (*tent of the high place*). [1] A Hittite woman of Mount Hor. She was one of the three wives of Esau, and in Gen. 26:34 is called Judith. Gen. 36:2, 5, 14, 18, 25. [2] A chief that sprang from Esau. Gen. 36:41; 1 Chron. 1:52.

Ahumai, a-hu´ma-i (*heated by Jehovah*), grandson of Shobal. 1 Chron. 4:2.

Ahu´zam (*a holding fast*), a son of Ashur. 1 Chron. 4:6.

Ahuz´zath (*holding fast*), friend of Abimelech. Gen. 26:26.

A´i (*the heap*). [1] **Aiath**, a-i´ath, **Ai´ja**, a-i´jah, or **Ha´i**, a royal city of the Canaanites, east of Bethel. Abraham built an altar near it. Ai is noted for Joshua's defeat on account of the sin of Achan and for his later victory. It is called HAI in Gen. 12:8, AIJA in Neh. 11:31, and AIATH in Isa. 10:28. [2] A city of the Ammonites, near Heshbon. Jer. 49:3.
Also see Gen. 13:3.
Josh. 7:2-5; 8:1-3, 9-12, 14, 16-18, 20, 21, 23-26, 28, 29; 9:3; 10:1, 2; 12:9.
Ezra 2:28.
Neh. 7:32.

Aiah, a-i´ah, or **A´jah** (*a vulture*). [1] A son of Zibeon. Gen. 36:24; 1 Chron. 1:40. [2] Father of Saul's concubine, Rizpah. 2 Sam. 3:7; 21:8, 10.

Aij´a-lon. See AJALON.

Aijeleth Shahar, ad´je-leth sha´har, is the title of Psalm 22, and is supposed to indicate the melody used in singing that Psalm.

A´in (*a fountain*) is spelled "En" in compound words like En-rogel, in the English Bible. [1] Ain is the name of a city of Judah. It was subsequently assigned to Simeon. Josh. 15:32. This city was given to the priests, and is called ASHAN in 1 Chron. 6:59. [2] A place west of Riblah, in the northern part of Canaan. Num. 34:11.

Air. In the Bible the air or atmosphere which surrounds the earth is often indicated by the word "heaven." "The fowls of heaven" means the birds of the air. To "beat the air" and to "speak in the air" means to speak or act without judgment. In Eph. 2:2 "the powers of the air" probably means demons. Many Jews and heathens thought that the lower part of the air was occupied by spirits, especially evil spirits.

A´jah. See AIAH.

Aj´alon or **Aij´alon**. [1] The name of a valley in the land of Dan. Josh. 10:12. Over this valley the moon stood still while Joshua was pursuing the five kings. [2] A Levitical city of Dan, in or near the valley of Ajalon. Josh. 19:42; 21:24; Judg. 1:35. [3] A place in the land of Zebulun. Judg. 12:12. [4] A town in the land of Benjamin or Judah, though there may be doubt whether it is not the same with Ajalon in Dan, or whether the texts quoted here all refer to the same city. 1 Sam. 14:31; 1 Chron. 8:13; 2 Chron. 11:10; 28:18. [5] A Levitical city supposed to be in the land of Ephraim, 1 Chron. 6:69, but is probably same as No. 2.

A´kan or **Ja´kan** (*acute*), one of the children of Ezer, Gen. 36:27, called JAKAN in 1 Chron. 1:42.

Ak´kub (*lain in wait*). [1] A son of Elioenai, who seems to have been of the family of David. 1 Chron. 3:24. [2] A porter for the sanctuary. 1 Chron. 9:17; Neh. 11:19. [3] A name applied to a family of hereditary porters for the sanctuary. Ezra 2:42; Neh. 7:45. [4] Head of a family of the Nethinims who returned to Jerusalem after the captivity. Ezra 2:45. [5] One of the priests who caused the people to understand the law when it was read to them by Ezra. Neh. 8:7.

Akrab´bim (*scorpions*), the name of a point in the southern boundary of Judah which was infested with scorpions and serpents. In Josh. 15:3 it is called Maaleh-acrabbim, the ascent of Akrabbim. Num. 34:4; Josh. 15:3.

Al´abaster, from Alabastron in Egypt, a name given to two kinds of white mineral substances different in composition, but similar in appearance. The true alabaster is a fine-grained kind of gypsum. The other variety is a crystalline carbonate of lime, harder than the first. Alabaster was commonly used for boxes or bottles to contain perfumes. Matt. 26:7; Mark 14:3; Luke 7:37. See CRUSE, SPIKENARD.

Al´ameth (*youthful vigor*), son of Becher. 1 Chron. 7:8. Another form of ALEMETH.

Alammelech, a-lam´me-lek (*the king's oak*), a town in Asher. Josh. 19:26.

Al´amoth (*soprano*), a musical term in the title of Ps. 46 and in 1 Chron. 15:20, is usually considered to refer to music for female voices. Some think it has reference to a kind of rhythm, and others to a certain variety of musical instrument.

Albeit, awl-be´it, in Ezek. 13:7, means although.

Alemeth, al´e-meth (*hiding-place*). [1] A Levitical city of Benjamin. 1 Chron. 6:60, called also ALMON. Josh. 21:18.

[2] A descendant of Jonathan, son of Saul. 1 Chron. 8:36; 9:42.

Aleph (A). The first letter of the Hebrew alphabet. Both the Hebrews and Greeks used their letters as numerals. The 119th Psalm is divided into twenty-two parts, the number of letters in the Hebrew alphabet. One of these letters is used as a heading for each of these parts, Aleph being used for the first part, and so on.

Alexan´der (*helper of men*). [1] Alexander the Great, king of Macedon, born B. C. 356. He was the son of King Philip, and succeeded his father as king, B. C. 336. He was generalissimo of the army of Greece, B. C. 334, conquered most of the then known world, and died at Babylon in his thirty-third year, B. C. 323. He is not mentioned by name in the canonical books, but in the apocryphal book of Maccabees, 1:1-9; 6:2, and in the prophecies of Daniel, where he is represented by the belly of brass in Nebuchadnezzar's dream of the colossal statue, Dan. 2:39, and in Daniel's vision. Dan. 7:6; 8:5-7; 11:3, 4. See ALEXANDRIA. [2] Son of Simon the Cyrenian, who was compelled to carry the cross of Jesus. Mark 15:21. [3] A leading man in Jerusalem when Peter and John were apprehended. Acts 4:6. [4] A Jewish convert who was with Paul when a tumult was raised by the Ephesians. Acts 19:33. Perhaps the same as No. 2. [5] A convert who afterward apostatized. 1 Tim. 1:20. [6] A man who hindered the work of Paul. 2 Tim. 4:14. Perhaps the same as No. 5.

Alexan´dria, Acts 6:9, a famous city of Egypt, was situated between the Mediterranean Sea and Lake Mareotis, twelve miles from the western mouth of the Nile. It was founded B. C. 332 by Alexander the Great, and named after him. It was the birthplace of Apollos. Acts 18:24. See ALEXANDER, No. 1. It became the capital of the Grecian kings reigning in Egypt, and was one of the largest and grandest cities in the world. It contained the greatest library of ancient times and the famous museum. In its best days it is supposed to have had six hundred thousand inhabitants, mostly Greeks and Jews. The modern city is near the site of the ancient one, and has a population of over two hundred thousand. See GREECE.

Alexan´drian, belonging to or coming from the city of that name. Acts 6:9.

Al´gum. See ALMUG.

Ali´ah or **Al´vah** (*sublimity*), a chief of Edom, Gen. 36:40, called ALIAH in 1 Chron. 1:51.

Ali´an, 1 Chron. 1:40, or **Al´van** (*sublime*), Gen. 36:23, son of Shobal.

Alien, ayl´yen, a foreign-born resident of a country. Many references are made in the Bible to aliens.
Exod. 18:3.
Deut. 14:21.
Job 19:15.
Ps. 69:8.
Isa. 61:5.
Lam. 5:2.
Eph. 2:12.
Heb. 11:34.

All, as the context shows, Exod. 9:6; Matt. 3:5; 10:22, is sometimes used in the Bible in a general and not a universal sense.

Alleging, al-lej´ing, in Acts 17:3, means showing; proving.

Al´legory, a story in which the literal or direct meaning is not the principal one, but sets forth some important truth. In Gal. 4:24 "which things are an allegory" signifies that the events referred to concerning the life of Isaac and Ishmael have been applied allegorically.

Allelu´ia (*Praise ye the Lord*). See HALLELUJAH.

Alli´ance. God's peculiar people were strictly forbidden to ally themselves with the heathen by family or by political ties, and especially as to the ancient Canaanites. Deut. 7:3-6. Hebrews sometimes married converts from heathenism, as in the case of Ruth.

Al´lon (*an oak*). [1] A city on the border of Naphtali. Josh. 19:33. See ZAANANNIM. [2] The chief of a family in Simeon. 1 Chron. 4:37.

Allon-bachuth, al´lon-bak´uth (*oak of weeping*), the place where Rebekah's nurse, Deborah, was buried. Gen. 35:8.

Allow´, Luke 11:48, means to praise; to approve.

All to, an old English expression which gives additional force to a verb. In Judges 9:53 "all to brake his skull" means thoroughly broke it.

Almo´dad (*the agitator*), a son of Joktan. Gen. 10:26; 1 Chron. 1:20.

Almon, ah´mun (*hiding-place*), a Levitical town in Benjamin. Josh. 21:18.

Almon-diblathaim, ah´mun-dib´la-tha´im, one of the last encampments of the Israelites between Mount Hor and the plains of Moab, Num. 33:46, 47, next preceding Abarim. See BETH-DIBLATHAIM.

Almond tree, ah´mund tree, is like a peach tree, but is larger. Its blossoms are pinkish-white and come out before the leaves; hence its Hebrew name, which signifies to *watch* and *hasten*. Aaron's rod was from an almond tree. Num. 17:8. In Palestine the almond blossoms in January and bears fruit in March. Eccles. 12:5; Jer. 1:11.

Alms, in Acts 3:3; 10:2, means a charitable gift. The word is not found in the Old Testament, but is frequently used in the New. The Jews were required by the law of Moses to provide for the poor. Lev. 19:9, 10; Deut. 15:11, etc. See POOR.

Al´mug or **Al´gum**, a kind of wood brought from Ophir by Hiram for Solomon, to be used for pillars in the Temple and for musical instruments. It was probably red sandal-wood. 1 Kings 10:11; 2 Chron. 2:8; 9:10, 11.

Al´oes. [1] A perfume spoken of in connection with "myrrh, cassia, and cinnamon," or a spice for embalming the dead. John 19:39, in which case it was the gum of the eagle-tree of China and North India. This perfume is not the aloes of modern apothecaries. [2] Lign-aloes, used by Balaam, Num. 24:6, with the cedars as an illustration of the noble situation of Israel planted in a choice land. It has nothing in common with our bitter aloes.

Aloof´, in Ps. 38:11, means afar off.

A´loth (*ascents*), a hilly region near Asher; but if the name is *Bealoth*, as some translate the original, it would mean a town in S. E. Judah. 1 Kings 4:16.

Alpha, al´fah, the first letter of the Greek alphabet, of which Omega, o´me-gah, or o-meg´ah, is the last. They signify the first and the last, and are used in Rev. 1:8 as a title of the Lord Jesus Christ.

Alphæus, al-fe´us (*leader*). [1] Father of the apostle James the Less, and possibly also of Jude. Matt. 10:3; Mark 3:18. In John 19:25 Alphæus is called CLEOPHAS, which is the same as CLEOPAS. [2] Father of Levi (or Matthew) the apostle and evangelist. Mark 2:14. Perhaps same as No. 1.

Altar, awl´ter, a table or elevated place on which sacrifices and incense were offered to some god. Altars were originally made of turf, and afterward of stone, wood or horn, and were of various forms.

Sacrifices were offered by Cain and Abel, but the first mention of altars in history is in Gen. 8:20, which states that Noah "builded an altar unto the Lord." Moses built an altar of earth. Exod. 20:24. The altars in the Jewish Tabernacle and in the Temple were: **[1]** THE ALTAR OF BURNT-OFFERINGS, which in the Tabernacle was a hollow box of shittim-wood about seven and a half feet square and four and a half feet high, covered with "brass" plates. At the corners were elevations called horns. It was movable, and had rings and staves for carrying it. The fire was a perpetual one, miraculously kindled and carefully kept. Lev. 6:12, 13; 9:24. On this altar the lamb of the daily morning and evening sacrifice was offered; also other sacrifices. See SACRIFICES. At this altar certain fugitives were allowed to find protection. In Solomon's Temple the altar of burnt-offerings was much larger, being at least thirty feet square and fifteen feet high. It is often called the "brazen altar." **[2]** THE ALTAR OF INCENSE, or GOLDEN ALTAR, which in the Tabernacle was a small table of shittim-wood, covered with plates of gold. Exod. 39:38. It was eighteen inches square and three feet high. At the corners were elevations called horns, and around its top was a border or crown. There were two rings on each side, in which staves were inserted to carry it. It stood in the Holy Place, before the Holy of Holies and between the golden candlestick and the table of show-bread. The priests burned incense on it morning and evening. See INCENSE, and TEMPLE. **[3]** THE TABLE OF SHEW-BREAD. See SHEW-BREAD. An altar at Athens was ascribed "to the unknown God." Acts 17:23. The name "altar" is applied to a part of the furniture of Christian churches.

Also see Gen. 12:7, 8; 13:4, 18; 22:9; 26:25; 33:20; 35:1, 3, 7.

Exod. 17:15; 20:25, 26. 21:14; 24:4, 6; 27:1, 5-7; 28:43; 29:12, 13, 16, 18, 20, 21, 25, 36-38, 44; 30:1, 18, 20, 27, 28; 31:8, 9; 32:5; 34:13; 35:15, 16; 38:1, 3, 4, 7, 30; 39:39; 40:5-7, 10, 26, 29, 30, 32, 33.

Lev. 1:5, 7-9, 11-13, 15-17; 2:2, 8, 9, 12; 3:2, 5, 8, 11, 13, 16; 4:7, 10, 18, 19, 25, 26, 30, 31, 34, 35; 5:9, 12; 6:9, 10, 14, 15; 7:2, 5, 31; 8:11, 15, 16, 19, 21, 24, 28, 30; 9:7-10, 12-14, 17, 18, 20; 10:12; 14:20; 16:12, 18, 20, 25, 33; 17:6, 11; 21:23; 22:22.

Num. 3:26, 31; 4:11, 13, 14, 26; 5:25, 26; 7:1, 10, 11, 84, 88; 16:38, 46; 18:3, 5, 7, 17; 23:1, 2, 4, 14, 29, 30.

Deut. 7:5; 12:3, 27; 16:21; 26:4; 27:5, 6; 33:10.

Josh. 8:30, 31; 9:27; 22:10, 11, 16, 19, 23, 26, 28, 29, 34.

Judg. 2:2; 6:24-26, 28, 30-32; 13:20; 21:4.

1 Sam. 2:28, 33; 7:17; 14:35.

2 Sam. 24:18, 21, 25.

1 Kings 1:50, 51, 53; 2:28, 29; 3:4; 6:20, 22; 7:48; 8:22, 31, 54, 64; 9:25; 12:32, 33; 13:1-5, 32; 16:32; 18:26, 30, 32, 35; 19:10, 14.

2 Kings 11:11, 18; 12:9; 16:10-15; 18:22; 21:3-5; 23:9, 12, 15-17, 20.

1 Chron. 6:49; 16:40; 21:18, 22, 26, 29; 22:1; 28:18.

2 Chron. 1:5, 6; 4:1, 19; 5:12; 6:12, 22; 7:7, 9; 8:12; 14:3; 15:8; 23:10, 17; 26:16, 19; 28:24; 29:18, 19, 21, 22, 24, 27; 30:14; 31:1; 32:12; 33:3-5, 15, 16; 34:4, 5, 7; 35:16.

Ezra 3:2, 3; 7:17.

Neh. 10:34.

Pss. 26:6; 43:4; 51:19; 84:3; 118:27.

Isa. 6:6; 17:8; 19:19; 27:9; 36:7; 56:7; 60:7; 65:3.

Jer. 11:13; 17:1, 2.

Lam. 2:7.

Ezek. 6:4-6, 13; 8:5, 16; 9:2; 40:46, 47; 41:22; 43:13, 15, 16, 18, 22, 26, 27; 45:19; 47:1.

Hos. 8:11; 10:1, 2, 8; 12:11.

Joel 1:13; 2:17.

Amos 2:8; 3:14; 9:1.

Zech. 9:15; 14:20.

Mal. 1:7, 10; 2:13.

Matt. 5:23, 24; 23:18-20, 35.

Luke 1:11; 11:51.

Rom. 11:3.

1 Cor. 9:13; 10:18.

Heb. 7:13; 13:10.

James 2:21.

Rev. 6:9; 8:3, 5; 9:13; 11:1; 14:18; 16:7.

Altaschith, al-tas´kith (*destroy not*), probably the first words of some common musical repetition, to which Psalms 57, 58, 59 and 75 were sung.

A´lush (*wild place*), the ninth encampment of the Israelites after they left Egypt. Num. 33:13, 14.

Al´vah. See ALIAH.

Al´van. See ALIAN.

A´mad (*a station*), a town in the border of the land of Asher. Josh. 19:26.

A´mal (*laboring*), a descendant of Asher. 1 Chron. 7:35.

Am´alek (*warlike*). [1] One of the princes of Edom; was the son of Eliphaz, and a grandson of Esau. Gen. 36:12, 16; 1 Chron. 1:36. The name Amalekites was not derived from him, as they existed long before his time. Gen. 14:7. [2] The name is also given to the people descended from him. See AMALEKITES.
Also see Exod. 17:8-11, 13, 14, 16.
Num. 24:20.
Deut. 25:17, 19.
Judg. 3:13; 5:14.
1 Sam 15:2, 3, 5, 20; 28:18.

2 Sam 8:12.

1 Chron. 18:11.

Ps. 83:7.

Amalekites, am´a-lek-ites, a wandering and warlike people, living, at the time of the Exodus, in the wilderness between Egypt and Palestine. They opposed the march of the Israelites and were defeated at Rephidim, and were destroyed by David hundreds of years afterward. See AGAG.

A´mam (*gathering-place*), a town in the south of Judah. Josh. 15:26.

Amana, am´a-nah, or a-ma´nah (*permanent*). [1] The northern ridge of Anti-Lebanon. The river Amana or Abana flowed swiftly from it toward Damascus. Song of Sol. 4:8. [2] In marginal notes, same as ABANA. 2 Kings 5:12. See ABANA.

Amari´ah (*Jehovah has said*). [1] The grandfather of Zadok, who was high-priest in the time of David. 1 Chron. 6:7; Ezra 7:3. [2] Son of Azariah, who was high-priest in the time of Solomon. 1 Chron. 6: 11. [3] A descendant of Kohath, the son of Levi. 1 Chron. 23:19; 24:23. [4] The chief priest in the time of Jehoshaphat. 2 Chron. 19:11. [5] A Levite who distributed tithes among his brethren in the time of Hezekiah. 2 Chron. 31:15. [6] A Jew who took a foreign wife during or after the captivity. Ezra 10:42. [7] One of the priests who sealed the covenant made by the Jews to serve the Lord. Neh. 10:3; 12:2, 13. [8] A descendant of Judah by Pharez. Neh. 11:4. [9] An ancestor of Zephaniah. Zeph. 1:1. Possibly the same as No. 4 or No. 5.

Amasa, am´a-sah (*burden-bearer*). [1] David's nephew, the son of David's sister, Abigail, and Jether, an Ishmaelite. He was general of Absalom's army, and was defeated by Joab, by whom he was subsequently treacherously murdered. 2 Sam. 20:4-10; 1 Chron. 2:17. [2] A chief of Ephraim. 2 Chron. 28:12.

Amasai, a-mas´a-i (*burden-bearer*). [1] A Levite, one of the sons of Elkanah. 1 Chron. 6:25. [2] A chief captain of Benjamin or Judah who went to David at Ziklag. 1 Chron. 12:18. [3] A priest who assisted in bringing the ark from the house of Obed-edom. 1 Chron. 15:24. [4] A Kohathite in Hezekiah's reign. 2 Chron. 29:12.

Amashai, a-mash´a-i (*carrying spoil*), a priest who dwelt in Jerusalem after the captivity. Neh. 11:13.

Am-a-si´ah (*Jehovah has strength*), one of the chief captains of the army of Judah in the time of Jehoshaphat. 2 Chron. 17:16.

Am-a-zi´ah (*Jehovah has strength*). [1] Eighth king of Judah. He succeeded Joash, his father. He was successful in war with the Edomites, reigned twenty-nine years, and was then killed by conspirators. [2] A man of Simeon. 1 Chron. 4:34. [3] A Levite descended from Merari. 1 Chron. 6:45. [4] An Israelite who was priest of the golden calf set up in Bethel. Amos 7:10, 12, 14.
Also see 2 Kings 12:21; 13:12; 14:1, 8, 9, 11, 13, 15, 17, 18, 21, 23; 15:1, 3.
1 Chron. 3:12.
2 Chron. 24:27; 25:1, 5, 9-11, 13-15, 17, 18, 20, 21, 23, 25-27; 26:1, 4.

Ambassador, am-bas´sa-dor. [1] An interpreter. 2 Chron. 32:31. [2] A messenger. Ambassadors were sent by the Jews only as occasion required, in peace or war. Ministers are Christ's ambassadors. 2 Cor. 5:20.
Also see Josh. 9:4.
2 Chron. 32:31; 35:21.
Prov. 13:17.
Isa. 18:2; 30:4; 33:7.
Jer. 49:14.

Ezek. 17:15.
Obad. :1.
Eph. 6:20.

Am´bas-sage. Luke 14:32. See AM-BASSADOR, No. 2.

Am´ber may mean either amber itself, which is a fossil resin, usually of a pale yellow color, and sometimes nearly transparent, or a very brilliant, amber-like metal, made of four parts gold and one part silver, much prized in ancient times. Ezek. 1:4, 27.

A-men´ (*steadfast, faithful, true*), meaning "so be it;" "so let it be;" "verily." In Rev. 3:14 our Lord is called "the Amen, the faithful and true witness." When used at the beginning of a sentence, it is translated "verily." In the Gospel of John it is often used thus double—"verily," "verily." In oaths, after the priest had repeated the words of the covenant or imprecation, all who said "amen" bound themselves by the oath.

Amerce, a-mers´, in Deut. 22:19, means to punish by a fine. The word implied that the debtor stood "at the mercy" of the creditor.

Am´e-thyst, a precious stone, so named from its reputed virtue of preventing intoxication, is transparent quartz, of a violet blue near to purple. Exod. 39:12; Rev. 21:20. The Oriental is more valuable than the common amethyst.

A´mi, a servant of Solomon whose descendants went up from Babylon with Zerubbabel after the captivity. Ezra 2:57. He is called AMON in Neh. 7:59.

A´mi-a-ble, in Ps. 84:1, means lovely.

A-min´a-dab (*my people is willing*), a son of Aram, Matt. 1:4; Luke 3:33, same as AMMIN´ADAB.

A-mit´tai (*truthful*), a Zebulonite,

father of Jonah the prophet. 2 Kings 14:25; Jonah 1:1.

Am´mah (*an aqueduct*), a hill near Gibeon of Benjamin, where Abner was defeated. 2 Sam. 2:24. See also METHEG-AMMAH.

Ammi, am´mi (*my people*), the style of address which the Lord directs his ransomed people to use. Hos. 2:1.

Ammiel, am´mi-el (*my people is strong*). [1] One of the spies sent into Canaan by Moses. Num. 13:12. [2] An Israelite of Lodebar in the time of David. 2 Sam. 9:4, 5; 17:27. [3] Father of Bathshua, a wife of David. 1 Chron. 3:5. The names Bathshua and Ammiel are given in 2 Sam. 11:3 *Bathsheba* and *Eliam*. [4] A Levite, son of Obed-edom, a porter in the tabernacle in the time of David. 1 Chron. 26:5.

Am-mi´hud (*my people is honorable*). [1] An Ephraimite whose son was appointed by the Lord chief of the tribe. Num. 1:10; 1 Chron. 7:26. [2] A Simeonite whose son Shemuel was appointed to divide the land. Num. 34:20. [3] A man of Naphtali whose son Pedahel was appointed to divide the land. Num. 34:28. [4] Father of Talmai, king of Geshur. 2 Sam. 13:37. [5] A man of Judah, a descendant of Pharez. 1 Chron. 9:4.

Am-min´a-dab (*my people is willing*). [1] An Israelite whose daughter was Aaron's wife. Exod. 6:23. [2] A Kohathite and chief of the sons of Uzziel. 1 Chron. 15:10-12. [3] Put for IZHAR in 1 Chron. 6:22; probably a copyist's error.

Am-mi-shad´da-i (*my people is mighty*), father of Ahiezer, the captain of the tribe of Dan in the time of Moses. Num. 1:12; 2:25.

Am-miz´a-bad (*my people is endowed*), a captain in David's army. 1 Chron. 27:6.

Am´mon (*a fellow-countryman*). The son of Lot by his younger daughter was called BEN-AMMI. Gen. 19:38. His descendants were called *Beni-Ammon, Children of Ammon*, or AMMONITES.

Am´mon-ites, the descendants of AMMON (which see). They lived on the east side of the Jordan and often made war on the Israelites, but were conquered by Jephthah, and later by David and Judas Maccabæus.
Deut. 2:20
1 Sam. 11:11
1 Kings 11:1, 5.
2 Chron. 20:1; 26:8; 27:5.
Ezra 9:1.
Neh. 4:7.
Jer. 27:3; 40:11, 14; 41:10, 15; 49:1, 2.
Ezek. 21:20, 28; 25:2, 3, 5, 10.

Am´mon-no. See NO.

Am´non (*tutelage*). [1] The eldest son of David by Ahinoam of Jezreel. 2 Sam. 3:2. Absalom caused him to be assassinated. 2 Sam. 13. [2] The son of Shimon. 1 Chron. 4:20.

A´mok (*deep*), a priest who came up with Zerubbabel from Babylon. Neh. 12:7, 20.

A´mon or **A´men** (*the hidden*), the name of an Egyptian god. Nah. 3:8, in the marginal notes.

A´mon (*workman*). [1] Governor of Samaria in the time of Ahab. 1 Kings 22:26; 2 Chron. 18:25. [2] A son of Manasseh, king of Judah, who succeeded his father. [3] One of the servants of Solomon whose descendants went up with Zerubbabel after the captivity. Neh. 7:59. It is given AMI in Ezra 2:57.
Also see 2 Kings 21:18, 19, 23-25.
1 Chron. 3:14.
2 Chron. 33:20-23, 25.
Jer. 1:2; 25:3.

Zeph. 1:1.

Matt. 1:10.

Am´o-rites (*mountaineers*), a warlike and powerful nation which in the time of Moses occupied the country on both sides of the Jordan and resisted the Israelites on their way to the Promised Land. Moses defeated their kings, Sihon and Og. The Amorites were subsequently conquered by Joshua, but he was unable to destroy them. The term AMORITE is often used in the Bible for CANAANITE in general.

Gen. 10:16; 14:7, 13; 15:16, 21; 48:22.

Exod. 3:8, 17; 13:5; 23:23; 33:2; 34:11.

Num. 13:29; 21:13, 21, 25, 26, 29, 31, 32, 34; 22:2; 32:33, 39.

Deut. 1:4, 7, 19, 20, 27, 44; 2:24; 3:2, 8, 9; 4:46, 47; 7:1; 20:17; 31:4.

Josh. 2:10; 3:10; 5:1; 7:7; 9:1, 10; 10:5, 6, 12; 11:3; 12:2, 8; 13:4, 10, 21; 24:8, 11, 12, 15, 18.

Judg. 1:34-36; 3:5; 6:10; 10:8, 11; 11:19, 21-23.

1 Sam. 7:14.

2 Sam. 21:2.

1 Kings 4:19; 9:20; 21:26.

2 Kings 21:11.

1 Chron. 1:14.

2 Chron. 8:7.

Ezra 9:1.

Neh. 9:8.

Pss. 135:11; 136:19.

Ezek. 16:3, 45.

Amos 2:9, 10.

A´mos (*burden-bearer*). [1] One of the minor prophets who lived B. C. about 780, in the time of Isaiah. He was a herdsman, and also gathered sycamore fruit in Tekoa, near Jerusalem. He prophesied in the time of Uzziah and Jeroboam to the ten tribes, and vigorously and eloquently denounced the prevailing idolatry, taking his illustrations from rural and pastoral life. He described the coming punishment of Israel and the advent of the Messiah. His prophecies seem to have been given in a single year, and to have brought against him a charge of conspiracy against the government because he alienated the people by his plain speaking. The authorship and genuineness of the book of Amos are not disputed. [2] One of the ancestors of Joseph, the husband of Mary. Luke 3:25.

A´moz (*strong*), the father of the prophet Isaiah. 2 Kings 19:2; Isa. 1:1.

Amphipolis, am-fip´o-lis (*on both sides the city*), an ancient and important city of Macedonia, was situated near the mouth of the Strymon, the waters of which are said to have once surrounded the city. Hence its name. It was founded B. C. about 437; was visited by Paul and Silas. Acts 17:1. *Neo-Khorio* now occupies part of the site of Amphipolis.

Am´pli-as, a short form of Ampliatus. Paul sends salutation to this person as "my beloved." Rom. 16:8.

Am´ram (*exalted people*). [1] A son of Kohath and father of Aaron, Miriam, and Moses. The faith of Amram and his wife Jochebed is commended in Heb. 11:23. [2] A son of Bani who had taken a foreign wife during the exile. Ezra 10:34.

Also see Exod. 6:18, 20.

Num. 3:19; 26:58, 59.

1 Chron. 1:41; 6:2, 3, 18; 23:12, 13; 24:20.

Am´ram, a descendant of Seir. 1 Chron. 1:41.

Amramites, am´ram-ites (*belonging to Amram*), descendants of Amram, the father of Moses. Num. 3:27; 1 Chron. 26:23.

Amraphel, am´ra-fel (*powerful people*), king of Shinar in Abraham's time. With other kings he made war on the tribes around the Dead Sea. Gen. 14:1, 9. Among his captives was LOT. Gen. 14:9-16.

Am´u-lets, small objects, of a variety of forms, worn as charms. They were supposed to protect the wearer against real and imaginary evils, and were common in ancient times in the form of earrings and necklaces. Precious stones were often thus used.

Am´zi (*my strength*). [1] A progenitor of Ethan whom David set over the service of song. 1 Chron. 6:46. [2] A priest, an ancestor of Adaiah, a returned exile. Neh. 11:12.

A´nab (*a hill*), a town or mountainous district in the south of Canaan, whose inhabitants, the Anakims, were cut off by Joshua. Josh. 11:21; 15:50. It is still called ANAB.

A´nah (*answering*), the father of Aholibamah, a wife of Esau. Gen. 36:2, 14, 24. He is said to have discovered some *warm springs*, translated *mules* in the Authorized Version. Gen. 36:24.

An-a-ha´rath (*narrow way*), a town in Issachar. Josh. 19:19.

An-a-i´ah (*Jehovah answers*). [1] A priest who was at the right hand of Ezra while he read the book of the law to the people. Neh. 8:4. [2] A Jew who, with Nehemiah, sealed the covenant. Neh. 10:22.

A´nak (*giant*), Num. 13:22; Deut. 9:2, the name of one of the Canaanite races, and not of an individual.

An´a-kim, plural of ANAK, a gigantic race descended from Arba, from whom Kirjath Arba (city of Arba), called Hebron by the Jews, was named. They lived in the south and west parts of the land of Canaan, were famous for their great stature, and hence were called giants. The Hebrew spies were terrified when they saw them. They were nearly destroyed by Joshua but a remnant was left in Gaza, Gad, and Ashdod. See GIANTS. Deut. 1:28; 2:10, 11, 21; 9:2. Josh. 11:21, 22; 14:12, 15.

An´a-mim (*rockmen*), the name of a son of Mizraim, or rather of his descendants. Gen. 10:13; 1 Chron. 1:11.

Anammelech, a-nam´me-lek (*the king's rock*), an idol worshipped by the people of Sepharvaim whom Shalmaneser placed in the cities of Israel after he had carried away the inhabitants. 2 Kings 17:31. See ADRAMMELECH.

A´nan (*he beclouds*), an exile who, with Nehemiah, sealed the covenant. Neh. 10:26.

A-na´ni (*my protector*), son of Elioenai. 1 Chron. 3:24.

An-a-ni´ah (*Jehovah is a protector*). [1] The grandfather of Azariah, who repaired part of the wall of Jerusalem after the return of Nehemiah from Shushan. Neh. 3:23. [2] A town where some Benjamites lived after returning from Babylon. Neh. 11:32.

Ananias, an-a-ni´as (*Jehovah is gracious*). [1] The husband of Sapphira. He was a Jew of Jerusalem who joined the Christians and pretended to give them the full price of his lands. Being convicted of falsehood by Peter, Acts 5:1-10, he died instantly. [2] A Christian of Damascus who restored the sight of Saul (Paul) after his vision of Christ. Acts 9:10; 22:12. [3] A high-priest of the Jews, A. D. 48. Before him and the Sanhedrin Paul was summoned. Acts 23:2; 24:1. **Ananias** is the Greek form of HANANIAH.

A´nath (*answer*), the father of Shamgar, a judge of Israel. Judg. 3:31; 5:6.

Anathema, a-nath´e-mah, word usually translated "a curse" or "accursed," but in one passage left untranslated. "Anathema Maranatha." 1 Cor. 16:22. Ecclesiastically, anathema means excommunicated, or cut off from the church. (It occurs in the Greek. Rom. 9:3; Gal. 1:8, 9).

An´a-thoth (*answers*). [1] A town of Benjamin given to the priests. It was the birthplace of Jeremiah the prophet. [2] A son of Becher the Benjamite. 1 Chron. 7:8. [3] A chief that sealed the covenant made by Nehemiah. Neh. 10:19.
Also see Josh. 21:18.
1 Kings 2:26.
1 Chron. 6:60.
Ezra 2:23.
Neh. 7:27; 11:32.
Isa. 10:30.
Jer. 1:1; 11:21, 23; 29:27; 32:7-9.

Ancient, ayn´shent (*aged*), when used as a name of any person, as in Isaiah 3:14 and in Job 12:12, means an elder.

An´cient of Days, the name given by Daniel to the supreme Judge he saw in vision. Dan. 7:9, 22.

And if, an obsolete expression used in Matt. 24:48, is a double form of if; thus, if, if.

An´drew (*manly*), John 1:40, one of the twelve apostles, was from Bethsaida and was a brother of Simon Peter. Both of them were fishermen. Andrew was a native of Bethsaida in Galilee and a disciple of John the Baptist. Matt. 4:18; 10:2; Mark 1:16, 29, etc. According to tradition, he preached the gospel in Greece and Scythia and suffered martyrdom at Patræ in Achaia, on a cross formed thus (X), commonly called "St. Andrew's cross."

An-dro-ni´cus (*conqueror*), a Jewish Christian living at Rome, was a fellow-prisoner and relative of Paul. Rom 16:7.

A´nem (*double fountain*), a Levitical city of Issachar. 1 Chron. 6:73. Probably same as EN-GANNIM, Josh. 19:21; 21:29, and has been identified with *Jenin*, on the plain of Jezreel. See EN-GANNIM, No. 2.

A´ner (*sprout*). [1] An Amorite ally of Abram in the pursuit of Chedorlaomer and rescue of Lot. Gen. 14:13, 24. [2] A Levitical city in Manasseh, west of Jordan. 1 Chron. 6:70. Some suppose it to be same as TAANACH, Judg. 1:27, and TANACH, Josh. 21:25.

Anethothite, an´e-thoth-ite, or **Anetothite**, an´e-toth-ite, a man of Anathoth in Benjamin. 2 Sam. 23:27; 1 Chron. 27:12. See ANTOTHITE.

An´gel (*messenger*), the name or title given to those beings whom the Lord employs as his messengers. The Jews believed there were several orders of angels. See ARCH-ANGEL. Angels that rebelled against God are angels of Satan, or the devil. See SATAN. The word angel is often used to denote an ordinary messenger to individuals, as in Job 1:14, etc.; to prophets, Isa. 42:19; to priests, Eccles. 5:6; and sometimes to objects without life, as in 2 Cor. 12:7. In a general sense it is applied to Christ as the Angel or Messenger of the covenant; also to the ministers of his gospel. **Angel of Light**, 2 Cor. 11:14, refers to a character assumed by Satan.

An´gel of the Lord, or the Angel Jehovah, is considered by some as one of the common titles of Christ in the Old Testament. Gen. 16:7-13.

An´ger, a strong emotion of indignation, usually called in the Bible a great sin, though sometimes it may be just. Anger is frequently ascribed to God because he punishes the wicked with the justice of a ruler provoked to anger.
Gen. 27:45; 30:2; 44:18; 49:6, 7.
Exod. 4:14; 11:8; 32:19, 22.

Num. 11:1, 10; 12:9; 22:22, 27; 24:10;
25:3, 4; 32:10, 13, 14.
Deut. 4:25; 6:15; 7:4; 9:18, 19; 13:17;
29:20, 23, 24, 27, 28; 31:17, 29; 32:16,
21, 22.
Josh. 7:1, 26; 23:16.
Judg. 2:12, 14, 20; 3:8; 6:39; 8:3; 9:30;
10:7; 14:19.
1 Sam. 11:6; 17:28; 20:30, 34.
2 Sam. 6:7; 12:5; 24:1.
1 Kings 14:9, 15; 15:30; 16:2, 7, 13, 26,
33; 21:22; 22:53.
2 Kings 13:3; 17:11, 17; 21:6, 15; 22:17;
23:19, 26; 24:20.
1 Chron. 13:10.
2 Chron. 25:10, 15; 28:25; 33:6; 34:25.
Neh. 4:5; 9:17.
Esther 1:12.
Job 9:5, 13; 18:4; 21:17; 35:15.
Pss. 6:1; 7:6; 21:9; 27:9; 30:5; 37:8; 38:3;
56:7; 69:24; 74:1; 77:9; 78:21, 38, 49,
50, 58; 85:3-5; 90:7, 11; 103:8; 106:29;
145:8.
Prov. 15:1, 18; 16:32; 19:11; 20:2; 21:14;
22:8; 27:4.
Eccles. 7:9.
Isa. 1:4; 5:25; 7:4; 9:12, 17, 21; 10:4, 5,
25; 12:1; 13:3, 9, 13; 14:6; 30:27, 30;
42:25; 48:9; 63:3, 6; 65:3; 66:15.
Jer. 2:35; 3:5, 12; 4:8, 26; 7:18-20; 8:19;
10:24; 11:17; 12:13; 15:14; 17:4;
18:23; 21:5; 23:20; 25:6, 7, 37, 38;
30:24; 32:29-32, 37; 33:5; 36:7; 42:18;
44:3, 6; 49:37; 51:45; 52:3.
Lam. 1:12; 2:1, 3, 6, 21, 22; 3:43, 66;
4:11, 16.
Ezek. 5:13, 15; 7:3, 8; 8:17; 13:13; 16:26;
20:8, 21; 22:20; 25:14; 35:11; 43:8.
Dan. 9:16; 11:20.
Hos. 8:5; 11:9; 12:14; 13:11; 14:4.
Joel 2:13.
Amos 1:11.
Jon. 3:9; 4:2.

Mic. 5:15; 7:18.
Nah. 1:3, 6.
Hab. 3:8, 12.
Zeph. 2:2, 3; 3:8.
Zech. 10:3.
Mark 3:5.
Rom. 10.19.
Eph. 4:31.
Col. 3:8, 21.

An´gle, in Isa. 19:8, means a fishing-hook.

A´ni-am (*lamentation of the people*) a descendant of Manasseh. 1 Chron. 7:19.

A´ nim (*fountains*), a town of Judah. Josh. 15:50.

An´i-mals were known to the Hebrews as either "clean" or "unclean," the use of the latter being forbidden. See the eleventh chapter of Leviticus for a list of them.

An´ise, a common herb of little value, resembling caraway, but more fragrant. It is the *dill*, which is found in Palestine and was tithed by the scribes and Pharisees. Matt. 23:23.

Ank´lets. See AMULETS, BRACELETS, RINGS.

An´na (*grace*), Luke 2:36-38, a prophetess, daughter of Phanuel, of the tribe of Asher, became a widow while still young, and devoted herself to God's service, being constant in attendance at the temple. At the age of eighty-four she saw the infant Saviour, heard the prophetic blessing of Simeon, and joined earnestly in it.

An´nas (*grace of Jehovah*), a Jewish high-priest along with Caiaphas, his son-in-law. Annas was appointed high-priest A. D. 7, but was removed from that office, which, after many changes, was given, A. D. 23, to Caiaphas, his son-in-law. Annas, having much influence and power, could properly be called high-priest along with Caiaphas. Christ, on the night of his seizure, was first taken before Annas. Annas also assisted in presiding over the Sanhedrin when Peter and John were brought before it. Luke 3:2; John 18:13, 24; Acts 4:6.

An-ni-hi-la´tion. See IMMORTALITY, and SADDUCEES.

A-noint´ed (*consecrated by anointing*). [1] Applied to a priest or a king. [2] Indicating the Redeemer. See CHRIST, and MESSIAH.

Exod. 29:2, 29.

Lev. 2:4; 4:3, 5, 16; 6:20, 22; 7:12, 36; 8:10-12.

Num. 3:3; 6:15; 7:1, 10, 84, 88; 35:25.

1 Sam. 2:10, 35; 10:1; 12:3, 5; 15:17; 16:6, 13; 24:6, 10; 26:9, 11, 16, 23.

2 Sam. 1:14, 16, 21; 2:4, 7; 3:39; 5:3, 17; 12:7, 20; 19:10, 21; 22:51; 23:1.

1 Kings 1:39, 45; 5:1.

2 Kings 9:3, 6, 12; 11:12; 23:30.

1 Chron. 11:3; 14:8; 16:22; 29:22.

2 Chron. 6:42; 22:7; 23:11; 28:15.

Pss. 2:2; 18:50; 20:6; 28:8; 45:7; 84:9; 89:20, 38, 51; 92:10; 105:15; 132:10, 17.

Isa. 45:1; 61:1.

Lam. 4:20.

Ezek. 16:9; 28:14.

Hab. 3:13.

Zech. 4:14.

Mark 6:13.

Luke 4:18; 7:38, 46.

John 9:6, 11; 11:2; 12:3.

Acts 4:27; 10:38.

2 Cor. 1:21.

Heb. 1:9.

A-noint´ing, a common act among the Hebrews and other Eastern nations. It was done by pouring or by rubbing olive oil or some precious ointment upon the hair, head, beard, or sometimes on the whole body. See OINTMENT. The omission of anointing was a sign of mourning. It was a common mark of respect to guests and a sign of prosperity. Dead bodies were often wrapped in spices and ointments to preserve them. Kings, high-priests, and sometimes prophets, were anointed when put into office; also the sacred vessels of the Temple. The anointing of sacred persons and objects indicated that they were set apart and consecrated to the service of God. The costly mixture then used was prohibited for all other uses.

A-non´, in Matt. 13:20, means quickly.

An´swer, in the Bible, besides the common meaning *reply*, often means, as in Zech. 3:4, *to speak*. It also means *to sing* in responses and to give one's account in judgment.

Also see Gen. 30:33; 41:16; 45:3.

Deut. 20:11; 21:7; 25:9; 27:15.

Josh. 4:7.

Judg. 5:29.

1 Sam. 2:16; 20:10.

2 Sam. 3:11; 24:13.

1 Kings 9:9; 12:6, 7, 9; 18:29.

2 Kings 4:29; 18:36.

2 Chron. 10:6, 9, 10.

Ezra 4:17; 5:5, 11.

Neh. 5:8.

Esther 4:13, 15.

Job 5:1; 9:3, 14, 15, 32; 13:22; 14:15; 19:16; 20:2, 3; 21:34; 23:5; 31:14, 35; 32:1, 3, 5, 14, 17, 20; 33:5, 12, 32; 34:36; 35:4, 12; 38:3; 40:2, 4, 5.

Pss. 27:7; 65:5; 86:7; 91:15; 102:2; 108:6; 119:42; 143:1.

Prov. 1:28; 15:1, 23, 28; 16:1; 22:21; 24:26; 26:4, 5; 27:11; 29:19.

Isa. 14:32; 30:19; 36:21; 41:28; 46:7; 50:2; 58:9; 65:12, 24; 66:4.

Jer. 5:19; 7:27; 22:9; 33:3; 42:4; 44:20.

Ezek. 14:4, 7; 21:7.

Dan. 3:16.

Joel 2:19.

Mic. 3:7.

Hab. 2:1, 11.

Zech. 13:6.

Matt. 22:46; 25:37, 40, 44, 45.

Mark 11:29, 30; 14:40.

Luke 2:47; 11:7; 12:11; 13:25; 14:6; 20:3, 26; 21:14; 22:68.

John 1:22; 19:9.

Acts 24:10; 25:16; 26:2.

Rom. 11:4.

1 Cor. 9:3.

2 Cor. 5:12.

Col. 4:6.

2 Tim. 4:16.

1 Pet. 3:15, 21.

Ant, a small insect remarkable for its industry, economy, social habits, and skill as a builder. It is referred to by Solomon in Prov. 6:6 and 30:24, 25.

An´te-lope. See ROE.

An´ti-christ (*opposed to Christ*), is found in the Bible only in the epistles of John, 1 John 2:18, 22; 4:3; 2 John 7, and signifies false Christians and heretical teachers, who denied the incarnation of Christ. There were many such in the days of John. The term was afterward used for an individual who was expected to precede the second advent.

An´ti-och. **[1]** A city of Syria, on the river Orontes. It was founded B. C. about 300 by Seleucus Nicator and named by him after his father Antiochus. It was the most splendid city of Syria, and had a population of at least 400,000. It was a great resort for Jews, and afterward for Christians. The name of Christians was here first given to the followers of Christ. Acts 11:26. It is famous as the place of Paul's first regular labors in the gospel and as the city from which he started on his missionary tours. It is now a small town called *Antakia*. **[2]** A city called "Antioch of Pisidia," so named because it was attached to the province of Pisidia in Asia Minor. Paul established a church in this city, which is now called *Yalobatch*. There were not less than six other Oriental towns called Antioch.

Also see Acts 6:5; 11:19, 20, 22, 27; 13:1, 14; 14:19, 21, 26; 15:22, 23, 30, 35; 18:22.

Gal. 2:11.

2 Tim. 3:11.

An´ti-pas. **[1]** See HEROD ANTIPAS. **[2]** The name of a martyr in Pergamos. Rev. 2:13. It is an abbreviation of Antipater.

An-tip´a-tris (*city of Antipater*), a city of Palestine about eight miles from the coast and sixteen miles north-east of Joppa, according to ancient authority was founded by Herod the Great and called Antipatris in honor of his father Antipater. It was visited by Paul. Acts 23:31.

An-to´ni-a, the name of a fortress on the east side of Jerusalem and north-west of the temple. It was rebuilt by Herod the Great and named after his friend Antony. It may be the castle mentioned in Acts 21:34.

An-to-thi´jah (*answers of Jehovah*), a son of Shashak, a descendant of Benjamin. 1 Chron. 8:24.

An´to-thite (*belonging to Anathoth*), a native of Anathoth. 1 Chron. 11:28; 12:3.

A´nub (*strong*), a descendant of Judah through Caleb. 1 Chron. 4:8.

Ape, an animal somewhat resembling man. Solomon imported apes from Ophir. They were worshipped in Egypt. 1 Kings 10:22.

A-pel´les, a Christian to whom Paul sent salutation. Rom. 16:10.

Apharsachites, a-far´sak-itz, **Apharsathchites**, a-far´sath-kitz, **Aphar´sites**, Assyrian colonists in Samaria. Ezra 4:9; 5:6; 5:6.

A´phek (*strength*) [1] A royal city of the Canaanites. Its king was slain by Joshua. Josh. 12:18. Probably same as APHEKAH. [2] A city of Asher, Josh. 19:30, near Sidon. Probably same as APHIK. [3] A place north-west of Jerusalem where the Philistines encamped before the ark was taken. 1 Sam 4:1. [4] A place in Issachar where the Philistines were before they defeated Saul. 1 Sam. 29:1. [5] A walled city of Syria, 1 Kings 20:26, 30, about six miles east of the Sea of Galilee.

A-phe´kah (*fortress*). Josh. 15:53. See APHEK, No. 1.

A-phi´ah (*refreshed*), one of Saul's ancestors. 1 Sam. 9:1.

A´phik. Judg. 1:31. See APHEK, No. 2.

Aph´rah, a city in the low country of Judah. Mic. 1:10.

Aph´ses (*the dispersed*), the head of the eighteenth course of priests in the time of David. 1 Chron. 24:15.

A-poc´a-lypse, the Greek word for Revelation, used in reference to the Revelation of John. See REVELATION.

A-poc´ry-pha (*hidden*). Under this title are comprised a number of books: two of Esdras, Tobit, Judith, some chapters of the book of Esther, the Wisdom of Solomon, Ecclesiasticus, or the Wisdom of Jesus the son of Sirach, Baruch, the Song of the Three Holy Children, the History of Susanna, the Destruction of Bel and the Dragon, the Prayer of Manasses, and the two Maccabees. They are not in the Hebrew Bible, but in the Septuagint, so called, or Greek translation of the Old Testament, dating from the third century B. C. From internal and external evidences it appears that they were not written by the men with whose names they are inscribed, but belong to a much later date, and probably originated in Alexandria. They are conse-

quently without divine authority, but they are by no means without interest, forming a transition, in many respects very instructive, from the Old to the New Testament. The Jews seem to have looked upon them in the same light, and so did most of the Christian Fathers. Jerome, A. D. 340–420, one of the most learned of the early Fathers, says: "The other books (the Apocrypha) the Church reads for example of life and instruction of manner, but it does not apply them to establish any doctrine;" and this verdict has been recognized by the Thirty-Nine Articles of the Church of England and the reformed churches generally. Nevertheless, from the Septuagint they were transferred to the Vulgate, the authorized Latin translation of the Bible, dating from the fourth century A. D., and from thence to other translations. Since the Council of Trent, A. D. 1545–63, recognized them as canonical, with the exception of the two books of Esdras and the Prayer of Manasses, they are found in all Roman Catholic Bibles, and for a long time they were also printed in Protestant Bibles. In 1826 the British and Foreign Bible Society decided to omit them, and the American Bible Society followed the example.

The New Testament may be said to have no Apocrypha, as the various apocryphal Gospels, Acts, and Revelation are generally of an altogether inferior character, but they confirm the canonical Gospels in the same way that counterfeit coins presuppose genuine ones.

Ap-ol-lo´ni-a (*place of Apollo*), a city of Macedonia, between Amphipolis and Thessalonica, mentioned in Acts 17:1.

A-pol´los (*a destroyer*), a learned and eloquent Jew of Alexandria who became a Christian. He preached in Achaia and Corinth with great success, especially among the Jews. He was with Paul at Ephesus. Apollos is said to have been Bishop of Corinth.

Acts 18:24; 19:1.

1 Cor. 1:12; 3:4-6, 22; 4:6; 16:12.

Titus 3:13.

A-pol´ly-on or **A-poll´yon**. See ABADDON.

A-pos´tle (*one who is sent*). This name is applied in Heb. 3:1 to Jesus Christ, but is commonly given to "the twelve," Matt. 10:2, and to Paul. Gal. 1:1, 12, 16; 2:9. It is the name translated "messenger" in 2 Cor. 8:23, where it means delegate on a charitable mission. It is also applied, in Rom. 16:7, to men of note among the apostles.

Also see Mark 6:30.

Luke 6:13; 9:10; 11:49; 17:5; 22:14; 24:10.

Acts 1:2, 26; 2:37, 42, 43; 4:33, 35-37; 5:2, 12, 18, 29, 34, 40; 6:6; 8:1, 14, 18; 9:27; 11:1; 14:4, 14; 15:2, 4, 6, 22, 23, 33; 16:4.

Rom. 1:1; 11:13.

1 Cor. 1:1; 4:9; 9:1, 2, 5; 12:28, 29; 15:7, 9.

2 Cor. 1:1; 11:5, 13; 12:11, 12.

Gal. 1:17, 19.

Eph. 1:1; 2:20; 3:5; 4:11.

Col. 1:1.

1 Thess. 2:6.

1 Tim. 1:1; 2:7.

2 Tim. 1:1, 11.

Titus 1:1.

1 Pet. 1:1.

2 Pet. 1:1; 3:2.

Jude :17.

Rev. 2:2; 18:20; 21:14.

A-pos´tles, Acts of. See ACTS OF THE APOSTLES.

A-pos´tles' Creed. This is the most universal creed of the Christian Church. According to a tradition of the fourth century, it was composed by the apostles, but this statement is now generally discredited. It is called also the Creed, or Confession of Faith, and is as follows: "I believe in God, the Father Almighty, Maker of heaven and earth. And in Jesus Christ, His only Son, our Lord; who was conceived by the Holy Ghost, born of the Virgin Mary; suffered under Pontius Pilate, was crucified, dead, and buried; he descended into hell [or hades]; the third day he rose from the dead; he ascended into heaven, and sitteth on the right hand of God the Father Almighty; from thence He shall come to judge the quick and the dead. I believe in the Holy Ghost; the Holy Catholic Church; the communion of Saints; the forgiveness of sins; the resurrection of the body; and the life everlasting. Amen."

The clause "He descended into hell" (that is, the place of departed spirits) first appeared in the Creed of Aquileia, A. D. 390, and then passed into the Roman Creed. The word "Catholic," in this creed, means "*Universal*."

A-pos-tol´ic Fa´thers, the disciples and fellow-laborers of the apostles, particularly those who left writings, namely, Clement, Barnabas, Polycarp, Ignatius, and Hermas.

A-poth´e-ca-ry, Exod. 30:25, one who prepared and sold anointing oil, sweet spices, etc.

Ap´pa-im, a son of Nadab. 1 Chron. 2:30.

Ap-par´el. See GARMENTS.

Ap-par´elled, in Luke 7:25, means dressed.

Ap-par´ent-ly, in Num. 12:8, means plainly; openly.

Ap-peal´. The Mosaic law, Deut. 17:8, 9, allowed appeals. They were also granted in the time of the Judges and the Kings. Paul, who was a Roman citizen, appealed for trial before the emperor. Acts 25:1-12.

Apphia, af´fi-a, Philem. 2, is supposed to have been the wife of Philemon.

Ap´pi-i Fo´rum (*market-place of Appius*), a market-town on the great road (*Via Appia*) from Rome to Capua, was founded by Appius Claudius. It was about forty-three miles from Rome and on the border of the Pontine marshes. Acts 28:15.

Ap´ple. The apple mentioned in Scripture is commonly supposed to have been different from the fruit now known by that name. The apple of the Bible was probably the apricot, which is common in Palestine; some say the citron is referred to, and some the quince. The apple is used in Prov. 25:11 as an illustration of "a word fitly spoken." Apple trees are several times mentioned in the Bible, and as there described are very much like the apricot.

Ap´ple of the Eye. Deut. 32:10. This phrase means, literally, "the little man," or "pupil" of the eye.

Ap´ple of Sod´om is found in the fertile spots near the Dead Sea, and has a thin yellow peel which crushes under pressure, leaving only worthless fragments.

Ap-point´ed, in Judg. 18;11, means armed; equipped.

Ap-pre-hend´, in Phil. 3:12, means to lay hold upon.

A´prons, mentioned in Gen. 3:7, were made of fig-leaves by Adam and Eve after they had sinned, and in Acts 19:12 aprons of another kind are referred to.

Aquila, ak´quil-lah (*an eagle*), a companion of Paul in his labors. He was a Jewish tent-maker who, with his wife Priscilla, joined the Christian Church at Rome. Acts 18:2, 18, 26.

Ar, and **Ar of Mo-ab**, Num. 21:28, on the east of the Dead Sea, is the principal city of Moab, and is called AROER. Deut. 2:36. The name AR, Deut. 2:29, is sometimes applied to the land of Moab.

A´ra (*strong*), son of Jether. 1 Chron. 7:38.

A´rab. [1] A city of Judah. Josh. 15:52. [2] A native of Arabia.

Ar´a-bah (*the plain*), a name applied to the valley of the Jordan north of the Dead Sea, and sometimes to that south of it. Josh. 18:18.

A-ra´bi-a (*wilderness*), the south-west part of Asia. It is situated south and east of Palestine. It extends about 1600 miles north and south and 1400 miles east and west, and is divided into three parts—ARABIA DESERTA (*the desert*), ARABIA PETRÆA (*the rocky*), and ARABIA FELIX (*the happy*). Arabia Petræa is south of Palestine. Its capital was Petra. See SELA. It was inhabited by the southern Edomites, the Amalekites, etc. Their successors are now called Arabs. It contained the peninsula of Mount Sinai, the land of Midian, etc. Here the Hebrews spent forty years of wandering on the way to the Promised Land. The queen of Sheba was probably from part of Arabia Felix, which was very rich and abounded with spices. It now contains the famous cities of Mecca and Medina. Southern Arabia contains descendants of Ham, Shem, Ishmael, of Abraham by Keturah, Gen. 25:2, also of Esau and Lot. See SINAI.

Also see 1 Kings 10:15.

2 Chron. 9:14.

Isa. 21:13.

Jer. 25:24.

Ezek. 27:21.

Gal. 1:17; 4:25.

A-ra´bi-ans, the Gentile name of the inhabitants of ARABIA. Acts 2:11.

A'rad (*fugitive*). [1] A Benjamite. son of Beriah. 1 Chron. 8:15. [2] A city in the south of Judea. Judg. 1:16. [3] A Canaanitish city. Josh. 12:14. [4] A king who attacked the Israelites near Mount Hor and was defeated. Num. 21:1; 33:40.

A'rah (*wayfarer*). [1] An Asherite and son of Ulla. 1 Chron. 7:39. [2] A man whose family returned from Babylon. His granddaughter married Tobiah the Ammonite. Ezra 2:5; Neh. 6:18; 7:10.

A'ram (*high*). [1] A son of Shem. Gen. 10:22, 23; 1 Chron. 1:17. [2] A descendant of Nahor, the brother of Abraham. Gen. 22:21. [3] Son of Shamer of Asher. 1 Chron. 7:34. [4] The son of Esrom, Matt. 1:3, 4; Luke 3:33, elsewhere called RAM. [5] The elevated country north-east of Palestine, toward the river Euphrates. Num. 23:7; 1 Chron. 2:23. It was nearly the same as SYRIA.

A'ram-na-ha-ra'im (*Aram of two rivers*), Ps. 60, title, the country between the Tigris and Euphrates Rivers, called in Greek Mesopotamia.

A'ram-zo'bah (*Aram of Tsobah*), Ps. 60, title, the country between the Orontes and Euphrates Rivers, near Damascus.

A-ram-i'tess (*the female Aramite*), Manasseh's concubine. 1 Chron. 7:14.

A'ran (*wild goat*), a descendant of Seir the Horite. Gen. 36:28; 1 Chron. 1:42.

Ar'a-rat (*holy land*). [1] A region of Armenia, between the river Araxes and the lakes Van and Urumiah. The name Ararat was sometimes applied to a larger portion of Armenia. 2 Kings 19:37; Jer. 51:27. [2] A grand volcanic mountain on the boundary between Persia, Turkey, and Russia; has two principal peaks. Greater Ararat is about seventeen thousand feet above the sea, and is covered with perpetual snow. Lesser Ararat is twelve thou-

sand eight hundred and forty feet high. Ararat is called by the Persians the "Mountain of Noah." Noah's ark rested "upon the mountains of Ararat." Gen. 8:4.

A-rau'nah (*Jehovah is firm*), a Jebusite of Mount Moriah. He is called ORNAN in 1 Chron. 21:18. David is said to have bought from Araunah his threshing-floor and oxen and the whole mount. 2 Sam. 24:16–24; 1 Chron. 21:25.

Ar'ba. See HEBRON.

Ar'bah. Gen. 35:27. See KIRJATH-ARBA, and HEBRON.

Ar'bath-ite (*belonging to Arabah*), descendants of Abialbon and Abiel. 2 Sam. 23:31; 1 Chron. 11:32.

Ar'bel. Hos. 10:14. See BETH-ARBEL.

Ar'bite, the (*a native of Arba*). 2 Sam. 23:35.

Arch'an-gel (*a chief angel*). 1 Thess. 4:16. Jude 9.

Archelaus, ar-ke-la'us (*people's chief*), a son of Herod the Great by his fourth wife, Malthace, was destined by his father to become his successor, but Augustus refused to make him a king. He ruled, however, for several years as ethnarch over Judea, Samaria. and Idumæa, but was cruel and tyrannical, with all his father's evil passions and none of his ability. He was deposed by Augustus in A. D. 6, and banished to Vienne in Gaul, where he died. He is mentioned in Matt. 2:22.

Arch'ers. See BOW.

Archevites, ar'ke-vites, inhabitants of Orchæ in Chaldea, removed to Samaria after the Israelites were carried away from there. Ezra 4:9.

Archi, ar'ki (*the long*), a city on the border of Ephraim. Josh. 16:2.

Archippus, ar-kip'pus (*chief groom*), a "fellow-soldier" of Paul. Col. 4:17; Philem. 2.

Archite, ar´kite (*the long*), the name applied to Hushai, David's friend. 2 Sam. 15:32; 1 Chron. 27:33.

Arc-tu´rus (*group*), a fixed star of the first magnitude in the constellation Bootes, so called because it is near the tail of the constellation called the Great Bear. In Job 38:32 the "sons" of Arcturus are probably stars in the Great Bear.

Ard (*fugitive?*), a Benjamite. He is called son of Benjamin in Gen. 46:21, and grandson of Benjamin in Num. 26:40. In 1 Chron. 8:3 he is called ADDAR.

Ard´ites, Num. 26:40, are the descendants of Ard.

Ar´don (*fugitive*), son of Caleb. 1 Chron. 2:18.

A-re´li (*heroic*), son of Gad. Gen. 46:16; Num. 26:17.

A-re´lites, descendants of Areli. Num. 26:17.

A-re-op´a-gite, a member of the council of the Areopagus. Acts 17:34.

A-re-op´a-gus (*hill of Mars*). [1] A rocky hill near the center of the city of Athens. Acts 17:19. See MARS' HILL. [2] The celebrated court of justice which was held at Areopagus. It was organized earlier than B. C. 740. Paul addressed the Athenians there. Acts 17:19-34.

Ar´e-tas, 2 Cor. 11:32, was king of north-western Arabia. He made war on Herod Antipas, and afterward appointed a governor over Damascus who attempted to put Paul in prison.

Ar´gob (*stony*), a small district of Bashan, east of the Jordan. It once contained sixty fortified cities, the ruins of many of them being still visible. It is now called the *Lejah*. Deut. 3:4; 1 Kings 4:13.

A-rid´a-i (*the strong*), a son of Haman. Esther 9:9.

A-rid´a-tha, another son of Haman.

Esther 9:8.

A-ri´eh (*lion of Jehovah*), a friend of Pekahiah. 2 Kings 15:25.

A´ri-el (*lion of God*). [1] One of the chief men of Ezra. Ezra 8:16. [2] In Isa. 29:1, 2, 7 it is applied to a city (Jerusalem) as the *hearth* on which burnt offerings and enemies of God were to be consumed.

Ar-i-ma-thæ´a (*heights*), a town in Judea. It was the home of Joseph, in whose new tomb the body of Jesus was laid. Matt. 27:57-60.
Also see Mark 15:43.
Luke 23:51.
John 19:38.

A´ri-och (*lion-like*). [1] King of Ellasar. Gen. 14:1-9. [2] A captain of Nebuchadnezzar's guard. Dan. 2:14, 15, 24, 25.

A-ris´a-i (*lion-like*), eighth son of Haman. Esther 9:9.

Aristarchus, ar-is-tar´kus (*best ruler*), a Macedonian and a faithful laborer with Paul, with whom he was a prisoner at Rome. Acts 19:29; Col. 4:10.

Ar-is-to-bu´lus (*best counsellor*), a resident of Rome whose household was saluted by Paul. Rom. 16:10.

Ark, a word meaning three structures. [1] NOAH'S ARK a vessel made at God's command, in which Noah and his family and the animals to be saved were preserved during the deluge which destroyed the rest of the human race for their sins. Gen. 6:14-16; 8:1-13. See DELUGE, and NOAH.

[2] MOSES' ARK, in which the infant Moses was hidden by his mother. Exod. 2:3-5. It was made of bulrushes, a kind of reed growing on the banks of the Nile.

[3] THE ARK OF THE COVENANT or TESTIMONY. Exod. 37:1-8. It was a covered chest of shittim-wood, overlaid within and with-

out with gold. In it were the stone tables on which the law or "covenant" made by God with the Hebrews was inscribed; also the pot of manna, Aaron's rod, and the books of the Law. The mercy-seat with the cherubim was on its lid. It was kept in the most holy place (the "Holy of Holies") of the sanctuary. No object was more sacred among the Jews than the "ark of God." In their journeys in the wilderness it was borne by the priests before the hosts of Israel. Before it the Jordan was divided and the walls of Jericho fell. It was brought to the Temple by Solomon, 2 Chron. 5:2, where it remained till the time of the later idolatrous kings. Its ultimate fate is unknown.

Also see Gen. 6:18, 19; 7:1, 7, 9, 13, 15, 17, 18, 23; 8:16, 19; 9:10, 18.

Exod. 25:10, 14-16, 21, 22; 26:33, 34; 30:6, 26; 31:7; 35:12; 39:35; 40:3, 5, 20, 21.

Lev. 16:2.

Num. 3:31; 4:5; 7:89; 10:33, 35; 14:44.

Deut. 10:1-3, 5, 8; 31:9, 25, 26.

Josh. 3:3, 6, 8, 11, 13-15, 17; 4:5, 7, 9-11, 16, 18; 6:4, 6, 8, 9, 11-13; 7:6; 8:33.

Judg. 20:27.

1 Sam. 3:3; 4:3-6, 11, 13, 17-19, 21, 22; 5:1-4, 7, 8, 10, 11; 6:1-3, 8, 11, 13, 15, 18, 19, 21; 7:1, 2; 14:18.

2 Sam. 6:2-4, 6, 7, 9-13, 15-17; 7:2; 11:11; 15:24, 25, 29.

1 Kings 2:26; 3:15; 6:19; 8:1, 3-7, 9, 21.

1 Chron. 6:31; 13:3, 5-7, 9, 10, 12-14; 15:1-3, 12, 15, 23-29; 16:1, 4, 6, 37; 17:1; 22:19; 28:2, 18.

2 Chron. 1:4; 5:4-10; 6:11, 41; 8:11; 35:3.

Ps. 132:8.

Jer. 3:16.

Matt. 24:38.

Luke 17:27.

Heb. 9:4; 11:7.

1 Pet. 3:20.

Rev. 11:19.

Ark´ites, descendants of Canaan that settled the town of Arka, at the northwest foot of Mount Lebanon. Gen. 10:17; 1 Chron. 1:15.

Arm, the symbol of power. Job 38:15.

Also see Gen. 49:24.

Exod. 6:6; 15:16.

Num. 31:3.

Deut. 4:34; 5:15; 7:19; 9:29; 11:2; 26:8; 33:20, 27.

Judg. 15:14; 16:12.

1 Sam. 2:31.

2 Sam. 1:10; 22:35.

1 Kings 8:42.

2 Kings 9:24; 17:36.

2 Chron. 6:32; 32:8.

Job 22:9; 26:2; 31:22; 35:9; 40:9.

Pss. 10:15; 18:34; 37:17; 44:3; 77:15; 89:10, 13, 21; 98:1; 136:12.

Prov. 31:17.

Song of Sol. 8:6.

Isa. 9:20; 17:5; 30:30; 33:2; 40:10, 11; 44:12; 48:14; 49:22; 51:5, 9; 52:10; 53:1; 59:16; 62:8; 63:5, 12.

Jer. 17:5; 21:5; 27:5; 32:17, 21; 48:25.

Ezek. 4:7; 13:20; 20:33, 34; 30:21, 22, 24, 25; 31:17.

Dan. 2:32; 10:6; 11:6, 15, 22, 31.

Hos. 7:15; 11:3.

Zech. 11:17.

Mark 9:36; 10:16.

Luke 1:51; 2:28.

John 12:38.

Acts 13:17.

1 Pet. 4:1.

Ar-ma-ged´don (*mountain of Megiddo*). Rev. 16:16. Megiddo is a city at the foot of Mount Carmel, and had been the scene of great slaughter. Hence the above reference to it in Revelation as the place in which God will collect his enemies for destruction.

Ar-me´ni-a, a large portion of Asia, between Media on the east, Cappadocia on the west, Colchis and Iberia on the north, Mesopotamia on the south, and the Euphrates and Syria on the south-west. It is between the Caucasus and Taurus ranges, contains Mount Ararat near its center, and is the source of the Euphrates, Tigris, and Araxes Rivers. 2 Kings 19:37; Isa. 37:38. See ARARAT.

Arm´let. See BRACELET.

Ar-mo´ni (*of the palace*), son of Saul by Rizpah. 2 Sam. 21:8.

Ar´mor and **Arms**. The armor used by the Hebrews consisted of helmets for the head, cuirasses for the body (called also coat of mail, habergeon, and breastplate), the shield, target or buckler, and greaves used to protect the legs. Armor was made of leather and metallic scales or plates. Their offensive arms were the bow and arrow, the battle-axe, the spear, dart, and javelin or short spear, the sling, and the sword. The sword was straight, short, and two-edged. See WAR, and SHIELD.

Ar´mor-bear´er, an attendant who bore the heavy arms, such as spear and shield, of a warrior of rank. Judg. 9:54; 1 Sam. 14:7. He was also employed to carry orders, and was expected to stand by his chief in time of danger.

Ar´nan (*strong*) is applied to a family apparently descended from David. 1 Chron. 3:21.

Ar´non (*roaring*), a river which rises in the mountains east of the Dead Sea, into which it empties, and in ancient times divided the territory of the Moabites from that of the Ammonites, Amorites, and Reubenites. Arnon is applied also to the valley through which the river Arnon flows.
Num. 21:13, 14, 24, 26, 28; 22:36.

Deut. 2:24, 36; 3:8, 12, 16; 4:48.
Josh. 12:1, 2; 13:9, 16.
Judg. 11:13, 18, 22, 26.
2 Kings 10:33.
Isa. 16:2.
Jer. 48:20.

A´rod (*descent*), a son of Gad. Num. 26:17. He is called ARODI in Gen. 46:16.

Ar´o-di (*my posterity*), a son of Gad, Gen. 46:16, the same who is called AROD in Num. 26:17.

A´rod-ites, a family of the Israelites whose ancestor was AROD, a son of Gad. Num. 26:17.

Ar´o-er (*ruins*) [1] A city of the Gadites near Rabbah. Num. 32:34; Josh. 13:25. [2] A city of the Amorites. Deut. 2:36; Jer. 48:19. [3] A town in the south of Judah, 1 Sam. 30:28, 11 miles south-east of Beersheba. It is now called *Ararah*. [4] Aroer, in Isa. 17:2, must be a region near Damascus if it is a proper name.

Ar´o-er-ite, an inhabitant of Aroer. 1 Chron. 11:44.

Ar´pad or **Ar´phad** (*resting-place*), a fortified city on the north side of Palestine. 2 Kings 18:34; Jer. 49:23. See ARVAD.

Ar-phax´ad, son of Shem, ancestor of Eber, and probably of the Chaldeans. Gen. 10:22, 24; 11:10-13; 1 Chron. 1:17, 18, 24.

Ar-ray´ed, Matt. 6:29, dressed or clothed.

Ar´row, 1 Sam. 20:36, was used in hunting and in war, and was in some instances only a sharpened reed; in others it was feathered, barbed, and sometimes poisoned. Arrows were used also to carry fire to the house or person of an enemy; the shield was sometimes wet as a protection.

Ar-tax-erx´es (*great king*). [1] A king of Persia, Ezra 4:7-24, in whose time the governor of Samaria obtained an order to stop the rebuilding of Jerusalem by Zerubbabel. He is supposed to have been Smerdis the Magian. [2] A king of Persia, in the seventh year of whose reign Ezra went up from Babylon to Jerusalem with some of his countrymen; fourteen years afterward Nehemiah was allowed by Artaxerxes to return and rebuild Jerusalem. Ezra 7:7; Neh. 2:1. He is supposed to be the same as Artaxerxes Longimanus, son of Xerxes, who reigned B. C. 464–425.

Ar´te-mas (*whole*), a faithful fellow-laborer with Paul. Titus 3:12.

Ar-tif´i-cers, workmen especially skillful in working in metals, carving wood and plating it with gold, setting precious stones, and designing embroideries. King Solomon procured many artificers from Hiram, king of Tyre. Gen. 4:22; 2 Chron. 34:11.

Ar-til´ler-y, in the Bible, means bows, arrows, javelins, darts, etc.; in 1 Sam. 20:40 it means bow and arrows.

Arts, in Acts 19:19, means pretended skill in astrology, magic, etc.

Ar´u-both (*courts*), one of Solomon's commissariat districts, including Sochoh. 1 Kings 4:10.

Ar´u-mah (*height*), a place where Abimelech lived. It was near Shechem. Judg. 9:41.

Ar´vad (*refuge*), a small island a short distance off the coast of Phoenicia. It is in the Mediterranean Sea, and closely related to Tyre. Ezek. 27:8, 11. See also Gen. 10:18; 1 Chron. 1:16. It is probably same as ARPAD and ARPHAD, and is now called *Ruad*.

Ar´vad-ites, a tribe descended from a son of Canaan. Gen. 10:18; 1 Chron. 1:16.

Ar´za, a steward of Elah. 1 Kings 16:9.

A´sa (*physician*). [1] Son and successor of Abijah as king of Judah. He reigned forty-one years, beginning B. C. 955, and fought a great battle with Zerah, an Ethiopian king, whom he defeated at Maresha. See 2 Chron. 14:8-15. Asa is said to have done "that which was good and right in the eyes of the LORD his God." 2 Chron. 14:2. [2] A Levite, the head of a family that dwelt near Jerusalem. 1 Chron. 9:16.

As´a-hel (*God is doer*). [1] A son of Zeruiah, David's sister. He was slain by Abner at the battle of Gideon. 2 Sam. 2:18-23. [2] A Levite. 2 Chron. 17:8. [3] A Levite employed under Hezekiah. 2 Chron. 31:13. [4] Father of one employed by Ezra. Ezra 10:15.

As-a-hi´ah (*Jehovah is doer*), a servant of King Josiah. 2 Kings 22:12, 14. Called ASAIAH (same name) in 2 Chron. 34:20.

As-a-i´ah (*Jehovah is doer*). [1] A descendant of Simeon. 1 Chron. 4:36, 41. [2] A Levite in the time of David. He was chief of the Merari, and assisted in bringing up the ark to Jerusalem. 1 Chron. 6:30, 31; 15:6, 11. [3] The firstborn of the Shilonite, according to 1 Chron. 9:5, and is called MAASEIAH in Neh. 11:5. [4] 2 Chron. 34:20. See ASAHIAH.

A´saph (*gatherer*). [1] A Levite, a chief leader of the choir of the Temple and a poet. 1 Chron. 6:39. Twelve Psalms are attributed to him—Ps. 50 and Pss. 73 to 83. In connection with David he is referred to as a "seer." 2 Chron. 29:30; Neh. 12:46. [2] Hezekiah's recorder. 2 Kings 18:18. [3] An officer appointed by the king of Persia to keep the forests in Judea. Neh. 2:8. [4] A Levite, an ancestor of Mattaniah. Neh. 11:17. Perhaps same as No. 1. [5] A Levite whose descendants dwelt in Jerusalem after the captivity. 1 Chron. 9:15. [6] A descendant of Kohath. 1 Chron. 26:1.

A-sar´e-el (*God is joined*), a descendant of Judah. 1 Chron. 4:16.

As-a-re'lah (*Jehovah is joined*), a musician. 1 Chron. 25:2. Called JESHAR-ELAH in 1 Chron. 25:14.

As'ca-lon. See ASHKELON.

As'e-nath (*favorite of Neith*), the wife of Joseph and daughter of Poti-pherah, an Egyptian priest. She was the mother of Ephraim and Manasseh. Gen. 41:45, 50; 46:20.

A'ser, Luke 2:36; Rev. 7:6, is the Greek form of ASHER. See ASHER.

Ash, a tree mentioned in Isa. 44:14, is supposed to be a variety of the pine. The true ash is not a native of Palestine.

A'shan (*smoke*), a city in the plain of Judah. Josh. 15:42; 1 Chron. 6:59. Ashan assigned to Simeon may be a different place. Josh. 19:7; 1 Chron. 4:32.

Ash'be-a (*I adjure*), a name in 1 Chron. 4:21. It is probably the name of a person; if of a place, it should be Beth-ashbea.

Ash'bel (*man of Baal*), a son of Benjamin, ancestor of the Ashbelites. Gen. 46:21; Num. 26:38.

Ashchenaz, ash'ke-naz. 1 Chron. 1:6; Jer. 51:27. See ASHKENAZ.

Ash'dod (*fortress*) or **A-zo'tus** was a stronghold of the Philistines, who defeated the people of Israel in Samuel's time and captured the ark of the covenant, which they took to the temple of Dagon in Ashdod. The place is called AZOTUS in the New Testament.
Josh. 11:22; 15:46, 47.
1 Sam. 5:1, 3, 5-7; 6:17.
2 Chron. 26:6.
Neh. 13:23, 24.
Isa. 20:1.
Jer. 25:20.
Amos 1:8; 3:9.
Zeph. 2:4.
Zech. 9:6
Acts 8:40.

Ash'doth-ites or **Ash'dod-ites**, inhabitants of Ashdod. Josh. 13:3; Neh. 4:7.

Ashdoth-pisgah, ash'doth-piz'gah (*springs of Pisgah*), a place or valley near Mount Pisgah. Deut. 3:17; 4:49; Josh. 12:3; 13:20. See SPRING.

Ash'er (*happy*). [1] The eighth son of Jacob. [2] One of the twelve tribes. See TRIBES. [3] A territory about sixty miles long, extending from Carmel to Lebanon, and from ten to twelve miles wide. The Phœnicians retained the plain by the sea, and Asher occupied the mountains. Josh. 19:24-31; Judg. 1:31, 32. [4] A town on the border of Ephraim and Manasseh. Josh. 17:7.
Gen. 30:13; 35:26; 46:17; 49:20.
Exod. 1:4.
Num. 1:13, 40, 41; 2:27; 7:72; 10:26; 13:13; 26:44, 46, 47; 34:27.
Deut. 27:13; 33:24.
Josh. 17:10, 11; 19:34; 21:6, 30.
Judg. 5:17; 6:35; 7:23.
1 Kings 4:16.
1 Chron. 2:2; 6:62, 74; 7:30, 40; 12:36.
2 Chron. 30:11.
Ezek. 48:2, 3, 34.

Ash'e-rah. See ASHTORETH.

Ash'er-ites, a name of the tribe of Asher. Judg. 1:32.

Ash'es. Ps. 102:9. This word is often used in the Bible in connection with SACKCLOTH (which see), and signifies penitence and grief. The ashes of a red heifer were used in ceremonial purification. Num. 19:17, 18; Heb. 9:13. See HEIFER.

Ash'i-ma, a god of the men of Hamath in Samaria. 2 Kings 17:30.

Ash'ke-lon or **As'ke-lon**, one of the five principal Philistine cities, was a seaport on the Mediterranean, about ten miles north of Gaza. It was captured by Judah, Judg. 1:18, and visited by Samson.

Judg. 14:19. It was the birthplace of Herod the Great and the seat of worship of the goddess Astarte. It was ruined in A. D. 1270 by Sultan Bibars, who filled its harbor with stones. Ruins abound there, and near them is the village of *Jûrah.*
Also see 1 Sam. 6:17.
2 Sam. 1:20.
Jer. 25:20; 47:5, 7.
Amos 1:8.
Zeph. 2:4, 7.
Zech. 9:5.

Ash´ke-naz (*strong*), the home of a tribe of the same name, probably in Armenia. In 1 Chron. 1:6; Jer. 51:27 it is called ASHCHENAZ.

Ash´ke-naz, Gen. 10:3, son of Gomer, and probable ancestor of the inhabitants of the country of the same name. Jer. 51:27. See MINNI.

Ash´nah (*fortification*). [1] A town of Judah, about sixteen miles north-west of Jerusalem. Josh. 15:33. [2] A town of Judah, sixteen miles south-west of Jerusalem. Josh. 15:43.

Ash´pe-naz, the master of the eunuchs of Nebuchadnezzar. He was very kind to Daniel and his three companions. Dan. 1:3.

Ash´ri-el (*vow of God*). See ASRIEL.

Ash´ta-roth or **As´ta-roth**. [1] A city of Bashan. It was east of the Jordan. Deut. 1:4; Josh. 9:10. Same as BEESHTERAH. Josh. 21:27. [2] An idol. See ASHTORETH.

Ash´te-rath-ite, an inhabitant of Ashtaroth, east of Jordan. 1 Chron. 11:44.

Ash´te-roth-Kar´na-im, an ancient city of the Rephaim, or giants. Gen. 14:5.

Ash´to-reth or **Ash´ta-roth**, a Syrian goddess whose worship was very ancient. It was common even among the Israelites. She is generally mentioned in connection with Baal, and is commonly identified with Astarte, the goddess of the moon.

See BAAL.

Ash´ur (*black*), father of Tekoa; that is to say, the founder of that city. 1 Chron. 2:24; 4:5.

Ash´ur-ites, a tribe occupying the whole country west of the Jordan, above Jezreel. They were descendants of Ashur. Ezek. 27:6.

Ash´vath, an Asherite. 1 Chron. 7:33.

A´sia, the largest of the continents, comprises nearly one-third of the land of the globe. The word *Asia* in the Bible refers to only a small part of the *continent* of Asia; in some instances to the whole of what is now known as *Asia Minor*, which lies between the Black Sea and the Mediterranean, but usually to only the western part of that country, namely, the region of which Ephesus was the chief city. The word *Asia* is used only in the New Testament.

A´si-el (*God is doer*), a Simeonite. 1 Chron. 4:35.

As´ke-lon. Judg. 1 18. See ASHKELON.

As´nah (*dweller in the thorn-bush*), one of the Nethinims. Ezra 2:50.

As-nap´per (*Asnap the great*), an Assyrian ruler who settled his people in the cities of Samaria. Ezra 4:10.

Asp, a serpent whose poison is deadly and very sudden in its operation. It is identified by modern naturalists with a species of hooded viper found in Egypt. On the Egyptian monuments it is a sacred and royal emblem, the sign of the protecting divinity.

As´pa-tha, the third son of Haman. Esther 9:7.

As´ri-el (*God is joined*), son of Gilead and founder of the Asrielites. Num. 26:31; Josh. 17:2; 1 Chron. 7:14.

Ass, one of the most common animals mentioned in the Bible, is found wild in Mesopotamia, and was introduced into

Palestine by Abraham. Asses were an important part of the wealth of ancient times. The ass and the ox were the principal beasts of burden among the Hebrews. Kings, judges, and prophets rode on the large Babylonian ass, an animal of a higher breed and very spirited. Judg. 12:14. The white variety was most prized. Judg. 5:10. Christ rode into Jerusalem on an ass. Zech. 9:9; Matt. 21:5. The wild ass is found in droves in desolate places in Asia, and is very shy and swift. Job 39:5; Jer. 2:24. It is seldom found now in Palestine.

As-say´, in Job. 4:2, means attempt.

As´shur, the second son of Shem. Gen. 10:22. He founded Assyria. Gen. 10:10, 11. See Assyria.

As´shur, a Hebrew form of Assyria. In the prophecies and historical books it refers to Assyria.

As-shu´rim, descendants of Dedan, grandson of Abraham. Gen. 25:3.

As´sir (*prisoner*). [1] A Levite, the son of Korah. Exod. 6:24; 1 Chron. 6:22. [2] A son of Ebiasaph. 1 Chron. 6:23, 37. [3] A son of Jeconiah. 1 Chron. 3:17.

As´sos or **As´sus**, also called Apollonia, a seaport of Mysia in Asia Minor, on the north shore of the Gulf of Adramyttium. Acts 20:13, 14. It is now desolate.

As´sur. Ezra 4:2; Ps. 83:8. See Assyria.

Asswaged, as-swajd´, in Job 16:6, means assuaged; eased.

As-syr´ia, the second of the four great Asiatic monarchies, was founded by Asshur, Gen. 10:10, 11, and peopled from Babylon. The mother-country, Assyria proper, corresponds nearly to the present Kurdistan, stretching west from the frontier of Persia to the Euphrates. But at the height of its power it comprised the whole of western Asia and parts of north-eastern Africa. The first Assyrian king mentioned in the Bible is Pul, who invaded Israel under the reign of Menakem and levied a heavy tribute. 2 Kings 15:19. The next is Tiglath-pileser, who aided Judah in its war against Israel and Syria. 2 Kings 16:7-9. The third is Shalmaneser, who under the reign of Hoshea took Samaria, B. C. 721, carried the Israelites away into captivity, and repeopled the country with Assyrian colonists. It is, however, first after that time that Assyria became a great empire. Under Sennacherib, B. C. 704-682, Egypt, Philistia, Armenia, Media, and Edom were conquered. But immediately after his defeat before Jerusalem, 2 Kings 19:35-37, the downfall seems to have begun, and in B. C. 625 the empire was overthrown by the Medes and Babylonians, and Nineveh, its capital, was destroyed. The Assyrians were of Shemitic origin, and during the last forty years excavations about Nineveh have shown that they were possessed of a civilization which in many respects surpassed even that of Egypt. Their language they had derived from Chaldea, and they put it into writing by means of some peculiar arrow-headed, wedge-shaped, cuneiform characters. Thousands and thousands of clay tablets, covered with inscriptions in those characters, have been dug up from the mounds of Nineveh, and they confirm the truth of the Bible narrative down to minute details. See Nineveh.

As´ta-roth. See Ashtaroth.

As-tar´te. See Ashtoreth.

As-ton´ied, Job 17:8, is an old form of the word astonished.

As-trol´o-gers pretended to prophesy future events by observations on the stars, which they fancied had an influence either good or bad upon human affairs. Isa. 47:13; Dan. 2:2, 27.

As-tron´o-my treats of the motions and appearances of the heavenly bodies, and also of their constitution. It was much studied in Asia in ancient times. The Chaldeans were proficient in it. The Hebrews seem to have had little knowledge of astronomy. Several heavenly bodies are mentioned in the Bible; for instance, in Isa. 14:12; Rev. 2:28; Job 9:9; 38:31.

A-sup´pim, in 1 Chron. 26:15, 17, means either the chambers of the Temple or some apartments of it where the stores were kept. It is translated *thresholds* in Neh. 12:25.

A-syn´cri-tus (*incomparable*), one whom Paul saluted. Rom. 16:14.

A´ tad (*thorn-bush*), a Canaanite who had a threshing-floor near the cave of Machpelah, where those who came from Egypt with the body of Jacob seemed to have halted, and which was called by the inhabitants ABEL-MIZRAIM (which see). Gen. 50:10, 11.

At´a-rah (*crown*), wife of Jerahmeel. 1 Chron. 2:26.

At´a-roth (*crowns*). [1] A town of Gad, east of Jordan, Num. 32:3, 34, now *Attarus*, a ruin. [2] A town of Ephraim. Josh. 16:2. It may be same as ATAROTH-ADAR and ATAROTH-ADDAR. Josh. 18:13. [3] Ataroth, the house of Joab, is found in the genealogy of Judah. 1 Chron. 2:54.

At´a-roth-ad´dar. See ATAROTH, No. 2.

A´ter (*lame*). [1] An Israelite whose descendants returned to Jerusalem after the captivity. Ezra 2:16; Neh. 7:21. [2] Head of a family whose descendants returned after the captivity. Ezra 2:42; Neh. 7:45.

Athach, a´thak (*inn*), a city of Judah. 1 Sam. 30:30.

Ath-a-i´ah (*Jehovah is helper*), a man of Judah. Neh. 11:4.

Ath-a-li´ah (*Jehovah is strong*).

[1] Daughter of Jezebel. She became the wife of Jehoram, king of Judah, and ruled in Judah after the death of her son Ahaziah. 2 Kings 8:26; 11:3. [2] Son of Jeroham, a Benjamite. 1 Chron. 8:26. [3] Father of Jeshaiah. Ezra 8:7. Also see 2 Kings 11:1, 2, 13, 14, 20. 2 Chron. 22:2, 10-12; 23:12, 13, 21; 24:7.

Ath´ens, capital of Attica, was the most celebrated city of ancient Greece. It was founded B. C. 1566, and was subsequently named from the goddess Minerva or Athene that was worshipped there. Athens is on the Saronic Gulf, forty-six miles east of Corinth, and was the perfection of ancient civilization, but given to idolatry. The apostle Paul preached there. Acts 17:22. It contained the AREOPAGUS (which see). Athens began to decline toward the end of the sixth century of the Christian era. In A. D. 1834 it became the capital of the new kingdom of Greece. It has a good harbor (now Drâko), the ancient Piræus, and a population of over eighty thousand. Acts 17:15, 16, 22; 18:1; 1 Thess. 3:1.

A-the´ni-ans, inhabitants of Athens. Acts 17:21.

Ath´lai (*Jehovah is strong*), a Jew of the family of Bebai. Ezra 10:28.

At one, in Acts 7:26, means reconciliation of two persons, and from those two words are derived "atone" (to reconcile), and "at-one-ment," or atonement.

A-tone´ment, the expiation of sin made by the obedience and sufferings of Christ.

A-tone´ment, Day of. Lev. 16; 23:27-32, the annual day of humiliation, and the only Jewish fast-day by the Mosaic law, was kept five days before the Feast of Tabernacles, or on the tenth day of Tisri, which was early in October.

At´roth (*crowns*) or "At´roth-

Sho´phan," Num. 32:35, was a city of Gad, near Dibon.

At´tai (*seasonable*). [1] Grandson of Sheshan. 1 Chron. 2:35. [2] A Gadite. 1 Chron. 12:11. [3] Son of Rehoboam. 2 Chron. 11:20.

At-ta-li´a, a seaport of Pamphilia, Acts 14:25, named from its founder, Attalus. It is now *Adalia*.

At-ten´dance, in 1 Tim. 4:13, means attention.

At-tent´, in 2 Chron. 6:40, means attentive.

Au-gus´tus (*venerable*), title of Octavius, who became emperor of Rome after the death of Julius Cæsar. Luke 2:1. In Acts 25:21-25 Nero is meant.

A´va (*ruin*), a district near Babylon. Its inhabitants were taken to Samaria in place of captive Jews. 2 Kings 17:24.

A´ven (*vanity*). [1] Egyptian city of ON, or Heliopolis. Ezek. 30:17. [2] A plain, probably of Lebanon. Amos 1:5. [3] Same as BETH-AVEN. Hos. 10:5, 8. See BAALBEC.

A-ven´ger of Blood, a person who pursued a murderer or a manslayer, by virtue of the ancient Jewish law, to avenge the blood of one who had been murdered or slain. Deut. 19:6; Josh. 20:3. See CITIES OF REFUGE.

A´vims or A´vites (*villagers*). [1] A tribe of the Philistines. Deut. 2:23; Josh. 13:3. [2] A city of Benjamin. Josh. 18:23. [3] A tribe transported to Samaria. 2 Kings 17:31.

A´vith, a city of Edom. Gen. 36:35; 1 Chron. 1:46.

A-void´, in 1 Sam. 18:11, means to retire or escape.

A-way´ with, in Isa. 1:13, means put up with, or endure.

A´zal (*declivity*), a place near Jerusalem. Zech. 14:5.

Az-a-li´ah (*Jehovah is noble*), father of Shaphan the scribe. 2 Kings 22:3; 2 Chron. 34:8.

Az-a-ni´ah (*Jehovah is hearer*), father of Jeshua the Levite. Neh. 10:9.

A-zar´e-el or A-zar´a-el (*God is helper*). [1] An Aaronite. 1 Chron. 12:6. [2] A Levite musician in the time of David. 1 Chron. 25:18. He is called UZZIEL in 1 Chron. 25:4. [3] A prince of Dan. 1 Chron 27:22. [4] A Jew who took a foreign wife. Ezra 10:41. [5] A priest of the family of Immer. Neh. 11:13; 12:36.

Az-a-ri´ah (*Jehovah is keeper*). [1] A descendant of Zadok. He was high-priest during the reign of Solomon. 1 Kings 4:2; 1 Chron. 6:9. [2] A chief officer of Solomon. 1 Kings 4:5. [3] A king of Judah, 2 Kings 14:21, generally called UZZIAH (which see). [4] Son of Ethan. 1 Chron. 2:8. [5] The son of Jehu, son of Obed. 1 Chron. 2:38, 39. [6] The son of Johanan, and high-priest under Abijah and Asa. 1 Chron. 6:10, 11. [7] In 1 Chron. 6:13 the name is probably wrongly inserted. [8] A Kohathite who was ancestor of Samuel. 1 Chron. 6:36. [9] A prophet who induced Asa to abolish idolatry. 2 Chron. 15:1. [10 and 11] Sons of King Jehoshaphat. 2 Chron. 21:2. [12] In 2 Chron. 22:6, by error of copyist, for Ahaziah. [13] A captain of Judah. 2 Chron. 23:1. [14] The high-priest in the reign of Uzziah. 2 Kings 14:21; 2 Chron. 26:17-20. [15] An Ephraimite chief. 2 Chron. 28:12. [16 and 17] Two Levites in the time of Hezekiah. 2 Chron. 29:12. [18] High-priest in the time of Hezekiah. 2 Chron. 31:10, 13. [19] One who helped repair the wall of Jerusalem. Neh. 3:23, 24. [20] A leader in Zerubbabel's company. Neh. 7:7. [21] A Levite who aided Ezra in the reading of the law. Neh. 8:7. [22] A priest who sealed the covenant. Neh. 10:2. He may be same with

Azariah who aided in dedicating the city wall. Neh. 12:33. [23] In Jer. 43:2, instead of Jezaniah. [24] The Hebrew original name of Abednego. Dan. 1:6, etc.

A´zaz (*strong*), father of a chief of Reuben. 1 Chron. 5:8.

Az-a-zi´ah (*Jehovah is strong*). [1] A Levite musician. 1 Chron. 15:21. [2] Father of Hoshea, the prince of Ephraim. 1 Chron. 27:20. [3] A Levite who had oversight of dedicated things. 2 Chron. 31:13.

Az´buk (*pardon*), father of Nehemiah (not the governor). Neh. 3:16.

A-ze´kah, a city in the north-west of Judah. Josh. 10:10; Jer. 34:7.

A´zel (*noble*), a Benjamite of the family of Saul. 1 Chron. 8:37; 9:43.

A´zem (*fortress*), a city in the south of Judah, Josh. 15:29, afterward a city of Simeon. 19:3. Same as EZEM in 1 Chron. 4:29.

Az´gad (*worship*). [1] A Jew, some of whose posterity returned from Babylon after the captivity. Ezra 2:12; Neh. 7:17. [2] A chief who sealed the covenant. Neh. 10:15.

A´zi-el (*God is might*), a Levite in the choral service of the Tabernacle. 1 Chron. 15:20. Shortened form of JAAZIEL. 1 Chron. 15:18.

A-zi´za (*strong*), a Jew who took a foreign wife. Ezra 10:27.

Az´ma-veth (*strong unto death*). [1] Probably a place in Benjamin, Ezra 2:24; Neh. 12:29, called also BETH-AZMAVETH. Neh. 7:28. [2] One of David's valiant men. 2 Sam. 23:31; 1 Chron. 11:33. [3] A descendant of Jonathan. 1 Chron. 8:36; 9:42. [4] A Benjamite. 1 Chron. 12:3. [5] A treasurer of David. 1 Chron. 27:25.

Az´mon (*fortress*), a place in the south-west of Palestine. Num. 34:4; Josh. 15:4.

Az´noth-ta´bor (*peaks of Tabor*), a place in Naphtali. Josh. 19:34.

A´zor (*a helper*), an ancestor of Christ. Mat. 1:13, 14.

A-zo´tus. Acts 8:40. See ASHDOD.

Az´ri-el (*God is helper*). [1] Head of a family of Manasseh. 1 Chron. 5:24. [2] Father of a ruler of Naphtali. 1 Chron. 27:19. [3] Father of Seraiah. Jer. 36:26.

Az´ri-kam (*my help has risen*). [1] Son of Neariah. 1 Chron. 3:23. [2] Son of Azel. 1 Chron. 8:38; 9:44. [3] A Levite. 1 Chron. 9:14; Neh. 11:15. [4] Governor of the house of Ahaz. 2 Chron. 28:7.

Az-u´bah (*forsaken*). [1] Mother of Jehoshaphat. 1 Kings 22:42; 2 Chron. 20:31. [2] Wife of Caleb. 1 Chron. 2:18, 19.

A´zur (*helper*). [1] Father of Hananiah, the false prophet of Gibeon. Jer. 28:1. [2] Father of Jaazaniah. Ezek. 11:1.

Az´zah (*fortress*). Deut. 2:23; Jer. 25:20. Same as GAZA (which see).

Az´zan (*very strong*), father of Paltiel. Num. 34:26.

Az´zur (*helper*), a Jew who sealed the covenant of Nehemiah. Neh. 10:17.

B

Ba´al or Ba´al-im (*master*), the chief male deity of the Phœnicians and Canaanites, as Ashtoreth was their principal female deity. [1] An idol of the Phœnicians and Tyrians. The worship of Baal, together with that of Astarte, was common among the Hebrews. The Babylonians worshipped Baal under the name of BEL. Human sacrifices were offered to Baal by the Jews. See Jer. 19:5. [2] A city of Simeon. 1 Chron. 4:33. [3] A descendant of Reuben. 1 Chron. 5:5. [4] A descendant of Benjamin. 1 Chron. 8:30; 9:36. In connection with other words, Baal denotes local idols, or some reference to them.

Also see Num. 22:41.

Judg. 2:11, 13; 3:7; 6:25, 28, 30-32; 8:33; 10:6, 10.

1 Sam. 7:4; 12:10.

1 Kings 16:31, 32; 18:18, 19, 21, 22, 25, 26, 40; 19:18; 22:53.

2 Kings 3:2; 10:18-23, 25-28; 11:18; 17:16; 21:3; 23:4, 5.

2 Chron. 17:3; 23:17; 24:7; 28:2; 33:3; 34:4.

Jer. 2:8, 23; 7:9; 9:14; 11:13, 17; 12:16; 23:13, 27; 32:29, 35.

Hos. 2:8, 13, 17; 11:2; 13:1.

Zeph. 1:4.

Rom. 11:14.

Ba′al-ah (*possessor*). **[1]** A name sometimes given to KIRJATH-JEARIM. Josh. 15:9; 1 Chron. 13:6. **[2]** A hill of Judah. Josh. 15:11. **[3]** A city of Judah. Josh. 15:29. Probably same as BALAH, Josh. 19:3, and BAAL in 1 Chron. 4:33.

Ba′al-ath (*belonging to Baal*), a town of Dan. Josh. 19:44; 2 Chron. 8:6.

Ba′al-ath-be′er (*lady of the well*), a city of Simeon. Josh. 19:8. See BEALOTH.

Baalbec or **Baalbek**, bahl-bek′, an ancient and magnificent city of Syria, was about forty miles north-west of Damascus. Nothing is known of its origin and early history. Its ruins are stupendous and wonderful. They include the remains of three beautiful temples, including the great temple of the sun. It was called by the Greeks HELIOPOLIS (*city of the sun*).

Ba′al-be′rith (*lord of the covenant*), an idol worshipped by the Israelites. Judg. 8:33; 9:4.

Ba′ale of Ju′dah (*possessors in Judah*), a place in Judah. 2 Sam. 6:2.

Another name for KIRJATH-JEARIM. See BAALAH, No. 1.

Ba′al-gad (*lord of fortune*), a town in the valley of Lebanon. Josh. 11:17; 13:5. Probably the modern *Banias*.

Ba′al-ha′mon (*lord of the multitude*), a place in Samaria. Song of Sol. 8:11.

Ba′al-ha′nan (*the lord is gracious*). **[1]** The seventh of the ancient kings of Edom. Gen. 36:38; 1 Chron. 1:50. **[2]** Superintendent of olive and sycamore trees under David. 1 Chron. 27:28.

Ba′al-ha′zor (*lord of Hazor*), a city of Benjamin, where Absalom killed Amnon. 2 Sam. 13:23.

Ba′al-her′mon (*lord of Hermon*), a town near Mount Hermon. Judg. 3:3; 1 Chron. 5:23.

Ba′al-i (*my lord*), a title rejected by the Lord. Hos. 2:16.

Ba′al-im, plural form of BAAL (which see).

Ba′a-lis (*lord of joy*), a king of the Ammonites. Jer. 40:14.

Ba′al-me′on (*lord of the habitation*), a city of Reuben, Num. 32:38; Ezek. 25:9, called also BETH-BAAL-MEON, Josh. 13:17, BETH-MEON, Jer. 48:23 and perhaps BEON. Num. 32:3.

Ba′al-pe′or (*lord of the opening*), an idol of the Moabites and the Israelites. Num. 25:3; Hos. 9:10. It is often called PEOR.

Ba′al-per′a-zim (*lord of breaches*), a place where David defeated the Philistines. 2 Sam. 5:20; 1 Chron. 14:11.

Ba′al-shal′i-sha (*lord of Shalisha*), a town of Ephraim. 2 Kings 4:42.

Ba′al-ta′mar (*lord of the palm*), a place in the land of Benjamin. Judg. 20:33.

Ba′al-ze′bub (*lord of the fly*), an idol of the Philistines. 2 Kings 1:2.

Ba′al-ze′phon (*lord of Typhon*), a

place on the border of Egypt, near the Red Sea. Exod. 14:2; Num. 33:7.

Ba´a-na or **Ba´a-nah** (*son of grief*). [1] A provider for Solomon. 1 Kings 4:12. [2] Another provider for Solomon. 1 Kings 4:16. [3] Father of Zadok. Neh. 3:4.

Ba´a-nah (*son of grief*). [1] The father of one of David's valiant men. 2 Sam. 23:29; 1 Chron. 11:30. [2] One of Ish-bosheth's captains. 2 Sam. 4:2, 5, 6, 9. [3] An Israelite who returned from Babylon. Ezra 2:2; Neh. 7:7. [4] Perhaps same as No. 3. Neh. 10:27.

Ba´a-ra (*daughter of the fresh*), a wife of Shaharaim. 1 Chron. 8:8.

Baaseiah, ba-a-se´yah (*Jehovah is bold*), a descendant of Gershom. 1 Chron. 6:40.

Ba´a-sha (*boldness*), a man of Issachar, and third king of Israel. He slew all the descendants of Jeroboam I. 1 Kings 15:16, 27; 16:3-11.

Ba´bel (*confusion*), a city in the plain of Shinar, which formed part of the dominions of Nimrod. Gen. 10:10; 11:9. See BABYLON.

Ba´bel, the Tow´er of, Gen. 11:4, 5, was destroyed, according to old Jewish tradition. Nevertheless, the captive Jews at Babylon thought that they recognized it in the famous temple of Belus, a huge mound about two hundred and fifty feet high and twenty-three hundred feet in circumference, situated west of Hillah, on the Euphrates. In this mound, consisting of bricks twelve inches square by four inches thick, it is easy to trace the outlines of a pyramidal or tower-like construction rising in terraces.

Bab´y-lon (*confusion*), the Greek form of the Hebrew word BABEL, is the name of an ancient kingdom and of its capital. The kingdom of Babylon comprised originally only an area of about thirty thousand square miles, situated in the lowlands around and between the Euphrates and the Tigris, and between Chaldea on the south and Assyria on the north. It was inhabited by a mixed population, half Chaldean and half Assyrian in its origin, and noted for its subtle wisdom, its commercial eagerness, its luxury, and its military valor. Babylonian civilization was very old, dating back more than two thousand years before our era. But the splendor of the Babylonian Empire was very short-lived, beginning with the fall of Nineveh, B C. 625, reaching its greatest power under Nebuchadnezzar, and becoming a province of Persia in B. C. 538. Of the four great monarchies of Asia, it occupies the third place, preceded by Chaldea and Assyria and succeeded by Persia. During this period the empire comprised, besides Babylonia proper, the provinces of Susiana, with the great city of Susa, Syria, Palestine, Phœnicia, Idumæa, and Lower Egypt. The principal cities of Babylonia proper were Babylon, Sippara, or Sepharvaim, Isa. 36:19. Cuthah, 2 Kings 17:24, etc.

Bab´y-lon, the Cit´y of, was the capital both of the Chaldean and of the Babylonian empires. It was built on both sides of the Euphrates River, about two hundred miles above its junction with the Tigris and three hundred miles from the Persian Gulf. According to the description of the Greek historian Herodotus, who had seen it himself, it was one of the largest and most magnificent cities which ever existed, fifty-six miles in circumference and covering an area of about two hundred square miles (London covers only one hundred and twenty-two square miles). Among its wonders were Nebuchadnezzar's palace, the temple of Belus, the hanging gardens, etc. It was founded by Nimrod, Gen. 10:10, taken by Cyrus, and again by Alexander the Great, and gradually fell into ruins so utterly that only "the wild beasts of the desert" came to lie down there. It is mentioned over two hundred and fifty times in the Bible, often with wonder and admiration, and often, too, as the doomed city. During the captivity it was the residence of the richest and most distinguished prisoners among the Jews, Dan. 1:1-4, and for a long time after the captivity it was one of the principal centers of Jewish learning and rabbinical lore. Its ruins are very extensive. The inscriptions upon its bricks confirm in many ways the statements of the Bible concerning it. See BABYLON, and BABYLONISH CAPTIVITY. The modern town of *Hillah* occupies part of the site of ancient Babylon.

Bab´ylon, mentioned in Rev. 14:8; 16:19, etc., is a symbolical name for heathen Rome. Reference is also made to Babylon in 1 Pet. 5:13. Various opinions are held concerning the place referred to.

Bab-y-lo´ni-ans (*sons of Babel*), inhabitants of Babylonia. Ezra 4:9; Ezek. 23:23.

Bab-y-lo´nish, anything belonging to the place where Babylon was. Josh. 7:21.

Bab-y-lo´nish Cap-tiv´i-ty. See CAPTIVITY.

Baca, ba´kah (*weeping*), a valley near Jerusalem. Its exact location is very uncertain, Ps. 84:6, the allusion here being to the joy of the worshippers going up to Jerusalem.

Bachrites, bak´rites, descendants of Becher, the son of Ephraim. Num. 26:35.

Badger, baj´er, a small burrowing animal of the bear kind, said to be plentiful in Palestine, but not found in Arabia. The outer covering of the Tabernacle was of "badgers' skins," which some suppose were the skins of a kind of seal found in the Red Sea. Various opinions are held concerning them. Exod. 25:5; Ezek. 16:10.

Bags were made of various sizes, and sometimes contained certain sums of money for which they passed current when the seal was not broken. 2 Kings 12:10. Bag is the translation of several entirely different words.

Ba-ha´ru-mite refers to one of David's valiant men. 1 Chron. 11:33. He is elsewhere called "the Barthumite."

Ba-hu´rim (*low grounds*), a town of Benjamin. 2 Sam. 3:16; 1 Kings 2:8.

Ba´jith (*house*) is in one place untranslated and used as the name of a place, although it may mean the idol temple of the Moabites. Isa. 15:2.

Bak-bak´kar (*diligent searcher*), a Levite. 1 Chron. 9:15.

Bak´buk (*waste*), a Nethinim whose descendants returned from Babylon. Ezra 2:51; Neh. 7:53.

Bak-bu-ki´ah (*wasted by Jehovah*), a Levite, leader in the temple worship. Neh. 11:17; 12:25.

Ba´ker. Among the ancient Hebrews baking was done in various ways; when for the family, the women usually did it. Gen. 18:6; 1 Sam. 8:13. There were public ovens in large towns in Eastern countries, and the bakers occupied a particular street. Jer. 37:21. Pharaoh had his chief baker. Gen. 40:2. See OVENS.

Balaam, ba´lam or ba´la-am (*glutton*), a prophet, a native of Mesopotamia, whom Balak, king of Moab, enticed by promise of great reward to come from a place near the Euphrates River to curse Israel when they were encamped on the plains of Moab. He seems to have been a worshipper of the one God. See his histo-

ry in Num. 22, 23, 24, 31. The Lord constrained him to bless Israel. The prophecies of Balaam are among the most remarkable in the Bible. Also see Deut. 23:4, 5.
Josh. 13:22; 24:9, 10.
Neh. 13:2.
Mic. 6:5.
2 Pet. 2:15.
Jude 11.
Rev. 2:14.

Ba´lac. Rev. 2:14. See BALAK.

Bal´a-dan (*having power*), father of Merodach- (or Berodach-) baladan. 2 Kings 20:12; Isa. 39:1.

Ba´lah (*withered*), a shorter form of BAALAH, a town of Simeon (called BILHAH in 1 Chron. 4:29). Josh. 19:3.

Ba´lak (*empty*), the king of Moab who hired Baalam to curse Israel.
Num. 22:2, 4, 7, 10, 13-16, 18, 35-41; 24:10, 12, 13, 25.
Josh. 24:9.
Judg. 11:25.
Mic. 6:5.

Bal´ance. Job 31:6. The balance is represented on Egyptian monuments. It was used to weigh money before coinage commenced. Gen. 23:16; 43:21.

Bald´ness, among the Israelites, was often treated with contempt, as it excited suspicion of leprosy. When voluntary, it was a sign of great distress. Ezek. 7:18. Natural baldness seems to have been uncommon.

Balm or **Bal´sam** was found in Judæa, especially in Gilead. The true balsam tree grows chiefly between Mecca and Medina in Arabia. Its gum is sometimes called the balm of Mecca. It is very costly and fragrant, and is used in the East as a medicine and as a cosmetic. Gen. 37:25; Jer. 8:22; 46:11. The balm-of-Gilead tree

of the United States is a different tree.

Ba´mah (*high place*), used by Ezekiel as the name of the place or places where the Israelites offered sacrifices to idols. Ezek. 20:29.

Ba´moth (*high places*), a city on the river Arnon. It is supposed to be the same place called BAMOTH-BAAL in Josh. 13:17. Num. 21:19, 20.

Ba´moth-ba´al (*high places of Baal*), a town of Moab; was afterward a city of Reuben. Josh. 13:17. Probably same place which is called, in Num. 21, BAMOTH.

Band, in Acts 10:1, means a body of Roman soldiers from Italy. A band was the tenth part of a legion, and contained from four hundred to six hundred men. Matt. 27:27; Acts 21:31.

Bands, the name applied by the prophet Zechariah to one of the two staves which symbolized the Lord's covenant with the seed of Jacob, and the brotherhood of Israel and Judah. Zech. 11:7, 14.

Ba´ni (*posterity*). [1] One of David's valiant men. 2 Sam. 23:36. [2] A descendant of Merari. 1 Chron. 6:46. [3] A descendant of Pharez. 1 Chron. 9:4. [4] An Israelite whose descendants returned from Babylon. Ezra 2:10; 10:29. In the parallel place in Neh. 7 the name given is BINNUI. [5] An Israelite whose descendants took foreign wives. Ezra 10:34. [6] A descendant of No. 5 who took a foreign wife. Ezra 10:38. [7] A Levite whose son repaired part of the wall of Jerusalem after the coming of Nehemiah. Neh. 3:17; 9:5. [8] A Levite who regulated the devotions of the people. Neh. 9:4; 10:13. [9] A chief man or a family who sealed the covenant of Nehemiah. Neh. 10:14. [10] May be same as No. 7 or No. 8. Neh. 11:22.

Ban´ner, Isa. 13:2, **Stand´ard,** Isa. 49:22, and **En´sign,** Isa. 5:26, probably have the same meaning. Each of the four grand divisions of the army of Israel had a different standard. None of these standards were flags.

Ban´quet, in Esther 7:1, means "to drink." Banquet is also used to denote a feast. See FEAST.

Bap´tism, the application of water as a religious ceremony by which a person is received into the visible Church of Christ, according to the command, Matt. 28:19. It was in use as a religious rite before the ministry of Christ. John baptized in the river Jordan, and the Jews baptized proselytes.

Bap´tist, the designation of John, the forerunner of Christ. Matt. 3:1; Luke 7:28.

Ba-rab´bas (*father's son*), a noted robber and murderer who was in prison when Christ was condemned, and whom the Jews, at the instigation of the priests, preferred to Jesus when Pilate would have released him. Mark 15:7, 11, 15; John 18:40.

Barachel, bar´a-kel (*blessed of God*), father of Elihu. Job 32:2, 6.

Barachiah, bar-a-ki´ah, or **Berechiah,** ber-e-ki´ah (*blessed of Jehovah*), father of the prophet Zechariah. Zech. 1:1, 7. See BERECHIAH, No. 7.

Barachias, bar-a-ki´as. Matt. 23:35. Same as BARACHIAH.

Ba´rak (*lightning*), an Israelite who, at the instigation of Deborah, led the tribes of Zebulun and Naphtali against Sisera, the leader of the Canaanites, and gained a notable victory. Judg. 4:6; 5:1; Heb. 11:32. See DEBORAH.

Bar-ba´ri-an, Bar´bar-ous, uncivilized, a title given to other nations by the Greeks. Acts 28:2, 4; Rom. 1:14.

Barb´ed, in Job 41:7, means fringed, or bearded with projecting points.

Bar-hu´mite (*belonging to young*

men), a name used in regard to one of David's valiant men. 2. Sam. 23:31. The name used in 1 Chron. 11:33 is Baharumite. See BAHURIM.

Ba-ri´ah (*fugitive*), a grandson of Shechaniah. 1 Chron. 3:22.

Bar-je´sus (*son of Joshua*), a false prophet, also called ELYMAS, who withstood Barnabas and Saul at Paphos. Acts 13:6. See SERGIUS PAULUS.

Bar-jo´na (*son of Johanan*), a name applied by Christ to Simon Peter the apostle. Matt. 16:17. See PETER.

Bar´kos (*partly-colored*), a Nethinim whose descendants returned to Jerusalem after the captivity. Ezra 2:53; Neh. 7:55.

Bar´ley was the common food of men, horses, asses, and oxen in Palestine. Oats were unknown. The Hebrews often used barley bread, though it was considered inferior to wheat. Barley was sown in Palestine from November to February, and reaped in March or April. Ruth 1:22; 2 Sam. 17:28.

Bar´na-bas (*son of consolation*), also called JOSES, a Levite and the companion of Paul in several journeys. Acts 4:36; Gal. 2:9. He is regarded by some as the author of the Epistle to the Hebrews.

Barns, in Palestine, were often caves in the rocks, the entrance being carefully concealed to prevent robbery. They were used for grain and other produce, rather than for hay. Caves are still used for this purpose on the hill of Jezreel. Domestic animals often occupy the ground floor of the owner's house in some parts of the East, and the family live in the rooms above. Job 39:12; Prov. 3:10.

Bar´rel, the word in Hebrew generally translated PITCHER. 1 Kings 17:12; 18:33.

Bar´ren-ness was peculiarly lamented in the East, especially among the Jewish women, who hoped for the honor of being the mother of the promised Messiah. Gen. 3:15.

Bar´sa-bas (*son of Saba*). [1] Joseph Barsabas, disciple of the Lord, who was nominated along with Matthias to succeed Judas Iscariot. Acts 1:23. Some consider him as the same person as BARNABAS. [2] Judas Barsabas, a disciple sent with Silas to Antioch. Acts 15:22.

Bar-thol´o-mew (*son of Tolmai*), one of the apostles. Matt. 10:3; Acts 1:13. Some suppose him to have been the same as Nathanael in John 1:45–51, and mentioned among the other apostles in John 21:2.

Bar-ti-mæ´us (*son of Timæus*), a blind beggar of Jericho, who received his sight at the word of Jesus. Mark 10:46.

Baruch, ba´rook (*blessed*). [1] A Jew who rebuilt part of the wall of Jerusalem. Neh. 3:20; 10:6. [2] A descendant of Pharez. Neh. 11:5. [3] A Jew whom Jeremiah the prophet employed as amanuensis when he was in prison. Jer. 32:12; 43:6, 7.

Bar-zil´la-i (*strong*). [1] A Gileadite who helped David when he was fleeing from Absalom. 2 Sam. 17:27; 19:31; 1 Kings 2:7. [2] An Israelite, father of Adriel. 2 Sam. 21:8. [3] A priest whose descendants returned from Babylon with Ezra. Ezra 2:61; Neh. 7:63.

Base, in 1 Cor. 1:28, means lowly; humble.

Ba´shan (*the fruitful*), the kingdom of Og the Amorite, on the east side of Jordan, extending northward from the river Jabbok, is famous, in the Bible, for stately oaks, fine cattle, and rich pastures. Num. 21:33; Deut. 1:4; 32:14.

Ba´shan-ha´voth-ja´ir, a name given by Jair to his villages in Mount Gilead. Deut. 3:14.

Bash´e-math (*fragrant*). [1] A daughter of Elon and wife of Esau. Gen. 26:34. [2] A daughter of Ishmael and wife of Esau. Gen. 36:3, 13.

Ba´sins or **Ba´sons** of various kinds are mentioned in the Bible; namely, a hand-basin, for washing of hands; a covered basin, used in the Sanctuary; the "omer," a common domestic vessel of Egypt, holding half a peck, for cooking; and the foot-basin, in which Christ washed the disciples' feet; probably same as wash-pot in the Psalms. Exod. 24:6; John 13:5.

Bas´kets of various forms, sizes, strength, and structure were used by the Jews, and were generally made of wicker-work, though sometimes of network or of ropework. 2 Kings 10:7; Jer. 24:1; Deut. 26:2; Amos 8:1; Gen. 40:16; 2 Cor. 11:33.

Bas´math (*fragrant*), a daughter of Solomon. 1 Kings 4:15.

Bat, a very common animal in Palestine, especially in the vaults under the Temple and in the caves of Galilee. It is included among the unclean fowls in Lev. 11:19, and among birds in Deut. 14:18.

Bath, the standard Hebrew measure for liquids, contained about seven gallons. 1 Kings 7:26; Isa. 5:10.

Bath´ing was practiced among the Hebrews mainly as a religious ceremony, or as the symbol of cleansing and repentance. In the hot climate of Egypt and in Babylonia it was a necessity, rather than a luxury. Lev. chapters 15, 16, 17; Num. chap. 19. See WASHING.

Bath-rab´bim (*daughter of many*), a gate of the city of Heshbon or a village near it. Song of Sol. 7:4.

Bath-she´ba (*daughter of an oath*), wife of Uriah the Hittite. who became the wife of David and the mother of Solomon. 2 Sam. 11:3; 1 Kings 1:15.

Bath-shua, bath´shoo-a. These words mean "the daughter of Shua," and are so translated in Gen. 38:12 and in 1 Chron. 2:3, but in 1 Chron. 3:5 they are used as the name of the mother of Solomon. She is there called the daughter of Ammiel.

Bat´ter-ing-Ram, an engine of war used to batter down walls in ancient times. It consisted of a long, solid wooden beam, armed at one end with a mass of metal in the shape of a ram's head, and suspended by the middle. The beam was swung repeatedly and with great violence against the wall of a city or fort until a breach was made. This beam was sometimes placed in the base of a wooden tower which was on wheels. About a hundred men were employed in working it. The top of the tower was filled with archers and slingers. 2 Sam. 20:15; Ezek. 4:2.

Bat´tle-axe, a powerful weapon of war. We have no knowledge of its form and manner of use in very ancient times. Jer. 51:20.

Bat´tle-ment, a structure around the flat roofs of Eastern houses to prevent persons from falling off. These roofs were much used for fresh air, retirement, and sleep. The Mosaic law required that a battlement should be built on every new house. Deut. 22:8. Battlements sometimes mean the fortifications of a city. Jer. 5:10.

Bavai, bav´a-i (*wisher*), a Jew who repaired part of the wall of Jerusalem after the coming of Jeremiah. Neh. 3:18.

Bay-tree, mentioned in Psalm 37:35, seems to mean only a green and vigorous native tree. It may have been the laurel, used from very ancient times for triumphal crowns.

Baz´lith or **Baz´luth** (*asking*), a Nethinim whose descendants returned from Babylon. Ezra 2:52; Neh. 7:54.

Bdellium, del´yum, may mean a fragrant gum or a precious stone; perhaps a pearl. Gen. 2:12; Num. 11:7.

Bealiah, be-a-li´ah (*Jehovah is lord*), an Israelite who joined David in Ziklag. 1 Chron. 12:5.

Be´a-loth (*ladies*), the plural feminine form of Baal, is a town of Judah. Josh. 15:24. Probably same as BAALATH-BEER, 19:8, the modern *Kurnub*.

Beans are grown in Palestine, and are still used for food as vegetables, and in flour. 2 Sam. 17:28; Ezek. 4:9.

Bears were common in Palestine, and resembled the common brown bear. They are still found in Galilee, Lebanon, and Mount Hermon. 1 Sam. 17:34; Prov. 17:12.

Beard. The Jews gave much attention to the beard, and regarded it, when long and full, as the noblest ornament of man. Ps. 133:2. To neglect, tear out, or cut off the beard were signs of deep mourning. Ezra 9:3. The Egyptians left a small tuft of beard on the chin. The Jews were forbidden in Lev. 19:27 to imitate this fashion. To be deprived of the beard was a mark of servility and infamy.

Beast. [1] This word is improperly given (in the Authorized Version) as the translation of the term used to designate the "living beings" that were round about the throne in heaven. Rev. 4:6; 6:1. [2] Another word, meaning wild beast, is given in Revelation to the antichristian power (probably heathen Rome). Rev. 11:7; 13:11.

Beat´en work, in Exod. 25:18, means not cast in a mold, but wrought or hammered.

Beauty, bu´ty, the name given by the prophet Zechariah to one of the two staves by which he symbolized the Lord's covenant with the house of Jacob, and the brotherhood of Israel and Judah. Zech. 11:7, 10.

Beb´a-i (*fatherly*). [1]An Israelite some of whose descendants returned from Babylon. Ezra 2:11; Neh. 7:16. [2] Perhaps same as No. 1. A Jew some of whose descendants went up with Ezra from Babylon. Ezra 8:11; 10:28. [3] The name of a family who sealed the covenant made by Nehemiah. Neh. 10:15.

Be-cause´, in Matt. 20:31, means in order that.

Becher, be´ker (*youth*). [1] A son of Benjamin. Gen. 46:21; 1 Chron. 7:6. [2] A son of Ephraim. Num. 26:35. He is called BERED in 1 Chron. 7:20.

Bechorath, be-ko´rath (*first birth*), an ancestor of Saul, the first king of Israel. 1 Sam. 9:1.

Bed, when used in the Bible, refers usually to a mattress like a thick quilt. It was rolled up during the day and spread only at night, often in the open air. The poorer people used skins for beds. Other kinds of beds, often like a low sofa, were used by wealthy people in the East. In Deut. 3:11 the iron bedstead of Og, king of Bashan, is mentioned. Beds are noticed in Exod. 8:3; John 5:11.

Be´dad (*son of Adad*), father of the fourth king of Edom. Gen. 36:35; 1 Chron. 1:46.

Be´dan (*son of judgment*). [1] A judge of the Israelites whose name is not in the book of Judges. 1 Sam. 12:11. It is probably a copyist's error for BARAK. [2] A descendant of Machir. 1 Chron. 7:17.

Bedeiah, be-de´ya (*servant of Jehovah*), a Jew who took a foreign wife. Ezra 10:35.

Bees, well-known insects common in Palestine; not only domesticated, but wild. Deut. 1:44; Matt. 3:4.

Beeliada, be-el-i´a-dah (*the lord knows*), a name given in one list to a son of David. 1 Chron. 14:7, who is called ELIADA in 2 Sam. 5:16; 1 Chron. 3:8.

Beelzebub, be-el´ze-bub (*lord of the fly*), an evil spirit whom the Pharisees called the prince of the devils. Matt. 10:25; Mark 3:22; Luke 11:15.

Be´er (*a wall*). [1] A station of the Israelites on the border of Moab. Num. 21:16. Probably BEER-ELIM. [2] A city of Israel. Judg. 9:21.

Beera, be-e´rah (*expounder*), a son of Zophar. 1 Chron. 7:37.

Beerah, be-e´rah (*expounder*), a prince of the Reubenites. 1 Chron. 5:6.

Be´er-e´lim (*well of Elim*), a place apparently on the border of Moab, Isa. 15:8, and commonly supposed to be same as BEER, No. 1.

Beeri, be-e´ri (*expounder*). [1] Father of Judith. Gen. 26:34. [2] Father of Hosea the prophet. Hos. 1:1.

Be´er-la-hai´roi (*well of the living one that beholds me*), the name of the fountain in the wilderness where the angel of the Lord found Hagar. Gen. 16:7, 14; 25:11.

Beeroth, be-e´roth (*wells*). [1] A station of Israel belonging to Jaakan. Deut. 10:6. Same as BENE-JAAKAN. Num. 33:31. [2] A city of the Hivites. It afterward belonged to Benjamin. Josh. 9:17; Neh. 7:29. See BEER, No. 2.

Beerothite, be-e´roth-ite, or **Be´roth-ite,** a native or inhabitant of Beeroth. 2 Sam. 4:2; 1 Chron. 11:39.

Be´er-she´ba (*well of the oath*), a name which Abraham gave to a well in the southern extremity of Palestine, dug when he and Abimelech swore friendship to each other. Gen. 21:31; Judg. 20:1. The town that was afterward situated here became quite noted. In Judges 20:1 "from Dan even to Beersheba" means the whole length of Palestine. Beersheba was a city of Judah, and afterward of Simeon. It was again occupied by the Jews after the captivity, and continued an important place many centuries after Christ. Neh. 11:27, 30. It is now in ruins.

Beeshterah, be-esh´te-rah (*house of Ashterah*), a Levitical city of Manasseh. Josh. 21:27. Same as ASHTAROTH. 1 Chron. 6:71.

Bee´tle, in Lev. 11:22, means a species of locust.

Beeves, Lev. 22:19, 21, is the ancient plural of *beef*, and, in its modern use, means cattle.

Beg´ging. See POOR.

Be´he-moth, a large beast, Job 40:15, is generally supposed to refer to the hippopotamus.

Be´kah, whether a weight or a coin (probably a piece of uncoined metal), was equal to half a shekel of the sanctuary, and was worth about twenty-seven cents. Exod. 38:26. See MONEY.

Bel (*lord*), the chief idol of the Babylonians. Isa. 46:1; Jer. 51:44. Another form of BAAL (which see).

Be´la or **Be´lah** (*consumption*). [1] A city, otherwise called Zoar, in the vale of Siddim. Gen. 14:2, 8. See ZOAR. [2] The first king of Edom mentioned in the Bible. Gen. 36:32; 1 Chron. 1:44. [3] The eldest son of Benjamin. Num. 26:38, 40; Gen. 46:21; 1 Chron. 7:6. [4] A son of Azaz. 1 Chron. 5:8.

Be´la-ites, descendants of BELA. Num. 26:38.

Be´li-al (*worthless*) is a term applied to vile and profligate persons. It is generally used with "man," "son," "daughter," or "children."
Deut. 13:13.
Judg. 19:22; 20:13.

1 Sam. 1:16; 2:12; 10:27; 25:17, 25; 30:22.
2 Sam. 16:7; 20:1; 23:6.
1 Kings 21:10, 13.
2 Chron. 13:7.
2 Cor. 6:15.

Bell. Small bells are still much used in the East. Bells of gold were fastened to the bottom of the robe of the high-priest, Exod. 28:33, and were attached to horses. Zech. 14:20.

Be-lov´ed, a title of Christ. Eph. 1:6.

Bel-shaz´zar (*Bel's prince*), son of Nebuchadnezzar and the last king of the Chaldeans. Dan. 5. He made an impious feast in Babylon. See DANIEL, and MENE.

Bel-te-shaz´zar (*the lord's leader*), the name given to Daniel when he was carried to Babylon. Dan. 1:7; 5:12. See DANIEL.

Ben (*son*), a Levite in the service of song. 1 Chron. 15:18. The word is a part of many Hebrew names.

Benaiah, be-na´yah (*whom Jehovah has built up*). [1] Son of Jehoiada, the chief priest. 2 Sam. 23:20, 22; 1 Kings 2:29-35. [2] One of David's valiant men. 2 Sam. 23, 30; 1 Chron. 27:14. [3] Head of a family of Simeon. 1 Chron. 4:36. [4] A priest in the service of the Tabernacle. 1 Chron. 15:18, 20; 16:5. [5] A priest in David's reign. 1 Chron. 15:24; 16:6. [6] Grandfather of Jahaziel. 2 Chron. 20:14. [7] A Levite overseer for the Temple. 2 Chron. 31:13 [8, 9, 10, 11] Four Jews who took foreign wives. Ezra 10:25, 30, 35, 43. [12] Father of Pelatiah. Ezek. 11:1, 13.

Ben-am´mi (*son of my people*), son of Lot by his younger daughter. He was the ancestor of the Ammonites. Gen. 19:38.

Ben´e-be´rak (*sons of lightning*), a city of Dan. Josh. 19:45.

Ben-e-fac´tor, a title of honor given to kings. Luke 22:25.

Bene-jaakan, ben´e-ja´a-kan (*sons of Ja-*

akan), the twenty-seventh station of the Israelites in their journey through the wilderness. Num. 33:31, 32. Same as BEEROTH.

Ben-ha´dad (*son of Hadad*), the title of kings of Syria. [1] King of Damascus in the time of Asa, king of Judah. 1 Kings 15:18; 2 Chron. 16:4. [2] A king of Damascus in the time of Ahab. 1 Kings 20:1; 2 Kings 6:24. [3] Son of Hazael. 2 Kings 13:3; Amos 1:4. [4] A general name of kings of Syria who reigned in Damascus. Jer. 49:27.

Ben-ha´il (*valiant*), a prince of Judah. 2 Chron. 17:7.

Ben-ha´nan (*very gracious*), a son of Shimon. 1 Chron. 4:20.

Ben´i-nu (*posterity*), a Levite who sealed the covenant of Nehemiah. Neh. 10:13.

Ben´ja-min (*son of the right hand*). [1] The twelfth and youngest son of Jacob and the second son of Rachel. He was born near Bethlehem B. C. about 1729. His mother, who died soon after his birth, named him Benoni (*son of my sorrow*), but his father gave him the name of Benjamin. He was greatly beloved by his father, who could hardly allow him to go to Egypt with his brethren. Gen. chapters 42 and 43. [2] The tribe of Benjamin had their part of the Promised Land adjoining Judah, and when the ten tribes revolted it became part of the kingdom of Judah. [3] A grandson of Jediael. 1 Chron. 7:10. [4] A descendant of Harim who took a foreign wife. Ezra 10:32. [5] A Jew who repaired part of the wall of Jerusalem. Neh. 3:23. [6] A Jew who took part in the ceremonial purifying of the wall of Jerusalem. Neh. 12:34. [7] A gate of Jerusalem. Jer. 20:2; Zech. 14:10. Also see Gen. 35:18, 24; 44:12; 45:12, 14, 22; 46:19, 21; 49:27.

Exod. 1:3.
Num. 1:11, 36, 37; 2:22; 7:60; 10:24; 13:9; 26:38, 41; 34:21.
Deut. 27:12; 34:12.
Josh. 13:11, 20, 21, 28; 21:4, 17.
Judg. 1:21; 5:14; 10:9; 19:14; 20:3, 4, 10, 12-15, 17, 18, 20, 21, 23-25, 28, 30-32, 35, 36, 39, 41, 44, 46, 48; 21:1, 6, 13-18, 20, 21, 23.
1 Sam. 4:12; 9:1, 16, 21; 10:2, 20, 21; 13:2, 15, 16; 14:16.
2 Sam. 2:9, 15, 25, 31; 3:19; 4:2; 19:17; 21:14; 23:29.
1 Kings 4:18; 12:21, 23; 15:22.
1 Chron. 2:2; 6:60, 65; 7:6; 8:1, 40; 9:3, 7; 11:31; 12:2, 16, 29; 21:6; 27:21.
2 Chron. 11:1, 3, 10, 12, 23; 14:8; 15:2, 8, 9; 17:17; 25:5; 31:1; 34:9, 32.
Ezra 1:5; 4:1; 10:9.
Neh. 11:4, 7, 31, 36.
Pss. 68:27; 80:2.
Jer. 1:1; 6:1; 17:26; 32:8, 44; 33:13; 37:12, 13; 38:7.
Ezek. 48:22-24, 32.
Hos. 5:8.
Obad. :19.
Acts 13:21.
Rom. 11:1.
Phil. 3:5.
Rev. 7:8.

Ben´jam-ite, a person of the tribe of Benjamin. Judg. 19:16; 1 Sam. 9:1. King Saul and Saul of Tarsus were Benjamites.

Be´no (*his son*), son of Jaaziah. 1 Chron. 24:26, 27.

Ben-o´ni (*son of my sorrow*), the name given by Rachel to her second son, Gen. 35:18, afterward called BENJAMIN (which see).

Ben-zo´heth (*strong*), son of Ishi. 1 Chron. 4:20.

Be´on (*lord or house of On*), a city and vicinity. It belonged to Reuben. Num.

32:3. See BAAL-MEON.

Be´or (*shepherd*). [1] Father of Bela, king of Edom. Gen. 36:32; 1 Chron. 1:43. [2] Father of Balaam the prophet. Num. 22:5; Josh. 13:22. He is called BOSOR in 2 Pet. 2:15.

Be´ra (*gift*), a king of Sodom in the time of Abram. Gen. 14:2.

Berachah, ber´a-kah (*blessing*). [1] An Israelite who aided David at Ziklag. 1 Chron. 12:3. [2] A valley of Judah. 2 Chron. 20:26.

Berachiah, ber-a-ki´ah. See BERECHI-AH, No. 2.

Beraiah, ber-a-i´ah (*Jehovah is maker*), a son of Shimhi. 1 Chron. 8:21.

Be-re´a, a city of Macedonia. Paul preached the gospel there with success when he first visited Europe. Acts 17:10-13.

Berechiah, ber-e-ki´ah (*blessed of Jehovah*). [1] A grandson of Pedaiah. 1 Chron. 3:20. [2] Father of Asaph, a chief singer, 1 Chron. 15:17; called BERACHIAH in 1 Chron. 6:39. [3] A Levite near Jerusalem. 1 Chron. 9:16. [4] A doorkeeper for the ark of the covenant in the Tabernacle. 1 Chron. 15:23. [5] An Ephraimite who opposed bringing captives from Judah as bondmen into Samaria. 2 Chron. 28:12. [6] Father of Meshullam. Neh. 3:4, 30; 6:18. [7] Father of Zechariah the prophet. Zech. 1:1, 7.

Be´red (*seed place*). [1] A place in the south of Canaan. Gen. 16:14. [2] A grandson of Ephraim. 1 Chron. 7:20. Same as BECHER, No. 2.

Ber-e-ni´ce. See BERNICE.

Be´ri (*expounder*), son of Zophah. 1 Chron. 7:36.

Be-ri´ah (*unfortunate*). [1] A son of Asher. Gen. 46:17; 1 Chron. 7:30. [2] A son of Ephraim. 1 Chron. 7:23. [3] Son of El-paal. 1 Chron. 8:13, 16. [4] A Levite descendant of Gershom. 1 Chron. 23:10, 11.

Be-ri´ites, a family of Israelites descended from BERIAH, son of Asher. Num. 26:44.

Be´rites, a family of Israelites in the north of Canaan. 2 Sam. 20:14.

Be´rith (*a covenant*), a word often used to designate the covenant which God made with his people, is found in Judges 9:46 as the name of an idol (otherwise called BAAL-BERITH) worshipped at Shechem.

Bernice, ber-ni´se, or Berenice, ber-e-ni´se, daughter of Herod Agrippa. Acts 25:13, 23; 26:30.

Berodach-baladan, be-ro´dak-bal´a-dan, or Merodach-baladan, me-ro´dak-bal´a-dan (*bold*), a king of Babylon. 2 Kings 20:12; Isa. 39:1. See MERODACH-BALADAN.

Be-ro´thah (*food*), a city in the north of Palestine. Ezek. 47:16.

Be-ro´thai (*cypresses of Jehovah*), a city of Hadadezer, king of Zobar. 2 Sam. 8:8.

Be´roth-ite, the native place of Naharai, Joab's armor-bearer. 1 Chron. 11:39. It would seem to mean a native of Berothai, but in 2 Sam. 23:37 Naharai is called a Beerothite.

Ber´yl, a precious stone used in the high-priest's breastplate. It is supposed to resemble the emerald. Exod. 28:20; Rev. 21:20.

Be´sai (*treading down*), a Nethinim who returned with Zerubbabel. Ezra 2:49; Neh. 7:52.

Besodeiah, bes-o-de´yah (*given to trust in Jehovah*), a repairer of the old gate of Jerusalem. Neh. 3:6.

Be´som, a broom made of twigs. Isa. 14:23.

Be´sor (*cool brook*), a brook which runs into the Mediterranean near Gaza. 1 Sam. 30:9, 21.

Be-stead´, in Isa. 8:21, means circumstanced; situated.

Be-stow´, in 2 Kings 5:24 and Luke 12:17, means to lay away safely.

Be´tah (*confidence*), a city of Hadadezer, king of Zobah. 2 Sam. 8:8. It is called TIBHATH in 1 Chron. 18:8.

Be´ten (*height*), a town of Asher, near Ptolemais. Josh. 19:25.

Beth (*house*), a part of many names of places.

Beth-ab´a-ra (*place of ford*), John 1:28, a place on the east side of Jordan, where John baptized. Perhaps the same as BETH-BARAH. Judg. 7:24. Some of the best manuscripts read BETHANY same as BETH-ABARA.

Beth-a´nath (*house of echo*), a fenced city of Naphtali. Josh. 19:38; Judg. 1:33.

Beth-a´noth (*house of echo*). A city of Judah. Josh. 15:59.

Beth´a-ny (*house of dates or figs*), a village on the Mount of Olives, about two miles east of Jerusalem, on the road to Jericho. It was the residence of Lazarus and his sisters Martha and Mary. Christ often visited it, and it was the scene of some of the most interesting events of his life. Matt. 21:17; 26:6; Mark 11:11, 12; 14:3; Luke 19:29; 24:50; John 11:1, 18; 12:1. [2] Some manuscripts read BETHANY for BETHABARA in John 1:28. See BETHABARA.

Beth-ar´a-bah (*house of the desert*), a city on north border of Judah. Josh. 15:6, 61. Same as a city of Benjamin, Josh. 18:22, and as ARABAH in Josh. 18:18, near the Dead Sea.

Beth-a´ram (*house or place of the height*), a city of Gad. Josh. 13:27. It is supposed to be same as BETH-HARAN.

Num. 32:36.

Beth-ar´bel (*house of God's court*), a town destroyed by Shalmaneser, king of Assyria. Hos. 10:14.

Beth-a´ven (*house of idols*), a town of Benjamin, near Bethel. Josh. 7:2; 18:12; 1 Sam. 13:5; 14:23. Used as a name for BETHEL (*house of God*); changed to BETH-AVEN (*house of idols*). Hos. 4:15; 5:8.

Beth-az´ma-veth (*house of Azmaveth*), a town of Benjamin. Neh. 7:28. It is called AZMAVETH in Ezra 2:24.

Beth-ba´al-me´on, a town of Moab given to Reuben. Josh. 13:17. See BAAL-MEON.

Beth-ba´rah (*fording-place*), a place in Gad, on the east side of Jordan. Judg. 7:24. See BETH-ABARA.

Beth-bir´e-i (*place of the city*), a town of Simeon. 1 Chron. 4:31. Probably same as BETH-LEBAOTH and LEBAOTH. Josh. 19:6; 15:32.

Beth´car (*place of pasture*), a stronghold of the Philistines in Judah. 1 Sam. 7:11.

Beth-da´gon (*house of Dagon*). [1] A town of Judah. Josh. 15:41. [2] A town of Asher. Josh. 19:27.

Beth-dib´la-tha´im, a town of the Moabites. Jer. 48:22. Same as ALMON-DIBLATHAIM. Num. 33:46.

Beth´el (*house of God*). [1] A town about twelve miles north of Jerusalem. It was visited by Abraham. Gen. 12:8; 13:3. Was the scene of Jacob's vision of the ladder from earth to heaven. Gen. 28:11-19. He named the place Bethel. Gen. 28:19. It was first called LUZ, Judg. 1:22, 23, was the dwelling-place of Jacob, Gen. 35:1-8, the home of prophets, 2 Kings 2:2, 3, and was called BETH-AVEN (*house of idols*). Hos. 10:5, 8. [2] A town in the south of Judah. Josh. 12:16. It is called also

CHESIL, BETHUL, and BETHUEL. [3] Mount Bethel, a hilly region near Bethel. Josh. 16:1; 1 Sam. 13:2.

Also see Gen. 31:13; 35:15, 16.

Josh. 7:2; 8:9, 12, 17; 12:9; 16:2; 18:13, 22.

Judg. 4:5; 21:19.

1 Sam. 7:16, 10:3; 30:27.

1 Kings 12:29, 32, 33; 13:1, 4, 10, 11, 32.

2 Kings 2:23; 10:29; 17:28; 23:4, 15, 17, 19.

1 Chron. 7:28.

2 Chron. 13:19.

Ezra 2:28.

Neh. 7:32; 11:31.

Jer. 48:13.

Hos. 10:15; 12:4.

Amos 3:14; 4:4; 5:5, 6; 7:10, 13.

Beth´el-ite, an inhabitant of Bethel. 1 Kings 16:34.

Beth-e´mek (*house of the valley*), a town of Asher. Josh. 19:27.

Be´ther (*depth*), a name either of a particular place of uncertain situation, or used as a descriptive term for any region of hills and valleys. Song of Sol. 2:17.

Bethesda, be-thez´dah (*house of mercy*), a pool or cistern in Jerusalem, near the sheep-market gate. Its location is doubtful. It was a great resort for the sick. See John 5:2-9.

Beth-e´zel (*place of declivity*), a town of Judah or of Israel, probably near the boundary-line. Mic. 1:11.

Beth-ga´der (*walled place*), a descendant of Caleb. 1 Chron. 2:51.

Beth-ga´mul (*place of the camel*), a town of the Moabites. Jer. 48:23.

Beth-gil´gal. See GILGAL.

Beth-haccerem, beth-hak´se-rem (*place of the vineyard*), a town of Judah. Neh. 3:14; Jer. 6:1.

Beth-ha´ran (*strong place*), a city built by the Gadites, near Gilead. Num. 32:36.

Same as BETH-ARAM in Josh. 13:27.

Beth-hog´lah (*place of magpies*), a town of Benjamin. Josh. 15:6; 18:19, 21.

Beth-ho´ron (*place of hollows*), the name of two towns, the upper and the nether, about three miles apart, in Ephraim. Josh. 10:10; 16:3, 5: 1 Chron. 6:68.

Beth-jesh´i-moth or **Beth-jes´i-moth,** a city of the Reubenites. Num. 33:49; Ezek. 25:9.

Beth-leb´a-oth (*place of lionesses*), a town in Simeon. Josh. 19:6. See BETH-BIREI.

Beth´le-hem (*house of bread*). [1] A village of Judah, originally called EPHRATH, Gen. 35:19, and which is more fully named BETHLEHEM JUDAH or BETHLEHEM EPHRATAH. It is about six miles south of Jerusalem, and was the birthplace of David, 1 Sam. 17:12, and of Christ. Matt. 2:1. Rachel was buried near it, and it was the home of Boaz, Naomi, and Ruth. It was visited by the shepherds, Luke 2:15-17, and by the wise men. Matt. 2. It has been a town for more than four thousand years, but was a small village till after the time of Christ. [2] A town in Zebulun, six miles west of Nazareth. Josh. 19:15. [3] A descendant of Caleb. 1 Chron. 2:51, 54; 4:4.

Also see Gen. 48:7.

Judg. 12:8, 10.

Ruth 1:19, 22; 2:4; 4:11.

1 Sam. 16:4; 17:15; 20:6, 28.

2 Sam. 2:32; 23:14-16, 24.

1 Chron. 11:16-18, 26.

2 Chron. 11:6.

Ezra 2:21.

Neh. 7:26.

Jer. 41:17.

Mic. 5:2.

Matt. 2:5, 6, 8, 16.

Luke 2:4.

John 7:42.

Beth´le-hem Eph´ra-tah. See BETH-LEHEM.

Beth´le-hem-ite, an inhabitant of Bethlehem in Judah. 1 Sam. 16:1; 2 Sam. 21: 19.

Beth´le-hem Ju´dah. See BETHLEHEM.

Beth-maachah, beth-ma´ah-kah (*place of oppression*), a town of the Manassites on the east side of Jordan. 2 Sam. 20:14; 2 Kings 15:29. Same as ABEL-BETH-MAACHAH, ABEL-MAIM, and ABEL.

Beth-mar´ca-both (*place of chariots*), a city of Simeon. Josh. 19:5; 1 Chron. 4:31.

Beth-me´on (*place of habitation*), a city of Moab, whose destruction was foretold by Jeremiah. Jer. 48:23. See BAAL-MEON.

Beth-nim´rah (*place of flowing water*), a fenced city of Gad, Num. 32:36; Josh. 13:27, evidently same as NIMRAH, Num. 32:3, and NIMRIM. Isa. 15:6.

Beth-pa´let or **Beth-phe´let,** a town in the south of Judah. Josh. 15:27; Neh. 11:26.

Beth-paz´zez (*place of destruction*), a town of Issachar. Josh. 19:21.

Beth-pe´or (*temple of Peor*), a place on Pisgah. Deut. 3:29; Josh. 13:20. See PISGAH.

Bethphage, beth´fa-je (*house of figs*), a village on the Mount of Olives, near Bethany. Matt. 21:1; Mark 11:1; Luke 19:29.

Beth-phe´let. See BETH-PALET.

Beth-ra´pha (*place of fear*), a great-grandson of Chelub. 1 Chron. 4:12.

Beth-re´hob (*house of Rehob*). A town or district in the north part of Canaan. Judg. 18:28; 2 Sam. 10:6, 8. Called REHOB in Num. 13:21.

Beth-sa´i-da (*place of nets*), a city on the west side and near the north end of the Sea of Galilee. Matt. 11:21; Luke 10:13; John 1:44. [2] It seems possible that there was another city of the same name on the east bank of the Jordan, near the Sea of Galilee. See Mark 8:22; Luke 9:10.

Beth´san, Beth´shan, or **Beth-she´an,** a city five miles west of the Jordan. It was called Scythopolis after the captivity, and was one of the principal cities of Decapolis. Josh. 17:11; 1 Chron. 7:29.

Beth-she´mesh (*house of the sun*). [1] A city of Judah. Josh. 15:10; 1 Sam. 6:9. [2] A city of Issachar. Josh. 19:22. [3] A city of Naphtali. Josh 19:38. [4] A name given by Jeremiah to a city of Egypt. Jer. 43:13. Same as Heliopolis, or On. See ON.

Beth-she´mite, an inhabitant of Bethshemesh. 1 Sam. 6:14, 18.

Beth-shit´tah (*place of acacia*), a town of Issachar. Judg. 7:22.

Beth-tap´pu-ah (*place of fruit trees*), a city of Judah. Josh 15:53.

Be-thu´el (*dweller in God*). [1] A son of Nahor. Gen. 22:22; 25:20. [2] A town of Simeon. 1 Chron. 4:30.

Be´thu-el, and **Be´thul.** See CHESIL, and BETHEL.

Beth´-zur (*place of rock*). [1] A city of Judah. Josh. 15:58; Neh. 3:16. [2] A name of the son of Maon. 1 Chron. 2:45.

Be-times´, in Gen. 26:31, etc., means early.

Bet´o-nim (*heights*), a city of Gad. Josh. 13:26.

Be-troth´ing or **espousing,** es-powz´-ing. In ancient times the Jews often betrothed their daughters without their consent and while they were quite young. A written contract was sometimes made, in which the bridegroom agreed to give a certain sum to the bride. The betrothal could not be dissolved, except by divorce or death. Deut. 20:7; Exod. 21:9.

Beu´lah (*married*), a term used by Isaiah to denote the intimate relation of the Jewish Church to God. Isa. 62:4.

Bewray, be-ray´, in Prov. 27:16; Matt. 26:73, means to disclose, and in Isa. 16:3, to betray.

Be´zai (*shining*). [1] An Israelite whose descendants returned with Zerubbabel from Babylon. Ezra 2:17; Neh. 7:23. [2] A family who sealed the covenant made by Nehemiah. Neh. 10:18.

Be-zal´e-el (*God is protection*). [1] A man of Judah fitted by God for work on the ark of the testimony and the Tabernacle. Exod. 31:2; 2 Chron. 1:5. [2] A Jew who returned from Babylon and had taken a foreign wife. Ezra 10:30.

Be´zek (*lightning*). [1] A city in the mountains of Judah. Judg. 1:3-5. [2] May be a district north of Tirzah. 1 Sam. 11:8.

Be´zer (*strong*). [1] A city of refuge in the wilderness east of Jordan. Deut. 4:43; Josh. 21:36. [2] An Israelite of Asher. 1 Chron. 7:37.

Be´ze-tha or **Be´zeth,** a hill in Jerusalem.

Bi´ble. The word *bible* is of Greek origin, and means simply "the book" or "the books." In the sense which it now has throughout the world, it was first used in the fourth century by the Greek Father, Chrysostom, but it was so natural to the Christians to designate the volume which contains the standard of their faith and duty and the foundation of their hope as "The Book," that the word was bodily transferred from Greek into Latin, and thence into all modern languages. Before that time the Christians generally designated the collection of their religious books by terms corresponding to our "Scriptures," "Holy Writ," "Sacred Writings," etc.

The Bible consists of the OLD and the NEW TESTAMENT. The word *testament* is of Latin origin, and a translation of the Greek word *diatheke*, used by Paul, 2 Cor. 3:14, meaning "covenant;" so that the terms OLD TESTAMENT and NEW TESTAMENT actually mean the books of the OLD and of the NEW COVENANT. A peculiar place, so to speak, between the Old and the New Testament, is occupied by the apocryphal books. What should be said about them is given under the special heading APOCRYPHA (which see).

I. THE OLD TESTAMENT consists of thirty-nine books arranged so as to correspond to the twenty-two letters of the Hebrew alphabet, the twelve minor prophets counting as one, Ruth being coupled with Judges, Ezra with Nehemiah, Lamentations with Jeremiah, and the two books of Samuel, Kings, and Chronicles counting as one each; and further, so that the five double books, Samuel, Kings, Chronicles, Ezra, and Jeremiah, correspond to the five double letters of the alphabet. The dates when these thirty-nine books were written, in whole or in part, vary from the age of Moses to the time of Ezra. The collection of them was consequently gradual. Moses ordered that the books of the Law should be put in the ark of the covenant, Deut. 31:26; Joshua and other annals, the Proverbs, and Prophecies were added, Zech. 7:12; Isa. 29:18; 34:16; and finally the collection was closed, according to Jewish tradition, in the time of Ezra and Nehemiah by the men of the Great Synagogue. At all events, the Hebrew Canon in its present shape existed at the time of Christ.

The existence of the APOCRYPHA, as well as the circumstance that several books unknown to us are mentioned both in the Old and New Testaments, proves that the Old Testament collection did not embrace the whole sacred literature of the

Jews, but only their *Canon*; that is, those books which were received among them as written by divine authority. The Greek word *canon* meant first a straight staff, then a measuring-rod, and finally, since the fourth century, the word has been used to denote the rule according to which the genuineness of the writings of the Old and the New Testament was defined, or those writings themselves. The Old Testament Canon is mentioned in the prologue to the Greek translation of Ecclesiasticus (B. C. 131), by Philo Judæus(B. C. 20–A. D. 40), by Josephus (A. D. 38–100), who, in speaking of the books of the Old Testament, adds that since the death of Artaxerxes (B. C. 424) no one had dared to add anything to them, to take anything from them, or to make any change in them. From the Synagogue the Canon passed into the Christian Church. The Jews generally arranged the books of their Canon into three classes: the *Law*, comprising the five books of Moses; the *Prophets*, divided into two groups: the former prophets, or the historical books of Joshua, Judges, Samuel, and Kings; and the later prophets, or the prophets proper (though with the exception of the book of Daniel, which they placed in the last class); and the *Hagiographa* (or Holy Writings), embracing the Psalms, Proverbs, Job, Canticles, Ruth, Lamentations, Ecclesiastes, Esther, Daniel, Ezra, Nehemiah, and Chronicles— an arrangement very similar to the common modern division, namely: [1] The PENTATEUCH (or five books of Moses); [2] THE HISTORICAL BOOKS (from Joshua to the end of Esther); [3] THE POETICAL or DEVOTIONAL BOOKS (from Job to the Song of Solomon); [4] THE PROPHETICAL BOOKS (from Isaiah to Malachi).

All the writings of the Old Testament Canon are in Hebrew, with the exception of a few minor portions, which are in Chaldee. Hebrew belongs to the Shemitic group of languages, and is very different from any language belonging to the Aryan group. It is somewhat lacking in that precision and flexibility which fit a language for philosophical and dialectical reasoning, but its great imaginative power and its depth of feeling have made it a wonderful vehicle for the expression of religious devotion. The books of the Old Testament are the only works extant in pure Hebrew. Each of these—namely, GENESIS, EXODUS, LEVITICUS, NUMBERS, DEUTERONOMY, JOSHUA, JUDGES, RUTH. I. SAMUEL, II. SAMUEL, I. KINGS, II. KINGS, I. CHRONICLES, II. CHRONICLES, EZRA, NEHEMIAH, ESTHER. JOB, PSALMS, PROVERBS, ECCLESIASTES, SONG OF SOLOMON, ISAIAH, JEREMIAH, LAMENTATIONS, EZEKIEL, DANIEL, HOSEA, JOEL, AMOS, OBADIAH, JONAH, MICAH, NAHUM, HABAKKUK, ZEPHANIAH, HAGGAI. ZECHARIAH, and MALACHI—will be treated separately under its own heading.

II. THE NEW TESTAMENT consists of four Gospels, the Acts of the Apostles, twenty-one Epistles, and the Revelation. All of these books were written within the first century after Christ, but between two and three more centuries passed before the Canon was finally settled. This was done by the councils of Laodicea (A. D. 369), Hippo Regius (A. D. 393). and Carthage (A. D. 397). All the Christian churches agree on this important point and have the same New Testament though in different versions.

All the books of the New Testament are further spoken of under their respective titles. See MATTHEW, MARK, LUKE, JOHN, ACTS, ROMANS, I. CORINTHIANS, II. COR-

INTHIANS, GALATIANS, EPHESIANS, PHILIP-
PIANS, COLOSSIANS, I. THESSALONIANS, II.
THESSALONIANS, I TIMOTHY, II. TIMOTHY,
TITUS, PHILEMON, HEBREWS, JAMES, I. PE-
TER, II. PETER, I. JOHN, II. JOHN, III. JOHN,
JUDE, REVELATION.

The books of the New Testament are
written in Hellenistic Greek as commonly
spoken and generally understood, not only
in Asia Minor, but also in Syria, Palestine,
Egypt, and even in Rome. It is not classi-
cal Greek; it shows influences of the
Hebrew, beside which it was used. But it
was best adapted for the expression of the
truths of the Christian religion and for the
Christians of the apostolic age. It admits of
easy translation into other languages without losing its force and beauty.

III. MANUSCRIPTS AND EDITIONS OF THE
BIBLE.—Before the invention of the art of
printing, in the middle of the fifteenth century, books were reproduced by rewriting
and existed only as manuscripts. These
manuscripts were generally made on finely prepared skin (parchment), or later on
paper made from the leaves of the
papyrus-plant or otherwise, and were generally in the form of rolls—just as we often
have maps rolled on sticks—or later in the
form of books consisting of leaves tied
together with strings.

Ancient Hebrew Books or Rolls.—The
"book" kept in the sacred place of the
Israelites was not such a book as the read-
er now holds in his hand, of paper, with
leaves and a cover, and opening by a flexible back; nor were the words and verses
and chapters arranged like ours. In those
days, and down to a period long after the
time of Christ, the "book" was a parchment roll made of skins fastened together
in a long strip; the text was written upon it
in narrow columns from top to bottom,

without any break between words, sentences, verses, or chapters; and the direction of its writing and reading was from
right to left, exactly the reverse of ours.
The same order is still used in the Hebrew
language, as any one may see who will
examine a Hebrew book as now printed.
To make this clear we will give the first
three verses of Genesis in the English
words and letters, but arranged as in the
ancient Hebrew roll:

gfotiripsehtdnapee   rcdoggninnigebehtnI
afehtnopudevomdo   htdnanevaehehtdetae
dnasretawehtfoec   htraeehtdnahtraee
eberehtteldiasdog   dnamroftuohtiwsaw
awerehtdnathgil   awssenkraddnadiov
               thgils   dehtfoecafehtnopus

The above example must be read from
right to left, beginning with the capital letter "I" in the first line of the righthand column. The two columns contain the following verses:

1. In the beginning God created the
heaven and the earth.

2. And the earth was without form, and
void; and darkness *was* upon the face of
the deep. And the Spirit of God moved
upon the face of the waters.

3. And God said, Let there be light: and
there was light.

Each ancient letter was probably an
eighth, or even a quarter of an inch high
and wide; the columns were a foot long
and four inches wide, or even considerably more. We copy from Horne the
description of a parchment roll now in
the British Museum, containing the
Pentateuch alone: "It is a large double roll,
containing the Hebrew Pentateuch, written with very great care on forty brown
African skins. These skins are of different

breadths, some containing more columns than others. The columns are one hundred and fifty-three in number, each of which contains about sixty-three lines, is about twenty-two inches deep, and generally more than five inches broad." With the prescribed margins above and below, and the spaces between the columns, this "roll," therefore, if unrolled and laid on the ground, would occupy a space seventy-six feet long and two feet two inches wide. It is thus evident that the rolls of those ancient times were extremely cumbrous and inconvenient compared with the books of the present day. The skins of parchment in such a roll were tied together with strings made of the skin of some clean animal, and the whole was rolled upon a round stick at each end, while a disk above and below the parchment on each stick, like the heads of a spool, served to guide the parchment in rolling up and to protect the edges of the skins. It was, of course, unavoidable, with this manner of reproduction, that errors, either from misunderstanding or from carelessness, should creep into the text, but no book from ancient times has come down to us better preserved than the Bible. Of small variations there are many, but few of them materially affect the sense and most of them can be corrected by collation of manuscripts.

The sacred original manuscripts of the Old Testament were lost when Nebuchadnezzar took Jerusalem (B. C. 597), and the original manuscripts of the collection and the manuscript arrangement by Ezra and Nehemiah were lost in the destruction of Jerusalem by Titus (A. D. 70). The text was, nevertheless, preserved with the most scrupulous care, both for service in the synagogues and for private use, and was regarded with extreme reverence.

Specially noteworthy in this connection are the Masoretes, from *masora*, "tradition," a body of scholars who lived at Tiberias and at Sora in the Euphrates Valley between the fifth and twelfth centuries. To them we owe the addition of the vowel-points in the writing down of the text; and the text, such as we now have it, is generally called the Masoretic, after them. The oldest manuscript extant dates from the tenth century. The Hebrew Bible was first printed in parts, the Pentateuch in 1482, the older Prophets in 1485, the later Prophets in 1486, the Hagiographa, or Sacred Writings, in 1487. The whole Old Testament in Hebrew appeared first in 1488 (Sorino: Abraham ben Chayin de'Tintori), in double columns, folio.

The manuscripts of the New Testament are both older and more numerous than those of the Old Testament. They are in two distinct groups: *uncials*, written in capitals throughout, and without any division of sentences or words; and *cursives*, written in running hand, as we now write. The former are the oldest, ranging from the fourth to the tenth century. The oldest two manuscripts extant, dating from the age of Constantine the Great, are [1] *Codex Vaticanus*, so called because it belongs to the Vatican library. A facsimile edition of the New Testament (one hundred copies) was published in Rome, 1889. [2] The *Codex Sinaiticus*, which was discovered by a German scholar, Tischendorf (A. D. 1859), in the monastery of Mount Sinai. It is now in St. Petersburg, and a quasi-facsimile was published in 1862, in four volumes. The original manuscripts of the apostles and evangelists were written on perishable Egyptian paper, and had therefore disappeared in the second century. But there are more copies of them than of any other ancient writings, and the materials for the restoration of original text are abundant—about two thousand manuscripts of all kinds, ancient versions, and patristic quotations. An immense amount of labor and skill has been spent, during the last and present centuries, upon the critical examination and collation of these sources. We have now a pure and reliable text of the Greek Testament, which has been utilized by the Committees of British and American Revisers of 1881 for the benefit of the English-reading community.

The division into chapters and verses was introduced very early in the Old Testament for liturgical purposes; first in the Law, then in the Prophets; first simply in fifty-four sections, to correspond to the Sabbaths in the Jewish intercalary year; then more elaborately in minor sections. As for the New Testament, the division was first applied to the Gospels by Ammonius of Alexandria (A. D. 220), in order to facilitate the comparison of corresponding portions of the several Gospels. The general application of it to all the books is of much later date, and due to Cardinal Hugo of St. Cher (died A. D. 1263), whose Concordance to the Vulgate has also a division into verses. The present system of verse-divisions was introduced by Robert Stephens in his edition of the Greek Testament (A. D. 1551).

The first published edition of the Greek text of the New Testament is that by Erasmus, Basel (A. D. 1516). The first printed edition of the original text of the whole Bible is that in the Complutensian Polyglot (A. D. 1514–20), six volumes folio, thus called from *Complutum*, the Latin name of the place where it was printed (Alcala in Spain), and the Greek word *polyglot*, "many-tongued," because the original Hebrew and Greek text was printed in parallel columns between the Greek and Latin translations.

IV.—VERSIONS OF THE BIBLE, or at least of parts of it, are now found in almost every language spoken on the globe. We mention below only those among the oldest versions which are important for the right understanding of the original text and the English versions.

OLD VERSIONS OF THE BIBLE.—*The Targums* are not exactly a translation, but rather a paraphrase of the Old Testament's Hebrew text into Chaldee, made after the return from the captivity, when the Jews had lost the ready command of their native tongue and had adopted the Aramaic dialect, a mixture of Hebrew and Chaldee. The word *targum* means "interpretation."

The Septuagint, or the LXX., a Greek translation of the Old Testament, made by seventy (a round number for seventy-two) Jewish scholars, whence its name, in Alexandria, under the patronage of Ptolemy Philadelphus, B. C. 285.

The Peshito, a translation of the Bible into Syriac, done by Christians, from the original text, Hebrew and Greek, probably in the beginning of the third or perhaps toward the close of the second century, and in general use throughout Syria during the fourth century. The word *peshito* means "simple."

Itala, the oldest Latin translation, but known to us only from fragments in the early Latin Fathers (Tertullian, Cyprian, etc.).

The Vulgate, the authorized Latin translation of the whole Bible, was made by Jerome (A. D. 385–405) from the original text, on the basis of an older Latin version called the *Itala*. It was generally adopted by the Western Church. The Council of Trent (A. D. 1563) ascribed to it the same authority as to the original text, and calls it "The old and commonly accepted version," whence its name, *Vulgate*.

ENGLISH VERSIONS OF THE BIBLE.— Translations of the Psalms and other parts of the Bible were made as early as the thirteenth century, and even in the Saxon period.

A. D. **1381.**—*Wycliffe's Translation* was made by John Wycliffe (about 1324–84) and Nicholas Hereford from the Latin Vulgate. The New Testament was printed in 1581; the whole work, in an authentic revision, not until 1850. But in manuscript it seems to have had a very wide circulation. It was the first translation of the whole Bible into the English language.

A. D. **1525.**—*Tyndale's Translation* of the New Testament was made by William Tyndale (born 1484; burnt at the stake 1536) from the original text as published by Erasmus. The New Testament was printed at Worms in 1525. Of the Old Testament he only translated the books of Moses, republished by Mombert (New York, 1884).

A. D. **1535.**—*Miles Coverdale's Translation* of the whole Bible was made from Tyndale, the Latin Vulgate, and the German. It was the first version of the whole Bible published in modern English (Wycliffe's translation being in mediæval English).

A. D. **1537.**—*Thomas Matthew's Bible* was made (under this assumed name) from the translations of Tyndale and Coverdale by John Rogers, the first martyr under Queen Mary (1555). It was published under the king's license, and was the first "Authorized Version."

A. D. **1539.**—*Taverner's* was a purified edition of Thomas Matthew's Bible, edited by Taverner.

A. D. **1539.**—*The Great Bible*, or *Cranmer's Bible*, was a new edition of Thomas Matthew's Bible, published in England under the authority of the English reformer, Thomas Cranmer, who was burned at the stake in 1556. It was the first edition in which the words not found in the original were printed in different type.

A. D. **1560.**—*The Geneva Version*, made in Geneva by refugees from the persecutions of Queen Mary, appeared 1560. It was the favorite version of the Puritans, and many copies were brought to America by the early settlers of New England.

A. D **1568.**—*Bishops' Bible*, a folio version based on Cranmer's, and executed by fifteen theologians, eight of whom were bishops, in opposition to the Geneva Bible. It was issued in three parts in 1568–72. It was large, costly, and short-lived.

A. D. **1582.**—*The Douai Bible*, or the *Rheims Version*, was made from the Latin Vulgate by English Roman Catholic divines who were at first connected with the college at Rheims, and later with that at Douai, a town of France. The New Testament was published in 1582; the Old Testament, in 1609–10.

A. D. **1611.**—*King James's Version*, or the *Authorized Version*, was proposed at the Hampton Court Conference, January, 1604, and begun in the same year by forty-seven Biblical scholars, who, at the invitation of King James I. of Great Britain, though not at his expense, assembled, formed themselves into six companies, and immediately went to work. It appeared in 1611, and has ever since been one of the mainstays of the religious life of the English-speaking race, "a sacred thing, which doubt has never dimmed and controversy never soiled." The Bible, or parts of it, is now printed in about two hundred and thirty different languages or dialects.

A. D. **1881; 1885.**—*The Revised Version* is a revision of King James's Version, and was made by an English and an American committee of Biblical scholars, of all the evangelical denominations, working together, 1870–85, for the purpose of bringing the Authorized Version into perfect harmony with the present state of the English language and the results of the latest Biblical researches in textual criticism, philology, archæology, and history. The New Testament was published by the University Presses of Oxford and Cambridge in 1881; the Old Testament, in 1885. The sacred text is arranged in paragraphs instead of chapters and verses. The chapters and verses of the Authorized Version are indicated in the Revised Version by figures on the margin. The poetical books of the Old Testament, and such quotations from them in the New Testament as extend to two or more lines, are arranged so as to agree with the metrical divisions of the Hebrew original. The hymns in the first two chapters of Luke are arranged in the same way.

Bichri, bik-ri (*youth*), a Benjamite whose son Sheba stirred up rebellion against David after Absalom died. 2 Sam. 20:1.

Bid´kar (*servant of Kar*), one of Jehu's captains. 2 Kings 9:25.

Bier, a frame on which a dead body is carried to the grave by men. Luke 7:14.

Big´tha (*given by fortune*), a chamberlain of Ahasuerus. Esther 1:10.

Big´than or **Big´tha-na,** a chamberlain who conspired with Teresh against Ahasuerus. Esther 2:21.

Big´vai (*happy*). [1] A chief man among the Jews who returned from Babylon. Ezra 2:2; Neh. 7:7. [2] An Israelite whose descendants returned from Babylon. Ezra 2:14; Neh. 7:19. [3] Perhaps same as No. 2. [4] A family of Jews who sealed the covenant made by Nehemiah. Neh. 10:16.

Bil´dad (*lord Adad*), one of Job's three friends that visited him in his affliction. Job 2:11; 42:9.

Bil´e-am (*place of conquest*), a city of Manasseh. 1 Chron. 6:70.

Bil´gah (*firstborn*). [1] A priest of the sanctuary. 1 Chron. 24:14. [2] A priest who returned from Babylon. Neh. 12:5, 18.

Bil´ga-i (*firstborn*), a priest or family of priests who sealed the covenant of Nehemiah. Neh. 10:8.

Bil´hah (*tender*). [1] The handmaid of Rachel. Gen. 29:29; 1 Chron. 7:13. [2] A town of Simeon. 1 Chron. 4:29. Probably same as BALAH in Josh. 19:3.

Bil´han (*tender*). [1] A son of Ezer. Gen. 36:27; 1 Chron. 1:42. [2] A son of Jediael. 1 Chron. 7:10.

Bil´shan (*searcher*), a prince of the Jews who returned with Zerubbabel. Ezra 2:2; Neh. 7:7.

Bim´hal (*circumcised*), son of Japhlet. 1 Chron. 7:33.

Bind, in Job 26:8 and Acts 9:14, means imprison or confine closely.

Bin´e-a (*wanderer*), a son of Moza. 1 Chron. 8:37; 9:43.

Bin-nu´i (*a building*). [1] Father of Noadiah. Ezra 8:33. [2 and 3] Jews who took foreign wives. Ezra 10:30, 38. [4] A Jew who repaired part of the wall of Jerusalem after the captivity. [5] An Israelite whose descendants returned from Babylon. Neh. 7:15. He is called BANI in Ezra 2:10. [6] A Levite who returned after the captivity. Neh. 12:8.

Bir'sha (*strong*), king of Gomorrah in Abram's time. Gen. 14:2.

Birth'day. Anniversaries of birthdays were celebrated in ancient times. Gen. 40:20. They are not mentioned among the Jews, except in the case of Herod. Matt. 14:6.

Birth'right, special privileges enjoyed among the Hebrews by the firstborn son.

Bir'za-vith (*olive-well*), a grandson of Beriah. 1 Chron. 7:31.

Bish'lam (*in peace*), a ruler in Israel who wrote to the king of Persia against the Jews who were rebuilding Jerusalem. Ezra 4:7.

Bish'op, an official title used interchangeably with "elder," and in Acts 20:28 translated OVERSEER. Phil. 1:1; 1 Pet. 2:25.

Bishops' Bible. See BIBLE.

Bi-thi'ah (*worshipper*), a daughter of Pharaoh. She was wife of Mered, a descendant of Judah. 1 Chron. 4:18.

Bith'ron (*broken place*), a district in Gad. 2 Sam. 2:29.

Bi-thyn'i-a, a Roman province in the north-west part of Asia Minor, bounded north by Pontus Euxinus (Black Sea) and west by Propontis (Sea of Marmora), was annexed to the Persian Empire B. C. 543, and afterward became an independent kingdom. Acts 16:7; 1 Pet. 1:1. It was conquered by the Turks in A. D. 1298.

Bit'tern, a bird of solitary habits found in ruins and other desolate places. It has a deep, hoarse cry. Isa. 14:23; Zeph. 2:14.

Bit'u-men. See SLIME.

Biz-joth'jah (*place of Jehovah's olives*), a town in the south of Judah. Josh. 15:28.

Biz'tha (*eunuch*), a chamberlain of Ahasuerus. Esther 1:10.

Black, a sign of affliction and mourn-ing. Job 30:30; Jer. 14:2.

Blains, in Exod. 9:9, means pimples, pustules, or swelling. It was the sixth plague, and is called in Deut. 28:27 "the botch of Egypt."

Blas'phe-my, reproachful, irreverent, or insulting language concerning God.

Blast'ing. See WINDS.

Blas'tus (*a bud*), the chamberlain of Herod Agrippa I. Acts 12:20.

Blaze abroad, in Mark 1:45, means to publish loudly.

Blem'ish-es, deformities or imperfections which made men unfit for priests, and animals not acceptable for sacrifice. Lev. 21:18-20; 22:20-24.

Bless'ed, the word used by the high-priest in asking Jesus if he was the son of God. Mark 14:61. It is used also as an adjective.

Blind'ness is very common in the East. Many cases of it were miraculously cured by Christ.

Blood. Blood often signifies the guilt of murder. 2 Sam. 3:28; Matt. 27:25. Also, relationship.

Blood Avenger. See AVENGER OF BLOOD

Blue. See COLORS.

Boanerges, bo-a-ner'jeez (*sons of thunder*), the surname given by Jesus to the sons of Zebedee. Mark 3:17.

Boar, the original stock of the common hog. In a wild state it is a furious and for-midable animal. It is found on Mount Carmel and near the Sea of Galilee. Ps. 80:13.

Bo'az (*fleetness, strength*). [1] A Bethlehemite of Judah. He was the hus-band of Ruth the Moabitess, and was an ancestor of David, B. C. 1312. See Ruth chaps. 2, 3, 4; 1 Chron. 2:11; Matt. 1:5; Luke 3:32. Boaz is called BOOZ in the

New Testament. [2] The name which Solomon gave to a brazen pillar he erected in the porch of the Temple. 1 Kings 7:21; 2 Chron. 3:17. Its companion was JACHIN (which see).

Bocheru, bok´e-roo (*youth*), a son of Azel. 1 Chron. 8:38; 9:44.

Bochim, bo´kim (*the weepers*), a place near Gilgal, where the Lord reproved the Israelites for disobeying his command to throw down the altars of the idolatrous inhabitants. Judg. 2:1, 5.

Bo´han (*stumpy*), a son or descendant of Reuben, from whom a boundary-stone between Judah and Benjamin was named. Josh. 15:6; 18:17.

Bol´led, in Exod. 9:31, means swollen out ready to blossom.

Bond, Bond´age, Bond´man, Bond´-wom´an, Bond´maid. See SERVANT.

Books, in ancient times, were rolls of papyrus, parchment, or leather, written on only one side, and fastened at each end to small rollers like those now used for wallmaps. Ezek. 2:9. See BIBLE.

Booths were usually made of poles set upright in the ground and covered with green boughs. The Jews were directed to dwell in booths in the seven days of the feast of tabernacles. Lev. 23:40-42; Neh. 8:14.

Boot´y, spoils captured in war. Num. 31:27-32.

Bo´oz, the Greek form of BOAZ (which see).

Bor´row. See LOAN.

Bor´rowed. In Exod. 3:22; 12:35 the Hebrews are said to have "borrowed" of the Egyptians. The original word means simply asked. As the Hebrews were taking final leave of Egypt, the Egyptians did not expect anything returned.

Bos´cath. 2 Kings 22:1. See BOZKATH.

Bo´som. The dress of the Jews was such that they carried in a fold in the bosom of their robes, above the girdle, such things as their hands could not hold. The word bosom also meant a place of rest and security. Isa. 40:11; Luke 6:38; 16:23.

Bo´sor. 2 Pet. 2:15. Same as BEOR, No. 2 (which see).

Bos´ses, in Job 15:26, means the strongest parts or projecting points of shields.

Botch, in Deut. 28:27, means an eruption of the skin. See LEPROSY.

Bot´tles, in ancient times, were made of goat-skins which were taken off without cutting, except in removing the head and feet. Sometimes the skins of larger animals were used in this way. Such bottles are still employed in the East. When used for new wine they were made of the freshest and most flexible skins, so that they might better endure the strain caused by the fermentation of the wine. Matt. 9:17. Ps. 119:83 mentions figuratively a "bottle in the smoke." Smoke would blacken and shrink a skin-bottle so that it would not hold water or wine. Most of the drinking-water used in Egypt is brought from the river Nile in skin-bottles by Arab water-carriers. The ancients made also elegant bottles of alabaster, porcelain, etc.

Bow, an instrument of war and hunting in ancient times. The Benjamites were noted for their skill in its use. 1 Chron. 12:2; 2 Chron. 14:8. Those who use the bow and arrow are called archers.

Bow´els. This word was used by Hebrew writers to represent the inner man, in the same way as we use the word "heart" as the seat of mercy, tenderness, etc. 1 Kings 3:26; Isa. 63:15.

Bow´ing. See SALUTE.

Box, in 2 Kings 9:1, 3, means flask or

bottle.

Box tree, a beautiful evergreen of Palestine. Isa. 41:19; 60:13.

Bo´zez (*shining*), a rock near Michmash. 1 Sam. 14:4.

Boz´kath and BOS´CATH (*height*), a place in Judah. Josh. 15:39; 2 Kings 22:1.

Boz´rah (*sheepfold*). [1] A city of the Edomites. Gen. 36:33; Jer. 49:13. [2] A city of Moab. Jer. 48:24.

Brace´let, an ornament in the form of a chain or a clasp worn on the wrist, except by royal persons, who wore them above the elbow. 2 Sam. 1:10. They were also called armlets.

Bram´bles. See THORNS.

Branch, a title of Messiah. Zech. 3:8; 6:12.

Brass. That mentioned in the Bible was a native production dug out from the hills of Canaan, Deut. 8:9, and probably like our copper. Gen. 4:22; Job 28:2. Brass is a mixed metal made of copper and zinc, and was unknown to the ancients.

Bra´very, in Isa. 3:18, means brilliance or finery.

Braw´ler, in Titus 3:2, means a noisy, quarrelsome person.

Bray, in Prov. 27:22, means pound or bruise.

Bra´zen or **Mol´ten Sea,** a copper or bronze laver made by Solomon for the Temple. It was seven and a half feet high and fifteen feet in diameter, and was supported by twelve metal oxen. It was filled with water for the ablutions of the priests. 2 Chron. 4:2-6.

Bra´zen Ser´pent, an image prepared by Moses and set up in the camp of the Israelites in the desert. It resembled the fiery serpents so destructive to Israel. See Num. 21:6-9. It was long preserved, but

being worshipped. it was broken in pieces by Hezekiah. It was a type of Christ. John 3:14, 15.

Breach´es, in Judg. 5:17, means harbors.

Bread, in the Bible, is often used for food in general. Gen. 3:19. Manna is called bread from heaven. Exod. 16:4. Bread, in the literal sense, usually means in the Bible cakes of wheaten flour. Gen. 14:18. Barley was used chiefly for the poor and for horses. The Hebrews did not cut their bread, but broke it. See SHEW-BREAD.

Breast´plate. [1] A piece of embroidery about ten inches square worn by the high-priest; it was set with twelve precious stones, on each of which was engraved the name of one of the twelve tribes of Israel. Exod. 28:15-30. See HIGH-PRIEST. [2] A piece of ancient armor worn by warriors to protect the breast. The word is figuratively used in Eph. 6:14; Isa. 59:17.

Breath´ed. John 20:22. Compare Gen. 2:7.

Breech´es, in Exod. 28:42, means short drawers worn by priests.

Breth´ren of the Lord. See BROTHERS OF CHRIST.

Brick, a building material among the Jews. Gen. 11:3. The size of their bricks was much larger than ours. They were made of clay and dried in the sun, but brick-kilns were sometimes used. 2 Sam. 12:31; Jer. 43:9; Nah. 3:14. Bricks found in the ruins of Babylon resemble tiles, and are often one foot square and over three inches thick. The Hebrews in Egypt were compelled to serve with rigor, and many pictures on the walls of Lower Egypt represent them making bricks under the lash of taskmasters. Straw was mixed with the clay used in making these bricks. Exod.

1:11; 5:7-14.

Bride, Bride´groom, Bride´-chamber. See MARRIAGE.

Bri´ers. See THISTLES.

Brig´an-dine, a light coat of mail. Jer. 46:4; 51:3.

Brim´stone, or sulphur, is washed ashore from the Dead Sea. Sodom and other cities of the plain were destroyed by brimstone and fire. Gen. 19:24.

Bring on the way means sometimes to accompany one a part of the way on a journey, and sometimes to furnish him the means for it. Gen. 18:16; 2 Cor. 1:16; Titus 3:13.

Broid´ed, in 1 Tim. 2:9, means braided or plaited.

Broth´er, Breth´ren, in Gen. 4:2 and 42:13, means sons of one man. It sometimes means persons of more remote kindred or of the same nation, Gen. 13:8; Acts 7:25, 37; 13:26, or even those closely united in affection. 2 Sam. 1:26. The word is also used to express the spiritual relationship which the true followers of Christ sustain to him and to each other.

Broth´ers of Christ, relations of Christ, either sons of Joseph from a former marriage, or younger sons of Mary, or cousins of Jesus. Matt. 12:46; 13:55; Mark 3:31.

Bruit, in Jer. 10:22 and Nah. 3:19, means rumor.

Buck´ler, a small shield. 1 Chron. 5:18.

Buf´fet, in Matt. 26:67; 1 Cor. 4:11; 1 Pet. 2:20, means to beat with the fist.

Buk´ki (*mouth of Jehovah*). [1] A chief of Dan appointed to divide the land west of Jordan. Num. 34:22. [2] A grandson of Eleazar. 1 Chron. 6:5; Ezra 7:4.

Buk-ki´ah (*mouth of Jehovah*), a son of Heman in service of song. 1 Chron. 25: 4, 13.

Bul (*rain-god*), the month from the new moon of November to that of December. 1 Kings 6:38. See MONTH.

Bulls of Ba´shan, symbols of fierce, numerous, and powerful foes. Bashan was noted for its fine cattle. Ps. 22:12, Isa. 34:7.

Bul´rush, or papyrus, a kind of reed which formerly grew on the banks of the Nile, and now found around the upper Jordan. The stalks were used in the construction of arks, Exod. 2:3, 5, and vessels of larger size. Isa. 18:2. Boats made of bulrushes were very common in Egypt. The inner bark of the bulrush was made into a kind of paper.

Bu´nah (*understanding*), son of Jerahmeel. 1 Chron. 2:25.

Bun´ni (*my understanding*). [1] A Levite who regulated the devotions of the people after Ezra read the law to them. Neh. 9:4. [2] A family of the Jews who sealed the covenant of Nehemiah. Neh. 10:15. [3] A Levite whose descendant Shemaiah dwelt in Jerusalem after the captivity. Neh. 11:15. Perhaps same as the person who gave his name to No. 2.

Bur´den is often used to denote afflictions, failings, sins, services under the law, and especially prophetic messages. Gen. 49:14.

Exod. 1:11; 2:11; 5:4, 5; 6:6, 7; 18:22; 23:5.

Num. 4:15, 19, 24, 27, 31, 32, 47, 49; 11:11, 17.

Deut. 1:12.

2 Sam. 15:33; 19:35.

1 Kings 5:15.

2 Kings 5:17; 8:9; 9:25.

2 Chron. 2:2, 18; 24:27; 34:13; 35:3.

Neh. 4:10, 17; 13:15, 19.

Job 7:20.

Pss. 38:4; 55:22; 81:6.

Eccles. 12:5.

Isa. 9:4; 10:27; 13:1; 14:25, 28; 15:1; 17:1; 19:1; 21:1, 11, 13; 22:1, 25; 23:1; 30:6, 27; 46:1, 2; 58:6.
Jer. 17:21, 22, 24, 27; 23:33, 34, 36, 38.
Lam. 2:14.
Ezek. 12:10.
Hos. 8:10.
Amos 5:11.
Nah. 1:1.
Hab. 1:1.
Zeph. 3:18.
Zech. 9:1; 12:1, 3.
Mal. 1:1.
Matt. 11:30; 20:12; 23:4.
Luke 11:46.
Acts 15:28; 21:3.
2 Cor. 12:16.
Gal. 6:2, 5.
Rev. 2:24.

Bur´i-al by the Jews was usually in tombs, but occasionally by interment. The body was sometimes anointed. It was wrapped in many folds of linen, with a profusion of aromatic spices— myrrh, aloes, etc. See MOURNING, and SEPULCHRE.

Burn´ing as a mode of execution was common in ancient times, and was some-times done by the Hebrews. Gen. 38:24; Lev. 20:14.

Burn´ing Bush, Exod. 3:2, may have been a kind of acacia now found at Sinai.

Burnt-of´fer-ings. See SACRIFICE.

Bush, in Mark 12:26; Luke 20:37, refers to that part of Scripture which gives an account of the burning bush, and not to the bush itself.

Bush´el, in the New Testament, is the Greek modius, about a peck. Matt. 5:15; Mark 4:21; Luke 11:33. See MEASURES.

But´ler or **Cup-bear´er,** an officer who attended Eastern monarchs and was obliged to taste their wines before serving

them as a pledge that they were not poi-soned. Gen. 40:1; Neh. 1:11.

But´ter, as the word is used in the Bible, probably means sour or curdled milk, which, when mixed with water, is considered an agreeable and refreshing beverage. Job 20:17. Their butter might sometimes have been clarified and pre-served in jars, as it now is in Asia. It resembles rich oil. Gen. 18:8.

Buz (*contempt*). [1] Son of Nahor. Gen. 22:21. [2] An Israelite of Gad. 1 Chron. 5:14. [3] A people and region whose situ-ation is uncertain, but who are supposed to have occupied part of Arabia Petræa. Jer. 25 23.

Bu´zi (*condemned of Jehovah*), an Aaronite, father of the prophet Ezekiel, B. C. 595, Ezek. 1:3.

Buz´ite, an inhabitant of the region called Buz. Job 32:2, 6.

By, in 1 Cor. 4:4, means of; against.

By and by, in Matt. 13:21, means immediately.

By-thin´i-a. See BITHYNIA.

By-word, in 2 Chron. 7:20, means a proverb.

C

Cab, the smallest definite measure for dry things that is mentioned in the Old Testament. It contained about three pints. 2 Kings 6:25. See MEASURES.

Cab´bon (*circle*), a town of Judah. Josh. 15:40.

Cab´ins, in Jer. 37:16, means cells within the dungeon; used for separate confinement of prisoners.

Ca´bul (*sandy*). [1] A border city of Asher. Josh. 19:27. [2] The name given by Hiram to the land containing twenty cities of Galilee which Solomon gave him. 1 Kings 9:13.

Cæsar, se´zer, in the New Testament, always means the Roman emperor. It is often improperly spelled CESAR. The Jews paid tribute to him, and those who were Roman citizens had the right of appeal to him. Paul availed himself of this right. Acts 25:11.

Cæ´sar Au-gus´tus. See AUGUSTUS.

Cæ´sar, Clau´di-us. See CLAUDIUS.

Cæsarea, ses-a-re´a, a city of Palestine on the Mediterranean, forty-four miles south of Acre and forty-seven miles north-west of Jerusalem, was built by Herod the Great B. C. 10, and was the principal center of Roman influence among the Jews. There Felix and Festus resided, Herod Agrippa I. died, Acts 12:19-23, and Vespasian was proclaimed emperor. Paul was kept in bonds at Cæsarea two years. Acts 24:27. The evangelist Philip lived there. Acts 8:40; 21:8.

Cæsarea Philippi, ses-a-re´a philip´pi, a city of Palestine, probably the BAAL-GAD of Old Testament history, certainly the Paneas of the Greek, thus called in honor of the god Pan, was rebuilt and much enlarged by Philip the tetrarch, and by him called Cæsarea Philippi to distinguish it from Cæsarea on the Mediterranean. It stood at the foot of Mount Hermon, about twenty miles north of the Sea of Galilee, and was the northern limit of our Lord's journeys. Matt. 16:13; Mark 8:27.

Caiaphas, ka´ya-fas (*depression*), the high-priest of the Jews. At a council of the chief priests and Pharisees he advised that Jesus should be put to death, John 11:49-52; 18:14, and presided at his trial. Matt. 26:57. Peter and John were brought before Caiaphas for trial. Acts 4:6.

Cain (*possession*), the first son of Adam. Gen. 4:1; 1 John 3:12. He slew his brother Abel. See ABEL.

Cain (*lance*), a town in the south of Judah. Josh. 15:57.

Cainan, ka-i´nan (*acquisition*). [1] The son of Enos. Gen. 5:9; Luke 3:37. He is called KENAN, which is the correct form, in 1 Chron. 1:2. [2] A son of Arphaxad. Luke 3:36.

Cake, a kind of bread, with or without leaven. Gen. 18:6; Exod. 29:2.

Cake of Figs, a lump of dry figs. 1 Sam. 25:18; 1 Chron. 12:40.

Ca´lah (*firm*), one of the most ancient cities of Assyria, was founded by Asshur. Gen. 10:11. It was probably for a time the capital of the Assyrian kingdom.

Cal´a-mus, Song of Sol. 4:14, or **Sweet Cal´a-mus,** Exod. 30:23, or **Sweet Cane,** Isa. 43:24; Jer. 6:20, were probably the same plant or belonged to the same genus. It is produced in Arabia and India. An inferior quality is found in Egypt and Syria. It is very fragrant, and was an ingredient of the sacred ointment.

Cal´col (*sustaining*), a son of Judah. 1 Chron. 2:6. Probably same as CHALCOL. 1 Kings 4:31.

Ca´leb (*capable*). [1] A son of Hezron. 1 Chron. 2:18, 42. Called also CHELUBAI in 1 Chron. 2:9. He was the father of Hur. [2] The son of Jephunneh, Num. 13:6, one of the twelve chiefs, one from each tribe, sent by Moses to spy out the land of Canaan. He and Joshua were the only spies that brought back a favorable report, and they were the only adults born in Egypt who entered Canaan as conquerors. Caleb was one of the princes that divided the land. Num. 34:19. He received as his share the city of KIRJATH-ARBA, with the adjacent hill country. This city was the stronghold of the giants, but Caleb drove them out and took possession of it.

It was afterward called HEBRON. [3] Caleb, the son of Hur, is mentioned in 1 Chron. 2:50. He may be CALEB the spy.

Also see Num. 13:30; 14:6, 24, 30, 38; 26:65; 32:12.

Deut. 1:36.

Josh. 14:6, 13, 14; 15:13, 14, 16-18; 21:12.

Judg. 1:12-15, 20; 3:9.

1 Sam. 25:3; 30:14.

1 Chron. 2:19, 42, 46, 48, 49; 4:15; 6:56.

Ca'leb (*a dog*), the region between Hebron and Carmel assigned to Caleb. 1 Sam. 30:14.

Ca'leb Eph'ra-ta, a place near Bethlehem-Judah, probably named after Caleb and his wife Ephratah. 1 Chron. 2:24.

Calf, a young animal much used among the Hebrews for sacrifice. The fatted or stall-fed calf was considered by them the choicest animal food. 1 Sam. 28:24; Luke 15:23. A *molten* or *golden calf* was prepared by Aaron from the earrings of the people, Exod. 32:4, and was worshipped by the Jews at Mount Sinai, Exod. 32:6, as a symbol of Jehovah. It was probably an imitation of an idol worshipped in Egypt.

Calkers, kawk'ers, in Ezek. 27:9, 27, means men who stop the seams or leaks of ships with tow.

Cal'neh (*fort of Ana*), a city of the kingdom of Nimrod. Gen. 10:10; Amos 6:2. Probably same as CALNO, Isa. 10:9, and CANNEH. Ezek. 27:23.

Cal'no. Isa. 10:9. Probably same as CALNEH, in Gen. 10:10.

Cal'va-ry (*skull*), an elevation in the shape of a skull. The word used in the original means a skull, and was properly rendered by the Latin translators *Calvarium*. The translators of the English Version retained the Latin word, giving it an English termination. Luke 23:33. Calvary, or GOLGOTHA, Matt. 27:33; Mark 15:22; John 19:17, the latter being the Hebrew term, is the place where Christ was crucified, near Jerusalem, John 19:20, but outside of its walls. Heb. 13:12. There is no sanction for the expression "*Mount Calvary.*" It is not found in the Bible. The exact location of Calvary is unknown.

Cam'el (*carrier*), an unclean animal among the Jews. It is very docile, is usually six or seven feet high, and is exceedingly strong and patient of labor. The feet of the camel have tough, elastic soles, which prevent them from sinking in the sand. Its stomach will contain a supply of water sufficient for many days. Its food is coarse, such as leaves, twigs, and thistles, and the animal is specially adapted to crossing the deserts. In the East the camel is called the *land-ship* or *ship of the desert*. The Arabian species commonly referred to in the Bible has only one hump. The dromedary is a lighter and swifter variety. It has been much used in the East from very early times, Gen. 12:16; Exod. 9:3; Gen. 37:25, for riding, drawing chariots, carrying burdens and messengers, and in war. Camels were formerly, and still are, in the East, among the chief possessions of the rich.

Also see Gen. 24:10, 11, 14, 19, 20, 22, 30-32, 35, 44, 46, 61, 63, 64; 30:43; 31:17, 34; 32:7, 15.

Lev. 11:4.

Deut. 14:7.

Judg. 6:5; 7:12; 8:21, 26.

1 Sam. 15:3; 27:9; 30:17.

1 Kings 10:2.

2 Kings 8:9.
1 Chron. 5:21; 12:40; 27:30.
2 Chron. 9:1; 14:15.
Ezra 2:67.
Neh. 7:69.
Esther 8:10, 14.
Job 1:3, 17; 42:12.
Isa. 21:7; 30:6; 60:6.
Jer. 49:29, 32.
Ezek. 25:5.
Zech. 14:15.
Matt. 3:4; 19:24; 23:24.
Mark 1:6; 10:25.
Luke 18:25.

Camel's hair was woven into cloth, usually coarse and rough, used for coats of shepherds and camel-drivers and for tent-coverings. Matt. 3:4. Some of the cloth was exceedingly soft and fine.

Ca-me´le-on. See CHAMELEON.

Ca´mon (*standing-place*), a town of Gilead. Judg. 10:5. Jair was buried there.

Camp, a word frequently used in accounts of the movements of the Israelites. Many passages in the Levitical law refer to things to be done within or without the camp. The different encampments or stations on the journey through the wilderness are mentioned in Num. 33.
Also see Exod. 14:19, 20; 16:13; 19:16, 17; 29:14; 32:17, 19, 26, 27; 33:7, 11; 36:6.
Lev. 4:12, 21; 6:11; 8:17; 9:11; 10:4, 5; 13:46; 14:3, 8; 16:26-28; 17:3; 24:10, 14, 23.
Num. 1:52; 2:3, 9, 10, 16-18, 24, 25, 31, 32; 4:5, 15; 5:2-4; 10:2, 5, 6, 14, 18, 22, 25, 34; 11:1, 9, 26, 27, 30-32; 12:14, 15; 14:44; 15:35, 36; 19:3, 7, 9; 31:12, 13, 19, 24.
Deut. 23:10-12, 14; 29:11.
Josh. 5:8; 6:11, 14, 18, 23; 9:6; 10:6, 15, 21, 43.

Judg. 7:17-19, 21; 13:25; 21:8, 12.
1 Sam. 4:3, 5-7; 13:17; 14:21; 17:4, 17; 26:6.
2 Sam. 1:2, 3.
1 Kings 16:16.
2 Kings 3:24; 6:8; 7:5, 7, 8, 10, 12; 19:35.
2 Chron. 22:1; 32:21.
Pss. 78:28; 106:16.
Isa. 29:3; 37:36.
Jer. 50:29.
Ezek. 4:2.
Joel 2:11.
Amos 4:10.
Nah. 3:17.
Heb. 13:11, 13.
Rev. 20:9.

Cam´phire, a plant of great beauty and fragrance found in Egypt and other Eastern countries, and called also *alhenna*. The ladies of the East are very fond of it, and use it as a dye in staining the lips and finger-nails a yellowish-red. Song of Sol. 1:14; 4:13. Our *camphor* is wholly different from it.

Ca´na, a village of Galilee a few miles north of Nazareth, noted as the scene of Christ's first miracle, John 2:1-11, and of a later one. John 4:46. It was the home of NATHANAEL. John 21:2.

Canaan, ka´nan or ka´na-an (*low*). [1] The name of the fourth son of Ham, Gen. 10:6; 1 Chron. 1:8, the father of the Canaanites who, before the arrival of the children of Israel, inhabited Canaan. [2] The land stretching from Lebanon on the north to the wilderness of Arabia on the south, and from the Dead Sea on the east to the frontiers of Phœnicia and Philistia on the west, with but little access to the Mediterranean or Great Sea. Abraham dwelt in the land, and it was promised to his descendants. But Jacob left it on account of famine, and went with his sons to Egypt. When the twelve tribes of Israel came out of Egypt under Moses, they found Canaan occupied by the HITTITES, JEBUSITES, AMORITES, and other tribes originally comprised under the common title CANAANITES, and after a terrible war they succeeded, under Joshua, in conquering it. See PALESTINE.

Canaanite, ka´nan-ite or ka´na-an-ite, a name used in reference to one of the apostles, who is otherwise called ZELOTES, "the zealous," Matt. 10:4; Mark 3:18.

Canaanites, ka´nan-ites or ka´na-an-ites, the national name of the descendants of Canaan, afterward confined to the inhabitants of the land of Canaan. Gen. 10:18, 19; 15:21; 24:3, 37; 34:30; 50:11.

Exod. 3:8, 17; 13:5, 11; 23:23.

Num. 13:29; 14:25, 43, 45; 21:3.

Deut. 1:7; 7:1; 11:30; 20:17.

Josh. 3:10; 5:1; 7:9; 12:8; 13:4; 16:10; 17:12, 13, 16, 18; 24:11.

Judg. 1:1, 3-5, 9, 10, 17, 27-30, 32, 33; 3:3, 5.

2 Sam. 24:7.

1 Kings 9:16.

Ezra 9:1.

Neh. 9:8, 24.

Obad. 20.

Candace, kan´da-se, a queen of Ethiopia, or, according to some, a general title. Acts 8:27.

Can´dle, a word often used in the Bible, Job 18:6; Prov. 31:18; Luke 15:8, for LAMP (which see). (Candles were not known in the East.) The word candle is often used figuratively in the Bible to denote light generally.

Can´dle-stick. The golden "candle-stick," or rather lamp-stand, of the tabernacle was on the left hand of one entering the Holy Place and opposite the table of shew-bread. It was made of fine gold, and consisted of a stem, supposed to have been five feet high, with six branches. The branches came out at three points, two at each point of the stem, and the width of the whole across the top was about three feet and a half. It was richly ornamented. At the extremity of each branch and at the top of the stem there was a socket for the lamp, making seven in all. The lamps were supplied with pure olive-oil and lighted every evening. In Solomon's Temple there were ten golden "candle-sticks" or lampstands. There was but one in the second Temple. It was carried to Rome when Jerusalem was destroyed, and is copied on the triumphal arch of Titus at Rome.

Cane. See CALAMUS.

Can´ker-worm, in the Authorized Version of the Bible, is used where the Hebrew word means a kind of locust, perhaps in the larva state. Joel 1:4; Nah. 3:15, 16.

Canon, kan´un, a Greek word, meant first a straight staff, then a measuring-rod, and finally, since the fourth century, the word has been used to denote the rule according to which the genuineness of the writings of the Old and the New Testament was defined, or those writings themselves. See BIBLE.

Can´neh. See CALNEH.

Can´ti-cles. See SONG OF SOLOMON.

Ca´per. See HYSSOP.

Ca-per´na-um (*village of Nahum*) is not mentioned in the Old Testament, but frequently in the four Gospels as the home of Jesus after he left Nazareth, and as the scene of many of his miracles and discourses. Matt. 8:5-14; 9:2; 17:24; John 4:46; 6:17-59, etc. It was a city of Galilee, on the shore of the Sea of Galilee, and had a custom-house and a noted synagogue.

Also see Matt. 4:13; 11:23.
Mark 1:21; 2:1; 9:33.
Luke 4:23, 31; 7:1; 10:15.
John 2:12.

Caph´tor (*cup*), the district or city where the Caphtorim lived. Deut. 2:23; Amos 9:7.

Caph´to-rim or **Caph´tho-rim,** a tribe or colony descended from Mizraim. Gen. 10:14; 1 Chron. 1:12.

Cap-pa-do´ci-a, a region in the eastern part of Asia Minor, adjoining Armenia. Acts 2:9; 1 Pet. 1:1.

Cap´tain. [1] The Jewish army had captains of different grades. The captain of the host was the commander of the whole army. Deut. 1:15, etc. [2] The commander of a thousand Roman soldiers. Mark 6:21; Acts 21:31. [3] A leader of Roman soldiers. Luke 22:4. A captain of a hundred soldiers was called a CENTURION. [4] The captain of the Temple, Acts 4:1, was the chief of the priests and Levites who guarded the Temple and its vicinity. In this sense it is applied to Christ in Heb. 2:10.

Cap´tives, in the Bible, usually means those taken in war. They were treated with great cruelty, and were often sold into slavery. The Romans sometimes joined a captive face to face with a dead body, until the horrible exhalations destroyed the life of the victim.
Gen. 31:26.
Num. 31:9, 12, 19.
Deut. 21:11; 32:42.
1 Sam. 30:2, 3, 5.
1 Kings 8:46, 47.
2 Kings 24:14.
2 Chron. 6:36, 38; 28:5, 11, 13-15, 17.
Ps. 106:46.
Isa. 14:2; 20:4; 45:13; 49:25; 61:1.
Jer. 28:4; 29:1, 4, 7; 43:3, 12; 48:46; 50:33.

Ezek. 1:1; 6:9; 16:53.
Dan. 2:25; 11:8.
Luke 4:18.

Cap-tiv´i-ty (*exile, removal*). Num. 21:29. The Jews were often punished by captivities or servitudes. See HEBREWS.

Car´bun-cle, a precious stone. The term represents two different Hebrew words. The one in Exod. 28:17; 39:10, and in Ezek. 28:13 is generally supposed to mean the emerald or the beryl. The other, in Isa. 54:12, may mean a kind of ruby.

Car´cas, a chamberlain of Ahasuerus, king of Persia. Esther 1:10.

Carchemish or **Charchemish**, kar´kemish (*citadel of Chemoth*), a city near the Euphrates. 2 Chron. 35:20; Jer. 46:2.

Ca-re´ah (*bald head*), given in one place as the name of the father of Johanan. 2 Kings 25:23. In other passages it is correctly given KAREAH.

Care´ful, in Dan. 3:16; Phil. 4:6, and elsewhere, means anxious.

Ca´ri-a, a small Roman province in south-west Asia Minor. Its cities CNIDUS and MILETUS are mentioned in Acts 20:15; 27:7.

Car´mel (*fruitful place*). [1] The name of that mountain-ridge, twelve miles long, which from the western highlands of Palestine juts out into the Mediterranean Sea. See PALESTINE. It is noted as the scene of the most remarkable events in the history of ELIJAH and ELISHA, and is kept sacred not only by the Jews and Christians, but also by the Mohammedans. The Carmelite monks had their first monastery there, and took their name from it. [2] A town where Saul set up a monument, 1 Sam. 15:12; 25:2, 5, 7, 40, and Uzziah had his vineyards. 2 Chron. 26:10. It was situated in the mountains of

Judah, ten miles south-east of HEBRON. Also see Josh. 12:22; 15:55; 19:26.
1 Kings 18:19, 20, 42.
2 Kings 2:25; 4:25; 19:23.
Song of Sol. 7:5.
Isa. 33:9; 35:2; 37:24.
Jer. 46:18; 50:19.
Amos 1:2; 9:3.
Mic. 7:14.
Nah. 1:4.

Car´mel-ite or **Car´mel-i-tess,** an inhabitant of Carmel. 1 Sam. 27:3; 1 Chron. 11:37.

Car´mi (*vine-dresser*). [1] A son of Reuben. Gen. 46:9; 1 Chron. 5:3. [2] An Israelite of Judah. His son Achan stole some of the spoils of Jericho. Josh. 7:1, 18; 1 Chron. 2:7. [3] A son of Judah. 1 Chron. 4:1.

Car´mites, a family of Israelites descended from Carmi. Num. 26:6.

Car´nal (*fleshly*), the opposite of spiritual and holy. Rom. 7:14; 1 Cor. 3:3.

Car´pen-ter. The original word signifies artisan or mechanic. When used alone it generally denotes one who works in wood. The trade of a carpenter or worker in wood was followed by Joseph, Matt. 13:55, the reputed father of Jesus, and by Jesus himself. Mark 6:3. Carpenters are often mentioned in the Bible.
Also see 2 Sam. 5:11.
2 Kings 12:11; 22:6.
1 Chron. 14:1.
2 Chron. 24:12.
Ezra 3:7.
Isa. 41:7; 44:13.
Jer. 24:1; 29:2.
Zech. 1:20.

Car´pus (*fruit*), a disciple at Troas who was a friend of Paul. 2 Tim. 4:13.

Car´riage, in Judg. 18:21; 1 Sam. 17:20, 22; Isa. 10:28; 46:1; Acts 21:15,

means baggage, or that which is carried.

Car-she´na (*slender*), one of the highest seven princes of Persia and Media in the time of Ahasuerus. Esther 1:14.

Carts are mentioned in the Bible. 1 Sam. 6:7, 8, 10, 11, 14; 1 Chron. 13:7, etc. They were often drawn by heifers.

Case´ment, in Prov. 7:6, means a lattice; a network or blind before a window.

Ca-siph´i-a (*shining*), the place where some of the principal Jews resided when Ezra went up to Jerusalem. It was probably near AHAVA. Ezra 8:17.

Cas´lu-him, a tribe descended from Mizraim, the son of Ham. Gen. 10:14; 1 Chron. 1:12.

Cas´si-a, the dried inner bark of an odoriferous tree of the same species with cinnamon. It was an ingredient of the holy anointing oil, and was probably always imported from India. Exod. 30:24; Ezek. 27:19.

Cast´a-way (*worthless*). 1 Cor. 9:27. Infants in heathen countries are frequently exposed in the fields and allowed to perish. Ezek. 16:5.

Cas´tle, in Acts 21:34, 37; 22:24; 23:10, 16, 32, means the tower of Antonia, which was a fortress at the northwest corner of the Temple in Jerusalem.

Cas´tor. Instead of retaining or translating the term which means "sons of Jupiter," the English Version uses the two names "Castor and Pollux." Acts 28:11.

Cast out, in John 9:34, means to deprive a person of the privileges of the Jewish Church.

Cat´er-pil-lar, an insect of the locust kind in an immature state. They are extremely destructive to vegetation, and were often employed to execute God's judgments. Pss. 78:46; 105:34. See LOCUST.

Cath´o-lic (*universal*), a name originally given to the Christian Church in general, but now claimed by the Roman Catholic Church. The "Catholic epistles"—namely, JAMES, PETER I., and II., JOHN I., and JUDE—are so called because they were addressed to the church *in general*.

Cat'tle, in the common scriptural use of the word, includes all tame quadrupeds employed by man, such as oxen, horses, sheep, camels, goats, etc. In ancient times wealth consisted mainly of cattle.

Gen. 1:24-26; 2:20; 3:14; 4:20; 6:20; 7:14, 21, 23; 8:1, 17; 9:10; 13:2, 7; 29:7; 30:29, 32, 39-43; 31:8-10, 12, 18, 41, 43; 33:14, 17; 34:5, 23; 36:6, 7; 46:6, 32, 34; 47:6, 16-18.

Exod. 9:3, 4, 6, 7, 19-21; 10:26; 12:29, 38; 17:3; 20:10; 34:19.

Lev. 1:2; 5:2; 19:19; 25:7; 26:22.

Num. 3:41, 45; 20:4, 19; 31:9; 32:1, 4, 16, 26; 35:3.

Deut. 2:35; 3:7, 19; 5:14; 7:14; 11:15; 13:15; 20:14; 28:4, 11, 51; 30:9.

Josh. 1:14; 8:2, 27; 11:14; 14:4; 21:2; 22:8.

Judg. 6:5; 18:21.

1 Sam. 23:5; 30:20.

1 Kings 1:9, 19, 25.

2 Kings 3:9, 17.

1 Chron. 5:9, 21; 7:21.

2 Chron. 14:15; 26:10; 35:8, 9.

Neh. 9:37; 10:36.

Job 36:33.

Pss. 50:10; 78:48; 104:14; 107:38; 148:10.

Eccles. 2:7.

Isa. 7:25; 30:23; 43:23; 46:1.

Jer. 9:10; 49:32.

Ezek. 34:17, 20, 22; 38:12, 13.

Joel 1:18.

Jon. 4:11.

Hag. 1:11.

Zech. 2:4; 13:5.

Luke 17.7.

John 4:12.

Caul, in Lev. 3:4, 10, 15; 4:9, probably means great lobe of the liver; in Hos. 13:8 it means membrane around the heart; and in Isa. 3:18, network for the hair.

Cause'way, in 1 Chron. 26:16, 18, is supposed to mean the ascent from Zion to the west side of the Temple area.

Caves are very numerous in Palestine, and the names of some parts of the country have been derived from this fact. HAURAN, Ezek. 47:16, is cave-land. The HORITES dwelt in caves. Caves were used for dwellings, Gen. 19:30, and for concealment, Josh. 10:16, etc., and as burial-places. Gen. 23:17, 19; 49:29; John 11:38. Several caves are named in the Bible. See ADULLAM, MACHPELAH.

Also see Gen. 23:9, 11, 20; 25:9; 49:30, 32; 50:13.

Judg. 6:2.

1 Sam. 13:6; 22:1; 24:3, 7, 8, 10.

2 Sam. 23:13.

1 Kings 18:4, 13; 19:9.

1 Chron. 11:15.

Job 30:6.

Pss. 57; 142.

Isa. 2:19.

Ezek. 33:27.

Heb. 11:38.

Ce'dar is used in the Bible in reference to the whole pine tree family, and specially to the cedar of Lebanon, which is a noble evergreen tree, greatly celebrated in the Scriptures. Ps. 92:12; Ezek. 31:3-6, etc. Everything about this tree has a strong odor of balsam, and is very pleasant. The wood is exceedingly durable, and was used in the noblest and most costly edifices, including Solomon's Temple.

Also see Lev. 14:4, 6, 49, 51, 52.

Num. 19:6; 24:6.

Judg. 9:15.
2 Sam. 5:11; 7:2, 7.
1 Kings 4:33; 5:6, 8, 10; 6:9, 10, 15, 16, 18, 20, 36; 7:2, 3, 7, 11, 12; 9:11; 10:27.
2 Kings 14:9; 19:23.
1 Chron. 14:1; 17:1, 6; 22:4.
2 Chron. 1:15; 2:3, 8; 9:27; 25:18.
Ezra 3:7.
Job 40:17.
Pss. 29:5; 80:10; 104:16; 148:9.
Song of Sol. 1:17; 8:9.
Isa. 2:13; 9:10; 14:8; 37:24; 41:19; 44:14.
Jer. 22:7, 14, 15, 23.
Ezek. 17:3, 22, 23; 27:5, 24.
Amos 2:9.
Zeph. 2:14.
Zech. 11:1, 2.

Cedron, se´dron, a brook in the valley between Jerusalem and the Mount of Olives. John 18:1. See KEDRON, or KIDRON.

Ceiled, seeld, in 2 Chron. 3:5; Jer. 22:14, etc., means paneled; wainscoted.

Ceil´ings were found only in the Temple, palaces of kings, or in princely residences. They were often very beautiful. 1 Kings 6:15; Hag. 1:4; Jer. 22:14.

Cel´lars, such as are common with us, were not known in the East. They had places used for storing wine, jars of which were buried to the neck.

Cel´o-Syr-i-a. See CŒLE-SYRIA.

Cen´chre-a, the eastern harbor of Corinth, is on the Saronic Gulf, about nine miles east of that city. A church was formed at Cenchrea. Rom. 16:1. Paul sailed from thence to Ephesus. Acts 18:18.

Cen´ser, Lev. 10:1, among the Jews, was a kind of pan used in the Temple service to carry the fire in which incense was burned to the altar of incense. The fire was taken from the perpetual supply on the altar of burnt-offering. Little is known of the form of the censer. The one used on the Day of Atonement was of pure gold. 1 Kings 7:50. The word translated "censer" in Heb. 9:4 means the golden altar of incense.

Cen´sus. The Old Testament mentions twelve censuses of the Jews. The first was taken in the third or fourth month after the exodus, and showed that there were 603,550 men. Exod. 38:26. The order for the second numbering is given in Num. 1:2. The third census was made directly after the Hebrews entered Canaan. Num. 26. King David made the fourth census. 2 Sam. 24:9; 1 Chron. 21:1. The last general census was made at the time of the return. Ezra 2:64; 8:1-14. The census of Cyrenius (or Quirinius) is mentioned in Luke 2:2.

Cen-tu´ri-on, an officer among the Romans commanding a hundred soldiers. Matt. 8:5; Acts 22:25.

Ce´phas (*rock*), a Syriac surname which Jesus gave to SIMON. John 1:42. See PETER.

Ce´sar. See CÆSAR.

Ces-a-re´a. See CÆSAREA.

Ces-a-re´a Philippi. See CÆSAREA PHILIPPI.

Chafed, in 2 Sam. 17:8, means heated; exasperated.

Chaff was separated from the grain, in ancient times, by throwing both together against the wind with the winnowing-shovel. The wind blew away the chaff and the grain fell to the ground. Notice the figurative use of the word chaff in Pss. 1:4; 35:5.

Chains, in Num. 31:50 and Isa. 3:19, is supposed to mean *foot-chains*. They were worn as ornaments around the ankles, and caused the wearer to observe a certain measured pace. The chains mentioned in Acts 12:6, 7 were fetters. Chains were part of the furnishing of the Temple and of the priestly dress.

Chalcedony, kal-sed´o-ny, Rev. 21:19, a precious stone found in the copper-mines of Chalcedon, near Constantinople, and elsewhere, is a species of quartz of various colors and resembling agate. It is used for cups and vases.

Chalcol or **Calcol,** kal´kol (*sustaining*), a son of Mahol. 1 Kings 4:31; 1 Chron. 2:6.

Chaldea, kal-de´a, a country comprising an area of about 23,000 square miles, occupied the southernmost part of the Mesopotamian plain along the Euphrates, down to the Persian Gulf. Abraham was born there, Gen. 11:31, but its native inhabitants were of Cushite descent. Their principal city was Ur; their great hero Nimrod, the son of Cush. The Chaldeans formed very early a great empire, the first of the four grand monarchies of Asia, extending north to the sources of the Euphrates. But B. C. about 1300 this empire was overthrown by the Assyrians, and from that time Chaldea became only a part or province, first of Assyria, afterward of Babylonia; the *Chaldeans* lost their Cushite nationality and became by amalgamation Shemites. After the establishment of the Babylonian Empire under Nabopalazzar, B. C. 625, CHALDEANS or CHALDEES became the generally accepted names for the subjects of that empire, Jer. 21:4; Hab. 1:6; Ezek. 23:14, and in the book of Daniel, 1:4; 2:2, etc., the name is evidently applied to only a peculiar portion of the Babylonian people—the learned class.

Chalk´stones, Isa. 27:9, a soft mineral substance resembling limestone. To make the Jewish altars like chalk-stones was to crumble and destroy them.

Cham´ber. Gen. 43:30. The private apartments of a house are usually called chambers. 2 Sam. 18:33; Ps. 19:5. In Job 9:9; Ps. 104:3, 13, chambers denotes constellations or regions in the heavens.

Cham´ber-ing, in Rom. 13:13, means licentiousness.

Cham´ber-lain, 2 Kings 23:11, an officer who has charge of the royal chambers, or the king's lodgings, wardrobes, etc. In Eastern courts eunuchs were commonly thus employed. Esther 1:10, 12, 15. In Rom. 16:23 the treasurer of the city is probably referred to.

Chameleon, ka-meel´yun, a lizardlike reptile whose color changes with that of objects about it or when its temper is disturbed. It feeds on insects which it catches by darting out its long, sticky tongue. It is mentioned in Lev. 11:30 among the unclean creeping things.

Chamois, sham´wa or sham´i, mentioned in Deut. 14:5, is not the well-known mountain-goat of Southern Europe, but probably a variety of wild sheep.

Cham-paign´, in Deut. 11:30, means plain; level country.

Cham´pion, in ancient warfare, was one who challenged a foe to single combat in the presence of contending armies. (See GOLIATH. 1 Sam. 17:4.) The issue of the battle was sometimes staked on such an encounter.

Chanaan, ka´nan or ka´na-an, Acts 7:11; 13:19, Greek form of Canaan. See CANAAN.

Chance, in 1 Sam. 6:9, might better be rendered *occurrence*, and is so rendered in several ancient versions.

Chan´cel-lor, in Ezra 4:8, 17, means counsellor.

Chap´i-ter, in Exod. 36:38, etc., means capital of a pillar.

Chap´men, in 2 Chron. 9:14, means travelling merchants.

Chapt, in Jer. 14:4, means cracked by heat and drought.

Charashim, kar´a-shim (*craftsmen*), a valley near Jerusalem. 1 Chron. 4:14; Neh. 11:35.

Charchemish, kar´ke-mish. 2 Chron. 35:20. Same as CARCHEMISH (which see).

Char´ger, in Num. 7:13; Ezra 1:9; Matt. 14:8, 11, means a large dish; a platter.

Charg´es. In Acts 21:24 "be at charges with them" means pay the cost of their rites and offerings.

Char´i-ots, mentioned in the Bible, were of two kinds, both of which were two-wheeled and drawn by horses. One kind was used for princes and generals to ride in, Gen. 41:43; 46:29; 2 Kings 5:9; Acts 8:28, or dedicated to idols. 2 Kings 23:11. Another kind was used in war: "chariots of iron," not made of iron, but armed with iron scythes or hooks extending from the ends of the axletrees. An archer or a spearman usually stood by the side of the charioteer as he drove furiously into the battle. Many chariots were used by the army of Pharaoh which pursued the Israelites at the time of the exodus. Exod. 14:28. In Song of Sol. 3:9 "chariot" seems to mean a kind of palanquin.

Char´i-ty (*love*). The Greek word means love, and is generally so translated. 1 Cor. 8:1; 13:1-4, 8, 13; 14:1; 16:14.
Col. 3:14.
1 Thess. 3:6.
2 Thess. 1:3.
1 Tim. 1:5; 2:15; 4:12.
2 Tim. 2:22; 3:10.
Titus 2:2.
1 Pet. 4:8; 5:14.
2 Pet. 1:7.
3 John 6.
Jude :12.
Rev. 2:19.

Charm´ers, people who claim to be able to tame and control serpents, even the most venomous kinds. Ps. 58:5; Jer. 8:17.

Charms. See AMULETS.

Charran, kar´ran. Acts 7:2, 4. Same as HARAN (which see).

Chebar, ke´bar (*joining*), a district and river in Chaldea, where Ezekiel the prophet saw the vision of the glory of the Lord. Ezek. 1:1, 3; 3:15, etc.

Chedorlaomer, ked´or-la´o-mer (*sheafband*), a king of Elam in the time of Abram. Gen. 14:1, 17. His name is found on Chaldean bricks.

Cheek Teeth, in Joel 1:6, means molars, or double teeth.

Cheese is several times mentioned in the Bible, and is an important article of food in the East. It is generally white, very salty, soft when new, but soon becomes hard and dry. Job 10:10; 1 Sam. 17:18.

Chelal, ke´lal (*completeness*), a Jew who married a foreign wife. Ezra 10:30.

Chelluh, kel´lu, a Jew who took a foreign wife. Ezra 10:35.

Chelub, ke´lub. [1] A descendant of Judah. 1 Chron. 4:11. [2] An Israelite whose son Ezri superintended the tillers of the ground in David's time. 1 Chron. 27:26.

Chelubai, ke-lu´bai, a name given in one place (1 Chron. 2:9) to the son of Hezron, who is in same chapter called CALEB.

Chemarims, kem´a-rimz. This word is usually translated "priests" or "idolatrous priests," but in one case it is left untranslated, as if it had been a proper name. 2 Kings 23:5 (margin); Hos. 10:5 (in the marginal notes); Zeph. 1:4.

Chemosh, ke´mosh (*fire*), the national idol of the Moabites. Num. 21:29; Jer. 48:7.

Chenaanah, ke-na´a-nah (*flat*). [1] Father of the false prophet Zedekiah. 1 Kings 22:11; 2 Chron. 18:10. [2] Brother of Ehud. 1 Chron. 7:10. Perhaps same as No. 1.

Chenani, ken´a-ni (*creator*), a Levite who conducted the devotions of the people after Ezra read to them the law. Neh. 9:4.

Chenaniah, ken´a-ni-ah. [1] A Levite leader of the singers when David brought up the ark from the house of Obed-edom. 1 Chron. 15:22, 27. [2] A descendant of Kohath. 1 Chron. 26:29.

Chephar-haammonai, ke´far-ha-am´-mo-nai, a small town of Benjamin. Josh. 18:24.

Chephirah, ke-fi´rah (*village*), a town of the Hivites which afterward belonged to the tribe of Benjamin. Josh. 9:17; Ezra 2:25.

Cheran, ke´ran (*union*), a child of Dishon. Gen. 36:26; 1 Chron. 1:41.

Cherethims, ker´eth-imz, or **Cherethites,** ker´eth-itz. [1] A tribe apparently of the Philistines. 1 Sam. 30:14; Zeph. 2:5. [2] A title of a class of officers who, with the Pelethites, formed David's guard. 2 Sam. 8:18; 1 Chron. 18:17.

Cherith, ke´rith (*gorge*), a brook or torrent which emptied into Jordan from the east, near Jericho. Elijah was commanded to hide himself near it from Ahab, and was there fed by ravens. 1 Kings 17:3-5.

Cher´ub, plural **Cher´u-bim,** beings of unknown nature, but not angels. The word "cherubim" occurs first in Gen. 3:24, where it is applied to the guard placed over Eden after Adam was driven out. Cherubim are the witnesses of God's presence, and representations of them were used in the Tabernacle and Temple. Two golden cherubim stood in the Holy of Holies, upon the mercy-seat in the Tabernacle. Exod 37:8. Precise directions are given in Exod. 25:18, etc. concerning their material, attitude, and position, and they are described in 2 Chron. 3:10–13, but nothing is said about their shape except that they had wings.

Also see Exod. 26:1, 31; 36:8, 35; 37:7-9.
Num. 7:89.
1 Sam 4:4.
2 Sam. 6:2; 22:11.
1 Kings 6:23-29, 32, 35; 7:29, 36; 8:6, 7.
2 Kings 19:15.
1 Chron. 13:6; 28:18.
2 Chron. 3:7, 14; 5:7, 8.
Pss. 18:10; 80:1; 99:1.
Isa. 37:16.
Ezek. 9:3; 10:1-9, 14-16, 18-20; 11:22; 28:14, 16; 41:18, 20, 25.
Heb. 9:5.

Cherub, ke´rub, a place in Babylonia perhaps Cheripha of Ptolemy. Ezra 2:59; Neh. 7:61.

Chesalon, kes´a-lon (*fortress*), a name sometimes given to Mount Jearim, in the north of Judah. Josh. 15:10.

Chesed, ke´sed, a son of Nahor, the brother of Abraham. Gen. 22:22.

Chesil, ke´sil (*fleshy*). [1] A town in south of Judah. Josh. 15:30. [2] Also a name given to one of the constellations, generally supposed to have been Orion. Job 9:9; Amos 5:8. In Isa. 13:10 the word occurs in the plural and is translated "constellations."

Ches´nut Tree, in Gen. 30:37; Ezek. 31:8, should be "plane tree." The chestnut tree is not found in Palestine.

Chest, the translation of two Hebrew words. The first is used in 2 Kings 12:9, 10; 2 Chron. 24:8, 10, 11, to denote the coffer into which the people put their contributions for repairing the Temple under

Joash. The original word in every other place except Gen. 50:26, where it denotes Joseph's coffin, means the ark of the covenant. An entirely different word is used for the ark of Noah and that of Moses. The second word is used only in Ezek. 27:24, where it means a treasure-chest.

Chesulloth, ke-sul´loth (*loins*), a town of Issachar. Josh. 19:18.

Chezib, ke´zib (*deceitful*), a town of the Canaanites, afterward in Judah. Gen. 38:5. It is probably same as ACHZIB in Judah.

Chidon, ki´don, 1 Chron. 13:9, is called also the threshing-floor of NACHON in 2 Sam. 6:6. It was near Jerusalem.

Chief Priest. See PRIEST.

Chil´dren. A large family of children was considered a great blessing in Bible times. See Ps. 127:3-5. They were subject to the father in all things, Gen. 22:21; Num. 30:5, and were liable to be sold into temporary bondage for his debts. Lev. 25:39-41; 2 Kings 4:1; Matt. 18:25. The firstborn son received a double portion of the father's estate; the daughters no portion, except in cases mentioned in Num. 27:1-11. At the age of thirty Benjamin is called a child in Gen. 44:20.

Chil´dren of the East, the name of the tribes who lived to the eastward of Canaan. Gen. 29:1; Judg. 6:3, 33; 7:12.

Chil´dren of E´den, the name of a tribe, probably in Mesopotamia. 2 Kings 19:12; Isa. 37:12.

Chil´dren of Is´ra-el. See HEBREWS.

Chileab, kil´e-ab, David's second son, whose mother was Abigail. 2 Sam. 3:3. He is called DANIEL in 1 Chron. 3:1.

Chilion, ki-li´on (*pining*), a son of Elimelech and Naomi. Ruth 1:2; 4:9.

Chilmad, kil´mad, a region supposed to have been between Assyria and Arabia. Ezek. 27:23.

Chimham, kim´ham (*longing*), an Israelite who was recommended to David's care by Barzillai. 2 Sam. 19:37, 38, 40; Jer. 41:17. Some infer from 1 Kings 2:7 that he was a son of Barzillai.

Chinnereth, kin´ne-reth, or **Chinneroth,** kin´ne-roth, Josh. 11:2, a fenced city of Naphtali, on the lake or sea of the same name. Num. 34:11. Called CINNEROTH in 1 Kings 15:20.

Chinnereth, kin´ne-reth, **Sea of.** See GALILEE, SEA OF.

Chios, ki´os, an island in the Grecian Archipelago, Acts 20:15, is about thirty miles long and ten miles wide, and is now called *Scio*. It has always been famous for its beauty and fertility.

Chisleu, kis´lu, the ninth month of the sacred year and the third month of the civil year of the Jews. Neh. 1:1; Zech. 7:1. This month begins with the new moon nearest the first of December. See MONTH.

Chislon, kis´lon (*confidence*), the father of Elidad. Num. 34:21.

Chisloth-tabor, kis´loth-ta´bor, denotes either a mountain or a place. Josh. 19:12. If a mountain, it is probably same as TABOR. If a city, is may be *Iksal*, about two miles west of TABOR.

Chittim, kit´tim, or **Kit-tim.** Num. 24:24; Isa. 23:1, 12; Jer. 2:10; Ezek. 27:6; Dan. 11:30. The "isles," "ships," "products," and "people" of Chittim are here mentioned or alluded to, and therefore the name has been supposed to mean the island of CYPRUS. Some think it applies to the islands and coasts west of Palestine. See CYPRUS.

Chiun, ki´un, Amos 5:26, an idol made and worshipped by the Israelites in the wilderness. See REMPHAN.

Chloe, klo´e, a female disciple apparently residing at the place from which

Paul sent his first Epistle to the Corinthians; generally supposed to be PHILIPPI. 1 Cor. 1:11.

Chor-ashan, ko-ra´shan (*smoking furnace*), a town of Judah which is supposed to be the same as ASHAN (Josh. 15:42), which afterward became a city of the Simeonites (Josh. 19.7). 1 Sam. 30:30.

Chorazin, ko-ra´zin, a city near the north end of the Sea of Galilee. It is mentioned with CAPERNAUM and BETHSAIDA, Matt. 11:20–23; Luke 10:13, in the woes spoken by Christ.

Chozeba, ko-ze´ba, a place in Judah. 1 Chron. 4:22.

Christ (*anointed*), the official name of the long-promised and long-expected Saviour. It is the Greek equivalent to the Jewish MESSIAH. Jesus was his personal name among men during his life on earth, and he is generally so called in the Gospels, while the CHRIST or JESUS CHRIST is generally used in the Epistles.

NAMES, TITLES, AND OFFICES OF CHRIST.

Adam, The Second. 1 Cor. 15:45, 47.
Advocate. 1 John 2:1.
Alpha and Omega. Rev. 1:8.
Amen. Rev. 3:14.
Author and Finisher of our faith. Heb. 12:2.
Author of eternal salvation. Heb. 5:9.
Beginning of the creation of God. Rev. 3:14.
Blessed and only Potentate. 1 Tim. 6:15.
Branch. Zech. 3:8.
Bread of God. John 6:33.
Bread of Life. John 6:35.
Captain of Salvation. Heb. 2:10.
Child, Little. Isa. 11:6.
Christ, the. Matt. 16:16.
Corner-stone. Eph. 2:20.

Counsellor. Isa. 9:6.
David. Jer. 30:9; Hos. 3:5.
Day-spring. Luke 1:78.
Deliverer. Rom. 11:26.
Desire of all nations. Hag. 2:7.
Emmanuel. Isa. 7:14; Matt. 1:23.
Everlasting Father. Isa. 9:6.
Faithful Witness. Rev. 1:5.
First and Last. Rev. 1:17.
First-begotten of the dead. Rev. 1:5.
God. Isa. 40:9.
God blessed for ever. Rom. 9:5.
Good Shepherd. John 10:11.
Governor. Matt. 2:6.
Great High-Priest. Heb. 4:14.
High-Priest. Heb 5:10.
Holy child Jesus. Acts 4:27.
Holy, the most. Dan. 9:24.
Holy One. Luke 4:34.
Holy Thing. Luke 1:35.
Horn of Salvation. Luke 1:69.
I AM. Exod. 3:14, with John 8:58.
Image of God. 2 Cor. 4:4.
Jehovah. Isa. 26:4.
Jesus. Matt. 1:21.
Just One. Acts 7:52.
King everlasting. Luke 1:33.
King of Israel. John 1:49.
King of the Jews. Matt. 2:2.
King of kings. 1 Tim. 6:15.
Lamb of God. John 1:29.
Lawgiver. Isa. 33:22.
Light of the world. John 8:12.
Light, True. John 1:9.
Lion of the tribe of Judah. Rev. 5:5.
Living stone. 1 Pet. 2:4.
Lord. Matt. 3:3.
Lord God Almighty. Rev. 15:3.
Lord of all. Acts 10:36.
Lord of Glory. 1 Cor. 2:8.
Lord of lords. Rev. 17:14.
Lord our Righteousness. Jer. 23:6.
Maker and Preserver of all things.

John 1:3.
Mediator. 1 Tim. 2:5.
Mediator of the new covenant.
  Heb. 12:24.
Messiah. Dan. 9:25.
Mighty God. Isa. 9:6.
Mighty One of Jacob. Isa. 60:16.
Morning Star. Rev. 22:16.
Nazarene. Matt. 2:23.
Our Passover. 1 Cor. 5:7.
Priest for ever. Heb. 5:6.
Prince. Acts 5:31.
Prince of Life. Acts 3:15.
Prince of Peace. Isa. 9:6.
Prince of the kings of the earth. Rev. 1:5.
Prophet. Deut. 18:15.
Redeemer. Job 19:25.
Righteous, the. 1 John 2:1.
Root and offspring of David. Rev. 22:16.
Root of David. Rev. 5:5.
Ruler in Israel. Mic. 5:2.
Same yesterday, today, and for ever.
  Heb. 13:8.
Saviour. Luke 2:11.
Shepherd and Bishop of souls. 1 Pet. 2:25.
Shepherd in the land. Zech. 11:16.
Shepherd of the sheep, Great. Heb. 13:20.
Shiloh. Gen. 49:10.
Son, a. Heb. 3:6.
Son, the. Ps. 2:12.
Son, My beloved. Matt. 3:17.
Son, only-begotten. John 1:18.
Son of David. Matt. 9:27.
Son of God. Matt. 8:29.
Son of man. Matt. 8:20.
Son of the Highest. Luke 1:32.
Star, bright and morning. Rev. 22:16.
Star and Sceptre. Num. 24:17.
Vine, the. John 15:5.
Vine, true. John 15:1.
Way, Truth, and Life. John 14:6.
Witness, faithful and true. Rev. 3:14.
Wonderful. Isa. 9:6.

Word. John 1:1.
Word of God. Rev. 19:13.

Chris´tians, the name given to the followers of Christ. It was first used, Acts 11:26, at Antioch in Syria, about A. D. 42.

Chron´i-cles, the First and Sec´ond Books of, are the thirteenth and fourteenth books of the Old Testament Canon. They give an account of the history of the Jewish people from their origin to their return from the captivity, embracing a period of nearly 3500 years. They were drawn from the same sources as FIRST and SECOND BOOKS OF KINGS, namely, the national diaries and journals and the living popular tradition, but were written from a specific sacerdotal point of view. They date from the time of Ezra or later. They were accepted in the Canon on account of the many additions to the BOOKS OF KINGS which they contain, but as they were of so recent date they were placed among the HAGIOGRAPHA (the holy writings of the Jews). See BIBLE.

Chro-nol´o-gy, the method of ascertaining the years when past events took place, and arranging them in order according to dates. B. C. before a date means before Christ; cir. means about; A. D. means the year of our Lord.

Chrys´o-lite (*golden stone*), Rev. 21:20, is the yellow topaz or the beryl of the Old Testament. It is supposed to be the Oriental topaz of modern times.

Chry-sop´ra-sus, Rev. 21:20, a precious stone of a greenish color.

Chub, kub, a people in alliance with Egypt in the time of Nebuchadnezzar. Ezek. 30:5.

Chun, kun, a town of Hadarezer, king of Zobah, which was pillaged by David. 1 Chron. 18:8. Same as BEROTHAI. 2 Sam. 8:8.

Church is the translation of a Greek word (*ecclesia*) which means an assembly, and denotes in the New Testament [1] a local congregation of Christian believers (as the church in Jerusalem, in Antioch, in Ephesus, in Corinth, in Rome, the churches in Asia, in Achaia, etc.); [2] the whole body of believers in Christ (as Matt. 16:18; Gal. 1:13; Eph. 1:22; 5:27). In Acts 7:38 church means the congregation of Israelites at Sinai.

Churl, in Isa. 32:5, 7, means a deceiver.

Churl´ish, in 1 Sam. 25:3, means coarse and rude.

Chusan-rishathaim, ku´shan-rish-a-tha´im, a king of Mesopotamia or Aram who oppressed the Israelites for eight years, and was subdued by Othniel. Judg. 3:8, 10.

Chuza, ku´za, the steward of Herod Antipas. Luke 8:3.

Cilicia, si-lish´i-a, a province of Asia Minor, bounded south by the Mediterranean Sea, north by Cappadocia, west by Pamphylia, east by Syria. Tarsus, its capital, was the home of Paul, and many Jews were living in the land. One of its chief industrial products was a kind of cloth made from goats' hair and used in tent-making, which was Paul's trade. The country is very frequently mentioned in the Acts, and is referred to in Gal. 1:21. See TARSUS.

Cin´na-mon´, Song of Sol. 4:14, the inner bark of a tree. The finest quality comes from Ceylon, and was obtained by the Jews by the way of Babylon. It was used by them in the perfumed oil with which the Tabernacle and its vessels were anointed. Exod. 30:23; Rev. 18:13.

Cinneroth, sin´ne-roth, a district in or adjacent to the territory of the tribe of Naphtali. 1 Kings 15:20. It is generally called CHINNERETH.

Cir´cle, in Isa. 40:22, means the line within which the earth revolves, and figuratively describes a position from which every part of its surface can be seen. In Prov. 8:27 the same word is rendered *compass*, and means the boundary within which the waters are restrained.

Cir-cum-cis´ion, a rite or ceremony of the Jewish religion.

Cis, sis, Acts 13:21, the father of King Saul. See KISH, No. 1.

Cis´terns, Prov. 5:15, were common in Judea. Some were merely holes dug in the ground to receive the water from a spring. When these pits were empty there was mire at the bottom. They were used for the most cruel and extreme punishments. Joseph was probably cast into such a pit. Gen. 37:24. See also Ps. 40:2; Jer. 38:6. Other cisterns were of various forms, and were sometimes hewn out of the rock. Large cisterns are found in various parts of Palestine, and were the chief dependence of the people for water; hence the force of the allusion in Jer. 2:13.

Cit´ies of Ref´uge, Num. 35:4, 5, 14, were six of the Levitical cities divinely appointed by the Jewish law as asylums, to which any one was commanded to flee, for safety and protection, who had been undesignedly accessory to the death of a human being. His offence was investigated, and if he was not within the provisions of the law, he was delivered to the avenger, and slain.

Cit´i-zen-ship, Phil. 3:20 (in the Revised Version), is CONVERSATION in the Authorized Version. Roman citizenship is referred to in the New Testament. It denoted the privileges enjoyed by certain Roman subjects in Palestime, and was secured by inheritance or by purchase.

Acts 22:28, by military service, by manumission, or by favor, and included the right of appeal unto Cæsar. Acts 25:11. Paul was a Roman citizen.

Cit´y of Con-fu´sion, applied prophetically to Jerusalem in describing the sinfulness and consequent calamities of the land. Isa. 24:10.

Cit´y of Da´vid, the name frequently given to that part of Jerusalem which was built on Mount Zion.

2 Sam. 5:7, 9; 6:10.
1 Kings 2:10; 3:1; 8:1; 9:24; 11:27, 43; 15:8, 24; 22:50.
2 Kings 8:24; 12:21; 14:20; 15:7, 38; 16:20.
1 Chron. 11:7; 13:13; 15:29.
2 Chron. 8:11; 9:31; 12:16; 14:1; 16:14; 21:1, 20; 24:16, 25; 27:9; 32:5, 30; 33:14.
Neh. 12:37.
Isa. 22:9.
Luke 2:4, 11.

Cit´y of De-struc´tion, the name prophetically given to one of the five cities in Egypt inhabited by Israelites. Isa. 19:18.

Cit´y of God, a name of ancient Jerusalem. Ps. 46:4.

Cit´y of Palm-trees, a name sometimes given to Jericho. Deut. 34:3; 2 Chron. 28:15.

Cit´y of Salt, a city in the south-east part of Judah, near the Dead Sea. Josh. 15:62.

Cit´y of Wa´ters, a name given by Joab to a part of RABBAH, the chief city of the Ammonites. 2 Sam. 12:27.

Clau´da, a small island in the Mediterranean Sea, a little south-west of Crete. Acts 27:16.

Clau´di-a, a female disciple at Rome. 2 Tim. 4:21.

Clau´di-us, the fourth Roman emperor, A. D. 41–54, was an intimate friend of Herod Agrippa I. Nevertheless, on account of their insubordination and aversion to all rule and discipline, he expelled the Jews from Rome, A. D. 53, and together with them the Christians, who were as yet considered a mere Jewish sect by the Romans. Acts 11:28; 18:2.

Clau´di-us Felix. See FELIX.

Clau´di-us Lys´i-as, a Roman officer who was chief captain of the army in Jerusalem when Paul was laid hold on by the Jews. Acts 23:26.

Clay was used by the ancients in many ways. See POTTER. It was used in sealing, as wax is with us. Job 38:14. A piece of clay was often put on the lock of a storehouse and sealed. Many impressions of seals are found on Babylonian bricks.

Clean and UNCLEAN are words often used in a ceremonial sense in the Bible.

Cleave, in Gen. 2:24; Rom. 12:9, means adhere; remain faithful.

Clem´ent, a fellow-laborer with Paul at Philippi. Phil. 4:3.

Cle´o-pas, one of the two disciples with whom Jesus conversed on the way to Emmaus, after he had risen from the dead. Luke 24:18. Some consider him same as CLEOPHAS.

Cle´o-phas, the husband of Mary, who is by some supposed to have been a sister of the mother of Jesus. John 19:25.

Cloak, Clothes. See GARMENTS.

Cloud, Pil´lar of, the miraculous sign of the divine presence and care which guided the Israelites in the desert.

Clouts, in Jer. 38:11. means pieces of old garments. "Clouted," in Josh. 9:5, means worn out and patched.

Cnidus, ni´dus, a Greek city on a promontory of Caria, at the south-west extremity of Asia Minor. Acts 27:7.

Coal, when mentioned in the Bible, usually means charcoal or the embers of a fire, often in a pan. John 18:18. Mines on Mount Lebanon supply a kind of coal somewhat sulphurous in quality, but there is no evidence that mineral coal was known and used by the Jews. Some passages seem to suggest it—namely, 2 Sam. 22:9, 13; Job 41:21; Prov. 26:21. In 2 Sam. 14:7 to "quench one's coal" means to destroy his last living child. The expression in Rom. 12:20, " heap coals of fire on his head," means melt him into kindness.

Coast, in the Authorized Version, is often used for border, and without reference to the sea. Judg. 11:20; Matt. 8:34.

Coat. See GARMENTS.

Coat of Mail. See ARMS, and HABERGEON.

Cock´a-trice, in Isa. 11:8, etc., is an old English word meaning a kind of crested venomous serpent.

Cock´-crow-ing, Mark 13:35, the third watch of the night in the time of Christ. It was between midnight and daybreak.

Cock´le (*stinking*), in Job 31:40, means an offensive wild plant found among grain and in the borders of fields.

Cœle-Syria, sel´e-syr´i-a (*hollow Syria*), the valley between the Lebanon and Anti-Lebanon ranges. See LEBANON, and SYRIA.

Cof´fer, in 1 Sam. 6:8, 11, 15, means a movable box on the side of a cart.

Cof´fin, in Gen. 50:26, means a mummy-chest cut out of stone or syca-more-wood. Such coffins were used in burying some noted persons, but not often among the Jews.

Col-ho´zeh (*wholly a seer*). [1] Father of Shallum. Neh. 3:15. [2] Perhaps the same person, grandfather of Maaseiah. Neh. 11:5.

Col´lege, in 2 Kings 22:14, probably one of the divisions of Jerusalem built on the hill Acra.

Col´lops, in Job 15:27, means slices or flakes of meat or fat.

Col´o-ny, in Acts 16:12, means a foreign town whose inhabitants were granted, for distinguished services, the same rights and privileges that the citizens of Rome enjoyed.

Col´ors. Gen. 37:3. The Jews understood the art of coloring cloth, though they did not originate it, but learned it from the Phœnicians and the Egyptians. The Bible mentions four artificial colors. [1] *Purple,* obtained from a shell-fish of the Mediterranean Sea. It was the royal and noble color. Judg. 8:26; Luke 16:19. [2] *Blue,* obtained from the same source as purple. Exod. 25:4; Esther 1:6. [3] *Scarlet* and *crimson* seem to indicate the same color, and were obtained from an insect resembling the cochineal. The above colors [1, 2, 3], in connection with white, were used in the curtains of the Tabernacle and the clothing of the priests. [4] *Vermilion* was used in fresco painting, Ezek. 23:14; also to color idols, decorate walls, etc. Jer. 22:14. The distinction between the natural colors *yellow* and *green* is not sharply defined in the Bible.

Co-los´se, Col. 1:2, or **Co-los´sæ,** a city of Phrygia, Asia Minor, now in ruins, may have been visited by Paul on his third missionary journey. Later on, however, the Colossian church was disturbed by the intrusion of Judaistic asceticism and Oriental mysticism, and in order to set things right again Paul wrote from Rome, A. D. 62, the Epistle to the Colossians.

Colossians, ko-losh´i-anz, **E-pis´tle to the,** has an introduction of rejoicing at the Christian attainments of the Colossians, with a description of the lofty character of Christ; also cautions and instructions against inclining toward the errors of Judaizing and over-philosophizing, together with sundry lessons in practical morals, especially in the various domestic relations.

Colt, a name given to the young of camels and asses in Gen. 32:15; 49:11; Judg 10:4, etc.

Come by the boat, in Acts 27:16, means secure the boat, so as to hoist it into the ship.

Com´fort-er, John 14:16, is the English rendering for PARACLETE (same as ADVOCATE), and is found only in the Gospel of John. It is applied to the HOLY GHOST in four out of the five passages in which it is used, and should be translated "advocate" or "helper." See ADVOCATE.

Com´fort-less, in John 14:18, literally means orphans.

Com-mand´ments. See Exod. 20, and LAW.

Com-mend´, in Rom. 3:5, means draw commendation upon.

Com-mune´, in Exod. 25:22; 1 Sam. 19:3; Ps. 4:4, means hold a conference.

Com´pass, fetch a, in 2 Sam. 5:23; 2 Kings 3:9; Acts 28:13, means to make a circuit.

Com-pel´, in Luke 14:23, means to urge vehemently. In Matt. 5:41 it has reference to the custom of Persian and Roman government couriers, who were authorized to press men and horses into their service for a certain time.

Com-pre-hend´ed, in Isa. 40:12; Rom. 13:9, means included.

Co-na-ni´ah (*Jehovah is founding*), a chief of the Levites in the time of King Josiah. 2 Chron. 35:9.

Con-cis´ion, in Phil. 3:2, means meaningless cutting; opposed to circumcision as a religious symbol.

Con´cu-bine, in the Bible, means a lawful wife of an inferior rank. Gen. 22:24; 25:6; 35:22; 36:12. Judg. 8:31; 19:1, 2, 9, 10, 24, 25, 27, 29; 20:4-6.
2 Sam. 3:7; 5:13; 15:16; 16:21, 22; 19:5; 20:3; 21:11.
1 Kings 11:3.
1 Chron. 1:32; 2:46, 48; 3:9; 7:14.
2 Chron. 11:21.
Esther 2:14.
Song of Sol. 6:8, 9.
Dan. 5:2, 3, 23.

Con-dem-na´tion. See DAMNATION.

Conduit, kon´dit or kun´dit, an aqueduct. 2 Kings 18:17; Isa. 36:2, etc.

Co´ney, in Lev. 11.5; Deut. 14:7; Ps. 104:18; Prov. 30:26, is an old English name for the rabbit. It is somewhat like the rabbit in shape and size, and is known in natural history as the Syrian *Hyrax*. It was an unclean animal according to Jewish law.

Con-fec´tion, in Exod. 30:35, means compound of various ingredients.

Con-gre-ga´tions, mentioned in the Bible, were of several kinds. See CHURCH.
Exod. 12:3, 6, 19, 47; 16:1, 2, 9, 10, 22; 17:1; 27:21; 28:43; 29:4, 10, 11, 30, 32, 42, 44; 30:16, 18, 20, 26, 36; 31:7; 33:7; 34:31; 35:1, 4, 20, 21; 38:8, 25, 30; 39:32, 40; 40:2, 6, 7, 12, 22, 24, 26, 29, 30, 32, 34, 35.
Lev. 1:1, 3, 5; 3:2, 8, 13; 4:4, 5, 7, 13-16, 18, 21; 6:16, 26, 30; 8:35, 31, 33, 35; 9:5, 23; 10:7, 9, 17; 12:6; 14:11, 23; 15:14, 29; 16:5, 7, 16, 17, 20, 23, 33; 17:4-6, 9; 19:2, 21; 24:3, 14, 16.
Num. 1:1, 2, 16, 18, 53; 2:2, 17; 3:7, 8, 25, 38; 4:3, 4, 15, 23, 25, 28, 30, 31, 33-35, 37, 39, 41, 43, 47; 6:10, 13, 18; 7:5, 89; 8:9, 15, 19, 20, 22, 24, 25; 10:3, 7;

11:16; 12:4; 13:26; 14:1, 2, 5, 10, 27, 35, 36; 15:15, 24-26, 33, 35, 36; 16:2, 3, 9, 18, 19, 21, 22, 24, 26, 33, 41-43, 45-47, 50; 17:4; 18:4, 6, 21-23, 31; 19:4, 9, 20; 20:1, 2, 4, 6, 8, 10-12, 22, 27, 29; 25:6, 7; 26:2, 9; 27:2, 14, 16, 17, 19-22; 31:12, 13, 16, 26, 27, 43, 54; 32:2, 4; 35:12, 24, 25.

Deut. 23:1-3, 8; 31:14, 30; 33:4.

Josh. 8:35; 9:15, 18, 19, 21, 27; 18:1; 19:51; 20:6, 9; 22:12, 16-18, 20, 30.

Judg. 20:1; 21:5, 10, 13, 16.

1 Sam. 2:22.

1 Kings 8:4, 5, 14, 22, 55, 65; 12:3, 20.

1 Chron. 6:32; 9:21; 13:2, 4; 23:32; 28:8; 29:1, 10, 20.

2 Chron. 1:3, 5, 6, 13; 5:5, 6; 6:3, 12, 13; 7:8; 20:5, 14; 23:3; 24:6; 28:14; 29:23, 28, 31, 32; 30:2, 4, 13, 17, 24, 25; 31:18.

Ezra 2:64; 10:1, 8, 12, 14.

Neh. 5:13; 7:66; 8:2, 17; 13:1.

Job 15:34; 30:28.

Pss. 1:5; 7:7; 22:22, 25; 26:5, 12; 35:18; 40:9, 10; 58:1; 68:10, 26; 74:2, 4, 19; 75:2; 82:1; 89:5; 107:32; 111:1; 149:1.

Prov. 5:14; 21:16; 26:26.

Isa. 14:13.

Jer. 6:18; 30:20.

Lam. 1:10.

Hos. 7:12.

Joel 2:16.

Mic. 2:5.

Acts 13:43.

Co-ni´ah (*Jehovah is creating*), a name given by Jeremiah to JEHOIACHIN, king of Judah. Jer. 22:24; 37:1. See JEHOIACHIN.

Co-no-ni´ah (*Jehovah is creating*), a Levite who was chief overseer of offerings, tithes, and dedicated things. 2 Chron. 31: 12, 13.

Con´science is the moral law within us which judges of the moral character of our actions, and condemns or justifies us accordingly.

John 8:9.

Acts 23:1; 24:16.

Rom. 2:15; 9:1; 13:5.

1 Cor. 8:7, 10, 12; 10:25, 27-29.

2 Cor. 1:12; 4:2; 5:11.

1 Tim. 1:5, 19; 3:9; 4:2.

2 Tim. 1:3.

Titus 1:15.

Heb. 9:9, 14; 10:2, 22; 13:18.

1 Pet. 2:19; 3:16, 21.

Con´se-crate, to devote to the service of God or to sacred purposes.

Exod. 28:3, 41; 29:9, 29, 33, 35; 30:30; 32:29.

Lev. 8:33; 16:32; 21:10.

Num. 3:3; 6:12.

Josh. 6:19.

Judg. 17:5, 12.

1 Kings 13:33.

1 Chron. 29:5.

2 Chron. 13:9; 26:18; 29:31, 33; 31:6.

Ezra 3:5.

Ezek. 43:26.

Mic. 4:13.

Heb. 7:28; 10:20.

Con-sort´ed, in Acts 17:4, means associated.

Con´trite, in Ps. 51:17, means bruised; ground to powder; so of one humbled to the dust.

Con-ve´ni-ent, in Prov. 30:8; Acts 24:25; Rom. 1:28; Eph. 5:4, means suitable; becoming; decorous.

Con-ver-sa´tion, in Phil. 3:20, means citizenship. In 1 Pet. 1:15 it means conduct and habits of life. Conversation is never used in its ordinary sense in the Authorized Version.

Con-ver´sion, a change of heart or disposition, in which the enmity of the heart to God and his law and the obstinacy of the will are subdued, and are succeeded by supreme love to God and a reformation of life.

Con-vince´, in Job 32:12; John 8:46, means convict.

Co´os, or **Cos,** a little island, now called *Stanchio,* in the Grecian Archipelago, near the south-west point of Asia Minor. It was passed by Paul on his voyage to Jerusalem. Acts 21:1.

Cop´per, often called brass, was known before the flood, and was worked by Tubalcain. Gen. 4:22. Palestine abounded in copper. Deut. 8:9. There is little doubt that copper is meant in the passages in the Bible which mention brass. Ezra 8:27 mentions "vessels of fine copper."

Cor, the largest measure for liquids which is mentioned in the Old Testament, was equal to the homer, used for things dry, and contained about seventy gallons. Ezek. 45:14; 1 Kings 4:22. See MEASURES.

Cor´al, a well-known marine production, can be made into beads and other ornaments, for which the red kind is the most valuable. It was an article of Tyrian merchandise, and is mentioned in Ezek. 27:16 and Job 28:18.

Cor´ban, a Syriac word which means "a gift," a thing vowed or consecrated to the use of the Temple. Mark 7:11. The Jews allowed this consecration to be abused. A child could withhold assistance from his parents under pretence that what they asked for was consecrated to God.

Co´re, Jude 11, the Greek form of KORAH (which see).

Co-ri-an´der Seed is mentioned in Exod. 16:31 and Num. 11:7. The plant is aromatic, and a native of China and the south of Europe. It is now widely cultivated. The manna which fell in the wilderness was like coriander seed in form.

Cor´inth, a city of Greece, now an insignificant town, but during the first three centuries of the Christian era one of the commercial centers of the world, stood on the narrow isthmus which connects Attica with Peloponnesus, between the Gulf of Corinth and the Gulf of Ægina, and with a good harbor on each. It was famous for its enterprise and wealth, its learning and elegance, its licentiousness and vice. Paul preached there, about A. D. 53, a year and a half, Acts 18:11; made another visit, A. D. 57, and spent three winter months there, till A. D. 58, during which he wrote the Epistle to the Romans. We have two epistles from Paul to the church he had founded in Corinth. Acts 18:1; 19:1; 1 Cor. 1:2; 2 Cor. 1:1. 23; 2 Tim. 4: 20.

Co-rinth´i-an, a native of, or dweller in, Corinth. Acts 18:3; 2 Cor. 6:11.

Co-rinth´i-ans, First Epistle to the, was written by Paul early in A. D. 57 from Ephesus, and gives a very vivid and instructive picture of the state of affairs in the young church. It had been founded by Paul and then left in the charge of Apollos. Consequently there immediately sprang up among the lively Corinthians a Paul party and an Apollos party. To these was added a Peter party, formed by judaizing Christians just from Jerusalem, who even went so far as to question the apostolic authority of Paul. The purpose of the epistle is to bring order out of this confusion, and it is as sharp in its analysis of that which is wrong as tender in its admonitions to that which is right. Another point: the somewhat lax state of morals among the members it was also necessary to treat at length.

Co-rinth´i-ans, Second Epistle to the, was written by Paul later in A. D. 57 than the first epistle, and from Macedonia. It was probably caused by the favorable reports Paul had received from Titus and Timothy concerning the effects of the previous epistle. The question of the apostolic authority of his ministry is here treated exhaustively in chapters 1–7.

Co-rin´thus, in the subscription to the Epistle to the Romans, is the Latin form of CORINTH.

Cor´mo-rant, Lev. 11:17, was an unclean bird. Its presence is used in the Bible as an emblem of ruin and desolation. Isa. 34:11; Zeph. 2:14. The original word for cormorant in the last two passages mentioned is elsewhere translated *pelican*. The reference is to some sea-bird. The cormorant known to us is an exceedingly greedy bird, about as large as a goose. It lives upon fish, and its name is often used to signify a glutton.

Corn is the general word used in the English Bible for grain of all kinds known to the Jews. It includes peas and beans, but *never means Indian corn (or maize),* which was unknown to the Hebrews. Palestine produced large quantities of grain. It was ususally reduced to meal by a hand-mill. See MILL.
Gen. 27:28, 37; 41:5, 35, 49, 57; 42:1-3, 5, 19, 25, 26; 43:2; 44:2; 45:23; 47:14.
Exod. 22:6.
Lev. 2:14, 16; 23:14.
Num. 18:27.
Deut. 7:13; 11:14; 12:17; 14:23; 16:9, 13; 18:4; 23:25; 25:4; 28:51; 33:28.
Josh. 5:11, 12.
Judg. 15:5.
Ruth 2:2, 14; 3:7.
1 Sam. 17:17; 25:18.
2 Sam. 17:19, 28.
2 Kings 4:42; 18:32.
2 Chron. 31:5; 32:28.
Neh. 5:2, 3, 10, 11; 10:39; 13:5, 12.
Job 5:26; 24:6, 24; 39:4.

Pss. 4:7; 65:9, 13; 72:16; 78:24.
Prov. 11:26.
Isa. 17:5; 21:10; 28:28; 36:17; 37:27; 62:8.
Lam. 2:12.
Ezek. 36:29.
Hos. 2:8, 9, 22; 7:14; 10:11; 14:7.
Joel 1:10, 17; 2:19.
Amos 8:5; 9:9.
Hag. 1:11.
Zech. 9:17.
Matt. 12:1.
Mark 2:23; 4:28.
Luke 6:1.
John 12:24.
Acts 7:12.
1 Cor. 9:9.
1 Tim. 5:18.

Cor-ne´li-us, a Roman centurion dwelling in Cæsarea, who was the first Gentile convert to Christianity. Acts 10.

Cor´ner-Stone, a title of Christ. Eph. 2:20; 1 Pet. 2:6.

Cor´net, a curved wind instrument of music. 1 Chron. 15:28; Dan. 3:5, 7.

Cos, an island in the Grecian Archipelago. See COOS.

Co´sam, an ancestor of Joseph, the husband of Mary, the mother of Jesus. Luke 3:28.

Cotes, in 2 Chron. 32:28, means sheepfolds.

Cot´tage, in Isa. 1:8; Zeph. 2:6, means a rustic tent often made of boughs. In Isa. 24:20 it signifies an elevated couch for a garden watchman.

Cot´ton, a word not found in the Authorized Version of the Bible. There is no proof that the Hebrews knew anything about it in ancient times. The cotton-plant is now largely cultivated in Palestine and Syria, and furnishes much of the clothing used there.

Coun´cil, in Matt. 10:17, means a judicial tribunal. It generally signifies the SANHEDRIM or SANHEDRIN (which see). In Matt. 12:14; Acts 25:12 council means the advisers of Festus, the Roman governor; in Matt 5:22; Mark 13:9, the lesser Jewish courts.

Coun´sel-lor (*judge*), a name or title applied to Messiah by the prophet Isaiah. Isa. 9:6.

Count, in Exod. 12:4, means reckoning.

Coun-ter-vail´, in Esther 7:4, means compensate for.

Court, 2 Sam. 17:18, means a yard enclosed by an Oriental house. See TEMPLE, for *courts of the temple.* The Tabernacle also had a court.

Cov´e-nant (*league, thing prepared*), a word expressing God's gracious purpose toward his people, and also the relation into which they are thereby brought to him. The Old and New Testaments denote the old and new covenants. See BIBLE, and TESTAMENT.

Coz (*thorn*), a descendant of Judah through Caleb. 1 Chron. 4:8.

Coz´bi (*deceitful*), a Midianitish woman whom Phinehas slew. Num. 25:15, 18.

Crack´nels, in 1 Kings 14:3, means hard, brittle, punctured cakes, so named on account of the peculiar noise made in breaking them.

Craft, in Acts 18:3, means trade or occupation. Jewish boys after the captivity were obliged to learn some useful craft, even if their parents were rich.

Crane, a bird mentioned in the Bible in Isa. 38:14; Jer. 8:7. Two birds are mentioned, one translated in our version *crane,* and the other *swallow.* Some think the stork is intended. The Numidian crane is also supposed to be referred to. Large flocks of cranes come in the winter to the wilderness of Beersheba in Palestine.

Cre-a´tion, the act of God in bringing this world into existence.

Cre-a´tor, the name used in two passages in the Bible to designate God as the Maker of all things. Rom. 1:25; 1 Pet. 4:19.

Crea´ture, in Rom. 1:25; 8:19, etc., means created thing; the creation.

Crescens, kres´senz, a disciple with Paul at Rome. 2 Tim. 4:10.

Crete, a large island in the Mediterranean, one hundred and forty miles long, thirty-five miles broad, on the route from Syria to Italy, nearly midway between Syria and Malta. Acts 27:7, 12, 13, 21. Cretans were present at Jerusalem on the day of Pentecost. Acts 2:11. Paul sailed by Crete on his voyage to Rome. Acts 27: 7, 13. He left Titus there to take charge of the church, either before or probably after his first Roman captivity. Titus 1:5. The people were proverbially untruthful.

Cretes or **Cretians,** kre´shi-ans, the inhabitants of Crete Acts 2:11; Titus 1:12.

Crib, in Isa. 1:3, etc., means a feeding-trough for cattle. It was a fixture in the stable, and was often made of stones and mortar.

Crim´son, a deep red color tinged with blue, is a deeper dye than scarlet; hence the force of the figure in Isa. 1:18.

Crisp´ing pins, in Isa. 3:22, is not correctly translated. It means a reticule or bag, probably finely decorated.

Cris´pus, the ruler of the Jewish synagogue at Corinth, converted under the preaching of Paul and baptized by him. Acts 18:8; 1 Cor. 1:14.

Cross, an ancient instrument used for capital punishment. After the crucifixion of Christ it became the Christian symbol of redemption. The New Testament gives no indication of the form of the cross on which Christ died. Tradition uniformly refers to the Roman cross. Other varieties were used. Crucifixion was regarded by the Romans as the basest and most ignominious death. It was an accursed death. Deut. 21:23; Gal. 3:13. As a Christian symbol the cross is in various forms, namely the Roman or Latin cross (†), the Saint Andrew's cross (X), the Greek cross (+). A double cross is used by the Pope, and a triple cross is used by the Raskolniks, a Russian sect.

Also see Matt. 10:38; 16:24; 27:32, 40, 42.
Mark 8:34; 10:21; 15:21, 30, 32.
Luke 9:23; 14:27; 23:26.
John 19:17, 19, 25, 31.
1 Cor. 1:17, 18.
Gal. 5:11; 6:12, 14.
Eph. 2:16.
Phil. 2:8; 3:18.
Col. 1:20; 2:14.
Heb. 12:2.

Crown, an emblem of sovereignty worn on the head by kings and queens. It was customary for a king to wear as many crowns as he had kingdoms. Another kind of crown was a sort of head-dress or coronet. Newly-married persons of both sexes wore crowns. Song of Sol. 3:11; Ezek. 16:12.

Also see Gen. 49:26.
Exod. 25:11, 24, 25; 29:6; 30:3, 4; 37:2, 11, 12, 26, 27; 39:30.
Lev. 8:9; 21:12.
Deut. 33:20.
2 Sam. 1:10; 12:30; 14:25.
2 Kings 11:12.
1 Chron. 20:2.
2 Chron. 23:11.
Esther 1:11; 2:17; 6:8; 8:15.
Job 2:7; 19:9; 31:36.
Pss. 21:3; 89:39; 132:18.

Prov. 4:9; 12:4; 14:24; 16:31; 17:6; 27:24.
Isa. 3:17; 28:1, 3, 5; 62:3.
Jer. 2:16; 13:18; 48:45.
Lam. 5:16.
Ezek. 21:26; 23:42.
Zech. 6:11, 14; 9:16.
Matt. 27:29.
Mark 15:17.
John 19:2, 5.
1 Cor. 9:25.
Phil. 4:1.
1 Thess. 2:19.
2 Tim. 4:8.
James 1:12.
1 Pet. 5:4.
Rev. 2:10; 3:11; 4:4, 10; 6:2; 9:7; 12:1, 3; 13:1; 14:14; 19:12.

Cruse, in 1 Sam. 26:11; 1 Kings 14:3; 17:12; 2 Kings 2:20, means a small cup or vessel for holding liquid. Cruses were made in various forms.

Crys´tal, a name applied to one of the most beautiful of precious stones, perfectly transparent, and now known as rock-crystal. It is ranked with gold in value, Job 28:17, and is alluded to in Rev. 4:6; 21:11; 22:1. The same word which is translated crystal in some passages is translated *frost* in Gen. 31:40, etc., and *ice* in Job 6:16, etc.

Cu´bit, a measure of different lengths. The common cubit was about eighteen inches. Matt. 6:27; John 21:8. See MEASURES.

Cuckoo, kook´oo, in Lev. 11:16; Deut. 14:15, probably means one of the larger kinds of petrels—sea-birds.

Cu´cum-bers are abundant in the East, particularly in Egypt. Num. 11:5. The Egyptian cucumber is superior to those of America. The cucumber is common now in Palestine.

Cum´ber, in Luke 10:40; 13:7, means encumber; occupy unprofitably.

Cum´min, a plant much like fennel An aromatic oil of a warm stimulating nature is produced from its seeds. Isa. 28:25, 27; Matt. 23:23. It was only inferentially included in the law concerning tithes.

Cun´ning, in Gen. 25:27; Exod. 28:15; 38:23; Ps. 137:5; 2 Pet. 1:16, means skilful; expert.

Cup is used in the Bible both in a figurative and in the usual sense. Cups were made of horn, earthenware, or of some precious metal.
Gen. 40:11, 13, 21; 44:2, 12, 16, 17.
2 Sam. 12:3.
1 Kings 7:26.
1 Chron. 28:17.
2 Chron. 4:5.
Pss. 11:6; 16:5; 23:5; 73:10; 75:8; 116:13.
Prov. 23:31.
Isa. 22:24; 51:17, 22.
Jer. 16:7; 25:15, 17, 28; 35:5; 49:12; 51:7; 52:19.
Lam. 4:21.
Ezek. 23:31-33.
Hab. 2:16.
Zech. 12:2.
Matt. 10:42; 20:22, 23; 23:25, 26; 26:27, 39, 42.
Mark 7:4, 8; 9:41; 10:38, 39; 14:23, 36.
Luke 11:39; 22:17, 20, 42.
John 18:11.
1 Cor. 10:16, 21; 11:25-28.
Rev. 14:10; 16:19; 17:4; 18:6.

Cup´-bear´er. See BUTLER.

Cu´rious, in Exod. 28:8; Acts 19:19, means that with which much care and trouble has been taken.

Curses are of different kinds.
Gen. 8:21; 12:3; 27:12, 13.
Exod. 22:28.
Num. 5:18, 19, 21-24, 27; 22:6, 11, 12, 17; 23:7, 8, 11, 13, 25, 27; 24:10.
Deut. 11:26, 28, 29; 23:4, 5; 27:13; 28:15,
45; 29:19-21, 27; 30:1, 7.
Josh. 6:18; 24:9.
Judg. 5:23; 9:57.
2 Sam. 16:9-11.
1 Kings 2:8.
2 Kings 22:19.
2 Chron. 34:24.
Neh. 10:29; 13:2.
Job 1:11; 2:5, 9; 3:8; 31:30.
Pss. 62:4; 109:28.
Prov. 3:33; 11:26; 24:24; 26:2; 27:14; 28:27; 30:10.
Eccles. 7:21; 10:20.
Isa. 8:21; 24:6; 34:5; 43:28; 65:15.
Jer. 15:10; 24:9; 25:18; 26:6; 29:18, 22; 42:18; 44:8, 12, 22; 49:13.
Lam. 3:65.
Dan. 9:11.
Zech. 5:3; 8:13.
Mal. 2:2; 3:9; 4:6.
Matt. 5:44; 26:74.
Mark 14:71.
Luke 6:28.
Acts 23:12, 14.
Rom. 12:14.
Gal. 3:10, 13.
James 3:9.
Rev. 22:3.

Cush (*black?*). [1] The oldest son of Ham, Gen. 10:6, 7, 8; 1 Chron. 1:8, 9, 10, brother of Mizraim, Phut, and Canaan, and, through his five sons, ancestor of the Cushites, who, moving in a south-western direction from Chaldea, through Arabia, crossed the Red Sea and formed an empire in the land south of Egypt, the present Nubia, but then called ETHIOPIA (which see). [2] The name is applied in the original to the people descended from Cush, but in the English Version it is translated ETHIOPIAN. [3] It is frequently used to denote the land where the descendants of Cush lived; in which case it is

generally translated ETHIOPIA. Isa. 11:11.
[4] A man of the tribe of Benjamin, who appears to have been an enemy of David. Ps. 7, title.

Cu´shan, a people generally admitted to be same as Cushites or Ethiopians. Hab. 3:7.

Cu´shi (*the Ethiopian*). [1] A man sent by Joab to tell David the issue of the battle with Absalom. 2 Sam. 18:21, 23. [2] The great-grandfather of Jehudi. Jer. 36:14. [3] Father of Zephaniah the prophet. Zeph. 1:1.

Cush´ite. See CUSH.

Custom. See TRIBUTE. In Acts 16:21 custom means a new religion.

Cu´thah or **Cuth,** a place subject to Assyria, from which Shalmaneser brought people to occupy the cities of Israel. 2 Kings 17: 24, 30.

Cut´tings or marks on the body were forbidden to the Jews. Lev 19:28; 21:5; 1 Kings 18:28.

Cym´bal, a musical instrument made of two broad convex metal plates, which, when struck together, produced a piercing noise. A smaller kind was used on the fingers. Ps. 150:5; 1 Cor. 13:1. Cymbals were used in the Temple and on occasions of public rejoicing.

Cy´press, an evergreen tree resembling the Lombardy poplar in form and size, and seems to have been used for making idols, Isa. 44:14, its wood being very durable. The cypress is thought to be intended in some passages where "fir-tree" occurs.

Cy´prus, a large island of the Mediterranean, one hundred and fifty miles long and fifty miles broad, has played a conspicuous part in history from the time when it was colonized by the Phœnicians, more than a thousand years before Christ, until it, in A. D. 1878, became a British possession. It had two large cities, Salamis at the east and Paphos at the west end, and seventeen towns. Barnabas was a native of Cyprus, and it is often mentioned in the Acts. Acts 4:36; 13:4; 15:39, etc.

Cy-re´ne was the capital of Libya, that part of northern Africa which lies between Egypt and Carthage. The city was Greek, but since the time of Alexander the Great the Jews held citizenship there on equal terms with the Greeks. They had a synagogue, and many of them accepted Christianity. Matt. 27:32; Acts 2:10; 11:20; 13:1. It was destroyed in the fourth century by the Saracens.

Cy-re´ni-an, a native of Cyrene or its neighborhood. Mark 15:21; Luke 23:26; Acts 6:9.

Cy-re´ni-us is the Greek form of the Latin name Quirinius. Publius Sulpicius Quirinius was Roman governor of Syria at the time of the birth of our Lord, and probably again, A. D. 6–11. Luke 2:2. Under his first term as governor the enrollment took place which compelled Mary and Joseph to go to Bethlehem, under the second census. Acts 5:37.

Cy´rus (*sun*), the founder of the last of the great Eastern monarchies, the Persian, allowed the Jews after the conquest of Babylon, B. C. 538, to return home to Judea, to rebuild the Temple, and reorganize a national existence on a theocratical basis. He was foretold by Isaiah as the deliverer of Judah. Isa. 44:28; 45:1-7. The prophet Daniel was highly favored at his court. Dan. 6:28. His reputed tomb is still shown near Murgab.

Also see 2 Chron. 36:22, 23.

Ezra 1:1, 2, 7, 8; 3:7; 4:3, 5; 5:13, 14, 17; 6:3, 14.

Dan. 1:21; 10:1.

D

Dab´a-reh (*pasture*), a town of Issachar. It became a Levitical city. Josh. 21:28. See DABERATH.

Dab´ba-sheth (*height*), a town of Zebulun. Josh. 19:11.

Dab´e-rath (*pasture*), a town of Zebulun and Issachar. It became a Levitical city. Josh. 19:12; 21:28. In the English version of Josh. 21:28 this name is erroneously given DABAREH.

Da´gon (*fish*), an idol of the Philistines, having the head and hands of a man with the body and tail of a fish. The chief seat of its worship was at ASHDOD. 1 Sam. 5:1-4; 1 Chron. 10:10.

Dal-a-i´ah (*Jehovah is deliverer*), a son of Elioenai. 1 Chron. 3:24. In the original this name is the same as that of several persons called DELAIAH.

Dal-ma-nu´tha, a small town on the Sea of Galilee, near Magdala. Mark 8:10.

Dal-ma´tia, a province on the eastern shore of the Adriatic Sea, between Illyricum and Macedonia. Titus was sent here by Paul to preach the gospel. 2 Tim. 4:10.

Dal´phon (*dropping*), a son of Haman. Esther 9:7.

Dam´a-ris, a woman of Athens, converted under the preaching of Paul. Acts 17:34.

Dam-a-scenes´, the inhabitants of Damascus. 2 Cor. 11:32.

Da-mas´cus, a city of Syria, called by the Arabs the "Eye of the Desert" or the "Pearl of the East," on account of its beautiful location, stands in a fertile plain surrounded by the desert, at the foot of the Anti-Lebanon range, at an elevation of twenty-two hundred and sixty feet, one hundred and thirty-three miles north-east of Jerusalem and fifty miles east of the Mediterranean. It is one of the oldest cities in the world, said to have been founded by Uz, a grandson of Shem, and well known to the patriarchs. Gen. 14:15; 15:2. David conquered it, but under Solomon it became an independent kingdom, which was overthrown by Tiglath-Pileser III. B. C. 732. By the conquest of Persia by Alexander the Great it became a Greek possession, B. C. 333, and by the conquest of Greece by Rome it became a Roman province, B. C. 63. In A. D. 635 it was taken by the Arabs and as the capital of a large Mohammedan empire it was raised to great splendor. Even under Turkish rule (1516-1918) it was still a place of considerable importance, and noted for the unquenchable hatred with which its Mohammedan inhabitants look upon their Christian townsmen, and which in A. D. 1860 caused a frightful massacre. It was ruled by the French until Syria gained independence in 1941. In the New Testament it is often mentioned in the Acts and in the Epistles. The conversion of Paul (then called Saul) took place, Acts 9:1-25, on his journey from Jerusalem to Damascus, A. D. 37, and tradition still points out the spot, at the crossing of the direct road from Jerusalem with that from Banias, where the miracle occurred. Several other places are shown as the scene of that event. The traditional window in the wall through which Paul was let down in a basket, 2 Cor. 11 33, and the houses of Ananias and Judas are also shown.
Also see 2 Sam. 8:5, 6.
1 Kings 11:24; 15:18; 19:15; 20:34.
2 Kings 5:12; 8:7, 9; 14:28; 16:9-12.
1 Chron. 18:5.
2 Chron. 16:2; 24:23; 28:5, 23.

Song of Sol. 7:4.
Isa. 7:8; 8:4; 10:9; 17:1, 3.
Jer. 49:23, 24, 27.
Ezek. 27:18; 47:16-18; 48:1.
Amos 1:3, 5; 3:12; 5:27.
Zech. 9:1.
Acts 9:27; 22:5, 6, 10, 11; 26:12, 20.
2 Cor. 11:32.
Gal. 1:17.

Dam-na´tion and **Con-dem-na´tion.**
At the time when the Authorized Version of the Bible was issued these words were equivalent terms. In Matt 23:33; John 5:29; Rom. 13:2; 1 Cor. 11:29 the word translated "damnation" means "judgment," and is so rendered in the Revised Version.
Also see Matt. 23:14.
Mark 3:29; 12:40.
Luke 20:47; 23:40.
John 3:19; 5:24.
Rom. 3:8; 5:16, 18; 8:1.
1 Cor. 11:34.
2 Cor. 3:9.
1 Tim. 3:6; 5:12.
James 3:1; 5:12.
2 Pet. 2:3.
Jude :4.

Dan (*judge*). [1] The name (afterward given) of a place to which Abram pursued the kings who had ravaged Sodom and carried away Lot. Gen. 14:14; Judg. 18:29; 1 Chron. 21:2. It is stated in Judg. 24:29 that a colony of the tribe of Dan settled there and changed the name of the city of which they took possession from Laish to DAN, which was the principal city of the northern part of the territory of the tribe of Dan. Judg. 20:1. It is now called *Tel-el-Kâdy*. [2] The fifth son of Jacob, and the first of Bilhah, Rachel's maid. Gen. 30:6; 49:16; 1 Chron. 2:2. [3] The name of the tribe descended from Dan, or the territory they occupied in the land of Canaan. [4] DAN, Ezek. 27:19, may be same as No. 1, but is identified with *Dedar* by some, and by others with *Aden* in Arabia.
Also see Gen. 35:25; 46:23; 49:17.
Exod. 1:4; 31:6; 35:34; 38:23.
Lev. 24:11.
Num. 1:12, 38, 39; 2:25, 31; 7:66; 10:25; 13:12; 26:42; 34:22.
Deut. 27:13; 33:22; 34:1.
Josh. 19:40, 47, 48; 21:5, 23.
Judg. 1:34; 5:17; 13:25; 18:2, 16, 22, 23, 25, 26, 30; 20:1.
1 Sam. 3:20.
2 Sam. 3:10; 17:11; 24:2, 15.
1 Kings 4:25; 12:29, 30; 15:20.
2 Kings 10:29.
1 Chron. 27:22.
2 Chron. 2:14; 16:4; 30:5.
Jer. 4:15; 8:16.
Ezek. 48:1, 2, 32.
Amos 8:14.

Dan´cing, among the Jews, was anciently an expression of religious joy and gratitude. It sometimes took place in honor of a conqueror. 1 Sam. 18:6, 7. It also took place on occasions of domestic joy and when the vintage was gathered.
Exod. 32:19.
Judg. 21:23.
1 Sam. 18:6; 30:16.
2 Sam. 6:14, 16.
1 Chron. 15:29.
Ps. 30:11.
Matt. 11:17; 14:6.
Mark 6:22.
Luke 7:32; 15:25.

Dan´iel (*God is judge*). [1] The second son of David by Abigail the Carmelitess. 1 Chron. 3:1. He is called CHILEAB in 2 Sam. 3:3. [2] A priest of the family of Ithamar, the son of Aaron, who went up from Babylon with Ezra. Ezra 8:2; Neh.

10:6. [3] The last of the greater prophets. The prophet DANIEL (called BELTESHAZ-ZAR by the Chaldeans), who was probably born at Jerusalem, Dan. 1:3; 9:24, of noble, perhaps of royal descent, and was in early youth carried by Nebuchadnezzar to Babylon, B. C. 604, where, on account of his comeliness and talents, he was educated at the court and for the royal service. Dan. 1:1-4. After interpreting a dream which the king had forgotten, Dan. 2, he was made "ruler of the whole province of Babylon and chief of the governors over all the wise *men* of Babylon," and he kept the position during the whole reign of Nebuchadnezzar. Under his successor, Belshazzar, he had the wisdom and the courage to interpret the mysterious handwriting on the wall, Dan. 5:25, and under Darius the Median, who took Babylon from Belshazzar, he was made one of the "three presidents" of the empire. One day, however, the king forbade all prayer save unto the king for thirty days, and when Daniel refused to obey he was thrown into the den of lions. Dan. 6:16. But when God delivered him out of this danger he was taken back to the court, retained in his office, and held in still higher esteem. In the third year of the reign of Cyrus he seems to have resigned and retired, perhaps returned to Judea, but of these later years of his life nothing is known. Ezek. 14:14, 20; 28:3; and the book of Daniel.

Dan´iel, the Book of, consists of two parts: the first, comprising chapters 1–6, is historical, and gives the narrative of the life of the author, in many points strongly reminding one of that of Joseph; the second, comprising chapters 7–12, is prophetic, and records his visions. To bring the historical part of the book into harmony with such facts as have been established from other evidences is not difficult, but to interpret rightly the visions of the prophetic part seems to require something of the very spirit of the author himself, and demands, at all events, a much more minute knowledge of those times than we have. It should be noticed. however, that as the deciphering of the Assyrian and Egyptian inscriptions progresses more and more light is thrown upon this, as upon many other portions of the Old Testament. The three apocryphal additions to the Book of Daniel: THE SONG OF THE THREE HOLY CHILDREN, THE HISTORY OF SUSANNA, and the HISTORY OF BEL AND THE DRAGON, which occur for the first time in the Septuagint and thence passed into the Vulgate, have never formed part of the Hebrew Canon of the Old Testament.

Dan´ites, descendants of Dan. Judg. 13:2; 1 Chron. 12:35.

Dan-ja´an (*Dan playing the pipe*). 2 Sam. 24:6. Probably *Danian,* a ruin north of ACHZIB.

Dan´nah (*low*), a town of Judah. Josh. 15:49.

Da´ra (*pearl of wisdom*), a son of Zerah. 1 Chron. 2:6. DARDA, in 1 Kings 4:31, is the same person.

Dar´da, an Israelite noted for wisdom. 1 Kings 4:31. See DARA.

Dar´ic, the common gold-piece of the empire of Persia, is translated DRAM in 1 Chron. 29:7; Ezra 2:69, etc. See DRAM.

Da-ri´us (*restrainer*) is a common name among the kings of Media and Persia. Those mentioned in the Bible are: [1] *Darius the Median,* Dan. 5:31, was the son of Ahasuerus. He took Babylon from Belshazzar the Chaldean. Only one year of his reign is spoken of. Dan. 9:1; 11:1, during which Daniel rose to the highest dignity. [2] *Darius Hystaspes,* B. C.

521–486, confirmed the decree of Cyrus concerning the building of the Temple. Ezra 4:5; Hag. 1:1; Zech. 1:1; 7:1. [3] *Darius Cadomannus,* Neh. 12:22, the last king of the ancient Persian monarchy, was conquered by Alexander the Great, B. C. 330, and thus the prophecy in Daniel, chapter 8, was fulfilled.

Dark´ness is sometimes used to express ignorance or absence of the truth. It was one of the plagues of Egypt. Exod. 10:21. Also see Gen. 1:2, 4, 5, 18; 15:12.
Exod. 10:22; 14:20; 20:21.
Deut. 4:11; 5:22, 23; 28:29.
Josh. 24:7.
1 Sam. 2:9.
2 Sam. 22:10, 12, 29.
1 Kings 8:12.
2 Chron. 6:1.
Job 3:4-6; 5:14; 10:21, 22; 12:22; 15:22, 23, 30; 17:12, 13; 18:18; 19:8; 20:26; 22:11; 23:17; 28:3; 29:3; 30:26; 34:22; 37:19; 38:9, 19.
Pss. 18:9, 11, 28; 82:5; 88:6, 18; 91:6; 97:2; 104:20; 105:28; 107:10, 14; 112:4; 139:11, 12; 143:3.
Prov. 2:13; 4:19; 20:20.
Eccles. 2:13, 14; 5:17; 6:4; 11:8.
Isa. 5:20, 30; 8:22; 9:2; 29:18; 42:7, 16; 45:3, 7; 47:5; 49:9; 50:10; 58:10; 59:9; 60:2.
Jer. 2:31; 13:16; 23:12.
Lam. 3:2.
Ezek. 32:8.
Dan. 2:22.
Joel 2:2, 31.
Amos 4:13; 5:18, 20.
Mic. 7:8.
Nah. 1:8.
Zeph. 1:15.
Matt. 4:16; 6:23; 8:12; 10:27; 22:13; 25:30; 27:45.
Mark 15:33.
Luke 1:79; 11:34, 35; 12:3; 22:53; 23:44.
John 1:5; 3:19; 8:12; 12:35, 46.
Acts 2:20; 13:11; 26:18.
Rom. 2:19; 13:12.
1 Cor. 4:5.
2 Cor. 4:6; 6:14.
Eph. 5:8, 11; 6:12.
Col. 1:13.
1 Thess. 5:4, 5.
Heb. 12:18.
1 Pet. 2:9.
2 Pet. 2:4, 17.
1 John 1:5, 6; 2:8, 9, 11.
Jude 6, 13.
Rev. 16:10.

Dar´kon (*scatterer*), a servant of Solomon. Ezra 2:56; Neh. 7:58.

Dar´ling, in Pss. 22:20; 35:17, means "my only one."

Dates, the fruit of the date-palm. See PALM TREE.

Da´than (*fount*), a son of Eliab, who with Korah and others conspired against Moses in the wilderness. Num. 16; 26:9; Ps. 106:17.

Daugh´ter, in the Bible, sometimes means a distant female relative, such as a niece or granddaughter or a more remote descendant. The word is also applied to women of a city or country, Gen. 36:2; women in general, Prov. 31:29; to female worshippers of an idol. Mal. 2:11. "Daughters of music," in Eccl. 12:4, means singing women.

Da´vid (*beloved*), born at Bethlehem B. C. 1085; died in Jerusalem B. C. 1015, was the youngest of Jesse's eight sons, of the tribe of Judah, and grew up as a shepherd in his father's field. Early in youth he was brought to the court of Saul to soothe the troubled spirit of the king by playing upon the harp, and he was made one of his armor-bearers. After his triumphal contest with GOLIATH (which see) he was even made a chieftain and married the king's daughter, Michal, but the brooding suspicion and open jealousy of Saul made life at the court dangerous to David, and he was at last compelled to flee for his life. He sought refuge in the cave of Adullam, 1 Sam. 22:1, and there gradually gathered a somewhat mercenary company around him, which, however, his craft and power of command enabled him to sway and by which he began a contest with Saul. After the battle of Gilboa, in which Jonathan fell and Saul slew himself, David was recognized king and took up his residence at Hebron. There he reigned for seven and a half years, but after the death of Isbosheth, a son of Saul, who exercised regal authority over the ten tribes, he became the sole king of all the Israelites, and then he moved his residence from Hebron to Jerusalem, which he made the political and religious capital of the Jewish nation. He enlarged the city, adorned it with many new buildings, fortified it, and laid the plan for a magnificent temple to take the place of the tabernacle. In Jerusalem he reigned thirty-three years, and his reign was a period of rapid development and great splendor. In spite of his many domestic troubles—not incidental, but the sure results of his own faults—in spite of the insurrections of his own sons Absalom and Adonijah, he succeeded in consolidating the twelve tribes of Israel into one compact nation and in subjugating the foreign tribes or peoples living in and around Palestine. Every year the whole people assembled in Jerusalem to celebrate the Passover, and when David died he was able to leave his crown and his treasures undisputed to his son Solomon. He was

buried in Jerusalem, and his tomb, still pointed out on Mount Zion, became the sepulchre of the subsequent kings and one of the sacred places of the people. David was one of the grandest and most brilliant characters of all human history, notwithstanding the small corner of the earth which was the field of his activity. No deed of human intrepidity has surpassed his encounter with the Philistine giant; no story of human affection is more famous or more touching than that of the friendship of David and Jonathan; no poems have ever so powerfully appealed to the hearts and souls of men as his psalms; and his wisdom as a ruler and his energy and valor as a commander raised a small, disorderly, disorganized, and half-subdued nation to the rank of a powerful kingdom. As a king he forms the central figure in the history of the Jews; as the author of some of the PSALMS (which see) his name is the grandest in Hebrew literature; and in his kingly character, notwithstanding all his faults and shortcomings, he is the type or symbol of the MESSIAH (which see). David was the ancestor of Joseph, the husband of Mary, Christ's mother. In Ezek. 34:23, 24 and Hos. 3:5 the word David is applied to the Messiah.
Also see Ruth 4.
1 Sam. 16–30.
2 Sam. 1–13; 15–24.
1 Kings 1–3; 5–9; 11–15; 22.
2 Kings 8; 9; 11; 12; 14–22.
1 Chron. 2–4; 6; 7; 9–29.
2 Chron. 1–3; 5–14; 16; 17; 21; 23; 24; 27–30; 32–35.
Ezra 3; 8.
Neh. 3; 12.
Pss. 3–9; 11–32; 34–41; 51–65; 68–70; 72; 78; 86; 89; 101; 103; 108–110; 122;

124; 131–133; 138–145.
Prov. 1.
Eccles. 1.
Song of Sol. 4.
Isa. 7; 9; 16; 22; 29; 37; 38; 55.
Jer. 13; 17; 21–23; 29; 30; 33; 36.
Ezek. 37.
Amos 6; 9.
Zech. 12; 13.
Matt. 1; 9; 12; 15; 20–22.
Mark 2; 10–12.
Luke 1–3; 6; 18; 20.
John 7.
Acts 1; 2; 4; 7; 13; 15.
Rom. 1; 4; 11.
2 Tim. 2.
Heb. 4; 11.
Rev. 3; 5; 22.

Day, a word used with various meanings. The Sabbath day of the Hebrews commenced in the evening. Lev. 23:32. The time when the sun is above the horizon was generally divided by the sacred writers into twelve hours. The sixth hour always ends at noon, and the twelfth hour is the last hour before sunset. The word day is often used for an undetermined period.
Also see Gen. 1–11; 14; 15; 17–19; 21; 22; 24–27; 29–35; 37; 39–42; 47–50.
Exod. 2; 3; 5; 6–8; 10; 12–16; 19–24; 29; 31; 32; 34; 35; 40.
Lev. 6–10; 12–16; 19; 22; 23; 25; 27.
Num. 1; 3; 6–15; 19; 20; 22; 24; 25; 28–31; 33.
Deut. 1–13; 15; 16–34.
Josh. 1–10; 13–16; 20; 22–24.
Judg. 1–6; 8–21.
Ruth 1–4.
1 Sam. 1–31.
2 Sam. 1–7; 11–16; 18–24.
1 Kings 1–5; 8–22.
2 Kings 2–4; 6–8; 10; 12–21; 23–25.
1 Chron. 1; 4; 5; 7; 9–13; 16; 17; 21–23;
26; 28; 29.
2 Chron. 3; 5–10; 13–15; 18; 20; 21; 24; 26; 28–30; 32; 34–36.
Ezra 3; 4; 6–10.
Neh. 1; 2; 4–6; 8–13.
Esther 1–5; 7–9.
Job 1–3; 7–10; 12; 14; 15; 17–21; 23; 24; 26; 29; 30; 32; 33; 36; 38; 42.
Pss. 1; 2; 7; 18–20; 21; 23; 25; 27; 32; 34; 35; 37–39; 42; 44; 49; 50; 55; 56; 59; 71–74; 77; 78; 81; 84; 86; 88–92; 94–96; 102; 103; 109; 110; 118; 119; 121; 128; 136–140; 143–146.
Prov. 3; 4; 6; 7; 9–11; 15; 16; 21–24; 27; 28; 31.
Eccles. 2; 5–9; 11; 12.
Song of Sol. 2–4; 8.
Isa. 1–5; 7; 9–14; 17; 19; 20; 22–32; 34; 37–39; 43; 47–49; 51–53; 56; 58–63; 65; 66.
Jer. 1–7; 9; 11–20; 22; 23; 25–27; 30–42; 44; 46–52.
Lam. 1–5.
Ezek. 1–5; 7; 8; 12; 13; 16; 20–24; 26–34; 36; 38–40; 43–46; 48.
Dan. 1; 2; 4–12.
Hos. 1–7; 9; 10; 12.
Joel 1–3.
Amos 1–6; 8; 9.
Obad. 8, 11-15.
Jon. 1; 3; 4.
Mic. 1–5; 7.
Nah. 1–3.
Hab. 1; 3.
Zeph. 1–3.
Hag. 1; 2.
Zech. 1–4; 6–9; 11–14.
Mal. 3; 4.
Matt. 2–4; 6; 7; 9–13; 15–17; 20–28.
Mark 1–6; 8–10; 13–16.
Luke 1; 2; 4–24.
John 1; 2; 4–9; 11; 12; 14; 16; 19; 20.
Acts 1–7; 9–17; 19–28.

Rom. 2; 8; 10; 11; 13; 14.
1 Cor. 1; 3–5; 10; 15; 16.
2 Cor. 1; 3; 4; 6; 11.
Gal. 1; 4.
Eph. 4–6.
Phil. 1–3.
Col. 1; 2.
1 Thess. 2; 3; 5.
2 Thess. 1–3.
1 Tim. 5.
2 Tim. 1; 3; 4.
Heb. 1; 3–5; 7; 8; 10–13.
James 4; 5.
1 Pet. 2; 3.
2 Pet. 1–3.
1 John 4.
Jude :6.
Rev. 1; 2; 4; 6–12; 14; 16; 18; 20; 21.

Day, Lord's. See SABBATH.

Day's Journey. An ordinary day's journey, in Bible times, was what was usually travelled on camel or horseback, or about twenty-five or thirty miles. A Sabbath day's journey was nearly a mile. Matt. 24:20; Acts 1:12.

Days'man, in Job 9:33, means one who appoints a day for arbitrating. When the Bible was translated *daysman* was commonly used in the sense of *umpire.*

Day'spring, Job 38:12; Luke 1:78, means the first light of dawn. Compare Isa. 60:1, 2; Rev. 22:16.

Dea'con (*servant*), an official title of one who superintends the temporal concerns of the Church. For the qualifications of deacons, see Acts 6:1-6; 1 Tim. 3:8-12.

Dea'con-ess-es, or servants of the Church, were employed in the apostolic and early Christian Church. Rom. 16:1, 12; 1 Tim. 5: 9-16.

Dead. No longer endowed with life. Gen. 20:3; 23:3, 4, 6, 8, 11, 13, 15; 42:38; 44:20; 50:15.

Exod. 4:19; 9:7; 12:30, 33; 14:30; 21:34-36.
Lev. 11:31, 32; 19:28; 21:1, 11; 22:4.
Num. 5:2; 6:6, 11; 9:6, 7, 10; 12:12; 15:48; 19:11, 13, 16, 18; 20:29.
Deut. 2:16; 14:1, 8; 25:5, 6; 26:14.
Josh. 1:2.
Judg. 2:19; 3:25; 4:1, 22; 5:27; 8:33; 9:55; 16:30; 20:5.
Ruth 1:8; 2:20; 4:5, 10.
1 Sam. 4:17, 19; 17:51; 24:14; 25:39; 28:3; 31:5, 7.
2 Sam. 1:4, 5; 2:7; 4:1, 10; 9:8; 11:21, 24, 26; 12:18, 19, 21, 23; 13:32, 33, 39; 14:2, 5; 16:9; 18:20; 19:10, 28.
1 Kings 3:20-23; 11:21; 13:31; 21:14-16.
2 Kings 3:5; 4:1, 32; 8:5; 11:1; 19:35; 23:30.
1 Chron. 1:44-50; 2:19, 24; 10:5, 7.
2 Chron. 20:24, 25; 22:10.
Esther 2:7.
Job 1:19; 26:5.
Pss. 31:12; 76:6; 79:2, 88:5, 10; 106:28; 110:6; 115:17; 143:3.
Prov. 2:18; 9:18; 21:16.
Eccles. 4:2; 9:3-5; 10:1.
Isa. 8:19; 14:9; 22:2; 26:14, 19; 37:36; 59:10.
Jer. 16:7; 22:10; 26:23; 31:40; 33:5; 34:20; 36:30; 41:9.
Lam. 3:6.
Ezek. 6:5; 24:17; 44:25, 31.
Amos 8:3.
Hag. 2:13.
Matt. 2:19, 20; 8:22; 9:18, 24; 10:8; 11:5; 14:2; 17:9; 22:31, 32; 23:27; 27:64; 28:4, 7.
Mark 5:35, 39; 6:14, 16; 9:9, 10, 26; 12:25-27; 15:44.
Luke 7:12, 15, 22; 8:49, 52, 53; 9:7, 60; 10:30; 15:24, 32; 16:30, 31; 20:35, 37, 38; 24:5, 46.
John: 2:22; 5:21, 25; 6:49, 58; 8:52, 53; 11:14, 25, 39, 41, 44; 12:1, 9, 17;

19:33; 20:9; 21:14.

Acts 2:29; 3:15; 4:2, 10; 5:10; 7:4; 10:41, 42; 13:30, 34; 14:19; 17:3, 31, 32; 20:9; 23:6; 24:15, 21; 25:19; 26:8, 23; 28:6.

Rom. 1:4; 4:17, 19, 24; 5:15; 6:2, 4, 7-9, 11, 13; 7:2-4, 6, 8; 8:10, 11; 10:7, 9; 11:15; 14:9.

1 Cor. 7:39; 15:12, 13, 15, 16, 20, 21, 29, 32, 35, 42, 52.

2 Cor. 1:9; 5:14.

Gal. 1:1; 2:19, 21.

Eph. 1:20; 2:1, 5; 5:14.

Phil. 3:11.

Col. 1:18; 2:12, 13, 20; 3:3.

1 Thess. 1:10; 4:16.

1 Tim. 5:6.

2 Tim. 2:8, 11; 4:1.

Heb. 6:1, 2; 9:14, 17; 11:4, 12, 19, 35; 13:20.

James 2:17, 20, 26.

1 Pet. 1:3, 21; 2:24; 4:5, 6.

Jude :12.

Rev. 1:5, 17, 18; 2:8; 3:1; 11:8, 9, 18; 14:13; 16:3; 20:5, 12, 13.

Dead Sea is not mentioned in the Bible by this name, but is called the SALT SEA, Gen. 14:3; Num. 34:12; Josh. 18:19; THE SEA OF THE PLAIN, Deut. 3:17; THE EAST or FORMER SEA, Ezek. 47:18; Joel 2:20; Zech. 14:8; and THE SEA, Ezek. 47:8. It is in the south part of Palestine, and is over thirteen hundred feet below the Mediterranean. It is about forty-five miles long and over ten miles wide in its broadest part, is fed by the Jordan and other streams, but has no apparent outlet. Its water is extremely salty. Pitch is found on its surface, and at the south end there is a remarkable mass of rock-salt. On its east and west sides are desolate cliffs. Large quantities of bitumen and sulphur are found on its shores. Its waters are so dense that a person can float on them without danger of sinking. It is said that no form of life is found in the Dead Sea.

Deal, in Exod. 29:40, means a part.

Death, a word used in the Bible with various meanings.

Gen. 21:16; 24:67; 25:11; 26:11, 18; 27:2, 7, 10.

Exod. 10:17; 19:12; 21:12, 15-17, 29; 22:19; 31:14, 15; 35:2.

Lev. 16:1; 19:20; 20:2, 9-13, 15, 16, 27; 24:16, 17, 21; 27:29.

Num. 1:51; 3:10, 38; 15:35; 16:29; 18:7; 23:10; 35:16-18, 21, 25, 28; 35:30-32.

Deut. 13:5, 9; 17:6, 7; 19:6; 21:22; 22:26; 24:16; 30:15, 19; 31:27, 29; 33:1.

Josh. 1:1, 18; 2:13; 20:6.

Judg. 1:1; 5:18; 6:31; 13:7; 16:16, 30; 20:13; 21:5.

Ruth 1:17; 2:11.

1 Sam. 4:20; 11:12, 13; 15:32, 35; 20:3; 22:22.

2 Sam. 1:1, 23; 6:23; 8:2; 15:21; 19:21, 22; 20:3; 21:9; 22:5, 6.

1 Kings 2:8, 24, 26; 11:40.

2 Kings 1:1; 2:21; 4:40; 14:6, 17; 15:5; 20:1.

1 Chron. 22:5.

2 Chron. 15:13; 22:4; 23:7; 24:17; 25:25; 26:21; 32:24, 33.

Ezra 7:26.

Esther 4:11.

Job 3:5, 21; 5:20; 7:15; 10:21, 22; 12:22; 16:16; 18:13; 24:17; 27:15; 28:3, 22; 30:23; 34:22; 38:17.

Pss. 6:5; 7:13; 9:13; 13:3; 18:4, 5; 22:15; 23:4; 33:19; 44:19; 48:14; 49:14; 55:4, 15; 56:13; 68:20; 73:4; 78:50; 89:48; 102:20; 107:10, 14, 18; 116:3, 8, 15; 118:18.

Prov. 2:18; 5:5; 7:27; 8:36; 10:2; 11:4, 19; 12:28; 13:14; 14:12, 27, 32; 16:14, 25; 18:21; 21:6; 24:11; 26:18.

Eccles. 7:1, 26; 8:8.

Song of Sol. 8:6.
Isa. 9:2; 25:8; 28:15, 18; 38:1, 18; 53:9, 12.
Jer. 2:6; 8:3; 9:21; 13:16; 15:2; 16:4;
 18:21; 21:8; 26:15, 19, 21, 24; 38:4, 15,
 16, 25; 43:3, 11; 52:11, 27, 34.
Lam. 1:20.
Ezek. 18:32; 28:8, 10; 31:14; 33:11.
Hos. 13:14.
Amos 5:8.
Jon. 4:9.
Hab. 2:5.
Matt. 2:15; 4:16; 10:21; 14:5; 15:4; 16:28;
 20:18; 26:38, 59, 66; 27:1.
Mark 5:23; 7:10; 9:1; 10:33; 13:12; 14:1,
 34, 55, 64.
Luke 1:79; 2:26; 9:27; 18:33; 21:16;
 22:33; 23:15, 22, 32; 24:20.
John 4:47; 5:24; 8:51, 52; 11:4, 13. 53;
 12:10, 33; 18:31, 32; 21:19.
Acts 2:24; 8:1; 12:19; 13:28; 22:4, 20;
 23:29; 25:11, 25; 26:10, 31; 28:18.
Rom. 1:32; 5:10, 12, 14, 17, 21; 6:3-5, 9,
 16, 21, 23; 7:5, 10, 13, 24; 8:2, 6, 38.
1 Cor. 3:22; 4:9; 11:26; 15:21, 26, 54-56.
2 Cor. 1:9, 10; 2:16; 3:7; 4:11, 12; 7:10;
 11:23.
Phil. 1:20; 2:8, 27, 30; 3:10.
Col. 1:22.
2 Tim. 1:10.
Heb. 2:9, 14, 15; 5:7; 7:23; 9:15, 16; 11:5.
James 1:15; 5:20.
1 Pet. 3:18.
1 John 3:14; 5:16, 17.
Rev. 1:18; 2:10, 11, 23; 6:8; 9:6; 12:11;
 13:3; 18:8; 20:6, 13, 14; 21:4, 8.

De-bate´, In Isa. 58:4, means strife.

De´bir (*sanctuary*). **[1]** A place in
Judah, near Hebron. It was taken by
Joshua, Josh. 10:38, 39, and was first
called KIRJATH-SEPHER, Josh. 15:15, and
KIRJATH-SANNAH. Josh. 15:49. **[2]** A place
near the Valley of Achor. Josh. 15:7. **[3]** A
place on the border of Gad, east of Jordan.

Josh. 13:26. May be same as LO-DEBAR.

De´bir, king of Eglon, Josh. 10:3, was
one of the five kings who fought against
Gibeon and was slain, with his companions, by Joshua. Josh. 10:26.

Deborah, deb´o-rah or de-bo´rah
(*bee*). **[1]** The name of the nurse of Rebekah. Gen. 35:8. **[2]** A prophetess and
judge of the people of Israel, whose history is told in the most charming manner in
Judges, and whose triumphal song after
the victory over Sisera is considered one
of the finest specimens of Hebrew poetry.
See Judg. 5.

Debt´or, in Rom. 1:14; Gal. 5:3, means
one under an obligation. The Hebrew law
authorized taking a debtor into slavery,
under merciful regulations. Lev 25:39-41.
The year of jubilee terminated Hebrew
bondage in all cases. Imprisonment for
debt had become customary in Christ's
time. Matt. 18:34 See LOAN.
Also see Ezek. 18:7.
Matt. 6:12; 23:16.
Luke 7:41; 16:5.
Rom. 8:12; 15:27.

Dec´a-logue, the ten commandments.
Exod. 20:3-17. See LAW.

De-cap´o-lis, Matt. 4:25; Mark 5:20;
7:31, a district (named from its containing
ten cities) which lay probably on both sides
of the Jordan. It was near the Sea of Galilee. Writers differ as to the names of the ten
cities. Decapolis was inhabited by many
foreigners, although it was within the limits of Israel. This may account for the herds
of swine (unclean under the Mosaic law)
which were kept there. Matt. 8:30.

De-cis´ion, Valley of. Joel 3:14. Supposed by Fürst to be same as Valley of Jehoshaphat. See JEHOSHAPHAT, VALLEY OF.

De´dan (*low*). **[1]** A grandson of Cush.
Gen. 10:7; 1 Chron. 1:9. **[2]** A son of Jok-

shan, Gen. 25:3; 1 Chron. 1:32. [3] A country in the Arabian peninsula, not far from the Edomites. Jer. 25:23; Ezek. 25:13.

Ded´a-nim, a tribe either named from, or which gave their name to, the country they inhabited. They are generally supposed to be descendants of Raamah. Isa. 21:13.

Ded-i-ca´tion, a religious ceremony by which any person or thing was set apart for the service of God.

Ded-i-ca´tion, Feast of the, John 10:22, was established to commemorate the purging of the Temple and the rebuilding of the altar after the Syrians were driven out by Judas Maccabæus. It lasted eight days at Jerusalem, and was a time of rejoicing. It began on the twenty-fifth day of Chisleu (December). Attendance was not obligatory.

Deemed, in Acts 27:27, means concluded.

Deep, in Luke 8:31; Rom. 10:7, means the *abyss* where lost spirits await their final doom. The same word is translated *bottomless pit* in Rev. 9:1, 2, 11; 11:7; 20:13.

Deer, reputed clean under the Mosaic law, is mentioned under the name of fallow deer in Deut. 14:5; 1 Kings 4:23. See HART, and ROE.

De-fenced´, in Isa. 36:1, means fenced or fortified.

De-gree´, in 1 Tim. 3:13, means an advance in spiritual life.

De-grees´, a word which occurs in the titles of several Psalms. The meaning of it is unknown. Pss. 120–134, both inclusive. Degrees of another but unknown kind are mentioned in 2 Kings 20:9, 10, 11, in connection with dial. See DIAL.

De-ha´vites, a tribe of which some were taken to people Samaria after the removal of the Israelites by Shalmaneser. Ezra 4:9.

De´kar (*lance-bearer*), father of an officer of Solomon. 1 Kings 4:9.

Delaiah, del-a-i´ah (*Jehovah is deliverer*). [1] Head of the twenty-third temple-course of priests in the time of David. 1 Chron. 24:18. [2] Founder of a family who, on their return from captivity, could not prove their genealogy. Ezra 2:60; Neh. 7:62. [3] Father of Shemaiah. Neh. 6:10. [4] A prince of Judah in the time of King Jehoiakim. Jer. 36:12, 25.

Del´i-cate-ly, in Deut. 28:56 and 1 Sam. 15:32, means tenderly; mincingly.

De-light´some, in Mal. 3:12, means delightful.

De-li´lah (*languishing*), a woman of the Philistines, who, being beloved by Samson, betrayed him to his enemies. Judg. 16:4-18. See SAMSON.

Del´uge, the, occurred B. C. 2500, and was a judgment upon the world for the wickedness of its inhabitants. For one hundred and fifty days the waters rose, until they stood fifteen cubits (about twenty-two feet) over the highest summits, and all human beings, save Noah and his family, perished. On the injunction of God Noah built the ark, and placed therein, besides himself, his wife, and their three sons with their wives, one pair of all land-animals. When the waters subsided the ark rested on Mount Ararat in Armenia, and when the dove sent out by Noah returned with an olive-leaf in its bill, all went out of the ark; the earth was dry and inhabitable again. The record of the flood in Genesis 6–8 is almost identical with that which has been deciphered from the Assyrian tablets, and very much like the records found in Chinese literature or among the Indians of Peru and Mexico.

See NOAH and ARK.

De´mas. [1] A disciple at Rome with Paul. Col. 4:14; Philem. 24. [2] Supposed to be the same as No. 1. 2 Tim. 4:10.

De-me´tri-us. [1] A silversmith at Ephesus who opposed Paul. Acts 19:24, 38. He was a manufacturer of silver shrines, small temples, and images of DIANA (which see). [2] A convert of whom nothing is recorded except the consistency of his character. 3 John 12.

De-na´ri-us, a Roman silver coin worth about fifteen cents. It was nearly equivalent to the Greek drachma, and is translated, in the Authorized Version, *penny,* which with us is of very small value, but it represents in the Bible a regular day's wages.

Dep´u-ty, in Acts 13:7, etc. means the proconsul of a senatorial province.

Der´be, a city of Lycaonia. Acts 14:6; 16:1. Paul and Barnabas fled to it from Lystra. Acts 14:20. See LYCAONIA.

De-scribe´, in Josh. 18:4, means to mark out. In Josh. 18:6 description has a similar meaning.

Des´ert, in the Bible, generally means an uncultivated place or grazing tract. Some deserts were dry and barren. Exod. 3:1; 5:3; 19:2; 23:31. Num. 20:1; 27:14; 33:16. Deut. 32:10. 2 Chron. 26:10. Job 24:5. Pss. 28:4; 78:40; 102:6; 106:14. Isa. 13:21; 21:1; 34:14; 35:1, 6; 40:3; 41:19; 43:19, 20; 48:21; 51:3. Jer. 2:6; 17:6; 25:24; 50:12, 39. Ezek. 7:27; 13:4; 47:8. Matt. 14:13, 15; 24:26. Mark 1:45; 6:31, 32, 35. Luke 1:80; 4:42; 9:10, 12. John 6:31.

Acts 8:26. Heb. 11:38.

Des´ert of the Sea, name of an uncertain part of the Desert of Arabia. Isa. 21:1. See WILDERNESS.

De-sired´, in 2 Chron. 21:20, means regretted.

Des´o-late, applied by Isaiah to the land of Judah while under the displeasure of the Lord on account of the rebellion of its people. Isa. 62:4.

De-u´el (*God is knowing*), father of Eliasaph. Num. 1:14; 7:42; 10:20. He is called REUEL in Num. 2:14.

Deu-ter-on´o-my (*repetition of the law*) is the fifth book of the Old Testament and of the PENTATEUCH (which see).

Dev´il, Dev´ils. Devils, in the New Testament, is often used for *demons,* or evil spirits, as in the phrases "possessed with devils" and "cast out devils."

Dev´ils, the name of certain idols worshipped by the Israelites while they were in Egypt, and also of those set up by Jeroboam. Lev. 17:7; Ps. 106:37. The original is translated *satyrs* in Isa. 13:21; 34:14.

De-vo´tions, in Acts 17:23, means objects of devotion.

Dews in the Holy Land and other Eastern countries are very heavy, and aid greatly in sustaining vegetation when little or no rain falls. Dew was especially heavy near the mountains. Gen. 27:28, 39. Exod. 16:13, 14. Num. 11:9. Deut. 32:2; 33:13, 28. Judg. 6:37-40. 2 Sam. 1:21; 17:12. 1 Kings 17:1. Job 29:19; 38:28. Pss. 110:3; 133:3. Prov. 3:20; 19:12.

Song of Sol. 5:2.
Isa. 18:4; 26:19.
Dan. 4:15, 23, 25, 33; 5:21.
Hos. 6:4; 13:3; 14:5.
Mic. 5:7.
Hag. 1:10.
Zech. 8:12.

Di´a-dem, in the New Testament, Rev. 12:3; 13:1; 19:12, means the crown of a king, in distinction from that of a conqueror.

Di´al, an instrument which shows the hour of the day by means of the progress of the shadow of the sun on the dial. The sun-dial is very ancient, and is mentioned in the Assyrian tablets. Dials are horizontal, vertical, or inclined. The form of the dial of Ahaz, mentioned in 2 Kings 20:11 and Isa. 38:8, is not known.

Di´a-mond, the most brilliant of gems and also the hardest, is supposed to have been unknown to the Jews. Exod. 28:18; Ezek. 28:13. ADAMANT is an old English name given to the diamond. The word diamond is used in several places in the Bible, and various meanings have been given to it.

Di-an´a, a heathen goddess extensively worshipped by the Greeks, had her most magnificent temple at Ephesus. It was one of the seven wonders of the world, four hundred and twenty-five feet long, two hundred and twenty feet broad, and had one hundred and twenty-seven columns sixty feet high. It was the treasury of the Pan-Ionian League, and the worship around the statue of the goddess was celebrated with great splendor. Small silver models of the temple enclosing the image of the goddess were spread all over the world, and her worship was so earnest by her devotees that the preaching of Paul in Ephesus led to a great uproar. Acts 19:23-

40. See EPHESUS.

Dib´la-im (*double cake*), father of Gomer, the wife of Hosea. Hos. 1:3.

Dib´lath (*circle*), Ezek. 6:14, has been identified with *Dibl,* a modern ruin. See RIBLAH.

Dib-la-tha´im. See ALMON-DIBLA-THAIM.

Di´bon (*wasting*). [1] Dibon in Moab. Num. 21:30; Isa. 15:2. It was built by Gad, Num. 32:34, and was therefore called DIBON-GAD; became a town of Reuben, and was also called DIMON, Isa. 15:9; was returned to Moab. Isa. 15:2. It was about twelve miles east of the Dead Sea and three miles north of the Amon. Its ruins cover a large space. The *Moabite Stone* was found here in 1868, and has an inscription of Mesha, king of Moab B. C. 900. It confirms 2 Kings, chapter 3, most remarkably by the thirty-four lines of Hebrew-Phœnician writing it contains. [2] A town in the south of Judah. Neh. 11:25. Same as DIMONAH. Josh. 15:22.

Di´bon-gad, the thirty-eighth station of the Israelites after they left Egypt. Num. 33:45, 46. See DIBON, No. 1.

Dib´ri (*eloquent*), a man of the tribe of Dan. Lev. 24:11.

Did´y-mus (*a twin*), John 11:16; 20:24; 21:2, the surname of the apostle THOMAS (which see).

Dik´lah (*palm grove*), a son of Joktan. Gen. 10:27; 1 Chron. 1:21.

Dil´e-an (*gourd*), a town in the plains of Judah. Josh. 15:38.

Dim´nah, a town of Zebulun which became a city of the Levites. Josh. 21:35. Same as RIMMON, 1 Chron. 6:77.

Di´mon (*river-bed*), a city of Moab. Isa. 15:9. Same as DIBON, No. 1.

Di-mo´nah, a town in the south of Judah. Josh. 15:22. Same as DIBON, No. 2.

Di´nah (*avenged*), daughter of Jacob. Gen. 30:21; 34:1, 13, 25, 26.

Di´na-ites, an Assyrian tribe transported to Samaria. Ezra 4:9.

Din´ha-bah, the seat of government of Bela, king of Edom. Gen. 36:32; 1 Chron. 1:43.

Dionysius, di-o-nish´i-us, an Athenian who was a member of the court of the Areopagus, and a convert under the preaching of Paul. Acts 17:34.

Diotrephes, di-ot´re-feez, a professing disciple, of whom nothing is known except what is told in 3 John 9.

Dis-an-nul´, in Job 40:8 and Gal. 3:15, is a stronger form of annul.

Dis-cern´ing of Spir´its, in 1 Cor. 12:10, means a miraculous gift of the Holy Ghost, by virtue of which the spirits of men were tried to show whether they were of God.

Dis-ci´ple. [1] The title given to those who afterward became apostles, and to all others who professed to be followers of Jesus. [2] Those who were baptized by John the Baptist, and followed his teaching.

Dis´ci-pline, in Job 36:10, means instruction.

Dis-cov´er, in Deut. 22:30; Mic. 1:6, means uncover.

Dis-cov´ered, in 2 Sam. 22:16; Isa. 22:8, means uncovered.

Dis-cov´er-eth, in Ps. 29:9, means uncovereth, or strips off the leaves.

Dis-eas´es came on account of sin. The plagues and pestilences of ancient times were often miraculous.

Di´shan (*antelope*), a son of Seir the Horite. Gen. 36:21; 1 Chron. 1:38.

Di´shon. [1] Another son of Seir the Horite. Gen. 36:21; 1 Chron. 1:38. [2] A son of Anah. Gen. 36:25; 1 Chron. 1:41.

Dis-persed´, in Isa. 11:12; John 7:35,

and **Dis-pers´ions,** in Jer. 25:34, are words usually applied to the Jews who after their captivity, and especially after the final destruction of Jerusalem, were scattered abroad. James 1:1; 1 Pet. 1:1.

Dis-po-si´tion, in Acts 7:53, means ordinance or ministration.

Dis-solve´, in Dan. 5:16, means solve.

Ditch, in Job 9:31; Isa. 22:11; Luke 6:39, means a pit or pool.

Di´ves is found in the Latin Version of the Bible, but not in the Authorized Version. It refers to the rich man in the parable. Luke 16:19-31.

Div-i-na´tion, the pretended divining or foretelling of future events.

Di-vorce´, Deut. 24:1-4, was tolerated by Moses. It was limited by Christ to the case of adultery. Matt. 5:32; 19:3-9.

Diz´a-hab (*golden*), a place in the wilderness of Sinai. Deut. 1:1.

Doc´tors, Luke 2:46, or teachers of the law of Moses, were highly esteemed by the Jews, and were usually, perhaps always, of the sect called Pharisees.

Doc´trine, in Matt. 7:28; Mark 4:2, means teaching.

Dod´a-i (*beloved of Jehovah*), one of David's captains. 1 Chron. 27:4.

Dod´a-nim indicates the family descended from a son of Javan. Gen. 10:4; 1 Chron. 1:7.

Dod´a-vah (*Jehovah is loving*), a man of Mareshah. 2 Chron. 20:37.

Do´do (*amatory*). [1] Grandfather of Tola. Judg. 10:1. [2] Father of Eleazar. 2 Sam. 23:9; 1 Chron. 11:12. [3] Father of Elhanan. 2 Sam. 23:24; 1 Chron. 11:26.

Do´eg (*fearful*), chief of King Saul's herdmen. 1 Sam. 21:7; Ps. 52; title. See AHIMELECH.

Dogs were unclean animals by the Jewish law, and were regarded with special contempt. Exod. 22:31. The dogs of Eastern countries are savage, much like wolves, are scavengers, and live wholly out of doors and in a wild state.

Doph´kah (*cattle-driving*), eighth encampment of the Israelites on their journey from Egypt to Canaan. Num. 33:12, 13.

Dor (*dwelling*), a royal city of the Canaanites. It was on the Mediterranean Sea, near Mount Carmel. Josh. 11:2; Judg. 1:27. There is now a small village there called *Tantûra,* eight miles north of Cæsarea.

Dor´cas or **Tab´i-tha** (*gazelle*), a charitable female disciple at Joppa whom Peter miraculously restored to life. Acts 9:36-40.

Do´than (*two cisterns*), a place near Mount Gilboa, Gen. 37:17, where Joseph found his brethren and where Elisha lived. 2 Kings 6:13. It was five miles south-west of *Jenin* and in the plain of Jezreel. Many cisterns hewn in the rock are still found there, which are thought to resemble the "pit," Gen. 37:24, into which Joseph was cast. Caravans on their way from Damascus to Egypt still pass this place.

Do you to wit, 2 Cor. 8:1, is rendered "make known to you" in the Revised Ver.

Doves, Gen. 8:9, were clean by the Mosaic law and often mentioned by the sacred writers. They were used in sacrifices. The dove is a symbol of simplicity. Matt. 10:16.
Also see Gen. 8:8, 10-12.
2 Kings 6:25.
Pss. 55:6; 68:13.
Song of Sol. 1:15; 2:14; 4:1; 5:2, 12; 6:9.
Isa. 38:14; 59:11; 60:8.
Jer. 48:28.
Ezek. 7:16.
Hos. 7:11; 11:11.
Nah. 2:7.
Matt. 3:16; 21:12.

Mark 1:10; 11:15.
Luke 3:22.
John 1:32; 2:14, 16.

Dove's Dung, mentioned in 2 Kings 6:25, is generally supposed to mean a kind of lentil or tare which appears much like dove's dung. The Arabs still call two or three vegetables by that name. Some think the use of dove's dung as *fuel* is referred to.

Dow´ry. The bridegroom in Eastern countries was required to pay the father of his betrothed a certain portion in money or otherwise, regulated by the rank of her family. Gen. 29:18-27; 34:12. Sometimes the father gave presents to his daughter. Judg. 1:15; 1 Kings 9:16.

Drachma, drak´ma, translated a *piece of silver* in Luke 15:8, 9, was a Greek silver coin worth about fifteen cents. Same as DENARIUS and PENNY (which see).

Drag, in Hab. 1:15, 16, means a suspended net drawn near the bottom of the water.

Drag´on, the name given to the devil in several passages in Revelation.
Deut. 32:33.
Neh. 2:13.
Job 30:29
Pss. 44:19; 74:13; 91:13; 148:7.
Isa. 13:22; 27:1; 34:13; 35:7; 43:20; 51:9.
Jer. 9:11; 10:22; 14:6; 49:33; 51:34, 37.
Ezek. 29:3.
Mic. 1:8.
Mal. 1:3.
Rev. 12:3, 4, 7, 9, 13, 16, 17; 13:2, 4, 11; 16:13; 20:2.

Drag´on-well (*the fountain of the jackals*), a fountain near the south wall of Jerusalem. Neh. 2:13.

Dram, a gold coin of Persia. Its value was about five dollars. 1 Chron. 29:7; Neh. 7:70; Ezra 2:69. See DARIC.

Draught, draft, in Matt. 15:17, means

drain. In Luke 5:9 it means all the fishes taken by once drawing the net.

Draught house, draft´-house, in 2 Kings 10:27, means cesspool; depository of drainage.

Dreams are often mentioned in the Bible.

Dress´es. See GARMENTS.

Drink-of´fer-ings consisted chiefly of wine, part of which was poured on the victim sacrificed and the rest was given to the priests.

Drink, Strong. See WINE.

Drom´e-da-ry, Isa. 60:6, a light and swift variety of CAMEL (which see).

Drought, drowt. The land of Judea was very dry from the end of April to September; the drought of summer. The grass was sometimes wholly withered, Ps. 102:4, and the ground parched and broken. Nothing but the copious dews preserved vegetable life.

Drunk´en-ness is often mentioned in the Bible.

Dru-sil´la, a daughter of Herod Agrippa I. who became wife of Felix, governor of Judea. Acts 24:24.

Dukes, in Gen. 36:15; Exod. 15:15; Josh. 13:21; 1 Chron. 1:51, means leaders or commanders, and not an order of nobility.

Dul´ci-mer, Dan. 3:5, was a musical instrument resembling the bagpipe. The modern dulcimer is entirely unlike it.

Du´mah (*silence*). [1] A son of Ishmael. Gen. 25:14; 1 Chron. 1:30. [2] A town of Judah ten miles south-west of Hebron. Josh. 15:52. [3] A city or a tribe. Isa. 21:11.

Dung, when dried, was used in Bible lands for fuel. It was also used for manure. Exod. 29:14.
Lev. 4:11; 8:17; 16:27.

Num. 19:5.
1 Kings 14:10.
2 Kings 6:25; 9:37; 18:27.
Neh. 2:13; 3:13, 14; 12:31.
Job 20:7.
Ps. 83:10.
Isa. 36:12.
Jer. 8:2; 9:22; 16:4; 25:33.
Ezek. 4:12, 15.
Zeph. 1:17.
Mal. 2:3.
Luke 13:8.
Phil. 3:8.

Dung´-gate or **port,** a gate of Jerusalem. Neh. 2:13; 3:14; 12:31.

Du´ra (*circle*), a plain near Babylon, where Nebuchadnezzar set up a golden image. Dan. 3:1.

Du-reth, in Matt. 13:21, means endureth.

Dust. Sitting in the dust was a sign of affliction. Dust or ashes put on the head was a sign of mourning. The word is used in the Bible with many different meanings.
Gen. 2:7; 3:14, 19; 13:16. 18:27; 28:14.
Exod. 8:16, 17; 9:9.
Lev. 14:41; 17:13.
Num. 5:17; 23:10.
Deut. 9:21; 28:24; 32:24.
Josh. 7:6.
1 Sam. 2:8.
2 Sam. 16:13; 22:43.
1 Kings 16:2; 18:38; 20:10.
2 Kings 13:7; 23:12.
2 Chron. 1:9; 34:4.
Job 2:12; 4:19; 5:6; 7:5, 21; 10:9; 14:19;
   16:15; 17:16; 20:11; 21:26; 22:24;
   27:16; 28:6; 30:19; 34:15; 38:38;
   39:14; 40:13; 42:6.
Pss. 7:5; 18:42; 22:15, 29; 30:9; 44:25;
   72:9; 78:27; 102:14; 103:14; 104:29;
   113:7; 119:25.

Prov. 8:26.
Eccles. 3:20; 12:7.
Isa. 2:10; 5:24; 25:12; 26:5, 19; 29:4, 5;
    34:7, 9; 40:12, 15; 41:2; 47:1; 49:23;
    52:2; 65:25.
Lam. 2:10; 3:29.
Ezek. 24:7; 26:4, 10, 12; 27:30.
Dan. 12:2.
Amos 2:7.
Mic. 1:10; 7:17.
Nah. 1:3; 3:18.
Hab. 1:10.
Zeph. 1:17.
Zech. 9:3.
Matt. 10:14.
Mark 6:11.
Luke 9:5; 10:11.
Acts 13:51; 22:23.
Rev. 18:19.

Dust, Rain of, is mentioned in Deut. 28:24. In the vicinity of Judea are plains or deserts of fine sand which is taken up by strong winds. One of the plagues of Egypt was caused by miraculously changing dust into lice. Exod. 8:16.

Dwell´ing. See HOUSE.

Dye´ing was well understood in Bible times, especially by the Phœnicians and the Egyptians. The Israelites evidently had some knowledge of the art at the time of the exodus. See Exod. 26:1, 14; 35:25. Lydia is mentioned in Acts 16:14 as "a seller of purple, of the city of Thyatira," which was famous for its dyers.

E

Ea´gle, an unclean bird, Lev. 11:13; Deut. 14:12, is often referred to in the Bible.

Also see Exod. 19:4.
Lev. 11:18.
Deut. 14:17; 28:49; 32:11.
2 Sam. 1:23.
Job 9:26; 39:27.
Ps. 103:5.
Prov. 23:5; 30:17, 19.
Isa. 40:31.
Jer. 4:13; 48:40; 49:16, 22.
Lam. 4:19.
Ezek. 1:10; 10:14; 17:3, 7.
Dan. 4:33; 7:4.
Hos. 8:1.
Obad. :4.
Mic. 1:16.
Hab. 1:8.
Matt. 24:28.
Luke 17:37.
Rev. 4:7; 12:14.

Ear, in 1 Sam. 8:12; Isa. 30:24, means plough.

Eared´, in Deut. 21:4, means ploughed.

Ear´ing, in Gen. 45:6; Exod. 34:21, means ploughing.

Ear´nest, a part paid beforehand, under a contract, as a pledge and security for the whole. It is of the same kind with the thing promised. 2 Cor. 1:22; 5:5; Eph. 1:14.

Ear´rings. See AMULETS, and RINGS. Earrings were worn by both sexes in Bible times, Exod. 32:2, and that fashion is often followed now in the East.
Also see Gen. 24:22, 30, 47; 35:4.
Exod. 32:3; 35:22.
Num. 31:50.
Judg. 8:24-26.
Job 42:11.
Prov. 25:12.
Isa. 3:20.
Ezek. 16:12.
Hos. 2:13.

Earth, a term used in Scripture to

denote—[1] The earth as distinguished from the heavens. Gen. 1:1. [2] The land as distinguished from the sea. Gen. 1:10. [3] A particular country or land; and in this case it is so translated. Gen. 2:11; 12:1.
Also see Gen. 1; 2; 4; 6–14; 18; 19; 22; 24; 26–28; 37; 41–43; 45; 48.
Exod. 8–10; 15; 19; 20; 31–34.
Lev. 11; 15; 26.
Num. 11; 12; 14; 16; 22; 26.
Deut. 3–7; 10–14; 26; 28; 30–33.
Josh. 2–5; 7; 23.
Judg. 3; 5; 6; 18.
1 Sam. 2; 4; 5; 14; 17; 20; 24–26; 28; 30.
2 Sam. 1; 4; 7; 12–15; 18; 22; 23.
1 Kings 1; 2; 4; 8; 10; 13; 17; 18.
2 Kings 5; 10; 19.
1 Chron. 1; 16; 17; 21; 22; 29.
2 Chron. 1; 2; 6; 9; 16; 20; 32; 36.
Ezra 1; 5.
Neh. 9.
Job 1–3; 5; 7–9; 11; 12; 14–16; 18–20; 22; 24; 26; 28; 30; 34; 35; 37–39; 41.
Pss. 2; 7; 8; 10; 12; 16–19; 21; 22; 24; 25; 33; 34; 37; 41; 44–48; 50; 57–61; 63; 65–69; 71–79; 82; 83; 85; 89; 90; 94–99; 102–106; 108; 109; 112–115; 119; 121; 124; 134–136; 138–141; 146–148.
Prov. 2; 3; 8; 10; 11; 17; 25; 30.
Eccles. 1; 3; 5; 7; 8; 10–12.
Song of Sol. 2.
Isa. 1; 2; 4–6; 8; 10–14; 18; 23–26; 28; 30; 33; 34; 37; 40–45; 48; 49; 51; 52; 54; 55; 58; 60–63; 65; 66.
Jer. 4; 6–10; 14–17; 19; 22–29; 31–34; 44; 46; 49–51.
Lam. 2–4.
Ezek. 1; 7–10; 26–28; 31; 32; 34; 35; 38; 39; 43.
Dan. 2; 4; 6–8; 12.
Hos. 2; 6.
Joel 2; 3.

Amos 2–5; 8; 9.
Jon. 2
Mic. 1; 4–7.
Nah. 1; 2.
Hab. 2; 3.
Zeph. 2; 3.
Hag. 1; 2.
Zech. 1; 4–6; 9; 12; 14.
Mal. 4.
Matt. 5; 6; 9–13; 16–18; 23–25; 27; 28.
Mark; 2; 4; 9; 13.
Luke 2; 5; 6; 10–12; 16; 18; 21; 23; 24.
John 3; 12; 17.
Acts 1–4; 7–11; 13; 14; 17; 22; 26.
Rom. 9; 10.
1 Cor. 3; 10; 15.
Eph. 1; 3; 4; 6.
Phil. 2.
Col. 1; 3.
2 Tim. 2.
Heb. 1; 6; 8; 11; 12.
James 5.
2 Pet. 3.
1 John 5.
Rev. 1; 3; 5–14; 16–21.
Earthquake.
1 Kings 19:11, 12.
Isa. 29:6.
Amos 1:1.
Zech. 14:5.
Matt. 24:7; 27:54; 28:2.
Mark 13:8.
Luke 21:11.
Acts 16:26.
Rev. 6:12; 8:5; 11:13, 19; 16:18.

East, a word used by the Hebrews for all countries around and beyond the rivers Tigris and Euphrates. Gen. 28:14. Also the country east or south-east of Mount Ararat. Gen. 11:2.
Also see Gen. 2:14; 3:24; 4:16; 10:30; 12:8; 13:11; 25:6; 29:1; 41:6, 23, 27.
Exod. 10:13; 14:21; 27:13; 38:13.

Lev. 1:16.

Num. 2:3; 3:38; 10:5; 23:7; 34:10, 11; 35:5.

Josh. 4:19; 7:2; 11:3; 12:1, 3; 15:5; 16:1, 5, 6; 17:10; 18:7, 20; 19:13.

Judg. 6:3, 33; 7:12; 8:10, 11; 11:18; 21:19.

1 Kings 4:30; 7:25.

1 Chron. 4:39; 5:10; 6:78; 9:24; 12:15.

2 Chron. 4:4, 10; 5:12; 29:4; 31:14.

Neh. 3:26, 29.

Job 1:3; 15:2; 27:21; 38:24.

Pss. 48:7; 75:6; 78:26; 103:12; 107:3.

Isa. 2:6; 11:14; 27:8; 41:2; 43:5; 46:11.

Jer. 18:17; 19:2; 31:40; 49:28.

Ezek. 8:16; 10:19; 11:1, 23; 17:10; 19:12; 25:4, 10; 27:26; 39:11; 40:6, 22, 23, 32, 44; 41:14; 42:9, 10, 12, 15, 16; 43:1, 2, 4, 17; 44:1; 45:7; 46:1, 12; 47:1, 8, 18; 48:1-8, 10, 16, 17, 21, 23-27, 32.

Dan. 8:9; 11:44.

Hos. 12:1; 13:15.

Joel 2:20.

Amos 8:12.

Jon. 4:5, 8.

Hab. 1:9.

Zech. 8:7; 14:4.

Matt. 2:1, 2, 9; 8:11; 24:27.

Luke 13:29.

Rev. 7:2; 16:12; 21:13.

East´er was originally the festival of *Eostre,* an Anglo-Saxon goddess, and in Acts 12:4 is a mistranslation for PASSOVER, the Jewish feast. See FEAST, and PASSOVER. Easter is now observed by many Christians in commemoration of our Saviour's resurrection, which occurred just after the PASSOVER and about the same time of the year as the heathen festival of *Eostre,* mentioned above.

East Sea, in Ezek. 47:18; Joel 2:20, is the same as DEAD SEA (which see).

East Wind is mentioned in Gen. 41:6, 23 as blasting the corn (grain), and in other places as very violent. See WIND. Also see Gen. 41:27.

Exod. 10:13; 14:21.

Job 15:2; 27:21; 38:24.

Pss. 48:7; 78:26.

Isa. 27:8.

Jer. 18:17.

Ezek. 17:10; 19:12; 27:26.

Hos. 12:1; 13:15.

Jon. 4:8.

Hab. 1:9.

Eat´ing with people of another religion or with those ceremonially unclean or dishonorable was considered by the Jews as defiling. Refusing to eat with any one implied an entire separation. Matt. 9:11; 1 Cor. 5:11. The Hebrews anciently *sat* while at their meals, Gen. 43:33, but afterward followed the fashion of the Persians, etc., and *reclined* on table-beds or divans. They rested on the left elbow with their heads toward the table, and used the right hand chiefly in taking food. This position makes the account in Luke 7:36–50 perfectly natural. See HOSPITALITY.

Also see Gen. 2; 3; 6; 9; 14; 18; 19; 24–28; 31; 32; 37; 39–41; 43; 45; 47.

Exod. 2; 10; 12; 13; 16; 18; 21–24; 29; 32; 34.

Lev. 3; 6–8; 10; 11; 14; 17; 19; 21–26.

Num. 6; 9; 11; 13; 15; 18; 23–25; 28.

Deut. 2; 4; 6; 8; 9; 11; 12; 14–16; 18; 20; 23; 26–29; 31; 32.

Josh 5; 24.

Judg. 9; 13; 14; 19.

Ruth 2; 3.

1 Sam. 1; 2; 9; 14; 20; 28; 30.

2 Sam. 3; 9; 11–13; 16; 17; 19.

1 Kings 1; 2; 4; 13; 14; 16–19; 21.

2 Kings 4; 6; 7; 9; 18; 19; 23; 25.

1 Chron. 12; 29.

2 Chron. 28; 30; 31.

Ezra 2; 6; 9; 10.

Neh. 5; 7–9.

Esther 4.

Job 1; 3; 5; 6; 13; 20; 21; 31; 40; 42.

Pss. 14; 22; 27; 41; 50; 53; 69; 78; 102; 105; 106; 127; 128; 141.

Prov. 1; 4; 9; 13; 18; 23–25; 27; 30; 31.

Eccles. 2–6; 8–10.

Song of Sol. 4; 5.

Isa. 1; 3–7; 9; 11; 21–23; 28–30; 36; 37; 44; 50; 51; 55; 59; 61; 62; 65; 66.

Jer. 2; 5; 7; 10; 15; 16; 19; 22; 24; 29; 31; 41; 52.

Lam. 2.

Ezek. 2–5; 12; 16; 18; 22; 24; 25; 33; 34; 39; 42; 44; 45.

Dan. 1; 4.

Hos. 2; 4; 8; 9; 10.

Joel 1; 2.

Amos 6; 7; 9.

Obad. :1.

Mic. 3; 6; 7.

Nah. 3.

Hab. 1.

Hag. 1.

Zech. 7; 11.

Matt. 6; 9; 11; 12; 14; 15; 24; 26.

Mark 1–3; 5–8; 11; 14.

Luke 4–7; 9; 10; 12–15; 17; 22; 24.

John 2; 4; 6; 13; 18.

Acts 2; 9–12; 20; 23; 27.

Rom. 14.

1 Cor. 5; 8–11; 15.

Gal. 2.

2 Thess. 3.

2 Tim. 2.

Heb. 13.

James 5.

Rev. 2; 10; 17; 19.

E´bal (*stone*). [1] A son of Shobal. Gen. 36:23; 1 Chron. 1:40. [2] A son of Joktan, 1 Chron. 1:22, called OBAL in Gen. 10:28.

E´bal (*stone*) and Ger´i-zim (*waste places*), the two mountains of Samaria from which the cursings and blessings were pronounced. Deut. 11:29; Josh. 8:30–35. Six tribes were placed on each of them, Deut. 27: 12, 13, and the ark in the valley between them. Joshua built an altar to the Lord on Mount Ebal. Josh. 8:30. He read the Law in the presence of the twelve tribes. The blessings were repeated by the Levites from Gerizim and the cursings from Ebal, and the people responded with Amen. EBAL is the northern mountain. It is rocky and bare, and rises twelve hundred feet above the plain. GERIZIM, the southern mountain, rises only eight hundred feet above SHECHEM (which see). Though it is nearly a mile and a half from one top to the other, experiments have proven that the human voice can be heard distinctly from top to top and down in the valley. Mount Gerizim became afterward the site of the Samaritan temple, and a Samaritan tradition makes it the place where Abraham offered Isaac.

E´bed (*servant*). [1] Father of Gaal. Judg. 9:26, 35. [2] A Jew who accompanied Ezra from Babylon to Jerusalem. Ezra 8.6.

Ebed-melech, e´bed-me´lek (*servant of the king*), an Ethiopian servant of King Zedekiah who was instrumental in saving the life of the prophet Jeremiah. Jer. 38:7; 39:16–18.

Eb-en-e´zer (*stone of help*), a place apparently in the west part of Judah, where the army of Israel was defeated by the Philistines and the ark was taken, and where Samuel set up a stone to which he gave this name, in remembrance of the subsequent victory obtained near it over the Philistines. 1 Sam. 4:1; 7:12.

E´ber or He´ber (*a shoot*). [1] The father of Peleg and the progenitor of the race of the Hebrews. Gen. 10:21; 1 Chron.

1:19. [2] The word is apparently used denoting, it may be, the Hebrews (descendants of Eber), but it may also be understood as referring to "those beyond the river" (Euphrates). Num. 24:24. [3] A head of a family in Gad. 1 Chron. 5:13. [4] A son of Elpaal, descendant of Benjamin. 1 Chron. 8:12. [5] Apparently a son of Shashak. 1 Chron. 8:22. [6] A priest of the family of Amok. Neh. 12:20.

E-bi´a-saph (*the father of gathering*), great-grandson of Korah. 1 Chron. 6:23; 9:19. See ABIASAPH.

Eb´on-y is mentioned in Ezek. 27:15. It is the wood of various trees found in India and Africa, and is hard, black, and heavy. It takes a fine polish.

E-bro´nah (*beach*), the thirtieth encampment of the Israelites after leaving Egypt. Num 33:34, 35.

Ec-bat´a-na, Ezra 6:2, in the marginal notes. [1] The capital city of northern Media, seventy-five miles south-west of the Caspian Sea. [2] The metropolis of lower Media. This city was larger than No. 1.

Ec-cle-si-as´tes, Hebrew *Koheleth,* **the Preach´er,** is a collection of experiences, impressions, and ideas derived from the contemplation of the follies of life, and consequently sad and almost depressing in its character, but nevertheless carrying with it a moral inspiration toward goodness and godliness as the chief end of life. According to an old tradition it was written by Solomon, and if so it corresponds to his old age as the SONG OF SOLOMON does to his youth and PROVERBS to his manhood. It contains the lesson of the life of Solomon.

Ed, in Josh. 22:34, means a witness.

E´den (*delight*). [1] The home of Adam and Eve before their fall; probably situated either in the highlands of Armenia or in the valley of the Euphrates, but notwithstanding the definite description in Gen. 2:8-15 its exact location has not yet been identified. [2] A son of Joah. 2 Chron. 29:12. [3] One of the Levites who, in the time of Hezekiah, were appointed to distribute the gifts among their brethren. 2 Chron. 31:15. May be same as No. 2. Also see Gen. 3:23, 24; 4:16.
Isa. 37:12; 51:3.
Ezek. 28:13; 31:9, 16, 18; 36:35.
Joel 2:3.
Amos 1:5.

E´den, a tribe or family who dwelt in Mesopotamia. 2 Kings 19:12; Ezek. 27:23.

E´dar or **E´der** (*flock*). [1] A place near which Jacob pitched his tent after leaving Ephrath, where Rachel was buried. Gen. 35:21. [2] A border city on the south side of Judah. Josh. 15:21. It may be same as No. 1. [3] A grandson of Merari. 1 Chron. 23:23; 24:30.

E´dom (*red*). [1] A name given to the elder son of Isaac in a few passages. Gen. 25:30; 36:1, 8, 19. [2] The word is also used to designate both the people who descended from Esau and the country in which they lived; but the latter is sometimes call IDUMEA (which see).
Also see Gen. 32:3; 36:16, 17, 21, 31, 32, 43.
Exod. 15:15.
Num. 20:14, 18, 20, 21, 23; 21:4; 24:18; 33:37; 34:3.
Josh. 15:1, 21.
Judg. 5:4; 11:17, 18.
1 Sam. 14:47.
2 Sam. 8:14.
1 Kings 9:26; 11:14-16; 22:47.
2 Kings 3:8, 9, 12, 20, 26; 8:20, 22; 14:7, 10.
1 Chron. 1:43, 51, 54. 18:11, 13.
2 Chron. 8:17; 25:20.

Pss. 60: 8, 9; 83:6; 108:9, 10; 137:7.

Isa. 11:14; 63:1.

Jer. 9:26; 25:21; 27:3; 40:11; 49:7, 17, 20, 22.

Lam. 4:21, 22.

Ezek. 25:12-14; 32:29.

Dan. 11:41.

Joel 3:19.

Amos 1:6, 9, 11; 2:1; 9:12.

Obad. 1, 8.

Mal. 1:4.

E´dom-ites, descendants of Esau. See IDUMEA.

Ed´re-i (*sown land*). [1] A chief city of the kingdom of Og. It was in the south of Bashan. Num. 21:33; Josh. 12:4. [2] A city of Naphtali. Josh. 19:37.

Eg´lah (*calf*), a wife of David. 2 Sam. 3:5; 1 Chron. 3:3.

Eg´la-im (*double spring*), a town of Moab. Isa. 15:8.

Eg´lon (*circle*). [1] A royal city of the Amorites (or Canaanites) which was taken by Joshua. Josh. 10:3; 12:12. It is now called *Ajlan.* [2] A king of Moab who oppressed the Israelites. Judg. 3:12, 17.

E´gypt is the Greek name of the land which the Hebrews called MIZR, or more frequently, using the dual form with reference to the distinction between Upper and Lower Egypt, MIZRA´IM. It consists of a long valley, from six to sixteen miles wide, which the Nile has excavated in the high, stony plateau occupying the northeastern corner of Africa, and which it has covered with its black deposit, which is the source of all Egypt's fertility. Lower Egypt, or Egypt proper, extends from the Mediterranean, 31° 37´ north latitude, to the first cataract of the Nile, 24° 2´ north latitude. On the south side of this cataract a high sandstone ledge between Upper and Lower Egypt crosses the whole valley

of the Nile. At 30° north latitude the rocky plateau recedes on both sides of the river, and here the Nile spreads out its delta, the eastern part of which forms the province of GOSHEN (which see).

Upper Egypt consists of a series of elevated plains, forming terraces over which the Nile descends between low mountain-ranges. Its soil is cultivable only in the valley of the Nile, which is much narrower here than in Lower Egypt. The climate is extremely hot. See NILE.

Both soil and climate contribute to make Egypt one of the most productive regions on earth. For centuries this land was the granary of the Roman Empire—or of the then civilized world—and long before there was any Roman Empire the nomadic tribes of Asia, when suffering from famine, used to go to Egypt for food: for instance, the visits of Abram and the sons of Jacob. Gen. 12:10; 42:3; 43:2. Not only cereals were produced there in abundance. but also fruits and vegetables of excellent quality, and all kinds of animals for food, such as cattle. sheep, swine, poultry, game, etc. The Israelites found it difficult to forget the fleshpots of Egypt, Exod. 16:3, and its melons, cucumbers, onions, etc. Num. 11:5. This productiveness of the country, together with its protected location, surrounded, as it was, on three sides by almost impenetrable deserts and on the fourth by the sea, made it a suitable home for the young race to grow in, and, indeed, in Egypt mankind made its first and one of its grandest attempts in civilization. When Joseph settled his brethren in Goshen the Egyptians had large and magnificent cities, an elaborate social organization, with a fully developed kingship, hierarchy, military establishment, and temple and palaces, the ruins of which fill the spectator with wonder and awe.

Egyptian history has been studied with great energy and marvellous results. The sources are few and precarious. They consist of half-ruined monuments with inscriptions half blotted out, incidental scraps of documents found in the temples or the sepulchres, and notices given by foreigners, Greeks and Hebrews. The first two sources, the inscriptions and the documents, were for a long time utterly inaccessible, as the language in which they were written was not understood and the method by which that language was reduced to writing, the hieroglyphics, was not known. Champollion, the French Egyptologist, 1790–1832, found the key to the latter, and thereby also to the former, and then the deciphering began. But it is slow work. Among the notices found in the Greek literature were some extracts from the historical work of Manetho. He was supreme pontiff at the temple of Hieropolis, and was commissioned by Ptolemy Philadelphus, who died B. C. 247, to write the history of Egypt, based upon the archives of the temples. He wrote his work in Greek, but it is lost, and only fragments of it have come down to us through Josephus, Africanus, and Eusebius, among which are his tables of the thirty dynasties that ruled over Egypt before its conquest by Alexander the Great, B. C. 332. Formerly the notices of Egypt contained in the Bible and in Herodotus were considered by many as fables, but they have been verified by modern discoveries.

The most difficult question with respect to the relation between Biblical and Egyptian history is one of chronology. But it must not here be overlooked that not only the Egyptian chronology before the Greek conquest but also the Biblical before Solomon are still in an unsettled state and perhaps not yet rightly understood. One point, however, and that a very important one, has been satisfactorily settled. Egyptian historians speak generally of the exodus of the Israelites as the expulsion of a rebellious tribe which was under the leadership of a Heliopolitan priest, Osarsiph, who afterward assumed the name of Moses and state that the event took place under a king whose father's name was Rameses and whose son's name was Sethos. But in the list of Manetho there is no other king who fits this description but Menephtha, belonging to the nineteenth dynasty, the son of Rameses II. and the father of Setho II. He should also be the king of the exodus and Rameses II. the king of the oppression, and so they are. Rameses II. was by far the greatest king of the nineteenth dynasty, and, so to speak, the culminating star of Egyptian power. No wonder, then, that he is very well known to us from the monuments. In the summer of 1881 his mummy, together with a number of papyrus rolls and objects of value, was discovered in a cave near Thebes in a perfect state of preservation. It was resting in a mummy-case of sycamore-wood carved to represent him as the god Osiris, wrapped in shrouds of rose-colored and yellow linen, with the arms crossed upon the breast, the right hand holding the royal whip and the left the royal hook, and with an inscription on the bands which pass across the shrouds to keep them in place stating that the body enclosed was that of Rameses II. Among the exploits of this famous king was the construction of the great canal in Goshen by which communication between the Nile and the Red Sea was finally completed and building at its eastern and western ter minations the two cities of Pi-Rameses and Pi-tum. But, according to Exod. 1:11, it was just the task of building those two cities, whose names are spelled Pithom and Raamses in the Bible, which filled the measure of oppression to overflowing and roused the Israelites to rebellion. With respect to Menephtha, the king of the ten. plagues and of the frightful disaster in the Red Sea, there is something connected with his name, not only in Egyptian history, but even in the notes of Herodotus, which reads like confused reminiscences of those events, and of the history of Joseph many traits have been distinctly verified by Egyptian discovery. The relations between the Israelites and the Egyptians after the exodus are of less interest. There has, however, been deciphered an inscription on the walls of the great temple at Karnak recording the capture of Jerusalem and the conquest of Judea by Shishak. 1 Kings 14:26. In this inscription is found a figure painted with very prominent Jewish features and with the superscription in Egyptian characters, "The king of Judah." The predictions of the prophets concerning the downfall of the Egyptian power are very remarkable, especially those of Isaiah and Daniel. Also see Gen. 12; 13; 15; 21; 25; 26; 37; 39–43; 45–48; 50. Exod. 1–14; 16–20; 22; 23; 29; 32–34. Lev. 11; 18; 19; 22; 23; 25; 26. Num. 1; 3; 8; 9; 11; 13–15; 20–24; 26; 32–34. Deut. 1; 4–11; 13; 15–17; 20; 23–26; 28; 29; 34. Josh. 2; 5; 9; 13; 15; 24. Judg. 2; 6; 11; 19. Sam. 2; 8; 10; 12; 15; 27; 30. Sam 7. Kings 3; 4; 6; 8–12; 14. Kings 17; 18; 21; 23–25.

1 Chron. 13; 17.
2 Chron. 1; 5–7; 9; 10; 12; 20; 26; 35; 36.
Neh. 9.
Pss. 68; 78; 80; 81; 105; 106; 114; 135; 136.
Prov. 7.
Isa. 7; 10; 11; 19; 20; 23; 27; 30; 31; 36; 43; 45; 52.
Jer. 2; 7; 9; 11; 16; 23–26; 31; 32; 34; 37; 41–44; 46.
Ezek. 17; 19; 20; 23; 27; 29–32.
Dan. 9; 11.
Hos. 2; 7–9; 11–13.
Joel 3.
Amos 2–4; 8; 9.
Mic. 6; 7.
Nah. 3.
Hag. 2.
Zech. 10; 14.
Matt. 2.
Acts. 2; 7; 13.
Heb. 3; 8; 11.
Jude 5.
Rev. 11.

E-gyp′tians. The name MIZ-RA′IM (*Egypt*) is the name most frequently used in the Hebrew for the people of Egypt.

E-gyp′tian Sea, Isa. 11:15, a name of either the whole or the northern part of the RED SEA (which see).

E′hi (*unity*), a son of Benjamin. Gen. 46:21. Supposed by some to be same with EHUD. 1 Chron. 8:6.

E′hud (*strong*). [1] A son of Gera who slew Eglon and delivered the Israelites from the oppression of the Moabites. He was one of the judges in Israel. Judg. 3:15, 16. [2] A grandson of Jediael. 1 Chron. 7:10. [3] A descendant of Benjamin. 1 Chron. 8:6. May be same as No. 1.

E′ker (*root*), a son of Ram. 1 Chron. 2:27.

Ek′ron (*emigration*), a chief city of the

Philistines. Josh. 13:3; Amos 1:8.

Ek´ron-ites, inhabitants of Ekron. Josh. 13:3; 1 Sam. 5:10.

El (*strength*), a name of God. It is very often a part of proper names, such as Bethel, Elijah, Eloi.

El´a-dah (*God is ornament*), a descendant of Ephraim. 1 Chron. 7:20.

E´lah (*oak*). [1] A duke (or chief) of Edom. Gen. 36:41; 1 Chron. 1:52. [2] A valley in Judah where Saul's army encamped when David slew Goliath. 1 Sam. 17:2; 21:9. [3] Father of one of Solomon's officers. 1 Kings 4:18. [4] Son of Baasha, king of Israel. 1 Kings 16:6, 8. [5] Father of Hoshea. 2 Kings 15:30; 18:1. [6] A son of Caleb. 1 Chron. 4:15. [7] An Israelite whose family dwelt in Jerusalem. 1 Chron. 9:8. Perhaps same as No. 3.

E´lam (*age*). [1] A son of Shem. His descendants settled in that part of Persia afterward often called by this name. Gen. 10:22; 1 Chron. 1:17. [2] Name of a province in Persia; applied also to the whole country and to its inhabitants. Gen. 14:1. [3] A son of Shashak. 1 Chron. 8:24. [4] A son of Meshelemiah. 1 Chron. 26:3. [5] The progenitor of a family who returned from Babylon. Ezra 2:7; Neh. 7:12. [6] Another Israelite whose posterity returned from Babylon. Ezra 2:31; Neh. 7:34. [7] An Israelite some of whose descendants returned from Babylon. Ezra 8:7. Perhaps same as either No. 5 or No. 6. [8] An ancestor of Shechaniah. Ezra 10:2, 26. Perhaps same as No. 5 or No. 6. [9] A chief or family of the Jews who sealed the covenant of Nehemiah. Neh. 10:14. [10] A priest who aided in the ceremony of purifying the rebuilt wall of Jerusalem. Neh. 12:42.

E´lam-ites, dwellers in Elam. Ezra 4:9; Acts 2:9.

El´a-sah (*God is doer*). [1] An ambassador whom Zedekiah sent to Nebuchadnezzar. Jer. 29:3. [2] A priest who took a foreign wife. Ezra 10:22.

E´lath or **E´loth** (*palm grove*), a place or city on the east gulf of the Red Sea. Deut. 2:8; 2 Kings 14:22; 16:6.

El-beth´el (*God of the house of God*), the name which Jacob gave to the place where God appeared to him when he fled from Esau. Gen. 35:7.

Eldaah, el´da-ah or el-da´ah (*whom God called*), a son of Midian. Gen. 25:4; 1 Chron. 1:33.

El´dad (*God is a friend*), an elder of Israel. Num. 11:26, 27.

Eld´ers. [1] Men among the Jews invested with authority (probably as counsellors or judges), and so named on account of their age. Matt. 15:2; Mark 7:3; Luke 7:3. [2] An official designation of those appointed to rule and teach in the church, interchangeably with "overseer," or "bishop." Acts 11:30; 1 Tim. 5:1; Rev. 4:4; 11:16.

E´le-ad (*God is witness*), a son of Ephraim. 1 Chron. 7:21.

E-le-a´leh (*God is exalted*), a city of Reuben. Num. 32:3; Jer. 48:34.

E-le´a-sah (*God is doer*). [1] A descendant of Sheshan. 1 Chron. 2:39, 40. [2] A descendant of Benjamin, apparently of the family of Saul. 1 Chron. 8:37; 9:43.

E-le-a´zar (*God is helper*). [1] The third son of Áaron, Exod. 6:23, and his successor in the office of high-priest, which he held for many years. [2] The son of Abinadab. 1 Sam. 7:1. [3] One of the three mighty men who aided David in smiting the Philistines. 2 Sam. 23:9; 1 Chron. 11:12 [4] A son of Mahli. 1 Chron. 23:21; 24:28 [5] A priest who went up with Ezra to Jerusalem. Ezra 8:33. [6] A priest in the

time of Nehemiah. Neh. 12:42. Perhaps same as No. 5. [7] A Jew who had taken a foreign wife. Ezra 10:25. [8] An ancestor of Joseph, the husband of Mary. Matt. 1:15. Also see Exod. 6:25; 28:1.
Lev. 10:6, 12, 16.
Num. 3:2, 4, 32; 4:16; 16:37, 39; 19:3, 4; 20:25, 26, 28; 25:7, 11; 26:1, 3, 60, 63; 27:2, 19, 21, 22; 31:6, 12, 13, 21, 26, 29, 31, 41, 51, 54; 32:2, 28; 34:17.
Deut. 10:6.
Josh. 14:1; 17:4; 19:51; 21:1; 22:13, 31, 32; 24:33.
Judg. 20:28.
1 Chron. 6:3, 4, 50; 9:20; 23:22; 24:1-5.
Ezra 7:5.

E-lect′ (*chosen*).
Isa. 42:1; 45:4; 65:9, 22.
Matt. 24:22, 24, 31.
Mark 13:20, 22, 27.
Luke 18:7.
Rom. 8:33.
Col. 3:12.
1 Tim. 5:21.
2 Tim. 2:10.
Titus 1:1.
1 Pet. 1:2; 2:6; 5:13.
2 John 1, 13.

El-e-lo′he-Is′ra-el (*God, the God of Israel*), the name which Jacob gave to the altar he built in the field he bought of the children of Hamor. Gen. 33:20.

E′leph (*union*), a town in Benjamin. Josh. 18:28.

El-ha′nan (*God is gracious*). [1] A man who slew Goliath's brother. 2 Sam. 21:19; 1 Chron. 20:5. [2] One of David's mighty men. 2 Sam. 23:24; 1 Chron. 11:26.

E′li (*Jehovah is high*). The high-priest and judge of Israel who immediately preceded Samuel.
1 Sam. 1:3, 9, 12-14, 17, 25; 2:11, 12, 20, 22, 27; 3:1, 2, 5, 6, 8, 9, 12, 14-16; 4:4,

11, 13-16; 14:3
1 Kings 2:27.
Matt. 27:46.

E′li, E′li, lama sabachthani? sa-bak-tha′ni, Matt. 27:46, or **Elo′i, Elo′i, lama sabachtha′ni?** Mark 15:34, the exclamation uttered by Christ on the cross, expressive of the acuteness of his sufferings and his horror at the hiding of his Father's countenance.

E-li′ab (*God is father*). [1] A captain of Zebulun. Num. 1:9; 10:16. [2] Father of Dathan and Abiram. Num. 16:1; Deut. 11:6. [3] A brother of David. 1 Sam. 16:6; 1 Chron. 2:13. Supposed to be same as ELIHU, who is named as one of the brethren of David in 1 Chron. 27:18. [4] A name given in one place as that of the grandfather of Elkanah, but in 1 Chron. 6:34 it is given ELIEL. 1 Chron. 6:27. [5] A valiant man of the Gadites. 1 Chron. 12:9. [6] A musician for the service of the Tabernacle. 1 Chron. 15:18; 16:5.

E-li′a-da (*God is knowing*). [1] A son of David. 2 Sam. 5:16. 1 Chron. 3:8. [2] (In the Authorized Version called **Eliadah.**) The father of Rezon. 1 Kings 11:23. [3] The chief captain of Benjamin in the time of Jehoshaphat. 2 Chron. 17:17.

E-li′ah (*God is Jehovah*). [1] A son of Jeroham 1 Chron. 8:27. [2] A Jew who had taken a foreign wife. Ezra 10:26.

E-li′ah-ba (*God hides*). one of David's valiant men. 2 Sam. 23:32; 1 Chron. 11:33.

E-li′a-kim (*God is setting up*). [1] The master of the king's household at Jerusalem in the time of Hezekiah. 2 Kings 18:18; Isa. 37:2. [2] A son of King Josiah. 2 Kings 23:34; 2 Chron. 36:4. His name was changed to JEHOIAKIM (which see). [3] A priest who officiated in purifying the rebuilt wall of Jerusalem. Neh. 12:41. [4] An ancestor of Joseph, the husband of

Mary, as given by Matthew. Matt. 1:13. [5] An ancestor of Joseph in the line given by Luke. Luke 3:30.

E-li´am (*God is founder of the people*). [1] Father of Bathsheba. 2 Sam. 11:3. [2] One of David's valiant men. 2 Sam. 23:34.

E-li´as, Matt. 11:14; Mark 6:15; Luke 1:17; John 1:21, the Greek form of ELIJAH (which see).

E-li´a-saph (*God is gatherer*). [1] A captain of the tribe of Gad. Num. 1:14; 10:20. [2] A descendant of Gershon. Num. 3:24.

E-li´a-shib (*God is requiter*). [1] A son of Elioenai. 1 Chron. 3:24. [2] The head of a family of priests. 1 Chron. 24:12. [3] A Levite, ancestor of Johanan. Ezra 10:6; Neh. 12:23. [4] A Levite who took a foreign wife. Ezra 10:24. [5] A son of Zattu who took a foreign wife. Ezra 10:27. [6] A son of Bani who took a foreign wife. Ezra 10:36. [7] The high-priest who began to rebuild the walls of Jerusalem. Neh. 3:1; 13:4.

E-li´a-thah (*God is come*), a son of Heman. 1 Chron. 25:4, 27.

E-li´dad (*God is a friend*), a chief of Benjamin. Num. 34:21.

E´li-el (*God is God*). [1] A head of the house of Manasseh in Bashan. 1 Chron. 5:24. [2] Great-grandfather of the prophet Samuel. 1 Chron. 6:34. In 1 Chron. 6:27 ELIAB is the name given. [3] A son of Shimhi. 1 Chron. 8:20. [4] A son of Sha-shak. 1 Chron. 8:22. [5] A captain of David's army. 1 Chron. 11:46. [6] One of David's valiant men. 1 Chron. 11:47. [7] May be same as No. 5 or No. 6. A man of Gad. 1 Chron. 12:11. [8] Perhaps same as No. 5. A chief apparently of the tribe of Judah in the time of David. 1 Chron. 15:9. [9] A chief among the Levites. 1 Chron.

15:11. [10] A Levite who had oversight of dedicated things. 2 Chron. 31:13.

E-li-e´na-i (*unto God are mine eyes*), a son of Shimhi. 1 Chron. 8:20.

E-li-e´zer (*God is help*). [1] A man of Damascus who was steward of Abram's house. Gen. 15:2. [2] A son of Moses. Exod. 18:4; 1 Chron. 23:15. [3] A son of Becher. 1 Chron. 7:8. [4] A priest who assisted in bringing up the ark out of the house of Obed-edom. 1 Chron. 15:24. [5] Ruler of the tribe of Reuben in the time of David. 1 Chron. 27:16. [6] A prophet who prophesied against Jehoshaphat. 2 Chron. 20:37. [7] A chief man who went with Ezra from Babylon to Jerusalem. Ezra 8:16. [8] A priest who took a foreign wife. Ezra 10:18. [9] A Levite who took a foreign wife. Ezra 10:23. [10] A Jew of the sons of Harim who took a foreign wife. Ezra 10:31. [11] An ancestor of Joseph, the husband of Mary. Luke 3:29.

E-li-ho-e´na-i (*toward Jehovah are my eyes*), one who returned with Ezra. Ezra 8:4.

E-li-ho´reph (*God of harvest rain*), one of Solomon's scribes or secretaries. 1 Kings 4:3. Supposed to be same as SERAIAH, David's scribe.

E-li´hu (*God himself*). [1] A descendant of Kohath. 1 Sam. 1:1. [2] A man of Manasseh who joined David in Ziklag. 1 Chron. 12:20. [3] A descendant of Kohath. 1 Chron. 26:7. [4] One of the brethren of David who was made ruler over the tribe of Judah. 1 Chron. 27:18. Supposed to be same as ELIAB. 1 Sam. 16:6. [5] A person who apparently had accompanied the friends of Job when they visited him. Job 32:2; 36:1.

E-li´jah (*my God is Jehovah*), Greek ELIAS. Matt. 17:3. [1] A native of Thisbeh, in the highlands of Gilead, east of the

Jordan, between Bashan and Moab. Although he wrote nothing, he stands out in the history of Israel as the greatest among the prophets. By his solitary life, far away from the noise of the world but close to God, and his sudden appearance with the message from the Lord, coming and going like the lightning on the sky; by the fearful promptness with which his prophecies of the drought, the doom of Ahab, the death of Ahaziah, etc. were fulfilled; by such deeds as the destruction by fire of the idolatrous prophets on Mount Carmel, the stopping of the drought by prayer, the destruction by fire of the soldiers sent against him, etc., he made an indelible impression on his age, which is renewed whenever the story of his life and death is read again. 1 Kings 17–21; 2 Kings 1, 2; 2 Chron. 21:12-15. In the New Testament he is mentioned as the prototype of John the Baptist and as present together with Moses at the transfiguration of Christ. Luke 9:28-35. [2] A Jew, apparently of the sons of the priests, who had taken a foreign wife during or after the captivity. Ezra 10:21.
Also see 2 Kings 3:11; 9:36; 10:10, 17. Mal. 4:5.

Elika, el´i-ka or e-li´ka (*God is rejector*), one of David's valiant men. 2 Sam. 23:25.

E´lim (*palm trees*), the second encampment of the Israelites after they crossed the Red Sea. Exod. 15:27; Num. 33:9.

Elimelech, e-lim´e-lek (*God is king*), the husband of Naomi. Ruth 1:3; 4:9.

E-li-o-e´na-i (*to Jehovah are mine eyes*). [1] A son of Neariah. 1 Chron. 3:23, 24. [2] An Israelite, apparently a chief of the tribe of Simeon. 1 Chron. 4:36. [3] A son of Becher. 1 Chron. 7:8. [4] A Jew, apparently a priest, who took a foreign wife. Ezra 10:22; Neh. 12:41. [5] A Jew of the family of Zattu who took a foreign wife. Ezra 10:27. [6] A Levite, the son of Meshelemiah. 1 Chron. 26:3.

El´i-phal (*God is judge*), a captain of David's army, 1 Chron. 11:35, called ELIPHELET in 2 Sam. 23:34.

E-liph´a-let (*God his deliverance*), a son of David, 2 Sam. 5:16; 1 Chron. 14:7, called ELIPHELET in 1 Chron. 3:8.

Eliphaz, el´i-faz or e-li´faz (*God his strength*). [1] A son of Esau. Gen. 36:4; 1 Chron. 1:35. [2] One of Job's friends. Job 2:11; 42:9.

E-liph´e-leh (*whom God makes distinguished*), a Levite in the choral service of the Tabernacle. 1 Chron. 15:18, 21.

E-liph´e-let (*God his deliverance*). [1] One of David's valiant men, 2 Sam. 23:34, called ELIPHAL in 1 Chron. 11:35. [2] A son of David, 1 Chron. 3:6, called ELPALET in 1 Chron. 14:5. [3] A son of David, 1 Chron. 3:8, called ELIPHALET in 2 Sam. 5:16; 1 Chron. 14:7. [4] A descendant of Saul. 1 Chron. 8:39. [5] One who returned from Babylon with Ezra. Ezra 8:13. [6] An Israelite who took a foreign wife. Ezra 10:33.

E-lis´a-beth (*worshipper of God*), the wife of Zacharias and mother of John the Baptist. Luke 1:5, 41.

El-i-se´us, the form in which the name ELISHA (which see) appears in the common version of the New Testament. Luke 4:27.

E-li´sha (*God is salvation*) was a native of Abel-meholah, a place in the Jordan Valley between the Sea of Galilee and the Dead Sea. He was anointed by Elijah, whom he then followed for eight years, and was present at his translation into heaven, B. C. about 896, after which he became his successor. But there was a striking difference between the master and the disciple in their exercise of the prophetic office. Elisha lived in the cities, was head of the prophetic school, and the intimate counsellor of four kings. This difference, however, was not simply the result of a difference of temper—Elisha was as tender and gentle as Elijah was stern and austere—but corresponded also to a difference in the surroundings. Elijah's task was to inaugurate a radical reform; Elisha's, to still the troubled waters; and probably the latter's ministration was as effective as the former's. The history of his life is recorded in 2 Kings chapters 2-9 and 13:14-21. He exercised the prophetic office for about sixty years. Also see 1 Kings 19:16, 17, 19.

E-li´shah (*God is salvation*), a son of Javan. Gen. 10:4; Ezek. 27:7.

E-li´shah, Isles of, Ezek. 27:7, are generally identified with Æolis, Lesbos, Tenedos, etc., in the Grecian Archipelago.

E-lish´a-ma (*God is hearer*). [1] A captain of Ephraim. Num. 1:10; 1 Chron. 7:26. [2] A son of David. 2 Sam. 5:16; 1 Chron. 14:7. [3] Grandfather of Ishmael, who slew Gedaliah. 2 Kings 25:25; Jer. 41:1. [4] An Israelite of Judah. 1 Chron. 2:41. [5] Another son of David, 1 Chron. 3:6, called ELISHUA in the lists given in 2 Sam. 5 and 1 Chron. 14. [6] A priest in the time of Jehoshaphat. 2 Chron. 17:8. [7] A scribe in the time of Jehoiakim. Jer. 36:12, 21.

E-lish´a-phat (*God is judge*), a captain by whose aid Jehoiada placed Joash on the throne of Judah. 2 Chron. 23:1.

E-lish´e-ba (*God is her oath*), daughter of Amminadab and wife of Aaron. Exod. 6:23.

E-lish´u-a (*God his salvation*), a son of David, 2 Sam. 5:15; 1 Chron. 14:5, called ELISHAMA in 1 Chron. 3:6.

E-li´ud (*God his praise*), an ancestor of Joseph, the husband of Mary. Matt. 1:14, 15.

E-li´za-phan (*God is protector*). [1] A Levite of the sons of Kohath. Num. 3:30; 1 Chron. 15:8. See ELZAPHAN. [2] Prince of Zebulun in the time of Moses. Num. 34:25.

E-li´zur (*God is a rock*), a chief of Reuben who assisted in numbering the people. Num. 1:5; 10:18.

El´ka-nah (*God is possessing*). There is much difficulty and uncertainty in the discrimination of the various individuals who bear this name. [1] A son or grandson of Korah. Exod. 6:24; 1 Chron. 6:23. [2] A descendant, as it appears, of No. 1. 1 Sam. 1:1; 1 Chron. 6:27. He was the husband of Hannah and father of Samuel. [3] A descendant of Kohath. 1 Chron. 6:25, 36. [4] Apparently a descendant of Kohath. 1 Chron. 6:26, 35. Perhaps same as No. 3. [5] A Levite whose descendants dwelt in the villages of the Netophathites. 1 Chron. 9:16. [6] An Israelite who joined David at Ziklag. 1 Chron. 12:6. [7] A Levite, one of the porters for the ark. 1 Chron. 15:23. [8] A chief officer of Judah in the time of Ahaz. 2 Chron. 28:7.

El´kosh-ite, a dweller in ELKOSH, which Jerome says was a village of Galilee. Others think it was in the territory of Simeon. Nah. 1:1.

El´la-sar, a country supposed to lay between Babylonia and Assyria, and which some consider the same as Telassar. Isa. 37:12; Gen. 14:1, 9.

Elm. Hos. 4:13. The original is elsewhere translated as OAK.

El-mo´dam, an ancestor of Joseph, the husband of Mary. Luke 3:28.

El´na-am (*God is pleasant*), father of Jeribai and Joshaviah. 1 Chron. 11:46.

El´na-than (*God is giving*). [1] Father

of Nehushta, the wife of Jehoiakim. 2 Kings 24:8. [**2, 3, 4**] Three Jews in the time of Ezra. Ezra 8:16.

Elo´i (*My God*), a name of the Most High, used by Christ on the cross. Mark 15:34.

E´lon (*oak, strong*). [**1**] Father of Bashemath, a wife of Esau. Gen. 26:34; 36:2. [**2**] A son of Zebulun. Gen. 46:14; Num. 26:26. [**3**] A town in Dan. Josh. 19:43. [**4**] A Zebulonite judge in Israel. Judg. 12:11, 12.

E´lon-beth´-ha-nan. 1 Kings 4:9. These words, which mean the oak or terebinth tree of the house of Hanan, are taken to be the full name of the town called ELON in Josh. 19:43.

E´lon-ites, Num. 26:26, a family of the Israelites whose founder was ELON.

E´loth (*oak or terebinth grove*), a place or city on the eastern gulf of the RED SEA. 1 Kings 9:26; 2 Chron. 8:17. In 2 Kings 16:6 the English Version has the name of this place ELATH.

El´pa-al (*God is working*), a son of Shaharaim. 1 Chron. 8:11, 18.

El´pa-let (*God is escape*), a name given to a son of David in one place. (Apparently same as the one called ELIPHALET in 1 Chron. 3:6, and who is omitted in the list in 2 Sam. 5.) 1 Chron. 14:5.

El-pa´ran (*oak of Paran*), a district south of Palestine and apparently westward from Edom. (Compare Gen. 21 with Num. 20:14, etc.). Gen. 14:6. See PARAN.

El´-te-keh (*God its fear*), a city of Dan. Josh. 19:44; 21:23.

El´-te-kon (*God is firm*), a city in the mountains of Judah. Josh. 15:59.

Eltolad, el-to´lad or el´to-lad (*God is begetter*), a town which belonged first to Judah, and subsequently to Simeon, Josh. 15:30; 19:4, called TOLAD in 1 Chron. 4:29.

E´lul (*the gleaning month*), the sixth month of the ecclesiastical year of the Jews beginning with the new moon of September. It is the twelfth month of their civil year. Neh. 6:15. See MONTH.

Eluzai, e-loo´za-i (*God is strong*), a valiant man of Benjamin or Judah. 1 Chron. 12:5.

El´y-mas (*a sorceror*), a false prophet who withstood Saul (who is also called Paul) and Barnabas at Paphos, and was struck with instant blindness. Acts 13:8. Elymas was also called BAR-JESUS. See SERGIUS PAULUS.

El´za-bad (*God is endowing*). [**1**] A Gadite warrior. 1 Chron. 12:12. [**2**] A son of Shemaiah. 1 Chron. 25:7.

El´za-phan (*whom God protects*), a son of Uzziel. Exod. 6:22; Lev. 10:4. See ELIZAPHAN.

Em-balm´ing, or preserving from decay the bodies of the dead, was practiced by the Egyptians at a very early period. The Hebrews learned the art from them, and made use of it occasionally in a less effectual way. The bodies of Jacob and Joseph were embalmed in Egypt.

Em´e-rald, a precious stone of a pure green color, to which it owes its chief value. Exod. 28:18; Rev. 4:3.

Em´e-rods, in 1 Sam. 5:6, means discharging piles.

E´mims (*the terrible*), a warlike and gigantic race who in Abraham's time occupied the country beyond Jordan afterward possessed by the Moabites. Gen. 14:5; Deut. 2:10.

Em-man´u-el, Matt. 1:23, a name applied in the New Testament to the MESSIAH. In the Old Testament the word IMMANUEL is used with the same meaning.

Em´ma-us (*hot spring*), a village about seven miles from Jerusalem, where Christ appeared to two of his disciples on the day of his resurrection. Luke 24:13. Its exact location is unknown.

Em´mor, Acts 7:16, a prince of the Hivites. See HAMOR.

En means a fountain, and is part of many names of towns and places.

En-a´bled, in 1 Tim. 1:12, means empowered.

En-a´jim (*gate of two eyes*), in marginal notes, Gen. 38:14, 21, may mean a place identical with ENAM.

E´nam (*double fountains*), a town of Judah. Josh. 15:34.

E´nan (*fountain*), father of Ahira. Num. 1:15; 10:27.

En-camp´ment. See CAMP.

En-chant´ments. Exod. 7:11. See DIVINATION.

En-dam´age, in Ezra 4:13, means injure.

En´-dor (*fountain of Dor*), a town where the woman lived whom King Saul consulted as having a familiar spirit. 1 Sam. 28:7-25. Endor was on the northern slope of Little Mount Hermon, eighteen miles south-east of Acre.

E´ne-as, a man of Lydda who had kept his bed eight years, and who was healed of the palsy by the Lord at the word of Peter. Acts 9:33, 34.

En-eg´la-im (*fountain of two calves*), a town near the Dead Sea. Ezek. 47:10.

En-gan´nim (*fountain of gardens*). [1] A city of Judah. Josh. 15:34. [2] A city of Issachar. Josh. 19:21; 21:29.

En-ge´di (*fountain of Gad*), a place in the east of Judah and near the Dead Sea. Josh. 15:62; Ezek. 47:10.

En-gra´ver, a carver in wood or stone, as well as an engraver on precious metals. Exod. 35:35; 38:23. The art of engraving in its various forms was well known to the ancient Egyptians.

En-had´dah (*swift fountain*), a town of Issachar. Josh. 19:21.

En-hak´ko-re (*fountain of the crier*), the name given by Samson to the fountain which God made to spring up in Lehi. Judg. 15:19.

En-ha´zor (*fountain of the village*), a fenced city of Naphtali. Josh. 19:37.

En-larged´, in Ps. 4:1, means set at liberty.

En-mish´pat, Gen. 14:7 (*fountain of judgment*), a place which was also called Kadesh, and seems to be the same as Kadesh in the wilderness of Paran, but different from Kadesh in the desert of Zin. See Num. 13:26 and 20:1.

E´noch or **He´noch** (*teacher*). [1] A son of Cain. Gen. 4:17, 18. [2] The name given by Cain to a city which he built. Gen. 4:17. [3] The son of Jared and father of Methuselah. Gen. 5:18, 21. He is called in Jude 14 "the seventh from Adam," to distinguish him from Enoch the son of Cain. He is said to have "walked with God," Gen. 5:22, and was translated to heaven—"God took him." Gen. 5:24.

E´non (*fountain*), a town, apparently on the west side of Jordan, where John baptized. John 3:23. It was near Salim. Same as ÆNON.

E´nos (*man*), a son of Seth and grandson of Adam. Gen. 4:26; 5:6, 9, 11; Luke 3:38. Called ENOSH in 1 Chron. 1:1.

E´nosh (*man*), 1 Chron. 1:1, a form of ENOS.

En-rim´mon (*fountain of Rimmon*), a town of Judah. Neh. 11:29.

En-ro´gel (*the fullers' fountain*), a fountain near Jerusalem, on the south side. Josh. 15:7; 1 Kings 1:9.

En-sam´ples, in 1 Cor. 10:11, means examples.

En-she´mesh (*fountain of the sun*), a

town in the north-east of Judah. Josh. 15:7; 18:17.

En´sign, as in Isa. 5:26; 30:17, sometimes means a signal or beacon, but is often used in the Bible in the same sense as BANNER or STANDARD.

En-sue´, in 1 Pet. 3:11, means pursue diligently.

En-tap´pu-ah (*fountain of Tappuah*), a town or fountain on the border of Manasseh. Josh. 17:7.

En-treat´ed, in Gen. 12:16; Acts 27:3, means treated. In Isa. 19:22 it means prevailed upon.

Epænetus, e-pen´e-tus, a disciple who had gone to Rome, and to whom Paul sends salutation. Rom. 16:5.

Ep´a-phras, a disciple of Colosse who accompanied Paul to Rome. Col. 1:7; Philem. 23.

E-paph-ro-di´tus, a Christian of Philippi who was sent by the churches of that place to Paul at Rome. Phil. 2:25; 4:18.

E´phah, a measure for things dry, equal in capacity to the BATH, used for things liquid. In contained about three pecks and a half. Exod. 16:36; Lev. 5:11.

E´phah (*obscurity*). [1] A son of Midian and grandson of Abraham. The name is apparently also applied to the district where he settled or to his posterity. Gen. 25:4; Isa. 60:6. [2] The concubine of Caleb the son of Hezron. 1 Chron. 2:46. [3] A son of Jahdai. 1 Chron. 2:47.

E´phai (*obscuring*), a Netophathite whose sons were among the captains whom Gedaliah tried to persuade to serve the Chaldeans. Jer. 40:8.

E´pher (*young deer or calf*). [1] A son of Midian. Gen. 25:4. [2] An Israelite of the tribe of Judah. 1 Chron. 4:17. [3] A head of the house of their fathers, in

Manasseh. 1 Chron. 5:24.

E-phes-dam´mim (*extension of brooks*), a place in Judah where the Philistines were encamped when David slew Goliath. 1 Sam. 17:1. See PAS-DAMMIM.

E-phe´sian, a native of Ephesus. Acts 19:28; 21:29.

E-phe´sians, the E-pis´tle of Paul to the, was, like that to the Colossians, which it resembles somewhat, written from Rome when Paul was a prisoner, between A. D. 61 and 63. It was not called forth by any special event, but was apparently written simply for the purpose of generally fortifying the Christian faith and practice of the church at Ephesus. The Epistle, aside from the brief beginning and ending, is in two parts: 1. Chapters 1–3. A very feeling exposition of Christian doctrine, especially of eternal election to holiness and salvation by Christ. 2. Chapters 4–6. An exhortation to apply the doctrines of Christianity to the duties of active life. The Epistle gives the fullest exposition of Paul's sublime idea of the Church as "the body of Christ, the fulness of him that filleth all in all" (1:23). It was a circular letter intended for all the churches of Asia Minor.

Eph´e-sus, now a desolate heap of ruins, thirty-five miles south-east of Smyrna, was in Paul's time the principal commercial city of Asia Minor, wealthy, elegant, and licentious, and the capital of the Ionian Confederacy, which had its treasury in the temple of Diana. That building was one of the wonders of the world, and looked upon by the Ionian race as Solomon's Temple was by the Jews. Thus the city was at once a center of wealth and a center of idolatry. Paul visited it twice, Acts 18:19-21 and Acts 19:1, and the last time he spent three years there. Afterward the Ephesian church was in charge of Timothy. It is addressed in Rev. 2:1-7. The excavations of J. T. Wood (1863 to 1874) brought to light remains of the temple of Diana, the theatre, the circus, and interesting Greek and Latin inscriptions.

Eph´lal (*judging*), a descendant of Jerahmeel. 1 Chron. 2:37.

Eph´od (*oracular*). [**1**] The father of Hanniel. Num. 34:23. [**2**] A part of the vesture which was directed to be worn by the high-priest when officiating. Exod. 39:2, 5, 7, 18, 21, 22; Hos. 3:4.

Eph´pha-tha, a Syriac word which means "be opened." It is the word spoken by Christ when he cured one that was deaf. Mark 7:34.

E´phra-im (*doubly fruitful*). [**1**] Joseph's second son by his wife Asenath. He was born in Egypt, Gen. 41:52, and although younger than Manasseh he was regarded with special favor. He was one of the Hebrew patriachs and the founder of one of the twelve tribes of Israel. [**2**] As in the case of the other tribes of Israel, the word is often used to denote the tribe which sprang from Ephraim or the territory which they occupied. [**3**] A city belonging to Benjamin. 2 Sam. 13:23; John 11:54. Supposed to be the same as EPHRAIN. [**4**] The name of one of the gates of Jerusalem. 2 Kings 14:13; Neh. 12:39. [**5**] Ephraim, Wood of. The name of a woody and rugged district in Gad. It is supposed to have been so named from the slaughter of the Ephraimites recorded in Judg. 12, which took place near it. 2 Sam. 18:6.

Also see Gen. 46:20; 48:1, 5, 13, 14, 17, 20; 50:23.

Num. 1:10, 32, 33; 2:18, 24; 7:48; 10:22; 13:8; 26:28, 35, 37; 34:24.

Deut. 33:17; 34:2.

Josh. 14:4; 16:4, 5, 8, 9; 17:8-10, 15, 17; 19:50; 20:7; 21:5, 20, 21; 24:30, 33.

Judg. 1:29; 2:9; 3:27; 4:5; 5:14; 7:24; 8:1, 2; 10:1, 9; 17:1, 8; 18:2, 13; 19:1, 16, 18.

1 Sam. 1:1; 9:4; 14:22.

2 Sam. 2:9; 20:21.

1 Kings 4:8; 12:25.

2 Kings 5:22.

1 Chron. 6:66, 67; 7:20, 22; 9:3; 12:30; 27:10, 14, 20.

2 Chron. 13:4; 15:8, 9; 17:2; 19:4; 25:7, 10, 23; 28:7, 12; 30:1, 10, 18; 31:1; 34:6, 9.

Neh. 8:16.

Pss. 60:7; 78:9, 67; 80:2; 108:8.

Isa. 7:2, 5, 8, 9, 17; 9:9, 21; 11:13; 17:3; 28:1, 3.

Jer. 4:15; 7:15; 31:6, 9, 18, 20; 50:19.

Ezek. 37:16, 19; 48:5, 6.

Hos. 4:17; 5:3, 5, 9, 11-14; 6:4, 10; 7:1, 8, 11; 8:9, 11; 9:3, 8, 11, 13, 16; 10:6, 11; 11:3, 8, 9, 12; 12:1, 8, 14; 13:1, 12; 14:8.

Obad. :19.

Zech. 9:10, 13; 10:7.

E´phra-im-ites. The name Ephraimite is sometimes used in the English when in the original the term is Ephraim, employed in a collective sense to denote the tribe. Josh. 16:10; Judg. 12:4.

E´phra-in (*hamlet*), a town apparently on the border of Benjamin, but possessed by Jeroboam, king of the ten tribes, from whom it was taken by Abijah, king of Judah. 2 Chron. 13:19.

Eph´ra-tah (*fertility*). [**1**] A town in Judah. Ruth 4:11; Mic. 5:2. Probably the same place elsewhere called EPHRATH. [**2**] The name apparently (but it may be a patronymic) of the father of Hur. 1 Chron. 2:50; 4:4.

Eph´rath. [**1**] The place near which Rachel died. Gen. 35:16, 19. It was in the land afterward allotted to Judah, and is elsewhere called BETHLEHEM. [2] One of the wives of Caleb, the son of Hezron. 1 Chron. 2:19.

Eph´rath-ite. [1] A native or an inhabitant of the town of BETH-LEHEM, otherwise called BETH-LEHEM-JUDAH or BETH-LEHEM-EPHRATAH, and sometimes simply EPH-RATH or EPHRATAH. Ruth 1:2; 1 Sam. 17:12. [2] The title was also given to the inhabitants of Mount Ephraim, a broad extent of hill-country partly in Ephraim and partly in Manasseh. 1 Sam. 1:1; 1 Kings 11:26.

E´phron (*strong*). [1] A son of Zohar the Hittite, from whom Abraham purchased the field and cave of Machpelah. Gen. 23:8; 49:30; 50:13. [2] A mountain between Judah and Benjamin. Josh. 15:9.

Epicureans, ep-i-ku-re´ans or ep-i-ku´-re-ans, a sect of philosophers founded by Epicurus of Attica. They were essentially atheists, and made pleasure the object of life. Acts 17:18.

E-pis´tles, the inspired letters addressed by the apostles or first preachers of Christianity to churches or individuals. Thirteen were by Paul, three by John, two by Peter, one by James, one by Jude, and the one to the Hebrews, which is anonymous. See BIBLE, and each epistle under its own title.

Er (*watcher*). [1] The eldest son of Judah by the daughter of Shua the Canaanite. Gen. 38:3; Num. 26:19. [2] A son of Shelah, the youngest son of Judah by the daughter of Shua the Canaanite. 1 Chron. 4:21. [3] An ancestor of Joseph, the husband of Mary. Luke 3:28.

E´ran (*watcher*), a son of Ephraim. Num. 26:36.

E´ran-ites, descendants of Eran. Num. 26:36.

E-ras´tus. [1] A Christian, apparently

of Ephesus, whom Paul sent into Macedonia. Acts 19:22; 2 Tim. 4:20. [2] The chamberlain of Corinth who was converted under Paul's preaching. Rom. 16:23.

Erech, e´rek (*size*), a city which formed part of the Kingdom of Nimrod. Gen. 10:10.

E´ri (*my watcher*), a son of Gad. Gen. 46:16; Num. 26:16.

E´rites, descendants of Eri, the son of Gad. Num. 26:16.

Esaias, e-za´yas, the Greek form of ISAIAH (which see).

E´sar-had´don (*victorious*), a son of Sennacherib, king of Assyria, who succeeded his father on the throne. 2 Kings 19:37; Isa. 37:38.

E´sau (*hairy*). [1] The elder son of Rebekah, the wife of Isaac. He sold his birthright to Jacob, his twin brother, for a mess of red pottage, Gen. 25:30-33, and in a few passages in the Bible is called EDOM. He was the progenitor of the Edomites. [2] The name is sometimes, but not often, used to denote the people who sprang from him or the country they dwelt in. Deut. 2:5; Obad. verse 6.

Also see Gen. 25:25-28, 34; 26:34; 27:1, 5, 6, 11, 15, 19, 21-24, 30, 32, 34, 37, 38, 41, 42; 28:5, 6, 8, 9; 32:3, 4, 6, 8, 11, 13, 17-19; 33:1, 4, 9, 15, 16; 35:1, 29; 36:1, 2, 4-6, 8-10, 12-15, 17-19, 40, 43.

Deut. 2:4, 8, 12, 22, 29.

Josh. 24:4.

1 Chron. 1:34, 35.

Jer. 49:8, 10.

Obad. 8, 9, 18, 19, 21.

Mal. 1:2, 3.

Rom. 9:13.

Heb. 11:20; 12:16.

Es-chew´, in 1 Pet. 3:11, means avoid.

Es-chewed´, in Job 1:1, means avoided.

Es-dra-e´lon, is the most fertile, picturesque, and historically important plain in Palestine, and lies between Tabor and Carmel and between the hills of Galilee and those of Samaria. In 2 Chron. 35:22 it is called the valley of MEGIDDO (which see). It has been the scene of many important battles. JEZREEL, VALLEY OF (which see), is in the south-eastern part of it, and its name is sometimes given to the whole.

E´sek (*contention*), a well dug by Isaac's servants in the valley of Gerar, for which Abimelech's servants strove. Gen. 26:20.

Esh-ba´al (*a man of Baal*), a son of King Saul. 1 Chron. 8:33; 9:39.

Esh´-ban (*man of understanding*), one of the children of Dishon. Gen. 36:26; 1 Chron. 1:41.

Esh´col (*cluster of grapes*). [1] An Amorite, brother of Mamre, in whose plain Abram dwelt when he rescued Lot. Gen. 14:13, 24. [2] A valley, and a brook which flowed through it. From this valley a cluster of grapes was taken by the Israelite spies as a specimen of the fruit of Canaan. Num. 13:23, 24; 32:9; Deut. 1:24.

E´she-an (*slope*), a town of Judah. Josh. 15:52.

E´shek (*strife*), a descendant of Jonathan, the son of King Saul. 1 Chron. 8:39.

Esh´ka-lon-ites, the inhabitants of Ashkelon. Josh. 13:3.

Esh´ta-ol (*hollow way*), a town included in the enumeration of the cities of Judah, but also mentioned among the cities of Dan. It was probably on the borders between these two tribes, and was ultimately assigned to the latter. Josh. 15:33; 19:41; Judg. 13:25.

Esh´ta-ul-ites, a family descended from Shobal, the son of Caleb, son of Hur, who inhabited Eshtaol. 1 Chron. 2:53.

Eshtemoa, esh-te-mo´a or esh-tem´o-a. [1] A city in Judah which was afterward assigned to the Levites. Josh. 15:50; 1 Chron. 6:57. [2] An Israelite of Judah, apparently the grandson of Ezra. 1 Chron. 4:17, 19. It is doubtful whether these two passages refer to the same person, and whether the former does not refer to the founder of the city of Eshtemoa.

Esh´te-moh. See ESHTEMOA.

Esh´ton (*rest*), a grandson of Chelub. 1 Chron. 4:11, 12.

Es´li, an ancestor of Joseph, the husband of Mary. Luke 3:25.

Es-pous´als. See BETROTHING.

Es´rom, son of Phares. Matt. 1:3; Luke 3:33.

Essenes, es-seenz´, **The,** formed a small party of mystical and ascetic character among the Jews in the time of our Lord. They are not mentioned in the New Testament, and disappeared after the destruction of Jerusalem. Some theologians have supposed that the heresy combated by Paul in the Epistle to the Colossians was of Essenic origin.

Es-tate´, in 1 Chron. 17:17; Esther 1:19; Luke 1:48; Rom. 12:16; Jude 6, means a settled condition in life. In Mark 6:21; Acts 22:5 it means a special class of men.

Esther, es´ter (*star*), Hebrew HADASSAH (*the myrtle*), a young Jewess of great beauty and careful education, an orphan child of the tribe of Benjamin adopted by her cousin Mordecai, became, in B. C. 479, the wife of Ahasuerus—that is, Xerxes—the king of Persia, and was by her position enabled to deliver the whole race to which she belonged from an overwhelming danger. Haman, the favorite and intimate counsellor of the king, had obtained from him a permit to kill all the Jews in the kingdom. Through Mordecai, whom Haman had persecuted with bitter hatred, Esther became aware of what was going on, and at the risk of her life succeeded in getting permission from Ahasuerus for the Jews to defend themselves on the appointed day of slaughter and to take vengeance on all who molested them. Haman was hanged and Mordecai took his place. In memory of this event the Purim feast was instituted by the Jews and each year celebrated with great rejoicing and gayety.

Esther, es´ter, **Book of,** is the record of the wonderful incidents of her life, some of which are mentioned in the above account of her. It reads like a novel. Of its truth, however, there can be no doubt. The existence of the Purim festival as part of the religious ritual of the nation is an incontestable evidence of the truth of the narrative, and its details correspond very closely to what is known from other sources about Xerxes and the Persian court. One peculiarity of the book deserves special mention: the name of God does not occur in it. The reason for this singular omission is probably that the festival at which the book was to be read aloud was one of national rather than religious character, and, at all events, one of gayety and glee. When it is remembered how cautious the Jews were of using the name of God the omission seems quite natural. Its author is unknown.

E´tam (*wild beasts' lair*). [1] A rock or rocky district in Judah. Judg. 15:8, 11. [2] A small town near Bethlehem. 2 Chron. 11:6. [3] Descendants of Judah. 1 Chron. 4:3. [4] A place in Simeon. 1 Chron. 4:32.

E´tham, the second station of the Israelites after leaving Egypt. Exod. 13:20; Num. 33:8.

E´than (*ancient*). [1] An Israelite renowned for his wisdom. 1 Kings 4:31;

Ps. 89, title. [2] A son of Zerah, the son of Judah 1 Chron. 2:6, 8. [3] A descendant of Gershon, the son of Levi. 1 Chron. 6:42. [4] A descendant of Merari, the son of Levi. 1 Chron. 6:44; 15:19.

Eth´a-nim (*the perennial*), 1 Kings 8:2, the first month of the civil year of the Jews and the seventh month of their sacred year. It was so called because the rains then begin. It corresponds nearly with October. It was also called TISHRI. See MONTH.

Eth´ba-al (*with Baal*), the name of a king (Josephus says a priest) of the Zidonians who was the father of Jezebel, wife of King Ahab. 1 Kings 16:31.

E´ther (*riches*), a town in that part of Judah which was afterward assigned to Simeon. Josh. 15:42; 19:7.

E-thi-o´pi-a, [1] called CUSH by the Hebrews, included Nubia, and was situated between Egypt on the north and Abyssinia on the south. Comprised also Sennaar and Kordofan. It partakes to some extent of the character of Egypt, but it is higher, reaching an elevation of eight thousand feet, and more rolling and mountainous. It was inhabited by the Cushites, a Hamitic people (See CUSH). About one thousand years before Christ they formed there a mighty empire and developed a high civilization. In the eighth century B. C. an Ethiopian dynasty ruled in Egypt, and afterward it often shared in the destinies of that empire. It was conquered by the Persians B. C. 536, by the Greeks B. C. 330, and by the Romans B. C. 22, when Augustus defeated Candace, queen of Ethiopia, and made her country tributary to Rome. In the Old Testament Ethiopia is often mentioned in connection with Egypt. Moses married an Ethiopian woman. Num. 12:1. There were Ethiopians in the army of Shishak. 2 Chron. 12:3, etc. It is also mentioned in the New Testament. Acts 8:27–38. [2] This name is sometimes used to denote the people who dwelt in Ethiopia or Cush. Ps. 68:31; Nah. 3:9. Also see Gen. 2:13.

2 Kings 19:9.

Esther 1:1; 8:9.

Job 28:19.

Ps. 87:4.

Isa. 18:1; 20:3, 5; 37:9; 43:3; 45:14.

Ezek. 29:10; 30:4, 5; 38:5.

Zeph. 3:10.

E-thi-o´pi-ans, the name generally given in the English Version to the descendants of Cush, the son of Ham. Num. 12:1.

2 Chron. 12:3; 14:9, 12, 13; 16:8; 21:16.

Isa. 20:4.

Jer. 13:23; 38:7, 10, 12; 39:16; 46:9.

Ezek. 30:9.

Dan. 11:43.

Amos 9:7.

Zeph 9:12.

Acts 8:27.

Eth´nan (*gift*), a grandson of Ashur. 1 Chron. 4:7.

Eth´ni (*my gift*), an ancestor of Asaph. 1 Chron. 6:41.

Eu-bu´lus, a Christian at Rome who saluted Timothy. 2 Tim. 4:21.

Eunice, u-ni´se or u´nis, the mother of Paul's disciple Timotheus. 2 Tim. 1:5.

Eunuch, u´nuk. [1] A person employed to take charge of the beds and lodging-rooms of the secluded princesses. 2 Kings 9:32. [2] An officer of a court in general. Acts 8:27.

Eu-o´di-as, a female disciple at Philippi. Phil. 4:2.

Eu-phra´tes, The (*the abounding*), the largest river of Western Asia, rises on the northern side of Mount Ararat in Armenia,

runs in a south-easterly direction, and discharges its waters into the Persian Gulf after a course of seventeen hundred and eighty miles and after uniting near its mouth with the Tigris. It is mentioned as one of the rivers of Eden, Gen. 2:14, and often afterward in the Old Testament, and is frequently called simply "the river," sometimes "the great river." On its banks stood Babylon.

Also see Gen. 2:14; 15:18.

Deut. 1:7; 11:24.

Josh. 1:4.

2 Sam. 8:3.

2 Kings 23:29; 24:7.

1 Chron. 5:9; 18:3.

2 Chron. 35:20.

Jer. 13:4-7; 46:2, 6, 10; 51:63.

Rev. 9:14; 16:12.

Eu-roc´ly-don, a tempestuous wind blowing from the east or north-east. Acts 27:14.

Eutychus, u´ti-kus, a young man of Troas whom Paul restored to life after he had fallen from a window and been taken up dead. Acts 20:9.

E-van´gel-ist, in Acts 21:8; Eph. 4:11; 2 Tim. 4:5, means one who announces good tidings. The writers of the four gospels are called "the evangelists." Evangelists were a special class of religious teachers who preached the gospel wherever they were called.

Eve. This term properly signifies *life*, and the first woman was named thus "because she was the mother of all living." Gen. 3:20; 4:1; 2 Cor. 11:3; 1 Tim. 2:13.

E´ven-ing. The Hebrews had two evenings in each day. See marginal reading, "between the two evenings," Exod. 12:6; Num. 9:3; 28:4. The time when each began and ended is uncertain.

Ev-er-last´ing Fa´ther, one of the titles

or names given to Messiah by the prophet Isaiah. Isa. 9:6.

E´vi (*desire*), a prince of Midian. Num. 31:8; Josh. 13:21.

Evil-merodach, e´vil-me-ro´dak, a king of Babylon. He was the son and successor of Nebuchadnezzar, and in the thirty-seventh year of the captivity released Jehoiachin, king of Judah, from prison and gave him a place of honor at his court. 2 Kings 25:27; Jer. 52:31.

Ex-ceed´ing, in Gen. 15:1; 2 Sam. 8:8, means surpassing description.

Ex´cel-lent, in Job. 37:23; Dan. 2:31; 2 Pet. 1:17, means surpassing description.

Ex-com-mu-ni-ca´tion, deprivation of church privileges.

Ex-e-cu´tion-er, in Mark 6:27, means a soldier of the king's guard.

Ex´o-dus (*a going forth*), the departure of the Israelites from Egypt under the leadership of Moses. See the book of EXODUS.

Ex´o-dus, the Book of, the second Book of the Old Testament, contains the Ten Commandments and the story of the escape of the children of Israel from their bondage. It is the second book of the PENTATEUCH (which see).

Ex´or-cists, in Acts 19:13, means those who pretended to cast out devils by adjuring.

Ex-pi-a´tion. See FEASTS, and ATONEMENT, DAY OF.

Eye-ser´vice, in Eph. 6:6, means service done only under supervision.

E´zar (*treasure*). 1 Chron. 1:38. See EZER.

Ez´ba-i (*shining*), father of Naarai. 1 Chron. 11:37.

Ez´bon (*splendor*). [1] A son of Gad. Gen. 46:16. [2] A son of Bela. 1 Chron. 7:7.

Ez-e-ki´as, Matt. 1:9, 10, the Greek

form of HEZEKIAH (which see).

E-ze´ki-el (*strength of God*), the third of the greater prophets and a contemporary of Jeremiah, was a son of a priest, Buzi, and was born and educated in Judea, but was in B. C. 598, eleven years before the destruction of Jerusalem, carried into captivity by Nebuchadnezzar and settled in a Jewish community on the river Chebar in Chaldea. In B. C. 595 he began his prophetic ministration and continued for twenty-two years, till B C. 573. We know that he had a house, Ezek. 8:1, lost his wife suddenly, Ezek. 24:16-18, conversed intimately with the elders of the community, Ezek. 8:1; 11:25, etc., and tradition adds that he was murdered, and points out his tomb near Baghdad. Also see Ezek. 1:3; 24:24.

E-ze´ki-el, Book of, consists of two parts: the first, chapters 1–24, written before the fall of Jerusalem, and the second, chapters 25–48, written after that event. They differ with respect to their contents, but not in reference to their character. Ezekiel was the son of a priest and a priest himself. His visions and prophecies are clear and unmistakable in their general bearing, but their details are often very obscure and many of his symbols and allegories were not understood until the modern excavations at Nineveh and Babylon brought to light those winged lions and human-headed bulls. The Jews reckoned his book among those which should not be read before the age of thirty. The grandest portion of it is the vision of the new Temple, the fulfillment of the Messianic promises, the church of Christ—chapters 40–48.

E´zel (*division*), the name given to a stone where Jonathan parted from David when obliged to flee from Saul. 1 Sam. 20:19.

E´zem (*strength*), a city or fortress of Judah, but afterward of Simeon. 1 Chron. 4:29. It is apparently the same which is called AZEM in Josh. 15:29.

E´zer (*help*). [1] A descendant of Judah through Caleb, the son of Hur. 1 Chron. 4:4. Supposed to be the same as Ezra, 1 Chron. 4:17, but uncertain. [2] A descendant of Ephraim. 1 Chron. 7:21. [3] One of the valiant men of Gad. 1 Chron. 12:9. [4] A Jew who repaired part of the wall of Jerusalem after the captivity. Neh. 3:19. [5] A priest who officiated in purifying the rebuilt wall of Jerusalem. Neh. 12:42.

E´zer (*union*), a son of Seir. Gen. 36:21; 1 Chron. 1:38.

E´zi-on-ga´ber or **E´zi-on-ge´ber** (*backbone of a mighty one*), a place on the shore of the eastern gulf of the Red Sea, where was the thirty-first encampment of the Israelites in their wandering through the wilderness. Num. 33:35; 2 Chron. 8:17. Here King Solomon equipped his vessels for the voyage to Ophir. 1 Kings 9:26.

Ez´nite (*the one belonging to Etsen*), patronymic of Adino, one of King David's worthies. 2 Sam. 23:8.

Ez´ra (*help*). [1] A Jewish priest and scholar living in Babylon, who obtained from the Persian king Artaxerxes Longimanus not only permission to lead a large company of Jewish exiles back to Jerusalem, B. C. 457, but substantial assistance in the undertaking. After a journey of four months he arrived at Jerusalem, and then undertook those reforms, especially in the intermarriage with foreign women, and that reorganization of public worship which have made his life a new departure in the history of the Jews. Of his later life nothing is known, but Jewish tradition credits him with the establish-

ment of the Old Testament Canon, the founding of the Great Synagogue, the introduction of Chaldee characters instead of the old Hebrew, and the authorship of the books of EZRA, NEHEMIAH and CHRONICLES. [2] A descendant of Judah, apparently through Caleb, the son of Jephunneh. 1 Chron. 4:17.

Also see Ezra 7:1, 6, 10-12, 21, 25; 10:1, 2, 5, 6, 10, 16.

Neh. 8:1, 2, 4-6, 9, 13; 12:1, 13, 26, 33, 36.

Ezra, the Book of, is in two parts: the first, chapters 1–6, narrates the return of the fifty thousand under Zerubbabel in the reign of Cyrus, and the second, chapters 7–10, the return of the colony under Ezra. The book may be considered a continuation of CHRONICLES. Of the authorship of the BOOK OF EZRA there can be no reasonable doubt. There exist "Two Books of Esdras," the Greek name of Ezra, and they have by some been ascribed to him, but they do not exist in Hebrew, and have never been recognized as authoritative by the Jews.

Ez´ra-hite, patronymic denoting the family of Ezrah, a name not in Scripture; but the term being applied to both Ethan and Heman, who are said in 1 Chron. 2:6 to be sons of Zerah, it has been supposed that in forming the patronymic a transposition had been used. 1 Kings 4:31; Ps. 88, title.

Ez´ri (*my help*), David's overseer of the tillers of the ground. 1 Chron. 27:26.

F

Fa´ble. The Old Testament contains two fables of a kind intended for instruction. Judg. 9:8-15; 2 Kings 14:9. It differs from the parable by drawing its illustrations from animal and vegetable life, while the parable teaches spiritual truths through pictures of human life. No fable occurs in the New Testament, but the word is used to denote the vain traditions of the Jews and the worthless legends of the heathen. 1 Tim. 1:4; 4:7; 2 Tim. 4:4.

Face, a word often used in reference to God.

Gen. 1–4; 6–9; 11; 16; 17–19; 24; 30–33; 35; 36; 38; 41–44; 46; 48; 50.

Exod. 2; 3; 10; 14; 16; 19; 20; 25; 32–34; 37.

Lev. 9; 13; 17; 19; 20; 26.

Num. 6; 11; 12; 14; 16; 19; 20; 22; 24.

Deut. 1; 5–9; 25; 28; 31; 32; 34.

Josh. 5; 7.

Judg. 6; 13; 18.

Ruth 2.

1 Sam. 5; 17; 20; 24–26; 28.

2 Sam. 2; 3; 9; 14; 18; 19; 24.

1 Kings 1; 2; 8; 13; 18–21.

2 Kings 4; 8; 9; 12–14; 18; 20.

1 Chron. 12; 16; 21.

2 Chron. 3; 6; 7; 20; 25; 29; 30; 32; 35.

Ezra 9.

Neh. 8.

Esther 1; 7.

Job 1; 2; 4; 9; 11; 13; 15; 16; 21–24; 26; 30; 33; 34; 37; 38; 40; 41.

Pss. 5; 10; 13; 17; 21; 22; 24; 27; 30; 31; 34; 41; 44; 51; 67; 69; 80; 83; 84; 88; 89; 102; 104; 105; 119; 132; 143.

Prov. 7; 8; 21; 24; 27.

Eccles. 8.

Isa. 3; 6; 8; 13; 14; 16; 23; 25; 27–29; 36; 38; 49; 50; 53; 54; 59; 64; 65.

Jer. 1; 2; 4; 5; 7; 8; 13; 16; 18; 21; 22; 25; 28; 30; 32; 33; 42; 44; 50; 51.

Lam. 2; 3; 5.

Ezek. 1; 3; 4; 6–15; 20; 21; 25; 28; 29; 34; 35; 38–41; 43; 44.

Dan. 1; 2; 8–11.

Hos. 5; 7.

Joel 2.

Amos 5; 9.

Mic. 3.

Nah. 2; 3.

Hab 1.

Zech. 5.

Mal. 2.

Matt. 6; 11; 16–18; 26.

Mark 1; 14.

Luke 1; 2; 5; 7; 9; 10; 12; 17; 21; 22; 24.

John 11.

Acts 2; 6; 7; 17; 20; 25.

1 Cor 13; 14.

2 Cor 3; 4; 11.

Gal. 1; 2.

Col. 2.

1 Thess. 2; 3.

James 1.

1 Pet. 3.

2 John 12.

3 John 14.

Rev. 4; 6; 7; 9–12; 20; 22.

Fain, in Job 27:22; Luke 15:16, means gladly.

Fair, in Isa. 54:11, means beautiful.

Fair Ha´vens, a harbor on the south coast of the island of Crete in the Mediterranean Sea. Paul wished to winter there, Acts 27:8, on his voyage to Rome. Fair Havens still retains the same name.

Fairs are mentioned in Ezek. 27:12, 14, 16, 19, 22, 27. The word may mean the periodical meetings of buyers and sellers, or the fixed places for such meetings, and sometimes the wares sold.

Faith, belief in and loyalty to God.

Deut. 32:20.

Hab. 2:4.

Matt. 6:30; 8:10, 26; 9:2, 22, 29; 14:31; 15:28; 16:8; 17:20; 21:21; 23:23.

Mark 2:5; 4:40; 5:34; 10:52; 11:22.

Luke 5:20; 7:9, 50; 8:25, 48; 12:28; 17:5,

6, 19; 18:8, 42; 22:32.

Acts 3:16; 6:5, 7, 8; 11:24; 13:8; 14:9, 22, 27; 15:9; 16:5; 20:21; 24:24; 26:18.

Rom. 1:5, 8, 12, 17; 3:3, 22, 25, 27, 28, 30, 31; 4:5, 9, 11-14, 16, 19, 20; 5:1, 2; 9:30, 32; 10:6, 8, 17; 11:20; 12:3, 6; 14:1, 22, 23; 16:26.

1 Cor. 2:5; 12:9; 13:2, 13; 15:14, 17; 16:13.

2 Cor. 1:24; 4:13; 5:7; 8:7; 10:15; 13:5.

Gal. 1:23; 2:16, 20; 3:2, 5, 7-9, 11, 12, 14, 22-26; 5:5, 6, 22; 6:10.

Eph. 1:15; 2:8; 3:12, 17; 4:5, 13; 6:16, 23.

Phil. 1:25, 27; 2:17; 3:9.

Col. 1:4, 23; 2:5, 7, 12.

1 Thess. 1:3, 8; 3:2, 5-7, 10; 5:8.

2 Thess. 1:3, 4, 11; 3:2.

1 Tim. 1:2, 4, 5, 14, 19; 2:7, 15; 3:9, 13; 4:1, 6, 12; 5:8, 12; 6:10-12, 21.

2 Tim. 1:5, 13; 2:18, 22; 3:8, 10, 15; 4:7.

Titus 1:1, 4, 13; 2:2; 3:15.

Philem. :5, 6.

Heb. 4:2; 6:1, 12; 10:22, 23, 38; 11:1, 3-9, 11, 13, 17, 20-24, 27-31, 33, 39; 12:2; 13:7.

James 1:3, 6; 2:1, 5, 14, 17, 18, 20, 22, 24, 26; 5:15.

1 Pet. 1:5, 7, 9, 21; 5:9.

2 Pet. 1:1, 5.

1 John 5:4.

Jude 3, 20.

Rev. 2:13, 19; 13:10; 14:12.

Faith´ful and **Faith´ful-ness.**

Num. 12:7.

Deut. 7:9.

1 Sam. 2:35; 22:14; 26:23.

2 Sam. 20:19.

Neh. 7:2; 9:8; 13:13.

Pss. 5:9; 12:1; 31:23; 36:5; 40:10; 88:11; 89:1, 2, 5, 8, 24, 33, 37; 92:2; 101:6; 119:75, 86, 90, 138; 143:1.

Prov. 11:13; 13:17; 14:5; 20:6; 25:13; 27:6, 28:20.

Isa. 1:21, 26; 8:2; 11:5; 25:1; 49:7.

Jer. 42:5.

Lam. 3:23.

Dan. 6:4.

Hos. 2:20; 11:12.

Matt. 24:45; 25:21, 23.

Luke 12:42; 16:10-12; 19:17.

Acts 16:15.

1 Cor. 1:9; 4:2, 17; 7:25; 10:13.

Gal. 3:9.

Eph. 1:1; 6:21.

Col. 1:2, 7; 4:7, 9.

1 Thess. 5:24.

2 Thess. 3:3.

1 Tim. 1:12, 15; 3:11; 4:9; 6:2.

2 Tim. 2:2, 11, 13.

Titus 1:6, 9; 3:8.

Heb. 2:17; 3:2, 5; 10:23; 11:11.

1 Pet. 4:19; 5:12.

1 John 1:9.

Rev. 1:5; 2:10, 13; 3:14; 17:14; 19:11; 21:5; 22:6.

Faith´less, in Mark 9:19, means unbelieving.

Fal´low-Deer. See ROE, and HART.

Fal´low Ground, in Jer. 4:3; Hos. 10:12, means land fit for cultivation, but not sowed.

Fal´low Year. See SABBATICAL YEAR.

Fame, in Gen. 45:16; Mark 1:28, means rumor; tidings.

Familiar, fa-mil´yar, **Spir´its.**

Lev. 19:31; 20:6, 27.

Deut. 18:11.

1 Sam. 28:3, 7-9.

2 Kings 21:6; 23:24.

1 Chron. 10:13.

2 Chron. 33:6.

Job 19:14.

Ps. 41:9.

Isa. 8:19; 19:3; 29:4.

Jer. 20:10.

Fam´ines are often mentioned in the Bible. The seven years' famine in Egypt, while Joseph was governor there, is the most remarkable. A spiritual famine is mentioned in Amos 8:11.

Gen. 12:10; 26:1; 41:27, 30, 31, 36, 50, 56, 57; 42:5, 19, 33; 43:1; 45:6, 11; 47:4, 13, 20.

Ruth 1:1.

2 Sam. 21:1; 24:13.

1 Kings 8:37; 18:2.

2 Kings 6:25; 7:4; 8:1; 25:3.

1 Chron. 21:12.

2 Chron. 20:9; 32:11.

Job 5:20, 22; 30:3.

Pss. 33:19; 37:19; 105:16.

Isa. 14:30; 51:19.

Jer. 5:12; 11:22; 14:12, 13, 15, 16, 18; 15:2; 16:4; 18:21; 21:7, 9; 24:10; 27:8, 13; 29:17, 18; 32:24, 36; 34:17; 38:2; 42:16, 17, 22; 44:12, 13, 18, 27; 52:6.

Lam. 5:10.

Ezek. 5:12, 16, 17; 6:11, 12; 7:15; 12:16; 14:13, 21; 36:29, 30.

Matt. 24:7.

Mark 13:8.

Luke 4:25; 15:14; 21:11.

Rom. 8:35.

Rev. 18:8.

Fan, in the Bible, means an implement for winnowing grain. It was made in two forms, one of which was used to produce wind during a calm, Isa. 30:24, and the other to throw the grain up to the wind, that the chaff might be blown away. The word is also used figuratively in many places. Isa. 41:16; Jer. 15:7; Matt. 3:12.

Far´thing, a Roman piece of copper money. Farthings were of two kinds: that mentioned in Matt. 10:29; Luke 12:6 was the *assarion*, and was worth a cent and a half; the other kind, mentioned in Matt. 5:26, was the *kodrantes*, worth about four mills. It was equal to two mites. See MONEY.

Fash´ion, in Phil. 2:8, means form.

Fast. Only one day was appointed in the Mosaic law for a fast. See ATONEMENT, DAY OF.

Fast´ing, or abstinence from food, was customary among the Jews as a religious duty.

Gen. 20:18.

Judg. 4:21; 15:13; 16:11; 20:26.

Ruth 2:8, 21, 23.

1 Sam. 7:6; 31:13.

2 Sam. 1:12; 12:15; 21–23.

1 Kings 21:9, 12; 27.

2 Kings 6:32.

1 Chron. 10:12.

2 Chron. 20:3.

Ezra 5:8; 8:21, 23.

Neh. 1:4; 9:1.

Esther 4:3, 16; 9:31.

Job 2:3; 8:15; 27:6; 38:38.

Pss. 33:9; 35:13; 38:2; 41:8; 65:6; 69:10; 89:28, 109:24; 111:8.

Prov. 4:13.

Isa. 58:3-6.

Jer. 8:5; 14:12; 36:6, 9; 46:14; 48:16; 50:33.

Dan. 6:18; 9:3.

Joel 1:14; 2:12, 15.

Jon. 1:5; 3:5.

Zech. 7:5; 8:19.

Matt. 4:2; 6:16, 18; 9:14, 15; 15:32; 17:21; 26:48.

Mark 2:18-20; 8:3; 9:29.

Luke 2:37; 5:33-35; 18:12.

Acts 10:30; 13:2, 3; 14:23; 16:24; 27:9, 33, 41.

1 Cor. 7:5; 16:13.

2 Cor. 6:5; 11:27.

Gal. 5:1.

Phil. 1:27; 4:1.

1 Thess. 3:8; 5:21.

2 Thess. 2:15.

2 Tim. 1:13.

Titus 1:9.

Heb. 3:6; 4:14; 10:23.

Rev. 2:13, 25; 3:3, 11.

    Fat. The use of fat was forbidden to the Jews, Lev. 3:16, 17, but did not mean that which was mixed with the lean. The fat parts of animals used for sacrifice were always consumed by fire on the altar, as being the choicest and especially sacred. Exod. 29:13, 22.

    Fat. See FATS.

    Fa´ther, the title by which God is distinguished as being the Father of the Lord Jesus Christ and of all his true disciples. In the time of the patriarchs the father was master and judge in his family. The word father is used in Gen. 45:8 to mean an adviser or counsellor. The word is also used in various other senses, as Jubal "was the father of all such as handle the harp and the organ." Gen. 4:21.

Also see Gen. 2; 4; 9–12; 15; 17; 19; 20; 22; 24; 26–29; 31–38; 41–50.

Exod. 2–4; 6; 10; 12; 13; 15; 18; 20–22; 34; 40.

Lev. 16; 18–22; 24–26.

Num. 1–4; 6; 7; 10–14; 17; 18; 20; 26; 27; 30–34; 36.

Deut. 1; 4–13; 19; 21; 22; 24; 26–33.

Josh. 1; 2; 4–6; 14; 15; 17–19; 21; 22; 24.

Judg. 1–4; 6; 8; 9; 11; 14–19; 21.

Ruth 2; 4.

1 Sam. 2; 4; 9; 10; 12; 14; 17–19; 20; 22–24.

2 Sam. 2; 3; 6; 7; 9; 10; 13–16; 17; 19; 21; 24.

1 Kings 1–3; 5–9; 11–16; 18–22.

2 Kings 2–6; 8–10; 12–24.

1 Chron. 2; 4–9; 12; 15; 17; 19; 21; 23–29.

2 Chron. 1–17; 19–36.

Ezra 1–5; 7–10.

Neh. 1; 2; 7–13.

Esther 2; 4.

Job 8; 15; 17; 29–31; 38; 42.

Pss. 22; 27; 39; 44; 45; 49; 68; 78; 89; 95; 103; 106; 109.

Prov. 1; 3; 4; 6; 10; 13; 15; 17; 19; 20; 22; 23; 27–30.

Isa. 7; 14; 22; 37; 39; 49; 64; 65.

Jer. 2; 3; 6; 7; 9; 11; 13; 14; 16; 17; 19; 20; 23–25; 30–32; 34; 35; 44; 47; 50.

Ezek. 2; 5; 16; 18; 20; 22; 36; 37; 44; 47.

Dan. 2; 5; 9; 11.

Hos. 9.

Joel 1.

Amos 2.

Mic. 7.

Zech. 1; 8; 13.

Mal. 1–4.

Matt. 23; 26.

Luke 1; 2; 6; 9; 11; 12; 15; 16.

John 2; 4–7; 10; 14; 15.

Acts. 3; 5; 7; 13; 15; 22; 24; 26; 28.

Rom. 1; 4; 6; 8; 9; 11; 15.

1 Cor. 1; 4; 5; 8; 10; 15.

2 Cor. 1; 6; 11.

Gal. 1; 4.

Eph. 1–6.

Phil. 1; 2; 4.

Col. 1–3.

1 Thess. 1–3.

2 Thess. 1; 2.

1 Tim. 1; 5.

2 Tim. 1.

Titus 1.

Philem. 3.

Heb. 1; 3; 7; 8; 12.

James 1–3.

1 Pet. 1.

2 Pet. 1; 3.

1 John 1–5.

2 John 3, 4, 9.

Jude 1.

Rev. 1–3; 14.

    Fath´om, a measure of length equal to about six and three-fourths feet. Acts

27:28. See MEASURES.

Fats, in Joel 2:24; 3:13, means vats, vessels for holding wine.

Fear, apprehension of incurring, or solicitude to avoid, God's wrath; the awe and reverence felt toward the Supreme Being. Also reverence for men of authority or worth.

Gen. 9; 15; 20; 21; 26; 31; 32; 35; 42; 43; 46; 50.
Exod. 9; 14; 15; 18; 20; 23.
Lev. 19; 25.
Num. 14; 21.
Deut. 1–6; 8; 10; 11; 13; 14; 17; 19–21; 28; 31.
Josh. 4; 8; 10; 22; 24.
Judg. 4; 6; 7; 9.
Ruth 3.
1 Sam. 4; 11; 12; 21–23.
2 Sam. 9; 13; 23.
1 Kings 8; 17; 18.
2 Kings 4; 6; 17; 25.
1 Chron. 14; 16; 28.
2 Chron. 6; 14; 17; 19; 20.
Ezra 3.
Neh. 1; 5; 6.
Esther 8; 9.
Job 1; 4; 6; 9; 11; 15; 21; 22; 25; 28; 31; 37; 39; 41.
Pss. 2; 5; 9; 14; 15; 19; 22; 23; 25; 27; 31; 33; 34; 36; 40; 46; 48; 49; 52; 53; 55; 56; 60; 61; 64; 66; 67; 72; 85; 86; 90; 96; 102; 103; 105; 111; 115; 118; 119; 135; 145; 147.
Prov. 1–3; 8–10; 14–16; 19; 20; 22–24; 29.
Eccles. 3; 5; 8; 12.
Song of Sol. 3.
Isa. 2; 7; 8; 11; 14; 19; 21; 24; 25; 29; 31; 33; 35; 41; 43; 44; 51; 54; 59; 60; 63; 66.
Jer. 2; 5; 6; 10; 20; 23; 26; 30; 32; 33; 35; 37; 40; 41; 46; 48–51.
Lam. 3.
Ezek. 3; 30.
Dan. 1; 6; 10.
Hos. 3; 10.
Joel 2.
Amos 3.
Jon. 1.
Mic. 7.
Zeph. 3.
Hag. 1; 2.
Zech. 8; 9.
Mal. 1–4.
Matt. 1; 10; 14; 21; 28.
Luke 1; 2; 5; 7; 8; 12; 13; 21; 23.
John 7; 12; 19; 20.
Acts 2; 5; 9; 13; 19; 27.
Rom. 3; 8; 11; 13.
1 Cor. 2; 16.
2 Cor. 7; 11; 12.
Eph. 5; 6.
Phil. 1; 2.
1 Tim. 5.
2 Tim. 1.
Heb. 2; 4; 11–13.
1 Pet. 1–3.
1 John 4.
Jude 12, 23.
Rev. 1; 2; 11; 14; 15; 18; 19.

Feasts are often mentioned in the Bible. They were usually given to celebrate some important or joyful event. A great feast was made by Abraham, Gen. 21:8, at the weaning of Isaac; also by Laban, Gen. 29:22, at the marriage of Jacob. Feasts were held to celebrate the end of harvest, of vintage, and of sheep-shearing. The Jews had also several festivals or seasons of ceremonial worship, which were established to commemorate great events. A list of the "feasts of the LORD" is given in Lev. 23. The three great feasts of the year were the *Feast of Unleavened Bread,* or *of the Passover;* the *Feast of Pentecost,* or *Feast of Weeks,* or *Feast of Harvest;* and the *Feast of Taber-*

nacles. The Jews had many other feasts. See also PASSOVER, PENTECOST, PURIM, and TABERNACLES, FEAST OF.

Also see Gen. 19:3; 21:8; 26:30; 40:20.

Exod. 5:1; 10:9; 12:14, 17; 13:6; 23:14-16; 32:5; 34:18, 22, 25.

Num. 15:3; 28:17; 29:12, 39.

Deut. 16:10, 13-16; 31:10.

Judg. 14:10, 12, 17; 21:19.

1 Sam. 25:36.

2 Sam. 3:20.

1 Kings 3:15; 8:2, 65; 12:32, 33.

1 Chron. 23:31.

2 Chron. 2:4; 5:3; 7:8, 9; 8:13; 30:13, 21, 22; 31:3; 35:17.

Ezra 3:4, 5; 6:22.

Neh. 8:14, 18; 10:33.

Esther 1:3, 5, 9; 2:18; 8:17.

Pss. 35:16; 81:3.

Prov. 15:15.

Eccles. 10:19.

Isa. 1:14; 5:12; 25:6.

Jer. 51:39.

Lam. 1:4; 2:6, 7.

Ezek. 36:38; 45:17, 21, 23, 25; 46:9, 11.

Dan. 5:1.

Hos. 2:11; 9:5; 12:9.

Amos 5:21; 8:10.

Nah. 1:15.

Zech. 8:19; 14:16, 18, 19.

Mal. 2:3.

Matt. 23:6; 26:2, 5, 17; 27:15.

Mark 14:1, 2; 12:39; 15:6.

Luke 2:41, 42; 5:29; 14:13; 20:46; 22:1; 23:17.

John 2:8, 9, 23; 4:45; 5:1; 6:4; 7:2, 8, 10, 11, 14, 37; 10:22; 11:56; 12:12, 20; 13:1, 29.

Acts 18:21.

1 Cor. 5:8; 10:27.

2 Pet. 2:13.

Jude 12.

Fe´lix (*happy*), the governor of Judea under the Romans, before whom Paul was accused by the Jews. Acts 23:24, 26; 24:22, 24, 25, 27.

Fel´loes, in 1 Kings 7:33, means the pieces composing the circumference of a wheel.

Fenced, in Num. 32:17, 36, means fortified.

Fences were used by the Jews for the protection of vineyards and gardens. They were often made of stones or of great lumps of dried earth, and sometimes a thorn hedge was added, Ps. 80:12; Mic. 7:4, which was frequently the habitation of serpents and locusts.

Fer´ret, an animal of the weasel family. The ferret mentioned in Lev. 11:30 is supposed to have been a kind of lizard called the *gecko*.

Fes´ti-vals, Re-lig´ous. See FEASTS.

Fes´tus, the Roman governor of Judea who succeeded Felix. Acts 24:27; 25:4, 9; 26:24, 25.

Fet´ters. See CHAINS.

Fields were cultivated portions of land. They were not enclosed, but their boundaries were marked by stones the removal of which was cursed. Deut. 27:17. Fields were often crossed by public roads. Luke 6:1.

Fi´er-y Ser´pents. See SERPENTS.

Figs abounded in Judea in ancient times, Deut. 8:8, and fig trees both wild and cultivated are now found in all parts of Palestine; they grow luxuriantly, are pleasant shade-trees, and the fruit is wholesome and much used. There are several varieties of fig trees. The fruit begins to show itself before the leaves and without apparent blossoms. Hence a fig tree in full leaf but without fruit may be known as barren for the season. Matt. 21:19.

File, in 1 Sam. 13:21, means literally

notchedness.

Fine, in Job 28:1, means refine.

Fin´er, in Prov. 25:4, means refiner.

Fin´ger, a measure of length supposed by some to be equal to the breadth of the joint of the thumb, and by others that of the first joint of the middle finger, equal to about three-fourths of an inch. Jer. 52:21.

Fin´ing, in Prov. 17:3; 27:21, means refining.

Fir, a well-known evergreen tree which flourished on Mount Lebanon and in other parts of Palestine. It was used for shipbuilding, Ezek. 27:5; in manufacturing musical instruments, 2 Sam. 6:5; and in costly buildings. 1 Kings 5:8, 10. It grew tall and straight, and in its top the storks built their nests. Ps. 104:17. The Hebrew word used for fir seems often to mean CYPRESS (which see).

Fire is often connected in the Bible with the presence of God, as in the burning bush and in the pillar of fire.
Gen. 19; 22.
Exod. 3; 9; 12–14; 19; 22; 24; 29; 30; 32; 35; 40.
Lev. 1–10; 13; 16; 18–24.
Num. 3; 6; 9; 11; 14–16; 18; 21; 26; 28; 29; 31.
Deut. 1; 4; 5; 7; 9; 10; 12; 13; 18; 32.
Josh. 6–8; 11; 13.
Judg. 1; 6; 9; 12; 14–16; 18; 20.
1 Sam. 2; 30.
2 Sam. 14; 22; 23.
1 Kings 9; 16; 18; 19.
2 Kings 1; 2; 6; 8; 16; 17; 19; 21; 23; 25.
1 Chron. 14; 21.
2 Chron. 7; 28; 33; 35; 36.
Neh. 1; 2; 9.
Job 1; 15; 18; 20; 22; 28; 31; 41.
Pss. 11; 18; 21; 29; 39; 46; 50; 57; 66; 68; 74; 78–80; 83; 89; 97; 104–106; 118; 140; 148.

Prov. 6; 16; 25; 26; 30.
Song of Sol. 8.
Isa. 1; 4; 5; 9; 10; 24; 26; 27; 29–31; 33; 37; 42–44; 47; 50; 54; 64–66.
Jer. 4–7; 11; 15; 17; 19–23; 29; 32; 34; 36–39; 43; 48–52.
Lam. 1; 2; 4.
Ezek. 1; 5; 8; 10; 15; 16; 19–24; 28; 30; 36; 38; 39.
Dan. 3; 7; 10.
Hos. 7; 8.
Joel 1; 2.
Amos 1; 2; 5; 7.
Obad. :18.
Mic. 1.
Nah. 1; 3.
Hab. 2.
Zeph. 1; 3.
Zech. 2; 3; 9; 11–13.
Mal. 1; 3.
Matt. 3; 5; 7; 13; 17; 18; 25.
Mark 9; 14.
Luke 3; 9; 12; 17; 22.
John 15; 18; 21.
Acts 2; 7; 28.
Rom. 12.
1 Cor. 3.
2 Thess. 1.
Heb. 1; 11; 12.
James 3; 5.
1 Pet. 1.
2 Pet. 3.
Jude 7, 23.
Rev. 1–4; 8–11; 13–21.

Fire´-pan, used in the Temple se
Exod. 27:3; 38:3. The same word, original. is elsewhere rendered S
DISH and CENSER.

Fir´kin, a measure of capacity. The English firkin contained about seven imperial gallons, but the Attic metretes held only about four and three-fourhs imperial gallons. It is therefore very evident that the substitution of the old English measure as a translation of the Greek name has the effect of increasing the stated capacity of the vessels by about one-half. John 2:6. See MEASURES.

Fir´ma-ment, the expanse or space surrounding the earth. Gen. 1:6, 7; Ezek. 1:22, 23.

First´-born. In order to commemorate the destruction of the first-born of the Egyptians God commanded that the first-born males of the Hebrews should be consecrated to him; also the first offspring of their cattle and the first-fruits of their ground. See also BIRTHRIGHT.

Gen. 10:15; 19:31, 33, 34, 37; 22:21; 25:13; 27:19, 32; 29:26; 35:23; 36:15; 38:6, 7; 41:51; 43:33; 46:8; 48:14, 18; 49:3.

Exod. 4:22, 23; 6:14; 11:5; 12:12, 29; 13:2, 13, 15; 22:29; 34:20.

Num. 3:2, 12, 13, 40-43, 45, 46, 50; 8:16-18; 18:15; 33:4.

Deut. 21:15-17; 25:6.

Josh. 6:26; 17:1.

Judg. 8:20.

1 Sam. 8:2; 14:49; 17:13.

2 Sam. 3:2.

1 Kings 16:34.

1 Chron. 1:13, 29; 2:3, 13, 25, 27, 42, 50; 3:1, 15; 4:4; 5:1, 3; 6:28; 8:1, 30, 39; 9:5, 31, 36; 26:2, 4, 10.

2 Chron. 21:3.

Neh. 10:36.

Job 18:13.

Pss. 78:51; 89:27; 105:36; 135:8; 136:10.

Isa. 14:30.

Jer. 31:9.

Mic. 6:7.

Zech. 12:10.

Matt. 1:25.

Luke 2:7.

Rom. 8:29.

Col. 1:15, 18.

Heb. 11:28; 12:23.

First´-fruits were offerings to God, brought in obedience to the law of Moses, Deut. 26:1–11, to the Tabernacle or to the Temple to express the thankfulness and dependence of the giver. They included every kind of produce of the earth, sometimes in a natural and sometimes in a prepared state.

Also see Exod. 23:16, 19; 34:22, 26.

Lev. 2:12, 14; 23:10, 17, 20.

Num. 18:12; 28:26.

Deut. 18:4.

2 Kings 4:42.

2 Chron. 31:5.

Neh. 10:35, 37; 12:44; 13:31.

Prov. 3:9.

Jer. 2:3.

Ezek. 20:40; 44:30; 48:14.

Rom. 8:23; 11:16; 16:5.

1 Cor. 15:20, 23; 16:15.

James 1:18.

Rev. 14:4.

First´ling, in Gen. 4:4; Neh. 10:36, means the first offspring of an animal.

Fishes of many varieties were abundant in Egypt in ancient times, and are also plentiful there now, in the river Nile and in Lake Moeris. Many kinds of fishing are represented on Egyptian monuments. Fish were abundant in the Sea of Galilee (where four of the disciples were fishermen, Matt. 4:18-21), and in Jabbok, Jordan, and Kishon Rivers in Palestine. All fishes which had scales and fins were clean under the Mosaic law, and were commonly used as food by the Jews.

See also Gen. 1:26, 28; 9:2.

Exod. 7:18, 21.

Num. 11:5, 22.

Deut. 4:18.

1 Kings 4:33.

2 Chron. 33:14.
Neh. 3:3; 12:39; 13:16.
Job 12:8; 41:7.
Pss. 8:8; 105:29.
Eccles. 9:12.
Isa. 19:10; 50:2.
Jer. 16:16.
Ezek. 29:4, 5; 38:20; 47:9, 10.
Hos. 4:3.
Jon. 1:17; 2:1, 10.
Hab. 1:14.
Zeph. 1:3, 10.
Matt. 7:10; 14:17, 19; 15:34, 36; 17:27.
Mark 6:38, 41, 43; 8:7.
Luke 5:6, 9; 9:13, 16; 11:11; 24:42.
John 6:9, 11; 21:6, 8-11, 13.
1 Cor. 15:39.

Fish´-gate, a gate in Jerusalem. 2 Chron. 33:14, etc.

Fish´-hooks, were used in very ancient times. Job 41:1; Amos 4:2. The usual way of taking fish was by nets.

Fish´-pools in Hesh´bon, in Song of Sol. 7:4, should be simply pools. There is no reference to fish. See HESHBON.

Fitch´es are a kind of wild pea in some instances. The word rendered *fitches* in Ezek. 4:9 is translated *rye* in Exod. 9:32. In Isa. 28:25, 27 it means a plant having black and aromatic seeds, commonly used for flavoring cakes, etc.

Flag, mentioned in Job 8:11, is a coarse kind of grass growing in wet lands. In Gen. 41:2, 18 the same thing is called *meadow*. In Exod. 2:3, 5 and Isa. 19:6 a different word is used in the original in a more general sense.

Flagon, flag´un, in 2 Sam. 6:19; 1 Chron. 16:3; Song of Sol. 2:5; Hos. 3:1, means a cake of dried grapes pressed into a special shape. The word in Isa. 22:24 translated *flagon* sometimes means a leather bottle.

Flax of the best quality was raised in Egypt, Isa. 19:9, and was an article of extensive commerce. It was also produced in Palestine. Josh. 2:6; Judg. 15:14. See LINEN. Also see Exod. 9:31.
Prov. 31:13.
Isa. 42:3.
Ezek. 40:3.
Hos. 2:5, 9.
Matt. 12:20.

Flea, mentioned in 1 Sam. 24:14; 26:20 as the most insignificant of creatures.

Flesh, a word used in Gen. 6:13, 17, 19 for everything living, except vegetables, and in Gen. 6:12 for mankind. In Col. 2:5; 1 Pet. 4:6 it denotes the body as distinguished from the soul. In the New Testament the word "flesh" often means the bodily propensities and passions.
Also see Gen. 2; 6–9; 17; 29; 37; 40.
Exod. 4; 12; 16; 21; 22; 29; 30.
Lev. 4; 6–9; 11–17; 19; 21; 22; 26.
Num. 8; 11; 12; 16; 18; 19; 27.
Deut. 5; 12; 14; 16; 28; 32.
Judg. 6; 8; 9.
1 Sam. 2; 17; 25.
2 Sam. 5; 6; 19.
1 Kings 17; 19; 21.
2 Kings 4–6; 9.
1 Chron. 11; 16.
2 Chron. 32.
Neh. 5.
Job 2; 4; 6; 7; 10; 13; 14; 19; 21; 31; 33; 34; 41.
Pss. 16; 27; 38; 50; 56; 63; 65; 73; 78; 79; 84; 109; 119; 135; 145.
Prov. 4; 5; 11; 14; 23.
Eccles. 4; 5; 11; 12.
Isa. 9; 17; 22; 31; 40; 44; 49; 58; 65; 66.
Jer. 7; 11; 12; 17; 19; 25; 32; 45; 51.
Lam. 3.
Ezek. 4; 11; 16; 20; 21; 23; 24; 32; 36; 37; 39; 40; 44.

Dan. 1; 2; 4; 7; 10.
Hos. 8.
Joel 2.
Mic. 3.
Zeph. 1.
Hag. 2.
Zech. 2; 11; 14.
Matt. 16; 19; 24; 26.
Mark 10; 13; 14.
Luke 3; 24.
John 1; 3; 6; 8; 17.
Acts 2.
Rom. 1–4; 6–9; 11; 13; 14.
1 Cor. 1; 5–8; 10; 15.
2 Cor. 1; 4; 5; 7; 10–12.
Gal. 1–6.
Eph. 2; 5; 6.
Phil. 1; 3.
Col. 1–3.
1 Tim. 3.
Philem. 16.
Heb. 2; 5; 9; 10; 12.
James 5.
1 Pet. 1; 3; 4.
2 Pet. 2.
1 John 2; 4.
2 John 7.
Jude 7, 8, 23.
Rev. 17; 19.

Flint is very abundant in Palestine and vicinity. Ps. 114:8. The word is used figuratively in Deut. 32:13 to represent the great abundance of oil, and in Isa. 50:7; Ezek. 3:9 to denote constancy and firmness.

Floats, in 1 Kings 5:9; 2 Chron. 2:16, means rafts for floating timber to Joppa, to be carried from there overland to Jerusalem for the Temple.

Flock. See SHEEP.

Flood, in Josh. 24:2, 3, means the river Euphrates. In Genesis it means DELUGE (which see).

Flute, a wind-instrument of music

mentioned in the Bible only in Dan. 3:5, 7, 10, 15. It was played like the modern clarinet, though there were different ways of making and using it.

Flux, Blood´y, in Acts 28:8, means dysentery.

Fly, the name of a great variety of insects, some of which are extremely annoying and destructive, found abundantly in Egypt and Judea. One of the plagues sent upon the Egyptians was "swarms of flies." Exod. 8:21.

Fold, in John 10:16, means flock.

Food is solid nourishment for the body.
Gen. 2:9; 3:6; 6:21; 41:35, 36, 48; 42:7, 10, 33; 43:2, 4, 20, 22; 44:1, 25; 47:24.
Exod. 21:10.
Lev. 3:11, 16; 19:23; 22:7.
Deut. 10:18.
1 Sam. 14:24, 28.
2 Sam. 9:10.
1 Kings 5:9, 11.
Job 23:12; 24:5; 38:41; 40:20.
Pss. 78:25; 104:14; 136:25; 146:7; 147:9.
Prov. 6:8; 13:23; 27:27; 28:3; 30:8; 31:14.
Ezek. 16:27; 48:18.
Acts 14:17.
2 Cor. 9:10.
1 Tim. 6:8.
James 2:15.

Fool, among other things, a person who lacks sense or judgment.
1 Sam. 26:21.
2 Sam. 3:33; 13:13.
Job 12:17; 30:8.
Pss. 14:1; 49:10; 53:1; 75:4; 92:6; 94:8; 107:17.
Prov. 1:7, 22, 32; 3:35; 7:22; 8:5; 10:8, 10, 18, 21, 23; 11:29; 12:15, 16, 23; 13:16, 19, 20; 14:8, 9, 16, 24, 33; 15:2, 5, 14; 16:22; 17:7, 10, 12, 16, 21, 24, 28; 18:2, 6, 7; 19:1, 10, 29; 20:3; 23:9; 24:7; 26:1, 3-12; 27:3, 22; 28:26;

29:11, 20; 30:22.

Eccles. 2:14-16, 19; 4:5; 5:1, 3, 4; 6:8; 7:4-6, 9; 9:17; 10:2, 3, 12, 14.

Isa. 19:11, 13; 35:8.

Jer. 17:11.

Hos. 9:7.

Matt. 5:22; 23:17, 19.

Luke 11:40; 12:20; 24:25.

Rom. 1:22.

1 Cor. 3:18; 4:10; 15:36.

2 Cor. 11:16, 19, 23; 12:6, 11.

Eph. 5:15.

Foot. In Deut. 11:10 the expression "wateredst with thy foot" is supposed to refer to some way of using the foot in irrigating the soil. Nakedness of the feet was a sign of mourning and of respect or reverence. Ezek. 24:17; Exod. 3:5. To wash the feet of a guest was a common mark of hospitality. Gen. 18:4. It was usually done by a servant. 1 Sam. 25:41; John 13:5, 6. Also see Gen. 8:9; 19:2, 24:32; 41:44; 43:24; 49:10, 33.

Exod. 4:25; 12:11, 37; 21:24; 24:10; 25:26, 29:20; 30:18, 19, 21, 28; 31:9; 35:16; 37:13; 38:8; 39:39; 40:11, 31.

Lev. 8:11, 23, 24; 11:21, 23, 42; 13:12; 14:14, 17, 25, 28.

Num. 20:19; 22:25.

Deut. 2:5, 28; 8:4; 11:24; 19:21; 25:9; 28:35, 56, 57, 65; 29:5; 32:35; 33:3, 24.

Josh. 1:3; 3:13, 15; 4:3, 9, 18; 5:15; 9:5; 10:24; 14:9.

Judg. 3:24; 4:10, 15, 17; 5:15, 27; 19:21.

Ruth 3:4, 7, 8, 14.

1 Sam. 2:9; 14:13; 24:3; 25:24.

2 Sam. 2:18; 3:34; 4:4, 12; 9:3, 13; 11:8; 14:25; 19:24; 21:20; 22:10, 34, 37, 39.

1 Kings 2:5; 5:3; 14:6, 12; 15:23.

2 Kings 4:27, 37; 6:32; 9:35; 13:21; 19:24; 21:8.

1 Chron. 20:6; 28:2.

2 Chron. 3:13; 16:12; 33:8.

Neh. 9:21.

Esther 8:3.

Job 2:7; 12:5; 13:27; 18:8, 11; 23:11; 28:4; 29:15; 30:12; 31:5; 33:11; 39:15.

Pss. 8:6; 9:15; 18:9, 33, 36, 38; 22:16; 25:15; 26:12; 31:8; 36:11; 38:16; 40:2; 47:3; 56:13; 58:10; 66:6, 9; 68:23; 73:2; 74:3; 91:12, 13; 94:18; 105:18; 115:7; 116:8; 119:59, 101, 105; 121:3; 122:2.

Prov. 1:15, 16; 3:23, 26; 4:26, 27; 5:5; 6:13, 18, 28; 7:11; 19:2; 25:17, 19; 26:6; 29:5.

Eccles. 5:1.

Song of Sol. 5:3; 7:1.

Isa. 1:6; 3:16, 18; 6:2; 7:20; 14:19, 25; 18:7, 20:2; 23:7; 26:6; 28:3; 32:20; 37:25; 41:2, 3; 49:23; 52:7; 58:13; 59:7; 60:13, 14.

Jer. 2:25; 12:10; 13:16; 14:10; 18:22; 38:22.

Lam. 1:13, 15; 3:34.

Ezek. 1:7; 2:1, 2; 3:24; 6:11; 16:25; 24:23; 25:6; 29:11; 32:2, 13; 34:18, 19; 37:10; 43:7.

Dan. 2:33, 34, 41, 42; 7:4, 7, 19; 8:13; 10:6.

Amos 2:15.

Nah. 1:3, 15.

Hab. 3:5, 19.

Zech. 14:4, 12.

Mal. 4:3.

Matt. 4:6; 5:13; 7:6; 10:14; 14:13; 15:30; 18:8, 29; 22:13; 28:9.

Mark 5:22; 6:11; 7:25; 9:45.

Luke 1:79; 4:11; 7:38, 44-46; 8:35, 41; 9:5; 10:39; 15:22, 17:16; 24:39, 40.

John 11:2, 32, 44; 12:3; 13:8-10, 12, 14; 20:12.

Acts 3:7; 4:35, 37; 5:2, 9, 10; 7:5, 33, 58; 10:25, 13:25, 51; 14:8, 10; 16:24; 21:11; 22:3; 26:16.

Rom. 3:15; 10:15; 16:20.

1 Cor. 12:15, 21; 15:25, 27.

Eph. 1:22; 6:15.
1 Tim. 5:10.
Heb. 2:8; 10:29; 12:13.
Rev. 1:13, 15, 17; 2:18; 3:9; 10:1, 2; 11:2, 11; 12:1; 13:2; 19:10; 22:8.

Foot´man sometimes means infantry. In other instances it refers specially to the king's guard. 1 Sam. 22:17. The word there translated *footman* is elsewhere rendered *guard*.

For´eign-er, Exod. 12:45, means any one not a Hebrew.

Fore-knowl´edge (*knowing beforehand*) is an attribute of God. Acts 2:23; 1 Pet. 1:2.

Fore-run´ner, in Heb. 6:20, used in reference to Christ's entrance within the veil, means not only one who goes before, but one who leads or prepares the way.

For´est. [1] The Forest of Hareth was apparently in the south of Judah. 1 Sam. 22:5. [2] Forest of Lebanon, in the north of Palestine, is mentioned only in connection with a house which was built by Solomon. 1 Kings 7:2; 2 Chron. 9:16. [3] Forest of Carmel. There seems to be no doubt that the Carmel here referred to was that on the sea-coast in the lot of Zebulun. 2 Kings 19:23; Isa. 37:24. [4] Forest in Arabia, only once alluded to, and that in a prophetical denunciation. Its situation is uncertain. Isa. 21:13.

For-give´ness.
Ps. 130:4.
Dan. 9:9.
Mark 3:29.
Acts 5:31; 13:38; 26:18.
Eph. 1:7.
Col. 1:14.

Forks, in 1 Sam. 13:21, means large flesh-hooks. Forks were not used by the Orientals in eating.

For´mer Sea, Zech. 14:8, is same as DEAD SEA (which see).

For-ni-ca´tion. It is often used figuratively with reference to idolatry.
2 Chron. 21:11.
Isa. 23:17.
Ezek. 16:15, 26, 29.
Matt. 5:32; 15:19; 19:9.
Mark 7:21.
John 8:41.
Acts 15:20, 29; 21:25.
Rom. 1:29.
1 Cor. 5:1; 6:13, 18; 7:2; 10:8.
2 Cor. 12:21.
Gal. 5:19.
Eph. 5:3.
Col. 3:5.
1 Thess. 4:3.
Jude :7.
Rev. 2:14, 20, 21; 9:21; 14:8; 17:2, 4; 18:3, 9; 19:2.

For-swear´. See OATH.

Forts are of very ancient origin. Deut. 1:28; 3:5.

For-tu-na´tus (*fortunate*), a Christian, apparently of Corinth, who is named in Paul's first Epistle to the church of the Corinthians. 1 Cor. 16:17.

Foun´tains are often mentioned in the Bible. They were of special value in the dry and thirsty land of Judea. Many places were named from some fountain in their vicinity. See EN (*a fountain*).
Gen. 7:11; 8:2; 16:7.
Lev. 11:36; 20:18.
Num. 33:9.
Deut. 8:7; 33:28.
Josh. 15:9.
1 Sam. 29:1.
1 Kings 18:5.
2 Chron. 32:3, 4.
Neh. 2:14; 3:15; 12:37.
Pss. 36:9; 68:26; 74:15; 114:8.
Prov. 5:16, 18; 8:24, 28; 13:14; 14:27; 25:26.

Eccles. 12:6.
Song of Sol. 4:12, 15.
Isa. 41:18.
Jer. 2:13; 6:7; 9:1; 17:13.
Hos. 13:15.
Joel 3:18.
Zech. 13:1.
Mark 5:29.
James 3:11, 12.
Rev. 7:17; 8:10; 14:7; 16:4; 21:6.

Fowl, a word used in Gen. 15:11; Job 28:7; Isa. 18:6 to denote birds of prey, and in Neh. 5:18; 1 Kings 4:23 for poultry. The word is also applied to birds in general, as in Luke 12:24.

Fox, a cunning and voracious animal well known generally and abundant in Palestine. The jackal is probably meant in several passages in which the word *fox* occurs.
Judg. 15:4.
Neh. 4:3.
Ps. 63:10.
Song of Sol. 2:15.
Lam. 5:18.
Ezek. 13:4.
Matt. 8:20.
Luke 9:58; 13:32.

Frank´in-cense, an exceedingly aromatic gum used in the sacred incense for the Temple service. It is distilled from a tree in Arabia. The substance generally used in modern times as frankincense is produced from the Norway pine.
Exod. 30:34.
Lev. 2:1, 2, 15, 16; 5:11; 6:15; 24:7.
Num. 5:15.
1 Chron. 9:29.
Neh. 13:5, 9.
Song of Sol. 3:6; 4:6, 14.
Matt. 2:11.
Rev. 18:13.

Frank´ly, in Luke 7:42, means freely.

Fray, in Deut. 28:26; Jer. 7:33; Zech.

1:21, means scare.

Fret, in Lev. 13:55, means corroded.

Friend, a word often used in the Bible. Abraham is called the "Friend of God" in James 2:23, and Christ in John 15:15 calls his disciples "friends." In Matt. 11:19 he is called "a friend of publicans and sinners." The word friend is often used where no affection or friendship is intended. Matt. 22:12; 26:50.
Also see Gen. 26:26; 38:12, 20.
Exod. 33:11.
Deut 13:6.
Judg. 14:20.
1 Sam. 30:26.
2 Sam. 3:8; 13:3; 15:37; 16:16, 17; 19:6.
1 Kings 4:5; 16:11.
2 Chron. 20:7.
Esther 5:10, 14; 6:13.
Job 2:11; 6:14, 27; 16:20; 17:5; 19:14, 19, 21; 32:3; 42:7, 10.
Pss. 35:14; 38:11; 41:9; 88:18.
Prov. 6:1, 3; 14:20; 16:28; 17:9, 17, 18; 18:24; 19:4, 6, 7; 22:11; 27:6, 9, 10, 14, 17.
Song of Sol. 5:1, 16.
Isa. 41:8.
Jer. 6:21; 19:9; 20:4, 6; 38:22.
Lam. 1:2.
Hos. 3:1.
Mic. 7:5.
Zech. 13:6.
Matt. 20:13.
Mark 3:21; 5:19.
Luke 7:6, 34; 11:5, 6, 8; 12:4; 14:10, 12; 15:6, 9, 29; 16:9; 21:16; 23:12.
John 3:29; 11:11; 15:13, 14; 19:12.
Acts 10:24; 12:20; 19:31; 27:3.
James 4:4.
3 John 14.

Fringes were attached to the hem or border of the outside garment worn by the Israelites, and contained, Num. 15:38, 39, "a ribband of blue," that they might remember and keep the commandments of the LORD. They became, in the course of time, objects of superstitious regard.

Frogs were noted as the second plague of Egypt. Exod. 8:1-14. They were worshipped by the Egyptians, but were unclean to the Hebrews. In Rev. 16:13 they represent uncleanness.

Front'lets were worn by male Jews from the age of thirteen when they went to the synagogue, in accordance with a literal interpretation of Exod. 13:9, 16. They were made of four pieces of parchment. Exod. 13:2-10 was written on the first; Exod. 13:11-21 on the second; Deut. 6:4-9 on the third; and Deut. 11:18-21 on the fourth. These were enclosed in a square form in a piece of tough skin on which the Hebrew letter *shin* was inscribed, and were bound around the forehead by a thong or ribband. See PHYLACTERIES.

Fro'ward, in Deut. 32:20, etc., means perverse.

Ful'ler, in Mal. 3:2; Mark 9:3, means a bleacher of cloth. Fullers also washed clothing that had been worn.

Ful'lers' Field, a place near the walls of Jerusalem, 2 Kings 18:17, 26; Isa. 36:2, where the fullers worked.

Fur'long, a measure of length. The furlong being the eighth part of a British mile, as the stadium was of the Greek and Roman mile, the name has been arbitrarily introduced into the English Version, although the length of it (six hundred and sixty feet) exceeds that of the stadium by about fifty-six feet. Luke 24:13; John 6:19; 11:18. See MEASURES.

Fur'nace, in the Bible, is translated from several different words, and means— [1] An oven for baking. Gen. 15:17; Neh. 3:11. [2] A smelting furnace or a lime-

kiln. Gen. 19:28; Exod. 9:8. [3] A refining furnace. Prov. 17:3; Isa. 48:10; Ezek. 22:18-22. [4] A crucible. Ps. 12:6. [5] The Chaldean furnace for capital punishment. Jer. 29:22; Dan. 3:19-26; Rev. 1:15; 9:2.

Fur'ni-ture, in Gen. 31:34, means equipment; in Exod. 31:7 it means the vessels of the Tabernacle.
Also see Exod. 31:8, 9; 35:14; 39:33.
Nah. 2:9.

Fu'ry is figuratively ascribed to God.
Gen. 27:44.
Lev. 26:28.
Job 20:23.
Isa. 27:4; 34:2; 42:25; 51:13, 17, 20, 22; 59:18; 63:3, 5, 6; 66:15.
Jer. 4:4; 6:11; 7:20; 10:25; 21:5, 12; 23:19; 25:15; 30:23; 32:31, 37; 33:5; 36:7; 42:18; 44:6.
Lam. 2:4; 4:11.
Ezek. 5:13, 15; 6:12; 7:8; 8:18; 9:8; 13:13; 14:19; 16:38, 42; 19:12; 20:8, 13, 21, 33, 34; 21:17; 22:20, 22; 24:8, 13; 25:14; 30:15; 36:6, 18; 38:18.
Dan. 3:13, 19; 8:6; 9:16; 11:44.
Mic. 5:15.
Nah. 1:6.
Zech. 8:2.

Fur'rows, in Hos. 10:10, means transgressions.

Fu'ry, in Jer. 10:25, is figurative expression for afflictive judgments.

G

G, when it comes before E and I in Hebrew Old Testament words, is pronounced hard, as in *give*. In Greek words it is pronounced soft, like J.

Ga'al (*rejection*), an Israelite, probably of the tribe of Ephraim, who rebelled against Abimelech, who had been made king in Shechem. Judg. 9:26-46.

Ga´ash (*quaking*), a mountain or hilly district forming part of Mount Ephraim; generally in the English Version called a hill, but in the original the term mount is applied to it. It contains Joshua's tomb. Josh. 24:30; Judg. 2:9.

Ga´ba (*height*), a city of Benjamin. Josh. 18:24. See GEBA.

Gab´ba-i (*ingatherer*), a chief man among the Benjamites. Neh. 11:8.

Gab´ba-tha (*elevated place*), the place of Pilate's judgment-seat; also called "the Pavement." John 19:13. The judgment-hall was the Prætorium, which was on the western hill of Jerusalem.

Ga´bri-el (*God is mighty*), an angel sent by God to Daniel, Dan. 8:16; 9:21; to Zacharias, Luke 1:19; and to Mary, Luke 1:26.

Gad (*the seer*). [1] The seventh son of Jacob. Gen. 30:11; Exod. 1:4. [2] The name is also used to denote the tribe which sprang from Gad and the land which they inhabited, which was east of the Jordan and between Reuben and Manasseh. [3] A prophet who lived in the time of David, and was his friend. 1 Sam. 22:5; 2 Sam. 24:13, 14.
Also see Gen. 35:26; 46:16; 49:19.
Num. 1:14, 24, 25; 2:14; 7:42; 10:20; 13:15; 26:15, 18; 32:1, 2, 6, 25, 29, 31, 33, 34; 34:14.
Deut. 27:13; 33:20.
Josh. 4:12; 13:24, 28; 18:7; 20:8; 21:7, 38; 22:9-11, 13, 15, 21, 25, 30-34.
1 Sam. 13:7.
2 Sam. 24:5, 11, 18, 19.
1 Chron. 2:2; 5:11; 6:63, 80; 12:14; 21:9, 11, 13, 18, 19; 29:29.
2 Chron. 29:25.
Jer. 49:1.

Ezek. 48:27, 28, 34.
Rev. 7:5.

Gad´a-ra, an ancient stronghold of Palestine about eight miles south-east of the Sea of Galilee and near the river Hieromax. Its ruins are called by the Arabs *Um Keis*, and are very extensive. Hot baths are found near by. Its inhabitants now live in old tombs in the rocks. See GADARENES.

Gad-a-renes´, inhabitants of a district on the east side of the Sea of Galilee, and east of the Jordan below that sea. Mark 5:1; Luke 8:26, 37.

Gad´di (*belonging to fortune*), one of the heads of the tribes whom Moses sent to search the land of Canaan. Num. 13:11.

Gad´di-el (*Gad is fortune-bringer*), another of the chief men who were sent to search the land of Canaan. Num. 13:10.

Ga´di (*fortunate*), an Israelite whose son Menahem rebelled against Shallum, the king of Israel, and killed him and usurped the throne. 2 Kings 15:14, 17.

Gad´ites (*haggadi*), the tribe of Gad. Deut. 3:12, 16; 1 Chron. 12:8; 26:32.

Ga´ham (*sunburnt*), a son of Nahor, the brother of Abraham. Gen. 22:24.

Ga´har (*prostration*), a Nethinim whose descendants went up from Babylon with Zerubbabel. Ezra 2:47; Neh. 7:49.

Gain-say´, in Luke 21:15, means contradict.

Gaius, ga´yus. [1] A Macedonian who accompanied Paul in some of his journeys and was with him at Ephesus. Acts 19:29. [2] A man of Derbe in Lycaonia who accompanied Paul on his return from Macedonia into Asia Minor. Acts 20:4. [3] A Corinthian whom Paul baptized. Rom. 16:23; 1 Cor. 1:14. [4] The person to whom John's third epistle is addressed. 3 John 1.

Ga´lal (*great*). [1] A Levite who dwelt in Jerusalem after the captivity. 1 Chron.

9:15. [2] A Levite whose descendants dwelt in Jerusalem after the return from Babylon. 1 Chron. 9:16; Neh. 11:17.

Galatia, ga-la´shi-a, a central division of Asia Minor, inhabited by Celts from the upper Rhine who in the third century B. C. had settled there and mingled with the Greeks and Jews. Paul visited this country twice, Acts 16:6 and 18:23, and was received with great enthusiasm, but the church was nevertheless afterward disturbed by Judaizing Christians who spoke slightingly of Paul's apostolic authority and asserted the obligation of the Mosaic code on all Christians.

Galatians, ga-la´shi-anz, inhabitants of Galatia. Gal. 3:1.

Ga-la´tians, E-pis´tle of Paul to the, was written by Paul from Ephesus, between A. D. 54 and 57. In it with fiery eloquence he vindicates the authority of his ministry and demonstrates the true relation between the Law of Moses and the Gospel of Christ. This epistle and that to the Romans were the chief authority for the doctrines of the Reformation of the sixteenth century, and form the Magna Charta of evangelical Protestantism. Considered simply as a piece of literature, the Epistle to the Galatians is one of the grandest and most perfect that exists. The "subscription" at the end of this epistle says it was written from *Rome;* but this "subscription" was added by some later hand and is without authority.

Gal´ba-num, a resinous gum used as an ingredient in the sacred incense burned at the golden altar, Exod. 30:34, and valuable for medicine.

Gal´e-ed (*heap of witness*), the name given by Jacob to the pillar or the heap of stones which he set up in Mount Gilead for a witness of the covenant which he made with Laban. Gen. 31:47, 48.

Gal-i-le´ans, the inhabitants of the district called Galilee. Mark 14:70; Luke 13:1, 2; 22:59; 23:6; John 4:45; Acts 2:7.

Gal´i-lee (*a circle*) is in the Old Testament the name of a small mountainous district of Naphtali including the twenty towns which Solomon gave to Hiram, king of Tyre, 1 Kings 9:11; 2 Kings 15:29, but having been repeopled by strangers during the period of the captivity, it became in the time of our Lord the name of the northernmost and most populous province of Palestine. The population was very much mixed, heathens, proselytes, and Jews living together, and though the Jews probably retained the dominant influence, they were, on account of their frequent intercourse with foreigners, less strict in the observation of the law than their brethren of Judea, and consequently not very much esteemed by them. One of the most salient features of the country was the Sea of Galilee, called Chinnereth or Chinneroth in the Old Testament, Num. 34:11; Josh. 12:3, and in the New Testament the Lake of Gennesaret, Luke 5:1, the Sea of Tiberias, John 6:1, etc. (See GALILEE, SEA OF). Among the towns were NAZARETH, CANA, TIBERIAS, CHORAZIN, BETHSAIDA, and CAPERNAUM (which see). Our Lord spent most of his time in Galilee, and all the twelve apostles, except Judas, were Galileans. See PALESTINE.

Also see Josh. 20:7; 21:32.

1 Chron. 6:76.

Isa. 9:1.

Matt. 2:22; 3:13; 4:12, 15, 18, 23, 25; 15:29; 17:22; 19:1; 21:11; 26:32, 69; 27:55; 28:7, 10, 16.

Mark 1:9, 14, 16, 28, 39; 3:7; 6:21; 7:31; 9:30; 14:28; 15:41; 16:7.

Luke 1:26; 2:4, 39; 3:1; 4:14, 31, 44; 5:17; 8:26; 17:11; 23:5, 6, 49, 55; 24:6.

John 1:43; 2:1, 11; 4:3, 43, 45-47, 54; 7:1

9, 41, 52; 12:21; 21:2.
Acts 1:11; 5:37; 9:31; 10:37; 13:31.

Gal′ilee of the Gentiles, and **of the nations.** See GALILEE.

Gal′i-lee, Sea of, Matt. 4:18, in Palestine, is called also SEA OF CHINNERETH or CHINNEROTH, Num. 34:11; Josh. 12:3; LAKE OF GENNESARET, Luke 5:1; SEA OF TIBERIAS, John 6:1; "the sea," Isa. 9:1; Matt. 4:13, 15; 17:27; and is about twenty-seven miles east of the Mediterranean Sea. It is about fourteen miles long from north to south and from four to seven miles wide, and its greatest depth is about one hundred and sixty feet. Its surface varies from six hundred to seven hundred feet below the level of the Mediterranean. The river Jordan enters the Sea of Galilee on the north-east and flows out at the south-west. This sea abounds in excellent fish of various kinds. It is enclosed by steep hills, broken or receding occasionally, from five hundred to seventeen hundred feet high, the eastern shore being much the highest. The Sea of Galilee is still liable to sudden tempests like that mentioned in Matt. 14:22-23.

Gall, in Job 16:13; 20:14, 25, means a bitter fluid secreted by the liver and generally called *bile.* In a great many other places the word gall is used for some bitter herb or plant. It was a common name for bitter substances. Gall was given to deaden the pain of persons suffering from crucifixion. It was offered to Christ. Matt. 27:34.

Gal′lant, in Isa. 33:21, means splendid. **Galley,** in the same verse, means a kind of vessel.

Gal′ler-y, in Ezek. 41:15, means colonnade, or else wainscoting; and in Song of Sol. 7:5, "tresses" or ringlets.

Gal′lim (*fountains* or *heaps*), a town of Benjamin. 1 Sam. 25:44; Isa. 10:30.

Gal′li-o, the proconsul or deputy of

Achaia before whom Paul was accused by the Jews. Acts 18:12, 14, 17.

Ga-ma′li-el (*God is recompenser*). [1] The captain of the tribe of Manasseh who was appointed to assist Moses in numbering the people. Num. 1:10; 2:20. [2] A celebrated rabbi among the Jews, the teacher of Paul. Acts 22:3. He was a prominent member of the Sanhedrin and a doctor of the law, and was very influential among the Jews. Acts 5:34. Gamaliel is famous for his wise counsel, Acts 5:38, 39, concerning the apostles when they were brought before the Sanhedrin.

Gam′ma-dims (*brave soldiers*), a word found only once, Ezek. 27:11, in the Bible. It is generally supposed to be descriptive of the men of Arvad, Ezek. 27:11, rather than the name of any special people.

Ga′mul (*matured*), leader of the twenty-second course of priests. 1 Chron. 24:17.

Gar′dens are often mentioned in the Bible, and were frequently places where trees and plants were more carefully cultivated than in the open field. Gethsemane was a garden or olive grove. Gardens sometimes consisted of fruit- and shade-trees with aromatic shrubs. Song of Sol. 5:1. The LORD God planted a garden in Eden. Gen. 2:8. A garden of herbs is mentioned in 1 Kings 21:2.
Also see Gen. 2:9, 10, 15, 16; 3:1-3, 8, 10, 23, 24; 13:10.
Num. 24:5.
Deut. 11:10.
2 Kings 9:27; 21:18, 26; 25:4.
Neh. 3:15.
Esther 1:5; 7:7, 8.
Job 8:16
Eccles. 2:5.
Song of Sol. 4:12, 15, 16; 6:2, 11; 8:13.
Isa. 1:8, 29, 30; 51:3; 58:11; 61:11; 65:3; 66:17.

Jer. 29:5, 28; 31:12; 39:4; 52:7.
Lam. 2:6.
Ezek. 28:13; 31:8, 9; 36:35.
Joel 2:3.
Amos 4:9; 9:14.
Luke 13:19.
John 18:1, 26; 19:41.

Ga´reb (*reviler*). [1] One of David's valiant men. 2 Sam. 23:28; 1 Chron. 11:40. [2] A hill near Jerusalem. Jer. 31:39.

Gar´lands, Acts 14:13, were probably to be used to decorate the oxen for sacrifice, according to the custom of the heathens.

Gar´lick, a well-known vegetable resembling the onion and much relished by the Jews in Egypt, Num. 11:5, and in Palestine.

Gar´ments made of skins, Gen. 3:21, were worn in very ancient times, but spinning and weaving were practiced quite early, Exod. 35:25, and garments of various kinds of cloth were then used. Many of the garments worn by the Hebrews were loose and flowing, and as the fashion of them changed but little from age to age, large quantities were laid up in store by the wealthy, Job 27:16, where the moth corrupts. Matt. 6:19. The outside garment or cloak was a large piece of cloth which was wrapped about the body and could be arranged so as to form a *bosom* for carrying things. It was also used by the poor as a bed. The inner garment or coat, Gen. 37:3, was sometimes woven without seam. John 19:23. See also FRINGES.
Also see Gen. 9:23; 25:25; 35:2; 38:14, 19; 39:12, 13, 15, 16, 18; 49:11.
Exod. 28:2-4; 29:5, 21, 29; 31:10; 35:19, 21; 39:1, 41; 40:13.
Lev. 6:10, 11, 27; 8:2, 30; 13:47, 49, 51-53, 56-59; 14:55; 15:17; 16:4, 23, 24, 32; 19:19; 21:10.
Num. 15:38; 20:26, 28.

Deut. 22:5, 11.
Josh. 7:21, 24; 9:5, 13.
Judg. 8:25; 14:12, 13, 19.
1 Sam. 18:4.
2 Sam. 10:4; 13:18, 19, 31; 20:8.
1 Kings 10:25; 11:29, 30.
2 Kings 5:22, 23, 26; 7:15; 9:13; 25:29.
1 Chron. 19:4.
Ezra 2:69; 9:3, 5.
Neh. 7:70, 72.
Esther 8:15.
Job 13:28; 30:18; 37:17; 38:9, 14; 41:13.
Pss. 22:18; 45:8; 69:11; 73:6; 102:26; 104:2, 6; 109:18, 19; 133:2.
Prov. 20:16; 25:20; 27:13; 30:4.
Eccles. 9:8.
Song of Sol. 4:11.
Isa. 9:5; 50:9; 51:6, 8; 52:1; 59:6, 17; 61:3, 10; 63:1-3.
Jer. 36:24; 43:12; 52:33.
Lam. 4:14.
Ezek. 16:16, 18; 18:7, 16; 26:16; 42:14; 44:17, 19.
Dan. 3:21; 7:9.
Joel 2:13.
Mic. 2:8.
Hag. 2:12.
Zech. 3:3-5; 13:4.
Mal. 2:16.
Matt. 9:16, 20, 21; 14:36; 21:8; 22:11, 12; 23:5; 27:35.
Mark 2:21; 5:27; 6:56; 10:50; 11:7, 8; 13:16; 15:24; 16:5.
Luke 5:36; 8:44; 19:35; 22:36; 24:4.
John 13:4, 12.
Acts 9:39; 12:8.
Heb. 1:11.
James 5:2.
Jude :23.
Rev. 1:13; 3:4; 16:15.

Gar´mite, The (*the strong*). Keilah the Garmite is mentioned in 1 Chron. 4:19.

Gar´ner, in Matt. 3:12, means granary

Gash´mu, Neh. 6:6, another form of GESHEM (which see).

Ga´tam (*burnt valley*), a son of Eliphaz, the son of Esau. Gen. 36:11, 16; 1 Chron. 1:36.

Gate. Many Eastern cities were surrounded with walls and were entered by means of strong gates. Jerusalem had many gates, each of which had a name. A city was generally considered as captured when its gates were taken, and the word sometimes means power. The gates of cities always had an open space near them which was used for judicial proceedings, public assemblies, a market-place, and a place of general resort.
Gen. 19; 22–24, 28; 34.
Exod. 20; 27; 32; 38–40.
Num. 4.
Deut. 3; 5; 6; 11; 12; 14–18; 21–26; 28; 31.
Josh. 2; 6–8; 20.
Judg. 5; 9; 16; 18.
Ruth 4.
1 Sam. 4; 9; 17; 21; 23.
2 Sam. 3; 10; 11; 15; 18; 19; 23.
1 Kings 16; 17; 22.
2 Kings 7; 9; 10; 11; 14; 15; 23; 25.
1 Chron. 9; 11; 19; 22; 26.
2 Chron. 8; 14; 18; 23–27; 31–33; 35.
Neh. 1–3; 6–8; 11–13.
Esther 2–6.
Job 5; 29; 31; 38.
Pss. 9; 24; 69; 87; 100; 107; 118; 122; 127; 147.
Prov. 1; 8; 14; 17; 22; 24; 31.
Song of Sol. 7.
Isa. 3; 13; 14; 22; 24; 26; 28; 29; 38; 45; 54; 60; 62.
Jer. 1; 7; 14; 15; 17; 19; 20; 22; 26; 31; 36–39; 49; 51; 52.
Lam. 1; 2; 4; 5.
Ezek. 8–11; 21; 26; 38; 40; 42–48.
Dan. 2.

Amos 5.
Obad. 11, 13.
Mic. 1; 2.
Nah. 2; 3.
Zeph. 1.
Zech. 3; 14.
Matt. 7; 16.
Luke 7; 13; 16.
Acts 3; 9; 10; 12; 14.
Heb. 13.
Rev. 21; 22.

Gath (*wine-press*), one of the cities from which Joshua did not fully cut off the Anakim. It was in the territory assigned to Dan, and was one of the five chief cities of the Philistines. It was the home of Goliath, 1 Sam. 17:14; a place to which the ark was carried, 1 Sam. 5:8; and where David sought refuge. 1 Sam. 21:10–15. Also see Josh 11:22.
1 Sam. 6:17; 7:14; 17:4, 23, 52. 27:2-4, 11.
2 Sam. 1:20; 15:18; 21:20, 22.
1 Kings 2:39-41.
2 Kings 12:17.
1 Chron. 7:21; 8:13; 18:1; 20:6, 8.
2 Chron. 11:8; 26:6.
Ps. 56.
Amos 6:2.
Mic. 1:10.

Gath-he´pher (*wine-press of the well*), 2 Kings 14:25, a town of Zebulun which is called GITTAH-HEPHER in Josh. 19:13. It was the birthplace of Jonah, and is now called *el-Meshed.*

Gath-rim´mon (*wine-press of Rimmon*). [1] A city of Dan. Josh. 19:45. [2] A city of the Levites, apparently on the boundary between Ephraim and Manasseh, Josh. 21:25; 1 Chron. 6:69, called BILEAM in 1 Chron. 6:70.

Gau-la-ni´tis. See GOLAN.

Ga´za (*the strong*), or **Az´zah,** as Gaza

No. 1 was sometimes called. [1] A strong city situated in the south-west corner of Palestine and about three miles from the Great or Mediterranean Sea. It is one of the oldest cities in the world, was peopled by the descendants of Ham, Gen. 10:19, by the Anakim, Josh. 11:22, and was the strongest of the five royal cities of the Philistines. It commanded the road to Egypt, and was the scene of many desperate struggles and of the exploits of Samson. Judg. 16. It was captured by Alexander the Great after a siege of nearly five months. [2] A city of Ephraim. Judg. 6:4; 1 Chron. 7:28.
Also see Josh. 10:41; 15:47.
Judg. 1:18.
1 Sam. 6:17.
2 Kings 18:8.
Jer. 47:1, 5.
Amos 1:6, 7.
Zeph. 2:4.
Zech. 9:5.
Acts 8:26.

Ga´zath-ites, the inhabitants of Gaza (Azzah). Josh. 13:3; Judg. 16:2.

Ga-zelle´. See ROE.

Ga´zer (*precipice*). 2 Sam. 5:25; 1 Chron. 14:16. See GEZER.

Ga´zez (*shearer*), the names of the son and grandson of Caleb. 1 Chron. 2:46. Some think the second is a repetition of the first.

Gaz´zam (*devourer*), one of the Nethinims whose posterity returned to Jerusalem with Zerubbabel. Ezra 2:48; Neh. 7:51.

Ge´ba (*height*), a Levitical city of Benjamin. Josh. 21:17; 1 Chron. 6:60. It is also called Gaba. Josh. 18:24. Geba and Gibeah seem to be sometimes confounded in the English Version. 1 Sam. 14:5. They were separate towns.

Ge´bal (*mountain*). [1] A city in Phœnicia, on the Mediterranean Sea, ten miles north of Beirut. Its inhabitants were noted for their skill in ship-building. It was called *Byblus* by the Greeks. Ezek. 27:9. [2] The name of a district of country in northern Edom, near the south end of the Dead Sea. Ps. 83:7.

Ge´ber (*strong*). [1] Father of one of Solomon's officers or purveyors. 1 Kings 4:13. [2] An officer or purveyor of Solomon. 1 Kings 4:19.

Ge´bim (*springs*), a small town near Jerusalem. Isa. 10:31.

Ged-a-li´ah (*Jehovah is great*). [1] The governor whom Nebuchadnezzar set over Judea when he had taken Jerusalem and carried the principal inhabitants away captive. 2 Kings 25:22; Jer. 39:14; 40:5. He was a friend of Jeremiah. Jer. 40:6. [2] One of the sons of Jeduthun. 1 Chron. 25:3, 9. [3] A priest who took a foreign wife. Ezra 10:18. [4] A prince of Judah in the time of Zedekiah. Jer. 38:1. [5] The grandfather of the prophet Zephaniah, who denounced the destruction of Judah in the time of Josiah. Zeph. 1:1.

Ged´e-on, Heb. 11:32, the Greek form of GIDEON (which see).

Ge´der (*walled*), a royal city of the Canaanites which was taken by Joshua. Josh. 12:13. Possibly same as GEDOR, No. 5.

Ge-de´rah (*sheep-cote*). [1] A town of the tribe of Judah, in the lowlands. Josh. 15:36.

Ged´e-rath-ite, an inhabitant of GEDERAH in Judah. 1 Chron. 12:4.

Ged´e-rite, a dweller in or native of GEDER. 1 Chron. 27:28.

Ge-de´roth (*sheep-cotes*), a city in the west of Judah. Josh. 15:41; 2 Chron. 28:18.

Ged-e-roth-a´im (*two sheep-folds*), a

town in the plain country of Judah. Josh. 15:36.

Ge´dor. [1 and 2] Two names in the genealogy of Judah. 1 Chron. 4:4, 18. [3] A Benjamite name in the genealogy of Saul. 1 Chron. 8:31; 9:37. [4] A town in the hill country of Judah. Josh. 15:58. [5] Apparently a town of Benjamin. 1 Chron. 12:7. Probably same as GEDER of Josh. 12:13. [6] Gedor of 1 Chron. 4:39 was probably between Judah and Mount Seir. It is called GERAR in the Septuagint.

Ge-ha´zi (*valley of vision*), the servant of Elisha the prophet. He was smitten with leprosy, 2 Kings 5:20–27, on account of his covetousness and falsehood when Elisha had refused to receive a reward from Naaman the Syrian.

Ge-hen´na. See HINNOM, VALLEY OF, and HELL.

Gel´i-loth (*circle*), one of the places which marked the boundary of Benjamin. Josh. 18:17. GILGAL is in place of GELILOTH in Josh. 15:7. They are considered to be the same. See GILGAL.

Ge-mal´li (*camel-driver*), father of the spy from Dan. Num. 13:12.

Gem-a-ri´ah (*whom Jehovah hath perfected*). [1] A son of Hilkiah the priest who was sent by Zedekiah, king of Judah, as an ambassador to Nebuchadnezzar, king of Babylon. Jer. 29:3. [2] A prince of Judah in the time of Jehoiakim, king of Judah. Jer. 36:10, 11, 12, 25.

Gems. See STONES, PRECIOUS.

Ge-ne-al´o-gy. The lineage of a family, or list of ancestors, was preserved with extreme care by the Jews, not only because the privileges of the Jewish Church were transmitted through Abraham, but because of the predictions concerning the Messiah.

Gen-er-a´tion, in Gen. 15:16, means a single succession in natural descent, as the children of the same parents; hence an age. In Luke 9:41 it means the people of the same period, or living at the same time. Generation or generations has the following secondary meanings: [1] A genealogical register, as in Gen. 5:1. [2] A family history. Gen. 6:9; 25:12. [3] A history of the origin of things and persons; for instance the earth.

Also see Gen. 2:4; 7:1; 9:12; 10:1, 32; 11:10, 27; 17:7, 9, 12; 25:13, 19; 36:1, 9; 37:2; 50:23.

Exod. 1:6; 3:15; 6:16, 19; 12:14, 17, 42; 16:32, 33; 17:16; 20:5; 27:21; 29:42; 30:8, 10, 21, 31; 31:13, 16; 34:7; 40:15.

Lev. 3:17; 6:18; 7:36; 10:9; 17:7; 21:17; 22:3; 23:14, 21, 31, 41, 43; 24:3; 25:30.

Num. 1:20, 22, 24, 26, 28, 30, 32, 34, 36, 38, 40, 42; 3:1; 10:8; 14:18; 15:14, 15, 21, 23, 38; 18:23; 32:13; 35:29.

Deut. 1:35; 2:14; 5:9; 7:9; 23:2, 3, 8; 29:22; 32:5, 7, 20.

Josh. 22:27, 28.

Judg. 2:10; 3:2.

Ruth 4:18.

2 Kings 10:30; 15:12.

1 Chron. 1:29; 5:7; 7:2, 4, 9; 8:28; 9:9, 34; 16:15; 26:31.

Esther 9:28.

Job. 42:16.

Pss. 12:7; 14:5; 22:30; 24:6; 33:11; 45:17; 48:13; 49:11, 19; 61:6; 71:18; 72:5; 73:15; 78:4, 6, 8; 79:13; 85:5; 89:1, 4; 90:1; 95:10; 100:5; 102:12, 18, 24; 105:8; 106:31; 109:13; 112:2; 119:90; 135:13; 145:4, 13; 146:10.

Prov. 27:24; 30:11-14.

Eccles. 1:4.

Isa. 13:20; 34:10, 17; 41:4; 51:8, 9; 53:8; 58:12; 60:15; 61:4.

Jer. 2:31; 7:29; 50:39.

Lam. 5:19.

Dan. 4:3, 34.
Joel 1:3; 2:2; 3:20.
Matt. 1:1, 17; 3:7; 11:16; 12:34, 39, 41, 42, 45; 16:4; 17:17; 23:33, 36; 24:34.
Mark 8:12, 38; 9:19; 13:30.
Luke 1:48, 50; 3:7; 7:31; 9:41; 11:29-32, 50, 51; 16:8; 17:25; 21:32.
Acts 2:40; 8:33; 13:36.
Col. 1:26.
Heb. 3:10.
1 Pet. 2:9.

    Gen´e-sis, the name of the first book of the Bible. The Hebrew name of the book is (in English) "in the beginning," according to the Hebrew custom of naming books by a title composed of their first words. The present name, "Genesis," is Greek, and means generation or creation, because the book tells the story of the Creation. It is the first book of the PENTATEUCH (which see).

    Gen-nes´a-ret, a district adjoining the Sea of Galilee (to which it sometimes gave its name), apparently on the west side and toward the north end; but its situation and extent are uncertain. Many of Christ's miracles were wrought there. Matt. 14:34; Mark 6:53; Luke 5:1.

    Gen-nes´a-ret, Lake of. See GALILEE, SEA OF.

    Gen´tiles was the name by which the Jews designated all people but themselves as idolaters. In the New Testament the name "Greeks" is sometimes used for Gentiles. Acts 16:1; Rom. 1:16.
Also see Gen. 10:5.
Judg. 4:2, 13, 16.
Isa. 11:10; 42:1, 6; 49:6, 22; 54:3; 60:3, 5, 11, 16; 61:6, 9; 62:2; 66:12, 19.
Jer. 4:7; 14:22; 16:19; 46:1.
Lam. 2:9.
Ezek. 4:13.
Hos. 8:8.
Joel 3:9.

Mic. 5:8.
Zech. 1:21.
Mal. 1:11.
Matt. 4:15; 6:32; 10:5, 18; 12:18, 21; 20:19, 25.
Mark 10:33, 42.
Luke 2:32; 18:32; 21:24; 22:25.
John 7:35.
Acts. 4:27; 7:45; 9:15; 10:45; 11:1, 18; 13:42, 46-48; 14:2, 5, 27; 15:3, 7, 12, 14, 17, 19, 23; 18:6; 21:11, 19, 21, 25; 22:21; 26:17, 20, 23; 28:28.
Rom. 1:13; 2:9, 10, 14, 24; 3:9, 29; 9:24, 30; 11:11-13, 25; 15:9-12, 16, 18, 27; 16:4.
1 Cor. 5:1; 10:20, 32; 12:2, 13.
Gal. 2:2, 8, 12, 14, 15; 3:14.
Eph. 2:11; 3:1, 6, 8; 4:17.
Col. 1:27.
1 Thess. 2:16; 4:5.
1 Tim. 2:7; 3:16.
2 Tim. 1:11; 4:17.
1 Pet. 2:12; 4:3.
3 John 7.
Rev. 11:2.

    Ge-nu´bath, son of Hadad the Edomite, who was an adversary of Solomon. 1 Kings 11:20.

    Ge´ra (*enmity*). [1] A son or grandson of Benjamin. Gen. 46:21; 1 Chron. 8:3, 5, 7. [2] A Benjamite, the father of Ehud. Judg. 3:15. [3] A Benjamite, the father of Shimei. 2 Sam. 16:5; 1 Kings 2:8.

    Ge´rah. This (which perhaps was properly a weight, not a coin) was the twentieth part of the shekel of the sanctuary, and was worth about three cents. Exod. 30:13; Ezek. 45:12. See WEIGHTS.

    Ge´rar (*circle*), a city belonging to the Canaanites which was afterward the residence of the kings of the Philistines. Gen. 10:19; 2 Chron. 14:13, 14.

    Ger´ge-sa, the country of the

Gergesenes, Matt. 8:28, on the south-east of the Sea of Galilee.

Ger´ge-senes, the inhabitants of Gergesa. The country of the Gergesenes was the scene of one of Christ's miracles, Matt. 8:28, in connection with the herd of swine.

Ger´i-zim (*waste places*), Deut. 11:29; Judg. 9:7, a mountain in Ephraim opposite EBAL. See EBAL AND GERIZIM.

Gershom, ger´shum (*expulsion*). [1] The eldest son of Moses and Zipporah. Exod. 2:22; 18:3. [2] A corruption of GERSHON. 1 Chron. 6:16, 17; 15:7. [3] A Levite who went up with Ezra from Babylon. Ezra 8:2. [4] Father of Jonathan, a Levite who became priest to a colony of Dan at Laish. Judg. 18:30.

Gershon, ger´shun (*explusion*), a son of Levi. Gen. 46:11; Exod. 6:16. He was founder of the Gershonites.

Gershonites, ger´shun-ites, descendants of Gershon, the son of Levi. Num. 3:21; Josh. 21:33.

Ger´zites. See GEZERITES or GEZRITES.

Ge´sham (*filthy*), 1 Chron. 2:47, a descendant of Judah. Gesham is improperly called GESHAN.

Ge´shem (*rain*), an Arabian who, with Sanballat and Tobiah, endeavored to prevent Nehemiah from rebuilding the walls of Jerusalem. Neh. 2:19; 6:1, 2. Called also GASHMU in Neh. 6:6.

Ge´shur (*bridge*), a district of Syria east of the Jordan. 2 Sam. 3:3; 1 Chron. 2:23.

Gesh´u-ri and the **Gesh´u-rites.** [1] The inhabitants of Geshur. Deut. 3:14; Josh. 12:5. [2] An ancient tribe bordering on the Philistines. Josh. 13:2.

Ge´ther, a son of Aram. Gen. 10:23; 1 Chron. 1:17.

Geth-sem´a-ne (*oil-press*), Matt. 26:36; Mark 14:32, an olive grove, called a garden, situated at the foot of the Mount of Olives, a little east of the brook Kedron and near Jerusalem. It was frequently visited by Christ and his disciples, and was the scene of his agony the last night before his crucifixion, and of his betrayal by Judas.

Ge-u´el (*God of salvation*), one of the men sent by Moses to search the land of Canaan. Num. 13:15.

Ge´zer (*a precipice*), a royal city of the Canaanites which was in Ephraim, and was afterward assigned to the Levites. Josh. 10:33; Judg. 1:29.

Ge´zer-ites, Gez´rites, or **Ger´zites,** the inhabitants of Gezer, a Canaanitish city. 1 Sam. 27:8.

Ghost, gōst, often used for spirit. In Gen. 25:8 "gave up the ghost" means *expired*; in Matt. 27:50 "yielded up the ghost" should be *gave up his spirit*. HOLY GHOST is the third person in the Holy Trinity. See SPIRIT.

Gi´ah (*waterfall*), a place near Gibeon in Benjamin. 2 Sam. 2:24.

Gi´ant. This word, to which the article *the* is prefixed, has been interpreted as meaning *formidable, heroic, gigantic, shadowy, powerless.* It is properly an appellation of the progenitor of the Rephaim, but it is translated *a giant* because the Rephaim are supposed to have been of gigantic stature. 2 Sam. 21:15; 1 Chron. 20:4.

Gi´ants, a word which has been variously understood, but its proper acceptation seems to be simply men of large stature. Gen. 6:4; Num. 13:33.

Gi´ants. [1] This term is, with doubtful propriety, used in the English Version to denote a people inhabiting some part of the land east of Jordan, and in the west among the Philistines. Deut. 2:11; Josh. 12:4. (The word is sometimes left untranslated. See "Rephaim," Gen. 14:5; 15:20.) [2] It is also, in one or two instances, used as the name of a valley near Jerusalem, more frequently called the Valley of Rephaim, Josh. 15:8; 2 Sam. 5:18; 1 Chron. 11:15; Isa. 17:5.

Gib´bar (*mighty*), an Israelite whose descendants went up from Babylon with Zerubbabel. Ezra 2:20.

Gib´be-thon (*height*), a town in Dan which was assigned as a Levitical city by Joshua, but remained long in possession of the Philistines. Josh. 19:44; 1 Kings 15:27.

Gib´e-a (*hill*), a name in the genealogy of Judah. 1 Chron. 2:49. Probably the name of a place, and not of a person. See GIBEAH, No. 1.

Gib´e-ah (*a hill*). [1] A town in the hill country of Judah. Josh. 15:57. [2] Gibeah of Benjamin. 1 Sam. 13:2. The tribe of Benjamin was nearly destroyed by a dreadful crime of some of its people. See Judg. chapters 19–21. This town is generally considered to be the same as Gibeah of Saul. [3] Gibeah of Saul, 1 Sam. 10:26; 11:4, the home of Saul, is held by many authorities to be the same as Gibeah of Benjamin. [4] Gibeah in Kirjath-jearim; doubtless a hill in that city. 2 Sam. 6:3, 4. [5] Gibeah in the field. Judg. 20:31. It was probably same as GEBA. [6] Gibeah-haaraloth, in the marginal notes, Josh. 5:3. See GILGAL.

Gib´e-ath (*hill*), Josh. 18:28, probably same as GIBEAH OF BENJAMIN, GIBEAH, No. 2.

Gib´e-ath-ite, an inhabitant of Gibeah. 1 Chron. 12:3.

Gib´e-on (*hill*), a city of the Hivites, whose inhabitants by a stratagem made peace with Joshua. It afterward belonged to Benjamin and was made a Levitical city. It is memorable for many important events recorded in the Bible, including the battle of the Israelites under Joshua with the five kings, during which "the sun

stood still upon Gibeon." Josh. 10:12, 13. Also see Josh. 9:3, 17; 10:1, 2, 4–6, 10, 41; 11:19; 18:25; 21:17.
2 Sam. 2:12, 13, 16, 24; 3:30; 20:8; 21:1–4, 9.
1 Kings 3:4, 5; 9:2.
1 Chron. 8:29; 9:35; 14:16; 16:39; 21:29.
2 Chron. 1:3, 13.
Neh. 3:7; 7:25.
Isa. 28:21.
Jer. 28:1; 41:12, 16.

Gib´e-on-ites, the inhabitants of Gibeon. 2 Sam. 21:1; Neh. 3:7.

Gib´lites, inhabitants of Gebal, a city near the coast of the Great (or Mediterranean) Sea, not far from Zidon. Josh. 13:5.

Gid-dal´ti (*I have magnified*), a son of Heman. 1 Chron. 25:4, 29.

Gid´del (*very great*). [1] One of the Nethinims whose descendants were among those that went up from Babylon with Zerubbabel. Ezra 2:47; Neh. 7:49. [2] A servant of Solomon whose descendants went up from Babylon with Zerubbabel. Ezra 2:56; Neh. 7:58.

Gid´e-on (*hewer*), an Israelite of Manasseh who defeated the Midianites and delivered Israel from the oppression under which they had been kept for seven years by them. He was also called JERUB-BAAL (*a contender against Baal*), because he had thrown down the altar of Baal. He was the fifth judge of Israel, held that office forty years, and was one of her greatest rulers.
Judg. 6:11, 13, 19, 22, 24, 27, 29, 34, 36, 39; 7:1, 2, 4, 5, 7, 13–15, 18–20, 24, 25; 8:4, 7, 11, 13, 21–24, 27, 28, 30, 32, 33, 35.

Gid-e-o´ni, a Benjamite, the father of Abidan. Num. 1:11; 10:24.

Gi´dom (*desolation*), a place in Benjamin where the Benjamites were defeated by the Israelites, so that only six hundred of the tribe were left. Judg. 20:45.

Gier-Eagle, jeer´-ea-gle, the Egyptian vulture, a comparatively small bird, very useful as a scavenger, and still common in Egypt and Palestine. In Lev. 11:18; Deut. 14:17 it is mentioned as unclean.

Gifts of many kinds and for various purposes have always been common in the East. The word is used in Eph. 4:8, 11, 12 to describe the graces or qualities with which Christ endues his disciples.
Also see Gen. 25:6; 34:12.
Exod. 23:8; 28:38.
Lev. 23:38.
Num. 8:19; 18:6, 7, 11, 29.
Deut. 16:19.
2 Sam. 8:2, 6; 19:42.
1 Chron. 18:2, 6.
2 Chron. 19:7; 21:3; 26:8; 32:23.
Esther 2:18; 9:22.
Pss. 45:12; 68:18; 72:10.
Prov. 6:35; 15:27; 17:8, 23; 18:16; 19:6; 21:14; 25:14; 29:4.
Eccles. 3:13; 5:19; 7:7.
Isa. 1:23.
Ezek. 16:33; 20:26, 31, 39; 22:12; 46:16, 17.
Dan. 2:6, 48; 5:17.
Matt. 2:11; 5:23, 24; 7:11; 8:4; 15:5; 23:18, 19.
Mark 7:11.
Luke 11:13; 21:1, 5.
John 4:10.
Acts 2:38; 8:20; 10:45; 11:17.
Rom. 1:11; 5:15-18; 6:23; 11:29; 12:6.
1 Cor. 1:7; 7:7; 12:1, 4, 9, 28, 30, 31; 13:2; 14:1, 12.
2 Cor. 1:11; 8:4; 9:15.
Eph. 2:8; 3:7; 4:7.
Phil. 4:17.
1 Tim. 4:14.
2 Tim. 1:6.
Heb. 2:4; 5:1; 6:4; 8:3, 4; 9:9; 11:4.
James 1:17.
1 Pet. 4:10.
Rev. 11:10.

Gihon (*stream*). [1] The name of one of the rivers of Eden. Gen. 2:13. [2] The name of a place near Jerusalem where there was a pool or watercourse. 1 Kings 1:33; 2 Chron. 32:30.

Gil´a-lai (*rolling*), one of the priests who officiated in the ceremony of purifying the people, the gates, and the walls of Jerusalem. Neh. 12:36.

Gil-bo´a or **Gil´bo-a** (*bubbling fountain*), a mountainous district in Manasseh west of Jordan (or of Issachar), where Saul was defeated and slain by the Philistines. 1 Sam. 28:4; 2 Sam. 21:12.

Gil´e-ad (*rocky*). [1] An extensive and mountainous district which formed the chief part of Manasseh east of Jordan and of Gad. Mount Gilead generally refers to that part of the district which lay in Manasseh, north of the river or brook Jabbok. When Gilead alone is used the whole district is commonly meant. The word sometimes means the inhabitants of GILEAD. [2] A grandson of Manasseh. Num. 26:29; Josh. 17:1. [3] The father of Jephthah, one of the judges of Israel. Judg. 11:1, 2. [4] One of the chiefs of the families of Gad. 1 Chron. 5:14.
Also see Gen. 31:21, 23, 25; 37:25.
Num. 26:30; 27:1; 32:1, 26, 29, 39, 40; 36:1.
Deut. 2:36; 3:10, 12, 13, 15, 16; 4:43; 34:1.
Josh. 12:2, 5; 13:11, 25, 31; 17:3, 5, 6; 20:8; 21:38; 22:9, 13, 15, 32.
Judg. 5:17; 7:3; 10:4, 8, 17, 18; 11:5, 7-11, 29; 12:4, 5, 7; 20:1.
1 Sam. 13:7.
2 Sam. 2:9; 17:26; 24:6.

1 Kings 4:13, 19; 17:1; 22:3.
2 Kings 10:33; 15:29.
1 Chron. 2:21-23; 5:9, 10, 16; 6:80; 7:14, 17; 26:31; 27:21.
Pss. 60:7; 108:8.
Song of Sol. 4:1; 6:5.
Jer. 8:22; 22:6; 46:11; 50:19.
Ezek. 47:18.
Hos. 6:8; 12:11.
Amos 1:3, 13.
Obad. :19.
Mic. 7:14.
Zech. 10:10.

Gil´e-ad-ites, a family among the Israelites which sprang from Gilead, the grandson of Manasseh. Num. 26:29; Judg. 10:3.

Gil´gal (*rolled*). [1] A place on the west side of Jordan, not far from Jericho, in Benjamin, and where the Israelites first encamped after miraculously passing over Jordan. Josh. 3:13-17. It was the resting-place of the Tabernacle for some time, and many important events recorded in the Bible took place there. [2] A place supposed to have been in the west part of Canaan, in the territory afterward possessed by the tribe of Dan; but it seems not quite certain that this Gilgal was not, as well as the other, in the east part of the land, near the Jordan. Josh. 12:23. [3] It is apparently agreed among the authorities of the present day that there was a place called Gilgal near the sea, a little to the north of Joppa, and to this reference is supposed to be made in Josh. 9:6; 10:6, 7, 9, 15, 43. [4] Some think another place bore the same name, Gilgal, about twelve miles south of Ebal and Gerizim, and that this is the place referred to in 2 Kings 2:1; 4:38. Also see Deut. 11:30.
Josh 4:19, 20; 5:9, 10; 14:6; 15:7.
Judg. 2:1; 3:19.

1 Sam. 7:16; 10:8; 11:14, 15; 13:4, 7, 8, 12, 15; 15:12, 21, 33.
2 Sam. 19:15, 40.
Neh. 12:29.
Hos. 4:15; 9:15; 12:11.
Amos 4:4; 5:5.
Mic. 6:5.

Gi´loh (*circle*), a town in the mountainous district of Judah. Josh. 15:21; 2 Sam. 15:12.

Gi´lo-nite, a native or an inhabitant of Giloh. 2 Sam. 15:12; 23:34.

Gim´zo (*sycamore*), a town in the north of Judah. 2 Chron. 28:18.

Gin, in Amos 3:5, means trap.

Gi´nath (*protection*), an Israelite whose son Tibni contested with Omri for the throne of Israel. 1 Kings 16:21, 22.

Gin´ne-tho or **Gin´ne-thon** (*great protection*), one of the princes or priests who sealed the covenant made by Nehemiah and the people to serve the Lord. Neh. 10:6; 12:4.

Gir´dles of various forms were worn by the Hebrews to confine their garments, which were loose and flowing, about the waist and to serve as a pouch in which to carry small articles. A girdle, when closely bound about the loins, was thought to increase the power of endurance. Girdles of fine quality were worn by the priests.
Exod. 28:4, 8, 27, 28, 39, 40; 29:5, 9; 39:5, 20, 21, 29.
Lev. 8:7, 13; 16:4.
1 Sam. 18:4.
2 Sam. 18:11; 20:8.
1 Kings 2:5.
2 Kings 1:8.
Job 12:18.
Ps. 109:19.
Prov. 31:24.
Isa. 3:24; 5:27; 11:5; 22:21.
Jer. 13:1, 2, 4, 6, 7, 10, 11.

Ezek. 23:15.

Matt. 3:4.

Mark 1:6.

Acts 21:11.

Rev. 1:13; 15:6.

Gir´ga-shites or **Gir´ga-sites,** a people descended from Canaan, the son of Ham. They are named in Gen. 15:21 among the nations whose land the posterity of Abraham should possess, and Josh. 24:11 mentioned them as one of the nations that fought against Israel. They are supposed to have lived on the east side of the Sea of Galilee. Gen. 10:16; Deut. 7:1; Josh. 3:10.

Gis´pa (*listening*), a Jew who was set over the Nethinims when the Jewish polity was restored by Nehemiah. Neh. 11:21.

Git´tah-he´pher, a town in Zebulun. It is called GATH-HEPHER in 2 Kings 14:25, which is apparently the proper name. Josh. 19:13.

Git´ta-im (*two wine-presses*), a town of Benjamin. 2 Sam. 4:3; Neh. 11:33.

Git´tites, the inhabitants of GATH. Josh. 13:3; 2 Sam. 6:10.

Git´tith (*from Gath*), a word generally regarded as denoting a musical instrument—but of what kind is uncertain—which was used at Gath, or a peculiar musical instrument used at the gathering of the vintage. Pss. 8, 81, 84, titles.

Gi´zo-nite, the patronymic applied to some of the valiant men of David's army. 1 Chron. 11:34.

Giz´rites. See GEZRITES.

Glass of some kind, probably semi-transparent, was made in very ancient times, and does not seem to have been used at that time for windows or mirrors, but for cups, bottles, vases, etc. It was made in Egypt as early as the exodus, and was doubtless known to the Jews. The "looking-glasses" mentioned in Exod. 38:8; Job 37:18 were made of polished metal. Many specimens of them are now in the British Museum. One of this kind is probably referred to in James 1:23 and in 1 Cor. 13:12 ("mirror" in the Revised Version).

Glis´ter-ing, in Luke 9:29 is rendered "dazzling" in the Revised Version.

Glean´ing. The poor had the right, under Mosaic law, to glean in harvest and vintage. Lev. 19:9, 10; Deut. 24:19-21. Ruth gleaned in the field of Boaz. Ruth 2:3.

Glede, in Deut. 14:13, an unclean bird of prey, probably means the buzzard, of which there are three kinds in Palestine.

Glo´ry, Glo´ri-fy. The glory of God refers to the peculiar and absolute perfection of all the divine attributes. To glorify is to exalt or make glorious.

Gen. 31; 45.

Exod. 8; 16; 24; 28; 29; 33; 40.

Lev. 9.

Num. 14; 16; 20.

Deut. 5; 33.

Josh. 7.

1 Sam 2; 4; 6.

1 Kings 8.

2 Kings 14.

1 Chron. 16; 22; 29.

2 Chron. 5; 7.

Esther 5.

Job 19; 29; 39; 40.

Pss. 3; 4; 8; 16; 19; 21; 22; 24; 29; 30; 45; 49; 50; 57; 62–64; 72; 73; 78; 79; 84–86; 89; 90; 96; 97; 102; 104–106; 108; 113; 115; 138; 145; 148; 149.

Prov. 3; 4; 16; 17; 19; 20; 25; 28.

Isa. 2–6; 8; 10; 13; 14; 16; 17; 20–25; 28; 35; 40–43; 45; 46; 48; 58–63; 66.

Jer. 2; 4; 9; 13; 14; 22; 30; 48.

Ezek. 1; 3; 8–11; 20; 24–26; 31; 39; 43; 44.

Dan. 2; 4; 5; 7; 11.

Hos. 4; 9; 10.

Mic. 1; 2.
Nah. 2.
Hab. 2; 3.
Hag. 2.
Zech. 2; 6; 11; 12.
Mal. 2.
Matt. 4–6; 16; 19; 24; 25.
Mark 8; 10; 13.
Luke 2; 4; 9; 12; 17; 19; 21; 24.
John 1; 2; 7; 8; 11–13; 16; 17; 21.
Acts 7; 12; 22.
Rom. 1–6; 8; 9; 11; 15; 16.
1 Cor. 1–4; 6; 9–11; 15.
2 Cor. 1; 3–5; 8–12.
Gal. 1; 5; 6.
Eph. 1; 3.
Phil. 1–4.
Col. 1; 3.
1 Thess. 2.
2 Thess. 1; 2.
1 Tim. 1; 3.
2 Tim. 2; 4.
Heb. 1–3; 9; 13.
James 2; 3.
1 Pet. 1; 2; 4; 5.
2 Pet. 1; 3.
Jude :24, 25.
Rev. 1; 4; 5; 7; 11; 14–16; 18; 19; 21.

Gnash, nash, **Gnashing,** nash'ing, grinding the teeth together in anguish or despair. Ps. 112:10; Matt. 8:12.

Gnat, nat, a word not found in the Old Testament. In Matt. 23:24 "strain at a gnat" means strain *out* a gnat, referring to the practice of straining wine before drinking, to avoid a breach of the ceremonial law, Lev. 11, concerning unclean things. Gnats are great pests on marshy land in Egypt and Palestine.

Go about, in John 7:19, 20, etc., means to "seek."

Go beyond, in 1 Thess. 4:6, means over-reach or cheat.

Go to, in Gen. 11:3, 4, 7, is used as an exhortation, and in Eccles. 2:1; Isa. 5:5; James 4:13; 5:1, a request for attention.

Goad, in Judg. 3:31; Eccles. 12:11, means a pole about two or three yards long with a sharp point on one end. It was used in guiding oxen and in urging them on. In Acts 26:14 the word *pricks* is used for *goads* in the expression concerning Saul (afterward Paul), "hard for thee to kick against the pricks."

Go'ath (*constance*), a place near Jerusalem. Jer. 31:39.

Goats in ancient times were among the chief possessions of rich people. Gen. 27:9. Their flesh and milk were used as food. They were regarded as clean for sacrifice, and on the Day of Atonement goats were used exclusively. Lev. 16:5-28. Goats' hair was used for weaving into cloth and the skins were made into bottles, etc. Several kinds of goats are kept in Palestine. The common goat of Palestine has very long hanging ears, and its horns are curved backward. Goats having long silky hair are referred to in Song of Sol. 4:1; 6:5. The wild goat is mentioned in 1 Sam. 24:2; Ps. 104:18; Job 39:1, etc., and resembles the chamois of the Alps. It is found among the high hills. The SCAPEGOAT is noticed in Lev. 16:8-26, and was used on the Day of Atonement. Two goats were set apart on that day, one of which was sacrificed to the Lord for a sin-offering; the other was the scapegoat. The high-priest laid his hands on its head, confessed "all the iniquities of the children of Israel," Lev. 16:21, and sent it away into the wilderness. The sins of the people were considered as transferred to the scapegoat, which became a type of Christ, who bore "the iniquities of us all." Isa. 53:6.

Also see Gen. 15:9; 27:16; 30:32, 33, 35;

31:38; 32:14; 37:31.

Exod. 12:5; 25:4; 26:7; 35:6, 23, 26; 36:14.

Lev. 1:10; 3:12; 4:23, 24, 28; 5:6; 7:23; 9:3, 15; 10:16; 17:3; 22:19, 27; 23:19.

Num. 7:16, 17, 22, 23, 28, 29, 34, 35, 40, 41, 46, 47, 52, 53, 58, 59, 64, 65, 70, 71, 76, 77, 82, 83, 87, 88; 15:24, 27; 18:17; 28:15, 22, 30; 29:5, 11, 16, 19, 25, 28, 22, 31, 34, 38; 31:20.

Deut. 14:4, 5; 32:14.

1 Sam. 19:13, 16; 25:2.

2 Chron. 17:11; 29:21, 23.

Ezra 6:17; 8:35.

Pss. 50:9, 13; 66:15.

Prov. 27:26, 27; 30:31.

Isa. 1:11; 34:6;

Jer. 50:8; 51:40.

Ezek. 27:21; 34:17; 39:18; 43:22, 25; 45:23.

Dan. 8:5, 8; 8:21.

Zech. 10:3.

Matt. 25:32, 33.

Heb. 9:12, 13, 19; 10:4.

Gob (*a pit*), a place, probably in the west of Judah, where several battles took place, in the time of David, between the Israelites and the Philistines. 2 Sam. 21:18, 19.

Gob'let. See Cup.

God (*Good*). There are four words used in the Hebrew which are translated *God*. [**1**] Adonai. [**2**] El. [**3**] Elohim. [**4**] Yehovah. The first and last are used exclusively with reference to the true God. The second and third are employed to designate the true God and also the false gods of the heathen. (The word "Zur" (*a rock*) is translated *God* in Isa. 44:8 and Hab. 1:12, but this is altogether exceptional.)

Also see Gen. 1–9; 14–17; 19–22; 24–28; 30–33; 35; 39–46; 48–50.

Exod. 1–10; 12–24; 29; 31; 32; 34; 35.

Lev. 2; 4; 10; 11; 18–26.

Num. 6; 10–12; 14–16; 20–25; 27; 33.

Deut. 1–33.

Josh. 1–4; 7–10; 13; 14; 18; 22–24.

Judg. 1–11; 13; 15; 16; 17; 18; 20; 21.

Ruth 1; 2.

1 Sam. 1–20; 22; 23; 25; 26; 28–30.

2 Sam. 2; 3; 5–7; 9; 10; 12; 14–16; 18; 19; 21–24.

1 Kings 1–5; 8–22.

2 Kings 1; 2; 4–11; 13; 14; 16–23.

1 Chron. 4–6; 9; 10–17; 19; 21–26; 28; 29.

2 Chron. 1–11; 13–36.

Ezra 1–10.

Neh. 1; 2; 4–13.

Job 1–6; 8–13; 15; 16; 18–25; 27–29; 31–40.

Pss. 3–5; 7; 9; 10; 13; 14; 16–20; 22; 24; 25; 27; 29–31; 33; 35–38; 40–92; 94; 95–100; 102; 104–109; 113–116; 118; 119; 122; 123; 132; 135; 136; 138–141; 143–147; 149; 150.

Prov. 2; 3; 21; 25; 26; 30.

Eccles. 1–3; 5–9; 11; 12.

Isa. 1–3; 5; 7–10; 12–14; 17; 21; 22; 24–26; 28–31; 35–38; 40–46; 48–62; 64–66.

Jer. 1–5; 7–11; 13–16; 19; 21–35; 37–40; 42–46; 48–51.

Lam. 3.

Ezek. 1–18; 20–40; 43–48.

Dan. 1–6; 9–11.

Hos. 1–9; 11–14.

Joel 1–3.

Amos 1–9.

Obad. 1.

Jon. 1–4.

Mic. 1; 3–7.

Nah. 1.

Hab. 1; 3.

Zeph. 1–3.

Hag. 1.

Zech. 6–14.
Mal. 1–3.
Matt. 1–6; 8; 9; 12; 14–16; 19; 21–23; 26; 27.
Mark 1–5; 7–16.
Luke 1–24.
John 1; 3–14; 16; 17; 19–21.
Acts 1–24; 26–28.
Rom. 1–16.
1 Cor. 1–12; 14–16.
2 Cor. 1–13.
Gal. 1–6.
Eph. 1–6.
Phil. 1–4.
Col. 1–4.
1 Thess. 1–5.
2 Thess. 1–3.
1 Tim 1–6.
2 Tim. 1–4.
Titus 1–3.
Philem. 3, 4.
Heb. 1–13.
James 1–4.
1 Pet. 1–5.
2 Pet. 1–3.
1 John 1–5.
2 John 3, 9, 10, 11.
3 John 11.
Jude 1, 4, 21, 25.
Rev. 1–22.

God'head, Col. 2:9, the nature or essential being of God. Acts 17:29; Rom. 1:20.

God'li-ness, piety and constant obedience to the commands of God. 2 Pet. 3:11. Godliness, in 1 Tim. 3:16, signifies the substance of revealed religion.
Also see 1 Tim. 2:2, 10; 4:7, 8; 6:3, 5, 6, 11.
2 Tim. 3:5.
Titus 1:1.
2 Pet. 1:3, 6, 7.

Gods. Rulers and judges are called gods in Exod. 22:28; Ps. 82:6; John 10:34

because they represent God.

Gog (*mountain*). [1] A son of Shemaiah, the grandson of Joel, who is named in the genealogy of Reuben, though not enumerated with his sons. 1 Chron. 5:4. [2] The name given by the prophet Ezekiel to the chief of the land of Magog, a region whose situation is supposed to correspond with some part of Tartary or Scythia. Ezek. 38:2; 39:1. The word Gog is also found in Rev. 20:8. See MAGOG.

Go'lan (*circle*), a city of Manasseh beyond Jordan, and which was appointed one of the cities of refuge and allotted to the Levites. Deut. 4:43; Josh. 20:8. It may have been in the center of Gaulanitis.

Gold is first mentioned in Gen. 2:11, 12. Several places are referred to in the Bible as abounding in gold, among which are Ophir, Job 28:16, Raamah and Sheba, Ezek. 27:22, and Parvaim, 2 Chron. 3:6, and it was much used by the Hebrews for the Temple and in other ways. It was very plentiful in the time of David and Solomon. It was not coined until after the reign of King David, but was an article of commerce and was sold by weight.
Also see Gen. 13; 24; 41; 44.
Exod. 3; 11; 12; 25; 26; 28; 30–32; 35–40.
Num. 7; 8; 22; 24; 31.
Deut. 7; 8; 17; 29.
Josh. 6; 7; 22.
Judg. 8.
1 Sam. 6.
2 Sam. 1; 8; 12; 21.
1 Kings 6; 7; 9; 10; 12; 14; 15; 20; 22.
2 Kings 5; 7; 12; 14; 16; 18; 20; 23–25.
1 Chron. 18; 20–22; 28; 29.
2 Chron. 1–5; 8; 9; 12; 13; 15; 16; 21; 24; 25; 32; 36.
Ezra 1; 2; 5; 7; 8.
Neh. 7.

Esther 1; 8.
Job 3; 22; 23; 28; 31; 36; 42.
Pss. 19; 21; 45; 68; 72; 105; 115; 119; 135.
Prov. 3; 8; 11; 16; 17; 20; 22; 25; 27.
Eccles. 2.
Song of Sol. 1; 3; 5.
Isa. 2; 13; 30; 31; 39; 40; 46; 60.
Jer. 4; 10; 52.
Lam. 4.
Ezek. 7:16; 28; 38.
Dan. 2; 3; 5; 10; 11.
Hos. 2; 8.
Joel 3.
Nah. 2.
Hab. 2.
Zeph. 1.
Hag. 2.
Zech. 4; 6; 9; 13; 14.
Mal. 3.
Matt. 2; 10; 23.
Acts 3; 17; 20.
1 Cor. 3.
1 Tim. 2.
2 Tim. 2.
Heb. 9.
James 2; 5.
1 Pet. 1; 3.
Rev. 3; 4; 9; 17; 18; 21.

Gol´den Can´dle-stick. See CANDLE-STICK.

Gol´go-tha (*a skull*), the Hebrew name of the place in which Christ was crucified, translated into Latin in the Vulgate: *Calvaria*. The site is by some supposed to be that on which now stands the church of the Holy Sepulchre. Matt. 27:33; Mark 15:22; John 19:17. See CALVARY.

Go-li´ath (*an exile*), a champion of the Philistines who was slain by David "with a sling and with a stone." 1 Sam. 17:4-51; 21:9; 22:10. Another Goliath was slain by Elhanan, and is mentioned in 2 Sam. 21:19.

Also see 2 Sam. 21:19.
1 Chron. 20:5.

Go´mer (*completion*). [1] A son of Japheth. Gen. 10:2, 3; 1 Chron. 1:5, 6. [2] The people descended from him, who are supposed to have lived on the north side of the Black Sea. Ezek. 38:6. [3] The wife of the prophet Hosea. Hos. 1:3.

Go-mor´rah (*fissure*), one of the boundary cities of the Canaanites, was situated in the plain or valley of Siddim. It is called GOMORRHA in Matt. 10:15; Mark 6:11; Rom. 9:29; 2 Pet. 2:6; Jude 7, and was miraculously destroyed with Sodom by God.

Also see Gen. 10:19; 13:10; 14:2, 8, 10, 11; 18:20; 19:24, 28.
Deut. 29:23; 32:32.
Isa. 1:9, 10; 13:19.
Jer. 23:14; 49:18; 50:40.
Amos 4:11.
Zeph. 2:9.

Good´man of the house, in Matt. 20:11, was a term in common use when the Authorized Version was made, and means master of the house.

Go´pher wood, the material of which Noah's ark was made, is mentioned only in Gen. 6:14. Nothing is known as to the kind of wood referred to. Many think it was *cypress*.

Go´shen. [1] The name of a district of Lower Egypt which lay apparently to the east of the Pelusiac, or eastern branch of the Nile, near to On or Heliopolis, and which Joseph assigned as the residence of his father and his brethren. Gen. 45:10; Exod. 8:22. See EGYPT. [2] A district in the hill country of Judah. It appears to have been a general name for the central part of the territory of the tribe, and perhaps to have been also applied to the south part of Benjamin. Josh. 10:41; 11:16. [3] A town enumerated among the cities of Judah. Josh. 15:51.

Gos′pel, the glad tidings of salvation through Jesus Christ. The *Gospels*, the first four books of the New Testament, were written by the evangelists Matthew, Mark, Luke, and John. Each portrayed the life and character of Christ in the manner natural to himself. They wrote for different classes: Matthew, for the Jews; Mark, for the Romans; Luke, for the Greeks; John, for advanced Christians of all nationalities. Matthew described Christ as the Messiah and king of the Jews; John, as the incarnate Son of God and Redeemer of the world; Mark displays his official and Luke his personal history. These four books together constitute the most important and best attested history. Two (Matthew and John) were written by eye-witnesses of the facts narrated; two by disciples of the apostles (Mark, a disciple of Peter; Luke, a disciple of Paul). See MATTHEW, MARK, LUKE, and JOHN.

Gos′pels, Har′mony of, is an arrangement of the four accounts of the life of Christ (MATTHEW, MARK, LUKE, and JOHN) in such a manner as to show their harmony with each other. The following condensed "Harmony of the Four Gospels" was prepared by William Thomson, D.D., late Lord Archbishop of York, for Smith's "Dictionary of the Bible." It places the events in the life of Christ in the order in which they took place, and gives the parallel passages for each from the separate Gospels. It also shows how the writers of the different Gospels have sometimes corroborated and sometimes supplemented each other.

CONDENSED HARMONY OF THE FOUR GOSPELS

NOTE.—In the following "Condensed Harmony of the Four Gospels," where all the references for any subject are in black-face type, some special difficulty besets the Harmony. When one or more references for any subject are in light-face type, and one or more are in black-face type, the former are given in their proper places, and it is more or less doubtful whether the references in black-face type are to be considered parallel narratives or not.

	Matthew.	Mark.	Luke.	John.
"The Word"	———	———	———	1:1-14
Preface, to Theophilus	———	———	1:1-4	
Annunciation of the Baptist's birth	———	———	1:5-25	
Annunciation of the birth of Jesus	———	———	1:26-38	
Mary visits Elizabeth	———	———	1:39-56	
Birth of John the Baptist	———	———	1:57-80	
Birth of Jesus Christ	1:18-25	———	2:1-7	
Two Genealogies	**1:1-17**	———	**3:23-38**	
The watching Shepherds	———	———	2:8-20	
The Circumcision	———	———	2:21	
Presentation in the Temple	———	———	2:22-38	
The wise men from the East	2:1-12	———	———	
Flight to Egypt	2:13-23	———	2:39	
Disputing with the Doctors	———	———	2:40-52	
Ministry of John the Baptist	3:1-12	1:1-8	3:1-18	1:15-31
Baptism of Jesus Christ	3:13-17	1:9-11	3:21, 22	1:32-34

	Matthew.	Mark.	Luke.	John.
The Temptation	4:1-11	1:12, 13	4:1-13	
Andrew and another see Jesus	——	——	——	1:35-40
Simon, now Cephas	——	——	——	1:41, 42
Philip and Nathanael	——	——	——	1:43-51
The water made wine	——	——	——	2:1-11
Passover (1st) and cleansing the Temple	——	——	——	2:12-22
Nicodemus	——	——	——	2:23-3:21
Christ and John baptizing	——	——	——	3:22-36
The woman of Samaria	——	——	——	4:1-42
John the Baptist in prison	4:12; 14:3	1:14; 6:17	3:19, 20	3:24
Return to Galilee	4:12	1:14, 15	4:14, 15	4:43-45
The synagogue at Nazareth	——	——	4:16-30	
The nobleman's son	——			4:46-54
Capernaum. Four Apostles called	4:18-22	1:16-20	5:1-11	
Demoniac healed there	——	1:21-28	4:31-37	
Simon's wife's mother healed	8:14-17	1:29-34	4:38-41	
Circuit round Galilee	4:23-25	1:35-39	4:42-44	
Healing a leper	8:1-4	1:40-45	5:12-16	
Christ stills the storm	8:18-27	4:35-41	8:22-25	
Demoniacs in the land of Gadarenes	8:28-34	5:1-20	8:26-39	
Jairus's daughter. Woman healed	9:18-26	5:21-43	8:40-56	
Blind men, and demoniac	9:27-34	——	——	
Healing the paralytic	9:1-8	2:1-12	5:17-26	
Matthew the publican	9:9-13	2:13-17	5:27-32	
"Thy disciples fast not"	9:14-17	2:18-22	5:33-39	
Journey to Jerusalem to 2nd Passover	——	——	——	5:1
Pool of Bethesda. Power of Christ	——	——	——	5:2-47
Plucking ears of corn on Sabbath	12:1-8	2:23-28	6:1-5	
The withered hand. Miracles	12:9-21	3:1-12	6:6-11	
The Twelve Apostles	**10:2-4**	3:13-19	6:12-16	
The Sermon on the Mount	**5:1-7:29**	——	6:17-49	
The centurion's servant	8:5-13	——	7:1-10	4:46-54
The widow's son at Nain	——	——	7:11-17	
Messengers from John	11:2-19	——	7:18-35	
Woe to the Cities of Galilee	11:20-24	——	——	
Call to the meek and suffering	11:25-30	——	——	
Anointing the feet of Jesus	——	——	7:36-50	
Second circuit round Galilee	——	——	8:1-3	
Parable of the Sower	13:1-23	4:1-20	8:4-15	
Parable of the Candle Under a Bushel	——	4:21-25	8:16-18	
Parable of the Sower	——	4:26-29	——	
Parable of the Wheat and Tares	13:24-30	——	——	
Parable of the Grain of Mustard-seed	13:31, 32	4:30-32	13:18, 19	
Parable of the Leaven	13:33	——	13:20, 21	
On teaching by parables	13:34, 35	4:33, 34	——	

	Matthew.	Mark.	Luke.	John.
Wheat and tares explained	13:36-43	————	————	
The treasure, the pearl, the net	13:44-52	————	————	
His mother and His brethren	**12:46-50**	**3:31-35**	**8:19-21**	
Reception at Nazareth	13:53-58	6:1-6	————	
Third circuit round Galilee	9:35-38;11:1	6:6	————	
Sending forth of the Twelve	10	6:7-13	9:1-6	
Herod's opinion of Jesus	14:1, 2	6:14-16	9:7-9	
Death of John the Baptist	14:3-12	6:17-29		
Approach of Passover (3rd)	————	————	————	6:4
Feeding of the five thousand	14:13-21	6:30-44	9:10-17	6:1-15
Walking on the sea	14:22-33	6:45-52	————	6:16-21
Miracles in Gennesaret	14:34-36	6:53-56	————	
The bread of life	————	————	————	6:22-65
The washen hands	15:1-20	7:1-23	————	
The Syrophœnician woman	15:21-28	7:24-30	————	
Miracles of healing	15:29-31	7:31-37	————	
Feeding of the four thousand	15:32-39	8:1-9	————	
The sign from heaven	16:1-4	8:10-13	————	
The leaven of the Pharisees	16:5-12	8:14-21	————	
Blind man healed	————	8:22-26	————	
Peter's profession of faith	16:13-19	8:27-29	9:18-20	**6:66-71**
The Passion foretold	16:20-28	8:30-9:1	9:21-27	
The Transfiguration	17:1-9	9:2-10	9:28-36	
Elijah	17:10-13	9:11-13	————	
The lunatic healed	17:14-21	9:14-29	9:37-42	
The Passion again foretold	17:22, 23	9:30-32	9:43-45	
Fish caught for the tribute	17:24-27	————	————	
The little child	18:1-5	9:33-37	9:46-48	
One casting out devils	————	9:38-41	9:49, 50	
Offences	18:6-9	9:42-48	17:2	
The lost sheep	18:10-14	————	15:4-7	
Forgiveness of injuries	18:15-17	————	————	
Binding and loosing	18:18-20	————	————	
Forgiveness. Parable	18:21-35	————	————	
"Salted with fire"	————	9:49, 50	————	
Journey to Jerusalem	————	————	9:51	7:1-10
Fire from heaven	————	————	9:52-56	
Answers to disciples	8:19-22	————	9:57-62	
The Seventy disciples	————	————	10:1-16	
Discussions at Feast of Tabernacles	————	————	————	7:11-53
Woman taken in adultery	————	————	————	8:1-11
Dispute with the Pharisees	————	————	————	8:12-59
The man born blind	————	————	————	9:1-41
The good Shepherd	————	————	————	10:1-21
The return of the Seventy	————	————	10:17-24	

	Matthew.	Mark.	Luke.	John.
The good Samaritan	———	———	10:25-37	
Mary and Martha	———	———	10:38-42	
The Lord's Prayer	6:9-13	———	11:1-4	
Prayer effectual	7:7-11	———	11:5-13	
"Through Beelzebub"	12:22-37	3:20-30	11:14-23	
The unclean spirit returning	12:43-45	———	11:24-28	
The sign of Jonah	12:38-42	———	11:29-32	
The light of the body	5:15; 6:22, 23	———	11:33-36	
The Pharisees	23	———	11:37-54	
What to fear	10:26-33	———	12:1-12	
"Master, speak to my brother"	———	———	12:13-15	
Covetousness	6:25-33	———	12:16-31	
Watchfulness	———	———	12:32-59	
Galileans that perished	———	———	13:1-9	
Woman healed on Sabbath	———	———	13:10-17	
The grain of mustard-seed	13:31, 32	4:30-32	13:18, 19	
The leaven	13:33	———	13:20, 21	
Toward Jerusalem	———	———	13:22	
"Are there few that be saved?"	———	———	13:23-30	
Warning against Herod	———	———	13:31-33	
"O Jerusalem, Jerusalem"	23:37-39	———	13:34, 35	
Dropsy healed on Sabbath-day	———	———	14:1-6	
Choosing the chief rooms	———	———	14:7-14	
Parable of the Great Supper	22:1-14	———	14:15-24	
Following Christ with the Cross	10:37, 38	———	14:25-35	
Parables of Lost Sheep, Piece of Money, Prodigal Son, Unjust Steward, Rich Man and Lazarus	———	———	15, 16	
Offences	18:6-15	———	17:1-4	
Faith and merit	17:20	———	17:5-10	
The ten lepers	———	———	17:11-19	
How the kingdom cometh	———	———	17:20-37	
Parable of the Unjust Judge	———	———	18:1-8	
Parable of the Pharisee and Publican	———	———	18:9-14	
Divorce	19:1-12	10:1-12	———	
Infants brought to Jesus	19:13-15	10:13-16	18:15-17	
The rich man inquiring	19 16-26	10:17-27	18:18-27	
Promises to the disciples	19 27-30	10:28-31	18:28-30	
Laborers in the vineyard	20 1-16			
Death of Christ foretold	20:17-19	10:32-34	18:31-34	
Request of James and John	20:20-28	10:35-45	———	
Blind men at Jericho	20:29-34	10:46-52	18:35-43	
Zacchæus	———	———	19:1-10	
Parable of the Ten Talents	25:14-30	———	19:11-28	
Feast of Dedication	———	———	———	10:22-39

	Matthew.	Mark.	Luke.	John.
Beyond Jordan	——	——	——	10:40-42
Raising of Lazarus	——	——	——	11:1-44
Meeting of the Sanhedrin	——	——	——	11:45-53
Christ in Ephraim	——	——	——	11:54-57
The anointing by Mary	26:6-13	14:3-9	**7:36-50**	12:1-11
Christ enters Jerusalem	21:1-11	11:1-10	19:29-44	12:12-19
Cleansing of the Temple (2nd)	21:12-16	11:15-18	19:45-48	**2:13-22**
The barren fig tree	21:17-22	11:11-14, 19-23		
Pray, and forgive	**6:14, 15**	11:24-26	——	
"By what authority," etc.	21:23-27	11:27-33	20:1-8	
Parable of the Two Sons	21:28-32	——	——	
Parable of the Wicked Husbandmen	21:33-46	12:1-12	20:9-19	
Parable of the Wedding Garment	22:1-14	——	**14:16-24**	
The tribute-money	22:15-22	12:13-17	20:20-26	
The state of the risen	22:23-33	12:18-27	20:27-40	
The great Commandment	22:34-40	12:28-34	——	
David's Son and David's Lord	22:41-46	12:35-37	20:41-44	
Against the Pharisees	23:1-39	12:38-40	20:45-47	
The widow's mite	——	12:41-44	21:1-4	
Christ's second coming	24:1-51	13:1-37	21:5-38	
Parable of the Ten Virgins	25:1-13	——	——	
Parable of the Talents	25:14-30	——	19:11-28	
The Last Judgment	25:31-46	——	——	
Greeks visit Jesus. Voice from Heaven	——	——	——	12:20-36
Reflections of John	——	——	——	12:36-50
Last Passover (4th). Jews conspire	26:1-5	14:1, 2	22:1, 2	
Judas Iscariot	26:14-16	14:10, 11	22:3-6	
Paschal Supper	26:17-29	14:12-25	22:7-23	13:1-35
Contention of the Apostles	——	——	22:24-30	
Peter's fall foretold	26:30-35	14:26-31	22:31-39	13:36-38
Last discourse. The departure; the Comforter	——	——	——	14:1-31
The vine and the branches. Abiding in love	——	——	——	15:1-27
Work of the Comforter in disciples	——	——	——	16:1-33
The prayer of Christ	——	——	——	17:1-26
Gethsemane	26:36-46	14:32-42	22:40-46	18:1
The betrayal	26:47-56	14:43-52	22:47-53	18:2-11
Before Annas (Caiaphas). Peter's denial	26:57, 58, 69-75	14:53, 54, 66-72	22:54-62	18:12-27
Before the Sanhedrin	26:59-68	14:55-65	22:63-71	
Before Pilate	27:1, 2, 11-14	15:1-5	23:1-3	18:28
The Traitor's death	27:3-10	——	——	
Before Herod	——	——	23:4-11	

	Matthew.	Mark.	Luke.	John.
Accusation and Condemnation .... {	27:15-26	15:6-15	23:13-25	18:29-40; 19:1-16
Treatment by the soldiers	27:27-31	15:16-20	**23:36, 37**	19:2, 3
The Crucifixion	27:32-38	15:21-38	23:26-34	19:17-24
The mother of Jesus	———	———	———	19:25-27
Mockings and railings	27:39-44	15:29-32	23:35-39	
The malefactor	———	———	23:40-43	
The death	27:50	15:37	23:46	19:28-30
Darkness and other portents	27:45-53	15:33-38	23:44, 45	
The bystanders	27:54-56	15:39-41	23:47-49	
The side pierced	———	———	———	19:31-37
The burial	27:57-61	15:42-47	23:50-56	19:38-42
The guard of the sepulchre .... {	27:62-66; 28:11-15	———	———	
The Resurrection	28:1-10	16:1-11	24:1-12	20:1-18
Disciples going to Emmaus	———	16:12, 13	24:13-35	
Appearances in Jerusalem	———	16:14-18	24:36-49	20:19-29
At the Sea of Tiberias	———	———	———	21:1-23
On the Mount in Galilee	28:16-20	———	———	
Unrecorded Works .... {	———	———	———	20:30, 31; 21:24, 25
Ascension	———	16:19, 20	24:50-53	

Gourd, gord, a rapidly growing plant with wide leaves common in the East, and used to make a shade for arbors. Jonah 4:6, 7, 9, 10. Another kind of gourd, the fruit of which is poisonous and easily mistaken for a wholesome melon, is mentioned in 2 Kings 4:39.

Gov´er-nor, in James 3:4, means helmsman; in Matt. 2:6 it is a title of Christ.

Go´zan (*food*), a province of Assyria to which Shalmaneser carried some of the people whom he removed out of the country of Israel. 2 Kings 17:6; Isa. 37:12.

Grace, the free and undeserved love and favor of God toward man as a sinner. Gen. 6:8; 19:19; 32:5; 33:8, 10, 15; 34:11; 39:4; 47:25, 29; 50:4.
Exod. 33:12, 13, 16, 17; 34:9.
Num. 32:5.
Judg. 6:17.
Ruth 2:2, 10.

1 Sam. 1:18; 20:3; 27:5.
2 Sam. 14:22; 16:4.
Ezra 9:8.
Esther 2:17.
Pss. 45:2; 84:11.
Prov. 1:9; 3:22, 34; 4:9; 22:11.
Jer. 31:2.
Zech. 4:7; 12:10.
Luke 2:40.
John 1:14, 16, 17.
Acts 4:33; 11:23; 13:43; 14:3, 26; 15:11, 40; 18:27; 20:24, 32.
Rom. 1:5, 7; 3:24; 4:4, 16; 5:2, 15, 17, 20, 21; 6:1, 14, 15; 11:5, 6; 12:3, 6; 15:15; 16:20, 24.
1 Cor. 1:3, 4; 3:10; 10:30; 15:10; 16:23.
2 Cor. 1:2, 12; 4:15; 6:1; 8:1, 6, 7, 9, 19; 9:8, 14; 12:9; 13:14.
Gal. 1:3, 6, 15; 2:9, 21; 5:4; 6:18.
Eph. 1:2, 6, 7; 2:5, 7, 8; 3:2, 7, 8; 4:7, 29; 6:24.

Phil. 1:2, 7; 4:23.
Col. 1:2, 6; 3:16; 4:6, 18.
1 Thess. 1:1; 5:28.
2 Thess. 1:2, 12; 2:16; 3:18.
1 Tim. 1:2, 14; 6:21.
2 Tim. 1:2, 9; 2:1; 4:22.
Titus 1:4; 2:11; 3:7, 15.
Philem. 3, 25.
Heb. 2:9; 4:16; 10:29; 12:15, 28; 13:9, 25.
James 1:11; 4:6.
1 Pet. 1:2, 10, 13; 3:7; 4:10; 5:5, 10, 12.
2 Pet. 1:2; 3:18.
2 John 3.
Jude :4.
Rev. 1:4; 22:21.

Gra´cious, in Prov. 11:16; Jer. 22:23, means courteous and winning.

Grain. See CORN.

Grapes were among the principal productions of Judea. Some localities, such as Eschol, were especially famous for their excellent grapes. Num. 13:23. Grapes, used in various ways, were a common article of food and were made into wine. They are still common in Palestine. See VINE, VINEYARD, and WINE. Also see Gen. 40:10, 11; 49:11.
Lev. 19:10; 25:5, 11.
Num. 6:3; 13:20, 24.
Deut. 23:24; 24:21; 28:30, 39; 32:14, 32.
Judg. 8:2; 9:27.
Neh. 13:15.
Job 15:33.
Song of Sol. 2:13, 15; 7:7, 12.
Isa. 5:2, 4; 17:6; 18:5; 24:13.
Jer. 8:13; 25:30; 31:29, 30; 49:9.
Ezek. 18:2.
Hos. 9:10.
Amos 9:13.
Obad. :5.
Matt. 7:16.
Luke 6:44.
Rev. 14:18.

Grass, a word often used in the Bible to denote herbage in general. Grass and small shrubs of all kinds are still used for fuel in Palestine, as wood is scarce.
Gen. 1:11, 12.
Num. 22:4.
Deut. 11:15; 29:23; 32:2.
2 Sam. 23:4.
1 Kings 18:5.
2 Kings 19:26.
Job 5:25; 6:5; 40:15.
Pss. 37:2; 72:6, 16; 90:5; 92:7; 102:4, 11; 103:15; 104:14; 106:20; 129:6; 147:8.
Prov. 19:12; 27:25.
Isa. 15:6; 35:7; 37:27; 40:6-8; 44:4; 51:12.
Jer. 14:5, 6; 50:11.
Dan. 4:15, 23, 25, 32, 33; 5:21.
Amos 7:2.
Mic. 5:7.
Zech. 10:1.
Matt. 6:30; 14:19.
Mark 6:39.
Luke 12:28.
John 6:10.
James 1:10, 11.
1 Pet. 1:24.
Rev. 8:7; 9:4.

Grass hop-pers were sometimes used as food by the Hebrews. Lev. 11:22. They are a kind of locust, and the original is translated *locust* in 2 Chron. 7:13. They often came to Palestine in very great numbers, and were extremely destructive to vegetation. Also see Num. 13:33.
Judg. 6:5; 7:12.
Job 39:20.
Eccles. 12:5.
Isa. 40:22.
Jer. 46:23.
Amos 7:1.
Nah. 3:17.

Grave, a word frequently employed

by the translators to denote the unseen state of the departed spirits, without any distinction of good and evil. When used in this sense, it is given as the equivalent of three words in the original, meaning —[1] *Sepulchre.* Job. 3:22; Ps. 88:11. [2] *Pit.* Job 33:22. [3] *Hades.* Gen. 37:35; 42:38; 44:29, 31; 1 Sam. 2:6; 1 Kings 2:6; Job 7:9; 14:13; 17:13; 21:13; 24:19; Pss. 6:5; 30:3; 31:17; 49:15; 88:3; 89:48; Eccles. 9:10; Isa. 38:10, 18; Hos. 13:14.

Gra´veth, in Isa. 22:16, means excavateth.

Great Sea, in Num. 34:6; Josh. 1:4, etc., means the Mediterranean Sea.

Greaves, in 1 Sam. 17:6, means armor for the legs.

Gre´cia or **Greece.** It being generally believed that the descendants of Javan, the son of Japheth, peopled the islands of the Ionian Archipelago, the translators of the English Version have sometimes substituted the ordinary for the scriptural name when the country is alluded to. Dan. 8:21; 10:20; 11:2; Zech. 9:13; Acts 20:2. See GREECE.

Gre´cians. [1] The names of the inhabitants of Ionia and the Grecian Islands, whom the Hebrews accounted to be descended from Javan. Joel 3:6. [2] Jews who, dwelling in Greece or a Grecian colony, had in some degree adopted the language and customs of Greece. Acts 6:1; 9:29; 11:20.

Greece or **Hel´las** was in prehistoric times settled by a people of Aryan stock, the Hellenes, allied to the Celts of Western Europe, the Italians of Italy, and the Teutons of Central and Northern Europe. They occupied the mainland of Greece and the islands of the Ægean Sea, and founded flourishing colonies in Gaul, Sicily, and Southern Italy to the west, and in Asia Minor to the east. Alexander the Great made the Greek influence predominant throughout the East. He founded a great empire which reached from the Adriatic Sea in Europe to the Indus River in Asia, though that empire split into many kingdoms immediately after his death, B. C. 323.

At the time of Christ the Greek language was spoken more or less throughout the whole Roman Empire. The Christian congregation of Rome used it till the end of the second century. In Jerusalem Greek was the language in which the Roman and the Jewish authorities communicated with each other. In Asia Minor and even in Syria the Greek language had so completely superseded the vernacular tongues, at least in the cities, that though Hebrew, or rather Aramaic, was the mother-tongue of Paul, since he was born a Jew, Greek was his native tongue, since he was born at Tarsus. Even the fishermen along the Sea of Galilee—John, Peter, etc.—understood and spoke Greek. The importance of this circumstance for the preaching of the gospel can hardly be overestimated.

A center of Greek influence, particularly interesting just in the present connection, was the city of ALEXANDRIA (which see), founded on the Mediterranean shore of Egypt, B. C. 330, by Alexander the Great. He induced a considerable number of Jews to settle in the new city, and the prosperity of that colony as well as the general prosperity of the city soon induced more to come. At the time of Christ Alexandria was one of the greatest Jewish cities in the world, and there the Jews came into daily and most intimate contact with the Greeks. Two remarkable events resulted from this circumstance. One was the translation of the Old Testament into Greek, the SEPTUAGINT, made by seventy (a round number for seventy-two) learned Jews. It was the only medium through which the Greeks obtained or could obtain any idea of the Old Testament. The other was the development of a peculiar combination of Jewish wisdom and Greek philosophy which not only led many Jews and Greeks to accept Christianity, but also had a certain influence on the development of Christianity itself, which otherwise would have been much more difficult. See GRECIA.

Greek. [1] A native of Greece. [2] The language spoken by the Greeks. Luke 23:38; John 19:20; Acts 21:37; Rev. 9:11. Also see Mark 7:26.
John 12:20.
Acts 14:1; 16:1, 3; 17:4, 12; 18:4, 17; 19:10, 17; 20:21; 21:28.
Rom. 1:14, 16; 10:12.
1 Cor. 1:22-24.
Gal. 2:3; 3:28.
Col. 3:11.

Grey´hound, in Prov. 30:31, is rendered in the marginal notes "girt in the loins," or, "a horse." It is generally agreed that "greyhound" is not the meaning of the original word. Many suppose it denotes a "wrestler" girded for the struggle; others consider it to mean the "horse."

Grind´ers, in Eccles. 12:3, means grinding teeth, or double teeth.

Grind´ing. Matt. 24:41; Luke 17:35. See MILL.

Griz´zled, in Gen. 31:10; Zech. 6:3, 6, means black and white mixed in small spots.

Groves were used for the worship of the true God in ancient times. Gen. 21:33.

It afterward became common to plant groves for the worship of idols, and, as these contained images of their gods, the words *grove* and *idol* were used interchangeably, and grove often means an image of a false god.
Also see Exod. 34:13.
Deut. 7:5; 12:3; 16:21.
Judg. 3:7; 6:25, 26, 28, 30.
1 Kings 14:15, 23; 15:13; 16:33; 18:19.
2 Kings 13:6; 17:10, 16; 18:4; 21:3, 7; 23:4, 6, 7, 14, 15.
2 Chron. 14:3; 15:16; 17:6; 19:3; 24:18; 31:1; 33:3, 19; 34:3, 4, 7.
Isa. 17:8; 27:9.
Jer. 17:2.
Mic. 5:14.

Guard´-cham-ber, in 1 Kings 14:28, means the room occupied by the king's guard.

Gud´go-dah, Deut. 10:7, a camping-place of the Israelites; apparently same as HOR-HAGIDGAD.

Guest, gest. See HOSPITALITY.

Guest´-cham-ber, Mark 14:14; Luke 22:11, probably a large unoccupied room, usually in the upper part of the house, used for guests and social meetings.

Guilty, gil´ty, **of Blood,** in Num. 35:27, 31, means guilty of shedding blood.

Guilty, gil´ty, **of Death,** in Matt. 26:66; Mark 14:64, means deserving of death.

Gu´ni (*protected*). [1] A son of Naphtali. Gen. 46:24; Num. 26:48. [2] An Israelite of Gad. 1 Chron. 5:15.

Gu´nites, the title of a family descended from Guni. Num. 26:48.

Gur (*lion's whelp*), the name of an ascent or of a place at the top of an ascent, in Issachar. 2 Kings 9:27.

Gur-ba´al (*dwelling of Baal*), the name of a place in Arabia whose situation is not known. 2 Chron. 26:7.

H

Ha-a-hash´ta-ri (*the courier*), a son of Asshur. 1 Chron. 4:6.

Habaiah, ha-ba´ya (*Jehovah is protection*), a priest whose descendants went up from Babylon with Zerubbabel, but, being unable to establish their genealogy, were put out from the priesthood. Ezra 2:61; Neh. 7:63.

Hab´ak-kuk or **Ha-bak´kuk** (*embrace*), one of the twelve minor prophets, lived in the reign of Jehoiakim or of Josiah, and was a contemporary of Jeremiah, but nothing further is known of him personally. Hab. 1:1; 3:1.

Hab´ak-kuk or **Ha-bak´kuk, the Book of,** consists of three chapters. The first is a prediction of the invasion by the Chaldeans; the second, a prediction of the punishment awaiting the Chaldeans themselves; and the third, a sublime psalm on the majesty of God.

Hab-a-zi-ni´ah, a Rechabite, the grandfather of Jaazaniah. Jer. 35:3.

Habergeon, ha-ber´je-un, an ancient piece of armor, called also COAT OF MAIL, covered the body from the neck to the middle, and was made of thick hide, of many thicknesses of quilted linen, of plates of metal arranged like fish-scales, or of small rings linked together. Neh. 4:16; Job 41:26.

Ha´bor (*united*), a place in Assyria where Shalmaneser settled part of the Israelites whom he had carried away captives. 2 Kings 17:6. See CHEBAR.

Hach-a-li´ah (*Jehovah is hidden*), father of Nehemiah, who in the time of Artaxerxes, king of Persia, went to succor the distressed Jews in Jerusalem. Neh. 1:1; 10:1.

Hach´i-lah (*drought*), a hill in the south of Judah. 1 Sam. 23:19; 26:3.

Hach´mo-ni (*the wise*), father of Jehiel. 1 Chron. 27:32.

Hach´mo-nite, son of Hachmoni. 1 Chron. 11:11.

Ha´dad (*sharpness*), a son of Ishmael, 1 Chron. 1:30, called HADAR in Gen. 25:15.

Ha´dad (*brave*), a different name (in Hebrew) from the preceding. [1] An early king of the Edomites. Gen. 36:35; 1 Chron. 1:46. [2] Another king of Edom, 1 Chron. 1:50, 51, called HADAR in Gen. 36:39. [3] One of the royal house of Edom. 1 Kings 11:14, 25.

Had-ad-e´zer or **Had-ar-e´zer** (*Hadad's help*), a king of Zobah who was defeated by David. 2 Sam. 8:3; 1 Kings 11:23; 1 Chron. 18:3.

Ha-dad-rim´mon (*Hadad of Rimmon*), a town near Megiddo in Issachar. Zech. 12:11.

Ha´dar (*room*). [1] A son of Ishmael, the son of Hagar, Gen. 25:15, called HADAD in 1 Chron. 1:30. [2] A king of Edom, Gen. 36:39, called HADAD in 1 Chron. 1:50, 51.

Had-ar-e´zer (*Hadar's help*). See HADADEZER.

Had´a-shah or **Ha-da´shah** (*new*), a city enumerated among those of Judah in the plain country. Josh. 15:37.

Ha-das´sah (*myrtle*), same as ESTHER (which see); a Jewess, the cousin of Mordecai, who became queen of Ahasuerus, king of Persia. Esther 2:7

Ha-dat´tah (*new*), a city of Judah. Josh. 15:25.

Ha´des, the under world, or realm of the dead. See HELL.

Ha´did (*peak*), a city of Benjamin. Ezra 2:33; Neh. 7:37.

Had′la-i (*lax*), the father of Amasa. 2 Chron. 28:12.

Ha-do′ram (*Hadar is high*). [1] A son of Joktan, of the family of Shem. Gen. 10:27; 1 Chron. 1:21. [2] A son of Tou, king of Hamath in the time of David. 1 Chron. 18:10. [3] An Israelite over the tribute in the time of Rehoboam. 2 Chron. 10:18.

Hadrach, ha′drak (*periodical return*), a place or district near Damascus. Zech. 9:1.

Haft, in Judg. 3:22, means handle.

Ha′gab (*bent*), one of the Nethinims whose posterity went up with Zerubbabel to Jerusalem. Ezra 2:46.

Hag′a-ba, a Nethinim whose posterity went up with Zerubbabel from Babylon. Neh. 7:48. Called HAGABAH in Ezra 2:45.

Ha′gar (*wandering*), the Egyptian maid-servant of Sarai (afterward Sarah), the wife of Abram (afterward Abraham). Hagar became the mother of Ishmael by Abram (afterward Abraham), and is mentioned in Gal. 4:24, 25 under the name AGAR, allegorically. Hagar's history is given in Gen. 16, 21, and 25:12.

Ha′gar-enes or **Ha′gar-ites,** a nation who dwelt apparently to the eastward of Gilead and were subdued by the tribes of Israel that settled in that land. 1 Chron. 5:10; Ps. 83:6.

Ha′ger-ite, usually understood to be a Gentile appellation denoting the same as HAGARITES. It is used to designate the origin of JAZIZ. 1 Chron. 27:31.

Hag′ga-i (*festive*), one of the twelve minor prophets, who lived at the time when the Jews returned to Jerusalem after the seventy years' captivity in Babylon. He exercised the prophetic office during the second year of the reign of Darius Hystaspes, Hag. 1:1, B. C. 520, but of his life nothing further is known.
Also see Ezra 5:1; 6:14.
Hag. 1:3, 12, 13; 2:1, 10, 13, 14, 20.

Hag′ga-i, the Book of, has reference principally to the rebuilding of the Temple and the glory which awaited it. The construction, begun by Zerubbabel, had been interrupted by a royal decree, but the accession of a new king brought with it the cancelling of that decree, and then the Jews showed themselves lukewarm in their ardor.

Hag′ge-ri (*wanderer*), father of Mibhar, one of David's valiant men. 1 Chron. 11:38.

Hag′gi (*festive*), a son of Gad. Gen. 46:16; Num. 26:15.

Hag′gi-ah, a descendant of Merari, the son of Levi. 1 Chron. 6:30.

Hag′gites, descendants of Haggi, a son of Gad. Num. 26:15.

Hag′gith (*festive*), a wife of David and mother of Adonijah. 2 Sam. 3:4; 1 Chron. 3:2.

Ha′i (*the heap*), a royal city of the Canaanites in the land which afterward fell to Benjamin. Gen. 12:8; 13:3. It is generally called AI.

Hail, in Luke 1:28, is a word used in salutation, and is the expression of a desire for the health and prosperity of the person to whom it is addressed. It was used in derision in reference to Christ in Matt. 27:29; Mark 15:18; John 19:3, and was spoken by Judas to Christ when he betrayed him. Matt. 26:49.

Hail′stones. One of the plagues of Egypt was a storm of hail. It is described in Exod. 9:23-26. A storm of hailstones was also used for the destruction of the Canaanites who fought against Joshua. Josh. 10:11.

Hair. In Egypt hair-cutting and shaving

were practiced, except in times of mourning. Joseph shaved himself. Gen. 41:14. The Hebrew men usually wore their hair moderately long and had full beards. The Nazarites allowed their hair to grow uncut. See NAZARITE.

Also see Gen. 42:38; 44:29, 31.
Exod. 25:4; 26:7; 35:6, 23, 26; 36:14.
Lev. 13:3, 4, 10, 20, 21, 25, 26, 30-32, 36, 37, 40, 41; 14:8, 9.
Num. 6:5, 18, 19; 31:20.
Deut. 32:25.
Judg. 16:22; 20:16.
1 Sam. 14:45; 19:13, 16.
2 Sam. 14:11, 26.
1 Kings 1:52.
Ezra 9:3.
Neh. 13:25.
Job 4:15.
Pss. 40:12; 69:4.
Song of Sol. 4:1; 6:5; 7:5.
Isa. 3:24; 7:20; 46:4; 50:6.
Jer. 7:29.
Ezek. 5:1; 16:7.
Dan. 3:27; 4:33; 7:9.
Hos. 7:9.
Matt. 3:4; 5:36; 10:30.
Mark 1:6; 21:18.
Luke 7:38, 44; 12:7.
John 11:2; 12:3.
Acts 27:34.
1 Cor. 11:14, 15.
1 Tim. 2:9.
1 Pet. 3:3.
Rev. 1:14; 6:12; 9:8.

Hak´ka-tan (*the little one*), the father of Johanan, one of the heads of families who went up from Babylon. Ezra 8:12.

Hak´koz (*the nimble*), one of the priests to whom the charges of the sanctuary were distributed by lot. 1 Chron. 24:10.

Ha-ku´phah (*incitement*), a Nethinim

whose descendants went up from Babylon after the captivity. Ezra 2:51; Neh. 7 53.

Ha´lah, a province of Assyria to which part of the Israelites were transported by Shalmaneser. 2 Kings 17:6; 1 Chron. 5:26.

Ha´lak, Mount, marked the southern limit of Joshua's conquests. Josh. 11:17; 12:7.

Hale, in Luke 12:58, means haul or drag.

Hal´hul (*trembling*), a city of Judah. Josh. 15:58.

Ha´li (*necklace*), one of the border cities of Asher. Josh. 19:25.

Ha´ling, in Acts 8:3, means hauling or dragging.

Hall, in Luke 22:55, means the uncovered space or courtyard enclosed by the house.

Hallelujah, hal-le-lu´yah, is translated in the English Version *Praise ye the Lord* or *Praise the Lord*, and is found in many of the Psalms in this form. Pss. 106; 111; 112; 113; 117; 135. In Rev. 19:1, 3, 4, 6 the word ALLELUIA is used with a similar meaning.

Hal´lo-hesh (*the enchanter*), one who sealed the covenant. Neh. 10:24.

Hal´low, in Exod. 29:1; 40:9, etc., means to consecrate; to make holy.

Ha-lo´hesh (*the enchanter*), one who helped repair the wall of Jerusalem. Neh. 3:12.

Halt, in Luke 14:21, means lame.

Halt´ed, in Gen. 32:31, means was lame.

Ham (*multitude*), a city or country where the people called Zuzim dwelt. Its situation is very uncertain Gen. 14:5.

Ham (*hot* or *multitude*). [1] The son of Noah and the father of Cush, Mizraim,

Phut, and Canaan. Gen. 10:6. From Cush descended the Cushites who inhabited Chaldea (Nimrod was his son. Gen. 10:8), parts of Arabia, and Ethiopia. From Mizraim, which is the Hebrew name of Egypt, descended the Egyptians; from Phut, another African people not further specialized; and from Canaan, the Canaanites; that is, those tribes which inhabited Canaan when the Israelites arrived there. All these nations are called Hamitic. [2] The patronymic of the descendants of Ham.

Also see Gen. 5:32; 6:10; 7:13; 9:18, 22; 10:1, 20; 14:5.

1 Chron. 1:4, 8; 4:40.

Pss. 78:51; 105:23, 27; 106:22.

Ha´man (*celebrated*), a courtier and favorite of Ahasuerus, the king of Persia, who devised persecution against the Jews. Esther chapters 3—9. He obtained a royal decree for the extermination of the Jews in Persia, but through the influence of Esther his plan was not carried out. He was hanged on the gallows that he had prepared for Mordecai. See MORDECAI, and PURIM.

Ha´math (*fortress*), one of the principal cities of Syria, and one of the oldest in the world. It was situated in the valley of the Orontes, and was founded by a son of Canaan. Gen. 10:18; Num. 34:8. It was visited by the spies, Num. 13:21, and is often noticed as the northern boundary of Palestine. Num. 34:8; Josh. 13:5. It is called "Hamath the great" in Amos 6:2. It is now called *Hamah*, and has about 30,000 inhabitants. The Hamath inscriptions are in very ancient characters, on four stones.

Also see Judg. 3:3.

2 Sam. 8:9.

1 Kings 8:65.

2 Kings 14:25, 28; 17:24, 30; 18:34; 19:13; 23:33; 25:21.

1 Chron. 18:3, 9.

2 Chron. 7:8; 8:4.

Isa. 10:9; 11:11; 36:19; 37:13.

Jer. 39:5; 49:23; 52:9, 27.

Ezek. 47:16, 17, 20; 48:1.

Amos 6:2.

Zech. 9:2.

Ha´math-ite, a tribe from a descendant of Canaan. Gen. 10:18; 1 Chron. 1:16.

Ha´math-zo´bah (*fortress of Zobah*), a city conquered by Solomon. 2 Chron. 8:3. It cannot have been "Hamath the great."

Ham´math (*warm springs*), a fenced city of Naphtali. Josh. 19:35. Probably same as HAMMON, No. 2, and HAMMOTH-DOR.

Ham-med´a-tha (*double ?*), father of Haman. Esther 3:1; 9:24.

Ham´me-lech (*the king*), in Jer. 36:26; 38:6, is translated "the king" in the Revised Version.

Ham´mer is the translation of four different words. In Isa. 44:12 it probably means a very heavy kind of hammer. The hammer used by Jael, Judg. 4:21, was doubtless a mallet. The "battle-axe" mentioned in Jer. 51:20 and the "maul" in Prov. 25:18 were a kind of hammers used in war. In Jer. 23:29; 50:23 "hammer" is used figuratively for mighty force.

Ham-mol´e-keth (*the queen*), sister of Gilead, the grandson of Manasseh. 1 Chron. 7:18.

Ham´mon (*hot spring*). [1] A town of Asher. Josh. 19:28. [2] A city of Naphtali which was assigned to the Levites, 1 Chron. 6:76, probably the same as HAMMATH and HAMMOTH-DOR.

Ham´moth-dor, a city of Naphtali which was made a Levitical city and a city of refuge. Josh. 21:32. See HAMMATH, and

HAMMON, No. 2.

Ham´o-nah or **Ha-mo´nah** (*multitude*), a city apparently adjacent to the place where the multitude of Gog should be buried. Ezek. 39:16.

Ha´mon-gog (*multitude of Gog*), the name which Ezekiel prophetically declares shall be given to the place where the great slaughter of Gog and his army shall take place. Ezek. 39:11, 15.

Ha´mor (*ass*), a prince of the Hivites in the time of Jacob, whose son Shechem appears to have given his name to the city in which they dwelt. They were killed by Jacob's sons. Gen. 34:26. Hamor is called EMMOR in Acts 7:16.
Also see Gen. 33:19; 34:2, 4, 6, 8, 13, 18, 20, 24.
Josh. 24:32.
Judg. 9:28.

Ha-mu´el (*wrath of God*), a descendant of Simeon, the son of Jacob. 1 Chron. 4:26.

Ha´mul (*pity*), a son of Pharez, the son of Judah. Gen. 46:12; 1 Chron. 2:5.

Ha´mul-ites, descendants of Hamul, the son of Pharez. Num. 26:21.

Ha-mu´tal (*God is fresh life*), wife of Josiah, king of Judah. 2 Kings 23:31; Jer. 52:1.

Ha-nam´e-el (*gift or grace of God*), son of Shallum, the uncle of Jeremiah the prophet. Jer. 32:7, 12.

Ha´nan (*merciful*). [1] A son of Shashak, a descendant of Benjamin. 1 Chron. 8:23. [2] A son of Azel, a descendant of Benjamin. 1 Chron. 8:38; 9:44. [3] A captain of David's army. 1 Chron. 11:43. [4] A Nethinim whose posterity went up from Babylon with Zerubbabel. Ezra 2:46; Neh. 7:49. [5] One of the priests who caused the people to understand the law when it was read to them by Ezra.

Neh. 8:7. [6] A Levite who sealed the covenant made by Nehemiah and the people to serve the Lord. Neh. 10:10; 13:13. Perhaps same as No. 5 [7] A chief man (or the patronymic of a family) who sealed the covenant made by Nehemiah. Neh. 10:22. [8] Another Jew (or the patronymic of another family) who sealed the covenant to serve the Lord. Neh. 10:26. [9] An officer about the Lord's house, whose sons had a chamber in the Temple. Jer. 35:4.

Ha-nan´e-el (*God is gracious*), the name of a tower near the sheep-gate of Jerusalem. Neh. 3:1; Zech. 14:10.

Ha-na´ni (*gracious*). [1] Father of Jehu the prophet. 1 Kings 16:1; 2 Chron. 19:2. [2] A son of Heman. 1 Chron. 25:4, 25. [3] A seer who reproved Asa for seeking help from the king of Syria. 2 Chron. 16:7. Perhaps same as No. 1. [4] A Jew (apparently a priest) who had taken a foreign wife. Ezra 10:20. [5] A brother of Nehemiah. Neh. 1:2; 7:2 [6] A priest, one of the musicians. Neh. 12:36.

Han-a-ni´ah (*Jehovah is gracious*). [1] A son of Zerubbabel. 1 Chron. 3:19, 21. [2] A son of Shashak. 1 Chron. 8:24. [3] A son of Heman. 2 Chron. 25:4, 23. [4] A captain of the army of Uzziah. 2 Chron. 26:11. [5] A Jew who had taken a foreign wife. Ezra 10:28. [6] A Jew who repaired part of the wall of Jerusalem. Neh. 3:8. [7] A Jew who, with Hanun, repaired part of the wall of Jerusalem. Neh. 3:30. [8] A Jew to whom Nehemiah gave in charge to keep the gates of Jerusalem. Neh. 7:2. [9] A Jew (or the designation of a family) who sealed the covenant made by Nehemiah. Neh. 10:23. [10, 11] Two priests. Neh. 12:12, 41. [12] A false prophet who opposed Jeremiah. Jer. 28:1, 17. [13] A young Jewish prince who was carried by Nebuchadnezzar to Babylon with Daniel. Dan. 1:6, 7, 19. Same as Shadrach. **[14]** Father of Zedekiah, a prince of Judah. Jer. 36:12. **[15]** Grandfather of Irijah, the captain of the guard at the gate of Benjamin. Jer. 37:13.

Hand, a symbol of skill, power, and many actions. The Hebrews in describing locations spoke as if facing the east. Hence "to the right hand" meant *to the south*; "to the left hand," *to the north*. 2 Sam. 24:5; Gen. 14:15; Job 23:9. The Hebrews at their meals picked up their foods with their fingers, using no forks; hence washing the hands was specially necessary. The scribes and Pharisees made this washing a religious ceremony, in accordance with "the tradition of the elders." Matt. 15:2.

Also see Gen. 3–5; 8; 9; 13; 14; 16; 19–22; 24; 25; 27; 30–33; 35; 37–44; 46–49.

Exod. 2–10; 12–19; 21–25; 29; 30; 32–35; 38; 40.

Lev. 1; 3; 4; 7–10; 14–16; 22; 24–26.

Num. 4–11; 15; 16; 20–22; 24; 25; 27; 31; 33; 35; 36.

Deut. 1–17; 19–21; 23–28; 30–34.

Josh. 1; 2; 4–11; 14; 17; 19–24.

Judg. 1–20.

Ruth 1; 4.

1 Sam. 2; 4–7; 9–14; 16–28; 30.

2 Sam. 1–6; 8; 10–16; 18–24.

1 Kings 2; 7; 8; 11; 13–18; 20; 22.

2 Kings 3–23.

1 Chron. 4–6; 11–14; 16; 18–22; 25; 26; 28; 29.

2 Chron. 3; 4; 6; 8; 10; 12; 13; 15–18; 20; 21; 23–26; 28–36.

Ezra 1; 4–10.

Neh. 1; 2; 4; 6; 8; 9; 11–13.

Esther 2; 3; 5; 6; 8; 9.

Job. 1; 2; 4–6; 9–17; 19–23; 26–31; 33–35; 37; 40; 41.

Pss. 7–10; 16–18; 20–22; 24; 26; 28; 31; 32; 36–39; 44; 45; 47; 48; 55; 58; 60; 63; 68; 71; 73–78; 80–82; 88–92; 95; 97; 98; 102; 104; 106–111; 115; 118; 119; 121; 123; 125; 127–129; 134–145; 149.

Prov. 1; 3; 4; 6; 10–12; 14; 16; 17; 19; 21; 22; 24; 26; 27; 30; 31.

Eccles. 2; 4; 5; 7; 9–11.

Song of Sol. 2; 5; 7; 8.

Isa. 1–3; 5; 6; 8–11; 13; 14; 17; 19; 22; 23; 25; 26; 28; 29; 31; 33–38; 40–45; 47–51; 53–57; 59; 60; 62–66.

Jer. 1; 2; 4; 6; 10–12; 15; 16; 18–23; 25–27; 29–34; 36–44; 46–48; 50; 51.

Lam. 1–5.

Ezek. 1–3; 6–14; 16–18; 20–23; 25; 27–31; 33–40; 43; 44; 46; 47.

Dan. 1–5; 7–12.

Hos. 2; 7; 12; 14.

Joel 1–3.

Amos 1; 5; 7; 9.

Obad. 13.

Jon. 3; 4.

Mic. 2; 4; 5; 7.

Nah. 3.

Hab. 2; 3.

Zeph. 1–3.

Hag. 1; 2.

Zech. 2–4; 8; 11–14.

Mal. 1; 2.

Matt. 3–6; 8–10; 12; 14; 15; 17–22; 25–27.

Mark 1; 3; 5–10; 12; 14–16.

Luke 1; 3–6; 8; 9; 13; 15; 20–24.

John 2; 3; 7; 8; 10; 11; 13; 18–21.

Acts 2–9; 11–14; 17; 19–24; 26–28.

Rom. 8; 10; 13.

1 Cor. 4; 12; 16.

2 Cor. 5; 6; 10; 11.

Gal. 2; 3; 6.

Eph. 1; 2; 4.

Phil. 4.

Col. 2–4.
1 Thess. 4.
2 Thess. 2; 3.
1 Tim. 2; 4; 5.
2 Tim. 1; 4.
Philem. 19.
Heb. 1; 2; 6; 8–10; 12.
James 4.
1 Pet. 3–5.
1 John 1.
Rev. 1; 2; 5–10; 13; 14; 17; 19; 20; 22.

Hand-breadth, Exod. 25:25; 1 Kings 7:26, a measure of length, reckoned to have been equal to the breadth of the four fingers across the first joint—about three inches.

Handkerchiefs, hank´er-chifs, were used in ancient times. Acts 19:12.

Hands, laying on of, a part of the ceremonial used in consecrating persons to high and holy service and in conferring spiritual gifts. Num. 27:18; Acts 8:15-17; 1 Tim. 4:14; 2 Tim. 1:6.

Hand´staves, in Ezek. 39:9, means darts or javelins.

Ha´nes (*Mercury*), a city in Egypt, Isa. 30:4.

Hang´ing. Under Jewish law criminals were first strangled and then hanged. Num. 25:4; Deut. 21:22. It was a special mark of infamy. Deut. 21:23. In Acts 5:30; Gal. 3:13, Jesus is said to have been "hanged on a tree," which means literally "on a beam of wood," and refers to his crucifixion.

Hang´ing (*a cover*), **Hang´ings** (*that which is in motion*), are translations of different words. Hanging is a word used for the curtain before the door of the Tabernacle, Exod. 26:36, and for the curtain before the entrance of the court. Exod. 27:16. Hangings were coverings upon the walls of the court of the Tabernacle. Exod.

27:9. Hangings, in 2 Kings 23:7, would be more properly translated *tents*.

Han´i-el (*grace of God*), a son of Ulla, of the tribe of Asher. 1 Chron. 7:39.

Han´nah (*grace*), a pious wife of Elkanah and the mother of the prophet Samuel, who was given to her in anwer to prayer. 1 Sam. 1, 2. Notice her song of praise in 1 Sam. 2:1-10.

Han´na-thon (*dedicated to grace*), a town named in describing the boundaries of Zebulun. Josh. 19:14.

Han´ni-el (*God is gracious*), a chief of Manasseh, one of those appointed to divide the land west of Jordan. Num. 34:23.

Hanoch, ha´nok (*dedicated*). [1] A son of Midian, Gen. 25:4, called HENOCH in 1 Chron. 1:33. [2] A son of Reuben. Gen. 46:9; Exod. 6:14.

Hanochites, ha´nok-ites, a family of the Israelites whose founder was Hanoch, a son of Reuben, Num. 26:5.

Ha´nun (*gracious*). [1] A king of the Ammonites who insulted the messengers whom David sent to comfort him after the death of his father. 2 Sam. 10:2; 1 Chron. 19:4. [2] A Jew who aided in repairing the walls of Jerusalem. Neh. 3:13. [3] A Jew who, with Hananiah, repaired part of the walls of Jerusalem. Neh. 3:30.

Haph-ra´im (*two pits*), a city of Issachar. Josh. 19:19.

Ha´ra (*hill-country*), a region in the kingdom of Assyria to which Tiglath-pileser carried away the trans-Jordanic tribes of Israel. 1 Chron. 5:26.

Har´a-dah (*terror*), the twentieth encampment of the Israelites in their wanderings through the wilderness. Num. 33:24, 25.

Ha´ran (*a mountaineer*). [1] Brother of Abraham and father of Lot. Gen. 11:26,

31. [2] A son of Shimei, of the tribe of Levi. 1 Chron. 23:9.

Ha´ran (*parched*), a son of Caleb, the son of Jephunneh. 1 Chron. 2:46.

Ha´ran (*parched, dry*), the place to which Abram removed after leaving Ur, and before he went into Canaan. Gen. 11:31; 2 Kings 19:12. The city was in Mesopotamia, and more definitely in Padan-aram. Gen. 24:10; 25:20. It is called CHARRAN in Acts 7:2, 4.

Ha´ra-rites (*mountaineers*), three persons connected with David's guard—namely AGEE, 2 Sam. 23:11; SHAMMAH, 2 Sam. 23:33; and SHARAR, 2 Sam. 23:33, called SACAR in 1 Chron. 11:35.

Har-bo´na or **Har-bo´nah** (*ass-driver*), one of the seven chamberlains of Ahasuerus. Esther 1:10; 7:9.

Hard, in Ps. 63:8; Matt. 25:24; Acts 18:7, means close.

Hardly, in Matt. 19:23, means with difficulty.

Hard´ness, in 2 Tim. 2:3 means hardship.

Hare, a well-known small animal, was prohibited to the Hebrews for food. Lev. 11:6; Deut. 14:7. Several varieties of the hare are found in Palestine.

Ha´reph (*early born*), a son of Caleb, the son of Hur. 1 Chron. 2:51.

Ha´reth (*thicket*), a piece of forest land in the hill-country of Judah. 1 Sam. 22:5. David fled to it from Saul.

Har-ha-i´ah (*Jehovah is angry*), a Jew whose son Uzziel repaired part of the walls of Jerusalem. Neh. 3:8.

Har´has (*very poor*), the grandfather of Shallum, the husband of Huldah the prophetess. 2 Kings 22:14. Called HASRAH in 2 Chron. 34:22.

Har´hur (*nobility*), a Nethinim whose descendants went up with Zerubbabel

from Babylon after the captivity. Ezra 2:51; Neh. 7:53.

Ha´rim (*snub-nosed*). [1] A priest in the time of David. 1 Chron. 24:8; Neh. 7:42. [2] Probably the name of a place in Judah or Benjamin. Ezra 2:32; Neh. 7:35. [3] A Jew some of whose descendants took foreign wives. Ezra 10:31. [4] A priest who sealed the covenant made by Nehemiah. Neh. 10:5. [5] The title of one of the families of the Jews who sealed the covenant. Neh. 10:27. [6] A priest who lived near the end of the captivity. Neh. 12:15. Perhaps same as No. 4.

Ha´riph (*plucking off*). [1] A Jew some of whose posterity went up from Babylon. Neh. 7:24. [2] The head of a family of Jews, who sealed the covenant made by Nehemiah. Neh. 10:19.

Har´lot, an abandoned woman. Prov. 29:3. Harlots are first mentioned in the case of Tamar. Gen. 38:15. Among the Hebrews harlots were often foreigners, hence their name, "strange women." The name is also applied figuratively to wicked cities, as Nineveh, Nah. 3:4, and Jerusalem, Isa. 1:21; also to Israel, referring to their idolatry.

Also see Gen. 34:31; 38:21, 22, 24.

Lev. 21:14.

Josh. 2:1; 6:17, 22, 25.

Judg. 11:1; 16:1.

1 Kings 3:16.

Prov. 7:10.

Isa. 23:15, 16.

Jer. 2:20; 3:1, 6, 8; 5:7.

Ezek. 16:15, 16, 28, 31, 35, 41; 23:5, 19, 44.

Hos. 2:5; 3:3; 4:14, 15.

Joel 3:3.

Amos 7:17.

Mic. 1:7.

Matt. 21:31, 32.

Luke 15:30.
1 Cor. 6:15, 16.
Heb. 11:31.
James 2:25.
Rev. 17:5.

Har´mony of the Gos´pels. See GOSPELS, HARMONY OF.

Har-ne´pher (*panting ?*), a son of Zophah, a descendant of Asher. 1 Chron. 7:36.

Har´ness, in 1 Kings 20:11; 22:34; 2 Chron. 18:33, means armor.

Ha´rod (*trembling*), a city or place in Manasseh, west of Jordan, near which Gideon encamped with the army of the Israelites. Judg. 7:1.

Ha´rod-ites, descendants of two of David's warriors. 2 Sam. 23:25.

Har´o-eh (*the seer*), a son of Shobal, the son of Caleb, the son of Hur. 1 Chron. 2:52. Same as REAIAH in 1 Chron. 4:2.

Ha´ro-rite, 1 Chron. 11:27, refers to one of David's valiant men. See HAROD-ITES.

Ha-ro´sheth (*forest*), a city in the north of Canaan which was under the dominion of Jabin, and in which Sisera, the captain of his army, dwelt. Judg. 4:2, 16. It was called HAROSHETH OF THE GENTILES on account of its mixed populaton.

Harps of various forms were used by the Hebrews. The harp was invented by Jubal, Gen. 4:21, and was used on joyful occasions. David was very skilful in its use and played on it before King Saul. 1 Sam. 16:23.
Also see Gen. 31:27.
1 Sam. 10:5; 16:16, 23.
2 Sam. 6:5.
1 Kings 10:12.
1 Chron. 13:8; 15:16, 21, 28; 16:5; 25:1, 3, 6.
2 Chron. 5:12; 9:11; 20:28; 29:25.

Neh. 12:27.
Job. 21:12; 30:31.
Pss. 33:2; 43:4; 49:4; 57:8; 71:22; 81:2; 92:3; 98:5; 108:2; 137:2; 147:7; 149:3; 150:3.
Isa. 5:12; 16:11; 23:16; 24:8; 30:32.
Ezek. 26:13.
Dan. 3:5, 7, 10, 15.
1 Cor. 14:7.
Rev. 5:8; 14:2; 15:2.

Har´row, in 2 Sam. 12:31; 1 Chron. 20:3, means a threshing instrument.

Har´sha (*deaf*), a Nethinim whose descendants went up from Babylon after the captivity. Ezra 2:52; Neh. 7:54.

Hart or **Stag,** an extremely graceful and beautiful animal of the deer kind; perhaps the red deer or the fallow-deer. It was a clean animal by the Levitical law, Deut. 12:15, and is often mentioned in the Bible. Ps. 42:1; Isa. 35:6, etc. The female has no horns, and is called a hind.

Ha´rum (*elevated*), a descendant of Coz, who sprang from Judah. 1 Chron. 4:8.

Harumaph, ha-roo´maf, a Jew whose son Jedaiah repaired part of the wall of Jerusalem. Neh. 3:10.

Haruphite, har´oo-fite, a patronymic or Gentile appellation, but of uncertain derivation. 1 Chron. 12:5.

Ha´ruz (*industrious*), a man of Jotbah whose daughter Meshullemeth was the wife of Manasseh. 2 Kings 21:19.

Har´vest usually commenced in Palestine about the beginning of April, and ended in June. In some elevated parts of the country it was later. It began with barley, and its first-fruits were taken to the Temple in Passover-week. The wheat harvest came next, and its first-fruits were offered at Pentecost. In Matt. 13:39 the

end of the world is referred to as the harvest.
Also see Gen. 8:22; 30:14; 45:6.
Exod 23:16; 34:21, 22.
Lev. 19:9; 23:10, 22; 25:5.
Deut. 24:19.
Josh. 3:15.
Judg. 15:1.
Ruth 1:22; 2:21, 23.
1 Sam. 6:13; 8:12; 12:17.
2 Sam. 21:9, 10; 23:13.
Job 5:5.
Prov. 6:8; 10:5; 20:4; 25:13; 26:1.
Isa. 9:3; 16:9; 17:11; 18:4, 5; 23:3.
Jer. 5:17, 24; 8:20; 50:16; 51:33.
Hos. 6:11.
Joel 1:11; 3:13.
Amos 4:7.
Matt. 9:37, 38; 13:30.
Mark 4:29.
Luke 10:2.
John 4:35.
Rev. 14:15.

Har′vest, Feast of. See PENTECOST.

Has-a-di′ah (*Jehovah is kind*), a son of Zerubbabel, who was a descendant of Jehoiakim, king of Judah. 1 Chron. 3:20.

Hasenuah, has-e-noo′a (*the hated*), an Israelite whose descendants dwelt in Jerusalem after the captivity. 1 Chron. 9:7.

Hash-a-bi′ah (*whom Jehovah regards*). [1, 2] Levite descendants of Merari. 1 Chron. 6:45; 9:14. [3] Head of a course of Levitical musicians. 1 Chron. 25:3, 19. [4] A Hebronite Levite. 1 Chron. 26:30. [5] A Levite, the son of Kemuel. 1 Chron. 27:17. [6] A chief of the Levites in the time of Josiah. 2 Chron. 35:9. [7] One of a family of priests who returned from Babylon. Ezra 8:19. [8] Another priest, Ezra 8:24, of the same family as No. 7. [9] A Levite who repaired part of the wall of Jerusalem. Neh. 3:17. [10] A Levite who sealed the covenant. Neh. 10:11. [11] A Levite, of the family of Asaph. Neh. 11:22. [12] Another Levite. Neh. 11:15. [13] A priest of the family of Hilkiah. Neh. 12:21.

Ha-shab′nah (*Jehovah is a friend*), the head of a family who sealed the covenant made by Nehemiah. Neh. 10:25.

Hash-ab-ni′ah (*Jehovah is a friend*). [1] A Levite whose son Hattush repaired part of the walls of Jerusalem. Neh. 3:10. [2] A Levite. Neh. 9:5.

Hash-bad′a-na (*considerate judge?*), one of the priests, Levites, or rulers who stood on Ezra's left hand while he read the book of law to the people. Neh. 8:4.

Ha′shem (*fat*), father of two or more of David's valiant men. 1 Chron. 11:34.

Hash-mo′nah (*fruitfulness*), the twenty-fifth encampment of the Israelites in their wandering through the wilderness. Num. 33:29, 30. Probably the same as HESHMON.

Ha′shub (*intelligent*). [1] A Levite whose family dwelt in Jerusalem after the captivity. Neh. 11:15. Called HASSHUB in 1 Chron. 9:14. [2] A Jew who repaired part of the wall of Jerusalem. Neh. 3:11. [3] A Jew who repaired the wall of Jerusalem in front of his house. Neh. 3:23. [4] The head of a family who sealed the covenant made by Nehemiah. Neh. 10:23.

Ha-shu′bah (*intelligent*), a son of Zerubbabel. 1 Chron. 3:20.

Ha′shum (*rich*). [1] A Jew whose descendants went up from Babylon with Zerubbabel. Ezra 2:19; Neh. 7:22. [2] One of the priests, Levites, or princes who stood beside Ezra while he read the book of the law to the people. Neh. 8:4. [3] The head of a family who sealed the covenant made by Nehemiah. Neh. 10:18.

Ha-shu′pha (*stripped*), a Nethinim

whose descendants returned with Zerubbabel. Neh. 7:46. Called HASUPHA in Ezra 2:43.

Has'rah (*very poor*), grandfather of Shallum. 2 Chron. 34:22. See HARHAS.

Has-se-na'ah (*thorn hedge*), a Jew whose sons built the fish-gate of Jerusalem. Neh. 3:3. If the name of a town, it must be same as SENAAH.

Has'shub, a Levite. See HASHUB, No. 1.

Ha-su'pha, a Nethinim. Ezra 2:43. See HASHUPHA.

Hatach, ha'tak, one of the chamberlains appointed to attend upon Esther. Esther 4:5, 10.

Hate sometimes means love in a less degree, as in Luke 14:26, which mentions father and mother, etc., as persons which must be hated if one would be a disciple of Christ.

Also see Gen. 24:60; 26:27; 27:41; 29:31, 33; 37:4, 5, 8; 49:23; 50:15.
Exod. 20:5; 23:5.
Lev. 19:17; 26:17.
Num. 10:35.
Deut. 1:27; 4:42; 5:9; 7:10, 15; 9:28; 12:31; 16:22; 19:4, 6, 11; 21:15-17; 22:13, 16; 24:3; 30:7; 32:41; 33:11.
Josh. 20:5.
Judg. 11:7; 14:16; 15:2.
2 Sam. 5:8; 13:15, 22; 19:6; 22:18, 41.
1 Kings 22:8.
2 Chron. 18:7; 19:2.
Esther 9:1, 5.
Job 8:22; 16:9; 31:29; 34:17.
Pss. 5:5; 9:13; 11:5; 18:17, 40; 21:8; 25:19; 26:5; 31:6; 34:21; 35:19; 38:19; 41:7; 44:7, 10; 45:7; 50:17; 55:3, 12; 68:1; 69:4, 14; 83:2; 86:17; 89:23; 97:10; 101:3; 105:25; 118:7; 119:104, 113, 128, 163; 120:6; 129:5; 139:21, 22.

Prov. 1:22, 29; 5:12; 6:16; 8:13, 36; 9:8; 11:15; 12:1; 13:5, 24; 14:17, 20; 15:10, 27; 19:7; 25:17; 26:24, 28; 28:16; 29:10, 24.
Eccles. 2:17, 18; 3:8.
Isa. 1:14; 60:15; 61:8; 66:5.
Jer. 12:8, 44:4.
Ezek. 16:27, 37; 23:28; 35:6.
Dan. 4:19.
Hos. 9:15.
Amos 5:10, 15, 21; 6:8.
Mic. 3:2.
Zech. 8:17.
Mal. 1:3; 2:16; 24:9.
Matt. 5:43, 44; 6:24; 10:22; 24:10.
Mark 13:13.
Luke 1:71; 6:22, 27; 16:13; 19:14; 21:17.
John 3:20; 7:7; 12:25; 15:18, 19, 23-25; 17:14.
Rom. 7:15; 9:13.
Eph. 5:29.
Heb. 1:9.
1 John 2:9, 11; 3:13, 15; 4:20.
Rev. 2:6, 15; 17:16.

Ha'thath (*fearful*), a son of Othniel, the son of Kenaz. 1 Chron. 4:13.

Hat'i-pha (*captive*), a Nethinim whose descendants went up with Zerubbabel from Babylon. Ezra 2:54; Neh. 7:56.

Hat'i-ta (*exploring*), a porter for the Tabernacle whose descendants went up with Zerubbabel from Babylon. Ezra 2:42; Neh. 7:45.

Hats, in Dan. 3:21, are turbans in the marginal notes. Hats were unknown to the Hebrews.

Hat'til (*wavering*), a servant of Solomon whose descendants went up from Babylon with Zerubbabel. Ezra 2:57; Neh. 7:59.

Hat'tush (*assembled*). [1] A grandson of Shechaniah. 1 Chron. 3:22. [2] A descendant of David who went up with Ezra from Babylon. Ezra 8:2. [3] A Jew who repaired part of the wall of Jerusalem. Neh. 3:10. [4] A priest who went up from Babylon with Zerubbabel and afterward sealed the covenant. Neh. 10:4; 12:2.

Haunt, in Ezek. 26:17, means frequent.

Hau´ran (*caves, caverns*), a country situated east of the Jordan and in the north-east corner of Palestine. Ezek. 47:16, 18. It is the *Auranitis* of the Greeks.

Hav´i-lah (*circle*). [1] A country supposed to lie on the east side of the river Indus—that is, in north-western India—or perhaps west of the Indus, along the shores toward the Persian Gulf. Gen. 2:11. [2] A descendant of Ham. Gen. 10:7; 1 Chron. 1:9. [3] A descendant of Shem. Gen. 10:29; 1 Chron. 1:23. [4] A country or district apparently east of the Amalekites. Gen. 25:18; 1 Sam. 15:7.

Ha´voth-ja´ir (*villages of Jair*), a name applied to those towns of the Amorites which Jair, the descendant of Manasseh, took in Mount Gilead. Num. 32:41; Deut. 3:14.

Hawk, an unclean bird, Lev. 11:16, of the falcon tribe. It was sacred among the Egyptians and the Greeks. Its migrations are referred to in Job 39:26.

Hay was not stored up by the Hebrews. Grass was cut by them green as it was wanted for use. In Prov. 27:25; Isa. 15:6 hay means the first blades of grass.

Haz´a-el (*God sees*), an officer of Ben-hadad, king of Syria, whom Elijah was commanded to anoint to be king in place of Ben-hadad. 1 Kings 19:15.
Also see 1 Kings 19:17.
2 Kings 8:8, 9, 12, 13, 15, 28, 29; 9:14, 15; 10:32; 12:17, 18; 13:3, 22; 24; 25.
2 Chron. 22:5, 6.

Amos 1:4.

Haz´a-el, House of, either the family or palace of Hazael. Amos 1:4.

Hazaiah, ha-za´yah (*Jehovah is seeing*), a descendant apparently of Pharez, the son of Judah whose posterity dwelt in Jerusalem after the return from Babylon. Neh. 11:5.

Ha´zar-ad´dar, a village on the south border of the land west of Kadesh-barnea. Num. 34:4. The same place is called ADAR in Josh. 15:3.

Ha´zar-e´nan (*court of the fountains*), a town in the region called Mount Hermon, at the east extremity of the north border of the Land of Promise. Num. 34:9; Ezek. 48:1.

Ha´zar-gad´dah (*court of Gad*), a village in the south of Judah. Josh. 15:27.

Ha´zar-hat´ti-con (*middle Hazar*), a town east of Jordan, near the border of Hauran. Ezek. 47:16.

Ha´zar-ma´veth (*court of death*), a son of Joktan, of the family of Shem. Gen. 10:26; 1 Chron. 1:20.

Ha´zar-shu´al (*fox* or *jackal village*), a village of Judah which afterward belonged to Simeon. Josh. 15:28; Neh. 11:27.

Ha´zar-su´sah or **Ha´zar-su sim** (*horse village*), a town of Simeon. Josh. 19:5; 1 Chron. 4:31.

Ha´zel, in Gen. 30:37, is supposed to mean wild almond.

Haz-e-lel-po´ni (*protection of the face of*), a female descendant of Judah through Caleb, the son of Hur. 1 Chron. 4:3.

Ha-ze´rim (*villages, courts*), a district apparently in the south of Palestine, or in the wilderness adjacent, extending to near Gaza. It was anciently inhabited by the Avims. Deut. 2:23.

Ha-ze´roth (*courts, villages*), the second encampment of the Israelites after they left Sinai. Num. 11:35; Deut. 1:1.

Haz´e-zon-ta´mar (*row of palms*), a town in the wilderness of Judah, Gen. 14:7, called HAZAZON-TAMAR in 2 Chron. 20:2. It was afterward better known as EN-GEDI.

Ha´zi-el (*God is seeing*), a son of Shimei. 1 Chron. 23:9.

Ha´zo (*vision, seer*), a son of Nahor, the brother of Abraham. Gen. 22:22.

Ha´zor (*enclosed*). **[1]** A royal city of the Canaanites situated in the north part of the land; afterward a city of Naphtali. Josh. 11:1; 1 Sam. 12:9. **[2]** A city of Judah. Josh. 15:23. **[3]** A town of Judah, Josh. 15:25, called HAZOR-HADATTAH or NEW HAZOR. **[4]** A city of Judah. Josh. 15:25. Same as HEZRON. **[5]** A town of Benjamin. Neh. 11:23. **[6]** A name given to certain countries in the east of Arabia. Jer. 49:28, 30, 33.

Head´bands, in Isa. 3:20, may mean little bands for the hair.

Head´stone, in Zech. 4:7, means chief stone.

Health. In Ps. 67:2 "saving health" means salvation.

Heap, in Deut. 13:16; Jer. 49:2, means ruin.

Heaps of stones were used to mark some signal providence of God. Josh. 4:4-7.

Heart, a word used in some parts of the Bible to denote the seat of the desires, affections, and motives of man, and in others to signify all his faculties and powers as an intellectual, moral and accountable being.
Gen. 6; 8; 17; 18; 20; 24; 27; 42; 45.
Exod. 4; 7–11; 14; 15; 23; 25; 28; 31; 35; 36.
Lev. 19; 26.
Num. 15; 32.
Deut. 1; 2; 4–11; 13; 15; 17–20; 24; 26; 28–30; 32.
Josh. 2; 5; 7; 11; 14; 22–24.
Judg. 5; 9; 16; 18; 19.
Ruth 3.
1 Sam. 1; 2; 4; 6; 7; 9; 10; 12–14; 16; 17; 21; 24; 25. 27; 28.
2 Sam. 3; 6; 7; 13–15; 17–19; 24.
1 Kings 2–4; 8–12; 14; 15; 18; 21.
2 Kings 5; 6; 9; 10; 12; 14; 20; 22; 23.
1 Chron. 12; 15–17; 22; 28; 29.
2 Chron. 1; 6; 7; 9; 11; 12; 15–17; 19; 20; 22; 25; 26; 29–32; 34; 36.
Ezra 6; 7.
Neh. 2; 6; 7; 9.
Esther 1; 5–7.
Job 1; 7–12; 15; 17; 22; 23; 27; 29; 31; 33; 34; 36–38; 41.
Pss. 4; 7; 9–17; 19; 20–22; 24–28; 31–41; 44; 45; 49; 51; 53; 55; 57; 58; 61; 62; 64; 66; 69; 73; 74; 77; 78; 81; 84; 86; 90; 94; 95; 97; 101; 102; 104; 105; 107–109; 111; 112; 119; 125; 131; 138–141; 143; 147.
Prov. 2–8; 10–28; 31.
Eccles. 1–3; 5; 7–11.
Song of Sol. 3–5; 8.
Isa. 1; 6; 7; 9; 10; 13–15; 19; 21; 29; 30; 32; 33; 35; 38; 42; 44; 47; 49; 51; 57; 59; 60; 63; 65; 66.
Jer. 3–5; 7–9; 11–18; 20; 22–24; 29–32; 42; 48; 49; 51.
Lam. 1–3; 5.
Ezek. 3; 6; 11; 13; 14; 16; 18; 20–22; 25; 27; 28; 31–33; 36; 40; 44.
Dan. 1; 2; 4–8; 10; 11.
Hos. 4; 7; 10; 11; 13.
Joel 2.
Obad. 3.
Nah. 2.
Zeph. 1–3.
Zech. 7; 8; 10; 12.
Mal. 2; 4.

Matt. 5; 6; 9; 11–13; 15; 18; 19; 22; 24.
Mark 2–4; 6–8; 10–12; 16.
Luke 1–3; 5; 6; 8–10; 12; 16; 21; 24.
John 12–14; 16.
Acts 1; 2; 4; 5; 7; 8; 11; 13–16; 21; 28.
Rom. 1; 2; 5; 6; 8–10.
1 Cor. 2; 4; 7; 14.
2 Cor. 1–9.
Gal. 4.
Eph. 3–6.
Phil. 1; 4.
Col. 2–4.
1 Thess. 2; 3.
2 Thess. 2; 3.
1 Tim. 1.
2 Tim. 2.
Heb. 3; 4; 8; 10; 13.
James. 1; 3–5.
1 Pet. 1; 3.
2 Pet. 1; 2.
1 John 3.
Rev. 2; 17; 18.

Hearth, harth or herth, in Ps. 102:3, means a fagot. It usually means, in the Bible, a stone on which a fire was made for baking bread and other uses. Abraham's wife Sarah made cakes (bread) upon the hearth. Gen. 18:6.

Heath, in Jer. 17:6; 48:6, probably means the dwarf juniper tree.

Heathen, he´thn (*nations*), a word sometimes used in the Bible to denote unbelievers, Jer. 10:25, but usually with the same meaning as GENTILES (which see). Also see Lev. 25:44; 26:33, 38, 45.
Deut. 4:27.
2 Sam. 22:44, 50.
2 Kings 16:3; 17:8, 11, 15; 21:2.
1 Chron. 16:24, 35.
2 Chron. 20:6; 28:3; 33:2, 9; 36:14.
Ezra 6:21.
Neh. 5:8, 9, 17; 6:6, 16.
Pss. 2:1, 8; 9:5, 15, 19; 10:16; 18:43,

49; 33:10; 44:2, 11, 14; 46:6, 10; 47:8; 59:5, 8; 78:55; 79:1, 6, 10; 80:8; 94:10; 96:3, 10; 98:2; 102:15; 105:44; 106:35, 41, 47; 110:6; 111:6; 115:2; 126:2; 135:15; 149:7.
Isa. 16:8.
Jer. 9:16; 10:2; 18:13; 49:14, 15.
Lam. 1:3, 10; 4:15, 20.
Ezek. 7:24; 11:12, 16; 12:16; 16:14; 20:9, 14, 22, 23, 32, 41; 22:4, 15, 16; 23:30; 25:7, 8; 28:25; 30:3; 31:11, 17; 34:28, 29; 36:3-7, 15, 19-24, 30, 36; 37:21, 28; 38:16; 39:7, 21, 23, 28.
Joel 2:17, 19; 3:11, 12.
Amos 9:12.
Obad. 1, 2, 15, 16.
Mic. 5:15.
Hab. 1:5; 3:12.
Zeph. 2:11.
Hag. 2:22.
Zech. 1:15; 8:13; 9:10; 14:14, 18.
Mal. 1:11, 14.
Matt. 6:7; 18:17.
Acts 4:25.
2 Cor. 11:26.
Gal. 1:16; 2:9; 3:8.

Heav´en. This word has a number of meanings in the *Old Testament*, which may be imperfectly classed thus: [1] The atmosphere, the region of clouds. [2] The region of the sun, moon, and stars. [3] The throne of God, and the habitation of the holy angels. [4] The word is frequently used in an indefinite, figurative, or metaphorical sense. In the *New Testament* also it has several meanings, which are imperfectly classed thus: [1] The Natural Heavens, frequently involving a reference to the next head, No. 2. [2] The Spiritual Heavens, the throne of God, the abode of the holy angels and the spirits of just men made perfect. [3] The word is sometimes used in an indefinite, figurative, or metaphorical sense.

Gen. 1; 2; 6–8; 11; 14; 15; 19; 21; 22; 24; 26–28; 49.

Exod. 9; 10; 16; 17; 20; 24; 31; 32.

Lev. 26.

Deut. 1–5; 7; 9–11; 17; 25; 26; 28–33.

Josh. 2; 8; 10.

Judg. 5; 13; 20.

1 Sam. 2; 5.

2 Sam. 18; 21; 22.

1 Kings 8; 18; 22.

2 Kings 1; 2; 7; 14; 17; 19; 21; 23.

1 Chron. 16; 21; 27; 29.

2 Chron. 2; 6; 7; 18; 20; 28; 30; 32; 33; 36.

Ezra 1; 5–7; 9.

Neh. 1; 2; 9.

Job. 1; 2; 9; 11; 14–16; 20; 22; 26; 28; 35; 37; 38; 41.

Pss. 2; 8; 11; 14; 18–20; 33; 36; 50; 53; 57; 68; 69; 73; 76–80; 85; 89; 96; 97; 102–105; 107; 108; 113; 115; 119; 121; 123; 124; 134–136; 139; 144; 146–148.

Prov. 3; 8; 23; 25; 30.

Eccles. 1–3; 5.

Isa. 1; 5; 13; 14; 34; 37; 40; 42; 44; 45; 48–51; 55; 63–66.

Jer. 2; 4; 7–10; 14; 15; 16; 19; 23; 31–34; 44; 49; 51.

Lam. 2–4.

Ezek. 1; 8; 29; 31; 32; 38.

Dan. 2; 4–9; 11; 12.

Hos. 2; 4; 7.

Joel 2; 3.

Amos 9.

Jon. 1.

Nah. 3.

Hab. 3.

Zeph. 1.

Hag. 1; 2.

Zech. 2; 5; 6; 8; 12.

Mal. 3.

Matt. 3–8; 10–14; 16; 18–26; 28.

Mark 1; 6–8; 10–14; 16.

Luke 2–4; 6; 9–12; 15–22; 24.

John 1; 3; 6; 12; 17.

Acts. 1–4; 7; 9–11; 14; 17; 22; 26.

Rom. 1; 10.

1 Cor. 8; 15.

2 Cor. 5; 12.

Gal. 1.

Eph. 1; 3; 4; 6.

Phil. 2; 3.

Col. 1; 4.

1 Thess. 1; 4.

2 Thess. 1.

Heb. 1; 4; 7–10; 12.

James 5.

1 Pet. 1. 3.

2 Pet. 1. 3.

1 John 5.

Rev. 3–6; 8–16; 18–21.

Heav´en, King´dom of. See KINGDOM OF HEAVEN.

Heave-of´fer-ing. See OFFERING.

He´ber (*alliance*). [1] The grandson of Asher. Gen. 46:17; 1 Chron. 7:31. [2] A Judite, a son of Ezra. 1 Chron. 4:18. [3] The head of a family in Gad. 1 Chron. 5:13. [4] A son of Elpaal, a Benjamite. 1 Chron. 8:17. [5] A son of Shashak, a Benjamite. 1 Chron. 8:22. [6] A Kenite, the husband of Jael, who killed Sisera, the captain of Jabin's army. Judg. 4:11, 17, 21, 22. See JAEL, and SISERA. [7] Heber, the father of Phalec. Luke 3:35. See EBER.

He´ber-ites, descendants of Heber, the grandson of Asher. Num. 26:45.

He´brew. [1] This word, which is used as a Gentile appellation for the descendants of Abraham, and applied to himself also, denotes one who comes from beyond, from the other side, or who has passed over, and is commonly regarded as having reference to Abraham's passing over the river Euphrates on his way to Canaan. [2] The language spoken by the Hebrews.

Gen. 14:13; 39:14, 17; 41:12.
Exod. 1:15, 16, 19; 2:7, 11; 21:2.
Deut. 15:12.
Jer. 34:9, 14.
Jon. 1:9.
Luke 23:38.
John 5:2; 19:13, 17, 20.
Acts 21:40; 22:2; 26:14.
Phil. 3:5.
Rev. 9:11; 16:16.

He´brew-ess, a Hebrew woman. Jer. 34:9.

He´brew Lan´guage. See BIBLE, and HEBREWS.

He´brews, The, were called ISRAELITES, Exod. 9:7; the CHILDREN OF ISRAEL, Exod. 1:13; the SEED OF ABRAHAM, Ps. 105:6; John 8:37; or the CHILDREN OF ABRAHAM, Gal. 3:7, until after the return from the captivity, when the name JEWS was adopted. The word "Jews" was formed from the same root as JUDEA. It referred to the purity of blood and strictness of religion by which those who reoccupied Judea were distinguished from the more mixed populations of Galilee and Samaria, with their laxer ideas of religion. The name HEBREWS was chosen because it was found that in the oldest times it had steadily been used by foreigners just in that sense. Gen. 14:13; 39:14; 41:12; 1 Sam. 4: 6.

The Hebrew race came from Chaldea, and Abraham from Ur, to which region he sent his servant to find a wife for Isaac, and Jacob went thither for the same purpose. But the home of the patriarchs was CANAAN (which see). That land was promised to them and their descendants, and Abraham bought the cave of Machʼelah, near Hebron, for a burial-place. It was on account of a famine that Jacob went down to Egypt, but when he found his son Joseph there as the favorite and first counsellor of the reigning Pharaoh, he remained there, and the Hebrews were settled in one of the best provinces of Egypt. How long they stayed there cannot be stated definitely on account of the uncertainty of both Egyptian and Biblical chronology, but they stayed, at all events, long enough to become thoroughly changed themselves and to see the circumstances under which they lived as thoroughly changed. They came a mere tribe, but they left a host, a people. They came as nomadic shepherds, but they had the arts of industry and the science of commerce at least as germs among them when they left. And they were compelled to leave. The great achievements of Joseph were forgotten long ago and the Hebrews were suppressed, almost enslaved, by the Egyptians, when Moses arose among them and led them across the Red Sea toward the Promised Land. For forty years they wandered about in the wilderness, but when they finally approached Canaan they possessed the Law, the Tabernacle, a social organization on a religious principle, and had become a nation. Moses died in sight of the Promised Land, and Joshua led the Hebrews into Canaan, conquered the country, and divided it among the tribes. Then followed, under the administration of the judges, a period in which pitiable failings and heroic deeds alternated until, under Saul, a national kingdom was formed, and under the reigns of David and Solomon the Hebrews became conspicuous in the history of the world. Jerusalem grew into a rich and splendid city, the Temple was built, commercial connections were formed with the Phœnicians, the Egyptians, etc., and in the interior nothing but order, industry, prosperity, and progress were to be seen, and a brilliant literature sprang up. Nevertheless, the very geographical position of the Hebrew kingdom was not without its peculiar dangers. There were great and ambitious empires, Egypt on one side of the Hebrews and Assyria and Babylonia on the other, and the war-path between those countries was inevitably through Palestine. Still worse, immediately after the death of Solomon the kingdom itself was divided, the ten tribes forming the kingdom of Israel, the other two (Judah and Benjamin) the kingdom of Judah. The jealousy between Israel and Judah led to wars, the wars to foreign alliances, the foreign alliances to a lowering of the national standard, and then came the doom. After the reign of nineteen rulers (in Israel), of seven different dynasties, some of them able men, Samaria was taken, B. C. 720, by Shalmaneser, the Hebrews carried away into captivity, and the land occupied by Assyrian settlers. After the reign of twenty rulers (in Judah), all from the house of David and some of them both able and good men, Jerusalem was taken, B. C. 588, by Nebuchadnezzar and the Hebrew inhabitants carried to Babylon as prisoners. One would think that such calamities must be the end of Hebrew history, but they were not. Babylon was conquered by the Persians B. C. 538, and Cyrus allowed the Hebrews to return home. One colony went back under Zerubbabel, another under Ezra, etc. The Temple was rebuilt, B. C. 520; the walls of Jerusalem, B. C. 445, under Nehemiah. Under the rule of the Persian governors it seems that the Hebrews were allowed to develop their theocratic form of government with considerable freedom and suc-

cess. Nor did their first contact with the Greeks cause any conflict. After the battle of Issus, B. C. 332, which meant the overthrow of the Persian monarchy, Alexander the Great visited Jerusalem, entered the Temple, had the book of Daniel with the prophecy of the downfall of Persia read to him, and treated the Hebrews with great friendliness. It should not be overlooked that he caused a considerable number of them to settle in the new city he built in Egypt, on the Mediterranean, for that event exercised a very great influence. (See ALEXANDRIA). Although Jerusalem continued to be the religious center of the Hebrew race, there now arose two foreign centers of Hebrew intelligence: one in Babylon, among the old exiles who had remained there and lived under a strongly pronounced Oriental influence, and one in Alexandria, among the recent colonists who lived there under a still more strongly pronounced Greek influence. The first conflict, however, between Greek philosophy and Hebrew religion took place in Jerusalem. After the death of Alexander the Great, B. C. 323, and the establishment of several kingdoms on the ruins of his empire, Palestine belonged first to Egypt, but afterward to Syria, and under Antiochus Epiphanes, B. C. 175–165, a great war began. He plundered the Temple, and erected in it a statue of Jupiter to which he tried to force the Hebrews to offer sacrifices. The result was a general rebellion under the leadership of the Maccabees, and after defeating and expelling the Syrians the Hebrews again established an independent kingdom under a native dynasty. The first of the Maccabees who assumed the royal title was Aristobulus I., B. C. 107, but with Antigonus, B. C. 40–37, a son of Aristobulus II., the dynasty ceased to reign and was followed by the Herodians. In the mean time Palestine had come under Roman sway, having been conquered by Pompey, B. C. 63. The Romans were as a rule not harsh masters in their conquered provinces. Especially in the East they were always willing to allow considerable religious and national liberty. But, unfortunately, the dynasty to which they confided the government of Palestine, the Herodian, was not of pure Hebrew descent: it came from Idumea. The Idumean rulers, sometimes bearing the title of king, sometimes other titles, tried to pass themselves off as Jews among the Jews, but they were in their hearts no more nor less than Greek-Roman pagans of the then prevailing type of religious indifference, and their policy was always to weaken and subdue the national feeling of the Hebrews by the introduction of Greek and Roman elements of civilization. As long as Herod the Great lived things went on with tolerable smoothness, but under his successors one insurrection followed the other, each increasing in fury and stubbornness. The Romans took a deep dislike to the Hebrews, baffled as they had been by them more than once in their undertakings, and finally their utter overthrow was decided upon. Vespasian was sent with a great army against them. Having been elected emperor, he left the command to his son Titus, who, with extreme cruelty, worked his way onward slowly, methodically, but irresistibly, broke down the walls around Jerusalem, burnt the Temple, and razed the city to the ground, A. D. 70. The state of Israel was established in 1948, and the Jewish homeland was restored as the Hebrew nation after nearly 2000 years. See JERUSALEM.

Also see Gen. 40:15; 43:32.
Exod. 2:6, 13; 3:18; 5:3; 7:16; 9:1, 13;
10:3.
1 Sam. 4:9; 13:3, 7, 19; 14:11, 21; 29:3.
Acts 6:1.
2 Cor. 11:22.
Phil 3:5.
Heb. 1–13.

He'brews, the E-pis'tle to the, is not addressed to any individual congregation, but generally to all the Jewish Christians in Palestine, who were suffering severely from the persecution of their Jewish countrymen and sorely tempted to apostasy from Christ. Its purpose is to strengthen those brethren in their faith by demonstrating to them the essential unity and at the same time the specific differences between the Old and the New Testament, the Old and the New Covenant, the Law of Moses, and the Gospel of Christ. It teaches the eternal priesthood and sacrifice of Christ. Its divine authority has never been doubted, but concerning its authorship there always has existed, and still exists, some uncertainty. It is anonymous, and has been ascribed to Paul, to Barnabas or Luke, and to Apollos. It is deeply impregnated with the genius of Paul, but the style and wording belong to somebody else, probably to Barnabas. It dates from A. D. 63 or 64, soon after Paul's first captivity in Rome.

He'bron (*friendship*). [1] A city of Palestine. It stands in a narrow but exceedingly fertile valley, at an elevation of three thousand feet above the level of the sea, midway between Jerusalem and Beer-sheba, is one of the oldest cities in the world, is mentioned before Damascus, Gen. 13:18, and was built seven years before Zoan (called by the Greeks TANIS), in Egypt. Num. 13:22. Its name while it was possessed by the Canaanites was KIRJATH-ARBA, Josh. 21:11; 15:13, 14, and this name was occasionally given to it long afterward. Hebron is often mentioned in the history of the Patriarchs. Abraham pitched his tent near it, under the oaks of Mamre, and bought the cave of Machpelah for a burial-place. After it had been conquered by Joshua, Josh. 10:36, 37; 12:10, it was made a Levitical city and a city of refuge. Josh. 20:7; 21:11. David resided there for seven and a half years. After the captivity it was speedily repeopled. Neh. 11:25. [2] One of the sons of Kohath, the son of Levi. Exod. 6:18; 1 Chron. 6:2. [3] The name (if it be not rather used as a patronymic) of the son of Mareshah. 1 Chron. 2:42; 15:9. [4] A city of Asher. Josh. 19:28.

Also see Gen. 23:2, 19; 35:27; 37:14.
Num. 3:19.
Josh. 10:3, 5, 23, 39; 11:21; 14:13-15; 15:13, 54; 21:13.
Judg. 1:10, 20; 16:3.
1 Sam. 30:31.
2 Sam. 2:1, 3, 11, 32; 3:2, 5, 19, 20, 22, 27, 32; 4:1, 8, 12; 5:1, 3, 5, 13; 15:7, 9, 10.
1 Kings 2:11.
1 Chron. 2:43; 3:1, 4; 6:18, 55, 57; 11:1, 3; 12:23, 38; 23:12, 19; 24:23; 29:27.
2 Chron. 11:10.

He´bron-ites, descendants of Hebron, the son of Kohath. Num. 3:27; 1 Chron. 26:23.

Hedge. In Hos. 2:6 a way or path hedged up with thorns is mentioned. In Job 1:10 hedge is figuratively used to denote protection.
Also see 1 Chron. 4:23.
Job 3:23.
Pss. 80:12; 89:40.
Prov. 15:19.
Eccles. 10:8.
Isa. 5:5.
Jer. 49:3.
Lam. 3:7.

Ezek. 13:5; 22:30.
Mic. 7:4.
Nah. 3:17.
Matt. 21:33.
Mark 12:1.
Luke 14:23.

Heg´a-i or **Hege,** he´je, the principal chamberlain of Ahasuerus, the king of Persia. Esther 2:3, 8, 15.

Heifer, hef´er, a young cow. A red heifer was used in sacrifice without the camp as a sin-offering. See Num. 19:1-10. Compare Heb. 9:13, 14.

Heir. See INHERITANCE.

He´lah (*tenderness*), a wife of Ashur, a descendant of Judah through Caleb, the son of Hur. 1 Chron. 4:5, 7.

He´lam, a place beyond the territory of Israel, toward the Euphrates. 2 Sam. 10:15, 17.

Hel´bah (*fertility*), a town of Asher. Judg. 1:31.

Hel´bon (*fruitful*), a city or district of Syria celebrated for the fine quality of its wine. Ezek. 27:18.

Hel´da-i (*worldly*). [1] A captain of David's army. 1 Chron. 27:15. [2] A chief man of the Jews who went up from Babylon at the end of the captivity. Zech. 6:10. Same as HELEM in Zech. 6:14.

He´leb (*milk*) or **He´led** (*transient*), one of David's valiant men. 2 Sam. 23:29; 1 Chron. 11:30.

He´lek (*portion*), a son of Gilead, the grandson of Manasseh. Num. 26:30; Josh. 17:2.

He´lek-ites, a family of the Israelites which descended from Helek, one of the sons of Gilead. Num. 26:30.

He´lem (*hammer*). [1] An Israelite descended from Asher. 1 Chron. 7:35. [2] The head of a family of the Jews who dwelt in Jerusalem when Darius gave permission to rebuild the Temple. Zech. 6:14. Same as HELDAI, No. 2.

He´leph (*exchange*), a place on the borders of Naphtali. Josh. 19:33.

He´lez (*strength*). [1] One of David's valiant men. 2 Sam. 23:26; 1 Chron. 11:27. [2] A descendant of Jerahmeel. 1 Chron. 2:39.

He´li (*elevation*), father of Joseph, the husband of Mary. Luke 3:23. Same word as ELI.

He-li-op´o-lis. [1] A city of Egypt. Ezek. 30:17, in the marginal notes. See AVEN, No. 1, and ON. [2] A city of Syria. Same as AVEN, No. 3. See BAALBEC.

Hel´ka-i (*whose portion is Jehovah*), a priest in Jerusalem in the time of Joiakim (Jehoiakim). Neh. 12:15.

Hel´kath (*portion*), a Levitical city of Asher. Josh. 19:25; 21:31.

Hel´kath-haz´zu-rim (*field of swords*), a place near the pool of Gibeon, where a kind of gladiatorial combat took place between twelve of the adherents of Ishbosheth and the same number of the servants of David. 2 Sam. 2:13-17.

Hell. In the Old Testament the Hebrew word for hell is *Sheol*, which corresponds to *Hades*, a Greek word which means the unseen under-world or the realm of the dead. In the English Bible *Sheol* is variously translated by the words *hell, pit,* and *grave.* 1 Sam. 2:6; Job 14:13, etc. In the New Testament the words translated "hell" are HADES and GEHENNA. In 1 Cor. 15:55 HADES is translated "grave," and in all other places "hell." HADES does not refer to the final abode of the impenitent, but to the disembodied state of man between death and the last judgment. Christ descended into *hades*, which was the place where he "preached unto the spirits in prison." 1 Pet. 3:19. GEHENNA, which cor-

responds nearly to our word "hell," means first the valley of Hinnom, on the south of Jerusalem. It was the seat of the worship of Moloch, and was afterward used as a place in which the filth and dead animals of the city were thrown; "where their worm dieth not, and the fire is not quenched." Mark 9:44. Hence the word Gehenna also denotes the final state and abode of lost souls. The rebellious angels were cast into hell. 2 Pet. 2:4. The cursed are to "go away into everlasting punishment" at the great judgment day. Matt. 25:46. See HINNOM, VALLEY OF.

Hel´len-ists, The, are called GRECIANS in the Authorized Version. Acts 6:1; 9:29; 11:20. They were Jews who spoke Greek and who by constant intercourse with the Gentiles had lost their exclusive spirit. The *Hellens* were a different people, native Greeks in religion as well as language.

Hel´met, defensive armor for the head. It was made of thick, tough hide or of metal. 1 Sam. 17:38.

He´lon (*strong*), a Zebulunite, the father of Eliab. Num. 1:9; 2:7.

Helps, in 1 Cor. 12:28, a gift of the Spirit, includes the various duties of the deacons and deaconesses of the Apostolic Church in the care of the sick, the poor, etc., and is also found among the laity in all ages where Christianity prevails.

Helps, in Acts 27:17, were cables, etc. which were, during a storm, passed under and around the vessel to strengthen it.

Helve, in Deut. 19:5, means handle.

Hem of His Gar´ment, the ancient fringe which Moses commanded the children of Israel to wear to remind them of the commandments of God. Num. 15:38, 40. See Matt. 9:20.

He´mam (*exterminating*), a son of Lotan. Gen. 36:22. Same as HOMAM in

Chron. 1:39.

He´man (*trusty*). [1] An Israelite noted for his wisdom. 1 Kings 4:31; 1 Chron. 2:6. [2] Grandson of the prophet Samuel. 1 Chron. 6:33; 2 Chron. 5:12. Psalm 88 is attributed to him.

He´math (*heat*), a person or place. 1 Chron. 2:55.

He´math (*fortress*). 1 Chron. 13:5; Amos 6:14. See HAMATH.

Hem´dan (*pleasant*), a son of Dishon, Gen. 36:26, called AMRAM in 1 Chron. 1:41.

Hem´lock, in Hos. 10:4; Amos 6:12, means a wild, noxious, and bitter plant which has not been identified. It is elsewhere translated "gall." Its figurative use is explained by comparing Amos 6:12 with Deut. 29:18; Amos 5:7; Heb. 12:15.

Hen (*favor*), a son of Zephaniah, a priest who had returned to Jerusalem and dwelt there at the time of the rebuilding of the Temple. Zech. 6:14.

Hen, a barnyard fowl, is touchingly mentioned in our Lord's lament over Jerusalem. Matt. 23:37; Luke 13:34. Hens must have been common in Palestine in New Testament times, and their eggs are probably referred to in Luke 11:12. The cock is mentioned in the account of Peter's denial of Christ. Matt. 26:34; Mark 14:30; Luke 22:60, 61.

He´na (*troubling*), a city which a king of Assyria subdued. 2 Kings 18:34; 19:13; Isa. 37:13.

Hen´a-dad (*favor of Hadad*), a Levite whose sons aided in rebuilding the Temple after the captivity. Ezra 3:9; Neh. 3:18.

Henoch, he´nok. [1] The son of Jared, a descendant of Seth. 1 Chron. 1:3. See ENOCH. [2] A son of Midian. 1 Chron. 1:33. See HANOCH.

He´pher (*a well*). [1] A descendant of Manasseh. Num. 26:32; Josh. 17:2. [2] A descendant of Judah. 1 Chron. 4:6. [3] A captain of David's army. 1 Chron. 11:36. [4] A district of Palestine, probably in Judah, taken by Joshua. Josh. 12:17.

He´pher-ites, descendants of HEPHER, No. 1. Num. 26:32.

Heph´zi-bah (*my delight is in her*). [1] The wife of Hezekiah and mother of Manasseh. 2 Kings 21:1. [2] A symbolic name for Jerusalem restored. Isa. 62:4.

Her´ald, a person who makes formal and public announcements in the name of a king or of the rulers of the Grecian games, etc.; mentioned in the Authorized Version only in Dan. 3:4.

Herbs of various kinds are found in Palestine. The variety mentioned in 2 Kings 4:39; Isa. 18:4; 26:19 is probably colewort or some kind of cabbage. The Jews were commanded, Exod. 12:8, to eat the Passover with bitter herbs. This was intended to remind them of the severe and cruel bondage in Egypt from which they had been delivered.

Also see Gen. 1:11, 12, 29, 30; 2:5; 3:18; 9:3.

Exod. 9:22, 25; 10:12, 15.

Num. 9:11.

Deut. 11:10; 32:2.

1 Kings 21:2.

2 Kings 19:26.

Job 8:12; 38:27.

Pss. 37:2; 104:14; 105:35.

Prov. 15:17; 27:25.

Isa. 37:27; 42:15; 56:14.

Jer. 12:4.

Matt. 13:32.

Mark 4:32.

Luke 11:42.

Rom. 14:2.

Heb. 6:7.

Herd, Herds´man. The chief part of the wealth of Abraham and his near descendants consisted of herds and flocks, Gen. 13:2; 26:14, and they were among the most valuable possessions of the Hebrews during their national life. Joseph's brethren were made Pharaoh's chief herdsmen. Gen. 47:6. See CATTLE.

Also see Gen. 13:5, 7, 8; 18:7; 24:35; 26:20; 32:7; 33:13; 45:10; 46:32; 47:1, 17, 18; 50:8.

Exod. 10:9, 24; 12:32, 38; 34:3.

Lev. 1:2, 3; 3:1; 27:32.

Num. 11:22; 15:3.

Deut. 8:13; 12:6, 17, 21; 14:23; 15:19; 16:2.

1 Sam. 11:5; 21:7; 30:20.

2 Sam. 12:2, 4.

1 Chron. 27:29.

2 Chron. 32:29.

Neh. 10:36.

Prov. 27:23.

Isa. 65:10.

Jer. 3:24; 5:17; 31:12.

Hos. 5:6.

Joel 1:18.

Amos 1:1; 7:14.

Jon. 3:7.

Hab. 3:17.

Matt. 8:30-32.

Mark 5:11, 13.

Luke 8:32, 33.

He´res (*sun*). [1] Mount Heres. Judg. 1:35. [2] Heres, in the marginal notes, Isa. 19:18. It is "city of destruction" in the text.

He´resh (*artificer*), the head of a family of Levites in Jerusalem. 1 Chron. 9:15.

Her´e-sy (*choice*), Acts 24:14, a word used in the Bible to denote a sect or party, and implies no judgment concerning the truth or error of their doctrines. It is sometimes translated "sect." The word heresy acquired its present meaning—departure from the fundamental truth of the Gospel—early in the history of the Christian Church.

Her´e-tick, in Titus 3:10, means a fractious person.

Her´mas (*of Mercury*), a Roman Christian greeted by Paul. Rom. 16:14.

Her´mes (*Mercury*), a Christian at Rome whom Paul saluted. Rom. 16:14. According to tradition, he was one of the Seventy and became bishop of Dalmatia.

Hermogenes, her-moj´e-neez, an Ephesian disciple who forsook Paul. 2 Tim. 1:15.

Her´mon or **Mount Her´mon** (*prominent summit*), the southern part of the mountain-range of Anti-Libanus, was called SIRION by the Sidonians, SHENIR by the Amorites, and is called SION in Deut. 4:48, which must not be mistaken for ZION. Mount Hermon was the northern limit of the territory of Israel beyond Jordan. Deut. 3:8; 4:48; Josh. 11:3, 17; 13:11. It has three summits and rises to an elevation of three thousand feet above the Mediterranean Sea. Its top is partly covered with snow or ice, which lies in the ravines during the whole year. Mount Hermon's majestic height and abundant dews were praised by the Hebrews. Pss. 89:12; 133:3. It is not mentioned in the New Testament, but is probably the site of Christ's transfiguration. Matt. 17; Mark 9.

Her´mon-ites, The, in Ps. 42:6, means the three summits of Mount Hermon.

Her´od was a common name in a numerous family which played a conspicuous and almost fatal part in Jewish politics in the times of our Lord and his apostles. It came from IDUMEA (which see). All its members were very zealous in professing the Mosaic law, though they did not keep it; very desirous to give no offence to

Jewish prejudices, though they despised them; and very painstaking in flattering Jewish vanity when thereby they could further their own plans. But as they could never hope to realize their great ambition to establish an Idumean dynasty in Judea without the support of the Romans, many of the Herod family were educated in Rome or had lived there for a long time. Thus they became a sort of middlemen between Greek-Roman civilization, Greek-Roman paganism, and Judaism, to the great injury of the Jews.

[1] HEROD THE GREAT was made king of Judea by the first Roman emperor, Augustus, and reigned for thirty-seven years. Christ was born near the end of his reign. Matt. 2:1–18. Herod rebuilt the Temple at Jerusalem. He also adorned Jerusalem with other splendid buildings, but they were theatres and amphitheatres, and were intended to aid in the introduction of pagan games and festivals among the Jews. Herod was despotic and cruel, and had ten wives, one after the other. One of them, Mariamne, he murdered B. C. 29, together with her mother, brother, and grandfather; later, B. C. 7, he killed two of his sons by her, Aristobulus and Alexander; and a few days before his death a third son, by Doris, Antipater. From his house his cruelty extended to his subjects. On their arrival in Jerusalem the Wise Men had an audience with him, and when they told him that a "King of the Jews" had been born at Bethlehem he ordered the Massacre of the Innocents. Matt. 2:16. While on his death-bed at Jericho he gathered a number of rich and distinguished people around him and gave a secret order that they should all be put to death immediately after his decease, in order that there might be mourning when he died.

[2] HEROD AN´TI-PAS, a son of Herod the Great by his fourth wife, Malthace, tried to become king of Judea after the death of his father, but had to content himself with the tetrarchy of Galilee, Luke 3:1, and Perea, over which he reigned B. C. 4–A. D. 39, when he was deposed by Caligula and banished to Lyons in Gaul. He married Herodias, though her legal husband, Herod Philip (not the tetrarch Philip, who married Salome), was still living. Denounced by John the Baptist for this open breach of the Mosaic law, he threw the prophet into a dungeon, and, taken by surprise by Salome, the daughter of Herodias, he had John the Baptist beheaded. Mark 6:16-28. He set Christ "at naught, and mocked him." Luke 23:7-12. Herod's character is described in Mark 6:16, 22 and in Luke 13:32, where he is called "that fox."

[3] ARCHELAUS, ar-ke-la´us, was the son of Herod the Great by Malthace, and was the elder brother of Herod Antipas. He was ethnarch of Judea, Samaria, and Idumea; was tyrannical; was banished to Vienne in Gaul; and is mentioned in the New Testament only in Matt. 2:22.

[4] PHIL´IP, B. C. 4–A D. 34, tetrarch of Gaulanitis, Auranitis, etc., was the son of Herod the Great, but was noted for moderation and justice. He married his niece Salome, the young woman that danced before Herod Antipas. Mark 6:22. He is mentioned in the New Testament only in Luke 3:1.

[5] HEROD PHIL´IP was the son of Herod the Great and Mariamne, and was the first husband of Herodias. He seems to have lived as a private citizen, and is called PHILIP in Mark 6:17.

[6] HEROD A-GRIP´PA I., king of Judea A. D. 37–44, was a grandson of Herod the Great and son of the murdered Aristobulus.

He was educated in Rome and was a friend of Caligula, but observed the ceremonial of the Pharisees, persecuted the apostles, beheaded James, and tried to execute Peter. Acts 12:1-19.

[7] HEROD A-GRIP'PA II., king of parts of Judea A. D. 50–100, was a son of Herod Agrippa I., and is noted in the history of Paul. Acts. 26:28.

Also see Matt. 2:12, 13, 15, 19; 14:1, 3, 6.

Mark 6:14; 8:15.

Luke 1:5; 3:19; 8:3; 9:7, 9; 13:31; 23:7, 15.

Acts 4:27; 12:20, 21; 13:1; 23:35.

He-ro'di-ans, the court party among the Jews in the time of Herod the Great. Matt. 22:16. They willingly submitted to the government of Rome and united with the Pharisees in attempting to destroy Christ. Matt. 22:16; Mark 3:6.

He-ro'di-as, a granddaughter of Herod the Great, and married first to her uncle, Herod Philip, to whom she bore Salome, Matt. 14:3, and then (during her first husband's life) to Herod Antipas, another uncle.

He-ro'di-on, a "kinsman" of Paul. Rom. 16:11.

Her'on, a well-known bird, several species of which are found in Palestine. Lev. 11:19; Deut. 14:18.

He'sed (*kindness*), father of one of Solomon's purveyors. 1 Kings 4:10.

Hesh'bon (*stronghold*), a city which originally belonged to the Moabites. It was afterward the capital of the Amorites, was captured by the Israelites, Num. 21:25, 26, and became a Levitical city on the borders of Reuben and Gad. It subsequently became a Moabitish town again.

Hesh'mon (*fertility*), a town in the south of Judah. Josh. 15:27.

Hes'ron, Hes'ron-ites. See HEZRON, HEZRONITES.

Heth (*terror*), one of the sons of Canaan, the son of Ham. Gen. 10:15; 1 Chron. 1:13. He was the progenitor of the HITTITES (which see).

Heth'lon (*stronghold*), a town on the northern border of Palestine. Ezek. 47:15; 48:1.

Hez'e-ki (*strong*), a son of Elpaal, a descendant of Benjamin. 1 Chron. 8:17.

Hez-e-ki'ah (*strength of Jehovah*). [1] A noted king of Judah, B. C. 726–697, the son and successor of the apostate Ahaz, but very unlike him. He was eminently godly, abolished idol-worship, tore down the "high places" dedicated to idolatry, and broke in pieces the brazen serpent of Moses, which had become an object of idolatrous worship. 2 Kings 18:4. He repaired the Temple, restored the Mosaic institutions to honor, and celebrated the Passover with a splendor and magnificence not seen since the days of David and Solomon. 2 Chron. 30:26. Under Ahaz Judah had become tributary to Assyria, but, having confidence in the promise and prophecy of Isaiah, Hezekiah claimed and asserted the independence of his kingdom, and the army of Sennacherib, by a sudden judgment of God, retired defeated from the walls of Jerusalem. 2 Kings 19:35. Sick unto death, he prayed to God to prolong his life, and Isaiah brought him the message that his prayer had been granted. 2 Kings 20:10. [2] A son of Neariah, of the house of David. 1 Chron. 3:23. [3] An Israelite whose descendants returned to Jerusalem with Zerubbabel. Ezra 2:16; Neh. 7:21. See ATER, No. 1.

Also see 2 Kings 16:20; 18:1, 9, 10,

13-17, 19, 22, 29-32, 37; 19:1, 3, 5, 9, 10, 14, 15, 20; 20:1, 3, 5, 8, 12-16, 19-21; 21:3.

1 Chron. 3:13; 4:41.

2 Chron. 28:27; 29:1, 18, 20, 27, 30, 31, 36; 30:1, 18, 20, 22, 24; 31:2, 8, 9, 11, 13, 20; 32:2, 8, 9, 11, 12, 15-17, 20, 22-27, 30, 32, 33; 33:3.

Prov. 25:1.

Isa. 1:1; 36:1, 2, 4, 7, 14-16, 18; 36:22; 37:1, 3, 5, 9, 10, 14, 15, 21; 38:1-3, 5, 9; 39:1-5, 8.

Jer. 15:4; 26:18, 19.

Hos. 1:1.

Mic. 1:1.

He´zi-on (*sight*), grandfather of Ben-hadad, king of Syria. 1 Kings 15:18.

He´zir (*returning home*). **[1]** A priest in the time of David. 1 Chron. 24:15. **[2]** One who sealed the covenant. Neh. 10:20.

Hez´ra-i (*enclosed*), one of David's valiant men. 2 Sam. 23:35. He is called HEZRO in 1 Chron. 11:37.

Hez´ro (*blooming*). 1 Chron. 11:37. Same as HEZRAI.

Hez´ron (*blooming*). **[1]** A son of Reuben. Gen. 46:9; Exod. 6:14. **[2]** A son of Pharez. Gen. 46:12; Ruth 4:18. **[3]** A town of Judah. Josh. 15:25. See HAZOR, No. 4.

Hez´ron-ites, a family in Reuben, and another in Judah. Num. 26:6, 21.

Hid´da-i (*joyful*), one of David's valiant men. 2 Sam. 23:30. He is called HURAI in 1 Chron. 11:32.

Hid´de-kel (*rapid Tigris*), the third of the rivers which flowed from the garden of Eden. Gen. 2:14; Dan. 10:4. It "goeth toward the east of Assyria."

Hi´el (*God lives*), an Israelite of Bethel, who rebuilt Jericho in the reign of Ahab. 1 Kings 16:34. Joshua's curse, Josh. 6:26, was fulfilled in HIEL.

Hi-e-rap´o-lis (*sacred city*), a city of Phrygia, Asia Minor, about twenty miles west of Colosse and six miles north of Laodicea. It contained the famous temple of Pluto, the ruins of which and of the city are still to be seen. Col. 4:13. The city was famous for its warm springs.

Higgaion, hig-ga´yon, Ps. 9:16, was probably originally a musical term which afterward acquired the additional meanings meditation and solemn sound.

High´est, a word used by the angel Gabriel (when announcing to Mary her miraculous conception) to indicate God the Father. Luke 1:32, 35, 76.

High Place. [1] The place where Saul met with Samuel. 1 Sam. 9:12, 13. **[2]** A name applied to Gibeon, where the Tabernacle was in the time of David. 1 Kings 3:4; 2 Chron. 1:3, 13. **[3]** The place "before Jerusalem" where Solomon set up idolatrous worship. 1 Kings 11:7. **[4]** A name applied to Bethel where Jeroboam set up the golden calf. 2 Kings 23:15. In the plural the term is used frequently, and generally denotes places where idolatrous worship was practiced.

High-Priest, the head of the priesthood of Israel. Lev. 21:10. The office was first held by AARON (which see), and afterward by his descendants. His immediate successor was Eleazar. The high-priest originally held office for life. Solomon disregarded this rule by deposing Abiathar and appointing Zadok, because Abiathar was disloyal. 1 Kings 2:35. The consecration services of the high-priest lasted seven days, and consisted of sacrifices, etc. Exod. 29; Lev. 21:10. The high-priest's dress was much more costly than that of the inferior priests. Exod. 39:1–9. He wore a breastplate, a piece of embroidery about ten inches square, which was set with twelve precious stones, on each of which was engraved the name of one of the twelve tribes of Israel. Exod. 28:15–40. His exclusive duty was to officiate in the most holy place on the great Day of Atonement. Lev. 16. He was the overseer of the Temple, and might at any time perform the duties of an ordinary priest. At the time of Christ the high-priest presided over the Sanhedrin. Acts 5:17; John 18:13, 14. Jesus is called the High-Priest. Heb. 4:14; 7:25–28; 9:11, etc.

High´ways. Palestine had roads in ancient times, as carts and chariots were used. Gen. 45:19, 20; Josh. 17:16, etc. The remains of the Roman roads are still to be seen. In Luke 14:23 Christ mentions highways in the parable of the Marriage Supper. See HEDGE, and FIELD.

Hi´len (*place of caves ?*), a city of Judah which was afterward assigned to the Levites. 1 Chron. 6:58. It is called HOLON in Josh. 15:51; 21:15.

Hil-ki´ah (*the Lord is my portion*). [1] The father of Eliakim. 2 Kings 18:18; Isa. 22:20. [2] The high priest in the reign of Josiah. He found the book of the law, 2 Kings 22:8, and is also mentioned in 2 Kings 23:4, 24; 2 Chron. 34:9, 14, 15, etc. [3, 4] Two descendants of Merari. 1 Chron. 6:45; 26:11. [5] A priest who stood beside Ezra while he read the book of the law to the people. Neh. 8:4; 11:11. [6] A priest who returned with Zerubbabel. Neh. 12:7, 21. [7] A priest who was the father of Jeremiah the prophet. Jer. 1:1. [8] Father of an ambassador from Zedekiah to Nebuchadnezzar. Jer. 29:3.

Hil´lel (*praise*), an Israelite of the tribe of Ephraim, who was the father of Abdon, a judge of Israel. Judg. 12:13, 15.

Hill, Hills. The words "hill" and "mountain" are used indefinitely in the Authorized Version. The "hill country," Luke 1:39, is the "mountain of Judah" in Josh. 20:7. In Luke 9:28 the same elevation is called "mountain" which in Luke 9:37 is named "hill." The original text is exact.

Hill coun´try. See HILL.

Hill of Zion. See ZION; JERUSALEM.

Hin, Exod. 29:40, a liquid measure containing twelve logs, or a little more than a gallon. A log was the smallest measure for liquids among the Israelites. See MEASURES.

Hind, the female of the HART (which see).

Hind´er Sea, Zech. 14:8, means the Mediterranean Sea.

Hinges, hinj´es, of "pure gold" for doors in Solomon's Temple are mentioned in 1 Kings 7:50. Hinges of another kind are referred to in Prov. 26:14.

Hin´nom, Val´ley of, is on the south and west of Jerusalem, and is also called "the valley of the son," "children of Hinnom," or "valley of the children of groaning." The south-eastern part of it is called Tophet, or "place of fire," Jer. 7:31, and Topheth in 2 Kings 23:10. That part is called the "valley of slaughter." Jer. 7:32; 19:6. The Valley of Hinnom is first mentioned in Josh. 15:8; 18:16 as the boundary between Judah and Benjamin. In this valley Ahaz and Manasseh made their children "pass through the fire." 2 Kings 16:3; 2 Chron. 33:6. The sacrifice of infants to the fire-gods was kept up here, and in order to put an end to this horrible practice King Josiah spread human bones, etc. over the place, 2 Kings 23:10, 13, 14, and it became a cesspool which received the sewage of Jerusalem. On account of its ceremonial defilement and its fires the later Jews used its name, *Ge Hinnom*, GEHENNA, to indicate the place of eternal suffering for lost angels and men. It is thus used in the

Gospels, and is translated "hell." Matt. 5:29; 10:28; 23:15; Mark 9:43; Luke 12:5. See HELL.

Hi´rah (*noble birth*), a citizen of Adullam and friend of Judah. Gen. 38:1, 12.

Hi´ram (*noble*). [1] The king of Tyre in the time of David and Solomon, with whom he was friendly. He furnished David with materials and workmen for his palace, 2 Sam. 5:11; 1 Chron. 14:1, and supplied Solomon with gold, timber, and men to build the Temple. 1 Kings 5:1-12; 9:11-14. He is called HURAM in 2 Chron. 2:3, 12, etc. [2] A famous artificer from Tyre who was employed by Solomon on the furniture of the Temple. 1 Kings 7:13. He is called HURAM in 2 Chron. 4:11, 16. Also see 1 Kings 5:18; 7:40, 45; 9:27; 10:11, 22.

Hire´ling, a laborer employed for a limited time. Job 14:6. He was to be paid promptly. Lev. 19:13; James 5:4. "The years of a hireling" signifies time exactly measured. Isa. 16:14; 21:16. A hireling had little interest in his flock compared with that of the permanent shepherd. See Christ's discourse in John 10:12, 13.

His is often used in the Authorized Version instead of "*its.*" Gen. 1:11, 12; Lev. 11:22; Deut. 14:15. In Matt. 6:33 "Seek ye first the kingdom of God, and his righteousness," "his" refers to God, and *not* to kingdom.

Hiss, an expression of contempt. 1 Kings 9:8; Jer. 19:8; Ezek. 27:36; Mic. 6:16. It also denotes a mode of calling an attendant still common in the East. Isa. 5:26; 7:18; Zech. 10:8.

Hit´tites, the descendants of Heth, the second son of Canaan. Abraham purchased Machpelah for a sepulchre from them. Gen. 23:3–13. Esau married two Hittite women. Gen. 26:34, 35.

Also see Gen. 15:20; 23:10; 25:9; 36:2; 49:29, 30; 50:13.
Exod 3:8, 17; 13:5; 23:23, 28; 33:2; 34:11.
Num. 13:29.
Deut. 7:1; 20:17.
Josh. 1:4; 3:10; 9:1; 11:3; 12:8; 24:11.
Judg. 1:26; 3:5.
1 Sam. 26:6.
2 Sam. 11:3, 6, 17, 21, 24; 12:9, 10; 23:39.
1 Kings 9:20; 10:29; 11:1; 15:5.
2 Kings 7:6.
1 Chron. 11:41.
2 Chron. 1:17; 8:7.
Ezra 9:1.
Neh. 9:8.
Ezek. 16:3, 45.

Hit´tites, Land of the, the territory occupied by the Hittites. It was in the south-eastern part of Canaan, in what was afterward called the hill country of Judah, and included Kirjath-arba (Hebron) and Machpelah. Gen. 23.

Hi´vites, a nation descended from Canaan, the son of Ham. Gen. 10:17; Exod. 3:8. They lived in various parts of the land of Canaan.

Hi´vites, Land of the, the territory in Canaan occupied by the Hivites. It included part of the east coast of the Mediterranean Sea and some of the adjacent hill country on the east. The Hivites voluntarily surrendered their country to Joshua, Josh. 9:7; 11:19, and subsequently paid tribute to Solomon. 1 Kings 9:20; 2 Chron. 8:7.

Hiz-ki´ah (*strength of Jehovah*), an ancestor of Zephaniah the prophet. Zeph. 1:1.

Hiz-ki´jah (*strength of Jehovah*), one who sealed the covenant. Neh. 10:17.

Ho´bab (*love*), son of Raguel, Num.

10:29, who is called REUEL in Exod. 2:18.

Ho'bah (*lurking-place*), a place near Damascus to which Abram pursued the confederate kings. Gen. 14:15.

Hod (*splendor*), a son of Zophah, a descendant of Asher. 1 Chron. 7:37.

Hod-a-i´ah (*splendor of Jehovah*), a son of Elioenai, a descendant of David. 1 Chron. 3:24.

Hod-a-vi´ah (*splendor of Jehovah*). [1] A chief of Manasseh. 1 Chron. 5:24. [2] A descendant of Benjamin. 1 Chron. 9:7. [3] A Levite whose descendants returned from Babylon. Ezra 2:40.

Ho´desh (*new moon*), a wife of Shaharaim, a descendant of Benjamin. 1 Chron. 8:9.

Ho-de´vah (*splendor of Jehovah*), a Levite, some of whose family returned from Babylon with Zerubbabel. Neh. 7:43.

Ho-di´ah (*splendor of Jehovah*), a wife of Ezra, a descendant of Judah through Caleb, the son of Jephunneh. 1 Chron. 4:19. May be same as JEHUDIJAH. 1 Chron. 4:18.

Ho-di´jah (*splendor of Jehovah*), three Levites in the time of Nehemiah and Ezra. Neh. 8:7; 9:5; 10:10, 13, 18.

Hog´lah (*partridge*), a daughter of Zelophehad. Num. 26:33; Josh. 17:3.

Ho´ham (*whom Jehovah incites*), an Amorite king of Hebron who was slain by Joshua. Josh. 10:3.

Hold, in Exod. 20:7; Job 9:28; Zech. 11:5; Matt. 21:26, means regard; treat.

Ho´lon (*sandy*). [1] A city in the mountains of Judah, Josh. 15:51; 21:15, called HILEN in 1 Chron. 6:58. [2] A city of Moab, east of the Jordan. Jer. 48:21.

Ho´ly, Ho´li-ness. Lev. 27:14; Exod. 15:11. Holiness is an attribute of the LORD. Isa. 6:3. The word "holy" is applied to angels in Matt. 25:31. It denotes comparative freedom from sin in the case of Christians. Heb. 3:1; Col. 3:12. "Holiness to the Lord" was inscribed on the golden plate which the high priest wore on his forehead. Exod. 28:36; 39:30.

Also see Exod. 3; 12; 15; 16; 19; 20; 22; 26; 28–31; 35; 37–40.

Lev. 2; 5–8; 10; 11; 14; 16; 19–25; 27.

Num. 4–6; 15; 16; 18; 28; 29; 31; 35.

Deut. 7; 12; 14; 23; 26; 28; 33.

Josh. 5; 24.

1 Sam. 2; 6; 21.

1 Kings 6–8.

2 Kings 4; 19.

1 Chron. 6; 16; 22; 23; 29.

2 Chron. 3–5; 8; 20; 23; 29–31; 35.

Ezra 2; 8; 9.

Neh. 7–12.

Job 6.

Pss. 2; 3; 5; 11; 15; 16; 20; 22; 24; 28; 29; 30; 33; 43; 46–48; 51; 60; 65; 68; 71; 78; 79; 86; 87; 89; 93; 96–99; 103; 105; 106; 108; 110; 111; 138; 145.

Prov. 9; 20; 30.

Eccles. 8.

Isa. 1; 4–6; 10–12; 17; 27; 23; 29–31; 35; 37; 40; 41; 43; 45; 47–49; 52; 54–58; 60; 62–66.

Jer. 2; 11; 23; 25; 31; 50; 51.

Ezek. 7; 20–22; 28; 36; 39; 41–46; 48.

Dan. 4; 5; 8; 9; 11; 12.

Hos. 11.

Joel 2; 3.

Amos 2; 4.

Obad. :16, 17.

Jon. 2.

Mic. 1.

Hab. 1–3.

Zeph. 3.

Hag. 2.

Zech. 2; 8; 14.

Mal. 2.
Matt. 1; 3; 4; 7; 12; 24; 25; 27; 28.
Mark 1; 3; 6; 8; 12; 13.
Luke 1–4; 9; 11; 12.
John 1; 7; 14; 17; 20.
Acts 1–11; 13; 15; 16; 19–21; 28.
Rom. 1; 5–7; 9; 11; 12; 14–16.
1 Cor. 2; 3; 6; 7; 9; 12; 16.
2 Cor. 6; 7; 13.
Eph. 1–5.
Col. 1; 3.
1 Thess. 1; 3–5.
1 Tim. 2.
2 Tim. 1; 3.
Titus 1–3.
Heb. 2; 3; 6; 7; 9; 10; 12.
1 Pet. 1–3.
2 Pet. 1–3.
1 John 2; 5.
Jude :20.
Rev. 3; 4; 6; 11; 14; 15; 18; 20–22.

Ho´ly City. See JERUSALEM.

Ho´ly Day. See FEASTS.

Ho´ly Ghost, Holy Spirit, the third person in the Trinity. See SPIRIT.

Ho´ly Land. See CANAAN, and PALESTINE.

Ho´ly One. This expression is used, either alone or in connection with appropriate words, to designate the Supreme God, and in a few cases is applied to the MESSIAH. "Thy holy one," in Ps. 89:19, is rendered "thy saints" in the Revised Version.
Also see Deut. 33:8.
2 Kings 19:22.
Job 6:10.
Pss. 16:10; 71:22; 78:41.
Isa. 1:4; 5:19, 24; 10:17, 20; 12:6; 17:7; 29:19, 23; 30:11, 12, 15; 31:1; 37:23; 40:25; 41:14, 16, 20; 43:3, 14, 15; 45:11; 47:4; 48:17; 49:7; 54:5; 55:5; 60:9, 14.

Jer. 50:29; 51:5.
Ezek. 39:7.
Hos. 11:9.
Hab. 1:12; 3:3.
Mark 1:24.
Luke 4:34.
Acts 2:27; 3:14; 13:35.
1 John 2:20.

Ho´mam (*extermination*). 1 Chron. 1:39. See HEMAM.

Ho´mer, Lev. 27:16; Ezek. 45:11, the largest measure for dry things, used by the Israelites, contained about eight bushels. See MEASURES.

Hon´est, Hon´est-y, Hon´est-ly are frequently used in the Authorized Version in the original sense of "honorable, comely." Rom. 12:17; 2 Cor. 13:17; Phil. 4:8; 1 Tim. 2:2; Heb. 13:18. Honest, in 1 Pet. 2:12, means morally beautiful.

Hon´ey, Hon´ey-comb. Palestine was anciently "a land flowing with milk and honey," Exod. 3:8, 17, and honey is still very abundant there. Honey and the honey-comb are beautifully alluded to figuratively in Ps. 19:10; Prov. 5:3; 27:7. Syrups from dates and grapes are sometimes included in the term "honey." Honey is mentioned in 2 Sam. 17:29; Isa. 7:15; Matt. 3:4, among articles of food. Also see Gen. 43:11.
Exod. 13:5; 16:31; 33:3.
Lev. 2:11; 20:24.
Num. 13:27; 14:8; 16:13, 14.
Deut. 6:3; 8:8; 11:9; 26:9, 15; 27:3; 31:20; 32:13.
Josh. 5:6
Judg. 14:8, 9, 18.
1 Sam. 14:25-27, 29, 43.
1 Kings 14:3.
2 Kings 18:32.
2 Chron. 31:5.
Job 20:17.

Pss. 81:16; 119:103.
Prov. 16:24; 24:13; 25:16, 27.
Song of Sol. 4:11; 5:1.
Isa. 7:22.
Jer. 11:5; 32:22; 41:8.
Ezek. 3:3; 16:3, 19; 20:6, 15; 27:17.
Mark 1:6.
Luke 24:42.
Rev. 10:9, 10.

Hood, in Isa. 3:23, means a turban.

Hooks of several kinds are mentioned in the Bible. [1] Fish-hooks. See FISH-HOOKS. [2] The "hook" of 2 Kings 19:28; Ezek. 29:4, which was probably a ring for the noses of wild beasts and used in leading them. Captives were sometimes thus led, as Assyrian sculptures show. [3] Pruning-hooks. Isa. 2:4; 18:5. [4] Flesh-hooks, Exod. 27:3; 1 Sam. 2:13, used to get flesh out of the caldrons. [5] Hooks which supported the curtains of the Tabernacle. Exod. 26:32, 37. [6] Perhaps hooks used for suspending carcasses while they were being skinned. Ezek. 40:43.

Hoph´ni (*a fighter*), a son of Eli the high-priest, was, like his brother PHINEHAS, licentious, exacting, and impious. They were slain in battle. 1 Sam. 1:3; 2:12-17, 22-26, 34; 4:11. See ELI.

Hor, Mount (*the mountain*). [1] A mountain "in the edge of the land of Edom." Num. 33:37. Edom, or Mount Seir, included the range of mountains which extends nearly from the south end of the Dead Sea to the Gulf of Akabah. About the middle of this range is its highest mountain, which is probably Mount Hor, on which Aaron died. Num. 20:24-29; 33:38, 39; Deut. 32:50. Its summit is 4800 feet above the Mediterranean. The mountain has two peaks, on the lower of which, 4360 feet above the Mediterranean, is "Aaron's tomb," so called, a small build-ing 28 by 33 feet, built over his supposed grave. Some suppose *Jebel Madurah* to be Mount Hor. [2] A mountain on the northern boundary of the Promised Land. It is mentioned only in Num. 34:7, 8, is probably the extreme northern summit of the Lebanon range, has an elevation of 10,000 feet, and is the highest mountain in Syria.

Ho´ram (*elevated*), the king of Gezer who went to help Lachish against Joshua, and was defeated by him. Josh. 10:33.

Ho´reb (*dry, desert*), a mountain or range often mentioned in the Bible. Some think that it is the name of the whole range of which Sinai is a special peak. Others consider Sinai as the range and Horeb a summit of it. In Leviticus and Numbers Sinai is exclusively used in reference to the giving of the Law. In Deuteronomy Horeb is used instead of Sinai. Sinai and Horeb are used indiscriminately in the Psalms. Sinai and its wilderness are the scene of events in the region of Horeb, and the whole of Horeb is called "the mountain of God." Exod. 3:1, 12; 4:27, etc. Hence "Sinai" is sometimes mentioned alone. Exod. 19:11, 20; 24:16, etc. But "Horeb" is often named alone, and the same events are spoken of as occurring on both "Horeb" and "Sinai." In the New Testament "Sinai" became a general name, and is so now. Acts 7:30, 38; Gal. 4:24, 25. See SINAI. Also see Exod. 17:6; 33:6.
Deut. 1:2, 6, 19; 4:10, 15; 5:2; 9:8; 18:16; 29:1.
1 Kings 8:9; 19:8.
2 Chron. 5:10.
Ps. 106:19.
Mal. 4:4.

Ho´rem (*devoted*), a fortified city of Naphtali. Josh. 19:38.

Hor-ha-gid´gad (*mountain of the cleft*), the twenty-eighth station of the

Israelites in their wanderings through the wilderness. Num. 33:32, 33. Supposed to be same as GUDGODAH. Deut. 10:7.

Ho´ri (*cave-dweller*). [1] A son of Lotan and grandson of Seir. Gen 36:22; 1 Chron. 1:39. [2] A man of Simeon. Num. 13:5.

Ho´rims, Ho´rites, a people who dwelt on the south and south-east of the Dead Sea, in the mountainous country about Petra, and who were, as is supposed, descended from Hori, the grandson of Seir. Gen. 14:6; Deut. 2:12.

Hor´mah (*place desolated*), a royal city of the Canaanites; was originally called ZEPHATH. Judg. 1:17. It was in the south part of the land, and was assigned to Simeon. Num. 14:45; 21:3; Deut. 1:44; 1 Sam. 30:30; 1 Chron. 4:30.

Horn, in the Old Testament, is an emblem of power, honor, or glory. Deut. 33:17; Lam. 2:3. It is also the symbol of victory, and is often used in the prophetic visions instead of "kings" and "kingdoms." Dan. 7:20-24; Zech. 1:18. Horns were used to contain liquids, notably oils and perfumes, 1 Sam. 16:1, and for trumpets. Josh. 6:8, 13. They were not always actual horns, but rather horn-shaped articles.

Horns of the Altar. See ALTAR.

Hor´net, a large wasp-like insect, noted for its irritability and the severity of its sting. Deut. 7:20. Hornets were used as instruments of divine judgment upon the enemies of the Israelites. Exod. 23:28; Josh. 24:12.

Hor-o-na´im (*two caverns*), a city of Moab. Isa. 15:5; Jer. 48:3.

Hor´o-nite, The, a name applied to Sanballat, who opposed Nehemiah when he rebuilt the wall of Jerusalem. Neh. 2:10, 19; 13:28. He may have come either from Horonaim or from Beth-horon.

Horse, Gen 49:17, a noble animal which is poetically described in Job 39:19-25. In very ancient times oxen and asses were generally used for labor. Horses were used chiefly in war. Exod. 14:9, 23; Esther 6:8. They were common among the Jews in the time of Solomon. Also see Gen. 47:17.
Exod. 9:3; 15:1, 19, 21.
Deut. 11:4; 17:16; 20:1.
Josh. 11:4, 6, 9.
2 Sam. 15:1.
1 Kings 4:26, 28; 10:25, 28, 29; 18:5; 20:1, 20, 21, 25; 22:4.
2 Kings 2:11; 3:7; 5:9; 6:14, 15, 17; 7:6, 7, 10, 13, 14; 9:33; 10:2; 11:16; 14:20; 18:23; 23:11.
1 Chron. 18:4.
2 Chron. 1:16, 17; 9:24, 25, 28; 23:15; 25:28.
Ezra 2:66.
Neh. 3:28; 7:68.
Esther 6:9-11.
Job 39:18.
Pss. 20:7; 32:9; 33:17; 76:6; 147:10.
Prov. 21:31; 26:3.
Eccles. 10:7.
Song of Sol. 1:9.
Isa. 2:7; 5:28; 30:16; 31:1, 3; 36:8; 43:17; 63:13; 66:20.
Jer. 4:13; 5:8; 6:23; 8:6, 16; 12:5; 17:25; 22:4; 31:40; 46:4, 9; 47:3; 50:37, 42; 51:21, 27.
Ezek. 17:15; 23:6, 12, 20, 23; 26:7, 10, 11; 27:14; 38:4, 15; 39:20.
Hos. 1:7; 14:3.
Joel 2:4.
Amos 2:15; 4:10; 6:12.
Mic. 5:10.
Nah. 3:2.
Hab. 1:8; 3:8, 15.
Hag. 2:22.
Zech. 1:8; 6:2, 3, 6; 9:10; 10:3, 5; 12:4;

14:15, 20.

James 3:3.

Rev. 6:2, 4, 5, 8; 9:7, 9, 17; 14:20; 18:13; 19:11, 14, 18, 19, 21.

Horse-leech ("Horseleach" in the Authorized Version), a well-known and blood-thirsty worm found in the stagnant waters of Palestine. Prov. 30:15.

Ho´sah (*place of refuge*). [1] A place mentioned in describing the borders of Asher. Josh. 19:29. [2] A Levite porter attached to the Tabernacle in the time of David. 1 Chron. 16:38; 26:10.

Ho-san´na (*save, we beseech!*), an exclamation used by the multitudes who welcomed Christ's entry into Jerusalem. Matt. 21:9–15.

Hosea, ho-ze´ah (*God is help*), one of the twelve minor prophets, called OSEE in Rom. 9:25, was a contemporary of Isaiah, and prophesied during the reign of Jeroboam II. in Israel and the reigns of Uzziah, Jotham, Ahaz, and Hezekiah in Judah, B. C. 790-725. Hosea is supposed to have been a native of the kingdom of Israel, as his prophecies are almost entirely addressed to that part of the Jewish nation. Nothing is known of his life, but his book reveals his sad and sympathetic heart in view of the sinfulness of his people. He was nevertheless full of hope.

Hosea, the Book of, consists of threats and denunciations against the wickedness of the Israelites, mingled with predictions of the final restoration of God's people to goodness and prosperity. His prophecies are obscure and difficult, from their brief and condensed style, their sudden transitions, the indistinctness of their allusions, and the great difficulty of rightly ascertaining to what precise period or transaction many of their passages refer. But he is remarkable for intensity of passion, both in wrath and in tenderness, and for poetic beauty of imagery and style. Hosea has been called "the prophet of tragic and elegiac sorrow." He is the most patriotic of all the prophets, confining himself to his own country and people, and referring less than they to the interests of the Gentiles.

His marriage, by divine command, with Gomer, "a wife of whoredoms," Hos. 1:2-9, is best explained figuratively as a symbol of the monstrous sin of spiritual whoredom or apostasy from the true God.

Ho´sen (old plural of *hose*) originally meant trousers and stockings in one piece. In Dan. 3:21 it means tunics.

Hosh-a-i´ah (*whom Jehovah saved*). [1] A prince of Judah who officiated in the ceremonial purifying of the people after their return to Jerusalem. Neh. 12:32. [2] The father of Jaazaniah or Jezaniah. Jer. 42:1; 43:2.

Hosh´a-ma (*whom Jehovah hears*), a son of Jeconiah (Jehoiachin), the last king of Judah. 1 Chron. 3:18.

Ho-she´a (*God is help*). [1] The name which Joshua, the servant and successor of Moses, bore before Moses changed it to Joshua. Deut. 32:44. See OSHEA. [2] The last of the kings of Israel, who was subdued and imprisoned by Shalmaneser, king of Assyria. 2 Kings 15:30; 17:1–6. [3] A ruler of the tribe of Ephraim. 1 Chron. 27:20. [4] A Jew who sealed the covenant. Neh. 10:23.

Hos-pi-tal´i-ty, receiving and entertaining strangers or guests without reward, is commanded in Lev. 19:33, 34; Deut. 15:7. Many instances of it are given in the Bible, as in the histories of Abraham, Gen. 18:2-8; Lot, Gen. 19:1-3; Jethro, Exod. 2:20; Manoah, Judg. 13:15, etc. The New Testament writers enjoin hospitality upon believers. Rom. 12:13; 1 Tim. 3:2; 5:10; 1 Pet. 4:9. Hospitality was so practiced by the early Christians as to win the admiration of the heathen. The abuse of it was a great crime. Ps. 41:9. To this day a fugitive, among the Arabs, is safe for the time if he gains the shelter of even an enemy's tent.

Host, a hospitable entertainer, Rom. 16:23; an inn-holder, Luke 10:35; or an army.
Also see Gen, 2; 21; 32.
Exod. 12; 14–16.
Num. 1; 2; 4; 10; 31.
Deut. 2; 4; 17; 23.
Josh. 1; 3; 5; 8; 10; 11; 18.
Judg. 4; 7; 8.
1 Sam. 1; 4; 11; 12; 14; 15; 17; 26; 28; 29.
2 Sam. 2; 3; 5–8; 10; 17; 19; 20; 23; 24.
1 Kings 1; 2; 4; 11; 15; 16; 18–20; 22.
2 Kings 3–7; 9; 11; 17–19; 21; 23; 25.
1 Chron. 9; 11; 12; 14; 17–19; 25–27.
2 Chron. 14; 16; 18; 23; 24; 26; 28; 33.
Neh. 9.
Pss. 24; 27; 33; 46; 48; 59; 69; 80; 84; 89; 103; 108; 136; 148.
Isa. 1–3; 5; 6; 8–10; 13; 14; 17–19; 21–25; 28; 29; 31; 34; 37; 39; 40; 44; 45; 47; 48; 51; 54.
Jer. 2; 3; 5–11; 15; 16; 19; 20; 23; 25–33; 35; 38; 39; 42–44; 46; 48–52.
Ezek. 1.
Dan. 8.
Hos. 12.
Amos 3–6; 9.
Obad. 20.
Mic. 4.
Nah. 2; 3.
Hab. 2.
Zeph. 1; 2.
Hag. 1; 2.
Zech. 1–10; 12–14.
Mal. 1–4.
Luke 2; 10.
Acts 7.
Rom. 16.

Hos′ta-ges are mentioned in 2 Kings 14:14; 2 Chron. 25:24.

Ho′tham (*signet ring*), a son of Heber, the grandson of Asher. 1 Chron. 7:32.

Ho′than (*signet ring*), father of Shama and Jehiel, two of David's valiant men. 1 Chron. 11:44. Same name as HOTHAM.

Ho′thir (*fulness*), a son of Heman appointed for the service of song. 1 Chron. 25:4, 28.

Hough, hock, in Josh. 11:6, 9; 2 Sam. 8:4, means to cut the hamstrings, or cords of the hind legs.

Hour sometimes denotes an indefinite period of time. Dan. 3:6; 4:19; Matt. 9:22. It also signifies a definite period. In the time of Christ the Jews divided the day, from sunrise to sunset, into hours, and the night into watches. The first hour began about 6 A. M.; the sixth at noon; and the twelfth about 6 P M. There were thus twelve hours between sunrise and sunset, and they varied in length in proportion to the length of day. "The eleventh hour" was a proverbial expression for lateness. Matt. 20:1-10 The Romans reckoned time from midnight to noon, and divided this into twelve equal parts, beginning with the first hour and ending with the twelfth. See DAY.

Houses. The Hebrews dwelt in tents, or occasionally in caves, until they entered the Promised Land and occupied the houses left by the Canaanites. Large and costly houses were built in Judea, Jer. 22:14; Amos 3:15; Hag. 1:4, but the houses of the mass of the people were rude and inconvenient. Eastern houses are built around an open court, called "the midst" in Luke 5:19, into which the windows open. Sometimes latticed windows or balconies open on the street. The roofs are usually flat, but in some cases have domes over one or more rooms, and they are surrounded by a battlement or wall, lest any one should fall to the ground. The roof was used as a place of repose, Neh. 8:16, and of resort. 2 Sam. 11:2; Luke 12:3. It was also a place of conference, 1 Sam. 9:25, and of worship. Acts 10:9. The word "house" is applied to a family, Gen. 12:17; 1 Tim. 5:8; to property, 1 Kings 13:8; to the earthly and the spiritual body, Eccles. 12:3; 2 Cor. 5:1; to the grave, Job 30:23; Isa. 14:18; to the Tabernacle, Exod. 23:19; to the Church, 1 Tim. 3:15; and to heaven. John 14:2.

House of God, Judg. 20:18, 26; 21:2, a name applied to BETHEL (which see).

House of the Rolls, Ezra 6:1, and **Treas´ure House,** Ezra 5:17, refer to the same place of deposit for public documents.

Huk´kok (*ditch*), a city on the borders of Asher and Naphtali. Josh. 19:34.

Hu´kok, 1 Chron. 6:75, a Levitical city of Asher. See HELKATH.

Hul (*circle*), one of the sons of Aram, the son of Shem. Gen. 10:23.

Hul´dah (*weasel*), a prophetess whom Josiah, king of Judah, consulted after he had read the denunciations of wrath against the people, contained in the book of the law which Hilkiah had found in the house of the Lord. 2 Kings 22:14; 2 Chron. 34:22. See 2 Kings 22:15-20 for her answer.

Hu-mil´i-ty is urged with great earnestness upon all who claim to be Christ's disciples. 1 Pet. 5:5. A perfect example of it is found in Christ. Phil. 2:5–8.

Also see Prov. 15:33; 18:12; 22:4.
Acts 20:19.
Col. 2:18, 23.

Hum´tah (*place of lizards*), a city of Judah. Josh. 15:54.

Hun´gred, preceded by "an," in Matt. 12:1, means hungry.

Hunt´ing. Nimrod was "a mighty hunter," Gen. 10:9, and Esau was "a cunning hunter." Gen. 25:27. The monuments show that hunting was pursued in Egypt as a sport. We know that Isaac was fond of venison. Gen. 27:3, 4. Various methods of capturing animals were practiced by the Hebrews.
Also see Gen. 27:5, 30.
Lev. 17:13.
1 Sam. 24:11; 26:20.
Job 10:16; 38:39.
Ps. 140:11.
Prov. 6:5, 26; 12:27.
Jer. 16:16.
Lam. 4:18.
Ezek. 13:18, 20, 21.
Mic. 7:2.

Hu´pham (*coast-dweller*), a son of Benjamin. Num. 26:39.

Hu´pham-ites, descendants of Hupham. Num. 26:39.

Hup´pah (*covering*), a priest who was head of the thirteenth course. 1 Chron. 24:13.

Hup´pim (*protection*), a Benjamite. Gen. 46:21; 1 Chron. 7:12.

Hur (*hole*). [1] One of the chief men of the Israelites, who with Aaron held up the hands of Moses on the mountain at the battle with Amalek. Exod. 17:10; 24:14. [2] A son of Caleb, the son of Hezron. Exod. 31:2; 35:30. [3] A king of Midian. Num. 31:8; Josh. 13:21. [4] Father of one of Solomon's officers. 1 Kings 4:8. [5] A man of Judah. 1 Chron. 2:50; 4:4. May be same as No. 2. [6] A son of Judah. 1 Chron. 4:1. [7] Father of one who helped to repair the wall of Jerusalem. Neh. 3:9.

Hu´rai (*linen-weaver*), one of David's valiant men. 1 Chron. 11:32.

Hu´ram (*noble-born*). [1] A son of Bela, the son of Benjamin. 1 Chron. 8:5. [2] The king of Tyre who is called HIRAM in 2 Sam. 5:11, etc. is in 2 Chron. 2:3, 12 called HURAM. [3] The Tyrian artificer HIRAM, whom Solomon employed to cast the vessels for the Temple, is called HURAM in 2 Chron. 4:11, 16.

Hu´ri (*linen-weaver*), a descendant of Gad. 1 Chron. 5:14.

Hus´band, a man betrothed, Matt. 1:16, 19, as well as one actually married. Gen. 3:6, 16. See MARRIAGE.
Also see Gen. 16:3; 29:32, 34; 30:15, 18, 20.
Exod. 4:25, 26; 21:22.
Lev. 19:20; 21:3, 7.
Num. 5:13, 19, 20, 27, 29; 30:6-8, 11-14.
Deut. 21:13; 22:22, 23; 24:3, 4; 25:11; 28:56.
Judg. 13:6, 9, 10; 14:15; 19:3; 20:4.
Ruth 1:3, 5, 9, 11–13; 2:11.
1 Sam. 1:8, 22, 23; 2:19; 4:19, 21; 25:19.
2 Sam. 3:15, 16; 11:26; 14:5, 7.
2 Kings 4:1, 9, 14, 22, 26.
Esther 1:17, 20.
Prov. 12:4; 31:11, 23, 28.
Isa. 54:5.
Jer. 3:20; 6:11; 29:6; 31:32.
Ezek. 16:32, 45; 44:25.
Hos. 2:2, 7.
Joel 1:8.
Mark 10:12.
Luke 2:36; 16:18.
John 4:16-18.
Acts 5:9, 10.
Rom. 7:2, 3.

1 Cor. 7:2-4, 10, 11, 13, 14, 16, 34, 39; 14:35.
2 Cor. 11:2.
Gal. 4:27.
Eph. 5:22-25, 33.
Col. 3:18, 19.
1 Tim. 3:2, 12.
Titus 1:6; 2:4, 5.
1 Pet. 3:1, 5, 7.
Rev. 21:2.

Hus´band-man, a cultivator of the ground. Cultivating the soil is one of the most ancient, useful, and honorable occupations of mankind. Gen. 9:20; Isa. 28:24-28. Christ uses the word figuratively, John 15:1, in parables and elsewhere to denote God's care for his people.
Also see 2 Kings 25:12.
2 Chron. 26:10.
Jer. 31:24; 51:23; 52:16.
Joel 1:11.
Amos 5:16.
Zech. 13:5.
Matt. 21:33-35, 38, 40, 41.
Mark 12:1, 2, 7, 9.
Luke 20:9, 10, 14, 16.
2 Tim. 2:6.
James 5:7.

Hu´shah (*haste*), a name in Judah's genealogy. 1 Chron. 4:4.

Hu´shai (*rapid*), an Archite and a faithful friend of David. 2 Sam. 16:16; 17:14.

Hu´sham (*haste*), a Temanite who became king of Edom before the Israelitish monarchy. Gen. 36:34, 35; 1 Chron. 1:45, 46.

Hu´shath-ite, the title of a family of Judah of which the progenitor was Hushah. 2 Sam. 21:18; 23:27.

Hu´shim (*haste*). [1] A son of Dan. Gen. 46:23. [2] A descendant of Benjamin. 1 Chron. 7:12. [3] A wife of Shaharaim, a descendant of Benjamin. 1 Chron. 8:8, 11.

Husks, Luke 15:16, in the parable of the Prodigal Son, are doubtless the fruit of the carob tree, which is a species of locust. Husks are commonly used in Palestine by the poor as food; cattle and swine are also fattened on them. When ripe the fruit resembles a bean-pod, is four to six inches long, and filled with seeds. It is imported into England and the United States as locust beans. Also called "St. John's bread," because some suppose that John the Baptist lived upon these "locusts."

Huz (*the strong*), the eldest son of Nahor, the brother of Abraham. Gen. 22:21.

Huz´zab. Nah. 2:7. The meaning of this word in the Authorized Version is obscure. The marginal notes give it thus: or, *that which was established,* or, *there was a stand made.*

Hy-æ´na, a carnivorous animal resembling a wolf in general appearance, but of a dirty gray color, with dark transverse stripes on the sides and limbs, is common in Palestine and feeds upon carrion. "Zeboim," in 1 Sam. 13:18; Neh. 11:34, means hyænas. "Speckled bird," in Jer. 12:9, according to some, should be translated "hyæna." Otherwise there is no reference to this animal in the Bible.

Hy-me-næ´us (*hymeneal*), a professed disciple, apparently of Ephesus, who had fallen into various errors and was denounced by Paul. 1 Tim. 1:20; 2 Tim. 2:17.

Hymns are mentioned in the New Testament with psalms and spiritual songs. Eph. 5:19; Col. 3:16. Christ and his disciples sang a hymn together after the Last Supper. Matt. 26:30.

Hypocrite, hip´o-krit, one who assumes the appearance of piety and virtue while destitute of true religion. Matt.

23:13-33.
Also see Job 8:13; 13:16; 15:34; 17:8; 20:5; 27:8; 34:30; 36:13.
Prov. 11:9.
Isa. 9:17; 33:14.
Matt. 6:2, 5, 16; 7:5; 15:7; 16:3; 22:18; 24:51.
Mark 7:6.
Luke 6:42; 11:44; 12:56; 13:15.

Hyr-ca´nus, John, was the son and successor (B. C. 135–105) of Simon Maccabæus. He restored the independence of Judea, and founded the monarchy that continued in his family until the accession of Herod.

Hys´sop, Exod. 12:22, a plant used in ceremonies of purification. Lev. 14:4, 6, 51; Ps. 51:7. It is mentioned in 1 Kings 4:33 as a small tree that "springeth out of the wall." See John 19:29.

I

I AM THAT I AM; I AM, the name by which God announced himself unto Moses in the bush at Horeb. Exod. 3:14.

Ib´har (*whom God chooses*), a son of David. 2 Sam. 5:15; 1 Chron. 3:6.

Ib´le-am (*consuming the people*), a city of Manasseh, in either Issachar or Asher. Josh. 17:11; Judg. 1:27. It is the same as BILEAM. 1 Chron. 6:70.

Ibneiah, ib-ne´yah (*Jehovah builds*), the head of a family of Benjamites. 1 Chron. 9:8.

Ib-ni´jah (*Jehovah builds*), a Benjamite. 1 Chron. 9:8.

Ib´ri (*Hebrew*), a descendant of Merari in the time of David. 1 Chron. 24:27.

Ib´zan (*beautiful ?*), a Bethlehemite and one of the judges of Israel. Judg. 12:8, 10.

Ice. See CRYSTAL.

Ichabod, ik´a-bod (*inglorious*), the name which was given by the wife of Phinehas, the son of Eli, to her son whom she bare soon after the ark of the covenant had been taken by the Philistines. 1 Sam. 4:21; 14:3.

I-co´ni-um (*place of images ?*), an important city of the province of Lycaonia in Asia Minor. It was situated in a fertile country, on the great Roman road from Ephesus to Tarsus, Antioch, and the Euphrates, and was visited by Paul on his first and second missionary journeys. Acts 13:51; 14:1, 19, 21; 16:2; 2 Tim. 3:11. Its present name is *Konieh,* and it has a population of about 30,000.

I-da´lah or **Id´a-lah,** a town of Zebulun. Josh. 19:15.

Id´bash (*stout*), a descendant of Judah. 1 Chron. 4:3.

Id´do (*timely*). **[1]** A prophet or seer who denounced the wrath of God against Jeroboam, the son of Nebat. 2 Chron. 9:29; 12:15. **[2]** Grandfather of the prophet Zechariah. Zech. 1:1, 7. **[3]** The father of Ahinadab. 1 Kings 4:14. **[4]** A descendant of Gershom, the son of Levi. 1 Chron. 6:21. **[5]** (*Calamity.*) A chief officer among the Jews of the captivity; a Nethinim. Ezra 8:17. **[6]** (*Favorite.*) Prince of Manasseh. 1 Chron. 27:21. **[7]** (*Timely.*) A priest who returned from Babylon with Zerubbabel. Neh. 12:4, 16.

I´dle, in Matt. 12:36, means morally useless.

I´dol, I-dol´a-try. Anything which is the object of the worship due only to God is an idol. In a literal sense an idol is an image consecrated to religious worship. Deut. 29:17. In a figurative sense it is anything which withdraws the affections from God. Col. 3:5.

Idolatry consists in worshipping as the true God some created object, or in worshipping the Deity by means of symbolic representations, such as statues and pictures. Its origin is obscure and it began in the most ancient times. It is strictly forbidden in the first and second commandments. Exod. 20:3, 4, 5; Deut. 5:7; 6:14, 15; 8:19, 20. The first chapter of Romans, beginning at the eighteenth verse, gives the best description of the progress and accompanying immorality of idolatry. The last verse of the First Epistle of John contains the warning, "Little children, keep yourselves from idols."

Also see Lev. 19:4; 26:1, 30.

1 Sam. 15:23; 31:9.

1 Kings 15:12, 13; 21:26.

2 Kings 17:12; 21:11, 21; 23:5, 24.

1 Chron. 10:9; 16 26.

2 Chron. 15:8, 16; 24:18; 33:7, 15; 34:7.

Pss. 96:5; 97:7; 106:36, 38; 115:4; 135:15.

Isa 2:8, 18, 20; 10:10, 11; 19:1, 3; 31:7; 45:16; 46:1; 48:5; 57:5; 66:3.

Jer. 22:28; 50:2, 38.

Ezek. 6:4-6, 9, 13. 8:10; 14:3-7; 16:36; 18:6, 12, 15; 20:7, 8. 16, 18, 24, 31, 39; 22:3, 4; 23:7. 30, 37, 39, 49; 30:13; 33:25; 36:18, 25; 37:23; 44:10, 12.

Hos. 4:17; 8:4; 13:2; 14:8.

Mic. 1:7.

Hab. 2:18.

Zech. 10:2; 11:17; 13:2.

Acts 7:41; 15:20, 29; 17:16; 21:25.

Rom. 2:22.

1 Cor. 5:10, 11; 6:9; 8:1, 4, 7, 10; 10:7, 14, 19, 28; 12:2.

2 Cor. 6:16.

Gal. 5:20.

Eph. 5:5.

Col. 3:5.

1 Thess. 1:9.

1 Pet. 4:3.

Rev. 2:14, 20; 9:20; 21:8; 22:15.

I-du-me´a is not the same land as EDOM (for which it is the Greek name), though the **Idumeans** are the same people as the EDOMITES. Edom was situated in the Sinaitic peninsula, south-west of Palestine, a wild and rugged tract of land, but quite fertile. Its original name was Seir, and its first inhabitants were cave-dwellers. These were expelled by the descendants of Esau, who was also called Edom, "red." Gen. 25:30. The Edomites were hunters, but after becoming domiciled in Seir, they built cities, engaged in trade, and had a social organization, with a king, long before the Israelites, their cousins. When the latter, on their way from Egypt to Palestine, reached the frontier of Edom, they were at first denied a passage through the land and generally treated very harshly by the people, though Moses recognized the common parentage of the two nations. Num. 20:14-17. But as soon as the Israelites became consolidated and settled they took revenge. Saul conquered Edom, 1 Sam. 14:47; David did likewise. 2 Sam. 8:14. The hostility continued, and when Nebuchadnezzar, B. C. 588, destroyed Jerusalem the Edomites were his allies and took part in the massacre and the pillage. It was at this time that the Edomites removed, leaving Seir, which was afterward occupied by an Arab tribe and was subsequently known in history as *Arabia Petræa*, and settling in the region south of the Dead Sea— Idumea. After the return of the Israelites from the captivity the hostility between them and the Idumeans was renewed. But John Hyrcanus, B. C. 135–105, not only subjugated the Idumeans, but compelled them to accept circumcision and the Mosaic law. They had hitherto been Baal-worshippers; now they became Jews. In B. C. 47 one of their great men, Antipater, was made procurator of Judea by Cæsar, and Antipater's son was HEROD THE GREAT (which see).

I´gal (*whom God redeems*). [1] One of the spies whom Moses sent to search the land of Canaan. Num. 13:7. [2] One of David's guard, 2 Sam. 23:36, called JOEL in 1 Chron. 11:38.

Ig-da-li´ah (*whom Jehovah makes great*), a prophet in the time of Jeremiah. Jer. 35:4.

Ig´e-al (*whom God redeems*), a son of Shemaiah. 1 Chron. 3:22.

I´im (*ruinous heaps*). [1] Num. 33:45. See IJE-ABARIM. [2] A town in the south of Judah. Josh. 15:29.

Ij-e-ab´a-rim (*ruins of Abarim*), the thirty-seventh encampment of the Israelites after they left Egypt. Num. 21:11; 33:44. Same as IIM, No. 1.

I´jon (*ruin*), a city of Naphtali which was plundered by Ben-hadad, 1 Kings 15:20, and again by Tiglath-pileser. 2 Kings 15:29.

Ik´kesh (*perverse*), a man of Tekoah whose son was one of David's guard. 2 Sam. 23:26; 1 Chron. 11:28.

I´lai (*exalted*), one of David's valiant men. 1 Chron. 11:29.

Il-lu´mi-na-ted, Heb. 10:32, means enlightened.

Il-lyr´i-cum, a Roman province on the eastern shore of the Adriatic, extending from Italy on the north to Epirus on the south. It was divided, and the northern part was called Dalmatia. The southern part remained a province of the Senate. Paul preached "round about unto Illyricum." Rom. 15:19.

Image, im´ej, a word generally used to

denote an object of idolatrous worship.
Gen. 1:26, 27; 5:3; 9:6; 31:19, 34, 35.
Exod. 20:4; 23:24; 34:13.
Lev. 26:1, 30.
Num. 33:52.
Deut. 4:16, 23, 25; 5:8; 7:5, 25; 9:12;
12:3; 16:22; 27:15.
Judg. 17:3, 4; 18:14, 17, 18, 20, 30, 31.
1 Sam. 6:5, 11; 19:13, 16.
2 Sam. 5:21.
1 Kings 14:9, 23.
2 Kings 3:2; 10:26, 27; 11:18; 17:10,
16, 41; 18:4; 21:7; 23:14, 24.
2 Chron. 3:10; 14:3, 5; 23:17; 28:2;
31:1; 33:7, 19, 22; 34:3, 4, 7.
Job 4:16.
Pss. 73:20; 78:58; 97:7; 106:19.
Isa. 10:10; 17:8; 21:9; 27:9; 30:22;
40:19, 20; 41:29; 42:8, 17; 44:9, 10,
15, 17; 45:20; 48:5.
Jer. 8:19; 10:14; 43:13; 50:2, 38; 51:17,
47, 52.
Ezek. 6:4, 6; 7:20; 8:3, 5, 12; 16:17;
21:21; 23:14; 30:13.
Dan. 2:31, 32, 34, 35; 3:1-3, 5, 7, 10,
12, 14, 15, 18.
Hos. 3:4; 10:1, 2; 11:2; 13:2.
Amos 5:26.
Mic. 1:7; 5:13.
Nah. 1:14.
Hab. 2:18.
Matt. 22:20.
Mark 12:16.
Luke 20:24.
Acts 19:35.
Rom. 1:23; 8:29; 11:4.
1 Cor. 11:7; 15:49.
2 Cor. 3:18; 4:4.
Col. 1:15; 3:10.
Heb. 1:3; 10:1.
Rev. 13:14, 15; 14:9, 11; 15:2; 16:2;
19:20; 20:4
Image of Jeal´ous-y, a general term

for idolatrous practices which excited
Jehovah's jealousy. Ezek. 8:3, 5.

Imagery, Cham´bers of, refers to an
Assyrian and Egyptian custom of painting
pictures of the gods on the walls of their
temples. Ezek. 8:12.

Im´la (*filled*), the father of Micaiah the
prophet, who predicted the fall of Ahab at
Ramoth-gilead. 2 Chron. 18:7, 8. Called
IMLAH in 1 Kings 22:8, 9.

Im´lah. Same as preceding.

Im-man´u-el (*God with us*), a title of
the MESSIAH. Isa. 7:14; 8:8. Same as
EMMANUEL. Matt. 1:23. See CHRIST.

Im´mer (*talkative*). [1] A priest whose
descendants dwelt in Jerusalem. 1 Chron.
9:12; Ezra 2:37; Neh. 11:13. [2] Father of
Zadok. Neh. 3:29. [3] A priest in the time
of Jeremiah, whose son Pashur smote Jeremiah and put him in the stocks. Jer. 20:1.

Im´mer, apparently a place in Babylonia. Ezra 2:59; Neh. 7:61.

Im-mor´tal. In 1 Tim. 1:17 God is said
to be "immortal." The word thus translated is the same as that rendered "uncor-
ruptible" in Rom. 1:23, and should be so
translated here.

Im-mor-tal´i-ty. Belief in immortality
is not specially taught in the Old
Testament, but is taken for granted. The
penitential and sacrificial system of the
Mosaic law would be unintelligible without the doctrine of immortality. It is definitely taught in the New Testament in connection with the resurrection of Christ.
Rom. 2:7.
1 Cor. 15:53, 54.
1 Tim. 5:16.
2 Tim. 1:10.

Im´na (*holding back*), a son of Helem,
who was of the tribe of Asher. 1 Chron.
7:35.

Im´nah (*success*) [1] Asher's eldest

son, 1 Chron. 7:30, called JIMNAH in Gen. 46:17. [2] A Levite, father of Kore. 2 Chron. 31:14.

Im-plead´, in Acts 19:38, means to sue at law.

Im-po´tent, in John 5:3; Acts 4:9; 14:8, means without strength, either on account of disease or malformation.

Im-pre-ca´tion. See OATH.

Im-pris´on-ment. See PUNISHMENT.

Im-pute´, the translation of a Greek word which is rendered by many different terms in the Authorized Version, such as "reckon," Rom. 4:4; "account," Gal. 3:6; "lay to one's charge," 2 Tim. 4:16. Impute means "to put to the account of a person that of which he is or is not possessed." God imputes *sin*, Rom. 4:8, and the righteousness of Christ is imputed to man on condition of faith in Christ's sacrifice. Rom. 4:11-24.

Also see Lev. 7:18; 17:4.
1 Sam. 22:15.
2 Sam. 19:19.
Ps. 32:2.
Hab. 1:11.
Rom. 4:6; 5:13.
2 Cor. 5:19.
James 2:23.

Im´rah (*obstinacy*), a son of Zophah, a descendant of Asher. 1 Chron. 7:36.

Im´ri (*eloquent*). [1] A descendant of Judah. 1 Chron. 9:4. [2] Father of Zaccur who rebuilt part of the wall of Jerusalem. Neh. 3:2.

In-can-ta´tions. See DIVINATION.

In´cense, Exod. 30:8, was a mixture of frankincense and other fragrant articles. Its materials and the method of preparing it are given in Exod. 30:34-36. Its preparation for common use was forbidden. The priest burned it morning and evening on the altar of incense. No other prepara-

tion could be used as incense, nor could any one but the priest offer it. Incense was offered as a symbol of prayer. See ALTAR, CENSER, and FRANKINCENSE.

Also see Exod. 25:6; 30:1, 7, 9, 27; 31:8, 11; 35:8, 15, 28; 37:25, 29; 39:38; 40:5, 27.
Lev. 4:7; 10:1; 16:12, 13.
Num. 4:16; 7:14, 20, 26, 32, 38, 44, 50, 56, 62, 68, 74, 80, 86; 16:7, 17, 18, 35, 40, 46, 47.
Deut. 33:10.
1 Sam. 2:28.
1 Kings 3:3; 9:25; 11:8; 12:33; 13:1, 2; 22:43.
2 Kings 12:3; 14:4; 15:4, 35; 16:4; 17:11; 18:4; 22:17; 23:5, 8.
1 Chron. 6:49; 23:13; 28:18.
2 Chron. 2:4; 13:11; 25:14; 26:16, 18, 19; 28:3, 4, 25; 29:7, 11; 30:14; 32:12; 34:25.
Pss. 66:15; 141:2.
Isa. 1:13; 43:23; 60:6; 65:3, 7; 66:3.
Jer. 1:16; 6:20; 7:9; 11:12, 13, 17; 17:26; 18:15; 19:4, 13; 32:29; 41:5; 44:3, 5, 8, 15, 17-19, 21, 23, 25; 48:35.
Ezek. 8:11; 16:18; 23:41.
Hos. 2:13; 4:13; 11:2.
Hab. 1:16.
Mal. 1:11.
Luke 1:9-11.
Rev. 8:3, 4.

In´di-a, Esther 1:1; 8:9, the region around the Indus River, perhaps including Scinde. Solomon opened a trade with India by his vessels, and through Hiram, king of Tyre. 1 Kings 10:10-22.

In-di´ting, in Ps. 45:1 (Hebrew, *bubbling up*), means dictating; composing.

In-gath´er-ing, Feast of. See TABERNACLES, FEAST OF.

In-her´it-ance. The sons had priority

of right, the eldest having a double portion. If there were no sons, the daughters inherited. Num. 27:8. There is no record of wills in the Old Testament; the law of Moses rendered them unnecessary. They were subsequently introduced, however. Gal. 3:15; Heb. 9:17. Believers have salvation for their inheritance, Heb. 1:14, and are "joint-heirs with Christ." Rom. 8:17.

Also see Gen. 31; 48.
Exod. 15; 34.
Lev. 25.
Num. 16; 18; 26; 27; 32–36.
Deut. 4; 9; 10; 12; 14; 15; 18–21; 24–26; 29; 32; 33.
Josh. 1; 11; 13–19; 21; 23; 24.
Judg. 2; 18; 20; 21.
Ruth 4.
1 Sam. 10; 26.
2 Sam. 14; 20; 21.
1 Kings 8; 12; 21.
2 Kings 21.
1 Chron. 16; 28.
2 Chron. 6; 10.
Ezra 9.
Neh. 11.
Job 31; 42.
Pss. 2; 16; 28; 33; 37; 47; 68; 74; 78; 79; 94; 105; 106.
Prov. 13; 17; 19; 20.
Eccles. 7.
Isa. 19; 47; 63.
Jer. 3; 10; 12; 16; 32; 51.
Lam. 5.
Ezek. 22; 33; 35; 36; 44–48.
Matt. 21.
Mark 12.
Luke 12; 20.
Acts 7; 20; 26.
Gal. 3.
Eph. 1; 5.
Col. 1; 3.

Heb. 1; 9, 11.
1 Pet. 1.

Iniquity, in-ik′we-ty, anything done contrary to the law of God.
Gen. 15; 19; 44.
Exod. 20; 28; 34.
Lev. 5; 7; 10, 16–20; 22; 26.
Num. 5; 14; 15; 18; 23; 30.
Deut. 5; 19; 32.
Josh. 22.
1 Sam. 3; 15; 20; 25.
2 Sam. 7; 14; 19; 22; 24.
1 Chron. 21.
2 Chron. 19.
Ezra 9.
Neh. 4; 9.
Job 4–7; 10; 11; 13–15 20–22; 31; 33; 34; 36.
Pss. 5–7; 14; 18; 25; 28; 31; 32; 36–41; 49; 51; 53; 55; 56; 59; 64–66; 69; 78; 79. 85; 89; 90; 92; 94; 103; 106; 107; 109; 119; 125; 130; 141.
Prov. 5; 10; 16; 19; 21; 22.
Eccles. 3.
Isa. 1; 5; 6; 13; 14; 22; 26; 27; 29–33; 40; 43; 50; 53; 57; 59; 64; 65.
Jer. 2; 3; 5; 9; 11; 13; 14; 16; 18; 25; 30–33; 36; 50; 51.
Lam. 2; 4; 5.
Ezek. 3; 4; 7; 9; 14; 16; 18; 21; 24; 28; 29; 32; 33; 35; 36; 39; 43; 44.
Dan. 4; 9.
Hos. 4–10; 12–14.
Amos 3.
Mic. 2; 3; 7.
Hab. 1; 2.
Zeph. 3.
Zech. 3.
Mal. 2.
Matt. 7; 13; 23; 24.
Luke 13.
Acts 1; 3; 8.
Rom. 4; 6.

1 Cor. 13.
2 Thess. 2.
2 Tim. 2.
Titus 2.
Heb. 1; 8; 10.
James 3.
2 Pet. 2.
Rev. 18.

Ink, Ink´horn. Jer. 36:18; Ezek. 9:2, 3, 11; 2 Cor. 3:3, etc. See WRITING.

Inn. An inn was sometimes only a station where caravans stopped for the night, near water if possible, but not necessarily having any buildings. At such an "inn" Joseph's brethren stopped, Gen. 42:27, and Moses met the LORD. Exod. 4:24. At such stations large buildings containing rooms for travellers and stalls for their animals were often erected around open square courts. No food was provided in them. In such a place our Saviour was born. Luke 2:7. Another kind of inn, in charge of a host, is mentioned in the parable of the Good Samaritan. Luke 10:35.

In-spi-ra´tion. The prophets and apostles spake "as they were moved by the Holy Ghost," 2 Pet. 1:21, but the divine Spirit influenced each author according to his individuality. Job. 32:8; 2 Tim. 3:16.

In´stant, In´stant-ly, in Luke 7:4; 23:23; Acts 26:7; Rom. 12:12; 2 Tim. 4:2, means urgent; earnest; or, urgently; earnestly.

In´stru-ments of Mu´sic. See MUSIC.

In-tend´ed, in Ps. 21:11, means also plotted.

In-ter-ces´sion, prayer in behalf of others. Abraham interceded for Sodom. Gen. 18:23-33. Paul exhorts that intercession be made for all men. 1 Tim. 2:1, 2. Christ is our Intercessor or Advocate. 1 John 2:1; John 17; Heb. 9:24; Rom. 8:34. The Holy Spirit also makes intercession. Rom. 8:26.

Also see Isa. 53:12; 59:16.
Jer. 7:16; 27:18; 36:25.
Rom. 8:27; 11:2.
Heb. 7:25.

In´ter-est. See LOAN, and USURY.

In-ter´pre-ter. See PROPHET.

In´ward, in Job 19:19, means familiar; confidential.

Iphedeiah, if-e-de´yah, (*whom Jehovah frees*) a son of Shashak, a descendant of Benjamin. 1 Chron. 8:25.

Ir (*a city*), an Israelite of the tribe of Benjamin, 1 Chron. 7:12, called IRI in verse 7.

I´ra (*watchful*). [1] One of David's chief rulers after the rebellion of Sheba was quelled. 2 Sam. 20:26. [2, 3] Two of David's valiant men. 2 Sam. 23:26, 38; 1 Chron. 11:28, 40; 27:9.

I´rad (*fleet*), the son of Enoch, a descendant of Cain. Gen. 4:18.

I´ram (*watchful*), one of the dukes (leaders) of Edom. Gen. 36:43; 1 Chron. 1:54.

Ir-ha-he´res, a city mentioned in Hebrew, Isa. 19:18, under the name "city of destruction," or of "Heres," or "of the sun" (Heliopolis), in the marginal notes.

I´ri (*watchful*), one of the sons of Bela, the son of Benjamin. 1 Chron. 7:7.

I-ri´jah (*Jehovah sees*), a captain of the ward in Jerusalem, who arrested Jeremiah. Jer. 37:13,14.

Ir-na´hash (*serpent city*), in the marginal notes called "the city of Nahash," 1 Chron. 4:12, was regarded by Jerome as the same as Bethlehem, which is not probable. It has been considered identical with the village and ruins *Deir Nahhaz*, on the road to Hebron.

I´ron. Some of the uses of iron were known in very ancient times. It is mentioned in Gen. 4:22. Iron tools are noticed

in Deut. 27:5; 2 Kings 6:6; spear heads, in 1 Sam. 17:7; agricultural implements, in 2 Sam. 12:31; Jer. 28:14. Abundance of iron-ore is found in northern Palestine. Also see Josh. 19:38.
Job 41:7.

I´ron (*pious*), one of the fenced cities of Naphtali. Josh. 19:38. Now *Yarun*.

Ir´pe-el (*God heals*), a town of Benjamin. Josh. 18:27.

Ir-she´mesh (*city of the sun*), a place in Dan. Josh. 19:41. See BETH-SHEMESH.

I´ru (*watch*), the eldest son of Caleb, who was one of the two faithful spies. 1 Chron. 4:15.

Isaac, i´zak (*laughter*), the second of the Hebrew patriarchs, was the son of Abraham and Sarah, and was born when his parents were very old, in fulfilment of God's promise. Gen. 17:4-17. The history of Isaac is found in Gen. 21:2-8; 22:2-13; chapters 24-28; 35:27-29. The only event of his early years which is recorded is the trial of his father's faith when, in obedience to God's command, Abraham was about to offer Isaac for a burnt offering. See Gen. 22:2-13. This is considered typical of the subsequent sacrifice of the only Son of God on Calvary. The intended sacrifice of Isaac is referred to in Heb. 11:17; James 2:21. Isaac was a prosperous farmer. Gen. 26:12, 14. He died at the age of one hundred and eighty. Gen. 35:28. See JACOB, and ESAU (his sons). Isaac is used in Amos 7:9, 16 as a poetic synonym for ISRAEL (the ten tribes).
Also see Gen. 17:19, 21; 21:10, 12; 26:1, 6, 8, 9, 12, 16, 17, 18, 27, 31, 35; 31:18, 42, 53; 32:9; 35:12, 27; 46:1; 48:15, 16; 49:31; 50:24.
Exod. 2:24; 3:6, 15, 16; 4:5; 6:3, 8; 32:13; 33:1.
Lev. 26:42.

Num. 32:11.
Deut. 1:8; 6:10; 9:5, 27; 29:13; 30:20; 34:4.
Josh. 24:3, 4.
1 Kings 18:36.
2 Kings 13:23.
1 Chron. 1:28, 34; 16:16; 29:18.
2 Chron. 30:6.
Ps. 105:9.
Jer. 33:26.
Matt. 1:2; 8:11; 22:32.
Mark 12:26.
Luke 3:34; 13:28; 20:37.
Acts 3:13; 7:8, 32.
Rom. 9:7, 10.
Gal. 4:28.
Heb. 11:9, 18, 20.

Isaiah, i-za´yah (*Jehovah's salvation*), the greatest of the prophets, was a son of Amoz, began his prophetic ministration probably in the last years of the reign of Uzziah, Isa. 6:1, B.C. 760 and continued it under Jotham, Ahaz, and Hezekiah, B.C. 698. We know from himself that he was a married man and had two sons; that his wife was called a prophetess and his sons bore prophetical names; that he lived on intimate terms with Hezekiah, etc. A Jewish tradition preserved in the Talmud tells us that when he was ninety years old he was sawn asunder in a hollow carob tree, in the reign of Manasseh, and that the "mulberry tree of Isaiah" in the Kedron valley, near Jerusalem, indicates the traditional spot of his martyrdom. The manner of his death is not mentioned in the Bible.
2 Kings 19:2, 5, 6, 20; 20:1, 4, 7-9, 11, 14, 16, 19.
2 Chron. 26:22; 32:20, 32.
Isa. 1:1; 2:1; 7:3; 13:1; 20:2, 3; 37:2, 5, 6, 21; 38:1, 4, 21; 39:3, 5, 8.

Isaiah, the Book of, which has fitly been characterized as the "Gospel of the

Old Testament," consists of two parts. The first part, chapters 1–39, contains a number of separate predictions and narratives referring to various nations—Assyria, Babylon, Moab, Ethiopia, etc. The second part, from chapter 40 to the end, refers to the close of the Babylonian captivity and the glory of the Messianic period, giving a most striking picture of the suffering Messiah, Isa. 53, as the "man of sorrows," who bore our sins and accomplished our salvation.

Is´cah (*she looks abroad*), a daughter of Haran, the brother of Abram. Gen. 11:29. She was a sister of LOT.

Is-car´i-ot. See JUDAS ISCARIOT.

Ish´bah (*praising*), a son of Ezra. 1 Chron. 4:17.

Ish´bak (*leaving behind*), a son of Abraham by Keturah. Gen. 25:2; 1 Chron. 1:32. The northern Arabians are his descendants.

Ish´bi-be´nob (*dwelling in rest*), a son of Rapha, a Philistine giant slain by Abishai. 2 Sam. 21:16, 17.

Ish-bo´sheth (*man of shame*), a son and successor of King Saul, was induced by Abner to assume the government while David reigned at Hebron. 2 Sam. 2:8, 11. All Israel, except Judah, acknowledged Ish-bosheth as king. A great battle was fought at Gibeon between the army of David under Joab and that of Ish-bosheth under Abner. The latter was totally defeated. Ish-bosheth was assassinated after a reign of two years. 2 Sam. 4:5, 7.

I´shi (*saving*). [1, 2] Judites. 1 Chron. 2:31; 4:20. [3] A man of Simeon. 1 Chron. 4:42. [4] Head of a family in Manasseh. 1 Chron. 5:24.

I´shi, the title by which the Lord declares that his people shall honor him when he shall renew his covenant of mercy with them and they shall return to him. Hos. 2:16.

I-shi´ah (*whom Jehovah lends*), a son of Izrahiah. 1 Chron. 7:3.

I-shi´jah (*whom Jehovah lends*), a Jew who had a foreign wife. Ezra 10:31.

Ish´ma (*desolation*), a descendant of Judah. 1 Chron. 4:3.

Ish´ma-el (*whom God hears*). [1] The son of Abraham by Hagar. He and his mother were expelled from the household of the patriarch at Sarah's request, Gen. 21:10, and went forth into the wilderness of Beer-sheba, where he became a hunter and married an Egyptian woman. From him descended the Ishmaelites, wild Bedouin tribes still roaming about in the same region and well known for their treachery and robberies. Ishmael, however, was present at the interment of his father's remains in the cave of Machpelah. Gen. 25:9. [2] A descendant of the royal family of Judah, who murdered Gedaliah, the governor appointed by Nebuchadnezzar, in the basest manner and then was compelled by Johanan to flee to the Ammonites. Jer. 41; 2 Kings 25:23, 25. [3] A son of Azel, a descendant of Benjamin. 1 Chron. 8:38; 9:44. [4] Father of Zebadiah, a ruler of the house of Judah. 2 Chron. 19:11. [5] One of the captains by whose aid Jehoiada the priest set Joash on the throne of Judah. 2 Chron. 23:1. [6] A priest who had a foreign wife. Ezra 10:22.

Also see Gen. 16:11, 15, 16; 17:18, 20, 23, 25, 26; 25:12, 13, 16, 17; 28:9; 36:3.

1 Chron. 1:28, 29, 31.

Jer. 40:8, 14-16.

Ish´ma-el-ites. See ISHMAEL.

Ish-ma-i´ah (*Jehovah hears*), prince

of Zebulun in the time of David. 1 Chron. 27:19.

Ish´me-el-ite. 1 Chron. 2:17. See ISHMAELITES.

Ish´me-rai (*whom Jehovah keeps*), a son of Elpaal, a Benjamite. 1 Chron. 8:18.

I´shod (*man of renown*), a son of Hammoleketh, the sister of Gilead. 1 Chron. 7:18.

Ish´pan (*bald*), a son of Shashak, a Benjamite. 1 Chron. 8:22.

Ish-tob (*men of Tob*), apparently a small kingdom, part of Aram. 2 Sam. 10:6, 8. See TOB.

Ish´u-ah (*quiet*), the second son of Asher, Gen. 46:17, called ISUAH. 1 Chron. 7:30.

Ish´u-ai (*quiet*), a son of Asher, 1 Chron. 7:30, called ISUI, Gen. 46:17, and JESUI, Num. 26:44.

Ish´u-i (*quiet*), a son of Saul. 1 Sam. 14:49.

Isles, Zeph. 2:11; Ps. 72:10; Ezek. 26:15. The Hebrew word signifies any land bordering on the sea. ISLES OF THE GENTILES, Gen. 10:5, refers to the coasts of the Mediterranean, Black, and Caspian Seas.

Ismachiah, is-ma-ki´ah (*whom Jehovah supports*), a Levitical overseer of offerings in the time of Hezekiah. 2 Chron. 31:13.

Is-ma-i´ah (*Jehovah hears*), a Gibeonite who joined David at Ziklag. 1 Chron. 12:4.

Is´pah (*bald*), a son of Beriah, a descendant of Benjamin. 1 Chron. 8:16.

Is´ra-el, Gen. 35:10, a name given to Jacob by the angel at Peniel, Gen. 32:28; Hos. 12:3, 4, meaning "the prince that prevails with God." The word is also used, Exod. 3:16, for all of Jacob's posterity; also for the kingdom of the ten tribes, 2 Kings 14:12; and, in a spiritual sense, for the whole body of true believers. Rom. 9:6; 11:26. See JACOB.

Also see Gen. 32; 34–37; 42; 43; 45–50.
Exod. 1–7; 9–20; 24; 25; 27–36; 39; 40.
Lev. 1; 4; 7; 9–12; 15–27.
Num. 1–11; 13–36.
Deut. 1–6; 9–11; 13; 17–27; 29; 31–34.
Josh. 1–14; 17–24.
Judg. 1–21.
Ruth 2; 4.
1 Sam. 1–20; 23–31.
2 Sam. 1–3; 5–8; 10–21; 23; 24.
1 King 1–6; 8–12; 14–22.
2 Kings 1–3; 5–10; 13–19; 21–24.
1 Chron. 1; 2; 4–7; 9–24; 26–29.
2 Chron. 1; 2; 5–13; 15–25; 27–36.
Ezra 1–10.
Neh. 1; 2; 7–13.
Pss. 14; 22; 25; 41; 50; 53; 59; 68; 69; 71–73; 76; 78; 80; 81; 83; 89; 98; 103; 105; 106; 114; 115; 118; 121; 122; 124; 125; 128–131; 135; 136; 147–149.
Prov. 1.
Eccles. 1.
Song of Sol. 3.
Isa. 1; 4; 5; 7–12; 14; 17; 19; 21; 24; 27; 29–31; 37; 40–49; 52; 54–56; 60; 63; 66.
Jer. 2–7; 9–14; 16–19; 21; 23–25; 27–39; 41–46; 48–51.
Lam. 2.
Ezek. 2–14; 17–22; 24; 25; 27–29; 33–40; 43–45; 47; 48.
Dan. 1; 9.
Hos. 1; 3–14.
Joel 2; 3.
Amos 1–9.
Obad. 20.
Mic. 1–3; 5; 6.
Nah. 2.
Zeph. 2; 3.

Zech. 1; 8; 9; 11; 12.
Mal. 1; 2; 4.
Matt. 2; 8–10; 15; 19; 27.
Mark 12; 15.
Luke 1; 2; 4; 7; 22; 24.
John 1; 3; 12.
Acts 1–5; 7; 9; 10; 13; 21; 28.
Rom. 9–11.
1 Cor. 10.
2 Cor. 3.
Gal. 6.
Eph. 2.
Phil. 3.
Heb. 8; 11.
Rev. 2; 7; 21.

Is´ra-el, Land of. See CANAAN.

Is´ra-el-ite, a person belonging to one of the tribes of Israel.

Is´ra-el, Kingdom of, a name often applied to the united kingdom before the revolt of the ten tribes. 1 Sam. 13:1, 4; 15:28. It was also used to designate the territory of the ten tribes. After the death of Solomon it was usually applied to the independent kingdom of the ten tribes, so that the kings of the ten tribes were called "kings of Israel," and David's descendants, who ruled Judah and Benjamin, were called "kings of Judah." The kingdom of Israel was about as large as New Hampshire and had a population of over three millions. The capitals were Shechem, Tirzah, and Samaria. It lasted B.C. 975– 721. See HEBREWS.
Also see 1 Sam. 24:20.
1 Kings 21:7.

Issachar, is´sa-kar (*God hath given me my hire*). **[1]** The fifth son of Jacob and Leah. Gen. 30:18; Exod. 1:3. A prophetical description of him in Gen. 49:14, 15 was fulfilled, as his descendants were laborious and subject to tributes from roving tribes. **[2]** A porter for the Tabernacle

in the time of David. 1 Chron. 26:5. See TRIBES.
Also see Gen. 35:23; 46:13.
Num. 1:8, 28, 29; 2:5; 7:18; 10:15; 13:7; 26:23, 25; 34:26.
Deut. 27:12; 33:18.
Judg. 5:15; 10:1.
1 Kings 4:17; 15:27.
1 Chron. 2:1; 6:62, 72; 7:1, 5; 12:32, 40; 27:18.
2 Chron. 30:18.
Ezek. 48:25, 26, 33.
Rev. 7:7.

Issachar, Territory of, comprised the great plain called Esdraelon or Jezreel, and extended from Mount Carmel to the Jordan and from En-gannim to Mount Tabor. It was one of the most fertile districts in Palestine and contained sixteen famous cities. Its boundaries are given in Josh. 19:17-23.
Also see Josh. 17:10, 11; 21:6, 28.

Is-shi´ah (*whom Jehovah lends*). **[1]** A descendant of Moses, 1 Chron. 24:21, called JESHAIAH in 1 Chron. 26:25. **[2]** A Kohathite Levite. 1 Chron. 24:25.

Is´u-ah (*quiet*), a son of Asher, 1 Chron. 7:30, called ISHUAH in Gen. 46:17.

Is´u-i (*quiet*), third son of Asher. Gen. 46:17. See ISHUAI.

Italian, i-tal´yan, **Band,** part of the Roman army. It was composed of Italians, Acts 10:1, and Cornelius was their centurion, or commander.

It´a-ly, a well-known country in the south of Europe, situated on the Mediterranean Sea. It is mentioned but four times in the Bible—namely, as the place from which Aquila and Priscilla were expelled, Acts 18:2; as the country for which Paul sailed, Acts 27:1, 6; and as the residence of some who joined in the salutations mentioned in Heb. 13:24.

Ith´a-i (*with Jehovah*), one of David's valiant men, a Benjamite, 1 Chron. 11:31, called ITTAI in 2 Sam. 23:29. See ITTAI, No. 2.

Ith´a-mar (*land of palms*), a son of Aaron. Exod. 6:23; Lev. 10:16; Ezra 8:2. Eli was the only high-priest of the line of Ithamar. 1 Chron. 24:6.

Ith´i-el (*God is with me*). [1] A man of the tribe of Benjamin. Neh. 11:7. [2] One of Agur's friends. Prov. 30:1.

Ith´mah (*orphanage*), a Moabite, one of David's valiant men. 1 Chron. 11:46.

Ith´nan (*bestowed*), a town near the south border of Judah. Josh. 15:23.

Ith´ra (*abundance*), father of Amasa, the captain of Absalom's host. 2 Sam. 17:25. Called JETHER in 1 Chron. 2:17. See JETHER, No. 3.

Ith´ran (*abundance*). [1] One of the Horites. Gen. 36:26; 1 Chron. 1:41. [2] A son of Zophah, an Asherite. 1 Chron. 7:37.

Ith´re-am (*residue of the people*), a son of David. He was born at Hebron. 2 Sam. 3:5; 1 Chron. 3:3.

Ith´rite, The, the name given to two of David's warriors. 2 Sam. 23:38; 1 Chron. 11:40.

It-tah-ka´zin, a landmark of Zebulun. Josh. 19:13.

It´tai (*in time*). [1] One of David's valiant men, a native of Gath. 2 Sam. 18:2. He was greatly attached to David. 2 Sam. 15:19-22. [2] A valiant Benjamite in David's army. 2 Sam 23:29. See ITHAI.

Ituræa, it-u-re´ah (*an enclosed region*), a small province in the north of Palestine, between the upper Jordan and Mount Hermon. Philip, brother of Herod, was "tetrarch of Ituræa and of the region of Trachonitis." Luke 3:1.

I´vah, a district near Babylon, 2 Kings 18:34, called AVA in 2 Kings 17:24.

I´vo-ry (*tooth*) has generally been defined as simply the tooth of the elephant, but is really a substance, between bone and horn, from the teeth or tusks of many animals. Solomon's throne was built of ivory, and it was lavishly used in ancient times in architecture, etc. Amos 3:15; 6:4; Ezek. 27:6. "Ivory palaces," mentioned in Ps. 45:8, were probably boxes richly wrought or inlaid with ivory, and used for keeping perfumes.

Iz´e-har. Num. 3:19. See IZHAR.

Iz´har (*oil*), a son of Kohath, the son of Levi. Exod. 6:18, 21; 1 Chron. 6:2. Called IZEHAR in Num. 3:19.

Iz´har-ites, 1 Chron. 24:22; 26:23, descendants of IZHAR, the son of Kohath. They are called IZEHARITES in Num. 3:27.

Iz-ra-hi´ah (*whom Jehovah causes to sparkle*), a grandson of Tola, the son of Issachar. 1 Chron. 7:3.

Iz´ra-hite, The, the designation of Shamhuth, a captain in David's army. 1 Chron. 27:8.

Iz´ri (*built*), a Levite leader in the service of song in David's time. 1 Chron. 25:11.

J

Ja´a-kan (*he shall adorn*), a son of Ezer, one of the sons of Seir. Deut. 10:6. Same as JAKAN in 1 Chron. 1:42, and AKAN in Gen. 36:27. See BENE-JAAKAN.

Ja-ak´o-bah (*supplanter*), a chieftain of Simeon. 1 Chron. 4:36.

Ja-a´la, Ja-a´lah (*a wild she-goat*), a servant of Solomon whose descendants returned with Zerubbabel. Ezra 2:56; Neh. 7:58.

Ja-a´lam (*whom God hides*), a son of Esau by Aholibamah. He was a chief of Edom. Gen. 36:5, 14, 18; 1 Chron. 1:35.

Jaanai, ja´a-na or ja-a´na (*whom Jehovah answers*), a chief of Gad. 1 Chron. 5:12.

Ja-ar´e-or´e-gim (*forests of the weavers*), the father of Elhanan, who slew Goliath's brother. 2 Sam. 21:19. Same as JAIR in 1 Chron. 20:5.

Ja´a-sau (*whom Jehovah has made*), a Jew who had taken a foreign wife. Ezra 10:37.

Ja-a´si-el (*whom God has made*), son of Abner and chief of Benjamin. 1 Chron. 27:21.

Ja-az-a-ni´ah (*whom Jehovah hears*). [1] A captain of the Jewish army. 2 Kings 25:23. [2] A chief man of the Rechabites in the time of Jeremiah. Jer. 35:3. [3] One of the seventy "men of the ancients" seen by Ezekiel in a vision. Ezek. 8:11. [4] A prince seen in a vision by Ezekiel, Ezek. 11:1, against whom he was directed to prophesy.

Ja-a´zer and **Ja´zer** (*Jehovah helps*), a city of Gilead situated east of the Jordan. It was conquered and assigned to Gad and the Levites. Num. 21:32; 32:1; Josh. 21:39. It was subject to Moab in later times, and is denounced in Isa. 16:8, 9; Jer. 48:32.

Ja-a-zi´ah (*whom Jehovah consoles*), a descendant of Merari, the son of Levi. 1 Chron. 24:26, 27.

Ja-a´zi-el (*whom God consoles*), a Levite in the choral service when the ark of the covenant was brought up from the house of Obed-edom. 1 Chron. 15:18. Same as AZIEL in verse 20.

Ja´bal (*a stream*), a son of Lamech, a descendant of Cain. Gen. 4:20. He was the "father of such as dwell in tents and have cattle."

Jab´bok (*emptying*), a small river which rises about twenty-five miles northeast of the north end of the Dead Sea, and, after flowing east, north, west, and southwest, empties into the Jordan about midway between the Dead Sea and the Sea of Galilee. Gen. 32:22; Num. 21:24; Deut. 2:37; 3:16.

Ja´besh (*dry*), the father of Shallum. 2 Kings 15:10, 13, 14. Shallum was a king of Israel.

Ja´besh and **Ja´besh-Gil´e-ad** (*dry Gilead*), a city of Gad east of the Jordan. It was destroyed by the Israelites, Judg. 21:8-14, and delivered by Saul from Nahash. 1 Sam. 11:1-11.

Ja´bez (*he causes pain*). [1] The head of a family of Judah. 1 Chron 4:9, 10. [2] Apparently a place. It is mentioned only in 1 Chron. 2:55, but its situation is not known.

Ja´bin (*whom God observes*). [1] A king of Hazor who was defeated by Joshua near the lake Merom. Josh. 11:1. [2] Another king of the same name and place, who oppressed the Israelites twenty years in the time of the judges. Judg. 4:2, 7, 17, 23, 24; Ps. 83:9.

Jab´ne-el (*Jehovah causes to be built*). [1] A town of Judah, Josh. 15:11, called also JABNEH in 2 Chron. 26:6. It was captured by Uzziah from the Philistines. [2] A border town of Naphtali; location uncertain. Josh. 19:33.

Jab´neh. See JABNEEL.

Jachin, ja´kin (*he shall establish*). [1] A son of Simeon. Gen. 46:10; Exod. 6:15. [2] Head of the twenty-first course of priests. 1 Chron. 9:10; 24:17; Neh. 11:10. [3] The name given by Solomon to the pillar which he set up on the right side of the porch of the Temple. 1 Kings 7:21;

2 Chron. 3:17. See BOAZ, No. 2.

Jachinites, ja'kin-ites, descendants of Jachin, son of Simeon. Num. 26:12. See JACHIN, No. 1.

Ja'cinth or **Hy'a-cinth,** probably same as LIGURE in Exod. 28:19. It was a yellowish-red or a dark-purple gem resembling the AMETHYST. Rev. 9:17; 21:20.

Ja'cob (*the supplanter*). [1] The third of the Jewish patriarchs, Gen. 25:26, the son of Isaac and Rebekah and the younger twin-brother of Esau. The relations between the two brothers were not good, and the fault was Jacob's. Gen. 27. He bought Esau's birthright from him, Gen. 25:29-34, was compelled to flee, and went to Laban, a brother of his mother, who lived in Padan-aram, and with whom he stayed for twenty years. See Gen. 28:12-22 for account of his vision at Bethel and subsequent vow. He married Laban's two daughters, Leah and Rachel, and he prospered. But he yearned after his native land, and as troubles continually arose between him and Laban they separated, though with a covenant of peace. Gen. 31:45-54. When he approached Canaan he felt anxious with respect to Esau, and then occurred that extraordinary event which made Israel, "the soldier of God," out of Jacob, "the supplanter." Gen. 32:24-32. The meeting with Esau was very friendly, and Jacob settled near Shechem, where he bought land, Gen. 33:19, and dug a well (see JACOB'S WELL). But new troubles overtook him and he decided to move to Hebron. On the way thither, at Bethlehem, Benjamin was born and Rachel died. After staying for some time at Hebron, where he and Esau buried their father, Isaac, in the cave of Machpelah, Gen. 35:29, Jacob moved to Egypt on account of famine. There he found Joseph, and there he died, rich and honored. Gen. 49:33. His remains were carried to Hebron and buried in the cave of Machpelah, Gen. 50:13, with his ancestors. [2] The father of Joseph, the husband of Mary. Matt. 1:15, 16.

Also see Gen. 25; 27-37; 42; 45-50.
Exod. 1-4; 6; 19; 33.
Lev. 26.
Num. 23; 24; 32.
Deut. 1; 6; 9; 29; 30; 32-34.
Josh. 24.
1 Sam. 12.
2 Sam. 23.
1 Kings 18.
2 Kings 13; 17.
1 Chron. 16.
Pss. 14; 20; 22; 24; 44; 46; 47; 53; 59; 75-79; 81; 84; 85; 87; 94; 99; 105; 114; 132; 135; 146; 147.
Isa. 2; 8-10; 14; 17; 27; 29; 40-46; 48; 49; 58-60; 65.
Jer. 2; 5; 10; 30; 31; 33; 46; 51.
Lam. 1; 2.
Ezek. 20; 28; 37; 39.
Hos. 10; 12.
Amos 3; 6-9.
Obad. :10, 17, 18.
Mic. 1-5; 7.
Nah. 2.
Mal. 1-3.
Matt. 1; 8; 22.
Mark 12.
Luke 1; 3; 13; 20.
John 4.
Acts 3; 7.
Rom. 9; 11.
Heb. 11.

Jacob's Well, at which Jesus sat and talked with the Samaritan woman, John 4:5, 6, is one and a half miles southeast of *Nabulûs*, the ancient Shechem, close to the highway from Jerusalem to Galilee, in the plain of Moreh, at the eastern base of Mount Gerizim. The wall which enclosed it and the church which once was built over it are now only heaps of ruins, but the well itself, seven and a half feet in diameter, seventy feet deep, and lined throughout with heavy masonry, is still intact except so far as it has doubtless been filled up to a considerable extent with the fragments of the church and the wall. According to Jewish tradition, the well was dug by Jacob (Gen. 33:19). Christians, Jews, Samaritans, and Mohammedans all agree in keeping the place sacred. It is one of the few ancient places in Palestine that can be certainly identified.

Ja´da (*knowing*), a grandson of Jerahmeel, the son of Hezron. 1 Chron. 2:28, 32.

Ja-da´u (*loving*), a Jew who had a foreign wife. Ezra 10:43.

Jad-du´a (*known*). [1] A Levite who sealed the covenant. Neh. 10:21. [2] Son of Jonathan, high-priest of the Jews. Neh. 12:11, 22. He is the last high-priest noticed in the Old Testament.

Ja´don (*judge*), a Jew who repaired part of the wall of Jerusalem. Neh. 3:7.

Ja´el (*mountain goat*), wife of Heber the Kenite, who killed Sisera, the Canaanitish leader, when he fled from the Israelites under Deborah and Barak. Judg. 4:17, 18, 21, 22; 5:6, 24.

Jaf´fa or **Yâ´fa** are modern names of JOPPA or JAPHO, the ancient seaport of Jerusalem. It is on the Mediterranean Sea. See JOPPA.

Ja´gur, a city in the south-east part of Judah. Josh. 15:21.

Jah, Ps. 68:4, is a contraction of JEHOVAH (which see), and is part of the words ADONIJAH and HALLELUJAH.

Ja´hath (*union*). [1] A descendant of Shobal, the son of Judah. 1 Chron. 4:2. [2] A descendant of Gershom, the son of Levi. 1 Chron. 6:20, 43. [3] Another descendant of Gershom. 1 Chron. 23:10, 11. [4] A descendant of Kohath, the son of Levi. 1 Chron. 24:22. [5] A descendant of Merari, the son of Levi. 2 Chron. 34:12.

Ja´haz (*place trodden down*), a Moabitish city afterward a Levitical city of Reuben. Num. 21:23; Deut. 2:32. Called JAHAZA, Josh. 13:18; JAHAZAH, Josh. 21:36; Jer. 48:21; and JAHZAH, 1 Chron. 6:78.

Ja-ha´za, Ja-ha´zah, Jah´zah. See JAHAZ.

Ja-ha-zi´ah (*whom Jehovah beholds*), a Jew who took account of those who had married foreign wives. Ezra 10:15.

Ja-ha´zi-el (*whom God beholds*). [1] An Israelite who came to David in Ziklag. 1 Chron. 12:4. [2] A priest who assisted in bringing up the ark of the covenant from the house of Obed-edom. 1 Chron. 16:6. [3] A son of Hebron, the son of Kohath. 1 Chron. 23:19; 24:23. [4] A Levite who encouraged the army of Jehoshaphat against the Moabites. 2 Chron. 20:14. [5] A chief man among the Jews, whose son went up with Ezra from Babylon. Ezra 8:5.

Jah´da-i (*whom Jehovah directs*), a man apparently of the family of Caleb, the son of Jephunneh. 1 Chron. 2:47.

Jah´di-el (*whom God makes joyful*), one of the heads of families of Manasseh. 1 Chron. 5:24.

Jah´do (*his union*), an Israelite of Gad. 1 Chron. 5:14.

Jah-le´el (*hoping in God*), a son of Zebulun, Gen. 46:14; Num. 26:26.

Jah´le-el-ites, descendants of Jahleel. Num. 26:26.

Jah´ma-i (*whom Jehovah guards*), a

son of Tola, the son of Issachar. 1 Chron. 7:2.

Jah´zah, a Moabitish city, 1 Chron. 6:78, same as JAHAZ (which see).

Jah´ze-el (*whom God allots*), a son of Naphtali. Gen. 46:24; Num. 26:48.

Jah´ze-el-ites, descendants of JAHZEEL. Num. 26:48.

Jah´ze-rah (*whom God leads back*), a priest of the family of Immer, whose descendants dwelt in Jerusalem. 1 Chron. 9:12. Called AHASAI in Neh. 11:13.

Jah´zi-el. 1 Chron. 7:13. Same as JAHZEEL.

Ja´ir (*whom Jehovah enlightens*). [1] A prominent warrior under Moses; was a descendant of the most powerful family of Judah and Manasseh. He conquered all the country of Argob east of Jordan; also villages in Gilead which he named Havoth-jair. Num. 32:41; Deut. 3:14; 1 Chron. 2:21-23. [2] One of the judges of Israel. Judg. 10:3-5. He judged Israel twenty-two years. [3] A Jew of the tribe of Benjamin, whose son Mordecai was cousin to Esther. Esther 2:5. [4] Father of Elhanan, 1 Chron. 20:5, called JAARE-OREGIM in 2 Sam. 21:19.

Ja´i-rites, descendants of Jair. 2 Sam. 20:26.

Ja-i´rus (*whom Jehovah enlightens*), a ruler of the synagogue in one of the towns of Galilee near the Lake of Tiberias. Luke 8:41, 42. He showed very strong faith. Christ went to his house with Peter, James, and John, and restored the daughter of Jairus to life. Mark 5:35-42.

Ja´kan (*sagacious*), a son of Ezer, 1 Chron. 1:42, same as JAAKAN in Deut. 10:6, and AKAN in Gen. 36:27.

Ja´keh (*pious*), the father of Agur. Prov. 30:1. The "words" of Agur are recorded in the thirtieth chapter of Proverbs.

Ja´kim (*whom God sets up*). [1] A son of Shimhi, a descendant of Benjamin. 1 Chron. 8:19. [2] Head of the twelfth course of priests. 1 Chron. 24:12.

Ja´lon (*abiding*), a son of Ezra, a descendant of Judah. 1 Chron. 4:17.

Jambres, jam´breez, a person mentioned by Paul, 2 Tim. 3:8, as having withstood Moses. He was an Egyptian magician at the court of Pharaoh. See JANNES and JAMBRES.

James, which is in Hebrew JACOB (*the supplanter*), is the name of two, or probably of three, persons in the New Testament.

[1] JAMES THE ELDER was a son of Zebedee and Salome, brother of John the Evangelist, probably a cousin of Jesus, and one of the three favorite apostles. His apostolic labors were confined to Jerusalem and Judea, and in A. D. 44 he was beheaded by order of King Herod Agrippa, thus becoming the first martyr among the apostles. Acts 12:2.

[2] JAMES THE LESS, or THE LITTLE, was a son of Alpheus and Mary, Mark 15:40; Matt. 10:3; Acts 1:13, and was also one of the twelve apostles. According to a tradition accepted by the Greek church, he labored in Egypt and was crucified there.

[3] JAMES, "THE BROTHER OF THE LORD," Gal. 1:19; compare Matt. 13:55; Mark 6:3, or simply JAMES. Acts 12:17; 15:13, is by some identified with JAMES THE LESS and regarded as a cousin of Jesus, while others distinguish between the two and take the designation "the brother of the Lord" in the strict sense of the words. At all events, he stood at the head of the Church in Jerusalem after the dispersion of the disciples and the departure of Peter, Acts 12:17, and he presided

at the Apostolical Council in Jerusalem, A. D. 50, whence he is generally styled by ecclesiastical writers "Bishop of Jerusalem." According to Josephus, the ancient Jewish historian, he was in A. D. 62 sentenced by the Sanhedrin to be stoned; according to Hegesippus, who was a Christian writer from the middle of the second century, he was thrown by the Pharisees from the pinnacle of the Temple and killed with a fuller's club while praying for his murderers.

Also see Matt. 4:21; 10:2; 17:1; 27:56.
Mark 1:19, 29; 3:17, 18; 5:37; 9:2; 10:35, 41; 13:3; 14:33; 16:1.
Luke 5:10; 6:14-16; 8:51; 9:28, 54; 24:10.
Acts 21:18.
1 Cor. 15:7.
Gal. 2:9, 12.
James 1:1.
Jude 1.

James, the Epistle of, was written by James, "the brother of the Lord," in Jerusalem, before A. D. 62; and is addressed to "the twelve tribes scattered abroad;" that is, to all Jewish converts to Christianity. It is moral rather than doctrinal, insisting upon the necessity of true faith manifesting itself in good works.

Ja'min (*prosperity, right hand*). [1] Second son of Simeon and founder of the Jaminites. Gen. 46:10; Exod. 6:15. [2] An Israelite of the tribe of Judah. 1 Chron. 2:27. [3] One of the priests who expounded the law with Ezra. Neh. 8:7.

Ja'min-ites, descendants of Jamin, son of Simeon. Num. 26:12.

Jamlech, jam'lek (*whom God makes king*), a descendant of Simeon. 1 Chron. 4:34.

Jang'ling, in 1 Tim. 1:6, means babbling; vain talking.

Jan'na (*whom Jehovah bestows*), one of the ancestors of Joseph, the husband of Mary. Luke 3:24.

Jannes, jan'neez, and **Jambres**, jam'breez, two noted magicians of Egypt, 2 Tim. 3:8, supposed to have used their art to deceive Pharaoh. Exod. 7:9-13.

Ja-no'ah (*rest*), a town of Naphtali taken by the king of Assyria. 2 Kings 15:29.

Ja-no'hah (*rest*), a town of Ephraim. Josh. 16:6, 7.

Ja'num (*slumber*), a city of Judah. Josh. 15:53. In the marginal notes it is JANUS (*flight*).

Ja'pheth (*enlargement*), one of the three sons of Noah. Gen. 5:32; 10:21. The prophetic blessing given him by his father, Gen. 9:27, was fully accomplished.

Ja'phi-a (*splendid*). [1] The Amorite king of Lachish who, with the neighboring kings, laid siege to Gibeon, but was defeated by Joshua. Josh. 10:3. [2] A son of David, born in Jerusalem. 2 Sam. 5:15; 1 Chron. 3:7; 14:6. [3] A town of Zebulun. Josh. 19:12.

Japh'let (*whom God delivers*), a grandson of Beriah, the son of Asher. 1 Chron. 7:32, 33.

Japh'le-ti, a landmark of Ephraim. Josh. 16:3.

Ja'pho, a city of Dan, on the coast of the Mediterranean Sea. Josh. 19:46. See JOPPA.

Ja'rah (*honey*), a Benjamite, the son of Ahaz, of the family of Saul. 1 Chron. 9:42. Called JEHOADAH in 1 Chron. 8:36.

Ja'reb (*an adversary*), Hos. 5:13; 10:6, is not the name of a king. He was a *hostile* king, *the king of Assyria*.

Ja'red (*descent*), the son of Mahalaleel, of the family of Seth. Gen. 5:15-20; Luke 3:37. He was the father of

Enoch and the grandfather of Methuselah. In 1 Chron. 1:2 Jared is called JERED.

Jar-e-si´ah (*whom Jehovah fattens*), a son of Jeroham, a descendant of Benjamin. 1 Chron. 8:27.

Jar´ha, an Egyptian servant to whom Sheshan gave his daughter Ahlai to wife. 1 Chron. 2:34, 35.

Ja´rib (*an adversary*). [1] One of the sons of Simeon, 1 Chron. 4:24, called JACHIN in Gen. 46:10. [2] A chief man among the Jews and a companion of Ezra. Ezra 8:16. [3] A priest who had taken a foreign wife. Ezra 10:18.

Jar´muth (*height*). [1] A town of Judah. Josh. 15:35; Neh. 11:29. [2] A Levitical city of Issachar, Josh. 21:29, called REMETH in Josh. 19:21, and RAMOTH in 1 Chron. 6:73.

Ja-ro´ah (*moon*), a descendant of Gad. 1 Chron. 5:14.

Ja´shen (*sleeping*), father of one of David's valiant men. 2 Sam. 23:32.

Ja´sher, Book of (*upright*), is mentioned in Josh. 10:13; 2 Sam. 1:18. It was probably a collection of national songs, and is now lost.

Ja-sho´be-am (*to whom the people turn*), a chief of David's captains. 1 Chron. 11:11; 27:2. Same as ADINO in 2 Sam. 23:8.

Jash´ub (*he turns*). [1] A son of Issachar and founder of the Jashubites. Num. 26:24; 1 Chron. 7:1. Called JOB in Gen. 46:13. [2] A Jew who married a foreign wife. Ezra 10:29.

Jash´u-bi-le´hem (*turner-back for food*), either a place or a descendant of Judah. 1 Chron. 4:22.

Jash´ub-ites, Num. 26:24, descendants of JASHUB, No. 1.

Ja´si-el (*whom God has made*), one of David's valiant men. 1 Chron. 11:47.

Same as JAASIEL.

Ja´son (*one who will heal*), a disciple of Thessalonica whom the Jews assaulted because he received Paul and Silas into his house. Acts 17:5, 6, 7, 9.

Jas´per, the last precious stone in the high-priest's breastplate, Exod. 28:20, and the first in the foundations of the New Jerusalem. Rev. 21:19. It is a kind of quartz of various colors and receives a high polish.

Jath´ni-el (*whom God bestows*), a Levite porter for the Tabernacle. 1 Chron. 26:2.

Jat´tir, a Levitical town in the hill country of Judah. Josh. 15:48; 21:14; 1 Sam. 30:27; 1 Chron. 6:57.

Ja´van. [1] Fourth son of Japheth and ancestor of the Grecians and Ionians. Gen. 10:2, 4; 1 Chron. 1:5, 7. [2] The name was also applied to the people descended from him and to the country which it is generally agreed that they inhabited (Ionia), and thus became afterward the name for the whole of Greece. Isa. 66:19; Ezek. 27:13. [3] A town of southern Arabia (*Yemen*). Ezek. 27:19.

Jav´e-lin, 1 Sam. 18:10; Num. 25:7, a light spear thrown from the hand.

Ja´zer, Josh. 21:39, or **Ja-a´zer,** Num. 21:32, a city of Gilead east of the Jordan. It was conquered and assigned to Gad and the Levites.

Ja´zer, Sea of, Jer. 48:32, was perhaps a lake which existed in ancient times near Jazer.

Ja´ziz (*whom God moves*), superintendent of the flocks in the time of David. 1 Chron. 27:31.

Jeal´ous, Exod. 34:14, a name of the LORD.

Jeal´ous-y generally means suspicion of conjugal infidelity. 2 Cor. 11:2. The word is also used for anger or indignation, Ps. 79:5; 1 Cor. 10:22, or for a deep interest for the prosperity and honor of another. Zech. 1:14; 8:2. Its various meanings are generally indicated by its connection.

Je´a-rim, Mount (*mount of forests*), mentioned in describing the northern boundary of Judah. Josh. 15:10.

Je-at´e-rai (*whom Jehovah leads*), a descendant of Gershom, the son of Levi. 1 Chron. 6:21. Called ETHNI in verse 41.

Jeberechiah, je-ber-e-ki´ah, father of the Zechariah whom Isaiah took as a witness. Isa. 8:2.

Je´bus (*threshing-floor*), an ancient name of Jerusalem. Judg. 19:10, 11. See JERUSALEM.

Je-bu´si, Josh. 15:8; 18:16, 28, a name for JEBUS, or JERUSALEM.

Jeb´u-sites, a tribe that lived in that part of Canaan about Jebus (afterward Jerusalem). The Israelites were commanded to destroy them. Deut. 7:1; 20:17. David conquered their stronghold. 2 Sam. 5:6, 8; 1 Chron. 11:4–6. The inhabitants of Jebus were called JEBUSITES.

Jecamiah, jek-a-mi´ah (*whom Jehovah gathers*), one of the line of David. 1 Chron. 3:18. Same as JEKAMIAH in 1 Chron. 2:41.

Jecholiah, jek-o-li´ah (*able through Jehovah*), the mother of Azariah, or Uzziah, king of Judah. 2 Kings 15:2. She is called JECOLIAH in 2 Chron. 26:3.

Jechonias, jek-o-ni´as, Matt. 1:11, 12, is the Greek form of JECONIAH, or JEHOIACHIN (which see).

Jecoliah, jek-o-li´ah. See JECHOLIAH.

Jeconiah, jek-o-ni´ah (*whom Jehovah establishes*). 1 Chron. 3:16; Jer. 24:1. See JEHOIACHIN.

Jedaiah, je-da´yah (*praise Jehovah*). [1] A descendant of Simeon. 1 Chron. 4:37. [2] A Jew who repaired part of the wall of Jerusalem. Neh. 3:10.

Jedaiah, je-da´yah (*Jehovah cares for him*), a different name, in the Hebrew, from the preceding. [1] Head of the second course of priests. 1 Chron. 9:10; Ezra 2:36. [2] A priest who came up from Babylon with Zerubbabel. Neh. 11:10; Zech. 6:10, 14. [3] Another priest who came up from Babylon with Zerubbabel. Neh. 12:7, 21.

Je-di´a-el (*known of God*). [1] A son or descendant of Benjamin; was progenitor of the most powerful family of the tribe. 1 Chron. 7:6, 10, 11. [2] One of David's valiant men. 1 Chron. 11:45. [3] May be same as the chief of Manasseh who joined David. 1 Chron. 12:20. [4] A Levite doorkeeper of the Temple in the time of David. 1 Chron. 26:2.

Jed´i-dah (*one beloved*), wife of Amon and mother of Josiah, kings of Judah. 2 Kings 22:1.

Jed-i-di´ah (*beloved of Jehovah*), the name which Nathan the prophet gave to Solomon by command of the Lord. 2 Sam. 12:25.

Jed´u-thun (*praising*), a Levite, one of the chief singers in the time of David, whose descendants dwelt in Jerusalem after the captivity. 1 Chron. 9:16; 16:38, 41, 42; 25:1, 3. Several of the Psalms are inscribed to him, among which are Pss. 39, 62, 77.

Je-e´zer (*father of help*), a shortened form of Abiezer, was a descendant of Manasseh through Gilead. Num. 26:30. See ABIEZER.

Je-e´zer-ites, descendants of JEEZER.

Je-gar-sa-ha-du´tha (*heap of testimony*), the name given by Laban to the heap of stones raised by Jacob as a witness of the covenant between them. Gen. 31:47.

Je-ha´le-le-el (*who praises God*), a descendant of Judah. 1 Chron. 4:16.

Je-hal´e-lel (*who praises God*), a descendant of Merari. 2 Chron. 29:12.

Jehdeiah, je-de´yah (*whom Jehovah makes joyful*). [1] The son of Shubael, a descendant of Levi. 1 Chron. 24:20. [2] The overseer of the asses in the time of David. 1 Chron. 27:30.

Je-hez´e-kel (*whom God makes strong*), head of the twentieth course of priests. 1 Chron. 24:16. Same name as EZEKIEL.

Je-hi´ah (*Jehovah lives*), a doorkeeper for the ark of the covenant. 1 Chron. 15:24.

Je-hi´el (*God lives*). [1] A Levite singer in the Tabernacle in the time of David. 1 Chron. 15:18, 20; 16:5. [2] A descendant of Gershon, the son of Levi. 1 Chron. 23:8; 29:8. [3] The tutor or companion of the sons of David. 1 Chron. 27:32. [4] A son of Jehoshaphat, king of Judah. 2 Chron. 21:2. [5] A son of Heman (the singer). 2 Chron. 29:14. [6] A ruler of the house of God in Josiah's reign. 2 Chron. 35:8. [7] A Levite overseer. 2 Chron. 31:13. [8] Father of Obadiah, who returned with Ezra. Ezra 8:9. [9] An Israelite whose son Shechaniah proposed to Ezra the putting away of foreign wives. Ezra 10:2. [10, 11] Jews who took foreign wives. Ezra 10:21, 26.

Je-hi´el (*treasured of God?*), a distinct name in Hebrew from Jehiel immediately preceding this one. [1] The father of Gibeon of Benjamin and an ancestor of Saul. 1 Chron. 9:35. [2] One of David's valiant men. 1 Chron. 11:44.

Je-hi´e-li, the descendants of Jehiel. 1 Chron. 26:21, 22.

Je-hiz-ki´ah (*whom Jehovah strengthens*), one of those who withstood the Israelites when they wished to make bond-slaves of the captives taken from Judah. 2 Chron. 28:12.

Je-ho´a-dah (*whom Jehovah adorns*),

a son of Ahaz, the great-grandson of Jonathan, 1 Chron. 8:36, called JARAH in 1 Chron. 9:42.

Je-ho-ad´dan, the queen of Joash and mother of Amaziah, king of Judah. 2 Kings 14:2; 2 Chron. 25:1.

Je-ho´a-haz (*whom Jehovah holds*). [1] Son and successor of Jehu, king of Israel. His reign was disastrous. 2 Kings 10:35; 13:1, 4, 7–10, 22, 25. [2] One of the sons of Josiah, king of Judah, whom the people made king after his father's death, but who, after a reign of three months, was deposed and imprisoned by Pharaoh-necho, king of Egypt. 2 Kings 23:30, 31, 34; 2 Chron. 36:1, 2, 4. [3] The son of Jehoram, king of Judah, who succeeded his father on the throne. 2 Chron. 21:17. Same as AHAZIAH and AZARIAH.

Je-ho´ash (*whom Jehovah bestowed*), the original form of JOASH, and applied to two kings. See JOASH, 3 and 4.

Jehohanan, je-ho-ha´nan or je-ho´hanan (*whom Jehovah gave*), a name contracted into JOHANAN and JOHN. [1] A son of Meshelemiah and a porter in the Tabernacle. 1 Chron. 26:3. [2] A chief captain under Jehoshaphat. 2 Chron. 17:15. [3] A Jew who had taken a foreign wife. Ezra 10:28. [4] A priest who went up with Zerubbabel from Babylon. Neh. 12:13. [5] A priest who was one of the singers at the dedication of the wall of Jerusalem. Neh 12:42.

Jehoiachin, je-hoi´a-kin (*whom Jehovah has appointed*), called JECONIAH in 1 Chron. 3:17, CONIAH in Jer. 22:24, and JECHONIAS in Matt. 1:12, was son and successor of Jehoiakim king of Judah. 2 Kings 24:8. After a reign of three months and ten days he, with the royal family, the chief men, and great treasures, was carried to Babylon by Nebuchadnezzar. 2 Kings 24:6-16.

Je-hoi´a-da (*whom Jehovah knows*). [1] The father of BENAIAH, one of David's chief officers. 2 Sam. 8:18; 1 Kings 1:8. This Jehoiada was the chief priest. 1 Chron. 27:5. By a copyist's error Benaiah is said to have been the father of Jehoiada instead of the son. 1 Chron. 27:34. [2] The high-priest who made Joash king after Athaliah had usurped the kingdom seven years. 2 Kings 11:4, 9, 15, 17; 2 Chron. 22:11; 23:1. [3] The second priest in the reign of Zedekiah. Jer. 29:25-29. [4] A Jew who repaired a gate of Jerusalem. Neh. 3:6. [5] The leader of the Aaronites who went to Ziklag to help David. 1 Chron. 12:27.

Je-hoi´a-kim (*whom Jehovah sets up*), the name which was given by Pharaoh-necho to Eliakim, the son of Josiah, king of Judah, whom he made king in place of his father, after Pharaoh-necho had deposed and imprisoned Jehoahaz, whom the people had made king. 2 Kings 23:34; 1 Chron. 3:15.

Also see 2 Kings 23:35, 36; 24:1, 5, 6, 19.

1 Chron. 3:16.

2 Chron. 36:4, 5, 8.

Jer. 1:3; 22:18, 24; 24:1; 25:1; 26:1, 21-23; 27:1, 20; 28:4; 35:1; 36:1, 9, 28-30, 32; 37:1; 45:1; 46:2; 52:2.

Dan. 1:1, 2.

Je-hoi´a-rib (*whom Jehovah defends*). [1] The head of the first course of priests. 1 Chron. 24:7. [2] A priest at Jerusalem. 1 Chron. 9:10.

Je-hon´a-dab or **Jon´a-dab** (*whom Jehovah incites*), the son of Rechab. 2 Kings 10:15.

Je-hon´a-than (*whom Jehovah gave*), very often **Jon´a-than**. [1] Overseer of David's storehouses. 1 Chron. 27:25. [2] A Levite whom Jehoshaphat sent to teach the law in the cities of Judah. 2 Chron. 17:8. [3] A priest in the time of Joiakim. Neh. 12:18.

Je-ho´ram, often **Jo´ram** (*whom Jehovah has exalted*). [1] The eldest son of Jehoshaphat, and his successor as king of Judah. 1 Kings 22:50; 2 Kings 8:16, 17. [2] A son of Ahab, king of Israel, who succeeded to the throne on the death of Ahaziah, who had no son. 2 Kings 1:17; 2 Chron. 22:5. [3] A priest employed by Jehoshaphat to instruct the people. 2 Chron. 17:8.

Je-ho-shab´e-ath (*her oath is Jehovah*). 2 Chron. 22:11. See JEHOSHEBA.

Je-hosh´a-phat (*whom Jehovah judges*). [1] The royal recorder under David and Solomon. 2 Sam. 8:16; 1 Kings 4:3. [2] One of Solomon's purveyors. 1 Kings 4:17. [3] The son of Asa who succeeded his father as king of Judah. He reigned B. C. 914-890, and was pious and prosperous. 2 Chron 17:3-6. [4] The father of King Jehu. 2 Kings 9:2, 14. [5] A priest in the time of David. 1 Chron. 15:24.

Also see 2 Sam. 20:24.

1 Kings 15:24; 22:2, 4, 5, 7, 8, 10, 18, 29, 30, 32, 41, 42, 44, 45, 48-51.

2 Kings 1:17; 3:1, 7, 11, 12, 14; 8:16; 9:14; 12:18.

1 Chron. 3:10; 18:15.

2 Chron. 17:1, 10-12; 18:1, 3, 4, 6, 7, 9, 17, 28, 29, 31; 19:1, 2, 4, 8; 20:1-3, 5, 15, 18, 20, 25, 27, 30, 31, 34, 35, 37; 21:1, 2, 12; 22:9.

Joel 3:2, 12.

Je-hosh´a-phat, Valley of (*valley of the judgment of Jehovah*), a place named only in Joel 3:2, 12. It is usually identified with the valley of the brook Kedron, between Jerusalem and Mount Olivet, but is probably an ideal place in the prophet's vision of the judgment.

Je-hosh´e-ba (*her oath is Jehovah*), wife of Jehoiada the high-priest, 2 Kings 11:2, 3, called JEHOSHABEATH in 2 Chron. 22:11. She saved her infant nephew Joash when Athaliah attempted the destruction of all the king's sons.

Je-hosh´u-a or **Je-hosh´u-ah** (*Jehovah is his help*), the full form for Joshua. It is used in Num. 13:16; 1 Chron. 7:27.

Je-ho´vah (*he will be*), a title of the Supreme Being. Exod. 6:3. Its meaning is similar to the title I AM. Exod. 3:14. In the English Bible it is generally translated "LORD" and printed in small capitals. It denotes the God of revelation and redemption. See JAH, and GOD.

Je-ho´vah-ji´reh (*The LORD will see*, or *provide*), the name given by Abraham to the place where, when he was about to sacrifice Isaac, he was stopped by an angel of the Lord. Gen. 22:14. It is probably the same as MOUNT MORIAH in Jerusalem.

Je-ho´vah-nis´si (*The LORD my banner*), the name which Moses gave to the altar which he built after the Israelites had defeated the Amalekites. Exod. 17:15.

Je-ho´vah-sha´lom (*The LORD send peace*), the name which Gideon gave to the altar which he built when the Lord said to him, "Peace be unto thee." Judg. 6:24.

Je-ho´vah-sham´mah (*The LORD is there*), the name given to the city spoken of in the prophetical description of the Holy Land communicated to Ezekiel. Ezek. 48:35, marginal notes.

Jehovah-tsidkenu, je-ho´vah-sid´ke-nu (*THE LORD OUR RIGHTEOUSNESS*), is found in the marginal notes in Jer. 23:6 and 33:16.

Je-hoz´a-bad is commonly contracted into **Joz´a-bad** (*whom Jehovah bestows*). [1] One of those who slew Joash. 2 Kings 12:21; 2 Chron. 24:26. [2] A Levite porter. 1 Chron. 26:4. [3] A chief captain of the tribe of Benjamin in the time of Jehoshaphat. 2 Chron. 17:18.

Je-hoz´a-dak (*whom God makes just*), son of the high-priest Seraiah. 1 Chron. 6:14, 15. He is more frequently called JOZADAK or JOSEDECH.

Je´hu (*Jehovah is he*). [1] The son of Hanani the seer. 1 Kings 16:1, 7, 12; 2 Chron. 19:2; 20:34. [2] The son of Jehoshaphat and grandson of Nimshi. Elisha was commanded to anoint him king over Israel, and he became the instrument of God's judgments on the house of Ahab. 1 Kings 19:16, 17; 2 Kings 9:1-10. Jehu was tyrannical and became idolatrous. 2 Kings 10:31. He reigned B. C. 884–856. [3] A descendant of Jerahmeel, the son of Hezron. 1 Chron. 2:38. [4] One of the tribe of Simeon. 1 Chron. 4:35. [5] A Benjamite who was with David at Ziklag. 1 Chron. 12:3.

Also see 2 Kings 9:11, 13-22, 24, 25, 27, 30, 31; 10:1, 5, 11, 13, 18-21, 23-25, 28-30, 34-36; 12:1; 13:1; 14:8; 15:12. 2 Chron. 22:7-9; 25:17.

Hos. 1:4.

Je-hub´bah (*he will be hidden*), a son of Shamer, who was a descendant of Asher. 1 Chron. 7:34.

Je´hu-cal or **Ju´cal** (*potent*), an officer under Zedekiah, king of Judah, whom the king sent to Jeremiah to entreat his prayers for the people. Jer. 37:3; 38:1.

Je´hud (*celebrated*), a town of Dan. Josh. 19:45.

Je-hu´di (*a Jew*), sent by the princes to tell Baruch to bring the roll of Jeremiah's prophecies. Jer. 36:14, 21, 23.

Je-hu-di´jah (*the Jewess*), a name applied to one of the wives of Mered to distinguish her from the other, an Egyptian. 1 Chron. 4:18.

Je´hush (*a collector*), a descendant of

Saul. 1 Chron. 8:39.

Je-i´el (*treasure of God*). [1] A Reubenite chief. 1 Chron. 5:7. [2] A Levite porter and musician for the Tabernacle. 1 Chron. 15:18, 21; 16:5. [3] A Levite of the sons of Asaph. 2 Chron. 20:14. [4] The principal scribe or recorder in the time of Uzziah, king of Judah. 2 Chron. 26:11. [5] A Levite who assisted in the reforms of Hezekiah. 2 Chron. 29:13. [6] A chief of the Levites in the time of Josiah. 2 Chron. 35:9. [7] One who returned with Ezra from Babylon. Ezra 8:13. [8] A Jew who had taken a foreign wife. Ezra 10:43.

Je-kab´ze-el (*which God gathers*), a town in the southern part of Judah, Neh. 11:25, called KABZEEL in Josh. 15:21; 2 Sam. 23:20.

Jek-a-me´am (*who gathers the people*), a son of Hebron, the grandson of Levi. 1 Chron. 23:19; 24:23.

Jek-a-mi´ah (*whom Jehovah gathers*), a descendant of Judah. 1 Chron. 2:41. Same as JECAMIAH. 1 Chron. 3:18.

Je-ku´thi-el (*piety towards God*), a son of Ezra, a descendant of Judah. 1 Chron. 4:18.

Jemima, je-mi´ma or jem´i-ma (*dove*), the eldest of Job's three daughters, born after he recovered. Job 42:14.

Je-mu´el (*day of God*), eldest son of Simeon, Gen. 46:10; Exod. 6:15, called NEMUEL in Num. 26:12; 1 Chron. 4:24.

Jeoparded, jep´ard-ed, in Judg. 5:18, means risked.

Jephthæ, jef´tha-e, Heb. 11:32, Greek form of JEPHTHAH (which see).

Jeph´thah, jef´thah (*whom God sets free*), a judge of Israel who delivered them from the Ammonites. Judg. 11:1-3. Jephthah made a vow, just before the battle, that if he gained the victory he would offer up for a burnt offering whatsoever

came forth from his house to welcome him on his return. This proved to be his daughter, an only child. Judg. 11:30-40.

Jephuuneh, je-fun´neh (*may he be regarded with favor!*). [1] A man of the tribe of Judah, father of Caleb the spy. Num. 13:6; Josh. 14:14; 1 Chron. 4:15. [2] Head of a family in Asher. 1 Chron. 7:38.

Je´rah (*moon*), a people descended from Joktan, from whom a region in Arabia was named. Gen. 10:26; 1 Chron. 1:20.

Je-rah´me-el (*on whom God has mercy*). [1] A son of Hezron, the grandson of Judah, 1 Chron. 2:9, 25, 26, 27, 33, 42, founder of the Jerahmeelites. [2] A descendant of Merari. 1 Chron. 24:29. [3] An officer under Jehoiakim, Jer. 36:26, employed to arrest Jeremiah and Baruch.

Je-rah´me-el-ites, descendants of Jerahmeel, son of Hezron. 1 Sam. 27:10; 30:29.

Je´red (*descent*). [1] 1 Chron. 1:2. See JARED. [2] A descendant of Judah. 1 Chron. 4:18.

Jer´e-mai (*dwelling in heights*), one who had a foreign wife. Ezra 10:33.

Jer-e-mi´ah (*whom Jehovah sets up*). [1] The father of Hamutal, wife of King Josiah. 2 Kings 23:31; 24:18; Jer. 52:1. [2] Head of a family in Manasseh. 1 Chron. 5:24. [3] A valiant man who joined David in Ziklag. 1 Chron. 12:4. [4, 5] Gadite warriors who joined David at Ziklag. 1 Chron. 12:10, 13. [6] A priest who sealed the covenant. Neh. 10:2; 12:1, 12, 34. [7] A descendant of Jonadab, the son of Rechab. Jer. 35:3. He was one of the Rechabites. [8] JEREMIAH (*whom Jehovah sets up*), one of the four great prophets, was of priestly descent, consecrated to the prophetic office before his birth, and was a son of Hilkiah of Anathoth, in the land of Benjamin. He began his prophetic ministrations at an early age, in the thirteenth year of the reign of Josiah, B. C. 626, and continued it for a period of forty-two years, until after the destruction of Jerusalem and the beginning of the captivity. He denounced the vices and the idolatry of the people, proclaimed the judgment of God which awaited them, and advised submission to Nebuchadnezzar as the only means of escaping destruction. But Jerusalem swarmed with false prophets who promised the king and the people the support of God in their undertakings, and then the end came. To the exiles he wrote that their captivity would be long–that, indeed it would last seventy years. After the murder of Gedaliah, Jeremiah was carried, against his will, to Egypt, and there he probably died.

Also see 2 Chron. 35:25; 36:12, 21, 22. Ezra 1:1.

Jer. 1:1, 11; 7:1; 11:1; 14:1; 18:1, 18; 19:14; 20:1-3; 21:1, 3; 24:3; 25:1, 2, 13; 26:7-9, 12, 20, 24; 27:1; 28:5, 6, 10-12, 15; 29:1, 27, 29, 30; 30:1; 32:1, 2, 6, 26; 33:1, 19, 23; 34:1, 6, 8, 12; 35:1, 12, 18; 36:1, 4, 5, 8, 10, 19, 26, 27, 32; 37:2-4, 6, 12-18, 21; 38:1, 6, 7, 9-17, 19, 20, 24, 27, 28; 39:11, 14, 15; 40:1, 2, 6; 42:2, 4, 5, 7; 43:1, 2, 6, 8; 44:1, 15, 20, 24; 45:1; 46:1, 13; 47:1; 49:34; 50:1; 51:59-61, 64.

Dan. 9:2.

Jeremi′ah, the Book of, contains the prophesies uttered under Josiah, B. C. 629–608, chapters 1–12; under Jehoiakim, B. C. 607–597, chapters 13, 20, 22, 23, 35, 36, 45–48, 49:1-33; under Zedekiah, B. C. 597–588, chapters 21, 24, 27–34, 37–39, 49:34-39; 50, 51; and under Gedaliah, chapters 40–44. See LAMENTATIONS OF JEREMIAH.

Jer-e-mi′as. Matt. 16:14. See JEREMIAH, No. 8, the prophet.

Jer′-e-moth (*heights*). [1] A son of Beriah, a descendant of Benjamin. 1 Chron. 8:14. [2] A Merarite Levite, 1 Chron. 23:23. called JERIMOTH in 1 Chron. 24:30. [3] Head of fifteenth course of musicians, 1 Chron. 25:22, in 1 Chron. 25:4 called JERIMOTH. [4, 5] Two Jews who had taken foreign wives. Ezra 10:26, 27.

Jer′e-my, Matt. 2:17; 27:9. See JEREMIAH, No. 8, the prophet.

Je-ri′ah (*founded by Jehovah*), a descendant of Hebron, the grandson of Levi. 1 Chron. 23:19; 24:23. Called JERIJAH in 1 Chron. 26:31.

Jer′i-bai (*whom Jehovah defends?*), one of David's valiant men. 1 Chron. 11:46.

Jer′i-cho (*fragrance*). an ancient strongly fortified and celebrated city of Palestine, stood in the valley of the Jordan, five miles west of that river and six miles north of the Dead Sea, in a very fertile plain watered by a large spring called the "Fountain of Elisha." 2 Kings 2:19-22. It was called the "city of palm trees." Deut. 34:3; Judg. 3:13; 2 Chron. 28:15. The Jericho mentioned in the New Testament was about a mile and a half south-east of the ancient city. Spies were sent into the ancient city and received by Rahab. Josh. 2; Heb. 11:31. It was the first city attacked by Joshua after crossing the Jordan. He was miraculously aided in capturing it, the wall "fell down flat," Josh. 6:20, and the city and its inhabitants, except Rahab and her kindred and all that she had, were destroyed. It was soon rebuilt and became prosperous again. It had a flourishing school of prophets which was often visited by Elijah. 2 Kings 2. After the Babylonian captivity it was immediately repeopled, Ezra 2:34; Neh. 7:36, and Herod the Great made it his winter residence, adorned it

with many splendid buildings, and died there. As the Jewish pilgrims going up to Jerusalem used to assemble at Jericho, Christ passed through it several times; there he met Zacchæus, Luke 19:1-9, and it is mentioned often in the New Testament. Matt 20:24-34; Mark 10:46–52, etc. At present it is only a miserable village. The scene of the parable of the Good Samaritan was on the road from Jericho to Jerusalem. It is still the haunt of robbers.
Also see Num. 22:1; 26:3, 63; 31:12; 33:48, 50; 34:15; 35:1; 36:13.
Deut. 32:49; 34:1.
Josh. 3:16; 4:13, 19; 5:10, 13; 6:1, 2, 25, 26; 7:2; 8:2; 9:3; 10:1, 28, 30; 12:9; 13:32; 16:1, 7; 18:12, 21; 20:8; 24:11.
2 Sam. 10:5.
1 Kings 16:34.
2 Kings 25:5.
1 Chron. 6:78; 19:5.
Neh. 3:2.
Jer. 39:5; 52:8.
Luke 10:30; 18:35.
Heb. 11:30.

Je´ri-el (*founded of God*), a son of Tola, the son of Issachar. 1 Chron. 7:2.

Je-ri´jah (*founded of Jehovah*), a descendant of Hebron. 1 Chron. 26:31. He is called JERIAH in 1 Chron. 23:19; 24:23.

Jer´i-moth (*heights*). [1] A son of Bela, the son of Benjamin. 1 Chron. 7:7. [2] A son of Becher, the son of Benjamin. 1 Chron. 7:8. [3] A valiant man who came to David in Ziklag. 1 Chron. 12:5. [4, 5] See JERE-MOTH, Nos. 2 and 3. [6] Ruler of Naphtali in the time of David. 1 Chron. 27:19. [7] A son of David. 2 Chron. 11:18. [8] An overseer in the Temple in the time of Hezekiah. 2 Chron. 31:13.

Je´ri-oth (*curtains*), wife of Caleb, son of Hezron. 1 Chron. 2:18.

Jer-o-bo´am (*whose people is many*) was the name of two kings of Israel. [1] JEROBOAM I., the founder of the kingdom of Israel, B. C. 975–954, came of the tribe of Ephraim, a son of Nebat, is noted as "the man who made Israel to sin," and was by Solomon made superintendent of all the workmen furnished by his tribe. It having been foretold by the prophet Ahijah that he should become king of the ten tribes, it aroused the suspicion of Solomon and Jeroboam fled to Egypt. After the death of the king he returned, placed himself at the head of the rebellion against Rehoboam, and fixed his residence at Shechem, which he fortified. Idolatry was part of his nature and also of his policy. In order to separate the ten tribes as far as possible from the two tribes which remained faithful to the house of David, he wished to prevent his subjects from going up to Jerusalem at the great festivals, and for that purpose he erected two idols, two golden calves, one at Bethel and the other at Dan, appointed priests out of the common people, and offered sacrifices himself at the altar. [2] JEROBOAM II., who reigned B. C. 825–784, was a son of Joash and great-grandson of Jehu. He was idolatrous, like Jeroboam I., 2 Kings 14:23-29, and as seen from the books of Hosea and Amos, but he was victorious over his enemies and raised the kingdom of Israel to its highest power. Not long after his death his family was cut off with the sword, 2 Kings 15:10, according to the predictions of the prophet Amos.
Also see 1 Kings 11:26, 28, 29, 31, 40; 12:2, 3, 12, 15, 20, 25, 26, 32; 13:1, 4, 33, 34; 14:1, 2, 4-7, 10, 11, 13, 14, 16, 17, 19, 20, 30; 15:1, 6, 7, 9, 25, 29, 30, 34; 16:2, 3, 7, 19, 26, 31;

21:22, 22:52.
2 Kings 3:3; 9:9; 10:29, 31; 13:2, 6, 11, 13; 14:16; 15:1, 8, 9, 18, 24, 28; 17:21, 22; 23:15.
1 Chron. 5:17.
2 Chron. 9:29; 10:2, 3, 12, 15; 11:4, 14; 12:15; 13:1-4, 6, 8, 13, 15, 19, 20.
Hos. 1:1.
Amos 1:1; 7:9-11.

Jer´o-ham (*who finds mercy*). [1] Grandfather of the prophet Samuel. 1 Sam. 1:1; 1 Chron. 6:27, 34. [2, 3] Benjamites. 1 Chron. 8:27; 9:8. [4] A priest, father of Adaiah. 1 Chron. 9:12. May be same person as in Neh. 11:12. [5] Father of some of David's warriors. 1 Chron. 12:7. [6] Father of Azareel, prince of Dan. 1 Chron. 27:22. [7] Father of a captain who assisted Jehoiada to place Joash on the throne of Judah. 2 Chron. 23:1.

Je-rub´-ba-al (*with whom Baal contends*), Judg. 6:32, and **Je-rub´-be-sheth** (*with whom the idol contends*), 2 Sam. 11:21, names given to GIDEON (which see).

Jer´u-el (*founded of God*), **Wil´derness of,** situated in the southern extremity of Judah, westward from the cliff of Ziz. 2 Chron. 20:16. Here the Ammonites, Moabites, and their allies were met and defeated by Jehoshaphat.

Je-ru´sa-lem (*the abode of peace*), the most important city in Biblical history, was the capital of the Hebrew monarchy and of the kingdom of Judah. It is the most sacred city of the world, and is called by the Psalmist "Beautiful for situation, the joy of the whole earth," and "the perfection of beauty." Pss. 48:2, 3; 50:2. Christ, in Matt. 23:37-39, speaks mournfully of it in view of its unfaithfulness and approaching destruction.

Names.—It is called JEBUSI, Josh.

18:28, and JEBUS, Judg. 19:10, 11, and is first mentioned as JERUSALEM in Josh. 10:1. It was also known as SALEM, CITY OF DAVID, CITY OF ZION, CITY OF JUDAH, CITY OF GOD, CITY OF THE GREAT KING, HOLY CITY, ARIEL, and prophetically, Isa. 24:10, as CITY OF CONFUSION. The word ZION sometimes denotes the whole of Jerusalem, but literally means its southwestern hill. In the Latin Version Jerusalem is called HIEROSOLYMA, and the Roman emperor Hadrian called it ÆLIA CAPITOLINA. Mohammedans, Arabs, and Turks called it *el-Khuds*, "the holy," and *Beit-el-Makhuddis*, "the holy house."

Situation and Extent.—It was built on four hills, Zion, Acra, Moriah, and Bezetha, and is in latitude 31° 46´ 35″ north and longitude 35° 13´ 30″ east from Greenwich. It is near the summit of the western mountain-range of Palestine; is thirty-two miles east of the Mediterranean and eighteen miles west of the Dead Sea. Its highest point is 2581 feet above the sea. The old walls of Solomon and Zerubbabel included only about 150 acres. At the time of its greatest extent, after the third wall had been built by Herod Agrippa, the city covered about 465 acres. The ancient city included territory now outside the walls and under cultivation. Jer. 26:18. Jerusalem is surrounded on all sides except the north by deep ravines which, before the invention of modern siege-guns, made it a place of great military strength. On the east is the valley of the Kedron, separating the city from the long ridge of the Mount of Olives, of which the central peak is called the Mount of the Ascension, 2665 feet high, and, still farther south, from the Mount of Offence, 2409 feet high, the seat of Solomon's idol-worship. On the west and south is the valley of Hinnom, separating the city from the Hill of Evil Counsel, 2552 feet high, where Judas is reputed to have made the bargain for the betrayal of our Lord, and where the traitor afterward hanged himself. On the side of this hill is the ACELDAMA (which see). The land on which the city itself is built comprises two parallel ridges, of which the eastern, Mount Moriah, 2440 feet high, was the site of the TEMPLE (which see), and the western, Mount Zion, 2550 feet high, the site of David's house and later of Herod's palace. These two ridges are separated by a depression called the Tyropœan Valley or the Valley of the Cheesemongers, which opens into the valley of the Kedron near the Pool of Siloam. North of Mount Zion was the Akra, or "lower city" of Josephus. The hill Bezetha was north of Mount Moriah.

History.—First or Jebusite Period, commencing B. C. 1450.—The first definite notice of Jerusalem is in Josh. 15:8; 18:16, 28. It was called JEBUSI, from the Jebusites who made it their stronghold, and JEBUS. Judg. 19:10. The Jebusites retained the city after the conquest of the land by Joshua. Josh. 15:63. After the death of Joshua the Israelites captured a part of the city, but the Jebusites retained the upper city for nearly four hundred years. In the eighth year of the reign of David (B. C. 1055–1015) over all Israel he organized an attack upon Jerusalem, the strong citadel was taken by his chief captain, Joab, and it was called "the stronghold of Zion" or "the city of David." 2 Sam. 5:7; 1 Chron. 11:7. The fame of Jerusalem commenced at this time.

Second Period: Jerusalem under the Kings.—David connected the fortress (which he used for his residence) with the city, enclosed them with a strong wall, brought up the ark of the covenant, 2 Sam. 5:2-16, and made the place the political and religious capital of the Israelites. From this time it was called JERUSALEM or ZION or the CITY OF DAVID. 2 Sam. 5:7; 1 Chron. 11:7. The choice of Jerusalem as the capital of the Israelites was made by David under divine direction. Deut. 12:5-21; 1 Kings 11:36. His son Solomon, who reigned B. C. 1015–975, made it one of the most magnificent cities of the world. He extended and strengthened the walls, built the TEMPLE (which see) and several palaces, among which were the "House of the Forest of Lebanon," 1 Kings 7:2-7, and a palace for the queen, the daughter of Pharaoh, 1 Kings 7:8, and gathered within its walls immense treasures. But under his son Rehoboam, B. C. 975–957, the separation between the ten tribes and the two tribes took place, B. C. 975, and Jerusalem became merely the capital of the kingdom of Judah, exposed to the jealousy and cupidity of the kings of Israel, Egypt, and Assyria. In the fifth year of the reign of Rehoboam, the Egyptian king Shishak invaded the kingdom of Judah, instigated by Jeroboam, king of Israel, captured Jerusalem B. C. 969, and pillaged the Temple. 1 Kings 14:25, 26; 2 Chron. 12:2-9. Under King Asa, thirty years later, Jerusalem again became independent after the great battle with Zerah (an Egyptian or Cushite king) at Mareshah. 2 Chron. 14:9-15. In spite of periods of idolatry and seasons of severe trouble which the city passed through, its prosperity under the reign of Hezekiah, B. C. 726–697, nearly equalled that which it enjoyed in the time of Solomon. Hezekiah made a great improvement both in the daily life of the city and in its strength in time of war. He provided it with an ample supply of water, and was eminently successful in repulsing the attacks of the Assyrians. But after that time the power of the kingdom of Judah rapidly declined, and in the frightful conflict between Pharoah-necho of Egypt and Nebuchadnezzar of Babylon the kingdom of Judah was destroyed and Jerusalem' was taken, B. C. 605, by Nebuchadnezzar. A number of its inhabitants, among whom was Daniel, were carried to Babylon as prisoners. After the revolt of Jehoiakim it was again taken by Nebuchadnezzar, B. C. 602, and ten thousand of the richest and most distinguished inhabitants, including the skilled artisans, were sent to Babylon. Finally, after the revolt of Zedekiah, the last king of Judah, the city was taken the third time by Nebuchadnezzar, B. C. 588, and this time nearly all its inhabitants (among whom was Zedekiah, whose eyes had been put out) were carried into captivity (only a few being left to be vine-dressers and husbandmen) and its Temple, palaces, houses, and walls were razed to the ground. The dreadful scenes of this seige and destruction are vividly described by Jeremiah in Lamentations, chapters 2 and 5. For fifty years it laid deserted, a mere heap of ruins.

Third Period: Jerusalem of Ezra and the Ptolemies.—Meanwhile the Babylonian empire had been overturned by Cyrus, king of Persia, B. C. 538, and he allowed the Jews to return to their native country and rebuild their capital and their Temple. The first returned under Zerubbabel, B. C. 536, some more under Ezra, B. C. 458, and the last under Nehemiah, B. C. 445. Under the Persian governors the Temple and the walls were rebuilt and the city arose from its ashes. The overturning of the Persian empire by Alexander the Great had no evil effect on the destiny of the city. According to Josephus, he visited it B. C. 332, after the battle of Issus, had

the book of Daniel and the prophecy of the downfall of Persia read to him, and showed the Jews many favors. Under the Ptolemies and Maccabees the city steadily progressed. Jerusalem was captured B. C. 63 by the Roman Pompey, who did not disturb the treasures of the Temple. Crassus plundered the Temple and the city of their treasures E. C. 54, and the city was captured B. C. 40 by the Parthians under Antigonus. Herod, afterward the Great (who died soon after Christ was born), laid siege to Jerusalem the next year, supported by a Roman army, and after a siege of five months the citadel and temple were captured by storm, the outer walls and lower city having been previously taken. Herod was afterward made king by the Romans, and at once began to improve and beautify the city, one of his principal works being the rebuilding and enlarging of the Temple, which occupied forty-six years. John 2:20. The work was begun B. C. 20, and continued long after his death. (See TEMPLE.) Jerusalem under the rule of Herod the Great was restored to much of its former magnificence.

Fourth Period: Jerusalem in the Time of Christ.—Very little can now be seen of the Jerusalem of the time of our Lord, the city of Zerubbabel and Herod. It lies buried twenty to eighty feet deep under ruins and rubbish. The city of David and Solomon lies still deeper, though it has been possible to trace its outlines, and even to touch the huge foundations upon which Solomon constructed the Temple. But it must be remembered that Jerusalem is more than thirty-five hundred years old, has suffered many sieges and captures, and has twice been razed to the ground and deserted. Herod was the representative of the Greek-Roman civilization, and national pride, exclusiveness, and moral indignation roused the Jews to resistance to him. With Herod began that hatred between the Jews and Romans which ended in the second total destruction of Jerusalem, A. D. 70, by the Romans under Titus—one of the most horrible events in the history of war. The besiegers were extremely cruel and the defenders very furious and desperate. The Jews suffered terribly during the siege and, according to Josephus, over 1,000,000 of them were killed and 97,000 made captives. The rebellion was continued about three years longer, when the Jewish power was totally destroyed.

Fifth Period: Jerusalem under Roman and Christian Emperors.—Jerusalem was again in ruins for half a century. A new Jerusalem was founded by the emperor Hadrian A. D. 118-138 (which he peopled with Romans), on the site of the ancient city, and named ÆLIA CAPITOLINA. A temple of Jupiter was built on the ruins of the Temple of Jehovah, and the Jews were not allowed to enter the city until the country was governed by the Christian emperors. Constantine the Great, A. D. 306–337, restored the name JERUSALEM, opened the gates of the city to the Jews, etc., and his mother, Helena, built the church of the Holy Sepulchre there. Julian, commonly called the Apostate, A. D. 363, vainly endeavored to rebuild the Jewish temple and restore Jewish worship. A fine church was founded by the emperor Justinian, A. D. 529, in honor of the Virgin. The Persians under Chosroes II. captured Jerusalem A. D. 614, killed large numbers of the monks and clergy, and destroyed the churches.

Sixth Period: Jerusalem of the Crusaders and Turks.—In A. D. 637 Jeru-salem was conquered by the Arabs under Caliph Omar, who made it a Mohammedan city, and, though retaken by the Crusaders A. D. 1099 and held by the Christians till A. D. 1187, when it was recaptured by the Mohammedans.

Modern Jerusalem.—The British, who had been awarded Palestine by the League of Nations at the close of the 1st World War, made Jerusalem their capital. On November 29, 1947, the United Nations recommended the partition of Israel between Arabs and Jews. But the Arab and Jewish peoples continued to fight. During the Arab–Israeli wars, the city was divided (1949–67) with the Old City becoming part of Jordan, and the New City the capital of Israel. In 1967 Israel took possession of the Old City. The Old City contains many places holy to Christians, Moslems and Jews.

Also see Josh. 10; 12; 15; 18.
Judg. 1; 19.
1 Sam. 17.
2 Sam. 5; 8–12; 14–17; 19; 20; 24.
1 Kings 2; 3; 8–12; 14; 15; 22.
2 Kings 8; 9; 12; 14–16; 18; 19; 21–25.
1 Chron. 3; 6; 8; 9; 11; 14; 15; 18–21;
    23; 28; 29.
2 Chron. 1–3; 5; 6; 8–13; 15; 17; 19–36.
Ezra 1–10.
Neh. 1–4; 6–8; 11–13.
Esther 2.
Pss. 51; 68; 79; 102; 116; 122; 125;
    128; 135; 137; 147.
Eccles. 1; 2.
Song of Sol. 1–3; 5; 6; 8.
Isa. 1–5; 7; 8; 10; 22; 24; 27; 28; 30; 31;
    33; 36; 37; 40; 41; 44; 51; 52; 62;
    64–66.
Jer. 1–9; 11; 13–15; 17–19; 22–25; 27;
    29; 32–40; 42; 44; 51; 52.
Lam. 1; 4.

Ezek. 4; 5; 8; 9; 11–17; 21–24; 26; 33; 36.
Dan. 1; 5; 6; 9.
Joel 2; 3.
Amos 1; 2.
Obad. :11, 20.
Mic. 1; 3; 4.
Zeph. 1; 3.
Zech. 1–3; 7–9; 12–14.
Mal. 2; 3.
Matt. 2–5; 15; 16; 20; 21.
Mark 1; 3; 7; 10; 11; 15.
Luke 2; 4–6; 9; 10; 13; 17–19; 21; 23; 24.
John 1; 2; 4; 5; 7; 10; 11; 12.
Acts 1; 2; 4–6; 8–13; 15; 16; 18–26; 28.
Rom. 15.
1 Cor. 16.
Gal. 1; 2; 4.
Heb. 12.
Rev. 3; 21.

Je-ru´sa-lem, New, a name used figuratively to denote the spiritual Church in its final triumph and glory. Rev. 3:12; 21:2.

Je-ru´sha (*possessed*), the mother of Jotham, king of Judah, 2 Kings 15:33, called JERUSHAH in 2 Chron. 27:1.

Jesaiah, je-sa´yah (*saving*). [1] A grandson of Zerubbabel. 1 Chron. 3:21. [2] A descendant of Benjamin. Neh. 11:7.

Jeshaiah, je-sha´yah (*help of Jehovah*). [1] A son of Jeduthun. 1 Chron. 25:3, 15. [2] A grandson of Eliezer, 1 Chron. 26:25, called ISSHIAH in 1 Chron. 24:21. [3] A chief man who returned with Ezra. Ezra 8:7. [4] A Levite of the family of Merari who returned with Ezra. Ezra 8:19.

Jesh´a-nah, a town of Palestine taken from Jeroboam by Abijah. 2 Chron. 13:19.

Je-shar´e-lah (*right toward God*), a Levite in the service of song, 1 Chron. 25:14, called ASARELAH in 1 Chron. 25:2.

Je-sheb´e-ab (*seat of one's father*), chief of a division of priests. 1 Chron. 24:13.

Je´sher (*uprightness*), a son of Caleb, the son of Hezron. 1 Chron. 2:18.

Jesh´i-mon (*the waste*) may be a general term for any wilderness. Pisgah and Peor are described in Num. 21:20; 23:28 as looking toward Jeshimon.

Je-shish´a-i (*offspring of an old man*), ancestor of a family of the Gadites. 1 Chron. 5:14.

Jesh-o-ha-i´a (*whom Jehovah bows down*), a descendant of Simeon. 1 Chron. 4:36.

Jesh´u-a (*whom Jehovah helps*). [1] Chief of a division of priests, Ezra 2:36; Neh. 7:39, called JESHUAH in 1 Chron. 24:11. [2] A Levite in charge of tithes. 2 Chron. 31:15. [3] A priest who returned from Babylon with Zerubbabel. Ezra 2:2; 3:2. He became a high-priest after the captivity, and is called JOSHUA in Zech. 3:1, 3, 8, 9, and in Hag. 1:1, 12, 14; 2:2, 4. [4] Head of a large family who returned from Babylon with Zerubbabel. Ezra 2:6; Neh. 7:11. [5] Head of a Levitical house. Ezra 2:40; Neh. 7:43. [6] A Levite. Ezra 8:33. [7] A Jew whose son repaired part of the wall of Jerusalem. Neh. 3:19. [8] A Levite who explained the law to the people. Neh. 8:7; 9:4. [9] JOSHUA, the son of Nun, is called JESHUA in Neh. 8:17.

Jesh´u-a (*Jehovah the salvation*), a town of Benjamin where some of the tribe of Judah dwelt after the captivity. Neh. 11:26.

Jesh´u-run (*dearly beloved*), a symbolical name for Israel. Deut. 32:15; 33:5, 26. Called JESURUN in Isa. 44:2. The word "he" in Deut. 33:5 does not refer to Moses, but to the LORD.

Je-si´ah (*whom Jehovah lends*). [1] An Israelite who came to David in Ziklag. 1 Chron. 12:6. [2] A Levite, 1 Chron. 23:20, same as JESHAIAH in 1 Chron. 26:25.

Je-sim´i-el (*whom God has set up*), a prince of Simeon. 1 Chron. 4:36.

Jes´se (*strong*), an Israelite of the tribe of Judah. He was the grandson of Ruth and the father of David. His genealogy is given in Ruth 4:18-22; 1 Chron. 2:5-12; Matt. 1:3-5; Luke 3:32-34. He had eight sons, of whom David was the youngest. Jesse is usually called "Jesse the Bethlehemite," and is announced in Isa. 11:1, 10 as the ancestor of Christ.
Also see Ruth 4:17.
1 Sam. 16:1, 3, 5, 8-11, 18-20, 22; 17:12, 13, 17, 20, 58; 20:27, 30, 31; 22:7-9, 13; 25:10.
2 Sam. 20:1; 23:1.
1 Kings 12:16.
1 Chron. 2:13; 10:14; 12:18; 29:26.
2 Chron. 10:16; 11:18.
Ps. 72:20.
Matt. 1:6.
Acts 13:22.
Rom. 15:12.

Jes´u-i (*level*), a descendant of Asher and founder of the Jesuites. Num. 26:44. He is called ISUI in Gen. 46:17, and ISHUAI in 1 Chron. 7:30.

Jes´u-ites, descendants of Jesui. Num. 26:44.

Jes´u-run. See JESHURUN.

Je´sus (*Saviour*) is the Greek form for the Hebrew word "Jehoshua," contracted to "Joshua," and is found only in the New Testament, and should be exclusively applied to CHRIST (which see). Jesus was the personal name of CHRIST among men during his life on earth. In Acts 7:45; Col. 4:11; Heb. 4:8, "Jesus" should be "Joshua," although these two names had

originally the same meaning.
Also see Matt. 1–4; 7–24; 26–28.
Mark 1–3; 5–16.
Luke 1–10; 13; 14; 17–20; 22–24.
John 1–14; 16–21.
Acts 1–11; 13; 15–22; 25; 26; 28.
Rom. 1–8; 10; 13–16.
1 Cor. 1–6; 8; 9; 11; 12; 15; 16.
2 Cor. 1; 4; 5; 8; 11; 13.
Gal. 1–6.
Eph. 1–6.
Phil. 1–4.
Col. 1–3.
1 Thess. 1–5.
2 Thess. 1–3.
1 Tim. 1–6.
2 Tim. 1–4.
Titus 1–3.
Philem. 1, 3, 5, 6, 9, 23, 25.
Heb. 2–4; 6; 7; 10; 12; 13.
James 1; 2.
1 Pet. 1–5.
2 Pet. 1–3.
1 John 1–5.
2 John 3, 7.
Jude 1, 4, 17, 21.
Rev. 1; 12; 14; 17; 19; 20; 22.

Je´sus, called JUSTUS, a disciple who was a fellow-worker with Paul and who sent salutations to the Christians of Colosse. Col. 4:11.

Je´ther (*excellence*). [1] In the marginal notes, Exod. 4:18. Same as JETHRO (which see). [2] The first-born son of Gideon. Judg. 8:20. [3] Father of Amasa, the nephew of David, 1 Chron. 2:17, called ITHRA in 2 Sam. 17:25. [4] An Israelite of the tribe of Judah. 1 Chron. 2:32. [5] Another member of the tribe of Judah. 1 Chron. 4:17. [6] A son of Asher 1 Chron. 7:38.

Je´theth (*a nail*), one of the dukes or princes of Edom. Gen. 36:40; 1 Chron. 1:51

Jeth´lah (*exalted*), a border city of Dan. Josh. 19:42.

Je´thro (*his excellence*), the priest of Midian who was father-in-law of Moses. He is called RAGUEL in Num. 10:29, REUEL in Exod. 2:18, and JETHER in the marginal notes in Exod. 4:18.

Je´tur (*an enclosure*), a son of Ishmael. Gen 25:15; 1 Chron. 1:31; 5:19. See ITURÆA.

Je´u-el (*treasured of God*), a descendant of Judah. 1 Chron. 9:6.

Je´ush (*to whom God hastens*). [1] A son of Esau. Gen 36:5; 1 Chron. 1:35. [2] A descendant of Benjamin. 1 Chron. 7:10. [3] A descendant of Shimei. 1 Chron. 23:10, 11. [4] A son of Rehoboam. 2 Chron. 11:19.

Je´uz (*counselling*), a son of Shaharaim, a descendant of Benjamin. 1 Chron. 8:10.

Jew´els, personal ornaments made of precious metals; among them were chains, bracelets, earrings, etc. They are mentioned in Gen. 24:22; Num. 31:50; Ezek. 23:26, etc. The word is figuratively used for anything peculiarly precious, as God's chosen people, Mal. 3:17, or wisdom. Prov. 20:15.
Also see Gen. 24:53.
Exod. 3:22; 11:2; 12:35; 35:22.
Num. 31:51.
1 Sam. 6:8, 15.
2 Chron. 20:25; 32:27.
Job 28:17.
Prov. 11:22.
Song of Sol. 1:10; 7:1.
Isa. 3:21; 61:10.
Ezek. 16:12, 17, 39.
Hos. 2:13.

Jew´ry, Dan. 5:13, is elsewhere translated JUDAH and JUDEA.

Jews, the people of the tribes of Judah and Benjamin, as distinguished from the revolted ten tribes. 2 Kings 16:6; Ezra 4:12. See HEBREWS.
Also see 2 Kings 18; 25.
2 Chron. 32.
Ezra 4–6.
Neh. 1; 2; 4–6; 13.
Esther 2–6; 8–10.
Isa. 36.
Jer. 32; 34; 38; 40; 41; 44; 52.
Dan. 3.
Zech. 8.
Matt. 2; 27; 28.
Mark 7; 15.
Luke 7; 23.
John 1–13; 18–20.
Acts 2; 9–14; 16–26; 28.
Rom. 1–3; 9; 10.
1 Cor. 1; 9; 10; 12.
2 Cor. 11.
Gal. 1–3.
Col. 3.
1 Thess. 2.
Rev. 2; 3.

Jez-a-ni´ah (*whom Jehovah hears*), a captain of the Jews, Jer. 40:8; 42:1, called AZARIAH in Jer. 43:2. See JAAZANIAH, No. 1.

Jez´e-bel (*chaste*), daughter of Ethbaal, king of the Zidonians, and wife of Ahab, king of Israel. She became infamous for her idolatries and her persecution of the prophets. 1 Kings 16:31; 18:4. She introduced the worship of Baal and other idols, and was virtually the ruler of Israel.
Also see 1 Kings 18:13, 19; 19:1, 2; 21:5, 7, 11, 14, 15, 23, 25.
2 Kings 9:7, 10, 22, 30, 36, 37.
Rev. 2:20.

Je´zer (*frame*), a son of Naphtali. Gen. 46:24; 1 Chron. 7:13.

Je´zer-ites, descendants of Jezer. Num. 26:49.

Je-zi´ah (*whom Jehovah sprinkles*), a Jew who took a foreign wife. Ezra 10:25.

Je´zi-el (*assembly of God*), a valiant man who joined David in Ziklag. 1 Chron. 12:3.

Jez-li´ah (*whom Jehovah delivers*), a descendant of Benjamin. 1 Chron. 8:18.

Jez´o-ar (*shining*), a son of Helah, the wife of Ashur. 1 Chron. 4:7

Jez-ra-hi´ah (*whom Jehovah brings forth*), the leader of the singers at the dedication of the wall. Neh. 12:42.

Jez´re-el (*God hath planted*). [1] A city of Issachar, in the valley of Jezreel, between Gilboa and Little Hermon, which Ahab chose for his residence; his "ivory house," 1 Kings 22:39, stood in the eastern part, while Jezebel lived by the city wall, near the temple and grove of Astarte. The city is now a village among ruins. [2] A town in Judah. Josh. 15:56; 1 Sam. 25:43; 29:1, 11. [3] A descendant of Judah. 1 Chron. 4:3. [4] Eldest son of Hosea the prophet. He was so named by command of God. Hos. 1:4. [5] The word is used figuratively in reference to the crimes of Ahab in Jezreel and the punishment threatened by God on account of them. Hos. 1:4, 11.
Also see Josh. 17:16; 19:18.
Judg. 6:33.
2 Sam. 2:9; 4:4.
1 Kings 4:12; 18:45, 46; 21:1, 23.
2 Kings 8:29; 9:10, 15-17, 30, 36, 37; 10:1, 6, 7, 11.
2 Chron. 22:6.
Hos. 1:5; 2:22.

Jez´re-el, the Valley of, is an exceedingly fertile plain of central Palestine which, south of the Carmel range, intersects the western highland, between the hills of Galilee and those of Samaria, and connects the low coast-land along the Mediterranean with the Jordan valley. See PALESTINE. It was the battle-field where Gideon triumphed, Judg. chapter 7, and Deborah sung her war-song. Judg. 5:2-31. Josiah was fatally wounded near it, by the Egyptians. Saul and Jonathan fell on the mountains of Gilboa near by. 1 Sam. 31:1-6. Its Greek name *Esdraelon* is not in the Bible. See ESDRAELON, and MEGIDDO.

Jez´re-el-ite, a male native or inhabitant of Jezreel. 1 Kings 21:1; 2 Kings 9:21.

Jezreelitess, jez´re-el-ite-es, a female inhabitant or native of Jezreel. 2 Sam. 2:2.

Jib´sam (*pleasant*), a son of Tola, the son of Issachar. 1 Chron. 7:2.

Jid´laph (*weeping*), a son of Nahor, the brother of Abraham. Gen 22:22.

Jim´na or **Jim´nah** (*good fortune*), a son of Asher, Num. 26:44, called JIMNAH in Gen. 46:17, and IMNAH in 1 Chron. 7:30.

Jim´nites, descendants of Jimna. Num. 26:44.

Jiphtah, jif´tah, a city of Judah. Josh. 15:43.

Jiphthah-el, jif´tha-el (*God opens*), a valley mostly in Zebulun, but bordering on Asher. Josh. 19:14, 27.

Jo´ab (*whose father is Jehovah*). [1] A son of Zeruiah, the sister of David, and the "chief and captain," 1 Chron. 11:6, of his army. He treacherously assassinated Abner, 2 Sam. 3:27, who had killed Joab's brother Asahel in self-defence. 2 Sam. 2:23. Joab killed Absalom, 2 Sam. 18:14, contrary to the express orders of David. After this event David made Amasa commander-in-chief in place of Joab, who soon after assassinated Amasa. 2 Sam. 20:10. David apparently took Joab again into favor, 2 Sam. 24:2, and Joab afterward combined with Abiathar and others to make Adonijah king instead of Solomon. The plot was defeated and Joab was put to death at the horns of the altar, 1 Kings 2:34, by Benaiah, by order of Solomon. [2] A grandson of Kenaz. 1 Chron. 4:14. [3] One whose descendants returned from Babylon. Ezra 2:6; 8:9. [4] A descendant of Caleb, the son of Hur. 1 Chron. 2:54.

Also see 1 Sam. 26:6.

2 Sam. 2:13, 14, 18, 22, 24, 26-28, 30, 32; 3:22-24, 26, 29-31; 8:16; 10:7, 9, 13, 14; 11:1, 6, 7, 11, 14, 16-18, 22, 25; 12:26, 27; 14:1-3, 19-23, 29-33; 17:25; 18:2, 5, 10-12, 15, 16, 20-22, 29; 19:1, 5, 13; 20:7-9, 11, 13, 15-17, 20-23; 23:18, 24, 37; 24:3, 4, 9.

1 Kings 1:7, 19, 41; 2:5, 22, 28-31, 33; 11:15, 16, 21.

1 Chron. 2:16; 11:8, 20, 26, 39; 18:15; 19:8, 10, 14, 15; 20:1; 21:2-6; 26:28; 27:7, 24, 34.

Neh. 7:11.

Ps. 60.

Jo´ah (*whose helper is Jehovah*). [1] A son of Asaph the recorder. 2 Kings 18:18, 37; Isa. 36:3. [2] A descendant of Gershom, the son of Levi. 1 Chron. 6:21. [3] A son of Obed-edom. 1 Chron. 26:4. [4] A Levite who aided Hezekiah in his reforms. 2 Chron. 29:12. [5] A Levite commissioned by Josiah to repair the house of the Lord. 2 Chron. 34:8.

Jo´a-haz (*whom Jehovah holds*), a Levite recorder in the time of Josiah. 2 Chron. 34:8.

Jo-an´na (*whom Jehovah has graciously given*). [1] An ancestor of Christ. Luke 3:27. [2] A female disciple, the wife of Chuza. Luke 8:3; 24:10.

Jo´ash, 2 Kings 13:1, or **Je-ho´ash,** 2 Kings 12:1 (*whom Jehovah bestowed*). [1] The father of Gideon. Judg. 6:11, etc. [2] A son of Ahab. 1 Kings 22:26; 2 Chron. 18:25. [3] Son and successor of Ahaziah,

king of Judah. He was the only son of Ahaziah that was not slain by order of Athaliah. He was hidden in the Temple six years by Jehosheba, his aunt, 2 Kings 11:2, 3, and became king of Judah when seven years old. 2 Kings 11:12. His kingdom was invaded by Hazael, but he redeemed his capital from plunder by a large sum of money and all the treasures and furniture of the Temple. 2 Kings 12:18. He reigned forty years, B. C. 878–839, and was murdered by his own servants. 2 Chron. 24:24-27. [4] Son of Jehoahaz, whom he succeeded as king of Israel. He reigned B. C. 840–825, including two years in which he was associated with his father. He was very successful in a war with Amaziah, king of Judah, and died soon afterward. 2 Kings 14:12-16. [5] A descendant of Judah. 1 Chron. 4:22. [6] One of David's heroes. 1 Chron. 12:3.

Also see Judg. 6:29-31; 7:14; 8:13, 29, 32.

2 Kings 11:21; 12:2, 4, 6, 7, 19, 20; 13:9, 10, 12-14, 25; 14:1, 3, 8, 9, 11, 17, 23, 27.

1 Chron. 3:11.

2 Chron. 22:11; 24:1, 2, 4, 22; 25:17, 18, 21, 23, 25.

Hos. 1:1.

Amos 1:1.

Jo´ash (*to whom Jehovah hastens*). [1] A son of Becher. 1 Chron. 7:8. [2] Keeper of the cellars of oil in the time of David. 1 Chron. 27:28.

Jo´a-tham, Matt. 1:9, an ancestor of Joseph, the husband of Mary. It is the Greek form of JOTHAM, No. 2 (which see).

Job (*desire?*), one of the sons of Issachar, Gen. 46:13, called JASHUB in 1 Chron. 7:1.

Job (*one persecuted*), the patriarch, Ezek. 14:14, 20; James 5:11, was of the land of Uz, Job 1:1, which was probably in eastern Edom. See JOB, BOOK OF.

Also see Job 1:5, 8, 9, 14, 20, 22; 2:3, 7, 10, 11; 3:1, 2; 6:1; 9:1; 12:1; 16:1; 19:1; 21:1; 23:1; 26:1; 27:1; 29:1; 31:40; 32:1-4, 12; 33:1, 31; 34:5, 7, 35, 36; 35:16; 37:14; 38:1; 40:1, 3, 6; 42:1, 7-10, 12, 15-17.

Job, the Book of, is a poem on a historical foundation, or history treated poetically. The person of Job is mentioned in Ezek. 14:14, 18, 20; James 5:11. He lives also in the tradition of the Arabs. The prologue (chaps. 1 and 2) and the epilogue (chap. 42:7-17) are written in narrative prose, the rest in Hebrew poetry. As a mere literary production it is one of the sublimest and most interesting works ever written, and fully equal to the greatest productions of genius. It has been called the Shakespeare in the Bible. The person of Job is represented as a prince of the patriarchal age, who from the highest prosperity was suddenly cast down to utter poverty and misery, deprived of all his property and children, stricken with a loathsome disease, forsaken and insulted by his wife and friends, but who after the severest trial of faith and patience was restored to more than his former prosperity and happiness. He was ignorant of the Mosaic law and Jewish worship, and lived outside of Palestine on the border line, but was nevertheless a worshipper of the true God, an inspired prophet, a hero of faith, a model of patience and endurance, with the assurance of a final victory over sin and sorrow. He was a holy outsider, as it were, of the order of Melchizedek, the friend of Abraham, "without father, without mother, without genealogy" (compare Heb. 7:3). The book wrestles with the problem of all ages—to harmonize the terrible fact

of sin and suffering with the government of an all-wise and merciful God. This problem is solved in the sufferings and death of Christ for the salvation of the world. The Book of Job has been called a Hebrew tragedy or Hebrew theodicy (a vindication of the justice of God in regard to the natural and moral evil that exists under his government). The authorship is unknown; some trace it to Moses or some earlier writer, others to the age of Solomon. The scenery is laid in the patriarchal age. The Book of Job has been and will continue to be a rich source of comfort to children of affliction.

Jo′bab (*a desert*). [1] A son of Joktan. Gen. 10:29; 1 Chron. 1:23. [2] A king of Edom. Gen. 36:33; 1 Chron. 1:44. [3] A king of Madon who was overcome by Joshua. Josh. 11:1. [4, 5] Descendants of Benjamin. 1 Chron. 8:9, 18.

Jochebed, jok′e-bed (*whose glory is Jehovah*), the wife of Amram and mother of Moses. Exod. 6:20; Num. 26:59.

Jo′ed (*his witness is Jehovah*), a descendant of Benjamin. Neh.11:7.

Jo′el (*Jehovah is his God*). [1] The eldest son of the prophet Samuel, 1 Sam. 8:2; 1 Chron. 6:33; 15:17, erroneously called VASHNI (which see) in 1 Chron. 6:28. [2] A descendant of Simeon. 1 Chron. 4:35. [3] A descendant of Reuben. 1 Chron. 5:4, 8. [4] Head of a Gadite family. 1 Chron 5:12. [5] A Levite of the family of Kohath, 1 Chron. 6:36, probably a corruption of SHAUL in 1 Chron. 6:24. [6] A descendant of Issachar. 1 Chron. 7:3. [7] One of David's valiant men, 1 Chron. 11:38, called IGAL in 2 Sam. 23:36. [8] A chief of the family of Gershom. 1 Chron. 15:7, 11. [9] One of the keepers of the treasure of the house of the Lord. 1 Chron. 23:8; 26:22. [10] A prince of Manasseh.

1 Chron. 27:20. **[11]** A descendant of Kohath in the time of Hezekiah. 2 Chron. 29:12. **[12]** A Jew who had a foreign wife. Ezra 10:43. **[13]** An overseer of the Benjamites that dwelt in Jerusalem. Neh. 11:9.

[14] JOEL, one of the minor prophets, a son of Pethuel; lived in Judah under the reign of Uzziah, but nothing further is known of his personal history. Joel 1:1.

Joel, the Book of, begins with the denunciation of the judgment of God which will strike the unrepentant people, and ends with the announcement of the blessings which will follow the coming of the Messiah. His prophecies are mentioned in Acts 2:16-21; Rom. 10:13.

Jo-e´lah (*whom Jehovah helps*), an Israelite of Judah who joined himself to David in Ziklag. 1 Chron. 12:7.

Jo-e´zer (*whose help is Jehovah*), a Korhite who came to David at Ziklag. 1 Chron. 12:6.

Jog´be-hah (*elevated*), a town in Mount Gilead built by the tribe of Gad. Num. 32:35; Judg. 8:11.

Jog´li (*exiled*), father of Bukki, a chief of Dan. Num. 34:22.

Jo´ha (*whom Jehovah revives*). **[1]** A descendant of Benjamin. 1 Chron. 8:16. **[2]** The Tizite, one of David's valiant men. 1 Chron. 11:45.

Jo-ha´nan (*to whom Jehovah is merciful*). **[1]** A captain of the Jews, at the time of the taking of Jerusalem, whom Gedaliah tried to persuade to serve the Chaldeans. 2 Kings 25:23-26; Jer. 40:7-16; chaps. 41, 42, 43. **[2]** A son of Josiah, king of Judah. 1 Chron. 3:15. **[3]** A descendant of David. 1 Chron. 3:24. **[4]** Son of Azariah, of the high-priestly line. 1 Chron. 6:9, 10. **[5, 6]** Valiant men who came to David at Ziklag. 1 Chron. 12:4, 12. **[7]** A man of Ephraim in the reign of Ahaz. 2 Chron. 28:12. **[8]** A chief man of the Jews who returned with Ezra from Babylon. Ezra 8:12. **[9]** A priest, a descendant of Eliashib. Ezra 10:6; Neh. 12:23. **[10]** A Jew who married the daughter of Meshullam. Neh. 6:18.

John, same as **Jo-ha´nan** (*whom Jehovah loves*). **[1]** A relation of Annas the high-priest. Acts 4:6. **[2]** The Hebrew name of the evangelist Mark. Acts 12:25; 13:5; 15:37. See MARK.

[3] JOHN THE BAPTIST, or, more properly, "the Baptizer," Matt. 3:1, son of Zacharias the priest and Elizabeth, a cousin of Mary, the mother of Jesus. He was born about six months before Christ. The angel Gabriel predicted his birth and work. Luke 1:5-15. His early life was spent in solitude, his raiment was of camel's hair, and his food was locusts and wild honey. When about thirty years old he began to preach in the wilderness of Judea, announcing the coming of the Messiah, calling all to repentance and reformation, pointing to Jesus as the Messiah, and baptizing with the baptism of repentance multitudes who came to him from all parts of the land and confessed their sins. Christ said of him, Matt. 11:11, "Among them that are born of women there hath not risen a greater than John the Baptist." He was the Elias (Elijah) of the New Testament, and was imprisoned and beheaded by Herod Antipas. Matt. 14:3–10.

[4] JOHN, THE APOSTLE AND EVANGELIST, was one of the first of the apostles, he "whom Jesus loved." He was a son of Zebedee and Salome, and if Salome was a sister of Mary, John 19:25, he was also a cousin of Jesus. He was probably born at Bethsaida, Matt. 4:18, 21, on the Sea of Galilee, and pursued, like his brother, the trade of a fisherman. Both brothers were followers of John the Baptist before they became apostles of Christ. John 1:37. After being called he seems to have been always with Christ during his whole ministry, and after the ascension he, together with Peter and James, took charge of the Christian church in Jerusalem, where he met with Paul, A.D. 50. Some years later he moved to Ephesus, and from that time till his death he was at the head of all the Christian churches in Asia Minor. He was banished to Patmos, a barren island in the Ægean Sea, by the Roman emperor, but was subsequently allowed to return to Ephesus, where he died full of days during the reign of Trajan, which began A.D. 98. Many beautiful traditions have clustered around his name.

Also see Matt. 3:4, 13, 14; 4:12; 9:14; 10:2; 11:2, 4, 7, 12, 13, 18; 14:2; 16:14; 17:1, 13; 21:25, 26, 32.

Mark 1:4, 6, 9, 14, 19, 29; 2:18; 3:17; 5:37; 6:14, 16-18, 20, 24, 25; 8:28; 9:2, 38; 10:35, 41; 11:30, 32; 13:3; 14:33.

Luke 1:60, 63; 3:2, 15, 16, 20; 5:10, 33; 6:14; 7:18-20, 22, 24, 28, 29, 33; 8:51; 9:7, 9, 19, 28, 49, 54; 11:1; 16:16; 20:4, 6; 22:8.

John 1:6, 15, 19, 26, 28, 29, 32, 35, 40; 3:23-27; 4:1; 5:33, 36; 10:40, 41.

Acts 1:5, 13, 22; 3:1, 3, 4, 11; 4:13, 19; 8:14; 10:37; 11:16; 12:2, 12; 13:13, 24, 25; 18:25; 19:3, 4.

Gal. 2:9.

Rev. 1:1, 4, 9; 21:2; 22:8.

John, the Gospel of, was written many years after the other gospels (between A.D. 80 and 90), and it is evident that John knew them when he undertook to write his own gospel. Quite naturally, therefore, though perhaps not intentionally, his gospel became a complement to the three earlier ones. He omits much which they contain, as, for instance, all the parables and most of the miracles, and concentrates his narrative on Christ's ministry in Judea, while the others are principally occupied with His ministry in Galilee. One-third of the whole book is devoted to what took place during the last twenty-four hours of Christ's life on earth. Its delineation of Christ is also an addition to what has been given by the others. It is not Christ the man or the teacher or the Messiah, but Christ the incarnate Son of God and redeemer of mankind who stood before the author, and there is in his word-painting a blend of love and awe which gives it a peculiarly sublime character. See GOSPELS, HARMONY OF.

John, the Epistles of, three in number, were all written in Ephesus and about the same time as his gospel. THE FIRST is a kind of doctrinal discourse addressed to believers in general, but more especially to the Gentiles of Asia Minor, for the purpose of confirming them in their faith and warning them against errors. THE SECOND and THIRD are very short, and addressed, it would seem, to private persons—the former to the "elect lady and her children" (the elect lady was probably some honorable woman well known to the churches as a disciple of Christ), the latter to one Gaius or Caius. For the REVELATION OF JOHN, see REVELATION.

Joi′a-da (*whom Jehovah favors*), a high-priest. Neh. 12:10, 11, 22.

Joi′a-kim (*whom Jehovah has set up*), Neh. 12:10, 12, 26, a contraction of JEHOIAKIM, a high-priest, son and successor of JESHUA.

Joi′a-rib (*whom Jehovah defends*) [1] A Jew whom Ezra sent to obtain ministers for the sanctuary to accompany him and the people. Ezra 8:16. [2] A descendant of Judah. Neh. 11:5. [3] A priest, father of Jedaiah. Neh. 11:10; 12:6. His full name

JEHOIARIB, is given in 1 Chron. 9:10.

Jok´de-am (*possessed by the people?*), a city in the mountains of Judah. Josh. 15:56.

Jo´kim (*whom Jehovah has set up*), a descendant of Shelah, the son of Judah. 1 Chron. 4:22

Jok´me-am (*gathered by the people*), a Levitical city of Ephraim. 1 Chron. 6:68. In 1 Kings 4:12 the Authorized Version incorrectly gives "Jokneam" for "Jokmeam."

Jok´ne-am (*gathered by the people*), a Levitical city of Zebulun. Josh. 12:22; 19:11; 21:34. See JOKMEAM.

Jok´shan (*a fowler*), one of the sons of Abraham by Keturah. Gen. 25:2, 3; 1 Chron. 1:32.

Jok´tan (*who is made small*), a son of Eber, of the family of Shem. Gen. 10:25-30; 1 Chron. 1:19-23. He was the ancestor of the Joktanite Arabs.

Jok´the-el (*subdued of God*). [1] A city in the plain country of Judah. Josh. 15:38. [2] The name given by Amaziah to Selah, a chief city of Edom. Perhaps the place now called *Petra*. 2 Kings 14:7.

Jo´na (*whom Jehovah bestows*), the father of the apostle Peter. John 1:42. See JONAS, No. 2.

Jon´a-dab (*whom Jehovah impels*). [1] A son of Shimeah, the brother of David. 2 Sam. 13:3, 5, 32, 35. [2] The form given several times in Jer. 35 for JEHONADAB (which see).

Jo´nah (*dove*), the fifth of the minor prophets, was a son of Amittai, and born at Gath-hepher, in the land of Lebanon, 2 Kings 14:25, but of his life nothing further is known except what is told in his book.

Jonah, the Book of, consists of two parts: the first contains the commission given him, his refusal, and his miraculous

escape from death out of the belly of "a great fish" (a whale or a shark; see WHALE); the second, the renewal of the commission, his obedience, the repentance of the Ninevites, and the hard spirit of Jonah. Some theologians have considered the book a parable, but its place in the Old Testament Canon, and still more the manner in which Christ refers to it, Matt. 12:39-41; 16:4; Luke 11:29-32, seem to give it the character of real history. An interesting feature of the book is the progress it evinces from a narrow Jewish spirit, in which it begins, to a thoroughly general view, in which it ends. It teaches the lesson that God's mercy and the working of his Spirit are not confined to the Jewish people and the visible Church, but extend also to the heathen. See NINEVEH, and WHALE.

Jo´nan (*whom Jehovah bestows*), an ancestor of Joseph, the husband of Mary, in the line recorded by Luke. Luke 3:30.

Jo´nas. [1] The Greek form of JONAH. Matt. 12:39-41; 16:4; Luke 11:30-32. [2] The father of the apostles Peter and Andrew, John 21:15-17, called also JONA in John 1:42.

Jon´a-than (*whom Jehovah gave*). [1] An Israelite of the tribe of Levi, who became a priest of the idol set up by Micah in Mount Ephraim and which was afterward taken away and set up at Laish by the Danites. Judg. 17:7-13; 18:30. [2] One of the sons of Saul, the first king of Israel. He was famous for his piety and valor. 1 Sam. 14:6-14. Jonathan loved David "as his own soul." 1 Sam. 18:1. Their remarkable friendship is minutely described in 1 Sam. 18:1-4; chapters 19, 20, etc. Jonathan, two of his brothers, and his father were slain in the battle of Gilboa. 1 Sam. 31:6. David's beautiful and pathetic lamentation for Jonathan is given in 2 Sam. 1:17–27.

[3] A son of Abiathar, one of the high-priests in the time of David. 2 Sam. 15:27; 1 Kings 1:42, 43. [4] A son of Shimeah, one of the brothers of David. 2 Sam. 21:21; 1 Chron. 20:7. [5] One of David's valiant men. 2 Sam. 23:32; 1 Chron. 11:34. [6] A descendant of Jerahmeel. 1 Chron. 2:32, 33. [7] An uncle of David. 1 Chron. 27:32. [8] A chief man of the Jews, whose son returned with Ezra to Babylon. Ezra 8:6. [9] A Jew who aided Ezra in the investigation of mixed marriages. Ezra. 10:15. [10] A high-priest for thirty-two years, Neh. 12:11, called JOHANAN in Neh. 12:22, 23. [11] A priest, the descendant of Melicuh. Neh. 12:14. [12] Another priest, a descendant of Shemaiah, Neh. 12:35, called JEHONATHAN in Neh. 12:18. [13] A scribe in whose house the prophet Jeremiah was imprisoned by the princes of Judah. Jer. 37:15, 20; 38:26. [14] A son of Kareah. Jer. 40:8.

Also see 1 Sam. 13: 2, 3, 16, 22; 14:1, 3, 4, 17, 21, 27, 29, 39-45, 49; 23:16, 18; 31:2.

2 Sam. 1:4, 5, 12; 4:4; 9:1, 3, 6, 7; 15:36; 17:17, 20; 21:7, 12-14.

1 Chron. 8:33, 34; 9:39, 40; 10:2.

Jonath-elem-rechokim, jo´nath-e-lem-re-ko´kim (*a dumb dove of distant places*), part of the title of Ps. 56. It is not found elsewhere in the Bible, and is probably the name of some melody to which the Psalm was to be sung.

Jop´pa (*beauty*), an old city of Palestine, in the territory of Dan, and called JAPHO in Josh. 19:46, stands upon a promontory one hundred and sixteen feet high which juts out into the Mediterranean Sea, thirty miles south of Cæsarea and thirty-five miles north-west of Jerusalem. It was the seaport into which the

cedar from Lebanon was brought for the building of Solomon's Temple, 2 Chron. 2:16, and for the rebuilding of the Temple after the captivity. Ezra 3:7. Jonah sailed from Joppa for Tarshish. Jonah 1:3. Here took place the raising of Tabitha to life by Peter, mentioned in Acts 9:36–43, and Peter's vision. Acts 10:11.

Jo´rah (*early rain*), an Israelite whose descendants returned from Babylon with Zerubbabel. Ezra 2:18.

Jo´ra-i (*whom Jehovah teaches*), one of the heads of families in Gad. 1 Chron. 5:13.

Jo´ram (*whom Jehovah has exalted*). [1] The son of Toi, king of Hamath, who was sent by his father to congratulate David on his victory over Hadadezer. 2 Sam. 8:10. [2] The son of Ahab. 2 Kings 8:16. See JEHORAM, No. 2. [3] The son of Jehoshaphat. 2 Kings 8:24. See JEHORAM, No. 1. [4] A descendant of Eliezer, the son of Moses. 1 Chron. 26:25.

Jor´dan (*the descender*), the principal river of Palestine, has four sources, which are situated among the mountains of Anti-Lebanon. The Jordan is first mentioned in Gen. 13:10; it was crossed by Jacob, Gen. 32:10, and passed over by the Israelites when entering the Promised Land. Josh. 3:14; Ps. 114:3. It is mentioned many times in the Old Testament, and wonderful miracles are connected with it, among which is the curing of Naaman. 2 Kings 5:14. The principal events associated with it in the New Testament are the baptism of the multitudes by John the Baptist, Matt. 3:6, and of Jesus. Mark 1:9. See PALE-STINE.

Also see Gen. 13; 32; 50.

Num. 13; 22; 26; 31–36.

Deut. 1–4; 9; 11; 12; 27; 30–32.

Josh. 1–5; 7; 9; 12–20; 22–24.

Judg. 3; 5; 7; 8; 10–12.
1 Sam. 13; 31.
2 Sam. 2; 10; 17; 19; 20; 24.
1 Kings 2; 7; 17.
2 Kings 2; 5–7; 10.
1 Chron. 6; 12; 19; 26.
2 Chron. 4.
Job 40.
Pss. 42; 114.
Isa. 9.
Jer. 12; 49; 50.
Ezek. 47.
Zech. 11.
Matt. 3; 4; 19.
Mark 1; 3; 10.
Luke 3; 4.
John 1; 3; 10.

Jo´rim (*Jehovah exalts*), an ancestor of Joseph, the husband of Mary. Luke 3:29.

Jor´ko-am (*paleness of the people*), probably a person; if a place, it is a town in Judah. 1 Chron. 2:44.

Jos´a-bad (*whom Jehovah gives*), one who joined David at Ziklag. 1 Chron. 12:4.

Josaphat, jos´a-fat, in Matt. 1:8, is the Greek form of Jehoshaphat. See JEHOSH-APHAT, No. 3.

Jo´se, in Luke 3:29, is the same person as JOSES (which see).

Josedech, jos´e-dek (*whom Jehovah makes just*), Hag. 1:1, father of Joshua (Jeshua). See JEHOZADAK, JOZADAK.

Joseph, jo´zef (*he will add*). [1] The eleventh son of Jacob, the first whom he had by Rachel. Gen. 30:24. His father's fondness for him excited the envy of his brothers, and they sold him for twenty pieces of silver to the Ishmaelites, who carried him to Egypt, where he became "governor over all the land of Egypt." The wonderful story of his life is contained in Genesis chapters 37, 39–50. He died at the age of one hundred and ten, and his bones were brought out of Egypt and buried in Shechem. Josh. 24:32. [2] The father of Igal the spy. Num. 13:7. [3] A Jew who married a foreign wife. Ezra 10:42. [4] A priest in the time of Joiakim. Neh. 12:14. [5] A son of Asaph. 1 Chron. 25:2, 9. [6, 7, 8] Three ancestors of Christ. Luke 3:24, 26, 30. [9] The husband of Mary, the mother of Jesus. He was a carpenter by trade, Matt. 13:55, and a "just man." Matt. 1:19. The account of his life is contained in Matt. 1:16-25; 2:13-23; Luke 1:27; 2:4-51; 3:23; 4:22; John 1:45; 6:42. Nothing is found in the Bible concerning Joseph after Jesus was twelve years old. He is generally supposed to have died before Christ began his public ministry. [10] Joseph of Arimathæa, a wealthy member of the Sanhedrin and a disciple of Christ. He went to Pilate and begged the body of Jesus and laid it in his own new tomb. Matt. 27:57-60. [11] A disciple called also BARSABAS, who was a candidate with Mathias to take the place of Judas among the apostles. Acts 1:23. Also see Gen. 30; 33; 35.
Exod. 1; 13.
Num. 1; 13; 26; 27; 32; 34; 36.
Deut. 27; 33.
Josh. 14; 16–18.
Judg. 1.
2 Sam. 19.
1 Kings 11.
1 Chron. 2; 5; 7.
Pss. 77; 78; 80; 81; 105.
Ezek. 37; 47; 48.
Amos 5; 6.
Obad. 18.
Zech. 10.
Mark 15.
Luke 23.
John 4; 19.

Acts. 7.
Heb. 11.
Rev. 7.

Joses, jo´zez (*whom Jehovah helps*). [1] One of the brothers of our Lord. Matt. 13:55; 27:56; Mark 6:3; 15:40, 47. See JAMES, No. 2. [2] Joses, Acts 4:36, also called BARNABAS (which see).

Jo´shah (*whom Jehovah lets dwell*), a descendant of Simeon. 1 Chron. 4:34.

Joshaphat, josh´a-fat (*whom Jehovah judges*), one of David's valiant men. 1 Chron. 11:43.

Josh-a-vi´ah (*whom Jehovah makes to dwell*), one of David's valiant men. 1 Chron. 11:46.

Josh-bek´a-shah (*seat in hardness*), head of a course of musicians. 1 Chron. 25:4, 24.

Jos´heb-bas´se-bet (*he who sits in the seat*), in the marginal notes of 2 Sam. 23:8, the chief of David's captains. See JASHOBEAM.

Josh´u-a. [1] The great leader of the Israelites in the conquest of Canaan; was the son of Nun, of the tribe of Ephraim, and was born in Egypt. His original name was OSHEA, Num. 13:8, or HOSHEA, Deut. 32:44, but it was changed to JEHOSHUA (*whose help is Jehovah*), Num. 13:16, of which JOSHUA is a contraction, and JESHUA or JESUS, which is the Greek form. He was one of the twelve spies, and he and Caleb were the only ones that told the truth. Num. 14:6–9. After the death of Moses he led the Israelites across the Jordan, defeated and subjugated six nations and thirty-one kings during a war of six years, and then divided the Promised Land among the twelve tribes. After ruling the people many years he caused them to renew their covenant with Jehovah, and made the vow "as for me

and my house, we will serve the Lord." Josh. 24:15. His influence on his generation was very great. Josh. 24:31. He died one hundred and ten years old, and was buried at Timnath-serah in Ephraim. Josh. 24:30. [2] An Israelite of Beth-shemesh. 1 Sam. 6:14, 18. [3] A governor of Jerusalem who gave his name to one of the gates. 2 Kings 23:8. [4] A high-priest after the captivity. Hag. 1:1; Zech. 3:1. He is called JESHUA by Ezra and Nehemiah. See JESHUA, No. 3.
Also see Exod. 17:9, 10, 13, 14; 24:13; 32:17; 33:11.
Num. 11:28; 14:30, 38; 26:65; 27:18, 22; 32:12, 28; 34:17.
Deut. 1:38; 3:21, 28; 31:3, 7, 14, 23; 34:9.
Josh. 1:1, 10, 12, 16; 2:1, 23, 24; 3:1, 5-7, 9, 10; 4:1, 4, 5, 8-10, 14, 15, 17, 20; 5:2-4, 7, 9, 13-15; 6:2, 6, 8, 10, 12, 16, 22, 25-27; 7:2, 3, 6, 7, 10, 16, 19, 20, 22-25; 8:1, 3, 9, 10, 13, 15, 16, 18, 21, 23, 26-30, 35; 9:2, 3, 6, 8, 15, 22, 24, 27; 10:1, 4, 6-9, 12, 15, 17, 18, 20-22, 24-29, 31, 33, 34, 36, 38, 40-43; 11:6, 7, 9, 10, 12, 13, 15, 16, 18, 21, 23; 12:7; 13:1; 14:1, 6, 13; 15:13; 17:4, 14, 15, 17; 18:3, 8-10; 19:49, 51; 20:1; 21:1; 22:1, 6, 7; 23:1, 2; 24:1, 2, 19, 21, 22, 24-29.
Judg. 1:1; 2:6-8, 21, 23.
1 Kings 16:34.
Hag. 1:12, 14; 2:2, 4.
Zech. 3:3, 6, 8, 9; 6:11.

Josh´u-a, the Book of, consists of three parts: the first, chapters 1 to 12, narrates the conquest of Canaan; the second, chapters 13 to 22, its partition; and the third, chapters 23, 24, contains the two addresses of Joshua to the people.

Jo-si´ah (*whom Jehovah heals*). [1] The son and successor of Amon; was eight years old when his father died, and reigned as king of Judah for thirty-one years, 641–610. He was noted for his piety and integrity. In his reign the high-priest found in the Temple a "book of the law of the Lord *given* by Moses," 2 Chron. 34:14, and when it was read to the king he was deeply grieved to see how far the people came short of living up to the law. He then assembled the people, read the book to them, and they made a solemn vow of obedience to it, after which every vestige of idolatry was swept out of the land and the feast of the Passover was celebrated with great solemnity. 2 Chron. 35:3-18. The book here spoken of was probably Deuteronomy. When the Egyptian king Pharaoh-necho, in his war with Assyria, invaded Judea, Josiah met him in battle at Megiddo, but was mortally wounded and brought to Jerusalem, where he died, thirty-nine years old, and "all Judah and Jerusalem mourned" for him. 2 Chron. 35:24, 25. His death ended the prosperity of Judah. [2] A priest who returned from Babylon. Zech. 6:10.

Also see 1 Kings 13:2.

2 Kings 21:24, 26; 22:1, 3; 23:16, 19, 23, 24, 28-30, 34.

1 Chron. 3:14, 15.

2 Chron. 33:25; 34:1, 33; 35:1, 19, 20, 22, 23, 26; 36:1.

Jer. 1:2, 3; 3:6; 22:11, 18; 25:1, 3; 26:1; 27:1; 35:1; 36:1, 2, 9; 37:1; 45:1; 46:2.

Zeph. 1:1.

Jo-si´as, in Matt. 1:10, 11, is the Greek form of JOSIAH.

Jos-i-bi´ah (*whom Jehovah lets dwell*), a descendant of Simeon. 1 Chron. 4:35.

Josiphiah, jos-i-fi´ah (*whom may Jehovah increase!*), the father of Shelomith, who returned with Ezra. Ezra 8:10.

Jot, Matt. 5:18, or **Yod** (in Greek *Iota*), is the name of the Hebrew letter *i*. It is the smallest letter of the alphabet, is shaped much like our comma (,), and is proverbially used by the Hebrews to denote the least imaginable thing.

Jot´bah (*goodness*), a place where Haruz resided. 2 Kings 21:19.

Jot´bath or **Jot´ba-thah** (*goodness*), the twenty-ninth encampment of the Israelites after they left Egypt, Num. 33:33, 34, "a land of rivers of waters." Deut. 10:7.

Jo´tham (*Jehovah is upright*). [1] The youngest son of Gideon, who escaped when his brothers were slain by Abimelech. Judg. 9:5, 7, 21, 57. [2] A son of Azariah (or Uzziah), king of Judah, who ruled during part of his father's life (because he had been smitten with leprosy), and on his death succeeded him as king. 2 Kings 15:5, 7. 30, 32, 36, 38. He reigned twenty-three years, including seven years he ruled during his father's life. [3] A descendant of Judah. 1 Chron. 2:47.

Jour´ney. People in Eastern countries travel early in the morning or in the evening, and often into the night. They rest during the day. A day's journey may mean simply the distance travelled on any particular day. See DAY'S JOURNEY.

Jour´ney-ings of Israel. Num. 9:17-23. See EXODUS, SINAI, and WILDERNESS OF THE WANDERINGS.

Joy is reckoned among the fruit of the Spirit. Gal 5:22, and is chiefly used in the Bible, especially in the New Testament, to signify religious emotion. Believers are commanded to rejoice. Phil. 3:1; 4:4.

Also see 1 Sam. 18:6.

1 Kings 1:40.

1 Chron. 12:40; 15:16, 25; 29:9, 17.

2 Chron. 20:27; 30:26.

Ezra 3:12, 13; 6:16, 22.
Neh. 8:10; 12:43.
Esther 8:16, 17; 9:22.
Job 8:19; 20:5; 29:13; 33:26; 38:7; 41:22.
Pss. 5:11; 16:11; 21:1; 27:6; 30:5; 32:11; 35:27; 42:4; 43:4; 48:2; 51:8, 12; 65:13; 67:4; 105:43; 126:5; 132:9, 16; 137:6.
Prov. 12:20; 14:10; 15:21, 23; 17:21; 21:15; 23:24.
Eccles. 2:10, 26; 5:20; 9:7.
Isa. 9:3, 17; 12:3; 16:10; 22:13; 24:8, 11; 29:19; 32:13, 14; 35:2, 10; 51:3, 11; 52:9; 55:12; 60:15; 61:3, 7; 65:14, 18, 19; 66:5, 10.
Jer. 15:16; 31:13; 33:9, 11; 48:27, 33; 49:25.
Lam. 2:15; 5:15.
Ezek. 24:25; 36:5.
Hos. 9:1.
Joel 1:12, 16.
Hab. 3:18.
Zeph. 3:17.
Zech. 8:19.
Matt. 2:10; 13:20, 44; 25:21, 23; 28:8.
Luke 1:14, 44; 2:10; 6:23; 8:13; 10:17; 15:7, 10; 24:41, 52.
John 3:29; 15:11; 16:20-22, 24; 17:13.
Acts 2:28; 8:8; 13:52; 15:3; 20:24.
Rom. 5:11; 14:17; 15:13, 32.
2 Cor. 1:24; 2:3; 7:13; 8:2.
Phil. 1:4, 25; 2:2, 17, 18; 4:1.
1 Thess. 1:6; 2:19, 20; 3:9.
2 Tim. 1:4.
Philem. 7, 20.
Heb. 12:2; 13:17.
James 1:2; 4:9.
1 Pet. 1:8; 4:13.
1 John 1:4.
2 John 12.
3 John 4.
Jude 24.

Joz´a-bad (*whom Jehovah bestows*). [1] An inhabitant of Gederah who joined David in Ziklag. 1 Chron. 12:4. [2] A man of Manasseh who came to David in Ziklag. 1 Chron. 12:20. [3] A Levite who aided Hezekiah in reforms. 2 Chron. 31:13. [4] A Levite chief in the time of Josiah. 2 Chron. 35:9. [5] A Levite who weighed the gold and silver vessels in the Temple. Ezra 8:33. [6] A priest who took a foreign wife. Ezra 10:22. [7] A Levite who took a foreign wife. Ezra 10:23. [8] A Levite who notably helped Ezra explain the law. Neh. 8:7; 11:16.

Jozachar, joz´a-kar (*whom Jehovah remembers*), one of the murderers of Joash, the king of Judah, 2 Kings 12:21, called ZABAD in 2 Chron. 24:26.

Joz´a-dak (*whom Jehovah makes just*), a contraction of JEHOZADAK, is used in Ezra 3:2, 8; 5:2; 10:18; Neh. 12:26. He was son of the high-priest Seraiah.

Ju´bal (*music*), a son of Lamech. He was the inventor of the harp and organ. Gen. 4:21.

Ju´bi-lee, the Year of, was the final consummation of the sabbatical system in use among the Jews, and according to which every seventh day was a Sabbath day, every seventh year a Sabbatical year, and every fiftieth year—that is, every year following after the close of seven sabbatical years, each of seven years—a jubilee year, beginning on the Day of Atonement and ushered in by the blast of trumpets. The principal feature of this jubilee, and one not entirely unknown to other people, was the return of all landed estates, except houses built with walled towers, Lev. 25:29-31, to the family whose inheritance it originally had been, irrespective of the manner in which it had been alienated. Minor features were the giving up of all pledges, the setting free of all servants, etc. No religious observances were prescribed. Also see Lev. 25:9-13, 15, 33, 40, 50, 52, 54; 27:17, 18, 21, 23, 24. Num. 36:4.

Ju´cal (*potent*), Jer. 38:1, a prince of Judah. See JEHUCAL.

Ju´da. [1] One of the brethren of Christ, Mark. 6:3, probably same as JAMES, No. 2. He is called JUDAS in Matt. 13:55. [2, 3] Two ancestors of our Lord. Luke 3:26, 30. [4] The patriarch Judah. Luke 3:33. [5] A name of the tribe of Judah. Heb. 7:14; Rev. 5:5; 7:5.

Ju´dah (*praise*). [1] The fourth son of Jacob and Leah, Gen. 29:35, one of the patriarchs. He saved the life of his brother Joseph by advising his sale, Gen. 37:26-28, and was surety for the safety of Benjamin. Gen. 43:3-10. His touching plea for Benjamin's liberty is contained in Gen. 44:14-34. His father's prophetic blessing on him is very remarkable. Gen. 49:8-12. [2] Father of two Levites who were overseers of the rebuilding of the Temple. Ezra. 3:9. [3] A Levite who took a foreign wife. Ezra 10:23. [4] A Benjamite. Neh. 11:9.

Also see Gen. 29; 35; 37; 38; 43; 44; 46; 49.
Exod. 1; 31; 35; 38.
Num. 1; 2; 7; 10; 13; 26; 34.
Deut. 27; 33; 34.
Josh. 7; 11; 14; 15; 18–21.
Judg. 1; 10; 15; 17; 18; 20.
Ruth 1; 4.
1 Sam. 11; 15; 17; 18; 22; 23; 27; 30.
2 Sam. 1–3; 5; 6; 11; 12; 19–21; 24.
1 Kings 1; 2; 4; 12–16; 19; 22.
2 Kings 1; 3; 8–10; 12–25.
1 Chron. 2; 4–6; 9; 12; 13; 21; 27; 28.
2 Chron. 2; 9–36.
Ezra 1–5; 7; 9; 10.
Neh. 1; 2; 4–7; 11–13.
Esther 2.
Pss. 48; 60; 63; 68; 69; 76; 78; 97; 108; 114.
Prov. 25.
Isa. 1–3; 5; 7–9; 11; 19; 22; 26; 36–38; 40; 44; 48; 65.
Jer. 1–5; 7–15; 17–40; 42–46; 49–52.
Lam. 1; 2; 5.
Ezek. 4; 8; 9; 21; 25; 27; 37; 48.
Dan. 1; 2; 5; 6; 9.
Hos. 1; 4–6; 8, 10–12.
Joel 3.
Amos 1; 2; 7.
Obad. 12.
Mic. 1; 5.
Nah. 1.
Zeph. 1; 2.
Hag. 1; 2.
Zech. 1; 2; 8–12; 14.
Mal. 2; 3.
Heb. 8.

Ju´dah, Land of. See CANAAN.

Ju´dah, King´dom of, embraced the territory of the tribe of Judah and also the greater part of that of Benjamin on the north-east, Dan on the north-west, and Simeon on the south. Edom, which was conquered by David, was faithful to Judah for a time. After the kingdom of Israel was divided, B. C. 975, Judah existed as a separate kingdom until B. C. 588. Jerusalem, its capital, was taken at that time by Nebuchadnezzar. See JERUSALEM, and PALESTINE.
2 Chron. 11:17.

Ju´dah, Ter´ri-to-ry of, occupied by the tribe of Judah in Canaan, is described, with its cities, in Josh. 15. It comprised western Palestine from the Dead Sea to the Mediterranean. Its northern boundary extended from Beth-hogla, a little southeast of Jericho, to Jabneel, about four miles below Joppa, on the Mediterranean. Its southern boundary extended from the south end of the Dead Sea westward to the river of Egypt, now called *Wady el Arish.* Part of this territory was afterward cut off for Simeon. The north-western part was given to Dan. See JUDAH, KINGDOM OF.

Ju´dah, Tribe of, was the largest which came out of Egypt. Num. 1:27. It was composed of descendants of the patriarch JUDAH (which see). King David was of that tribe.
Also see Exod. 31:2; 35:30; 38:22.
Num. 7:12; 13:6; 34:19.
Josh. 7:1, 16, 18; 21:4.
2 Kings 17:18.

Ju´dah, City of, is mentioned in 2 Chron. 25:28, and is probably the city of David, a name of Mount Zion at Jerusalem.

Ju´dah upon Jor´dan, a town of Naphtali. Josh. 19:34.

Ju´das (*praise*). [1] JUDAH, the patriarch. Matt 1:2, 3.

[2] JUDAS, the betrayer of Christ. He was the son of Simon, was one of the apostles, the treasurer of the first Christian community, and was surnamed "Iscariot," which probably means *Ish Kerioth,* "the man from Kerioth," a town of Judah. Josh. 15:25. After being with the Lord during nearly his whole public ministry he betrayed him, Matt. 26:15, for thirty shekels or pieces of silver, the price of a slave. After being present at the beginning of the last paschal meal (though not at the institution of the Lord's Supper) he led the Temple guard and attendant mob to the garden of Gethsemane, and by a kiss showed them Christ, whom they wanted to seize. Matt. 26:48. But after the deed was done Judas "brought again the thirty pieces of silver to the chief priests and elders, saying I have

sinned in that I have betrayed the innocent blood," and went to the southern hill-side of the valley of Hinnom, to the place now called Aceldama, and hanged himself. Matt. 27:3-10.

[3] The one called JUDA in Mark 6:3. See Matt. 13:55.

[4] One of the apostles, John 14:22, and a brother of James. Jude 1. He is called LEBBÆUS in Matt. 10:3, THADDÆUS in Mark 3:18, and JUDE in Jude 1.

[5] JUDAS OF GALILEE, the leader of an insurrection against the Roman enrolment under Augustus, successful at first, but finally defeated. Acts 5:37.

[6] JUDAS in whose house Paul found shelter in Damascus during his blindness. Acts 9:11-17.

[7] JUDAS, surnamed Barsabas, who, together with Paul, Barnabas, and Silas, was chosen to carry the decisions of the Council of Jerusalem, A. D. 50, to Antioch. Acts 15:22-33.

Jude, one of the apostles, Jude 1, is called JUDAS in Luke 6:16; John 14:22; Acts 1:13, and surnamed LEBBÆUS in Matt. 10:3, and THADDÆUS in Mark 3:18.

Jude (called a brother of James), **the Epis´tle of,** was written about A. D. 65, and bears in its general aspect a strong resemblance to the Second Epistle of Peter. It was probably addressed to the same persons and for the same reasons. Some of its details, however—the prophecy of Enoch and the dispute between the archangel Michael and Satan—are not mentioned anywhere else.

Ju-de´a or **Ju-dæ´a** is a name applied to that part of Canaan in which those Jews settled who returned from captivity. In the New Testament it sometimes means the province of Judea, and sometimes the whole country inhabited by the Jews. See

CANAAN, JUDAH, and PALESTINE.
Ezra 5:8.
Matt. 2:1, 5, 22; 3:1, 5; 4:25; 19:1; 24:16.
Mark 1:5; 3:7; 10:1; 13:14.
Luke 1:5, 65; 2:4; 3:1; 5:17; 6:17; 7:17; 21:21.
John 3:22; 4:3, 47, 54; 7:3; 11:7.
Acts 1:8; 2:9, 14; 8:1; 9:31; 10:37; 11:1, 29; 12:19; 15:1; 21:10; 26:20; 28:21.
Rom. 15:31.
2 Cor. 1:16.
Gal. 1:22.
1 Thess. 2:14.

Ju-de´a or **Ju-dæ´a, the Hill country of,** extends from north to south through the province of Judea. Luke 1:65.

Ju-de´a or **Ju-dæ´a, the Wilderness of,** is wild and desolate, and extends from the hill country near Jerusalem to the Dead Sea. Its average width is about fifteen miles. It is a rough and barren country, having only small places covered with grass, and was the scene of the temptation of Christ. Matt. 4:1; Mark 1:13.

Judg´es. [1] A class of magistrates originally appointed by Moses, Exod. 18:13-26, as his assistants. [2] Those judges whose history is given in the book of Judges. They were raised up for special emergencies, had extraordinary civil and military powers, and were given to the Israelites about four hundred and fifty years, until Samuel the prophet. Acts 13:20.
Also see Exod. 21:6, 22; 22:8, 9.
Num. 25:5.
Deut. 1:16; 16:18; 19:17, 18; 21:2; 25:1; 32:31.
Josh. 8:33; 23:2; 24:1.
Judg. 2:16-18.
Ruth 1:1.
1 Sam. 8:1, 2.
2 Sam. 7:11.

2 Kings 23:22.
1 Chron. 17:6, 10; 23:4; 26:29.
2 Chron. 1:2; 19:5, 6.
Ezra 7:25; 10:14.
Job 9:24; 12:17; 31:11.
Pss. 2:10; 141:6; 148:11.
Prov. 8:16.
Isa. 1:26; 40:23.
Dan. 3:2, 3; 9:12.
Hos. 7:7; 13:10.
Zeph. 3:3.
Matt. 12:27.
Luke 11:19.
James 2:4.

Judg´es, the Book of, is so called because it narrates the history of the Israelites from about twenty years after the death of Joshua to the time of Saul, the first king of Israel, during which period they were governed by fifteen judges. The author is not known, nor the time when it was written, but it is evidently compiled from trustworthy materials. The book consists of an introduction, chapter 1 to chapter 3:8; an account of God's successive deliverances of the Israelites, chapter 3:8 to chapter 17; and an account of the invasion of Laish by the Danites, connected with the story of Micah, an idolater in Mount Ephraim, and Jonathan his priest, chapters 17 and 18; also a narrative of the revenge of the insult to "a certain Levite," chapters 19 to 21.

Judg´ment, Judg´ments, are words often mentioned in the Bible. Their meaning is generally determined by the connection in which they are used.
Gen. 18.
Exod. 6; 7; 12; 21; 23; 24; 28.
Lev. 18–20; 25; 26.
Num. 27; 33; 35; 36.
Deut. 1; 4–8; 10–12; 16; 17; 24; 25–27; 32; 33.

Josh. 20.
Judg. 4; 5.
1 Sam. 8.
2 Sam. 8; 22; 15.
1 Kings 2; 3; 6–11; 20.
2 Kings 25.
1 Chron. 16; 18; 22; 28.
2 Chron. 7; 9; 19; 20; 22; 24.
Ezra 7.
Neh. 1; 9; 10.
Esther 1.
Job 8; 9; 14; 19; 22; 27; 29; 32; 34–37; 40.
Pss. 1; 7; 9; 10; 18; 19; 25; 33; 35–37; 48; 72; 76; 89; 94; 97; 99; 101; 103; 105; 106; 111; 119; 122; 143; 146; 147; 149.
Prov. 1; 2; 8; 13; 16–21; 24; 28; 29; 31.
Eccles. 3; 5; 8; 11; 12.
Isa. 1, 3–5; 9; 10; 16; 26; 28; 30; 32–34; 40–42; 49; 51; 53; 54; 56; 59; 61.
Jer. 1; 4; 5; 7–10; 12; 21–23; 33; 39; 48; 49; 51; 52.
Ezek. 5; 11; 14; 16; 18; 20; 23; 25; 28; 30; 34; 36; 37; 39; 44; 45.
Dan. 4; 7; 9.
Hos. 2; 5; 6; 10; 12.
Amos 5; 6.
Mic. 3; 7.
Hab. 1.
Zeph. 2; 3.
Zech. 7; 8.
Mal. 2–4.
Matt. 5; 7; 10–12; 23; 27.
Mark 6.
Luke 10; 11.
John 5; 7–9; 12; 16; 18; 19.
Acts 8; 18; 23–25.
Rom. 1; 2; 5; 11; 14.
1 Cor. 1; 4; 6; 7.
2 Cor. 5.
Gal. 5.
Phil. 1.

2 Thess. 1.
1 Tim. 5.
Heb. 6; 9; 10.
James 2.
1 Pet. 4.
2 Pet. 2; 3.
1 John 4.
Jude :6, 15.
Rev. 14–20.

Judg´ment Hall, a room in the palace of the Roman governor, used for the trial of causes and the administration of justice. John 18:28.

Judg´ment Seat, Matt. 27:19, was an elevated place in the judgment hall. Sentence was pronounced from it.

Judg´ment, Breast´plate of, Exod. 28:15, a name given to the breastplate of the high-priest. See HIGH-PRIEST.

Judg´ment of U´rim. See URIM.

Judg´ment, Day of, the day when Christ shall judge the world in righteousness. Acts 17:31.
Also see Matt. 10:15; 12:36.
Mark 6:11.
2 Pet. 2:9; 3:7.
1 John 4:17.

Judith (*Jewess*), a wife of Esau. Gen. 26:34.

Ju´li-a, a female disciple at Rome, saluted by Paul. Rom. 16:15.

Ju´li-us, the centurion under whose charge Paul was sent to Rome. Acts 27:1, 3.

Ju´ni-a, a kinsman of Paul, saluted in Rom. 16:7.

Ju´ni-per, a shrub about twelve feet high when full grown, especially abundant in the desert of Sinai, where it is often the only shelter. It grows also in the sandy regions of Arabia and northern Africa. Elijah laid and slept under a juniper tree after a long journey. 1 Kings 19:4, 5.

Ju´ni-per, Coals of, are mentioned in Ps. 120:4 in connection with "sharp arrows of the mighty." Fire was often kindled by these coals, which were carried by arrows on to the combustible baggage, etc. of an enemy.

Ju´piter, in the mythology of Greek-Roman paganism the highest and mightiest of the Olympian gods, the father and ruler of gods and men, is mentioned twice in the New Testament. Acts 14:12, 13; 19:35.

Ju´shab-he´sed (*whose love is returned*), a descendant of David. 1 Chron. 3:20.

Just, applied as an epithet to the Lord Jesus Christ. Acts 3:14; 7:52; 22:14.

Jus´ti-fi-ca´tion, Rom. 4:25, an act of free grace by which God pardons the sinner and accepts him as righteous on account of the atonement of Christ. Faith is the only means of justification. Also see Rom. 5:16, 18.

Jus´tus (*just*). [1] The surname of Joseph, a disciple nominated with Matthias to take the place of Judas Iscariot. Acts 1:23. [2] A disciple at Corinth, in whose house Paul preached. Acts 18:7. [3] A surname of Jesus, a disciple and fellow-worker of Paul. Col. 4:11.

Jut´tah, a city in the mountains of Judah. Josh. 15:55. It afterward became a Levitical city. Josh. 21:16.

K

Kab or Cab, 2 Kings 6:25, a measure for dry things. See CAB, and MEASURES.

Kab´ze-el (*gathered by God*), a city in the extreme south of Judah. Josh. 15:21; 2 Sam. 23:20.

Ka´desh (*sacred*) or **Ka´desh-Bar´ne-a,** on the southern frontier of Canaan, often mentioned in the Old Testament, has been identified with Ain Gadîs, about fifty miles south of Beersheba. The Israelites encamped there the second summer after they left Egypt. Num. 33:18. It is the same as MERIBAH-KADESH, Ezek. 47:19, EN-MISHPAT, Gen. 14:7, and RITHMAH, Num. 33:18. On account of the rebellion of the Israelites as they were about to enter Canaan they were obliged to remain forty years in the wilderness, and seem to have made Kadesh their principal camp. At this place the rock was smitten for water. Num. 20:1-21. Here Miram died. Gen. 14:7; 16:14; 20:1. Num. 13:26; 20:1, 14, 16, 22; 27:14; 33:8; 33:36, 37; 34:4. Deut. 1:2, 19, 46. 2:14; 9:23. Josh. 10:41; 14:6, 7; 15:3. Judg. 11:16, 17. Ps. 29:8. Ezek. 47:19; 48:28.

Kad´mi-el (*before God*), a Levite who returned with his descendants from captivity with Zerubbabel. Ezra 2:40; 3:9; Neh. 9:4; 10:9; 12:8. Two persons may possibly be referred to in these texts.

Kad´mon-ites (*eastern*), a tribe in the land of Canaan in the time of Abraham. Gen. 15:19.

Ka´in (*dance*), in the marginal notes, Num. 24:22, and "the Kenite" in the text of that verse. See KENITES.

Kal´la-i (*swift runner of Jehovah*), a priest in the time of Joiakim. Neh. 12:20.

Ka´nah (*place of reeds*). [1] A town in Asher. Josh. 19:28. [2] A river, part of the boundary-line between Ephraim and Manasseh. Josh. 16:8; 17:9.

Ka-re´ah (*bald*), father of Johanan and Jonathan, Jer. 40:8; 41:11; 42:1; 43:2

called CAREAH in 2 Kings 25:23.

Karkaa, kar´ka-ah (*foundation*), a place on the south border of Judah. Josh. 15:3.

Kar´kor (*foundation*), a place where Gideon finally scattered the defeated hosts of Zebah and Zalmunna. Judg. 8:10.

Kar´tah (*city*), a city of Zebulun assigned to the Levites. Josh. 21:34.

Kar´tan (*double city*), a city of Naphtali assigned to the Levites. Josh, 21:32. Called KIRJATHAIM in 1 Chron. 6:76.

Kat´tath (*small*), a town of Zebulun. Josh. 19:15.

Ke´dar (*dark-skinned*), a son of Ishmael. Gen. 25:13; 1 Chron. 1:29. Some of the principal tribes of Arabia descended from him. They and the country in which they lived are called Kedar. Isa. 21:16; Jer. 49:28.
Also see Ps. 120:5.
Song of Sol. 1:5.
Isa. 21:17; 42:11; 60:7.
Jer. 2:10.
Ezek. 27:21.

Ked´e-mah (*eastward*), a son of Ishmael. Gen. 25:15; Chron.1:31.

Ked´e-moth (*easternmost*), a city east of the Dead Sea, belonging to the tribe of Reuben. Josh. 13:18. It was assigned to the Levites. Josh 21:37; 1 Chron. 6:79. Moses encamped in the surrounding wilderness. Deut. 2:26.

Ke´desh (*sanctuary*). [1] A town in the south of Judah. Josh. 15:23. [2] A city of Issachar assigned to the Levites. 1 Chron. 6:72. Called KISHON in Josh. 21:28. [3] A city of Naphtali assigned to the Levites. It became a city of refuge and was the residence of Barak, Judg. 4:6, where it is called KEDESH-NAPHTALI. It was the place where the tribes of Zebulun and Naphtali were assembled by Deborah. Judg. 4:11.

Tiglath-pileser captured it. 2 Kings 15:29. The city of the Canaanites mentioned in Josh. 12:22; 19:37 is probably the same place.

Ke´dron or **Kid´ron** (*black brook*), a noted brook, dry in the summer, but a torrent in the rainy season. It rises about a mile and a half north-west of Jerusalem, and flows near the east side of the city, between it and Mount Olivet, through the deep valley of Jehoshaphat and the wilderness of Judea, into the north-west part of the Dead Sea. This brook is called CEDRON in John 18:1. David crossed over Kidron when fleeing from Absalom. 2 Sam. 15:23. Christ also crossed it on his way to Gethsemane, John 18:1, the night before his crucifixion. It is mentioned also in 1 Kings 2:37; 15:13; 2 Kings 23:4, 6, 12; 2 Chron. 15:16; 29:16, etc.

Keep´er, a word used for shepherd, armor-bearer, jailer, etc. In Ps. 121:5 the LORD is called our keeper.

Ke-hel´a-thah (*assembly*), the eighteenth encampment of the Israelites after they left Egypt. Num. 33:22, 23.

Keilah, ke´lah (*fortress*). [1] A city of Judah. Josh 15:44; 1 Sam. 23:1; Neh. 3:17, 18. [2] A descendant of Judah. 1 Chron. 4:19.

Kelaiah, ke-la´yah (*swift messenger of God*), a Levite who took a foreign wife. Ezra 10:23. Called also KELITA in Ezra 10:23; Neh. 8:7; 10:10. He aided Ezra in expounding the law, and also sealed the covenant made by Nehemiah.

Kel´i-ta (*dwarf*). see KELAIAH.

Ke-mu´el (*helper*). [1] A son of Nahor, the brother of Abraham. Gen. 22:21. [2] A prince of Ephraim, one of those who divided Canaan. Num. 34:24. [3] A Levite, the father of Hashabiah. 1 Chron. 27:17.

Ke′nan, the son of Enos, 1 Chron. 1:2, called CAINAN in Gen. 5:9; Luke 3:37.

Ke′nath (*possession*), Num. 32:42; 1 Chron. 2:23, a city of the Amorites taken by Nobah, and by him called NOBAH.

Ke′naz (*a hunt*). [1] A son of Eliphaz, the son of Esau. Gen 36:11, 42; 1 Chron. 1:36. [2] Father of Othniel, who was a judge of Israel. Josh. 15:17; 1 Chron. 4:13. [3] A grandson of Caleb, the son of Jephunneh. 1 Chron. 4:15. The marginal note for "Kenaz" in this verse is "or, *Uknaz.*" See UKNAZ.

Ken′ez-ite (*hunter*), a title used to designate Jephunneh, the father of Caleb. Num. 32:12.

Ken′ites (*smith*), one of the tribes which occupied Canaan in the time of Abraham, to whom their land was promised. Gen. 15:19. They were mentioned in Balaam's prophecy. Num 24:21. Part of the tribe joined Israel. Judg. 1:16.
Also see Num. 24:22.
Judg. 4:11, 17; 5:24.
1 Sam. 15:6; 27:10; 30:29.
1 Chron. 2:55.

Ken′iz-zites (*hunter*), a tribe in Canaan. Gen. 15:19. The same word in Hebrew as KENEZITE.

Kept, in John 17:12, means safely guarded.

Kerchiefs, ker′chifs (*spread out*), a kind of veil worn by the idolatrous women of Israel. Ezek. 13:18, 21.

Keren-happuch, ker′en-hap′puk (*paint-horn*), a daughter of Job born after his prosperity was restored. Job 42:14.

Ke′ri-oth (*cities*). [1] A town of Judah. Josh. 15:25. [2] A strong city of Moab. Jer. 48:24, 41; called KIRIOTH, Amos 2:2.

Kern′els (*acrid*), seeds of grapes. Num. 6:4.

Ke′ros (*curved*), one of the Nethinims

whose descendants returned from Babylon with Zerubbabel. Ezra 2:44; Neh. 7:47.

Ket′tle (*boiling*), a vessel used in cooking and also for sacrificial purposes. 1 Sam. 2:14. The same word in the original is translated "basket" in Jer. 24:2; "caldron" in 2 Chron. 35:13. and "pot" in Job 41:20.

Ke-tu′rah (*incense*), the wife of Abraham after the death of Sarah. Gen. 25:1; 1 Chron. 1:32.

Key, an instrument for opening or for fastening a lock. Judg. 3:25. Keys were sometimes made very large, and carried on the shoulder as an emblem of office. Isa. 22:22. The word "key" is used figuratively in many ways.
Also see Matt. 16:19.
Luke 11:52.
Rev. 1:18; 3:7; 9:1; 20:1.

Kezia, ke-zi′ah (*cassia*), the second daughter of Job, born after his prosperity was restored. Job. 42:14.

Ke′ziz, a town of Benjamin. Josh. 18:21.

Kib′roth-hat-ta′a-vah (*graves of lust*), Num. 33:16, 17; Deut. 9:22, the first encampment of the Israelites after they left Sinai. It was so called on account of the plague with which the people were smitten because of their lust for the flesh they had been accustomed to eat in Egypt. Great flocks of quails were miraculously sent to this encampment, Num. 11:31-35, on which the people fed for a month.

Kib′za-im (*two heaps*), a city of Ephraim assigned to the Levites. Josh 21:22. It is called JOKMEAM in 1 Chron. 6:68.

Kid, a young goat, was one of the luxuries of ancient times. Gen. 38:17; 1 Sam. 16:20. Kids were also used for sacrifices. Num. 7:16, 22, 28.

Kid´ney (*longing?*), the supposed seat of desire. See marginal note, Job 19:27. The fat upon the kidneys of sacrifices was to be burned. Exod. 29:13. In Deut. 32:14 "kidneys" is used for kernels of wheat because of their richness and shape. See REINS.

Kid´ron, a brook near Jerusalem. See KEDRON.

Ki´nah (*dirge*), a city in the south of Judah. Josh. 15:22.

Kin´dred, a word used in the Bible to denote the following: **[1]** Relatives by birth. Luke 1:61; Acts 7:13. **[2]** Family in a larger sense. Acts 4:6; 7:19. **[3]** A tribe. Rev. 5:9; 14:6. **[4]** Descendants in a direct line. Acts 3:25. "Kinsfolk," "kinsman," and "kinswoman" are used in the same way.

Kine is the old English word for cows. Gen. 32:15; 41:2-27.

King. **[1]** God, "the King eternal." 1 Tim. 1:17. See GOD. **[2]** Christ, "the King of kings," 1 Tim. 6:15, and the king of the Jews. Matt. 27:11; Luke 19:38; John 1:49. See CHRIST. **[3]** The title "king" is applied to human rulers without regard to the extent of their dominions. The kings of the Hebrews were considered to be God's representatives. Saul was their first king, and was succeeded by DAVID (which see). The word "king" is also applied to the tetrarch Herod, Matt. 14:9; to the people of God, Rev. 1:6; to the devil, Rev. 9:11; to death, Job 18:14, etc.

King´dom of Christ. Matt. 13:41; Eph. 5:5, etc. King´dom of God. Matt. 6:33; Mark 1:14, etc. King´dom of Heav´en. Matt. 3:2; 4:17, etc. These terms have nearly the same meaning, and denote the blessedness of the followers of Christ, partially attained in this life, and perfectly in the world to come.

See also Matt. 5:3, 10, 19, 20; 6:33; 7:21; 8:11; 10:7; 11:11, 12; 12:28; 13:11, 24, 31, 33, 44, 45, 47, 52; 16:19; 18:1, 3, 4, 23; 19:12, 14, 23, 24; 20:1; 21:31, 43; 22:2; 23:13; 25:1, 14.
Mark 1:15; 4:11, 26, 30; 9:1, 47; 10:14, 15, 23-25; 12:34; 14:25; 15:43.
Luke 4:43; 6:20; 7:28; 8:1, 10; 9:2, 11, 27, 60, 62; 10:9, 11; 12:31, 32; 13:20, 28, 29; 14:15; 16:16; 17:20, 21; 18:16, 17, 24, 25, 29; 19:11; 21:31; 22:16, 18; 23:51.
John 3:3, 5.
Acts 1:3; 8:12; 14:22; 19:8; 20:25; 28:23, 31.
Rom. 14:17.
1 Cor. 4:20; 6:9, 10; 15:24, 50.
Gal. 5:21.
Col. 4:11.
2 Thess. 1:5.

King´dom of Is´ra-el. See ISRAEL.

King´dom of Ju´dah. See JUDAH.

King's Dale, an ancient name of the valley on the east side of Jerusalem, which was afterward called the valley of Jehoshaphat. Gen. 14:17; 2 Sam. 18:18.

King's Pool, the name of a large reservoir (otherwise called the Upper or the Old Pool) which was on the west side of Jerusalem. Neh. 2:14; Isa. 7:3; 22:11.

Kings, First and Second Books of, like the two books of Samuel, were anciently one unbroken narrative. Their Hebrew name was their first words, "Now King David." The Septuagint Version called them the third and fourth books of the Reigns or Kingdoms, the two books of Samuel being the first two.

The First Book of Kings covers the history of one hundred and twenty-six years, from the anointing of Solomon, B. C. 1015, to the death of Jehoshaphat, B. C. 889.

The Second Book of Kings contains the history of about three hundred years, from the death of Jehoshaphat, B. C. 889, to the destruction of Jerusalem by Nebuchadnezzar, B. C. 588. The last three verses of First Kings ought to be the first three of Second Kings. There is added to the second book a brief notice of the setting free of Jehoiachin, king of Judah, from prison by the king of Babylon and of his kind treatment of the captive for the rest of his life. The description of the reign of Solomon, the building of the Temple and the palaces, etc., is very minute and exact. Then follows the separation of the ten and the two tribes, forming the two kingdoms of Israel and Judah, and their respective histories. The style is simple and the narrative is interesting and instructive. The author is not known. A Jewish tradition in the Targum mentions Jeremiah as their author. Some think they were written by Ezra. The books have always had a place in the Old Testament Canon, and the discoveries of modern science in Babylon, Nineveh, Moab, and Egypt bear witness to their accuracy.

Kins´folk, Kins´man, Kins´wom-an. See KINDRED.

Kir (*wall*), a city from which the Syrians came forth to settle in the country north of Palestine. Its location is unknown. Tiglath-pileser sent the captive Syrians to it after the conquest of Damascus. 2 Kings 16:9; Amos 1:5; 9:7.

Kir-har´a-seth (*brick fortress*), 2 Kings 3:25, or **Kir-har´e-seth,** Isa. 16:7, or **Kir-ha´resh,** Isa. 16:11, or **Kir-he´res,** Jer. 48:31, 36, or **Kir of Moab,** Isa. 15:1, a strong fortress near the south-east shore of the Dead Sea. It is now called *Kerak.*

Kir-i-a-tha´im (*double city*), Jer. 48;1, 23; Ezek. 25:9, or **Kir-jath-a´im,** Num.

32:37; Josh. 13:19, a strong town east of the Jordan. It belonged to Reuben, but was afterward occupied by the Moabites.

Kir´i-oth, a strong city of Moab. See KERIOTH, No. 2.

Kir´jath (*city*), a city of Benjamin. Josh. 18:28, probably same as KIRJATH-JEARIM.

Kir-jath-a´im, a strong town east of the Jordan. See KIRIATHAIM.

Kir´jath-ar´ba (*the city of Arba*), a city in the hill country of Judah. Gen. 23:2; Josh. 14:15. Is the same as HEBRON (which see).

Kir´jath-a´rim, a city of Judah. Ezra 2:25. Same as KIRJATH-JEARIM (which see).

Kir´jath-ba´al (*the city of Baal*), a city of Judah. Josh. 15:60; 18:14. Same as KIRJATH-JEARIM.

Kir´jath-hu´zoth (*the city of streets*), a city of Moab. Num. 22:39.

Kir´jath-je´a-rim, a city of the Gibeonites, Josh. 9:17, was on the border of Judah and Benjamin. The ark of the LORD was brought here from the Philistines. 1 Sam. 6:21.

Kir´jath-san´nah (*palm city*), a city of Judah. Josh. 15:49. Same as DEBIR, No. 1, and as KIRJATH-SEPHER.

Kir´jath-se´pher (*city of books*), a city of Judah. Josh. 15:15; Judg. 1:11. Same as DEBIR, No. 1, and KIRJATH-SANNAH.

Kir of Mo´ab, a strong fortress. See KIR-HARASETH.

Kish (*a bow*). [1] Father of King Saul. 1 Sam. 9:1, 3; 10:11, 21. In Acts 13:21 he is called CIS. [2] A Levite, the grandson of Merari. 1 Chron. 23:21; 24:29. [3] A Benjamite. 1 Chron. 8:30; 9:36. [4] A Levite. 2 Chron. 29:12. [5] A Benjamite who was an ancestor of Mordecai. Esther 2:5.

Kish´i (*bow of Jehovah*), a Levite of the family of Merari, 1 Chron. 6:44, called

KUSHAIAH in the marginal notes of this verse.

Kish´i-on (*hardness*), Josh. 19:20, or **Ki´shon,** Josh. 21:28, a city of Issachar allotted to the Levites.

Ki´shon (*curved*), Judg. 4:7; 1 Kings 18:40, called **Kison** in Ps. 83:9, a river which rises in Mount Tabor and flows into the Great or Mediterranean Sea. Sisera was totally defeated there, Judg. 4:7; 5:21, and the idol priests were executed by Elijah. 1 Kings 18:40.

Kiss, a salutation especially common in the East, was used to express reverence as well as affection. It was practiced between parents and children, Gen 27:26; between near male relations and friends, Gen. 33:4; 45:15. King Saul received the kiss of allegiance from the prophet Samuel. 1 Sam. 10:1. In the early days of the Church it was a pledge of Christian brotherhood and love. Rom. 16:16; 1 Cor. 16:20.

Also see Gen. 27:27; 29:11, 13; 31:28, 55; 48:10; 50:1.
Exod. 4:57; 18:7.
Ruth 1:9, 14.
1 Sam. 20:41.
2 Sam. 14:33; 15:5; 19:39; 20:9.
1 Kings 19:18, 20.
Job 31:27.
Pss. 2:12; 85:10.
Prov. 7:13; 24:26; 27:6.
Song of Sol. 1:2; 8:1.
Hos. 13:2.
Matt. 26:48, 49.
Mark 14:44, 45.
Luke 7:38, 45; 15:20; 22:47, 48.
Acts 20:37.
2 Cor. 13:12.
1 Thess. 5:26.
1 Pet. 5:14.

Kite, a bird of prey of the hawk family, unclean by the ceremonial law. Lev. 11:14.

Kith´lish, a town of Judah. Josh 15:40.

Kit´ron (*knotty*), a town of Zebulun. Judg. 1:30.

Kit´tim, Gen. 10:4; 1 Chron. 1:7, supposed to mean the island of Cyprus. See CHITTIM.

Knead´ing-troughs, -trawfs, used in making bread, are mentioned in Exod. 8:3; 12:34. They were either circular pieces of leather made so that they could be drawn up into a kind of bag, or were small wooden bowls. The Arabs now use both kinds. The same word in the original is translated "store" in Deut. 28:5, 17.

Knee and **Kneel´ing.** The word "knee" is often used figuratively. The knees are the seat of strength. Deut. 28:35; Isa. 35:3. Kneeling was a sign of subjection, and became a customary posture in prayer. 2 Kings 1:13; Isa. 45:23; Dan. 6:10, 11; Luke 22:41; Acts 9:40; Rom. 11:4.

Knife, a word used as the translation of several different Hebrew words meaning cutting instruments of various kinds. Knives were not generally used in eating. Gen. 22:6.

Knock, a sign of importunity, Matt. 7:7, 8, or a summons to open a door. Judg. 19:22. It is the custom in the East to knock or to call out at the outer gate, but not at room-doors. Creditors were obliged to stand outside of the house and call. Deut. 24:10, 11.

Knop, in Exod. 25:31, 33, is the carved imitation of the bud of a flower or of the fruit of the almond. The word *knop* is now spelled "knob." Knops were used in ornamenting the golden candlestick, etc.

Koa, ko-ah (*he-camel*), probably means a prince, but may denote a city of Babylonia, an enemy of Jerusalem. Ezek. 23:23.

Ko´hath (*assembly*), a son of Levi,

ancestor of the large Kohathite family of priests. Gen. 46:11; Exod. 6:16, 18; Num. 3:17, 27; 26:57, 58; Josh. 21:5; 1 Chron. 6:1.

Ko´hath-ites were Levites of the highest rank, and descendants of Kohath the son of Levi. 2 Chron. 20:19.

Kol-a-i´ah (*voice of Jehovah*). [1] An Israelite of the tribe of Benjamin. Neh. 11:7. [2] The father of Ahab, the false prophet. Jer. 29:21.

Ko´rah (*baldness*). [1] A son of Esau and Aholibamah, Gen. 36:5; 1 Chron. 1:35, named as son of Eliphaz in Gen. 36:16. [2] A son of Izhar, the grandson of Levi. He was leader in the rebellion against Moses and Aaron, and was destroyed, with many of his companions, by the Lord. Exod. 6:18, 21, 24; Num. 16:1-35; 26:9, 10.

Ko´rah-ites, descendants of Korah. Among them were famous singers. Several Psalms bear their names. Some of them were doorkeepers. 1 Chron. 9:19, 31.

Ko-rath-ites. Num. 26:58. See KORAHITES.

Ko´re (*partridge*). [1] A Levite, a descendant of Korah. 1 Chron. 9:19; 26:1. [2] A Levite who had charge of free-will offerings. 2 Chron. 31:14.

Kor´hites. Exod. 6:24; 1 Chron. 12:6; 26:1. See KORAHITES.

Koz (*thorn*). [1] A descendant of Judah. He is called COZ in 1 Chron. 4:8. [2] The head of one of the courses of priests. 1 Chron. 24:10. See HAKKOZ. The descendants of Koz, No. 2, were probably those who could not show their genealogy and were put out of the priesthood. Ezra 2:61; Neh. 7:63. Part of the wall of Jerusalem was repaired by Meremoth, of the family of Koz. Neh. 3:4, 21.

Kushaiah, kush-a´yah, the father of Ethan. 1 Chron. 15:17. See KISHI.

L

La´a-dah (*order*), a son of Shelah, the son of Judah. 1 Chron. 4:21.

La´a-dan (*put in order*). [1] A descendant of Ephraim. He was an ancestor of Joshua. 1 Chron. 7:25. [2] Son of Gershon. 1 Chron. 23:7, 8, 9. He is called LIBNI in the marginal notes of 1 Chron. 23:7 and elsewhere.

La´ban (*white*). the son of Bethuel and brother of Rebekah. He was the father of Leah and Rachel. Rebekah sent her son Jacob to him, Gen. 27:43, so that he might escape from the anger of his brother Esau, whom he had wronged. Jacob served Laban seven years for Rachel. Laban deceived him and gave him Leah as a wife, and afterward Rachel, for whom he served seven years more. Gen. 29:18-28. See JACOB.

Also see Gen. 24:29, 50; 25:20; 28:2, 5; 29:5, 10, 13-16, 29; 30:25, 27, 34, 36, 40, 42; 31:1, 2, 12, 19, 20, 22, 24-26, 31, 33, 34, 36, 43, 47, 48, 51, 55; 32:4, 46:18, 25.

La´ban (*white*), the name of a place, perhaps LIBNAH, near the Arabian desert. Deut. 1:1.

Lace (*twisted*) was the blue cord which bound the high-priest's breastplate to the ephod. Exod. 28:28. Also called "wires" in Exod. 39:3, "thread" in Judg. 16:9, and "line" in Ezek. 40:3.

Lachish, la´kish (*invincible*), a royal city of the Amorites. It was captured by Joshua and included in Judah. It was besieged by Sennacherib. 2 Kings 18:13,

14, and was reoccupied after the captivity. Neh. 11:30.

Lack, in Exod. 16:18, means deficiency. In Mark 10:21 "thou lackest" means "thou art deficient in."

Lad´der, from earth to heaven, seen by Jacob in a vision. The Hebrew word "ladder" means *a staircase.* Gen. 28:12–17. Compare John 1:51.

La´dy, in Isa. 47:5, 7, is applied to Babylon as mistress of nations. In Judg. 5:29; Esther 1:18 "ladies" means princesses. In 2 John 1:5 "lady" is used as a title, or possibly as a proper name.

La´el (*of God*), a Levite of the family of Gershon. Num. 3:24.

La´had (*oppression*), a great-grandson of Shobal, the son of Judah. 1 Chron. 4:2.

La-hai´-roi, a well (called a fountain in Gen. 16:7) where the angel of the Lord found Hagar. Gen. 24:62; 25:11. It is the same place as BEER-LAHAIROI.

Lah´mam (*provisions*), a town of Judah. Josh. 15:40.

Lah´mi (*warrior*), a brother of Goliath. 1 Chron. 20:5.

La´ish (*lion*), father of Phalti, 1 Sam. 25:44, called PHALTIEL in 2 Sam. 3:15, to whom King Saul gave David's wife Michal.

La´ish or **Le´shem.** [1] A town in the north border of Canaan. Judg. 18:7. It is called LESHEM in Josh. 19:47, and was afterward called DAN (which see). [2] Laish, noticed in Isa. 10:30, is probably not the same place as No.1. Its situation is uncertain.

Lake. The Sea of Galilee is called "the lake of Gennesaret" in Luke 5:1, and "the lake" in Luke 5:2; 8:22, 23, 33.

La´kum (*fortress*), a place on the border of Naphtali. Josh. 19:33.

Lamb, a title given to the Lord Jesus Christ as the atoning sacrifice for the sins of his people. Rev. 5:6, 8, 12, 13. In John 21:15 "lambs" means disciples of Christ.

Lamb. See SHEEP.

La´mech, la´mek (*strong*). [1] The son of Methuselah and father of Noah. Gen. 5:25, 31; 1 Chron. 1:3; Luke 3:36. [2] The son of Methusael, a descendant of Cain. He was the father of Jabal, Jubal, and Tubalcain. Gen. 4:18-24.

Lam-en-ta´tions of Jer-e-mi´ah, the book following immediately after Jeremiah's prophecies, contains a series of poems artistically composed, in which the fate of Jerusalem is described. The first, second, and fourth chapters consist of twenty-two verses each, corresponding to the twenty-two letters of the Hebrew alphabet, each verse beginning with the corresponding letter. The third chapter has three verses under each letter, but in the fifth chapter, though it also has twenty-two verses, the alphabetical order is not observed.

Lamp. The lamps used in ancient times are sometimes called candles in the Authorized Version. See CANDLE. They were made in various forms, and from clay, terracotta, bronze, etc. They were filled generally with olive-oil, which was abundant in Palestine. Pitch, tallow, wax, etc. were also used for the same purpose. The lamps of the Hebrews were probably kept burning all night. A darkened house denoted the extinction of its former occupants, Job 18:5, 6; Prov. 13:9; 20:20, or its desertion, but a constant light in the night was a sign of prosperity. Prov. 31:18. As the streets were not lighted at night in ancient times, lamps were carried by persons passing through them after dark, and it was necessary to fill the lamps frequently from vessels which the travellers carried. See Matt. 25:3, 4, 8, in the parable of the Ten Virgins.

Lance, a kind of spear. Jer. 50:42.

Lan´cet, a light spear or a pointed knife. 1 Kings 18:28.

Land´marks. Fences and walls were not common in Judea. Mark 2:23. The boundaries of fields were sometimes indicated by rows of trees, but in many instances by heaps of stones at the corners. In Deut. 27:17 a curse is pronounced upon him "that removeth his neighbor's landmark."

Also see Deut. 19:14.

Job 24:2.

Prov. 22:28; 23:10.

Lanes, mentioned in Luke 14:21, were narrow streets on which were the houses of poor people.

Lan´guage. In Gen. 2:20 it is stated that Adam "gave names to all cattle," etc. In Gen. 11:1 it is mentioned that "the whole earth was of one language, and of one speech." This language was used until about a hundred years after the deluge. When the tower of Babel was commenced the "Lord confounded the language" then used. Gen. 11:6-9. See BIBLE for an account of the languages in which it was written.

Lan´terns are mentioned in John 18:3. They were used by the men that arrested Jesus on the night before his crucifixion.

Laodicea, la-od-i-se´ah, the old city of Diospolis, Asia Minor, which the Syrian king Seleucus II. enlarged and beautified and renamed after his wife Laodice. It became a great commercial center. A Christian church was established there at an early date, probably from Ephesus. Rev. 1:11; 3:14-18. From the Epistle to the Colossians, 4:15, 16, it appears that it was a Christian church at Laodicea to which Paul wrote a letter. Some refer this passage to the Epistle to the Ephesians, which was a circular letter. Laodicea is now an insignificant village.

Laodiceans, la-od-i-se´anz, inhabitants of Laodicea. Col. 4:16; Rev. 3:14.

Lap´peth, in Judg. 7:5, mentioned in the account of the testing of the alertness of Gideon's men, refers to a method of drinking still practiced by Eastern people with wonderful rapidity. They take up the water in the hollow of their hands while sitting on their heels, with their faces close to the water and with their tongues extended to meet it.

Lap´i-doth (*torches*), an Israelite of the tribe of Ephraim. He was the husband of the prophetess Deborah. Judg. 4:4.

Lap´wing, a small bird of singular appearance, mentioned in Lev. 11:19. It is probably the hoopoe, which is so named from its call-note and was abundant in Palestine.

Lasea, la-se´ah, a city near the eastern end of the island of Crete. Acts 27:8.

La´sha (*fissure*), a place on the southeastern boundary of Canaan. Gen 10:19.

La-sha´ron, a district near Tabor. Josh. 12:18. Its king was killed by Joshua.

Latch´et, a strap or string used to fasten a sandal to the foot. Mark 1:7.

Lat´in, the language of the Romans, is mentioned in Luke 23:38. For an account of the Latin Version of the Bible see BIBLE.

Lat´tice, a kind of latticed window or balcony fronting the street in Eastern houses, 2 Kings 1:2, and used only on public days.

Laud, in Rom. 15:11 means to extol by words of praise or by song.

Laugh, as used in Prov. 1:26; Pss. 2:4; 37:13, with reference to God, denotes that he pays no respect to the person referred to.

La´ver, a vessel containing water for the priests to wash their hands and feet with before they offered sacrifices. It stood without the Tabernacle, near the altar of burnt-offering. Exod. 30:18, 21. The Temple of Solomon had ten brazen lavers. 1 Kings 7:27–39.

Law, The, a term applied in the New Testament to the Mosaic legislation, and sometimes to the whole old dispensation as distinguished from the dispensation under the Gospel. "The law and the prophets" means the Scriptures of the Old Testament.

Law´yers. The Hebrew lawyers were expounders of the law (see LAW) in the synagogues and schools. They did not plead in courts, and were entirely different from lawyers of the present time. Matt. 22:35.

Lay´ing on of hands. See HANDS, LAYING ON OF.

Laz´a-rus, an abbreviation of **El-e-a´zer** (*whom God helps*). [1] A man of Bethany, the brother of Martha and Mary. Jesus raised him from the dead. John 11:1 to 12:11. [2] The name given by Christ to a beggar who was the subject of one of his parables. Luke 16:19-31.

Lead was known in ancient times, and is mentioned in Exod. 15:10, etc. The words "graven with an iron pen and lead in the rock for ever" refer to letters cut in the rock and filled with melted lead to make them more conspicuous.

Leaf. A fresh leaf of a tree is used to denote prosperity, Ps 1:3; Ezek. 47:12, and a faded leaf as a symbol of decay. Job. 13:25; Isa. 64:6. The word is figuratively used in other ways.
Also see Gen. 3:7; 8:11.
Lev. 26:36.
1 Kings 6:34.
Isa. 1:30; 6:13; 34:4.
Jer. 8:13; 17:8; 36:23.

Ezek. 17:9; 41:24.
Dan. 4:12, 14, 21.
Matt. 21:19; 24:32.
Mark 11:13; 13:28.
Rev. 22:2.

Leagues (alliances for mutual aid) were made by Joshua with Gibeon, Josh. 9:15, 16; by David with the elders of Israel, 2 Sam. 5:3; by Hiram and Solomon, 1 Kings 5:12; and by others. No league was to be made with the Canaanites, Exod. 23:32, 33; with the Amalekites, Exod. 17:8, 14; or the Moabites. Deut. 2:9-19.

Le´ah (*wearied*), Laban's elder daughter, whom he substituted instead of Rachel as a wife for Jacob. Gen. 29:16-25.

Leas´ing, in Pss. 4:2; 5:6, means lies; falsehood.

Leath´er. The Jews used leather for clothing, Job 31:20; Heb. 11:37; for girdles, 2 Kings 1:8; Matt. 3:4; and for covering, Exod. 26:14. Simon the tanner lived at Joppa. Acts 9:43.

Leav´en is sour dough used to raise the new dough with which it is mixed. Exod. 12:15. The Jews were forbidden to use leaven or have it in their houses during the seven days of the Passover. For this reason this festival was sometimes called the "feast of unleavened bread." Luke 22:1. The word leaven is often used figuratively. Matt. 13:33; 16:6.

Le-an´noth, in the title of Ps. 88, is a word used to indicate that the Psalm is to be sung in a subdued manner. See MAHALATH.

Leb´a-na, Neh. 7:48, or **Leb´a-nah,** Ezra 2:45, a Nethinim whose descendants returned with Zerubbabel.

Leb´a-non and **An´ti-Leb´a-non** (*exceeding white*), referring to the snow-capped peaks, form a double mountain-range which, enclosing the valley of the

Orontes, runs through Syria from north to south, and gives that country a configuration of four parallel belts very similar to that of Palestine. The highest peak of Lebanon is Jebel Mukhmel, ten thousand two hundred feet. The highest point of Anti-Lebanon is Mount Hermon, nine thousand feet above the Mediterranean. The country was promised to the Israelites, but was never conquered by them. Josh. 13:2-6; Judg. 3:1-3. The western part, Lebanon, was under Phœnician rule; the eastern, Anti-Lebanon, under the sway of the king of Damascus. In the southern part of Anti-Lebanon the wild tribes remained independent for a long time and occasionally caused much trouble to their neighbors. With the Phœnicians in the eastern part the Israelites maintained very friendly relations in the reigns of David and Solomon, and they became well acquainted with Lebanon, its cedars, Song of Sol. 5:15, its cool breezes, its magnificent springs, etc. When, after the death of Alexander the Great, B. C. 323, a Syrian monarchy was established in Lebanon under the dynasty of the Seleucidæ, Palestine became for a time a dependency of that kingdom. See CEDAR, and HEBREWS.

Leb´a-oth (*lionesses*), a town in the south of Judah. Josh. 15:32.

Lebbæus, leb-be´us, one of the apostles who was surnamed Thaddeus. Matt. 10:3.

Le-bo´nah (*frankincense*), a town of Ephraim, near Shiloh. Judg. 21:19.

Lecah, le´kah (*walking*), is found only in the genealogies of Judah, 1 Chron. 4:21, where it seems to mean a son of Er. It may be the name of a town.

Leek, a vegetable resembling an onion. One kind of leek has been raised in Egypt from very ancient times. Num. 11:5. The original word is often translated "grass," and in one case "herb."

Lees, the grosser parts or dregs of any liquor, which have settled to the bottom of the vessel containing it. In Isa. 25:6 "wines on the lees" means good wine. In Ps. 75:8 drinking the dregs (lees) of wine indicates great distress.

Left hand. In Gen. 14:15; Job 23:9 left hand means "the north." In Judg. 3:15; 20:16 "lefthanded" means able to use the left hand as effectively as the right hand. Many of the tribe of Benjamin were left-handed, that is ambidextrous.

Leg, in 1 Sam. 17:6, means the lower limb from the knee to the foot. The legs of crucified persons were sometimes broken to hasten their death. John 19:31-33.

Le´gion, a body of Roman soldiers, originally composed of about three thousand, and subsequently of between six thousand and seven thousand men. In Matt. 26:53; Mark 5:9, 15 the word refers to a large but indefinite number of angels or of devils.

Le´ha-bim (*flaming*), Gen. 10:13; 1 Chron. 1:11, **Lu´bim,** or **Lib´ya-no,** Dan. 11:43; Nah. 3 9, a people of Hamitic descent, called "Libyans" in classic and modern literature, and "Lebu" in Egyptian inscriptions.

Le´hi (*jaw-bone*), a place in Judah where Samson slew "a thousand" Philistines. Judg. 15:9-16.

Lem´u-el (*dedicated to God*), a king to whom Prov. 31:2-9 was addressed by his mother. Nothing is known concerning Lemuel except that he was a king.

Lend, Lend´er. See LOAN.

Len´tiles, a plant of the same family as the garden pea but smaller. 2 Sam. 23:11; Gen. 25:34. Lentiles are still common in Palestine, and are used in making pottage, and, when mixed with barley, beans, etc., are made into bread. Ezek. 4:9.

Leopard, lep´ard, a fierce animal which pounces upon and destroys cattle, etc., is still found in the forests of Gilead, in parts of the Jordan valley, and elsewhere in Palestine. It is mentioned in Jer. 5:6; Hos. 13:7, etc.

Lep´er, a person afflicted with leprosy, a disgusting disease still common in Egypt, Syria, and other Eastern countries. Its progress and effects are described in Job 2:7, 8, 12; 6:2; 7:3-5; 19:14-21. Many cases of leprosy are mentioned in the Bible.

Also see Lev. 13:2, 3, 8, 9, 11-13, 15, 20, 25, 30, 42, 43, 45, 47, 49, 51, 52, 59; 14:2, 3, 7, 32, 34, 44, 54, 55, 57; 22:4.

Num. 5:2.

Deut. 24:8.

2 Sam. 3:29.

2 Kings 5:1, 3, 6, 7, 11, 27; 7:8; 15:5.

2 Chron. 26:19, 21, 23.

Matt. 8:2, 3; 10:8; 11:5; 26:6.

Mark 1:40, 42; 14:3.

Luke 4:27; 5:12, 13; 7:22; 17:12.

Lep´ro-sy. See LEPER.

Les´bos, an island in the Mediterranean. Its capital is Mitylene, Acts 20:14, where Paul stopped.

Le´shem, the ancient name of the city of Laish, on the west side of Mount Hermon. Josh. 19:47. It was afterward called DAN (which see).

Let, in 2 Thess. 2:7, means hinder; prevent.

Lethech, le´thek, in the marginal notes of Hos. 3:2, means a measure of grain, about four bushels—half a homer. See HOMER.

Let´ters sent in ancient times were in the form of rolls. 2 Sam. 11:14; Ezra 4:11.

Also see 2 Sam. 11:15.

1 Kings 21:8, 9, 11.

2 Kings 5;5-7; 10:1, 2, 6, 7; 19:14; 20:12.

2 Chron. 30:1, 6; 32:17.

Ezra 4:7, 8, 18, 23; 5:5-7; 7:11.

Neh. 2:7-9; 6:5, 17, 19.

Esther 1:22; 3:13; 8:5, 10; 9:20, 25, 26, 29, 30.

Isa. 37:14; 39:1.

Jer. 29:1, 25, 29.

Luke 23:38.

John 7:15.

Acts 9:2; 15:23; 22:5; 23:25, 34; 28:21.

Rom. 2:27, 29; 7:6.

1 Cor. 16:3.

2 Cor. 3:1, 6; 7:8; 10:9-11.

Gal. 6:11.

2 Thess. 2:2.

Heb. 13:22.

Le-tu´shim (*sharpened*), a tribe descended from Dedan and living in Arabia. Gen 25:3.

Le-um´mim (*nations*), Gen. 25:3, is same as LETUSHIM.

Le´vi (*joining*). [1] The third son of Jacob by Leah. Gen. 29:34; 34:25–31. [2] The tribe descended from Levi, No. 1. Exod. 2:1; Num. 1:49. [3, 4] Two ancestors of Joseph, the husband of Mary. Luke 3:24, 29. [5] The original name of Matthew the publican and apostle. Matt. 9:9; Mark 2:14; Luke 5:27, 29. See MATTHEW.

Also see Gen. 35:23; 46:11; 49:5.

Exod. 1:2; 2:1; 6:16, 19; 32:26, 28.

Num. 3:6, 15, 17; 4:2; 16:1, 7, 8, 10; 17:3, 8; 18:2, 21; 26:59.

Deut. 10:8, 9; 18:1; 21:5; 27:12; 31:9; 33:8.

Josh. 13:14, 33; 21:10.

1 Kings 12:31.

1 Chron. 2:1; 6:1, 38, 43, 47; 9:18; 12:26; 21:6; 23:6, 14, 24; 24:20.

Ezra 8:15, 18.
Neh. 10:39; 12:23.
Ps. 135:20.
Ezek. 40;46; 48:31.
Zech. 12:13.
Mal. 2:4, 8; 3:3.
Heb. 7:5, 9.
Rev. 7:7.

Le-vi′a-than, an animal described in Job 41, may be the crocodile, which was once common in the Zerka or Crocodile River in Palestine, which flowed into the Mediterranean Sea. The word "leviathan," in Ps. 74:14; Isa. 27:1, seems to mean crocodile, but in Ps. 104:26 some sea monster is evidently referred to. Perhaps the whale.

Le′vites, in Num. 35:2; Josh. 21:3, 41, etc., means all the descendants of Levi, or the whole tribe of Levi. The term "Levites" is generally used to designate those descendants of Levi who were not priests. 1 Kings 8:4; Ezra 2:70; John 1:19, etc. The Levites were employed in the lower services of the Tabernacle and of the Temple and as special servants of the Lord. Deut. 10:8, 9; 18:1, 2; 33:8-11. Many cities were allotted to the Levites. Also see Exod. 6; 38.
Lev. 25.
Num. 1–4; 7; 8; 18; 26; 31; 35.
Deut. 17; 18; 24; 27; 31.
Josh. 3; 8; 14; 18; 21.
1 Sam. 6.
2 Sam. 15.
1 Kings 8.
1 Chron. 6; 9; 13; 15; 16; 23; 24; 26–28.
2 Chron. 5–8; 11; 13; 17; 19; 20; 23; 24; 29–31; 34; 35.
Ezra 1–3; 6–10.
Neh. 3; 7–13.
Isa. 66.
Jer. 33.

Ezek. 43–45; 48.
John 1.

Le-vit′i-cus, the third book of the Pentateuch and of the Old Testament. In Hebrew the book is named from the first words, "And he called." The present name refers to its contents as a book of Levitical or ceremonial regulations. The historical extent of Leviticus is very small, being only one month, the first month of B. C. 1490. See PENTATEUCH.

Lev′y, a body of men forced into service on public works. 1 Kings 5:13, 14; 9:15.

Lewd, in Acts 17:5, means bad; and **Lewdness,** in Acts 18:14, means wickedness; crime. These words elsewhere refer to licentiousness.

Lib′er-tines, in Acts 6:9, means those Jews who were taken prisoners in the Syrian wars, carried to Rome, reduced to slavery, and afterward set free. They had a synagogue in Jerusalem.

Lib′nah (*whiteness*). [1] The sixteenth encampment of the Israelites after they left Egypt. Num. 33:20, 21. [2] A city of Judah. It was nearly south of Jerusalem, and had been a chief royal city of the Canaanites. It became a Levitical city. Josh. 10:29; 15:42; 2 Kings 19:8.

Lib′ni (*white*). [1] A Levite, a son of Gershon, the son of Levi. Exod. 6:17; Num. 3:18. [2] A grandson of Merari, the son of Levi. 1 Chron. 6:29.

Lib′nites, descendants of Libni, the son of Gershon. Num. 3:21; 26:58.

Libya, lib′i-ah, a name applied, in Ezek. 30:5; 38:5; Acts 2:10, to that part of northern Africa which is west of Egypt. It was peopled by a Hamitic race mentioned in the Old Testament as LEHABIM (which see).

Lib′y-ans, inhabitants of Libya. Jer. 46:9; Dan. 11:43.

Lice, the third plague of Egypt, were miraculously sent to induce Pharaoh to let the Israelites go out of Egypt. Exod. 8:16, 17; Ps. 105:31. These lice were probably ticks which live in the sand.

Lies of all kinds are condemned in the Bible. Lev. 19:11; John 8:44.

Also see Deut. 33:29.

Judg. 16:10.

Job 11:3; 13:4; 24:25.

Pss. 40:4; 58:3; 62:4; 63:11; 101:7; 116:11.

Prov. 6:19; 14:5, 25; 17:4; 19:5, 9, 22; 29:12; 30:6, 8.

Isa. 9:15; 16:6; 28:15, 17; 44:25; 59:3, 4.

Jer. 9:3, 5; 14:14; 15:18; 16:19; 20:6; 23:14, 25, 26, 32; 48:30; 50:36.

Ezek. 13:8, 9, 19, 22; 22:28; 24:12.

Dan. 11:27.

Hos. 7:3, 13; 10:13; 11:12; 12:1.

Amos 2:4.

Mic. 6:12.

Nah. 3:1.

Hab. 2:18.

Zeph. 3:13.

Zech. 13:3.

John 8:55.

Rom. 3:4.

1 Tim. 1:10; 4:2.

Titus 1:12.

1 John 1:10; 2:4, 22; 4:20; 5:10.

Rev. 2:2; 21:8.

Lieu-ten′ants is a general name for viceroys (governors with royal authority) of Persian provinces. Ezra 8:36. They are called princes in Dan. 3:2; 6:1.

Life, a word used both in a natural and spiritual sense.

Gen. 1–3; 6; 7; 9; 18; 19; 23; 25; 27; 32; 42; 44; 45; 47; 48.

Exod. 4; 6; 21.

Lev. 17; 18.

Num. 35.

Deut. 4; 6; 12; 16; 17; 19; 20; 24; 28; 30; 32.

Josh. 1; 2; 4.

Judg. 9; 12; 16; 18.

Ruth 4.

1 Sam. 1; 7; 18–20; 22; 23; 25; 26; 28.

2 Sam. 1; 4; 14–16; 18; 19.

¹ Kings 1–4; 11; 15; 19; 20.

␣ Kings 1; 4; 7; 8; 10; 25.

2 Chron. 1.

Ezra 6.

Neh. 6.

Esther 7; 8.

Job 2; 3; 6; 7; 9; 10; 13; 24; 31; 33; 36.

Pss. 7; 16; 17; 21; 23; 26; 27; 30; 31; 34; 36; 38; 42; 61; 63; 64; 66; 78; 88; 91; 103; 128; 133; 143.

Prov. 1–16; 18; 19; 21; 22; 31.

Eccles. 2; 3; 5–9.

Isa. 15; 38; 43; 57.

Jer. 4; 8; 11; 21; 22; 34; 38; 39; 44; 45; 49; 52.

Lam. 2; 3.

Ezek. 3; 7; 13; 32; 33.

Dan. 12.

Jon. 1; 2; 4.

Mal. 2.

Matt. 2; 6; 7; 10; 16; 18–20; 25.

Mark 3; 8–10.

Luke 1; 6; 8–10; 12; 14; 17; 18; 21.

John 1; 3–6; 8; 10–15; 17; 20.

Acts 2; 3; 5; 8; 11; 13; 17; 20; 26; 27.

Rom. 2; 5–8; 11; 16.

1 Cor. 3; 6; 14; 15.

2 Cor. 1–5.

Gal. 2; 3; 6.

Eph. 4.

Phil. 1; 2; 4.

Col. 3.

1 Tim. 1; 2; 4; 6.

2 Tim. 1–3.

Titus 1; 3.

Heb. 7; 11.
James. 1; 4.
1 Pet. 3; 4.
2 Pet. 1.
1 John 1–3; 5.
Jude :21.
Rev. 2; 3; 8; 11; 13; 17; 20–22.
   Light, a word often used and with various meanings.
Gen. 1; 44.
Exod. 10; 13; 14; 25; 27; 35; 39; 40.
Lev. 24.
Num. 4; 8; 21.
Deut. 27.
Judg. 9; 19.
Ruth 2.
1 Sam. 14; 18; 25; 29.
2 Sam. 2; 17; 21; 23.
1 Kings 6; 7; 11; 16.
2 Kings 3; 7; 8; 20.
2 Chron. 21.
Neh. 9.
Esther 8.
Job 3; 10; 12; 17; 18; 22; 24; 25; 28–30; 33; 36–38; 41.
Pss. 4; 18; 27; 36–38; 43; 44; 49; 56; 74; 78; 89; 90; 97; 104; 105; 112; 118; 119; 136; 139; 148.
Prov. 4; 6; 13;15; 16.
Eccles. 2; 11; 12.
Isa. 2; 5; 8–10; 13; 30; 42; 45; 49–51; 58–60.
Jer. 4; 13; 25; 31.
Lam. 3.
Ezek. 8; 22; 32.
Dan. 2; 5.
Hos. 6.
Amos 5.
Mic. 2; 7.
Hab. 3.
Zeph. 3.
Zech. 14.
Matt. 4–6; 10; 11; 17; 22; 24.

Mark 13.
Luke 1; 2; 8; 11; 12; 15; 16.
John 1; 3; 5; 8; 9; 11; 12.
Acts 9; 12; 13; 16; 20; 22; 26.
Rom. 2; 13.
1 Cor. 4.
2 Cor. 4; 6; 11.
Eph. 5.
Phil. 2.
Col. 1.
1 Thess. 5.
1 Tim. 6.
2 Tim. 1.
James 1.
1 Pet. 2.
2 Pet. 1.
1 John 1; 2.
Rev. 7; 18; 21; 22.
   Light'ning.
Exod. 19:16; 20:18.
2 Sam. 22:15.
Job 28:26; 37:3; 38:25.
Pss. 18:14; 77:18; 97:4; 135:7; 144:6.
Jer. 10:13; 51:16.
Ezek. 1 13, 14.
Dan. 10:6.
Nah. 2:4
Zech. 9:14.
Matt. 24:27; 28:3.
Luke 10:18; 17:24.
Rev. 4:5; 8:5; 11:19; 16:18.
   Lign Aloes, Num. 24:6, or wood aloes, a kind of tree referred to by Balaam.
   Lig'ure, a precious stone in the high-priest's breastplate. Exod. 28:19. Nothing more is known about it,
   Lik'hi (*learned*), a son of Shemidah. 1 Chron. 7:19.
   Lik'ing, in Job 39:4, means condition; and in Dan. 1:10, conditioned.
   Lil'y. Only one true lily, the scarlet martagon, is now found in Palestine. A white and fragrant kind was probably

once found on the coast, and may have been the one referred to in Song of Sol. 2:1. The word "lily" is probably used in the Bible for any beautiful flower resembling a lily. Matt. 6:28; Luke 12:27.

Lime, as it is now prepared and employed for plaster or cement, was probably known to the ancients. Deut. 27:2; Isa. 33:12.

Line, in Amos 7:17; Zech. 1:16, refers to the method of measuring land with a cord. Lines naturally came to mean a piece of land or an inheritance. Ps. 16:6. In Ezek. 40:3 it means a measuring-line about one hundred and forty feet long.

Lin′e-age, in Luke 2:4, means family or race.

Lin′en, Exod. 28:42, was well known and much used in ancient times, especially in Egypt, where the finest quality of it was made.

Lines. Ps. 16:6. See LINE.

Lin′tel, the top piece of a door-frame, that which rests on the two side-posts. On the Passover night the Hebrews were commanded to strike it with the blood of the sacrificial lamb. Lintel, in Amos 9:1; Zeph. 2:14, means the projecting capital of a column.

Li′nus, a Roman disciple from whom Paul sent salutation to Timothy. 2 Tim. 4:21.

Li′on of the tribe of Jud′a, a title given on one occasion to the glorified Saviour. Rev. 5:5.

Li′ons, probably of the Asiatic species, smaller and less formidable than the African lion, were found in Palestine as late as the twelfth century, but have now disappeared in that country. The lion was the emblem of the tribe of Judah.

Liq′uor, in Num. 6:3, means drink made from steeped grapes. In Song of Sol.

7:2 it means highly flavored wine. In Exod. 22:29 "liquors" means the juice of the olive and grapes.

List′ed, in Matt. 17:12; Mark 9:13, means pleased.

List′eth, in John 3:8; James 3:4, means desires.

Lit′ter, a covered chair so made as to shelter the occupant from the rain and sun. It was carried by men or by animals. Isa. 66:20.

Live′ly, in 1 Pet. 2:5, means living. In Exod. 1:19 it means vigorous; full of life.

Liv′er is often mentioned in the Pentateuch with reference to sacrifices. The phrase "the caul above the liver" means one of the lobes of the liver, which was to be burned on the altar, and not eaten. Exod. 29:13, 22; Lev. 3:4, etc.

Liv′ing Crea′tures. These words were applied by Ezekiel to certain beings which he saw in vision by the river Chebar. Ezek. 1:5, 13-15, 19-22; 10:15, 17, 20. See BEAST.

Liz′ard (*that which clings to the ground*), an unclean animal. Lev. 11:30. There are many kinds of lizards in Palestine.

Loaf. 1 Chron. 16:3. Loaves of bread were made shaped like a plate, and when leavened were usually about as thick as one's little finger.

Lo-am′mi (*not my people*), the name which the prophet Hosea was commanded to give to his son as a token of the rejection of Israel by the LORD. Hos. 1:9. See LORUHAMAH.

Loan. The Mosaic law required the rich to relieve the poor by loans as well as by alms. Exod. 22:25; Lev. 25:35-37. No interest was to be taken. Exod. 22:25; Lev. 25:36; Deut. 23:19. These laws had no reference to foreigners. The Jews took interest from them.

Locks of a clumsy kind were used in ancient times. 1 Kings 4:13; Song of Sol. 5:5; Judg. 3:24.

Lo´cust, an insect of the grasshopper kind, remarkable for its voracity and numbers. When mature it can fly to a considerable height. The locusts of Eastern countries are not exactly like those of America. In an immature state they are sometimes called caterpillars. Locusts were often instruments of divine judgment. Exod. 10:4-15; Deut. 28:38-42; Joel 1:4; 2:25. Also see Exod. 10:19.
Lev. 11:22.
1 Kings 8:37.
2 Chron. 6:28; 7:13.
Pss. 78:46; 105:34; 109:23.
Prov. 30:27.
Isa. 33:4.
Nah. 3:15, 17.
Matt. 8:4.
Mark 1:6.
Rev. 9:3, 7.

Lod, 1 Chron. 8:12, is the Hebrew name for a village called LYDDA in Acts 9:32.

Lo-de´bar, a town of Manasseh beyond Jordan. 2 Sam. 9:4, 5; 17:27.

Lodge, in Isa. 1:8, denotes a small hut or booth on an elevated place in a garden. It is occupied by a keeper, day and night, while the fruits are ripening.

Log, Lev. 14:10, the smallest measure for liquids that was used among the Israelites, was the seventy-second part of a bath, and contained about two-thirds of a pint. See MEASURES.

Loins, the lower part of a man's back and the parts within, represented the seat of strength. Deut. 33:11; Job 40:16. When working or travelling the Hebrews girded up their loose garments about the loins. In 1 Pet. 1:13 this custom is referred to figuratively.

Lo´is, the grandmother of Timothy. She was commended by Paul on account of her faith. 2 Tim. 1:5.

Looked, in Acts 28:6, means expected.

Look´ing-glass. That which is thus translated was a plate of highly polished metal. Exod. 38:8; Job 37:18.

Lord, a title used—[1] To denote the Godhead generally. Matt. 1:22; Mark 5:19; Luke 1:6, etc. [2] With personal reference to the Lord Jesus Christ. Matt 7:21; Mark 1:3; Luke 1:43; John 1:23. [3] Applied as a title of respect to men. Matt. 10:24; Mark 12:9; Luke 12:36; John 13:16, etc. "Lord" is the translation of two Hebrew words, "Jehovah" and "Adonai." When it represents the former it is printed in capitals. Gen. 15:4. When it is the translation of Adonai it is printed with a capital initial. Ps. 97:5, etc.

Lord's Day. Since the time of the apostles the first day of the week has been kept sacred by Christians in commemoration of the resurrection of Christ. Rev. 1:10.

Lord's Supper. This was instituted by Christ on the night preceding his crucifixion. It is a memorial of Christ's atoning death and a visible token of Christian fellowship. Matt. 26:19-30; Mark 14:16-26; Luke 22:13-20; 1 Cor. 11:23-26.

Lo-ru´ha-mah (*the uncompassionated*), the name which the prophet Hosea was directed to give his daughter in token of the withdrawal of God's mercy from Israel. Hos. 1:6, 8.

Lot (*a covering*) was the nephew of Abraham and the son of Haran. Gen. 11:27. He had many flocks and herds, and dwelt in Sodom, although he abhorred the sinfulness of its inhabitants. When Sodom was destroyed by God on account of sin Lot and his family were saved by means of a special messenger from the Lord; but his "wife looked back from behind him, and she became a pillar of salt." Gen. 19:26. The Ammonites and Moabites descended from Lot.

Also see Gen. 11:32; 12:4, 5; 13:1, 5, 7, 8, 10-12, 14; 14:12, 16; 19:1, 5, 6, 9, 10, 14, 15, 18, 23, 29, 30, 36.

Deut. 2:9, 19.

Ps. 83:8.

Luke 17:28, 29, 32.

2 Pet. 2:7.

Lo´tan (*covering*), a son of Seir the Horite. Gen. 36:20; 1 Chron. 1:38.

Lots. Decision by lots was often made by the Hebrews, but always with strict reference to God's interposition, as in the case of the apostle Matthias. Acts 1:26. The Promised Land was divided by lot among the tribes of Israel. Num. 26:55.

Also see Lev. 16:8.

Josh. 18:6, 8, 10.

1 Sam. 14:42.

1 Chron. 24:31; 25:8; 26:13, 14.

Neh. 10:34; 11:1.

Ps. 22:18.

Joel 3:3.

Obad. :11.

Jon. 1:7.

Nah. 3:10.

Matt. 27:35.

Mark 15:24.

Luke 23:34.

John 19:24.

Lots, Feast of. See PURIM.

Love. The perfect exercise of love includes our whole duty to God and our fellow-creatures. Matt. 22:37-40; Rom. 13:8, 10. The love of God to man is manifested in Jesus Christ. Rom. 5:8.

Also see Gen. 24; 25; 27; 29; 34; 37.

Exod. 20; 21.

Lev. 19.

Deut. 4–7; 10; 11; 13; 19; 23; 30; 33.

Josh. 22; 23.

Judg. 5; 16.

1 Sam. 1; 16; 18; 20.

2 Sam. 1; 12; 13.

1 Kings 3; 10; 11.

2 Chron. 2; 9; 11; 19; 26.

Neh. 1.

Esther 2.

Pss. 4; 5; 18; 26; 31; 40; 45; 47; 69; 70; 78; 91; 97; 109; 116; 119; 122; 145.

Prov. 1; 4; 5; 7–10; 15–18; 20; 27.

Eccles. 3; 9.

Song of Sol. 1–8.

Isa. 38; 43; 48; 56; 61; 63; 66.

Jer. 2; 5; 8; 14; 31.

Ezek. 16; 23; 33.

Dan. 1; 9.

Hos. 3; 4; 9; 11; 14.

Amos 5.

Mic. 3; 6.

Zeph. 3.

Zech. 8.

Mal. 1; 2.

Matt. 5; 6; 19; 22-24.

Mark 10; 12.

Luke 6; 7; 10; 11; 16; 20.

John 3; 5; 8; 10–17; 19–21.

Rom. 5; 8; 9; 12; 13; 15.

1 Cor. 2; 4; 8; 16.

2 Cor. 2; 5; 6; 8; 11–13.

Gal. 2; 5.

Eph. 1–6.

Phil. 1; 2.

Col. 1–3.

1 Thess. 1; 3–5.

2 Thess. 2; 3.

1 Tim. 1; 6.

2 Tim. 1; 4.

Titus 2; 3.

Philem. 5, 7, 9.

Heb. 1; 6; 10; 13

James 1; 2.

1 Pet. 1–3.

2 Pet. 2.
1 John 2–5.
2 John :1, 3, 5, 6.
3 John :1.
Jude :2, 21.
Rev. 1–3; 12.

Love feasts were held in connection with the Lord's Supper. 2 Pet. 2:13; Jude 12. Compare 1 Cor. 11:20-22.

Lov´er, in Scripture, often means an intimate friend. 1 Kings 5:1; Ps. 38:11.

Low´er parts of the earth, in Isa. 44:23, means valleys. In Ps. 63:9; Eph. 4:9 it means the abode of disembodied spirits secluded from view. In Ps. 139:15 it means the womb.

Lu´bim (*thirsty*), a people. 2 Chron. 12:3; 16:8. See LEHABIM and LIBYA.

Lu´cas. Philem. 24. See LUKE.

Lu´ci-fer (*light-giver*) is found in the Bible only in Isa. 14:12, where it is applied to the king of Babylon to denote his glory, like a morning star. Some suppose the passage refers to the fall of Satan.

Lucius, lu´shi-us. [1] A disciple and prophet or teacher, a native of Cyrene, whom Paul met at Antioch. Acts 13:1. [2] A disciple whom Paul calls his kinsman, and from whom he sends salutations to the brethren at Rome. Rom. 16:21. He may be same as No. 1.

Lu´cre, gain in money or goods; "filthy lucre," in 1 Tim. 3:3, 8; Titus 1:7, 11, means ill-gotten and base gain.

Lud, a son of Shem. Gen 10:22. The Lydians of Asia Minor are supposed to be descended from him.

Lu´dim, a son of Mizraim. Gen. 10:13; 1 Chron. 1:11. His posterity, called also Lydians, Jer. 46:9, probably settled in Africa.

Lu´hith (*made of boards*), a town of Moab. Isa. 15:5; Jer. 48:5.

Luke the Evangelist (Greek, *Lucas*), 2 Tim. 4:11; Philem. 24, was not of Jewish but of Gentile descent, and was by profession a physician. Col. 4:14. Tradition adds that he was also an artist, a painter. The date and place of his birth and death are not known. He was the true and trusted companion of Paul in his later journeys. He joined him at Troas on his second journey, Acts 16 10, and accompanied him to Philippi. Some years later he again met him at Troas, Acts 20:5, and remained with him until the close of his first Roman captivity. Acts 28:30. He was the author of the Gospel which bears his name, and of the Acts of the Apostles, both of which are addressed to one Theophilus, probably a Christian convert of distinguished character and position.

Luke, the Gospel of, was written from the oral traditions of eye-witnesses and earlier documents (Luke 1:1-4), which a liberal education enabled the author to use with discretion and discrimination. It was written for the Gentiles (as Matthew's Gospel was for the Jews), and corresponds to the teaching of Paul. It carries the genealogy of Christ back to Adam, and exhibits Christ as the Healer of all diseases and Saviour of all men. As a narrative it is more complete than any of the other Gospels, and, on account of its chronological notices, more firmly constructed. Chapters 1 and 2 and the whole section from chapter 9:51 to 18:4, including the account of the Nativity, the presentation in the Temple, the sending out of the Seventy, etc., and the parables of the Good Samaritan, the Lost Sheep, the Prodigal Son, etc., are peculiar to it. It was probably written at Cæsarea about A. D. 58–60. For the Acts of the Apostles, see ACTS. See GOSPELS, and GOSPELS, HARMONY OF.

Luke´warm, in Rev. 3:16, denotes indifferent persons who remain entirely unimpressed by the call from the Lord.

Lu´na-tic, in Matt. 4:24; 17:15, seems to mean epileptic.

Lust, in Exod. 15:9; 2 Tim. 4:3, means desire of any kind.

Lust´y, in Judg. 3:29, means vigorous.

Luz. [1] A city of the Canaanites which was afterward called Bethel. Gen. 28:19; Josh. 16:2. [2] A city of the Hittites. Judg. 1:26.

Lycaonia, lik-a-o´ni-ah, a province of Asia Minor, bounded south by Cilicia, north by Galatia, east by Cappadocia, west by Phrygia and Pisidia, was twice visited by Paul. Acts 14:1-23; 16:1-6. Its principal cities were Iconium, Derbe, and Lystra.

Lycia, lish´i-ah, a part of Asia Minor. It extended along the Mediterranean Sea, opposite the island of Rhodes and south-west of Pamphylia. Acts 27:5.

Lydda, lid´dah, a city in the territory of Dan, about ten miles east of Joppa. Acts 9:32, 35, 38. Lydda is the Greek name for the Hebrew LOD.

Lydia, lid´i-ah, a woman of Thyatira with whom Paul lodged when he was at Philippi. Acts 16:14, 40. She was baptized together with her household. Acts 16:15.

Lydia, lid´i-ah, a part of Asia Minor situated on the Mediterranean Sea, and extending from the mouth of the Hermas to the promontory of Mycale. Sardis, Thyatira, and Philadelphia were its principal cities.

Lyre, a kind of harp.

Ly-sa´ni-as, the tetrarch or governor of Abilene when John the Baptist began to preach. Luke 3:1.

Lysias, lish´i-as, a Roman officer in Jerusalem. See CLAUDIUS LYSIAS.

Lystra, lis´trah, a city of eastern Lycaonia, was twice visited by Paul, Acts 14 and 16, the first time with Barnabas, the second time with Silas. Timothy was probably born there. 2 Tim. 3:11.

M

Ma´a-cah (*oppression*), 2 Sam. 3:3, or **Maachah,** ma´a-kah, 1 Chron. 3:2, a wife of King David and the mother of Absalom.

Ma´a-cah, 2 Sam. 10:6, or **Maachah,** ma´a-kah, 1 Chron. 19:6, 7, a small district of Syria on the north-east of Palestine.

Maachah, ma´a-kah. [1] A daughter of Nahor, the brother of Abraham. Gen. 22:24. [2] The father of Achish, king of Gath. 1 Kings 2:39. He is called MAOCH in 1 Sam. 27:2. [3] The mother of King Abijah. 1 Kings 15:2; 2 Chron. 11:20. [4] The concubine of Caleb, the son of Hezron. 1 Chron. 2:48. [5] A Benjamitess who became the wife of Machir. 1 Chron. 7:15, 16. [6] The wife of Jehiel, the founder of Gibeon. 1 Chron. 8:29; 9:35. [7] The father of Hanan, who was one of David's warriors. 1 Chron. 11:43. [8] The father of Shephatiah, a ruler of the Simeonites. 1 Chron. 27:16.

Maachathi, ma-ak´a-thi, Deut. 3:14, or **Maachathites,** ma-ak´a-thites, the inhabitants of Maachah. Josh. 12:5; 13:11, 13.

Maadai, ma-ad´a (*the ornament of Jehovah*), a Jew of the family of Bani who had taken a foreign wife. Ezra 10:34.

Ma-a-di´ah, a priest who returned to Jerusalem with Zerubbabel. Neh. 12:5. Called MOADIAH in Neh. 12:17.

Ma-a´i (*compassionate*), a priest who

aided in the ceremonial of purifying the people after their return from Babylon. Neh. 12:36.

Ma-al´eh-a-crab´bim (*the ascent of scorpions*). Josh. 15:3. It is called elsewhere ACRABBIM and AKRABBIM.

Ma´a-rath (*open place*), a city in the mountainous district of Judah. Josh. 15:59.

Maaseiah, ma-a-se´yah (*the work of Jehovah*). [1, 2, 3] Three priests who had taken foreign wives. Ezra 10:18, 21, 22. [4] A descendant of Pahath-moab who took a foreign wife. Ezra 10:30. [5] The father of Azariah. Neh. 3:23. [6] A priest or Levite who assisted Ezra when he read the law to the people. Neh. 8:4. [7] A Levite who expounded the law to the people. Neh. 8:7. [8] A Jew whose descendants sealed the covenant made by Nehemiah. Neh. 10:25. [9, 10] Two Jews whose descendants lived in Jerusalem after the captivity. Neh. 11: 5, 7. [11, 12] Two priests who assisted in the ceremonial of purifying the wall of Jerusalem. Neh. 12:41, 42. [13] A priest, the father of Zephaniah. Jer. 21:1; 29:25. [14] The father of Zedekiah the false prophet. Jer. 29:21. [15] A Levite porter for the ark. 1 Chron. 15:18, 20. [16] A captain who assisted Jehoiada in making Joash king of Judah. 2 Chron. 23:1. [17] One of the principal officers under Uzziah, king of Judah. 2 Chron. 26:11. [18] A son of Ahaz, king of Judah. 2 Chron. 28:7. [19] The governor of Jerusalem in the time of King Josiah. 2 Chron. 34:8. [20] An officer of the Temple. Jer. 35:4.

Maaseiah, ma-a-se´yah, (*refuge of Jehovah*), the grandfather of Baruch. Jer. 32:12; 51:59.

Maasiai, ma-as´i-a (*work of Jehovah*), a descendant of Aaron through Immer. 1 Chron. 9:12.

Ma´ath (*small*), an ancestor of Joseph, the husband of Mary. Luke 3:26.

Ma´az (*anger*), a son of Ram. He was a descendant of Judah. 1 Chron. 2:27.

Ma-a-zi´ah (*Jehovah's consolation*). [1] The head of the twenty-fourth course of priests in the time of David. 1 Chron. 24:18. [2] A priest who sealed the covenant made by Nehemiah. Neh. 10:8.

Mac´ca-bees, the Family of the, properly called "Asmonæans" or "Hasmonæans," from Chasmon, the great-grandfather of Mattathias, of the sons of Jehoiarib. 1 Chron. 24:7. Judas, one of the sons of Mattathias, was surnamed Maccabæus, and became the leader in a general revolt against the despotism of Antiochus Epiphanes, who was king of Syria B. C. 175–154, plundered the Temple, and persecuted the Jews. Judas Maccabæus conquered Lysias, the Antiochian general, and the Jews re-entered Jerusalem, B. C. 165. Judas was killed in the battle of Eleasa, and the contest for independence was successfully continued by his brothers Jonathan and Simon until B. C. 135.

Mac-e-do´ni-a (*extended land*), an ancient kingdom of Europe north of Greece, and bounded east by Thrace, west by Illyricum, and north by the Balkan mountains, between it and Mœsia, became known in the history of the Jews through Alexander the Great. (See HEBREWS.) The great Macedonian empire was named from this small kingdom. In New Testament history it plays quite a conspicuous part, being the first European country which was visited by the apostles. Paul was there twice, Acts chapters 16 and 20, and perhaps a third time. Compare 1 Tim. 1:3; Phil. 2:24. Thessalonica and Philippi were two of its principal cities. In both of them Paul founded flourishing Christian churches, as his epistles to the Thessalonians and Philippians show.

Machbanai, mak´ba-nay (*thick*), a Gadite warrior. 1 Chron. 12:13.

Machbenah, mak´be-nah (*hillock*), a name in the genealogical list of Judah. 1 Chron. 2:49.

Machi, ma´ki (*decrease*), father of one of the men sent by Moses to spy out the land of Canaan. Num. 13:15.

Machir, ma´kir (*sold*). [1] A son of Manasseh and the father of Gilead. Gen. 50:23; 1 Chron. 7:14. [2] A son of Ammiel. 2 Sam. 9:4, 5; 17:27.

Machirites, ma´kir-ites, descendants of Machir, the son of Manasseh. Num. 26:29.

Machnadebai, mak-na-de´ba (*what like the liberal?*), a Jew who took a foreign wife. Ezra 10:40.

Machpelah, mak-pe´lah (*double cave*), the cave in Hebron which Abraham bought (including the field in which it was situated) for a burying-place for his family. See Gen. 23:16-20. The cave is positively known, and became the burial-place of Abraham and Sarah, Isaac and Rebekah, Jacob and Leah, and perhaps of Joseph. It is the oldest burial-place in the world. It is mentioned only in Genesis chapters 23, 25, 49, 50. It is now covered by a famous Mohammedan mosque.

Mad sometimes means insane, as in 1 Cor. 14:23, but generally denotes uncontrollable excitement. Harmless madmen in the East are revered and allowed to do as they please. Hence David was able to escape from Achish by pretended madness. 1 Sam. 21:13-15.
Also see Deut. 28:34.
2 Kings 9:11.
Ps. 102:8.
Prov. 26:18.

Eccles. 2:2; 7:7.
Isa. 44:25.
Jer. 25:16; 29:26; 50:38; 51:7.
Hos. 9:7.
John 10:20.
Acts 12:15; 26:11, 24, 25.

Mad´a-i (*middle land*), a son of Japheth. Gen. 10:2; 1 Chron. 1:5.

Made, in Luke 24:28, means appeared.

Ma´di-an, Acts 7:29, the country to which Moses fled. Same as MIDIAN (which see).

Mad-man´nah (*dunghill*), a town of Judah. Josh. 15:31. In 1 Chron. 2:49 Shaaph is called the father of Madmannah.

Mad´men (*dunghill*), a town of Moab whose destruction was foretold by Jeremiah. Jer. 48:2.

Mad-me´nah (*dunghill*), a town of Benjamin. Isa. 10:31.

Ma´don (*contention*), a royal city of the Canaanites. Josh. 11:1; 12:19.

Mag´bish (*gathering*) was probably the name of a place in Benhamin. Ezra. 2:30.

Mag´da-la (*tower*), a town of Galilee near the south end of the Sea of Galilee. It is mentioned only in Matt. 15:39.

Mag´da-la, Coasts of, on the Sea of Galilee. Matt. 15:39.

Mag-da-le´ne, a female native of Magdala, is a word used to denote a woman named Mary who was relieved of "seven devils" by Christ and became his devoted disciple. Luke 8:2, 3. See MARY, No. 5.

Mag´di-el (*the praise of God*), a chief of Edom descended from Esau. Gen. 36:43; 1 Chron. 1:54.

Magi, ma´ji, was the Chaldean name of the priests or wise men who in the ancient Eastern empires, Media, Persia, Babylonia, and Assyria, occupied the place next to the king. They were generally his advisers, but sometimes became his judges. In Persia the Magi were, as priests, the only ones allowed to perform the sacred religious rites, and, as scholars, were the only persons supposed to be able to explain the past and predict the future. The Jews, who had known them well since the days of the captivity, always spoke of them with respect. Dan. 1:20; 2:24; 5:11. The Magi or Wise Men who came to worship Christ at his birth, Matt. 2:1-14, may have received the first germs of the Messianic idea from Jews in exile. They were the forerunners of the heathen converts and gave rise to the legend of the three kings. See STAR OF THE WISE MEN.

Mag´ic, superstitious ceremonies practiced to hurt or to benefit mankind. The Hebrews were forbidden to consult magicians. Lev. 19:31; Deut. 18:9-14. Magicians are often mentioned in the Bible. Notice the case of Pharaoh. Exod. chapters 7, 8, and 9.

Ma-gi´cian, one who practiced magic. Gen. 41:8; Exod. 7:11.
Gen. 41:24.
Exod. 7:22; 8:7, 18, 19; 9:11.
Dan. 1:20; 2:2, 10, 27; 4:7, 9; 5:11.

Mag´is-trate, a word used to denote civil officers with legal authority, as in Ezra 7:25; Luke 12:11, and to signify Roman colonial officers. Acts 16:20, 22, 35, 36, 38.

Mag-nif´i-cal in 1 Chron. 22:5, means magnificent.

Ma´gog (*region of Gog*). [1] A son of Japheth. Gen. 10:2; 1 Chron. 1:5. [2] The word is used to denote the people descended from him. Ezek. 38:2; 39:6. [3] It is used prophetically to denote one of the parties in the last assault on the camp of the saints and the beloved city. Rev. 20:8.

Ma´gor-mis´sa-bib (*terror on every side*), the symbolical name which

Jeremiah gave to Pashur, the son of Immer. Jer. 20:3.

Mag´pi-ash (*moth-killer*), a Jew who sealed the covenant made by Nehemiah. Neh. 10:20.

Ma-ha´lah or **Ma´ha-lah** (*sickness*), a son of Hammoleketh, the sister of Gilead. 1 Chron. 7:18.

Ma-ha´la-le-el (*praise of God*). [1] The son of Cainan. Gen. 5:12; 1 Chron. 1:2. He is called MALELEEL in Luke 3:37. [2] An Israelite whose descendants lived in Jerusalem after the captivity. Neh. 11:4.

Ma´ha-lath (*stringed instrument*). [1] A daughter of Ishmael and a wife of Esau. Gen. 28:9. [2] A granddaughter of David and a wife of Rehoboam. 2 Chron. 11:18.

Ma´ha-lath, Ps. 53, and **Ma´ha-lath-le-an´noth,** Ps. 88, are found only in the titles of Pss. 53 and 88. The meanings of the words are not known

Ma´ha-li (*sick*), a son of Merari. Exod. 6:19. Same as MAHLI.

Ma-ha-na´im (*two camps*), the place where Jacob, when returning from Padan-aram, met the angels of God, and where he divided his company into two bands. It was afterward a Levitical city of Gad. Gen. 32:2; Josh. 13:26.

Ma´ha-neh-dan (*the camp of Dan*), a place in Judah, so called because the Danites encamped there. Judg. 18:12.

Ma-har´a-i (*impetuous*), one of David's valiant men. 2 Sam. 23:28; 1 Chron. 11:30; 27:13.

Ma´hath (*grasping*). [1] A descendant of Kohath, the son of Levi. 1 Chron. 6:35. [2] Another descendant of Kohath. 2 Chron. 29:12; 31:13.

Ma´ha-vite, a name applied to Eliel, one of David's warriors. 1 Chron. 11:46.

Ma-ha´zi-oth (*vision*), a son of

Heman. He was chief of a course of musicians. 1 Chron. 25:4, 30.

Ma'her-shal'al-hash'-baz (*hasting to the spoil*), a symbolical name applied to a son of Isaiah, Isa. 8:1, 3, in reference to the plunder of Damascus and Samaria by the Assyrian king.

Mah'lah (*disease*), a daughter of Zelophehad. Num. 26:33; Josh. 17:3.

Mah'li (*sickly*). [1] A son of Merari, the son of Levi. Num. 3:20; 1 Chron. 6:19. Called MAHALI in Exod. 6:19. [2] A son of Mushi, the son of Merari. 1 Chron. 6:47; 23:23.

Mah'lites, descendants of Mahli, the son of Merari. Num. 3:33; 26:58.

Mah'lon (*sickly*), a son of Elimelech and Naomi. Ruth 1:2, 5; 4:9, 10.

Ma'hol (*dance*), the father of Israelites famous in the time of Solomon for their wisdom. 1 Kings 4:31.

Mail, coat of, in 1 Sam. 17:5, means armor which covered the upper part of the body, that is, the breast and back.

Ma'kaz (*end*), a place where an officer of Solomon resided. Its situation is not known. 1 Kings 4:9.

Mak-he'loth (*place of assemblies*), the twenty-first station of the Israelites after they left Egypt. Num. 33:25, 26.

Mak-ke'dah (*place of shepherds*), one of the royal cities of the Canaanites. It was taken by Joshua, and was in the territory alloted to Judah. Josh. 10:10, 16, 17, 21, 28, 29.

Mak'tesh (*mortar*), a place in Jerusalem denounced in Zeph. 1:11.

Malachi, mal'a-ki (*messenger of Jehovah*), the last of the prophets of the Old Testament, lived after the captivity, later than Haggai and Zechariah, and after the completion of the Temple. He was probably a contemporary of Nehemiah, B. C. 433.

Malachi, the Book of, contains a prophecy of the coming of Messiah and the announcement that Elijah will return as his forerunner. It is called the "seal," because it is the last book of the Old Testament.

Malcham, mal'kam (*their king*). [1] A son of Shaharaim, a Benjamite. 1 Chron. 8:9. [2] An idol of the Ammonites and Moabites. Zeph. 1:5.

Malchiah, mal-ki'ah (*Jehovah's king*). [1] An ancestor of Asaph. 1 Chron. 6:40. [2, 3] Two Jews who had taken foreign wives. Ezra 10:25, 31. The last mentioned is probably same as MALCHIJAH in Neh. 3:11. [4, 5] Two Jews who repaired the wall of Jerusalem. Neh. 3:14, 31. [6] A priest who stood beside Ezra while he read the law to the people. Neh. 8:4. [7] A priest who was the father of Pashur. Neh. 11:12. [8] An officer into whose dry cistern the prophet Jeremiah was thrown. Jer. 38:6. Dry cisterns were used as dungeons in Palestine.

Malchiel, mal'ki-el (*God's king*), a son of Beriah, the son of Asher. Gen. 46:17; Num. 26:45.

Malchielites, mal'ki-el-ites, descendants of Malchiel. Num. 26:45.

Malchijah, mal-ki'jah (*Jehovah's king*). [1] 1 Chron. 9:12. The same as MALCHIAH, No. 7. [2] Chief of fifth course of priests in the time of David. 1 Chron. 24:9. [3] A Jew who took a foreign wife. Ezra 10:25. [4] A Jew who aided in repairing the walls of Jerusalem. Neh. 3:11. [5] A Jew who aided in the dedication of the walls of Jerusalem. Neh. 12:42.

Malchiram, mal-ki'ram (*king of altitude*), a descendant of Jehoiachin, king of Judah. 1 Chron. 3:18.

Malchishua, mal-ki-shu'ah (*king of help*), 1 Chron. 8:33; 9:39, or **Melchishua,** mel-ki-shu'ah, 1 Sam. 14:49; 31:2, a son of King Saul.

Malchus, mal´kus (*reigning*), the high-priest's servant, whose ear Peter cut off when Jesus was apprehended. John 18:10.

Ma-le´le-el, Luke 3:37. Same as MAHALALEEL, No. 1 (which see).

Mal´lo-thi (*my fulness*), a son of Heman engaged in the service of song. 1 Chron. 25:4, 26.

Mal´lows, a vegetable, several species of which grow in Palestine and are used as pot-herbs by the poor. Job 30:4.

Malluch, mal´luk (*reigning*). [1] A Levite of the family of Merari. 1 Chron. 6:44. [2, 3] Two Jews who had taken foreign wives. Ezra 10:29, 32. [4] A priest who returned with Zerubbabel, Neh. 12:2, and sealed the covenant made by Nehemiah. Neh. 10:4.

Mam´mon, a word signifying riches, employed by Christ to indicate worldly goods or the desire for them. Matt. 6:24; Luke 16:9, 11, 13.

Mam´re (*strength*), a chief of the Amorites. Gen. 14:13, 24.

Mam´re, a place near Hebron, named after an Amorite chief. Gen. 14:13, 24. Also the name of a plain and a grove near which Abraham dwelt and where he entertained three angels. Gen. 13:18; 18:1.

Man, a word used in the declaration of God's purpose to create a human being. It is also frequently employed as the name of the first man (Adam), and is used to denote mankind in a general sense. Gen. 1:26, 27; 2:5, 7.
Also see Gen. 1–7; 9; 13; 16–20; 24–27; 29–32; 34; 37–45; 47; 49.
Exod. 1; 2; 7–13; 15; 16; 19; 21–25; 30; 32–36; 38.
Lev. 1; 5; 6; 7; 12–22; 24; 25; 27.
Num. 1–3; 5–9; 11–19; 21; 23–27; 30–32; 35; 36.

Deut. 1; 3–5; 7; 8; 11; 12; 15–17; 19–25; 27–29; 32–34.
Josh. 1–8; 10; 11; 14;17; 21–24.
Judg. 1–11; 13; 16–21.
Ruth 1–4.
1 Sam. 1; 2; 4; 8–11; 13–18; 20; 21; 24–28; 30.
2 Sam. 1–3; 7; 12–24.
1 Kings 1; 2; 4; 7–14; 17; 20; 22.
2 Kings 1; 3–15; 18; 21–23.
1 Chron. 11; 12; 16; 17; 20–23; 27–29.
2 Chron. 2; 6–11; 14; 15; 17–20; 23; 25; 28; 30–32; 34; 36.
Ezra 3; 8.
Neh. 1; 2; 5–9; 12.
Esther 1; 4–6; 8; 9.
Job 1–5; 7–17; 20–22; 24; 25; 27; 28; 32–38; 40; 42.
Pss. 1; 5; 8–10; 18; 19; 22; 25; 31–34; 36–40; 43; 49;52; 55; 56; 58; 60; 62; 65; 71; 74; 76; 78; 80; 84; 87–90; 92; 94; 103–105; 107–109; 112; 118; 119; 127; 128; 135; 140; 142–144; 146; 147.
Prov. 1–3; 5–30.
Eccles. 1–12.
Song of Sol. 3; 8.
Isa. 2–7; 9; 10; 13; 14; 17; 19; 24; 29; 31–33; 35; 36; 38; 41; 42; 44–47; 49–53; 55–60; 62; 65; 66.
Jer. 2–5; 7–18; 20–23; 26; 27; 29–38; 40; 41; 44; 46; 49–51
Lam. 3, 4.
Ezek. 1–18; 20–41; 43; 44; 46; 47.
Dan. 2; 3; 5–10; 12.
Hos. 3; 4; 6; 9; 11.
Amos 2; 4; 5.
Jon. 1; 3.
Mic. 2; 4–7.
Nah. 3.
Hab. 1; 2.
Zeph. 1; 3.
Hag. 1

Zech. 1–4; 6–10; 12; 13.
Mal. 2; 3.
Matt. 1; 4–13; 15–27.
Mark 1–16.
Luke 1–24.
John 1–16; 18; 19; 21.
Acts 1–14; 16–26; 28.
Rom. 1–10; 12–14.
1 Cor. 2–16.
2 Cor. 2; 4; 5; 7–12.
Gal. 1–3; 5; 6.
Eph. 2–6.
Phil. 2; 3.
Col. 1–4.
1 Thess. 3–5.
2 Thess. 2; 3.
1 Tim. 1–6.
2 Tim. 2–4.
Titus 2; 3.
Heb. 2–5; 7; 8; 10; 12; 13.
James 1–3; 5.
1 Pet. 1–4.
2 Pet. 1; 2.
1 John 2–5.
Rev. 1–7; 9; 11-16; 18–22.

Man´a-en (*consoler*), a teacher of the church at Antioch. Acts 13:1.

Man´a-hath (*rest*). [1] A descendant of Seir. Gen. 36:23; 1 Chron. 1:40. [2] A place in the territory of Benjamin. 1 Chron. 8:6.

Ma-nah´eth-ites, the name of a people composed of the descendants of Shobal and of his brother Salma. 1 Chron. 2:52, 54.

Ma-nas´seh (*forgetting*). [1] Joseph's first-born son. Gen. 41:51; 46:20; Num. 26:28, 29. [2] A king of Judah. 2 Kings 20:21; 1 Chron. 3:13; 2 Chron. 32:33. He was the son and successor of King Hezekiah, and became king B. C. 696, when twelve years old. He was taken captive by an Assyrian king and carried to Babylon, but was allowed to return to Jerusalem. He died B. C. 641. He is called MANASSES in Matt. 1:10. [3] A Levite whose grandson Jonathan became an idolatrous priest of the tribe of Dan. Judg. 18:30. [4] A Jew who married a foreign wife. Ezra 10:30. [5] Another Jew who marked a foreign wife. Ezra 10:33.
Also see Gen. 48:1, 5, 13, 14, 17, 20; 50:23.
Num. 1:10, 34, 35; 2:20; 7:54; 10:23; 13:11; 26:34; 27:1; 32:33, 39-41; 34:14, 23; 36:1, 12.
Deut. 3:13, 14; 29:8; 33:17; 34:2.
Josh. 1:12; 4:12; 12:6; 13:7, 29, 31; 14:4; 16:4, 9; 17:1-3, 5-12, 17; 18:7; 20:8; 21:5, 6, 25, 27; 22:1, 7, 9, 13, 21, 20, 31.
Judg. 1:27; 6:15, 35; 7:23; 11:29.
1 Kings 4:13.
2 Kings 21:1, 9, 11, 16-18, 20; 23:12, 26; 24:3.
1 Chron. 5:18, 23, 26; 6:61, 62, 70, 71; 7:14, 17, 29; 9:3; 12:19, 20, 31, 37; 26:32; 27:20, 21.
2 Chron. 15:9; 30:1, 10, 11, 18; 31:1; 33:1, 9-11, 13, 18, 20, 22, 23; 34:6, 9.
Pss. 60:7; 80:2; 108:8.
Isa. 9:21.
Jer. 15:4.
Ezek. 48:4, 5.

Ma-nas´seh. The name is often applied to the tribe descended from Manasseh, the son of Joseph. Num. 1:10, 34; Deut. 3:13. Their territory was divided into two portions, one lying east of the river Jordan and the other west of it. The latter is frequently joined with the territory of Ephraim in Biblical references.

Ma-nas´ses, king of Judah. Matt. 1:10. Same as MANASSEH, No. 2 (which see). Also a tribe of Israel. Rev. 7:6.

Ma-nas´sites, The, descendants of Manasseh, the son of Joseph. Deut. 4:43;

Judg. 12:4; 2 Kings 10:33.

Man´drake (*love-plant*), a plant with a root like a beet and a sweet fruit about the size of a large plum. The smell of the plant is enjoyed by the people of the East, Song of Sol. 7:13, and it is still believed in Eastern countries, as it was in Rachel's time, that eating its fruit will render barren women fruitful. Gen. 30:14–16.

Ma´neh, Ezek. 45:12, a Hebrew weight of one hundred shekels, equal to about three pounds. See WEIGHTS.

Man´ger, crib or feeding-trough, Luke 2:7, 12, 16, in which the infant Saviour was laid. See INN.

Man´na (*what is this?*), miraculous food which God gave to the Israelites during their wanderings in the wilderness. Its history and nature are fully described in Exodus, chapter 16. It was called *bread from heaven,* and was furnished daily for forty years. Deut. 29:5, 6. A different substance called "manna" drops from various trees, principally the tamarisk, in the valleys around Sinai. The manna now used as a medicine is the dried juice of the manna ash found in southern Europe. Also see Num. 11:6, 7, 9.
Deut. 8:3, 16.
Josh. 5:12.
Neh. 9:20.
Ps. 78:24.
John 6:31, 49, 58.
Heb. 9:4.
Rev. 2:17.

Ma-no´ah (*rest*), an Israelite of the tribe of Dan. He was the father of Samson. Judg. 13:2, 8, 9.

Man´sions, in John 14:2, means rooms, resting-places, or dwelling-places.

Man´slay-er, Num. 35:6, 12, one who had killed another; could flee to a city of refuge. See CITIES OF REFUGE.

Man´tle is the translation of four Hebrew words, and means, in Judg. 4:18, a coarse cloth used for making beds in tents; in 1 Sam. 15:27, a garment like the official priestly robe; in Isa. 3:22, a lady's wrapper with sleeves; and in 1 Kings 19:13, 19; 2 Kings 2:8, 13, 14, the principal garment of the prophet Elijah.

Maoch, ma´ok (*breast-band?*), the father of Achish, king of Gath. 1 Sam. 27:2.

Ma´on (*habitation*), a descendant of Caleb, the son of Hezron. 1 Chron. 2:45.

Ma´on, a city of Judah. Josh. 15:55; 1 Sam. 25:2.

Ma´on-ites, a people mentioned in Judg. 10:12.

Mar, in Ruth 4:6, means injure or despoil.

Ma´ra (*bitter*), the name which Naomi, in reference to her misfortunes, Ruth 1:20, said was more appropriate to her than her own (which signified *my delight*).

Ma´rah (*bitterness*), the first station of the Israelites after they left Egypt. Exod. 15:23; Num. 33:8. They found there a spring of bitter water, which was afterward miraculously sweetened. Exod. 15:23-35.

Mar´a-lah (*trembling*), a place in the boundary of Zebulun. Josh. 19:11.

Mar-a-nath´a, a Syriac or an Aramaic expression, meaning "the Lord cometh." 1 Cor. 16:22.

Mar´ble is mentioned in 1 Chron. 29:2; Esther 1:6; Song of Sol. 5:15; Rev. 18:12. The word "marble" is used sometimes to denote almost any kind of shining stone.

Mar´cus, Col. 4:10. See MARK.

Ma-re´shah (*possession*), a descendant of Caleb, the son of Hezron. 1 Chron. 2:42.

Ma-re´shah (*top of a hill*), a fortified city of Judah. Josh. 15:44. 2 Chron. 11:8.

Ma´rish-es, Ezek. 47:11. means marshes.

Mark, or **John Mark,** as he is also

called, Acts 12:12; 15:37, was a Jew, probably a native of Jerusalem, where his mother, Mary, resided. He was a cousin of Barnabas, Col. 4:10, and closely connected with Peter, who calls him his (spiritual) son. 1 Pet. 5:13. Mark accompanied Paul and Barnabas on their first missionary journey, but left them at Perga. Acts 13:13. Afterward, however, he was again with Paul in Rome. Col. 4:10; Philem. 24. Ancient writers call him "the interpreter of Peter," and his gospel "the Gospel of Peter." He is called Marcus in Col. 4:10.

Mark, the Gos´pel of, has something in its general character and in its details which seems to show that it in some manner came from the lips of Peter. It describes the power of Christ's ministry and the impression it produced on the people with striking rapidity and energy, and with many pictorial details which have been traced to the preaching of Peter. See Gospels, and Gospels, Harmony of.

Mar´ket or **Mar´ket-place** in Hebrew cities was usually just within the gate, and was the principal place for trade. Laborers also came to it to find employment. Ezek. 27:13, 17, 19, 25; Matt. 23:7; Mark 12:38; Luke 11:43.

Ma´roth (*bitterness*), a place in Judah. Mic. 1:12.

Mar´riage was instituted in Paradise, Gen. 2:18-25, and was confirmed by Christ. Matt. 19:5, 6; Mark 10:5-10. He was present at the marriage feast in Cana. John 2:1. In the time of Christ weddings were often celebrated with great feasting and rejoicing. When the marriage feast was to take place the bridegroom went to the house of the bride with his friends, called "the children of the bridechamber" in Matt. 9:15. A great procession was formed, which with torches and lamps

accompanied the bride to the house of the bridegroom. Matt. 25:1-10. There is no instance of polygamy after the captivity on record in the Old Testament. Also see Gen. 34:9.
Exod. 21:10.
Deut. 7:3.
Josh. 23:12.
Ps. 78:63.
Matt. 22:2, 4, 9, 30; 24:38.
Mark 12:25.
Luke 17:27; 20:34, 35.
John 2:2.
1 Cor. 7:38.
Heb. 13:4.
Rev. 19:7, 9.

Mars' Hill is in the city of Athens in Greece. Paul addressed the "men of Athens" from it. Acts 17:22-31. See Areopagus, No. 1.

Mar´se-na (*worthy*), one of the seven princes of Persia and Media in the time of Ahasuerus. Esther 1:14.

Mar´tha, the sister of Mary and Lazarus. Luke 10:38, 40, 41; John 11:1, 5. She and her sister Mary were devoted friends and disciples of Christ and were much beloved by him. She was a good housekeeper, and represents the practical life, while Mary was contemplative.

Mar´tyr. This word is found in the Bible only in Acts 22:20, where mention is made of Stephen, and in Rev. 2:13; 17:6.

Ma´ry. This name corresponds to the Old Testament name Miriam.

[1] Mary, the mother of Jesus, Acts 1:14; Matt. 1:16-25; 2:11-23; Mark 6:3; Luke 1:26-56; 2:4-51. She was, by marriage, connected with Elisabeth, the mother of John the Baptist, and was at the marriage in Cana of Galilee, John 2:3; is mentioned in Matt. 12:46; Mark 3:31-35; Luke 8:19; and was present at the cruci-

fixion of Christ, John 19:25-27, where she was commended to the care of the beloved John. She was one of the praying company in the upper room at Jerusalem, Acts 1:14, after the ascension of Christ. According to tradition, she died in Jerusalem after A. D. 50. As the mother of our Lord, she will always be "blessed among women," as Elizabeth greeted her. Luke 1:42.

[2] MARY, the wife of Cleophas. John 19:25. She was present at the crucifixion and the burial of Christ, Matt. 27: 56, 61; went with others to anoint him, Mark 16:1-10; received the news of his resurrection, Luke 24:6, 10; met and worshipped him. Matt. 28:1, 9.

[3] MARY, the mother of John Mark, Acts 12:12, and aunt of Barnabas. Col. 4:10. She was a pious woman, and lived in Jerusalem. The disciples met at her house on the night when Peter was miraculously delivered from prison. Acts 12:7-12.

[4] MARY, the sister of Lazarus and Martha. Luke 10:39. She was a devoted disciple and friend of Christ, and heard from him the words, "Mary hath chosen that good part, which shall not be taken away from her." Luke 10:42. See also John 11:1; 12:3.

[5] MARY MAGDALENE, Matt. 27:56, a woman of Magdala in Galilee. She was relieved of "seven devils" (demons) by Christ, and followed him. Luke 8:2, 3. She was a woman of good character, and was prominent among those who ministered to Christ and his disciples. She was present at the crucifixion of Christ, John 19:25; was at his burial, Mark 15:47; was with those who went to anoint him, Mark 16:1; and was the first to whom Christ appeared after his resurrection. Mark 16:9. See also John 20:11-18. The popular belief

that Mary Magdalene was a woman of unchaste character rests merely on tradition, which identifies her with the unnamed, "woman that was a sinner" and that kissed the Saviour's feet. Luke 7:37.

[6] MARY, a disciple at Rome to whom Paul sends salutation. Rom. 16:6.

Maschil, mas'kil, a word in the title of many Psalms, among which are Pss. 32 and 42, is supposed by some to refer to the melody used in singing them.

Mash, Gen. 10:23, or **Meshech,** me'shek, 1 Chron. 1:17, a son of Aram, the son of Shem.

Ma'shal (*entreaty*), a city of Asher assigned to the Levites. 1 Chron. 6:74.

Ma'son-ry. The Hebrews doubtless learned this trade in Egypt. Exod. 1:11, 14. Phœnicians were also employed in masonry by Solomon. 1 Kings 5:17, 18. Plastering with mortar was used for common buildings. Lev. 14:40-42; Matt. 23:27.

Mas're-ka (*vineyard of noble vines*), probably a city in Idumæa. Gen. 36:36; 1 Chron. 1:47.

Mas'sa (*gift*), a son of Ishmael. Gen. 25:14; 1 Chron. 1:30.

Mas'sah (*temptation*). a place where the Israelites murmured against Moses for want of water. Exod. 17:7; Deut. 6:16. It is called MERIBAH in same verse.

Mas'ter, a word which often means "teacher." Luke 6:40; John 3:10, and hence is often applied to Christ. Matt. 22:16, 24, etc. The word is used also to denote ownership, as a term of respect to superiors, etc.

Ma-thu'sa-la, Luke 3:37, is another form of METHUSELAH (which see).

Ma'tred (*propelling*), the mother of Mehetabel, who was wife of a king of Edom. Gen. 36:39; 1 Chron. 1:50.

Ma´tri (*rain of Jehovah*), the head of a family of Benjamin from which King Saul descended. 1 Sam. 10:21.

Mat´tan (*a gift*). [1] A priest of Baal. He was slain before his altar. 2 Kings 11:18; 2 Chron. 23:17. [2] The father of Shephatiah. Jer. 38:1.

Mat´ta-nah (*gift*), a station of the Israelites. It was between the desert and Moab. Num. 21:18, 19.

Mat-ta-ni´ah (*gift of Jehovah*). [1] The original name of a son of Josiah. Nebuchad-nezzar made him king of Judah, 2 Kings 24:17, and changed his name to ZEDEKIAH (which see). [2] A Levite singer. 1 Chron. 9:15. [3] A Levite who was chief of the ninth division of singers. 1 Chron. 25:4, 16. [4] A descendant of Asaph and an ancestor of Jahaziel. 2 Chron. 20:14. [5] A descendant of Asaph who assisted in purifying the temple. 2 Chron. 29:13. [6] An ancestor of Hanan. Neh. 13:13. [7, 8, 9, 10] Four Jews who had taken foreign wives. Ezra 10:26, 27, 30, 37.

Mat´ta-tha (*gift of Jehovah*), a grandson of David and an ancestor of Joseph, the husband of Mary. Luke 3:31.

Mat´ta-thah (*gift of Jehovah*), a Jew who took a foreign wife. Ezra 10:33.

Mat-ta-thi´as. [1, 2] Two ancestors of Joseph, the husband of Mary. Luke 3:25, 26. [3] The head of the family of the Maccabees. See MACCABEES, THE FAMILY OF.

Mat-te-na´i (*gift of Jehovah*). [1, 2] Two Jews who took foreign wives. Ezra 10:33, 37. [3] A priest of the family of Joiarib. Neh. 12:19.

Mat´than, an ancestor of Joseph, the husband of Mary. Matt. 1:15.

Mat´that (*gift of God*), two ancestors of Joseph, the husband of Mary. Luke 3:24, 29.

Mat´thew (*gift of God*) was a Jew by birth and was the son of Alphæus. His original name, before he was converted and called to the apostleship, was LEVI, Mark 2:14; Luke 5:27, and he was a publican, or collector of taxes and customs on persons and goods crossing the Sea of Galilee, at Capernaum, on the route between Damascus and the Phœnician seaports. He was present in the upper room at Jerusalem after the ascension of Christ, Acts 1:13, and tradition tells us that he suffered martyrdom in Ethiopia.

Mat´thew, the Gos´pel of, occupies, very appropriately, the first place in the New Testament Canon. Matthew wrote first a Gospel in Hebrew (Aramaic) for Jewish readers, which consisted chiefly of discourses of the Saviour, but which has been lost. The Greek Gospel of Matthew, as we have it, is not a translation, but an original work on a larger scale. It represents Christ as the Messiah and King of Israel, and constantly points to the fulfilment of prophecy. Its arrangement is according to topics, and groups together the discourses, parables, and miracles. It gives us the fullest record of the Sermon on the Mount (chapters 5 to 7), the parables (chapter 13), the prophecies of the destruction of Jerusalem and the end of the world (chapters 24 and 25). The style is simple, dignified, and majestic. It was written while Jerusalem, which is called "the holy city," "the city of the Great King," was still standing, between A. D. 60 and 70. The destruction of Jerusalem is foretold as an impending event, without any hint of the fulfilment of the prophecy. See GOSPELS, and GOSPELS, HARMONY OF.

Matthias, math-thi´as (*gift of Jehovah*), a disciple who was chosen by lot to take the place of Judas Iscariot among the apostles. Acts 1:23, 26.

Mat-ti-thi´ah (*gift of Jehovah*). [1] A Levite of the family of Korah. 1 Chron. 9:31. [2] A Levite in the musical service of the Tabernacle. 1 Chron. 15:18, 21; 16:5. [3] A Jew who took a foreign wife. Ezra 10:43. [4] A priest who stood by Ezra when he read the book of the law to the people. Neh. 8:4.

Mat´tock, an agricultural implement for loosening the ground. Isa. 7:25. It resembles a heavy hoe.

Maul, in Prov. 25:18, means a heavy club or hammer used in war.

Mauz´zim (*fortresses*) is found in the margin of Dan. 11:38. Its meaning is doubtful.

Maw, in Deut. 18:3, means the stomach of an animal that chews the cud.

Maz´za-roth, Job 38:32, means the twelve signs of the Zodiac.

Mead´ow, in Gen. 41:2, is the translation of a word meaning rushes or water-plants generally. In Judg. 20:33 the word "meadows" probably means caves.

Me´ah (*a hundred*), a tower in Jerusalem. Neh. 3:1; 12:39.

Me-a´rah (*a cave*), Josh. 13:4, is called "the cave" in the marginal notes. It is in the north part of Canaan.

Mean, in Prov. 22:29; Isa. 2:9; Acts 21:39, means obscure or lowly, but not base.

Meas´ure. This word is used as the translation of Hebrew and Greek words denoting different capacities. The exact measure referred to is often mentioned in the marginal notes. As indicating a certain quantity in the household, the measure contained about a peck and a half. Gen. 18:6; Matt. 13:33; Luke 13:21.

Meas´ures. No specimens of the Hebrew system of measures survive, and we cannot hope to reconstruct it. We know, however, that their measures of length were nearly all borrowed from the human body. It should be borne in mind that the following lengths and capacities are only approximately correct.

Measures of Length.

A finger was about three-fourths of an inch.

A hand-breadth (four fingers) was about three inches.

A span (three hand-breadths) was about nine inches.

A cubit (two spans) was about eighteen inches.

A fathom was a little over six feet.

A reed was about one hundred and twenty feet.

A furlong was about six hundred feet.

A mile (Roman), about four thousand eight hundred feet, was over nine-tenths of an English mile. Another Eastern mile was about one-fifth longer than an English mile.

A day's journey was about twenty-five or thirty miles.

A Sabbath day's journey was nearly one mile.

Measures of Quantity.

A log was about two-thirds of a pint.

A cab was abut three pints.

An omer (ten ephahs) was nearly five pints.

A hin (twelve logs) was a little over a gallon.

A bushel, the Greek *modius,* was about a peck.

The measure, equal to about a peck and a half (see MEASURE, above), is the translation of the Hebrew *seah.*

An ephah or bath was about seven gallons.

A firkin was between nine and ten gallons.

A lethech was about four bushels.

A homer or cor was about eight bushels.

Meat, when mentioned in the Bible, rarely means flesh. The word is used to denote any other kind of food. It is first mentioned in Gen. 1:29. The "meat-offering" was always a vegetable offering, a cake made of flour and oil. Lev. 2:1.

Also see Gen. 1; 9; 27; 45.

Exod. 29; 30; 40.

Lev. 2; 5–7; 9–11; 14; 22–25.

Num. 4; 6–8; 15; 18; 28; 29.

Deut. 2; 20; 28.

Josh. 22.

Judg. 1; 13; 14.

1 Sam. 20.

2 Sam. 3; 11–13.

1 Kings 8; 10; 19.

2 Kings 3; 16.

1 Chron. 12; 21; 23.

2 Chron. 7; 9.

Ezra 3; 7.

Neh. 10; 13.

Job 6; 12; 20; 30; 33; 34; 36; 38.

Pss. 42; 44; 59; 69; 74; 78; 79; 104; 107; 111; 145.

Prov. 6; 23; 30; 31.

Isa. 57; 62; 65.

Jer. 7; 16; 17; 19; 33; 34.

Lam. 1; 4.

Ezek. 4; 16; 29; 34; 42; 44–47.

Dan. 1; 4; 11.

Hos. 11.

Joel 1; 2.

Amos 5.

Hab. 1; 3.

Hag. 2.

Mal. 1; 3.

Matt. 3; 6; 9; 10; 14; 15; 24–26.

Mark 2; 7; 8; 14; 16.

Luke 3; 7–9; 11; 12; 14; 17; 22; 24.

John 4; 6; 21.

Acts 2; 9; 15; 16; 27.

Rom. 14.

1 Cor. 3; 6; 8; 10.

Col. 2.

1 Tim. 4.

Heb. 5; 9; 12; 13.

Mebunnai, me-bun´nay (*building of Jehovah*), one of David's valiant men. 2 Sam. 23:27. He is called SIBBECHAI in 2 Sam. 21:18; 1 Chron. 20:4, and SIB-BECAI in 1 Chron. 11:29; 27:11.

Mecherathite, mek´e-rath-ite, a name applied to one of David's warriors. 1 Chron. 11:36. He is also called the MAACHATHITE.

Me´dad (*love*), an elder of Israel who prophesied in the camp. Num. 11:26, 27.

Me´dan (*contention*), a son of Abraham by Keturah. Gen. 25:2; 1 Chron. 1:32.

Medeba, me´de-bah (*waters of quiet*), a city of Moab. Num. 21:30; Isa. 15:2. It was taken by the Israelites and allotted to Reuben. Josh. 13:16.

Medes, 2 Kings 17:6; Acts 2:9, the inhabitants of MEDIA (which see).

Media, me´di-ah (*middle land*), Esther 1:3; Isa. 21:2, was bounded north by the Caspian Sea, east by Parthia, south by Persia, and west by Assyria. For a long time it seems to have been a dependent of Assyria, but in B. C. 633 it became an independent kingdom under Cyaxares, who conquered Assyria and destroyed Nineveh. In B. C. 558 Media was united to Persia under Cyrus—the "Medes and Persians" of Dan. 5:28; 6:8, etc.—and from that time it shared the destinies of that empire. The Medes are mentioned in connection with the Parthians. Acts 2:9.

Me´di-an, a native of Media. Dan. 5:31.

Me´di-a-tor, one that interposes between persons who are at variance for the purpose of reconciling them. It is a title of Christ, 1 Tim. 2:5; Heb. 12:24, who is the only mediator between God and man.

Med´i-cine. The medical skill of the Egyptians was widely celebrated. Medicine is mentioned in Prov. 17:22; Jer. 30:13; 46:11; Ezek. 47:12. Luke was a physician.

Meek´ness is a Christian grace, and means humble serenity of spirit and submission to the divine will. Eph. 4:2; 1 Tim. 6:11.
Also see Ps. 45:4.
Zeph. 2:3.
1 Cor. 4:21.
2 Cor. 10:1.
Gal. 5:23; 6:1.
Col. 3:12.
2 Tim. 2:25.
Titus 3:2.
James 1:21; 3:13.
1 Pet. 3:15.

Meet, in Exod. 8:26; Matt. 3:8; Heb. 6:7, means fit; suitable; worthy.

Me-gid´do (*place of troops?*), a royal city of the Canaanites, whose king was conquered by Joshua. Josh. 12:21. It was afterward a city of Manasseh in the borders of Issachar, and was on the southwest border of the plain of Esdraelon, which includes the valley of Jezreel. King Josiah was defeated and mortally wounded there by Pharoah-necho. 2 Kings 23:29.

Me-het´a-beel (*whom God does good to*), the father of Delaiah. Neh. 6:10.

Me-het´a-bel, wife of Hadar, a king of Edom. Gen. 36:39; 1 Chron. 1:50.

Me-hi´da (*famous*), one of the Nethinims whose descendants returned with Zerubbabel. Ezra 2:52; Neh. 7:54.

Me´hir (*price*), a descendant of Judah. 1 Chron. 4:11.

Me-hol´ath-ite, a native of Abel-meholah. 1 Sam. 18:19; 2 Sam. 21:8.

Me-hu´ja-el (*smitten of God*), a son of

Irad. Gen. 4:18.

Me-hu´man (*faithful*), one of the seven chamberlains of Ahasuerus. Esther 1:10.

Me-hu´nim (*habitations*), Ezra 2:50, a family of Nethinims that returned with Zerubbabel. 2 Chron. 26:7 may refer to same.

Me-jar´kon (*waters of yellowness*), a town of Dan. Josh. 19:46.

Mek´o-nah (*standing-place*), a town of Judah. Neh. 11:28.

Mel-a-ti´ah (*delivered by Jehovah*), a Gibeonite who repaired part of the wall of Jerusalem. Neh. 3:7.

Melchi, mel´ki (*Jehovah's king*), two ancestors of Joseph, the husband of Mary. Luke 3:24, 28.

Melchiah, mel-ki´ah. See MALCHIAH.

Melchishua, mel-ki-shu´ah, a son of King Saul. See MALCHISHUA.

Melchizedek, mel-kiz´e-dek, or **Melchisedec,** mel-kiz´e-dek, the New Testament form of the name (*king of righteousness*), is mentioned three times in the Bible: first in Gen. 14:18-20, where, as king of Salem and priest of the Most High God, he meets Abram in the valley of Shaveh, blesses him, and receives tithes from him; next in Ps. 110:4, where Messiah is described as a priest "after the order of Melchizedek;" and finally in Heb. 5:6, 7, where an analogy is drawn between him and Christ.

Melea, me´le-ah (*fulness?*), an ancestor of Joseph, the husband of Mary. Luke 3:31.

Melech, me´lek (*king*), a son of Micah, a descendant of King Saul. 1 Chron. 8:35; 9:41.

Mel´i-cu. a priest. Neh. 12:14. See MALLUCH, No. 4.

Melita, mel´i-tah (*honey*), now MALTA, is an island in the Mediterranean, seventeen miles long and nine miles broad, situated sixty-two miles south of Sicily, and is an English possession. The bay where Paul was shipwrecked on his voyage to Rome, Acts 27:1–44, is still called St. Paul's Bay.

Mel´ons of many kinds are common in the East and grow luxuriantly in Egypt. The Hebrews remembered and longed for them in the desert. Num. 11:5. Melons are abundant in Palestine, especially the watermelon, which grows to a very large size.

Mel´zar, probably a word of Persian origin, was the title of an officer at the court of Nebuchadnezzar, and corresponded to the English words "steward" and "tutor." Dan. 1:11, 16.

Me-mo´ri-al, in Esther 9:28; Ps. 9:6, means remembrance.

Mem´phis, Hos. 9:6, a chief city of ancient Egypt. Its ruins are on the west bank of the river Nile, about ten miles south of Cairo. It was founded by Menes, the first king of Egypt, contained the temples of Apis, Isis, and Serapis, and was the capital of that country for many centuries. It is mentioned under the name of NOPH in Isa. 19:13; Jer. 2:16; 44:1; 46:14, 19; Ezek. 30:13, 16. Its overthrow was predicted by Isaiah and Jeremiah B. C. about 600. Its ruins were used in building Cairo, the capital of modern Egypt, about A. D. 630.

Me-mu´can, one of the seven princes of Persia and Media in the court of Ahasuerus. Esther 1:14, 16, 21.

Men´a-hem (*consoler*), an Israelite who rebelled against Shallum, king of Israel, killed him, and reigned in his stead. 2 Kings 15:14-20.

Me´nan, an ancestor of Joseph, the husband of Mary. Luke 3:31.

Me´ne, Me´ne, Te´kel, U-phar´sin, Dan. 5:25, a Chaldee sentence miracu-

lously traced on the wall at the impious feast of Belshazzar, Dan. 5:1-5, and signifying his impending doom. Mene means "he is numbered;" Tekel, "he is weighed;" Upharsin. "they are divided."

Me´ni (*fortune*), in the marginal notes, Isa. 65:11, denotes an idol which the Jews worshipped in Babylon.

Men of war, in Luke 23:11, mean soldiers.

Menuchah, me-nu´kah (*rest*), in the marginal notes, Judg. 20:43, is supposed by some to be a place, and the same as MANAHATH.

Menuchites, me-nu´kites, in the marginal notes, 1 Chron. 2:52, is the same as MANAHETHITES.

Me-on´e-nim, Plain of (*oak of soothsayers*), means an oak or terebinth. It was in the territory of Ephraim. Judg. 9:37.

Me-on´o-thai (*my dwelling*), a descendant of Judah. 1 Chron. 4:14.

Meph´a-ath (*lofty place*), a Levitical city of Reuben. Josh. 13:18; 1 Chron. 6:79.

Me-phib´o-sheth (*extermination of idols*). [1] A son of King Saul. David delivered him into the hands of the Gibeonites, who hanged him. 2 Sam. 21:8, 9. [2] A son of Jonathan and grandson of King Saul. 2 Sam. 4:4; 9:6; 21:7. He is called MERIB-BAAL in 1 Chron. 8:34; 9:40.

Me´rab, the eldest daughter of King Saul. 1 Sam. 14:49; 18:17, 19.

Mer-a-i´ah (*rebellion*), a priest in the time of Joiakim. Neh. 12:12.

Meraioth, me-ra´yoth (*rebellious*). [1, 2] Two priests in the line of Eleazar. 1 Chron. 6:6, 7, 52; Ezra 7:3; 1 Chron. 9:11; Neh. 11:11. [3] A priest who returned with Zerubbabel. Neh. 12:15. He is called MEREMOTH in Neh. 12:3.

Mer´a-ri or **Me-ra´ri** (*bitter*), a son of Levi and head of the Merarites. Gen.

45:11; Num. 3:17.

Mer´a-rites, descendants of Merari, the son of Levi, Num. 26:57, were one of the three great families of the tribe of Levi.

Mer-a-tha´im (*double rebellion*), is a symbolic or prophetic name for the city of Babylon. Jer. 50:21.

Mer´chant man, in Matt. 13:45, etc., means merchant.

Mer´chants, Gen. 23:16; 1 Kings 10:28, carried on their business in ancient times principally by caravans or travelling companies which had their regular seasons and routes. Joseph was sold to the merchants of an Egyptian caravan. There was also considerable trade by water.

Mer-cu´ri-us, one of the false gods of the Greeks and Romans. Acts 14:12.

Mer´cy is a distinguishing attribute of God, and signifies the divine goodness exercised toward the guilty and wretched, in harmony with truth and justice. Ps. 85:10. Also see Gen. 19; 24; 32; 39; 43.
Exod. 15; 20; 25; 26; 30; 31; 33–35; 37; 39; 40.
Lev. 16.
Num. 7; 14.
Deut. 5; 7; 13.
Judg. 1.
2 Sam. 7; 15; 22; 24.
1 Kings 3; 8.
1 Chron. 16; 17; 21; 28.
2 Chron. 1; 5–7; 20.
Ezra 3; 7; 9.
Neh. 1; 9; 13.
Job 37.
Pss. 4–6; 9; 13; 18; 21; 23; 25; 27; 30–33; 36; 37; 40; 44; 51; 52; 57; 59; 61; 62; 69; 77; 79; 85; 86; 89; 90; 94; 98; 100–103; 106–109; 115; 118; 119; 123; 130; 136; 138; 143; 145; 147.
Prov. 3; 12; 14; 16; 20; 21; 28.
Isa. 9; 14; 16; 27; 30; 47; 49; 54; 55; 60;

63.
Jer. 6; 13; 16; 21; 30; 31; 33; 42; 50.
Lam. 3.
Ezek. 39.
Dan. 2; 4; 9.
Hos. 1; 2; 4; 6; 10; 12. 14.
Jon. 2.
Mic. 6; 7.
Hab. 3.
Zech. 1; 7; 10.
Matt 5; 9; 12; 15; 17; 20; 23.
Mark 10.
Luke 1; 10; 16–18.
Acts 13.
Rom. 9; 11; 12; 15.
1 Cor. 7.
2 Cor. 1; 4.
Gal. 6.
Eph. 2.
Phil. 2.
Col. 3.
1 Tim. 1.
2 Tim. 1.
Titus 1; 3.
Heb. 4; 10.
James 2; 3; 5.
1 Pet. 1; 2.
2 John :3.
Jude :2. 21.

Mercy-seat, the name given to the lid or covering of the ark of the covenant. On the ends of it were the cherubim. It was of pure gold. See ARK. No. 3. On the Day of Atonement the high-priest sprinkled the blood of the sin-offerings before and upon the mercy-seat as a propitiation. Lev. 16:11-16. God was believed to be present in a peculiar manner at the mercy-seat to make known His holy will and to hear and answer prayer. Exod. 25:22. Compare Heb. 9:5; Rom. 3:25.
Also see Exod. 25 17-21; 26:34; 30:6; 31:7; 35:12; 37:6-9; 39:35; 40:20.

Lev. 16:2, 13-15.

Num. 7:89.

Me´red (*rebellion*), a son of Ezra. 1 Chron. 4:17, 18.

Mer´e-moth (*heights*). [1] A son of Uriah, the priest. He weighed and registered the gold and silver vessels of the Temple in the time of Ezra, and aided in repairing the walls of Jerusalem. Ezra 8:33; Neh. 3:4. [2] A Jew who took a foreign wife. Ezra 10:36. [3] A priest who sealed the covenant. Neh. 10:5. See MERAIOTH.

Me´res (*worthy*), one of the seven princes of Persia and Media in the court of Ahasuerus. Esther 1:14.

Mer´i-bah (*strife*). [1] The name which Moses gave to a place between the wilderness of Sin and Sinai, where he struck the rock and water came out of it for the people. Exod. 17:7; Ps. 81:7. [2] A place near the desert of Zin, near Kadesh, where Moses struck the rock and water came out abundantly. Num. 20:11-13; Deut. 33:8.

Mer´ib-ba´al, a son of Jonathan, the son of King Saul. 1 Chron. 8:34; 9:40. He is called MEPHIBOSHETH in 2 Sam. 4:4, etc.

Merodach, me-ro´dak (*slaughter*), an idol of the Babylonians. Jer. 50:2. The word Merodach is often used as a surname for Babylonish kings. See MERODACH-BALADAN.

Merodach-baladan, me-ro´dak-bal´a-dan (*Merodach, worshipper of Baal*), a Babylonian king who sent ambassadors to King Hezekiah. Isa. 39:1. In 2 Kings 20:12 he is called BERODACH-BALADAN.

Me´rom, Wa´ters of (*waters of the high place*), a small lake in the course of the river Jordan, about eleven miles north of the Sea of Galilee. Josh. 11:5, 7.

Me-ron´o-thite, a name given to JEHDEIAH in 1 Chron. 27:30, and to JADON in Neh. 3:7.

Me´roz (*refuge*), a place in the northern part of Palestine. Its inhabitants were cursed because they did not aid Barak against Sisera. Judg. 5:23.

Mer´ry, in 2 Chron. 7:10; Prov. 17:22; Luke 15:32; James 5:13, means joy and happiness, not noisy mirth.

Mesech, me´sek, Ps. 120:5, or **Meshech,** me´shek. Ezek. 32:26. [1] A son of Japheth. Gen. 10:2; 1 Chron 1:5. [2] A son of Shem. 1 Chron. 1:17. [3] A district inhabitated by descendants of Meshech, the son of Shem. Ps. 120:5. [4] The tribe descended from Meshech, the son of Japheth. Ezek. 32:26.

Me´sha (*deliverance*). [1] A king of Moab in the time of Ahab. 2 Kings 3:4. [2] A son of Caleb. 1 Chron. 2:42. [3] A descendant of Benjamin. 1 Chron. 8:9.

Me´sha (*retreat*), a place mentioned as one of the boundaries of the Joktanites. Gen. 10:30.

Meshach, me´shak, the name given by the chief of Nebuchadnezzar's eunuchs to Mishael, a companion of Daniel. Dan. 1:7. Meshach was thrown into a fiery furnace, by command of Nebuchadnezzar, with Shadrach and Abednego, Dan. 3:20-30, but came out unhurt.

Meshech, me´shek, a tribe that descended from Japheth. Ezek. 27:13. See MESECH, No. 1, and MASH.

Me-shel-e-mi´ah (*whom Jehovah repays*), a descendant of Kohath. 1 Chron. 9:21; 26:1. He is called SHELEMIAH in 1 Chron. 26:14.

Me-shez´a-beel (*delivered by God*). [1] A Jew whose descendant Meshullam repaired part of the wall of Jerusalem. Neh. 3:4. [2] A Jew who sealed the covenant made by Nehemiah. Neh. 10:21. [3] A descendant of Zerah. Neh. 11:24.

Me-shil´le-mith (*retribution*), a priest whose descendants dwelt in Jerusalem. 1 Chron. 9:12. He is called MESHIL-LEMOTH in Neh. 11:13.

Me-shil´le-moth. [1] An Ephraimite, father of Berechiah. 2 Chron. 28:12. [2] A priest of the family of Immer. Neh. 11:13. Same as MESHILLEMITH in 1 Chron. 9:12.

Me-sho´bab, a descendant of Simeon. 1 Chron. 4:34.

Me-shul´lam (*friend*). [1] The grandfather of Shaphan. 2 Kings 22:3. [2] A son of Zerubbabel. 1 Chron. 3:19. [3] A descendant of Gad. 1 Chron. 5:13. [4, 5, 6] Three descendants of Benjamin. 1 Chron. 8:17; 9:7, 8. [7] High-priest, of the family of Zadok, 1 Chron. 9:11; Neh. 11:11, called SHALLUM in 1 Chron. 6:12; Ezra 7:2. [8] A priest whose descendants dwelt in Jerusalem. 1 Chron. 9:12. [9] A descendant of Kohath, the son of Levi. 2 Chron. 34:12. [10] A chief man among the Jews who went up with Ezra. Ezra 8:16. [11] A Jew who aided in taking account of those who had taken foreign wives. Ezra 10:15. [12] A Jew who took a foreign wife. Ezra 10:29. [13, 14] Two Jews who aided in repairing the wall of Jerusalem. Neh. 3:4, 6, 30; 6:18. [15] A priest who sealed the covenant made by Nehemiah. Neh. 10:7, 20. [16, 17] Two priests in the time of Joiakim. Neh. 12:13, 16. [18] A Levite, one of the porters for the sanctuary. Neh. 12:25. [19] One who aided in dedicating the walls of Jerusalem. Neh. 12:33.

Me-shul´le-meth (*friend*), the wife of Manasseh and mother of Amon. 2 Kings 21:19.

Mes´o-ba-ite, a name applied to Jasiel, one of David's valiant men. 1 Chron. 11:47.

Mes-o-po-ta´mi-a (*between the rivers*) was the Greek name of the fertile plain between the Euphrates and the Tigris. Acts 2:9; 7:2. The Hebrew name was Aram-naharaim (*Aram of the two rivers*), Gen. 24:10, or Padan-aram (*the plain of Aram*). Gen. 25:20. It was inhabited by independent tribes, mostly of Chaldean origin, until conquered by Assyria.

Mess, in Gen. 43:34; 2 Sam. 11:8; means a dish of meat. See PORTION.

Mes´sen-gers were sent to distant towns and provinces by Jewish kings to proclaim laws and edicts. 1 Sam. 11:7; 2 Chron. 36:22. Messengers were sent by many others besides kings. John the Baptist is called a messenger in Matt. 11:10.

Also see Gen. 32:3, 6; 50:16.

Num. 20:14; 21:21; 22:5; 24:12.

Deut. 2:26.

Josh. 6:17, 25; 7:22.

Judg. 6:35; 7:24; 9:31; 11:12-14, 17, 19.

1 Sam. 4:17; 6:21; 11:3, 4, 9; 16:19; 19:11, 14-16, 20, 21; 23:27; 25:14, 42.

2 Sam. 2:5; 3:12, 14, 26; 5:11; 11:4, 19, 22, 23, 25; 12:27; 15:13.

1 Kings 19:2; 20:2, 5, 9; 22:13.

2 Kings 1:2, 3, 5, 16; 5:10; 6:32, 33; 7:15; 9:18; 10:8; 14:8; 16:7; 17:4; 19:9, 14, 23.

1 Chron. 14:1; 19:2, 16

2 Chron. 18:12; 36:15, 16.

Neh. 5:3.

Job 1:14; 33:23.

Prov. 13:17; 16:14; 17:11; 25:13.

Isa. 14:32; 18:2; 37:9, 14; 42:19; 44:26; 57:9.

Jer. 27:3; 51:31.

Ezek. 23:16, 40; 30:9.

Nah. 2:13.

Hag. 1:13.

Mal. 2:7; 3:1.

Mark 1:2.
Luke 7:24, 27; 9:52.
2 Cor. 8:23; 12:7.
Phil. 2:25.
James 2:25.

Mes-si´ah, the name by which Daniel indicates the Redeemer. Dan. 9:25, 26. Same as MESSIAS. John 1:41; 4:25. The word "Messiah" is often used in the Old Testament in its literal sense, signifying one who has been anointed. 1 Sam. 24:6; Ps. 105:15. It has the same meaning in Hebrew as Christ has in Greek. It generally refers to CHRIST (which see).

Mes-si´as, the Greek form of MESSIAH (which see). John 1:41; 4:25.

Met´als. The principal metals were well known to the Hebrews from very early times. Copper and iron are abundant in Syria and Palestine. Gold and silver were brought to Palestine in large quantities from other countries.

Mete, in Matt. 7:2, means measure.

Mete´yard, in Lev. 19:35, means a measuring-rod.

Me´theg-am´mah, 2 Sam. 8:1, is translated in the marginal notes "the bridle of Ammah," and may denote that David subdued the metropolis of the Philistines, probably Gath.

Me-thu´sa-el (*man of God*), the son of Mehujael and father of Lamech, was a descendant of Cain. Gen. 4:18.

Me-thu´se-lah (*man of dart,* or *he dies and it is sent*—namely, the flood) was the son of Enoch and the grandfather of Noah. Gen. 5:27; 1 Chron. 1:3. He was the longest-lived man, and died at the age of nine hundred and sixty-nine years.

Me-u´nim, a Nethinim whose descendants returned with Zerubbabel. Neh. 7:52. Same as MEHUNIM. Ezra 2:50.

Me-u´zal, in the marginal notes, Ezek.

27:19, may mean "from Uzal," the later Sanaa, the metropolis of Yemen.

Mez´a-hab (*waters of gold*), the grandfather of Mehetabel, the wife of Hadar, king of Edom. Gen. 36:39; 1 Chron. 1:50.

Mi´a-min (*from the right hand*). [1] A Jew who took a foreign wife. Ezra 10:25. [2] A priest who returned with Zerubbabel. Neh. 12:5. Called MIJAMIN in Neh. 10:7, and MINIAMIN in Neh. 12:17.

Mib´har (*choice*), one of David's valiant men. 1 Chron. 11:38.

Mib´sam (*sweet odor*). [1] A son of Ishmael. Gen. 25:13; 1 Chron. 1:29. [2] One of the sons of Simeon. 1 Chron. 4:25.

Mib´zar (*a fortress*), one of the chiefs of Edom. Gen. 36:42; 1 Chron. 1:53.

Mi´cah (*who is like Jehovah?*) [1] An Ephraimite who, having fallen into idolatry, hired a Levite to be his priest. His idols were stolen from him by the Danites. Judg. chapters 17 and 18.
[2] The sixth of the minor prophets, a native of Moresheth-gath, west of Jerusalem, in Gath. He was a contemporary of Isaiah, and prophesied during the reigns of Jotham, Ahaz, and Hezekiah, B. C. 750–698.
[3] Micah, a Reubenite. 1 Chron. 5:5. [4] The son of Merib-baal. 1 Chron. 8:34, 35. Called MICHA in 2 Sam. 9:12. [5] A Levite of the family of Asaph. 1 Chron. 9:15. He is called MICHA in Neh. 11:17, 22, and MICHAIAH in Neh. 12:35. [6] A Levite of the family of Kohath, 1 Chron. 23:20, called MICHAH in 1 Chron. 24:24, 25. [7] The father of Abdon, 2 Chron. 34:20, and called MICHAIAH in 2 Kings 22:12.

Mi´cah, the Book of (see MICAH, No. 2, above), refers with great definiteness to Samaria and Jerusalem, the complete devastation of the former and the temporary destruction of the latter. His prophecies of Messiah have the same character, and he predicted that Christ should be born at Bethlehem. Mic. 5:2.

Micaiah, mi-ka´yah, the prophet who predicted the fall of Ahab at the siege of Ramoth-gilead. 1 Kings 22:8-28; 2 Chron. 18:7, 27.

Micha, mi´kah. [1] A Levite who sealed the covenant made by Nehemiah. Neh. 10:11. See MICAH, No. 5. [2] The son of Merib-baal. 2 Sam. 9:12. See MICAH, No. 4.

Michael, mi´ka-el or mi´kel (*who like God?*). [1] The father of Sethur the spy, from Asher. Num. 13:13. [2, 3] A man of Gad and one of his ancestors. 1 Chron. 5:13, 14. [4] A Levite of the family of Gershom. 1 Chron. 6:40. [5] A chief man of Issachar. 1 Chron. 7:3. [6] A descendant of Benjamin. 1 Chron. 8:16. [7] A captain of Manasseh who joined David at Ziklag. 1 Chron. 12:20. [8] The father of Omri. 1 Chron. 27:18. [9] A son of King Jehoshaphat. 2 Chron. 21:2. [10] The father of Zebadiah. Ezra 8:8. [11] The angel who is called by Daniel the prince of the people of Judah. Dan. 10:13, 21; 12:1. Also, the archangel mentioned in Jude 9, and the leader of the hosts of the angels. Rev. 12:7-9.

Michah, mi´kah. 1 Chron 24:24, 25. See MICAH, No. 6.

Michaiah, mi-ka´yah. [1] See MICAH, No. 7. [2] 2 Chron. 13:2. See MAACHAH, No. 3. [3] One of Jehoshaphat's officers. 2 Chron. 17:7. [4] See MICAH, No. 5. [5] One of the priests who assisted in dedicating the walls of Jerusalem. Neh. 12:41. [6] One of Jehoiakim's officers. Jer. 36:11, 13.

Michal, mi´kal, a daughter of King Saul and wife of David. 1 Sam. 14:49; 18:20, 27.

Michmas, mik´mas, or **Michmash,**

mik´mash (*something hidden*), a town of Benjamin. 1 Sam. 13:2. It became famous in the Philistine war of Saul and Jonathan. 1 Sam. 13:11.

Michmethah, mik´me-thah (*rocky?*), a town on the borders of Ephraim and Manasseh. Josh. 16:6; 17:7.

Michri, mik´ri (*prize of Jehovah*), a Benjamite. 1 Chron. 9:8.

Michtam, mik´tam, a word in the titles of Pss. 16 and 56 to 60. Its meaning is unknown.

Mid´din (*measures*), a city in the south of Judah. Josh. 15:61.

Mid´dle Wall of Par-ti´tion, in Eph. 2:14, refers to the sacred barrier between the court of the Gentiles and the inner parts of the Temple.

Mid´i-an (*strife*). [1] A son of Abraham by Keturah. Gen. 25:2, 4; 1 Chron. 1:32, 33. [2] The country which the descendants of Midian occupied. Gen. 36:35; Exod. 2:15, 16. See MIDIANITES.
Also see Exod. 3:1; 4:19; 18:1.
Num. 22:4, 7; 25:15, 18; 31:3, 8, 9.
Josh. 13:21.
Judg. 6:1, 2; 7:8, 13-15, 25; 8:3, 5, 12, 22, 26, 28; 9:17.
1 Kings 11:18.
1 Chron. 1:46.
Isa. 9:4; 10:26; 60:6.
Hab. 3:7.

Mid´i-an-ites, the descendants of Midian, were the inhabitants of the region from the Sinaitic peninusula to the banks of the Euphrates. They traded much with Palestine, Lebanon, and Egypt. It was probably the Midianites and the Ishmaelites who bought Joseph. They at first joined Moab against the Israelites. Num. chapters 22, 24, 25, and afterward attempted hostilities on their own account, Judg. 6:1-40, but failed in both instances. They were finally incor-

porated with the Moabites and the Arabs. Also see Gen. 37:28, 36.
Num. 10:29; 31:2, 3, 7.
Judg. 7:1, 2, 7, 12, 23-25; 8:1.
Ps. 83:9.

Midianitish, mid´i-an-ite-ish, a female descendant of Midian. Num. 25:6, 14, 15.

Mid´wives. The two midwives, Shiphrah and Puah, mentioned in Exod. 1:15 were probably the superintendents or representatives of a class. Midwives are also mentioned in Gen. 35:17; 38:28.

Mig´dal-el (*tower of God*), one of the fortified cities of Naphtali. Josh. 19:38.

Mig´dal-gad (*tower of God*), one of the towns of Judah. Josh. 15:37.

Mig´dol (*tower*). [1] A place situated near the north end of the Red Sea. Exod. 14:2; Num. 33:7. [2] A city in the northeast part of Egypt, near Palestine. It contained a colony of Jews. Jer. 44:1; 46:14.

Might´y, a title which is sometimes given to the true God. Gen. 49:24; Pss. 132:2, 5; Isa. 1:24; 49:26; 60:16.

Mig´ron (*precipice*), a city of Benjamin. 1 Sam. 14:2; Isa. 10:28.

Mij´a-min (*on the right hand*). [1] A priest in the time of David. 1 Chron. 24:9. [2] One who sealed the covenant made by Nehemiah. Neh. 10:7. See MIAMIN, No. 2.

Mik´loth (*staves*). [1] A descendant of Benjamin. 1 Chron. 8:32; 9:37, 38. [2] A ruler in David's guard. 1 Chron. 27:4.

Mikneiah, mik-ne´yah (*possession of Jehovah*), a Levite engaged in the musical service connected with the removal of the ark of the covenant. 1 Chron. 15:18, 21.

Mil-a-la´i (*eloquent*), one of the priests who aided in purifying the people after their return from Babylon. Neh. 12:36.

Mil´cah (*queen* or *counsel*). [1] A daughter of Haran. She was the wife of Nahor, a brother of Abraham. Gen. 11:29;

22:20, 23. [2] A daughter of Zelophehad. Num. 26:33; Josh. 17:3.

Mil´com, an idol worshipped by the Ammonites. 1 Kings 11:5, 33; 2 Kings 23:13. Same as MOLECH and MOLOCH. See MOLECH.

Mile. A Roman mile, about 4800 feet, is over nine-tenths of an English mile. Another kind of Eastern mile is about one-fifth longer than an English mile. The English mile is the same as the United States mile. Matt. 5:41. See MEASURES.

Mil-le´tum, in 2 Tim. 4:20, is the same as MILETUS (which see).

Mi-le´tus, a seaport of Ionia, Asia Minor, on the south-western side of the Latmian Gulf, directly opposite the mouth of the river Meander, was visited by Paul on his return from his third missionary journey. He met there the elders from Ephesus and made the parting address which is recorded in Acts 20:15-38.

Milk of cows, camels, sheep, and goats was used in Palestine, and is frequently mentioned in the Old Testament. Gen. 18:8; 49:12; Exod. 3:8, 17.
Also see Gen. 49:12.
Exod. 13:5; 23:19; 33:3; 34:26.
Lev. 20:24.
Num. 13:27; 14:8; 16:13.
Deut. 6:3; 11:9; 14:21; 26:9; 27:3; 31:20; 32:14.
Josh. 5:6.
Judg. 4:19; 5:25.
Job 10:10; 21:24.
Prov. 27:27; 30:33.
Song of Sol. 4:11; 5:1, 12.
Isa. 7:22; 28:9; 55:1; 60:16; 66:11.
Jer. 11:5; 32:22.
Lam. 4:7.
Ezek. 20:6; 25:4.
Joel 3:18.

1 Cor. 3:2; 9:7.
Heb. 5:12, 13.
1 Pet. 2:2.

Mill. Exod. 11:5; Num. 11:8. The mills mentioned in the Bible were not buildings, but pairs of round millstones about 2 feet in diameter and about six inches thick. The lower or "nether" millstone was slightly convex on the top and was stationary. The upper stone was correspondingly concave on the lower side, and in its center was a hold through which the grain was poured into the mill. The top of the upper stone had an upright handle by which it was rapidly turned. The meal came out around the outside of the mill and fell upon a cloth or a board on which the mill stood. These mills were operated by women, Matt. 24:41, and were used by each family every morning. No man was allowed to take "the nether or the upper millstone to pledge: for he taketh *a man's* life to pledge." Deut. 24:6. The stopping of the noise of these mills in the morning was a sign of desolation. Jer. 25:10; Rev. 18:22.

Mil-len´ni-um means a period of one thousand years, and is, in its religious use, applied to the era prophetically mentioned in Rev. 20:1–7.

Mil´let, a kind of grain cultivated in Palestine and elsewhere. Ezek. 4:9. The name "millet" is applied to two kinds of grain—namely, the seeds of panic-grass and the durah or Egyptian corn, which somewhat resembles maize.

Mil´lo (*a mound*). [1] A part of the citadel or fortress of Jerusalem. 2 Sam. 5:9; 1 Kings 9:15. [2] Those who lived in the fortress of Shechem. Judg. 9:6, 20.

Mil´lo, House of, the place where Joash was murdered. 2 Kings 12:20. See MILLO, No. 1.

Mina, mi´nah, a weight, in the margin-

al notes of Luke 19:13, is translated "pound" in the text. It is twelve ounces and a half, and is worth about sixteen dollars.

Min´cing, in Isa. 3:16, means walking with very short steps.

Mines. The remains of ancient Egyptian mines are still to be seen on the edge of the Ethiopian desert and in the peninsula of Sinai. In Deut. 8:9 Moses refers to the mineral wealth of Canaan. The Jews understood how to extract metals from the earth.

Min´gled Peo´ple, a name given to some tribe or tribes whose origin and location are uncertain Jer. 25:20, 24; Ezek. 30:5. They apparently lived near the Arabians. In 1 Kings 10 15 the same word in the original is translated "Arabia."

Mi-ni´a-min (*from the right hand*). [1] A Levite in the time of Hezekiah. 2 Chron. 31:15. [2] A priest who returned with Zerubbabel. Neh. 12:17, 41. See MIAMIN.

Min´ish, in Exod. 5:19, means diminish; lessen.

Min´is-ter. This word, when used in the Bible, sometimes means one who is in voluntary attendance upon another person. Joshua was the minister of Moses. Exod. 24:13. Elisha was the minister of Elijah. 1 Kings 19:21. In Heb. 8:2 Christ is called "A minister of the sanctuary;" that is, as our High-Priest.

Also see Exod. 28:1, 3, 4, 35, 41, 43; 29:1, 30, 44; 30:20, 30; 31:10; 35:19; 39:26, 41; 40:13, 15.
Lev. 7:35; 16:32.
Num. 1:50; 3:3, 4, 6, 31; 4:9, 12, 14; 8:26; 16:9; 18:2.
Deut. 10:6, 8; 17:12; 18:5, 7; 21:5.
Josh. 1:1.
1 Sam. 2:11, 18; 3:1.

2 Sam. 13:17.
1 Kings 1:4, 15; 8:11; 10:5.
2 Kings 25:14.
1 Chron. 6:32; 9:28; 15:2; 16:4, 37; 23:13; 26:12; 28:1.
2 Chron. 5:14; 8:14; 9:4; 13:10; 22:8; 23:6; 24:14; 29:11; 31:2.
Neh. 10:36, 39.
Esther 2:2; 6:3.
Ps. 9:8.
Isa. 60:7, 10.
Jer. 33:22; 52:18.
Ezek. 40:46; 42:14; 43:19; 44:11, 12, 15-17, 19, 27; 45:4, 5; 46:24.
Dan. 7:10.
Joel 1:9, 13; 2:17.
Matt. 4:11; 8:15; 20:26, 28; 25:44; 27:55.
Mark 1:13, 31; 10:43, 45; 15:41.
Luke 1:2; 4:20, 39; 8:3.
Acts 13:2, 5; 19:22; 20:34; 24:23; 26:16.
Rom. 12:7; 13:4, 6; 15:8, 16, 25, 27.
1 Cor. 3:5; 4:1; 9:13.
2 Cor. 3:3, 6; 6:4; 8:4; 9:1, 10; 11:15, 23.
Gal. 2:17.
Eph. 3:7; 4:29; 6:21.
Phil. 2:25.
Col. 1:7, 23, 25; 2:19; 4:7.
1 Thess. 3:2.
1 Tim. 1:4; 4:6.
2 Tim. 1:18.
Philem. :13.
Heb. 1:7, 14; 6:10; 10:11.
1 Pet. 1:12; 4:10, 11.
2 Pet. 1:11.

Min´ni, a province of Armenia. Jer. 51:27.

Min´nith (*divisions*), a place belonging to the Ammonites. Wheat was sent from it to Tyre. Judg. 11:33; Ezek. 27:17.

Min´strel, a singer or musician.

Minstrels were employed at funerals and in time of death, as in the case of Jairus' daughter, Matt. 9:23, and also on other occasions. 2 Kings 3:15.

Mint, a common herb of little value, resembling garden sage. Various species of it are found in Palestine. It was used in ancient times for seasoning and in medicine. The Jews were required to pay tithes on all produce of the earth. Deut. 14:22, but were more careful concerning trifles than about important matters. Matt. 23:23.

Miphkad, mif´kad (*appointed place*), one of the gates of Jerusalem. Neh. 3:31.

Mir´a-cle, an act or event produced by supernatural or divine agency. The New Testament uses three terms to denote miracles—namely, signs, wonders, and power or mighty works.
Exod. 7:9.
Num. 14:22.
Deut. 11:3; 29:3.
Judg. 6:13.
Mark 6:52; 9:39.
Luke 23:8.
John 2:11, 23; 3:2; 4:54; 6:2, 14, 26; 7:31; 9:16; 10:41; 11:47; 12:18, 37.
Acts 2:22; 4:16, 22; 6:8; 8:6, 13; 15:12; 19:11.
1 Cor. 12:10, 28, 29.
Gal. 3:5.
Heb. 2:4.
Rev. 13:14; 16:14; 19:20.

Mir´i-am (*rebellion*). [1] A daughter of Amram and the sister of Moses and Aaron. 1 Chron. 6:3. She was watching the ark of bulrushes in which the infant Moses was laid, and when the daughter of Pharaoh discovered it Miriam called her mother as a nurse for Moses. Exod. 2:4-10. She led the women of Israel in a triumphant song after the passage of the

Red Sea. Exod. 15:20. She was smitten with leprosy for murmuring against Moses, but was restored to health in answer to Moses' prayer. Num. 12:1-15. She died at Kadesh and was buried there. Num. 20:1. [2] A descendant of Judah. 1 Chron. 4:17.

Mir´ma, mer´mah (*fraud*), a descendant of Benjamin. 1 Chron. 8:10.

Mir´ror. See LOOKING-GLASS.

Mis´chief, in Ezek. 7:26; Acts 13:10, means serious harm.

Mis´gab (*high place*), a place in Moab. Jer. 48:1.

Mish´a-el (*who is what God is?*). [1] One of the sons of Uzziel. Exod. 6:22; Lev. 10:4. [2] One of those who stood at Ezra's left hand when he read the law to the people. Neh. 8:4. [3] The Babylonian name given to MESHACH, one of the three companions of Daniel who were thrown into a fiery furnace and miraculously delivered. Dan. 1:6, 7; 3:20-30.

Mi´shal and **Mi´she-al** (*entreaty*), a town of Asher. Josh. 21:30; 19:26.

Mi´sham (*purification* or *swift-going*), a descendant of Benjamin. 1 Chron. 8:12.

Mishma, mish´mah (*a report, a hearing*). [1] One of the sons of Ishmael. Gen. 25:14; 1 Chron. 1:30. [2] A son of Simeon. 1 Chron. 4:25.

Mish-man´nah (*fatness*), a descendant of Gad. 1 Chron. 12:10.

Mish´ra-ites, a family from Kirjath-jearim which founded towns. 1 Chron. 2:53.

Mis´per-reth, a Jew who returned with Zerubbabel. Neh. 7:7. Called MIZPAR in Ezra 2:2.

Misrephoth-maim, mis´re-foth-ma´im (*burnings of water*), a place situated in the northern part of Palestine. Josh. 11:8;

13:6.

Mite, the least valuable Jewish coin, worth about two mills of United States money. Mark 12:42. See MONEY.

Mith´cah (*sweetness*), one of the stations of the Hebrews in the desert. Num. 33:28, 29.

Mith´nite, a name applied to Joshaphat, one of David's warriors. 1 Chron. 11:43.

Mith´re-dath (*given by Mithra*, the sun-god). [1] The treasurer of Cyrus, king of Persia. Ezra 1:8. [2] A Persian who opposed the Jews in the time of Artaxerxes, king of Persia. Ezra 4:7.

Mi´tre, the head-dress of a Jewish priest. It was made of fine linen and in the form of an Eastern turban, and had on its front a gold plate containing the inscription "Holiness to the Lord." Exod. 28:4, 36-39.

Mit-y-le´ne, the capital and principal town of the island of Lesbos in the Mediterranean Sea. Paul spent a night there. Acts 20:14.

Mix´ed Mul´ti-tude, mentioned in Exod. 12:38; Neh. 13:3, were people living among the Israelites, but who were not of pure Hebrew blood.

Mi´zar (*smallness*), a hill, probably near Mount Hermon. Ps. 42:6.

Miz´pah and **Miz´peh** (*watch-tower*). [1] The place on Mount Gilead where Jacob made a covenant with Laban and put up a heap of stones as a witness. Gen. 31:43-49. It is called Mizpeh of Gilead in Judg. 11:29. Jephthah met his daughter there. Judg. 11:34. [2] A city of Moab. 1 Sam. 22:3. [3] The land of Mizpeh, in northern Palestine, occupied by the Hivites. Josh. 11:3. It may be the same as No. 4. [4] The valley of Mizpeh. Josh. 11:3, 8. [5] A city of Judah. Josh. 15:38. [6] A city of Benjamin. Josh. 18:26. Saul may include various rats and weasels.

Molech, mo'lek (*the ruler*), Lev. 18:21, or **Mil'com,** 1 Kings 11:5, or **Moloch,** mo'lok, an idol of the Ammonites and of the Jews. 2 Kings 23:10; Ezek. 20:26. Human sacrifices, especially children, were offered to it. The Jews set up a tabernacle to Molech (Moloch) in the valley of Hinnom and sacrificed their children to that idol.

Mo'lid (*begetter*), a descendant of Judah. 1 Chron. 2:29.

Mon'ey. The first money was not coined, but was in the form of wedges, rings, etc. Money mentioned in the Old Testament before the captivity means a particular weight of some precious metal. After the captivity Persian, Greek, Syrian, Roman, and national Jewish coins were used by the Jews. The first Jewish coins were made in the time of Simon Maccabæus, B. C. about 139. Shekels, half-shekels, etc. of gold, silver, and copper were then produced. No image of any man was allowed on them.

Mon'ey-chang'ers are mentioned in Matt. 21:12; Mark 11:15. They exchanged foreign for Jewish money, which was to be used in paying Temple dues. The money-changers Jesus drove out of the Temple were guilty of charging a large premium for making this exchange.

Month. The Hebrews usually designated their months by numbers—namely, first month, second month, etc. They also had a special name for each of them. The length of their month was regulated by the changes of the moon, and was reckoned from one new moon to the next one. A thirteenth month, called VE-ADAR, was inserted among the months about once in three years, or seven times in nineteen years, to make up for the differ-

ence between the Jewish year and the solar year, the one now used. See SEASONS.

HEBREW MONTHS IN ONE YEAR

Months of the Sacred Year	Corresponding Months of the Civil Year	Beginning with the New Moon
Abib or Nisan	Seventh ..	March or April
Zif or Ziv ...	Eighth ...	April or May
Sivan	Ninth	May or June
Tammuz	Tenth	June or July
Ab	Eleventh ..	July or August
Elul	Twelfth ...	Aug. or Sept.
Ethanim or Tishri	First	Sept. or Oct.
Bul	Second ...	Oct. or Nov.
Chislieu or Kislieu	Third	Nov. or Dec.
Tebeth	Fourth ...	Dec. or Jan.
Shebat	Fifth	Jan. or Feb.
Adar	Sixth	Feb. or March

Moon is called "the lesser light" in Gen. 1:16. Many of the feasts and sacred services observed by the Jews were regulated by the new moon, which was always the beginning of the month and was celebrated with special sacrifices. Num. 28:11-15. The moon was worshipped under various names by the heathen. The idolatrous Jews burned incense to it. 2 Kings 23: 5; Jer. 8:2.

Mo'ras-thite, a name applied to a native of Moresheth-gath, the birthplace of the prophet Micah. Jer. 26:18; Mic. 1:1.

Mordecai, mor'de-kay (*little man,* or *worshipper of Mars*). [1] A chief man among the Jews who returned from Babylon with Zerubbabel. Ezra 2:2; Neh. 7:7. [2] A Jew of the tribe of Benjamin. He was the cousin and guardian of Esther, whose Hebrew name was Hadassah and who became queen of Ahasuerus, king of Persia. Mordecai was despised and abused by Haman, a chief officer of Ahasuerus. Haman devised a plan for the extermination of the Jews in the territory ruled by that king, but Mordecai, aided by Esther, defeated his purpose. Haman was hanged and Mordecai was raised to power and wealth. See Esther 2:5 to 10:3; also ESTHER, and HAMAN.

Mo´reh. [1] The plain, plains, or oaks of Moreh, near Shechem. Abram stopped there after entering Canaan, Gen. 12:6, and it is mentioned in Deut. 11:30 as "the plains of Moreh." [2] The name of a hill in the valley of Jezreel, where the Midianites and Amalekites were encamped before Gideon attacked them. Judg. 7:1. It is the same as the "Little Hermon."

Mor´esh-eth-gath (*possession of wine-press*), a town in the western part of Judah. It was the birthplace of the prophet Micah. Mic. 1:14.

Mo-ri´ah (*chosen of Jehovah?*). [1] The land to which Abraham was commanded to go to offer up Isaac for a burnt-offering. Gen. 22:2. [2] The mount on which Solomon built the Temple in Jerusalem. 2 Chron. 3:1. See JERUSALEM.

Morn´ing Star, a title of Christ. See STARS.

Morn´ing watch. See WATCHES OF THE NIGHT.

Mor´tar. Gen. 11:3. See LIME, PITCH.

Mor´tars, vessels in which grain and spices were pounded (pulverized), were used by the Hebrews. Num. 11:8; Prov. 27:22.

Mor´ti-fy, in Rom 8:13; Col. 3:5, means put to death (figuratively).

Mosera, mo-se´rah, and **Mo-se´roth** (*bond, bonds*) are commonly supposed to

be the same station (the twenty-sixth) of the Israelites in their wanderings in the wilderness. Deut. 10:6; Num. 33:30, 31.

Mo´ses (*drawn out*), the great leader and lawgiver of the Israelites and the moulder of their national character, was the youngest child of Amram and Jochebed. Their other children were Miriam and Aaron, Miriam being the oldest. The life of Moses falls naturally into three periods, of forty years each. Acts 7:23, 30, 36. Hid by his mother in the "ark of bulrushes," Exod. 2:3, he was found and adopted by the daughter of Pharaoh, and was educated in the splendor of the Egyptian court, trained in all the skill of Egyptian life and civilization, initiated in the secret wisdom of the priesthood, and placed in a prominent and conspicuous position close to the ruler. In his fortieth year he slew an Egyptian taskmaster who was ill-treating a Hebrew, Exod. 2:12, and to escape the wrath of Pharaoh he fled to Midian, where he spent the next forty years in tending the flocks of the Midianite priest Jethro, whose daughter Zipporah he married. Exod. 2:21. The Egyptian court with its associations had afforded Moses a rich field for practical observation, but the rugged life he now led as a shepherd had its own advantages, and the solitude of the desert proved inviting for deep meditations and for maturing great plans. At the age of eighty Moses received the divine commission to deliver his people from their bondage. Exod. 3:3-10. This task was accomplished in forty years that were full of troubles, but also full of the most extraordinary events. (See the books of Exodus, Leviticus, Numbers, and Deuteronomy for a detailed account of their wanderings in the wilderness.) When, finally, the Israelites approached the land of Canaan, ready to enter upon their national life, Moses, forbidden by God to accompany them because he had *struck* the rock at Meribah instead of *speaking* to it, as God had commanded him, ascended Mount Nebo, and from Pisgah's top the LORD showed him the Promised Land. With his eye not dim nor his natural force abated, he was one hundred and twenty years old when he died in the land of Moab, and "there arose not a prophet since in Israel like unto Moses, whom the LORD knew face to face." Deut. 34:7, 10. He was the author of parts of the PENTATEUCH (which see), and of the ninetieth Psalm, which was probably written in the wilderness.

Also see Exod. 2–20; 24; 25; 30–36; 38–40.
Lev. 1; 4–27.
Num. 1–21; 25–36.
Deut. 1; 4; 5; 27; 29; 31–34.
Josh. 1; 3; 4; 8; 9; 11–14; 17; 18; 20–24.
Judg. 1; 3; 4.
1 Sam. 12.
1 Kings 2; 8.
2 Kings 14; 18; 21; 23.
1 Chron. 6; 15; 21–23; 26.
2 Chron. 1; 5; 8; 23–25; 30; 33–35.
Ezra 3; 6; 7.
Neh. 1; 8–10; 13.
Pss. 77; 90; 99; 103; 105; 106.
Isa. 63.
Jer. 15.
Dan. 9.
Mic. 6.
Mal. 4.
Matt. 8; 17; 19; 22; 23.
Mark 1; 7; 9; 10; 12.
Luke 2; 5; 9; 16; 20; 24.
John 1; 3; 5–9.
Acts 3; 6; 7; 13; 15; 21; 26; 28.
Rom. 5; 9; 10.
1 Cor. 9; 10.
2 Cor. 3.
2 Tim. 3.
Heb. 3; 7–12.
Jude :9.
Rev. 15.

Most High, a name often applied to God. Num. 24:16; Ps. 21:7, etc.

Mote, in Matt. 7:3, means a very small particle of anything.

Moth means the common insect which, in its caterpillar form, is very destructive to woollen cloths and garments. Many references are made in the Bible to the destructiveness of this insect. Job 13:28; Isa. 50:9. The ancient Hebrews had much treasure laid up in the form of costly garments. See Matt. 6:19, 20.

Also see Job 4:19; 27:18.
Ps. 39:11.
Isa. 51:8.
Hos. 5:12.
Luke 12:33.

Moth´er is sometimes used in the Old Testament in place of grandmother. 1 Kings 15:10. In Gen. 3:20 Eve is called "the mother of all living." The name is applied to Deborah as a political leader. Judg. 5:7.

Mo´tions, in Rom. 7:5, means impulses, or, as in the marginal notes, passions.

Mould´y, in Josh. 9:5, 12, means crumbled.

Mount, in Jer. 6:6, 32:24, 33:4, means a mound or embankment made for use in besieging a city.

Mount of the A-mal´e-kites, a mountain in Ephraim where one of the Judges of Israel was buried. Judg. 12:15.

Moun´tains. Among the principal mountains and mounts mentioned in the Bible are those of Ararat, Ebal, Hermon, Hor, Horeb, Lebanon, Moriah, Nebo, Olivet or Olives, Sinai, Tabor, and Zion.

was elected king there. 1 Sam. 10:17-21.

Miz´par (*number*), a chief man among the Jews who returned with Zerubbabel. Ezra 2:2. He is called MISPERETH in Neh. 7:7.

Miz-ra´im (*limits*). [1] One of the sons of Ham. Gen. 10:6; 1 Chron. 1:8. [2] The name generally given to Egypt by the Hebrews. See EGYPT.

Miz´zah (*fear*), one of the sons of Reuel, the son of Esau. Gen. 36:13, 17; 1 Chron. 1:37.

Mnason, na´son (*remembering*), a man of Cyprus. He was a disciple with whom Paul lodged at Jerusalem. Acts 21:16.

Mo´ab (*of the father*). [1] The son of Lot and his eldest daughter. Gen. 19:37. [2] The same name is also used to denote the descendants of Moab and the land in which they lived. Gen. 36:35; Exod. 15:15. The territory of the Moabites was in three parts, having different names: 1. *The Land of Moab,* lying east of the Jordan and the Dead Sea and between the rivers Arnon and Jabbok. Deut. 1:5; 2. *The Field of Moab,* a district east of the Dead Sea and south of the river Arnon. Ruth 1:2, 3. *The Plains of Moab,* a district in the Jordan valley east of that river and opposite Jericho. Num. 22:1. See DIBON, No. 1, for an account of the *Moabite stone.* Also see Exod. 15:15.

Num. 21:11, 13, 15, 20, 26, 28, 29; 22:3, 4, 7, 8, 10, 14, 21, 36; 23:6, 7, 17; 24:17; 25:1; 26:3, 63; 31:12; 33:44, 48-50; 35:1; 36:13.

Deut. 2:8, 18; 29:1; 32:49; 34:1, 5, 6, 8.

Josh. 13:32; 24:9.

Judg. 3:12, 14, 15, 17, 28-30; 10:6; 11:15, 17, 18, 25.

Ruth 1:1, 4, 6, 22; 2:6; 4:3.

1 Sam. 12:9; 14:47; 22:3, 4.

2 Sam. 8:2, 12; 23:20.

1 Kings 11:7.

2 Kings 1:1; 3:4, 5, 7, 10, 13, 23, 26.

1 Chron. 1:46; 4:22; 8:8; 11:22; 18:2, 11

2 Chron. 20:1, 10, 22, 23.

Neh. 12:23.

Pss. 60:8; 83:6; 108:9.

Isa. 11:14; 15:1, 2, 4, 5, 8, 9; 16:2, 4, 6, 7, 11-14; 25:10.

Jer. 9 26; 25:21; 27:3; 40:11; 48:1, 2, 4, 9, 11, 13, 15, 16, 18, 20, 24-26, 28, 29, 31, 33, 35, 36, 38-47.

Ezek. 25:8, 9, 11.

Dan. 11:41.

Amos 2:1, 2.

Mic. 6:5.

Zeph. 2:8, 9.

Mo´ab-ites, the descendants of Moab, the son of Lot's eldest daughter. Gen. 19:37; Num. 22:4.

Also see Deut. 2:9, 11, 29.

Judg. 3:28.

2 Sam. 8:2.

1 Kings 11:1, 33.

2 Kings 3:18, 21, 22, 24; 13:20; 23:13; 24:2.

1 Chron. 18:2.

Ezra 9 1.

Moabitess, mo´ab-ite-ess, a female inhabitant of Moab. Ruth 1:22; 2 Chron. 24:26.

Mo-a-di´ah, a priest. Neh. 12:17. See MAADIAH.

Mod-er-a´tion, in Phil. 4:5, means conciliatory spirit.

Mol´a-dah (*birth*), a city of Judah which afterward became a city of the Simeonites. Josh. 15:26; 1 Chron. 4:28.

Mole. In Lev. 11:30 the Hebrew word is believed to mean the chameleon. Another word translated "mole" in Isa. 2:20 means "the burrower." No true moles have been found in Palestine, and the term

Each of these and many others are mentioned in separate articles (which see).

Mourn, Mourn´ers. The Hebrews made great manifestations of their grief at the death of friends and relations. Gen. 50:10. The usual period of mourning was seven days, but the mourning for Moses and for Aaron continued thirty days. Num. 20:29; Deut. 34:8. Special mourning was made for an only son. Zech. 12:10. Hired mourners were often employed.
Also see Gen. 23:2; 37:34; 50:3.
Exod. 33:4.
Num. 14:39.
1 Sam. 15:35; 16:1.
2 Sam. 1:12; 3:31; 11:26; 13:37; 14:2.
1 Kings 13:29, 30; 14:13, 18.
1 Chron. 7:22.
2 Chron. 35:24.
Ezra 10:6.
Neh. 1:4; 8:9.
Job 2:11; 5:11; 14:22; 29:25.
Ps. 55:2.
Prov. 5:11; 29:2.
Eccles. 3:4; 12:5.
Isa. 3:26; 16:7; 19:8; 38:14; 57:18; 59:11; 61:2, 3; 66:10.
Jer. 4:28; 12:4; 48:31.
Lam. 1:4.
Ezek. 7:12, 27; 24:16, 23; 31:15.
Hos. 4;3; 9:4; 10:5.
Joel 1:9.
Amos 1:2; 8:8; 9:5.
Zech. 7:5; 12:12.
Matt. 5:4; 9:15; 11:17; 24:30.
Mark 16:10.
Luke 6:25; 7:32.
1 Cor. 5:2.
James 4:9.
Rev. 18:11.

Mouse (*the corn-eater*), Lev. 11:29, an unclean animal. Many species of mice were found in Palestine, and were very destructive.

Mouth is sometimes used in the Bible in place of the speaker. Exod. 4:16; Jer. 15:19.

Mow´ing, in Ps. 129:7, means reaping with a sickle.

Mow´ings, King's. Grass was cut, green, with a sickle for cattle, but was never cut with a scythe. The king probably had a special right to the first grass in certain districts for his horses. Amos 7:1.

Moza, mo´zah, (*a going forth*). [1] A son of Caleb, the son of Jephunneh. 1 Chron. 2:46. [2] One of the descendants of King Saul. 1 Chron. 8:36, 37; 9:42, 43.

Mo´zah (*going forth*), a city of Benjamin. Josh. 18:26.

Muf´flers, in Isa. 3:19, means flowing, out-door veils.

Mul´ber-ry trees, in 2 Sam. 5:23, 24, is generally agreed to be a mistranslation. Many different meanings are suggested, among which is aspen or poplar.

Mules, the offspring of the horse and the ass, were ridden by distinguished men among Jews. 2 Sam. 13:29. In Gen. 36:24 mules means hot springs. See ANAH.

Munitions, mu-nish´uns, in Isa. 33:16, means fortress.

Mup´pim (*serpent?*), a descendant of Benjamin. Gen. 46:21. Called SHUPHAM in Num. 26:39.

Mur´der. Under the Jewish law one who slays another from enmity, hatred, or by lying in wait is called a murderer. There was no pardon for intentional murder.
Num. 35:16-19, 21, 30, 31.
2 Kings 6:32; 14:6.
Job 24:14.
Pss. 10:8; 94:6.
Isa. 1:21.
Jer. 4:31; 7:9.

Hos. 6:9; 9:13.
Matt. 15:19; 19:18; 22:7.
Mark 7:21; 15:7.
Luke 23:19, 25.
John 8:44.
Acts 3:14; 7:52; 21:38; 28:4.
Rom. 1:29.
Gal. 5:21.
1 Tim. 1:9.
1 Pet. 4:15.
1 John 3:15.
Rev. 9:21; 21:8; 22:15.

Mur´rain, an infectious and fatal disease which attacked the horses, asses, camels, oxen, and sheep of the Egyptians, and not those of the Israelites. It was one of the plagues of Egypt sent by the LORD. Exod. 9:1-7.

Mu´shi (*forsaking*), a son of Merari. Exod. 6:19; 1 Chron. 6:47.

Mu´shites, descendants of Mushi. Num. 3:33; 26:58.

Mu´sic, 1 Sam 18:6, formed an important part of the religious services and festivities of the Hebrews. The sons of Asaph, Heman, and Jeduthun were appointed by David for the musical service. Musical instruments were invented by Jubal. Gen. 4:21. Among those used by the Jews were the harp, the sackbut, the psaltery, cymbals, trumpets, organs (see ORGAN), etc.
Also see 1 Chron. 15:16; 16:42.
2 Chron. 5:13; 7:6; 23:13; 34:12.
Neh. 12:36.
Pss. 4–6; 8; 9; 11–14; 18–22; 31; 36; 39–42; 44–47; 49; 51–62; 64–70; 75–77; 80; 81; 84; 85; 88; 109; 139; 140.
Eccles. 2:8; 12:4.
Lam. 3:63; 5:14.
Dan. 3:5, 7, 10, 15; 6:18.
Amos 6:5.

Luke 15:25.
Rev. 18:22.

Mus´tard, mentioned in Matt. 13:31, 32; 17:20; Luke 17:6, is the black mustard, which grows to a very large size in Palestine.

Muth-lab´ben is found in the title of Ps. 9. Its meaning is unknown.

Myra, my´rah (*flowing, weeping*), an ancient city and seaport of Lycia, on the south-west coast of Asia Minor. Acts 27:5.

Myrrh, mer, a precious gum from a low thorny tree found chiefly in Arabia. It was one of the ingredients of the holy ointment, Exod. 30:23, and of the embalming substance. John 19:39. It is also used in medicine and as a perfume.
Also see Gen. 37:25; 43:11.
Esther 2:12.
Ps. 45:8.
Prov. 7:17.
Song of Sol. 1:13; 3:6; 4:6, 14; 5:1, 5, 13.
Matt. 2:11.
Mark 15:23.

Myr´tle, a fragrant and beautiful shrub common in northern Palestine. It is used in contrast with the brier to illustrate the glory of the Church. Isa. 41:19; 55:13. The myrtle was used for wreaths for ancient victors.

Mysia, mizh´iah (*beech region?*), a province at the north-western extremity of Asia Minor. Acts 16:7, 8.

Mys´te-ry, in the New Testament, means a spiritual truth which cannot be discovered by mere reason, but which is now revealed, although its full comprehension is beyond our finite understanding. The Gospel is called a mystery. Eph. 3:9; Col. 1:26.
Also see Matt. 13:11.
Mark 4:11.
Luke 8:10.

Rom. 11:25; 16:25.
1 Cor. 2:7; 4:1; 13:2; 14:2; 15:51.
Eph. 1:9; 3:3, 4; 5:32; 6:19.
Col. 1:27; 2:2; 4:3.
2 Thess. 2:7.
1 Tim. 3:9, 16.
Rev. 1:20; 10:7; 17:5, 7.

N

Na´am (*pleasantness*), one of the sons of Caleb, the son of Jephunneh. 1 Chron. 4:15.

Na´a-mah (*pleasing*). [1] A daughter of Lamech and Zillah. Gen. 4:22. [2] The mother of King Rehoboam. 1 Kings 14:21; 2 Chron. 12:13.

Na´a-mah (*pleasing*), one of the cities of Judah. Josh. 15:41.

Na´a-man (*pleasantness*). [1] The "captain of the host" of the king of Syria. He was highly esteemed by the king for his mighty deeds, but he was a leper. He heard of the fame of the prophet Elisha through a captive Jewish girl, went to him, and was miraculously cured of his leprosy after washing seven times in the river Jordan, according to the direction of the prophet. 2 Kings 5:1–19. Naaman promised Elisha that he would "henceforth offer neither burnt-offering nor sacrifice unto other gods, but unto the LORD." [2] One of the sons of Benjamin. Gen. 46:21. [3] A son of Bela, the son of Benjamin. Num. 26:40; 1 Chron. 8:4. [4] The name apparently of a son of Ehud (or Abihud?). 1 Chron. 8:7.

Na´a-math-ite, a name given to Zophar, who was one of the friends of Job. Job 2:11; 11:1.

Na´a-mites, descendants of Naaman, a grandson of Benjamin. Num. 26:40.

Na´a-rah (*girl*), a wife of Ashur. 1 Chron. 4:5, 6.

Naarai, na´a-ray (*God reveals*), one of David's valiant men, 1 Chron. 11:37, called PAARI in 2 Sam. 23:35.

Na´a-ran (*juvenile*), a town of Ephraim. 1 Chron. 7:28.

Na´a-rath (*handmaid*), a town of Ephraim. Josh. 16:7.

Na-ash´on, one of the leaders of the tribe of Judah, and a brother of Elisheba, Aaron's wife. Exod. 6:23.

Na-as´son, in Matt. 1:4; Luke 3:32, is the Greek form of NAHSHON, one of the leaders of Judah. See NAHSHON.

Na´bal (*fool*), a wealthy inhabitant of Maon whose possessions were in Carmel. He was unfeeling and "evil in his doings," and refused in the most insulting manner to aid David, who had protected him from robbers. David immediately undertook to destroy him and his property, but was prevented from doing so by the discreet intervention of Abigail, the wife of Nabal. See 1 Sam. 25:2-38. Nabal died suddenly soon afterward, and Abigail subsequently became a wife of David.

Na´both (*fruits*), an inhabitant of Jezreel in Issachar whose vineyard Ahab, the king of Israel, coveted and obtained by the wicked artifice of his wife Jezebel, who had Naboth put to death. 1 Kings 21:1-19.

Nachon, na´kon, the name of the threshing-floor, between Kirjath-jearim and Jerusalem, near which Uzzah was slain for touching the ark of God. 2 Sam. 6:6. It is called CHIDON in 1 Chron. 13:9, and PEREZ-UZZA in 1 Chron. 13:11.

Nachor, na´kor, an ancestor of Joseph, the husband of Mary. Luke 3:34. See NAHOR, No. 1.

Na´dab (*liberal*). [1] One of the sons of

Aaron. He and his brother Abihu were miraculously destroyed for offering strange fire to the Lord. Lev. 10:1-3. [2] A son of Jeroboam I., whom he succeeded as king of Israel. 1 Kings 14:20; 15:25-31. [3] A son of Shammai. 1 Chron. 2:28. [4] A son of Gibeon. He was the uncle of King Saul. 1 Chron. 8:30.

Nag´ge (*shining*), one of the ancestors of Joseph, the husband of Mary. Luke 3:25.

Na´ha-lal, Na-hal´lal, and **Na´ha-lol** (*pasture*), one of the towns of Zebulun belonging to the Levites. Josh. 19:15; Judg. 1:30.

Na-ha´li-el (*valley of God*), one of the stations of the Israelites in their wanderings in the desert. Num. 21:19.

Na´ha-lol. Judg. 1:30. See NAHALAL.

Na´ham (*consolation*), a brother of Hodiah. 1 Chron. 4:19.

Na-ham´a-ni (*compassionate*), a Jew who returned with Zerubbabel from Babylon. Neh. 7:7.

Na-har´a-i or **Na´ha-ri** (*snorer*), an armor-bearer of Joab. 1 Chron. 11:39; 2 Sam. 23:37.

Na´hash (*serpent*). [1] One of the Ammonite kings. 2 Sam. 10:2. [2] A man (or woman) whose daughter Abigail was the mother of Amasa. 2 Sam. 17:25.

Na´hath (*rest*). [1] A grandson of Esau. He was a duke (chief) in Edom. Gen. 36:13; 1 Chron. 1:37. [2] One of the Levites, a descendant of Kohath. 1 Chron. 6:26. [3] A Levite who lived in Hezekiah's reign. 2 Chron. 31:13.

Nah´bi (*hidden*), one of the twelve spies sent by Moses to search the land of Canaan. Num. 13:14.

Na´hor (*snorting*), Gen. 11:23, or **Na-chor,** na´kor, Josh. 24:2. [1] The grandfather of Abraham. Gen. 11:23; 1 Chron.

1:26 [2] A brother of Abraham. Gen. 11:26.

Nah´shon (*enchanter*), one of the leaders of the tribe of Judah in the wilderness. Num. 1:7; 10:14. His name in the Greek form, NAASSON, is in the list of ancestors of Joseph, the husband of Mary.

Na´hum (*consolation*), one of the twelve minor prophets, of whose private life nothing is known except what is stated in Nah. 1:1, where he is called "the Elkoshite." He prophesied B. C. about 713, and probably during the reign of Hezekiah.

Na´hum, the Book of, consists of one poem of such eloquence, sublimity, and ardor of thought and language that it places its author in the highest rank of Hebrew poets. Its theme is "the burden of Nineveh"—that is the coming punishment of that city and the Assyrian empire for the cruel treatment of the Jews.

Nails of various kinds are mentioned in the Bible. In Deut. 21:12 finger-nails are mentioned. The nail used by Jael in killing Sisera, Judg. 4:21, 22, was a tent-pin, such as is driven into the ground to hold the cords of a tent. Nails of iron are mentioned in 1 Chron. 22:3, and nails of gold in 2 Chron. 3:9. Nails are mentioned in John 20:25; Col. 2:14, in connection with the crucifixion of Christ.

Na´in (*beauty*), a city of Galilee where Christ raised to life the only son of a widow. Luke 7:11-16.

Naioth, na´yoth (*habitations*), a place situated in Ramah, on Mount Ephraim. It was the residence of the prophet Samuel. 1 Sam. 19:18-23; 20:1.

Na´ked. This word is used in its literal sense in reference to Adam and Eve, Gen. 2:25, and in Job 1:21 in reference to himself. In 1 Sam. 19:24; John 21:7 it signi fies that the usual outer garments were not worn. The word "naked" is often used figuratively, meaning spiritual destitution. Rev. 3:17.

Names are first mentioned in Gen. 2:11. In Gen. 2:20 it is mentioned that Adam gave names "to all cattle, and to the fowl of the air, and to every beast of the field." Names of persons and places referred to in the Bible have generally special meanings which have reference to some particular circumstance connected with them. Many highly significant names are applied to Christ. See CHRIST, NAMES OF.

Also see Gen. 2–5; 10–13; 16; 17; 19; 21; 22; 24–26; 28–33; 35; 36; 38; 41; 46; 48; 50.

Exod. 1–3; 5; 6; 9; 15–18; 20; 23; 28; 31; 33–35; 39.

Lev. 18–22; 24.

Num. 1; 3; 4; 6; 11; 13; 17; 21; 25–27; 32; 34.

Deut. 3; 5–7; 9; 10; 12; 14; 16; 18; 21; 22; 25; 26; 28; 29; 32.

Josh. 5; 7; 9; 14; 15; 17; 19; 21; 23.

Judg. 1; 2; 8; 13; 15–18.

Ruth 1; 2; 4.

1 Sam. 1; 7–9; 12; 14; 16–18; 20; 21; 24; 25; 28.

2 Sam. 3–9; 12–14; 16–18; 20; 22; 23.

1 Kings 1; 3–5; 7–11; 13–16; 18; 21; 22.

2 Kings 2; 5; 8; 12; 14; 15; 18; 21–24.

1 Chron. 1; 2; 4; 6–9; 11–14; 16; 17; 21–23; 28; 29.

2 Chron. 2; 3; 6; 7; 12–14; 18; 20; 22; 24–29; 31; 33; 36.

Ezra 2; 5; 6; 8; 10.

Neh. 1; 7; 9.

Esther 2; 3; 8; 9.

Job 1; 18; 42.

Pss. 5; 7–9; 16; 18; 20; 22; 23; 25; 29; 31; 33; 34; 41; 44; 45; 48; 49; 52; 54; 61; 63; 66; 68; 69; 72; 74–76; 79; 80; 83; 86; 89; 91; 92; 99; 100; 102; 103; 105; 106; 109; 111; 113; 115; 116; 118; 119; 122; 124; 129; 135; 138–140; 142; 143; 145; 147–149.

Prov. 10; 18; 21; 22; 30.

Eccles. 6; 7.

Song of Sol. 1.

Isa. 4; 7–9; 14; 18; 24–26; 29; 30; 40–45; 47–52; 54–57; 59; 60; 63–66.

Jer. 3; 7; 10–16; 20; 23; 25–27; 29; 31–34; 37; 44; 46; 48; 50-52.

Lam. 3.

Ezek. 20; 23; 24; 36; 39; 43; 48.

Dan. 1; 2; 4; 9; 10.

Hos. 1; 2.

Joel 2.

Amos 2; 4–6; 9.

Mic. 4–6.

Nah. 1.

Zeph. 1; 3.

Zech. 5; 6; 10; 13; 14.

Matt. 1; 6; 7; 10; 12; 18; 19; 21; 23; 24; 27; 28.

Mark 5; 6; 9; 11; 13; 16.

Luke 1; 2; 6; 8–11; 13; 19; 21; 24.

John 1–3; 5; 10; 12; 14–18; 20.

Acts 1–5; 7–10; 13; 15; 16; 18; 19; 21; 22; 26; 28.

Rom. 1; 2; 9; 10; 15.

1 Cor. 1; 5; 6.

Eph. 1; 5.

Phil. 2; 4.

Col. 3.

2 Thess. 1; 3.

1 Tim. 6.

2 Tim. 2.

Heb. 1; 2; 6; 13.

James 2; 5.

1 Pet. 4.

1 John 2; 3; 5.

3 John :7, 14.

Rev. 2; 3; 6; 8; 9; 11; 13–17; 19; 21; 22.

Na-o´mi (*my delight*), the wife of Elimelech and the mother-in-law of RUTH (which see). Naomi, with her husband and two sons, moved from Bethlehem to Moab on account of a famine in their native land. Ruth 1:1, 2. Elimelech and his two sons died in Moab. Naomi returned to Bethlehem with her daughter-in-law Ruth, a native of Moab. See Ruth, chapters 1 to 4:17.

Naphish, na´fish (*recreation*), one of the sons of Ishmael. Gen. 25:15; 1 Chron. 1:31.

Naph´ta-li (*my wrestling*), Gen. 30:8, or **Neph´tha-lim,** Matt. 4:15, a son of Jacob and Bilhah.

Naph´ta-li, Tribe of, Num 1:42, 43, descendants of Naphtali. The chief hero of the tribe was Barak. Judg. 4:10.
Also see Num. 2:29; 13:14.
Josh. 21:6, 32.
1 Kings 7:14.
1 Chron. 6:62, 76; 27:19.

Naph´ta-li, Territory of, was in the north-east part of Palestine. Its boundaries are described in Josh. 19:32-39.

Naph´tu-him, a tribe of Egyptians, descendants of Mizraim. Gen. 10:13; 1 Chron. 1:11.

Nap´kin, in Luke 19:20; John 11:44; 20:7, means a little cloth. In Acts 19:12 the same word in the original is translated handkerchief. The word napkin had a much wider meaning in ancient times than at present.

Narcissus, nar-sis´sus (*daffodil*), one of the Christians at Rome. Paul sends greeting to him in Rom. 16:11.

Nard, a fragrant plant highly valued by the ancients both as an article of luxury and as a medicine. It is usually called spikenard. The word nard is in the marginal notes of Mark 14:3, and corresponds to spikenard in the text of that verse.

Na´than (*given*). [1] A prophet in the times of David and Solomon. He was highly esteemed by them. David conferred with him concerning the building of a house for the Lord. 2 Sam. 7:1-17. In a fine allegory Nathan rebuked David for his sin against Uriah. 2 Sam. 12:1-10. See Ps. 51, referring to David's repentance for this act. Nathan was one of the biographers of David, 1 Chron. 29:29, and also of Solomon. 2 Chron. 9:29. [2] A son of David by Bathsheba. 1 Chron. 3:5. [3] Father of one of David's valiant men. 2 Sam. 23:36. [4] A chief man who returned to Jerusalem with Ezra. Ezra 8:16. [5] A descendant of Judah, of the family of Jerahmeel. 1 Chron. 2:36. [6] Father of Solomon's principal officer. 1 Kings 4:5. [7] The brother of one of David's valiant men. 1 Chron. 11:38. [8] A Jew who took a foreign wife. Ezra 10:39.

Na-than´a-el (*gift of God*), a native of Cana in Galilee who confessed the Messiahship of Jesus and was with the apostles after the resurrection. John 1:45-49; 21:2. Christ called him 'an Israelite indeed, in whom is no guile!" Some suppose Nathanael to be the same as the apostle Bartholomew.

Nathan-melech, na´than-me´lek, a chamberlain of Josiah, King of Judah. 2 Kings 23:11.

Na´tion, in Phil. 2:15, means generation.

Naught, in 2 Kings 2:19; Prov. 20:14, means bad; worthless; nothing.

Naught´i-ness, in 1 Sam. 17:28; James 1:21, means wickedness.

Naught´y, in Prov. 6:12, means wicked

Na´um, an ancestor of Joseph, the husband of Mary. Luke 3:25.

Naves, in 1 Kings 7:33, means the centers of wheels which have spokes.

Naz-a-rene´, a native of Nazareth. Matt. 2:23; Acts 24:5.

Naz´a-reth (*separated?*), a city of lower Galilee, about sixty-five miles north of Jerusalem, nearly half-way from the river Jordan to the Mediterranean Sea, and about fourteen miles from the Sea of Galilee. It is not mentioned in the Old Testament (except by an indirect allusion of prophecy, Matt. 2:23), or by any writer before the time of Christ, and had a bad reputation among the Jews, John 1:46, but "Jesus of Nazareth" has made it a household word throughout Christendom. It was the home of Jesus from his childhood until he commenced his public ministry and was rejected by his own townsmen. Luke 4:28-31. "In Bethlehem we feel the joy of our Saviour's birth; in Jerusalem, the awe and anguish of his crucifixion, but also the glory of his resurrection; in Nazareth we look at the humble abode of his youth and early manhood. Talent and character are matured in quiet seclusion for the great battle of public life."

Also see Matt. 4:13; 21:11; 26:71.

Mark 1:9, 24; 10:47; 14:67; 16:6.

Luke 1:26; 2:4, 39, 51; 4:16, 34; 18:37; 24:19.

John 1:45; 18:5, 7; 19:19.

Acts 2:22; 3:6; 4:10; 6:14; 10:38; 22:8; 26:9.

Naz´a-rite, one who consecrated himself to the Lord for a time, during which he abstained from certain things. Num. 6:2; Judg. 13:5.

Also see Num. 6:13, 18-21.

Judg. 13:7; 16:17.

Lam. 4:7.

Amos 2:11, 12.

Ne´ah (*shaking*), a town on the border of Zebulun. Josh. 19:13.

Ne-ap´o-lis (*new city*), a city on the seacoast of Macedonia, about ten miles southeast from Philippi. Acts 16:11. It was the place where Paul first landed in Europe.

Ne-a-ri´ah (*servant of Jehovah*). [1] A grandson of Shechaniah. 1 Chron. 3:22, 23. [2] A captain of the Simeonites. 1 Chron. 4:42.

Neb´a-i (*fruitful*), a Jew who sealed the covenant made by Nehemiah. Neh. 10:19.

Nebaioth, ne-ba´yoth, Isa. 60:7, or **Ne-ba´joth** (*heights*), Gen. 25:13, the eldest son of Ishmael, the son of Hagar. His descendants were a pastoral people. Isa. 60:7.

Ne-bal´lat (*hidden folly*), a town of Judah. Neh. 11:34.

Ne´bat (*aspect*), the father of Jeroboam, king of Israel. 1 Kings 11:26; 12:2; 2 Kings 3:3.

Ne´bo (*proclaimer*), an Assyrian god. Isa. 46:1.

Ne´bo (*prophet*), a mountain on the east side of the river Jordan, and part of the range of Abarim. It is in the land of Moab and "over against Jericho," and from it Moses beheld the land of Canaan. Deut. 32:49. See Pisgah.

Ne´bo. [1] A city on the east side of the river Jordan. It was rebuilt by the Gadites, Num 32:3, 38, and was captured by the Moabites. Isa. 15:2; Jer. 48:1. [2] A town of Benjamin. Neh. 7:33.

Nebuchadnezzar, neb-u-kad-nez´zar, or **Nebuchadrezzar,** neb-u-kad-rez´zar (*may Nebo protect the crown!*), the greatest of kings of Babylon, was the son of Nabopolassar, the founder of the Babylonian empire, and he reigned B C. 605-561. Sent by his father against the Egyptian king Pharaoh-necho, he defeated the latter in a great battle on the Euphrates River, Jer. 46:2, conquered all the countries in

Asia which Pharaoh-necho had occupied—namely, Syria, Phœnicia, Palestine, etc.—captured Jerusalem, and carried away as captives a part of its inhabitants, among them Daniel and his companions. Dan. 1:1-4. On the death of Nabopolassar, B. C. 605, Nebuchadnezzar ascended the throne. Jehoiakim, king of Judah, who had been made a vassal of Nebuchadnezzar, revolted in B. C. 602. Nebuchadnezzar made him a prisoner, but afterward released him. His son Jehoiachin also revolted, but this time Nebuchadnezzar inflicted a heavy punishment. Jehoiachin, with a number of the principal inhabitants of Jerusalem and all the treasures of the Temple and palace, were carried to Babylon, 2 Kings 24:12-16, and Jehoiachin's uncle Mattaniah, whose name was changed to Zedekiah, was made king of Judah. Zedekiah also revolting, Nebuchadnezzar broke down the walls of Jerusalem, destroyed the Temple, razed the whole city to the ground, put out the eyes of Zedekiah, and carried him and the inhabitants of Judea captives to Babylon, in B. C. 588. See JERUSALEM. The first four chapters of the book of Daniel contain an account of events during the reign of Nebuchadnezzar, including the divine infliction of madness which he for a time suffered. During his reign he rebuilt all the cities of upper Babylonia and constructed vast temples, palaces, etc., including the famous hanging gardens of Babylon.
Also see 2 Kings 24:1, 10, 11; 25:1, 8, 22.
1 Chron. 6:15.
2 Chron. 36:6, 7, 10, 13.
Ezra 1:7; 2:1; 5:12, 14; 6:5.
Neh. 7:6.
Esther 2:6.
Jer. 21:2, 7; 22:25; 24:1; 25:1, 9; 27:6, 8, 20; 28:3, 11, 14; 29:1, 3, 21; 32:1; 34:1; 35:11; 37:1; 39:1, 5, 11; 43:10; 44:30; 46:13, 26; 49:28, 30; 50:17; 51:34; 52:4, 12, 28-30.
Ezek. 26:7; 29:18, 19; 30:10.
Dan. 1:18; 2:1, 28, 46; 3:1-3, 5, 7, 9, 13, 14, 16, 19, 24, 26, 28; 4:1, 4, 18, 28, 31, 33, 34, 37; 5:2, 11, 18.

Nebuchadrezzar, neb-u-kad-rez´zar, in Jer. 21:2, 7, etc. Ezek. 26:7, is the more correct form for the name NEBUCHADNEZZAR (which see).

Neb-u-shas´ban (*Nebo saves me*), the chief of Nebuchadnezzar's eunuchs. Jer. 39:13.

Neb-u-zar-a´dan (*Nebo sends posterity*), captain of Nebuchadnezzar's bodyguard, who conducted the siege of Jerusalem. 2 Kings 25:8-21. Jeremiah was treated very kindly by this captain. Jer. 39:11; 40:1.

Necho, ne´ko, a king of Egypt in the time of Josiah, king of Judah. 2 Chron. 35:20, 22; 36:4.

Nec´ro-man-cer, one who pretends to reveal future events by the communication with the dead. This pretense is forbidden in Deut. 18:11.

Ned-a-bi´ah (*whom Jehovah impelled*), a son of Jeconiah, the son of Jehoiakim, king of Judah. 1 Chron. 3:18.

Nees´ings, in Job 41:18, is used to describe the violent breathing of the enraged leviathan, and is translated "sneezed" in 2 Kings 4:35.

Neg´i-nah (*a stringed instrument*) is the singular of NEGINOTH, and is found in the title of Ps. 61. See NEGINOTH.

Neg´i-noth is found in the titles of Pss. 4, 6, 54, 55, 67, 76, and in the marginal notes, Hab. 3:19. It appears to be a general name for musical instruments, and is translated "stringed instruments" in Hab. 3:19.

Ne-hel´a-mite, a name applied to

Shemaiah, Jer. 29:24, and translated in the marginal notes "dreamer." No town of Nehelam is known. Nehelamite is also found in Jer. 29:31, 32.

Ne-he-mi´ah (*consoled by Jehovah*). [1] The son of Hachaliah, Neh. 1:1; was the pious restorer and governor of Jerusalem after the Babylonian exile. He lived in the fifth century B. C., and was cup-bearer, a very high position, to the Persian king Artaxerxes, who afterward appointed him governor of Jerusalem and permitted him to rebuild that city. Neh. 2:1-6. Nehemiah was the model of a Hebrew patriot and statesman. See NEHEMIAH, THE BOOK OF. [2] A chief man among the Jews who went up to Jerusalem with Zerubbabel after the captivity. Ezra 2:2; Neh. 7:7. [3] The son of Azbuk who repaired part of the wall of Jerusalem after the captivity. Neh. 3:16.

Ne-he-mi´ah, the Book of, the sixteenth of the Old Testament Canon, is a continuation of the book of Ezra, and narrates how Nehemiah (No. 1, mentioned above) returned to Jerusalem, rebuilt the walls in spite of the insidious opposition of some of his countrymen, and, in conjunction with Ezra, re-established the law and the Sabbath in the country and introduced other necessary reforms.

Ne´hi-loth, in the title of Ps. 5, is a word commonly applied to a flute or to a similar musical instrument.

Ne´hum (*comfort*), a leader among the Jews that returned with Zerubbabel from Babylon. Neh. 7:7. He is called REHUM in Ezra 2:2.

Nehushta, ne-hush´tah (*brass*), the wife of Jehoiakim and mother of Jehoiachin, kings of Judah. 2 Kings 24:8.

Ne-hush´tan (*a piece of brass*), the name which King Hezekiah gave in con-

tempt to the brazen serpent that Moses had formerly set up, Num. 21:8, 9, in the wilderness (see BRAZEN SERPENT), and which the Israelites had preserved, worshipped, and offered incense to. It was therefore broken in pieces and destroyed by King Hezekiah. 2 Kings 18:4.

Ne-i´el or **Ne´i-el** (*treasured of God*), a place which was one of the landmarks on the boundary-line between Asher and Zebulun. Josh. 19:27.

Neigh´bor. Luke 10:29. The Pharisees confined the meaning of this word to people of their own nation or to their own friends. Christ taught them, in the parable of the Good Samaritan, that all men are neighbors. Luke 10:30-37.

Also see Exod. 3:22; 11:2; 12:4; 20:16, 17; 21:14; 22:7-9, 10, 11, 14, 26; 32:27.

Lev. 6:2; 18:20; 19:13, 15-18; 20:10; 24:19; 25:14, 15.

Deut. 4:42; 5:20, 21; 15:2; 19:4, 5, 11, 14; 22:24, 26; 23:24, 25; 27:17, 24.

Josh. 9:16; 20:5.

Ruth 4:7, 17.

1 Sam. 15:28; 28:17.

2 Sam. 12:11.

1 Kings 4:3; 8:31; 20:35.

2 Chron. 6:22.

Job 12:4; 16:21; 31:9.

Pss. 12:2; 15:3; 101; 5.

Prov. 3:28, 29; 6:29; 11:9, 12; 12:26; 14:20, 21; 16:29; 18:17; 19:4; 21:10; 24:28; 25:8, 9, 17, 18; 26:19; 27:10; 28:3; 29:5; 31:11; 44:13; 79:4, 12; 80:6; 89:41.

Eccles. 4:4.

Isa. 3:5; 19:2; 41:6.

Jer. 5:8; 6:21; 7:5; 9:4, 5, 8, 20; 12:14; 22:8, 13; 23:27, 30, 35; 29:23; 31:34; 34:15, 17; 49:10, 18; 50:40.

Ezek. 16:26; 18:6, 11, 15; 22:11, 12;

23:5, 12; 33:26.
Hab. 2:15.
Zech. 3:10; 8:10, 16, 17; 11:6; 14:13.
Matt. 5:43; 19:19; 22:39.
Mark 12:31, 33.
Luke 1:58; 10:27, 36; 14:12; 15:6, 9.
John 9:8.
Acts 7:27.
Rom. 13:9, 10; 15:2.
Gal. 5:14.
Eph. 4:25.
Heb. 8:11.
James 2:8.

Ne´keb (*cavern*), a town on the boundary of Naphtali. Josh. 19:33.

Nekoda, ne-ko´dah (*distinguished*), one whose descendants returned from Babylon with Zerubbabel. Ezra 2:48, 60.

Ne-mu´el (*day of God*). [1] A descendant of Reuben. Num. 26:9. [2] One of the sons of Simeon. Num. 26:12; 1 Chron. 4:24. He is called JEMUEL in Gen. 46:10; Exod. 6:15.

Ne-mu´el-ites, the descendants of Nemuel, a son of Simeon. Num. 26:12.

Ne´pheg (*sprout*). [1] One of the brothers of Korah. Exod. 6:21. [2] One of David's sons. 2 Sam. 5:15; 1 Chron. 14:6.

Neph´ew. This word, in the Authorized Version, always means either "grandchild" or "descendant" generally, which was its old English meaning. Job 18:19; Isa. 14:22.

Ne´phish, 1 Chron. 5:19, is an improper form of NAPHISH, one of the sons of Ishmael.

Ne-phish´e-sim, Neh. 7:52, an incorrect form of NEPHUSIM (which see).

Neph´tha-lim, Matt. 4:13, 15; Rev. 7:6, another name for the land and tribe of NAPHTALI (which see).

Neph´to-ah (*opening*), **the Water of.** Its fountain was one of the landmarks

between Benjamin and Judah. Nephtoah was a small stream near Jerusalem. Josh. 15:9; 18:15.

Ne-phu´sim, Ne-phish´e-sim (*expansions*), a family whose descendants returned from Babylon with Zerubbabel. Ezra 2:50.

Ner (*light, lamp*) was the father of Kish and the grandfather of King Saul. 1 Chron. 8:33.

Nereus, ne´rews, a disciple to whom Paul sent salutation. Rom. 16:15.

Ner´gal (*great hero*), a god of the Assyrians which was similar to Mars. 2 Kings 17:30. Monuments containing his name and titles have been found.

Ner´gal-sha-re´zer (*fire-prince*), a name applied to two princes of Babylon when Jerusalem was taken by Nebuchadnezzar. Jer. 39:3, 13.

Ne´ri (*lamp of Jehovah*), an ancestor of Joseph, the husband of Mary. Luke 3:27.

Ne-ri´ah (*lamp of Jehovah*), the father of Baruch, Jeremiah's messenger. Jer. 32:12; 36:4.

Ne-than´e-el (*given of God*). [1] One of the captains of Issachar in the wilderness. Num. 1:8; 10:15. [2] A son of Jesse. 1 Chron. 2:14. [3] A priest in the time of King David. 1 Chron. 15:24. [4] One of the Levites. 1 Chron. 24:6. [5] A son of Obed-edom. 1 Chron. 26:4. [6] One of the princes in the reign of Jehoshaphat. 2 Chron. 17:7. [7] A Levite in the time of King Josiah. 2 Chron 35:9. [8] A Jew who took a foreign wife. Ezra 10:22. [9] A priest in the time of Joiakim. Neh. 12:21. [10] One of the players on musical instruments when the wall of Jerusalem was dedicated. Neh. 12:36.

Neth-a-ni´ah (*given of Jehovah*). [1] A son of Elishama. 2 Kings 25:25. [2] One of the sons of Asaph. 1 Chron. 25:2, 12.

[3] A Levite in the reign of Jehoshaphat. 2 Chron. 17:8. [4] Jehudi's father. Jer. 36:14.

Neth´er, in Deut. 24:6, Exod. 19:17; Ezek. 32:18, means lower.

Neth´i-nim, a class of persons who were employed as servants to the Levites in their ministrations in the Tabernacle and in the Temple. 1 Chron. 9:2; Ezra 2:43, 58; Neh. 3:26.

Ne-to´phah (*dropping*), the name of a town apparently in Judah. Ezra 2:22; Neh. 7:26.

Ne-toph´a-thi, in Neh. 12:28, is elsewhere called NETOPHATHITE.

Ne-toph´a-thite, an inhabitant of Netophah. 2 Sam. 23:28; 2 Kings 25:23.

Nets are often mentioned in the Bible, especially in connection with the first disciples of Christ, several of whom were fishermen. Matt. 13:47, 48; Luke 5:1-10. Nets were also used in hunting animals and in catching birds.

Net´tles, in Job 30:7; Prov. 24:31; Zeph. 2:9, probably refers to a shrub resembling the common nettle, but larger.

New Je-ru´sa-lem. Rev. 21:2. See JERUSALEM, NEW.

New Moon. Each of the Hebrew months commenced with the new moon. Moses appointed special sacrifices for that time. Num. 28:11–15. See MOON, and MONTH.

New Tes´ta-ment. See BIBLE.

New Year. See TRUMPETS, FEAST OF.

Ne-zi´ah (*famous*), one of those whose children returned to Jerusalem from the captivity. Ezra 2:54; Neh. 7:56.

Ne´zib (*statue*), one of the cities of Judah. Josh. 15:43.

Nib´haz (*barker*), one of the idols of the Avites. 2 Kings 17:31.

Nib´shan (*light, soft soil*), a city in the wilderness of Judah. Josh. 15:62.

Ni-ca´nor (*conqueror*) was one of the first seven deacons of the early Church in the time of the apostles. Acts 6:5.

Nic-o-de´mus (*victor of the people*), a noted Pharisee and Jewish ruler who "came to Jesus by night" and conversed with him concerning his doctrine. John 3:1-20. He defended Christ against the Pharisees, John 7:50, 51, and brought spices to anoint his body. John 19:39.

Nic-o-la´i-tanes, a sect condemned by the Lord in Rev. 2:6, 15.

Nic´o-las (*victor of the people*), a native of Antioch who was one of the first seven deacons of the early Church in the time of the apostles. Acts 6:5.

Ni-cop´o-lis (*city of victory*). There were several cities of this name in ancient times. The one at which Paul determined to winter, Titus 3:12, was probably the noted Nicopolis in Epirus.

Niger, ni´jer (*black*), the surname of Simeon, one of the prophets and teachers who were at Antioch. Acts 13:1.

Night is first mentioned in Gen. 1:5. In John 9:4 it is figuratively used to signify death, and in 1 Thess. 5:5 to denote sin. Its meaning is evident in Rev. 21:25; 22:5.

Night´hawk is mentioned in Lev. 11:16 and Deut. 14:15 as an unclean bird. It is not the bird known in the United States by that name, but is probably a kind of owl common in Egypt and Syria.

Nile (*blue, dark*), the famous river of Egypt, is formed by the junction of the White Nile and the Blue or Black Nile. The White Nile is the principal stream, and rises in Lake Victoria, most of which is south of the equator. The Blue Nile rises in the mountains of Abyssinia. The whole length of the Nile is about four thousand miles. Its course below the junction of the Blue and the White Nile is nearly north, and it flows into the Mediterranean Sea by two principal mouths, forming a delta which commences one hundred miles from the Mediterranean Sea and extends one hundred sixty miles along its shore. As rain seldom falls in Egypt proper, its fertility depends entirely on the annual overflow of the Nile, which generally commences in June and begins to decrease in October. It leaves a deposit of mud which fertilizes the valley. The overflow of the Nile is distributed by numerous canals and by the use of buckets with which it is raised above the water-level. The Nile was worshipped as a god by the ancient Egyptians. Its greatest width is about three thousand three hundred feet. The word "Nile" is not found in the Bible, but that river is referred to as SIHOR in Josh. 13:3; Isa. 23:3; Jer. 2:18; as SHIHOR in 1 Chron. 13:5; as "the river" in Gen. 41:1; Exod. 1:22; 2:3, 5; and as "the flood of Egypt" in Amos 8:8; 9:5. See EGYPT.

Nim´rah (*limpid, pure*), one of the cities of Gad east of the Jordan. Num. 32:3. It is evidently the same as BETH-NIMRAH in Num. 32:36.

Nim´rim (*limpid, pure*) is the plural form of NIMRAH. "The waters of Nimrim," mentioned in Isa. 15:6; Jer. 48:34, refer to a stream or brook in Moab.

Nim´rod (*strong*). [1] One of the sons of Cush, the son of Ham. In Gen. 10:9 he is mentioned as a "mighty hunter before the LORD." He was also noted as a conqueror and as the founder of Babylon. [2] The name is also used to denote the kingdom he founded, "the land of Nimrod." Mic. 5:6.

Nim´shi (*drawn out, saved*), father of King Jehu. 1 Kings 19:16; 2 Kings 9:2.

Nin´e-ve, Luke 11:32, is another form of NINEVEH (which see).

Nin´e-veh (*dwelling of Nin?*) stood on the eastern shore of the Tigris, two hundred and fifty miles north of Babylon and five hundred and fifty miles north-west of the Persian Gulf. It was founded by Asshur, Gen. 10:11, or, according to another translation, by Nimrod (who "went out into Assyria). Nineveh became the capital of Assyria, probably during the reign of Sennacherib, and remained so till its destruction, after a siege of two years, by the combined forces of the Medes and the Babylonians, B. C. 606. Its site is marked by a number of huge mounds. In Scripture it is mentioned principally in the books of Jonah and Nahum. Concerning its extent scholars are not agreed. It was at all events one of the largest cities that ever existed, having within its walls not only gardens and groves, but also vast pastures. Up to the middle of the nineteenth century very little was known about the city, but since that time excavations have disclosed large portions of the city walls, three temples of various dates, the palace of Shalmaneser, three palaces of Sennacherib, a palace of Tiglath-pileser II., and a temple of Nebo. These architectural monuments, with numerous pieces of sculpture and various specimens of industrial art in metal, glass, alabaster, etc. which have been found in the mounds of Nineveh, show that Assyrian civilization exercised a decided influence on Persia and Greece. The most precious discovery, however, is that of vast remnants of the library of Tiglath-pileser, consisting of tablets and cylinders of burnt clay covered with arrow-headed or wedge-shaped characters (see ASSYRIA). These curious inscriptions have been deciphered, and they furnish a complete confirmation of the truth of the Biblical records.

Nin´e-vites, inhabitants of Nineveh. Luke 11:30.

Ni´san, Neh. 2:1, the name given, after the Babylonian captivity, to the first month of the Hebrew sacred year and the seventh month of the civil year. It was previously called ABIB, and corresponded nearly with our April. See MONTH.

Nisroch, nis´rok (*great eagle?*), one of the Assyrian gods, in whose temple at Nineveh the Assyrian king Sennacherib was murdered by his sons. 2 Kings 19:37; Isa. 37:38.

Ni´tre, mentioned in Prov. 25:20 and Jer. 2:22, means an earthy and alkaline salt which resembles, and is used like, soap. It rises from the bottom of Lake Natron in Egypt, and is not in any respect like the nitre used in manufacturing gunpowder.

No, an ancient city of Egypt. Ezek. 30:14–16; Jer. 46:25. See NO-AMON.

No-a-di´ah (*whom Jehovah meets*). [1] One of the Levites. Ezra 8:33. [2] A prophetess who attempted to hinder Nehemiah in his work of reconstruction. Neh. 6:14.

No´ah (*rest*), the son of Lamech. He was the ninth after Adam, and was preserved with his family in the ark (see ARK) from the flood which destroyed the rest of the human race. He "found grace in the eyes of the LORD," Gen. 6:8, and was "a preacher of righteousness." 2 Pet. 2:5. He built an altar immediately after leaving the ark and offered sacrifices unto the LORD. Gen. 8:20. His history and that of the flood is given in Genesis, chapters 5 to 9. He died at the age of nine hundred and fifty years. Gen. 9:29. He is mentioned in Heb. 11:7 among the heroes of faith. See DELUGE.

Also see Gen. 10:1, 32.
Num. 26:33; 27:1; 36:11.
Josh. 17:3.
1 Chron. 1:4.

Isa. 54:9.
Ezek. 14:14, 20.
1 Pet. 3:20.

No´ah (*motion*), a daughter of Zelophehad. Num. 26:33; Josh. 17:3.

No-A´mon (*place of Amon?*), in the marginal notes, Nah. 3:8, translated "populous No" in the text of that verse. It was the capital of Upper Egypt, and was named after the god Amon. It was situated on both sides of the Nile, about four hundred fifty miles from its mouth. It was also called *Diospolis* and *Thebes*.

Nob (*height*), one of the cities of the priests. It was situated in Benjamin, near Jerusalem. 1 Sam. 22:19; Neh. 11:32. It was destroyed by King Saul. 1 Sam. 22:9-19.

No´bah (*barking*), an Israelite, the conqueror of Kenath, a city of the Amorites. Num. 32:42.

No´bah (*barking*), the name given by Nobah to Kenath and its adjacent villages when he conquered that place. Num. 32:42; Judg. 8:11. See KENATH.

No´ble-man, John 4:46-54, came to Christ to beseech him to heal his son, lying "at the point of death." This nobleman, according to the marginal notes, John 4:46, may have been a courtier or a ruler connected with the court of Herod.

Nod (*flight*), the land in which Cain dwelt. It was east of Eden. Gen. 4:16.

No´dab (*nobility*), a name given to a descendant of Ishmael and founder of a tribe of Arabs. 1 Chron. 5:19.

No´e, Matt. 24:37; Luke 3:36, and elsewhere in the New Testament the patriarch NOAH (which see).

No´gah (*brightness*), one of the sons of David. 1 Chron. 3:7; 14:6.

No´hah (*rest*), a son of Benjamin. 1 Chron. 8:2.

Noi´some, in Ps. 91:3; Ezek. 14:15, 21,

means noxious; hurtful.

Non (*fish*), 1 Chron. 7:27, the father of Joshua, called Nun in Exod. 33:11.

Noph, a famous city of Egypt, Isa. 19:13; Jer. 2:16; afterward called Memphis (which see).

No´phah (*blast*), one of the towns of Moab. Num. 21:30.

Nose Jew´els were strung upon a ring of gold or some other metal, which was put through one of the nostrils. Isa. 3:21.

Nov´ice, in 1 Tim. 3:6, means, as in the marginal notes, one newly come to the faith; one recently converted and received into the Christian Church.

Num´bers. Among the Hebrews special significance was given to certain numbers. *Seven* implies perfection, and is often used in the Bible. There are seven days in the week; the Revelation of John mentions seven churches, seven angels, seven golden vials; also seven heads and seven crowns of the dragon. See Seven.

Num´bers, the fourth book of the Old Testament and of the Pentateuch, is so named because it gives an account of the numbering of Israel. It also contains sundry laws given to the Israelites and interesting facts connected with their journey through the wilderness, notably the sedition of Miriam and Aaron, the report of the spies sent to search out Canaan, the brazen serpent raised by Moses, Balaam and his ass, etc. See Pentateuch.

Nun (*fish*), the father of Joshua, Exod. 33:11; Num. 11:28, called Non in 1 Chron. 7:27.

Nurse. The nurse of Rebekah went with her to Canaan, and was buried with great mourning. Gen. 24:59; 35:8. Nurses were highly esteemed in ancient times.

Nur´ture, in Eph 6:4, means education; training.

Nuts, in Gen. 43:11, probably means pistachio-nuts. They resemble almonds but taste like walnuts. In Song of Sol. 6:11 nuts means English walnuts.

Nym´phas (*bridegroom*), one of the members of the church of Laodicea to whom Paul sent salutation. Col. 4:15.

O

Oak stands in the English Bible for six Hebrew words (most of which mean *strong*), and sometimes denotes any strong tree or a grove of trees rather than any particular tree. In many instances, Gen. 35:4; Judg. 6:11, it represents the elm tree of Hos. 4:13, and the Teil Tree (which see) of Isa. 6:13. It often served as a landmark and to designate the locality of great events. Gen. 35:4; Josh. 24:26. The word translated "plains," Gen. 12:6; Deut. 11:30, means places noted for groves of the oak. The wood of the oak was used for idols. Isa. 44:14. See Hebron.

Oath. To take an oath is to call God to witness what we affirm. The custom was observed in the days of the patriarchs. Gen. 21:23. God also bound himself by oaths. Acts 2:30; Gen. 26:3. The taking of an oath was accompanied by the raising of the hand toward heaven, also by putting the hand under the thigh. Gen. 24:2, 3. Our Lord prohibited the use of profane and careless oaths. Matt. 5:34-36.
Also see Gen. 24:8, 41; 26:28; 50:25.
Exod. 22:11.
Lev. 5:4.
Num. 5:19, 21; 30:2, 10, 13.
Deut. 7:8; 29:12, 14.
Josh. 2:17, 20; 9:20.
Judg. 21:5.

1 Sam. 14:26-28.
2 Sam. 21:7.
1 Kings 2:43; 8:31; 18:10.
2 Kings 11:4.
1 Chron. 16:16.
2 Chron. 6:22; 15:15.
Neh. 5:12; 10:29.
Ps. 105:9.
Eccles. 8:2; 9:2.
Jer. 11:5.
Ezek. 16:59; 17:13, 16, 18, 19; 21:23.
Dan. 9:11.
Hab. 3:9.
Zech. 8:17.
Matt. 5:33; 14:7, 9; 26:72.
Mark 6:26.
Luke 1:73.
Acts 23:21.
Heb. 6:16, 17; 7:20, 21, 28.
James 5:12.

O-ba-di´ah (*servant of Jehovah*). [1] The head of a family which apparently descended from David. 1 Chron. 3:21. [2] A descendant of Tola, the son of Issachar. 1 Chron. 7:3. [3] A son of Azel, a Benjamite. 1 Chron. 8:38; 9:44. [4] A Levite, the son of Shemaiah. 1 Chron. 9:16. [5] A Gadite who joined David in Ziklag. 1 Chron. 12:9. [6] The governor of the house of Ahab, king of Israel. He hid and fed many of the Lord's prophets during the persecution of Jezebel. 1 Kings 18:3-16. [7] One of the princes of Judah who taught the people the law in the reign of Jehoshaphat. 2 Chron. 17:7. [8] The father of Ishmaiah. 1 Chron. 27:19. [9] A Levite overseer of repairs of the house of the Lord in the time of Josiah. 2 Chron. 34:12. [10] A son of Jehiel. Ezra 8:9. [11] A priest who sealed the covenant made by Nehemiah. Neh. 10:5. [12] A porter for the sanctuary. Neh. 12:25. [13] OBADIAH, the fourth of the minor prophets, lived after the destruction of Jerusalem, B. C. 588, but nothing more is known about him. Obad. verse 1.

O-ba-di´ah, the Book of, begins with the denunciation of the Edomites for their wicked and cruel conduct toward the Jews in the days of their misfortune, and closes with predicting the discomfiture of the Edomites and the restored glory and happiness of the descendants of Jacob. The striking resemblance between the first nine verses of Obadiah and Jeremiah 49:7-16 seems to indicate that one of these prophets had read the other's prophecy.

O´bal (*bare*), a son of Joktan, Gen. 10:28, called EBAL in 1 Chron. 1:22.

O´bed (*serving*). [1] A son of Boaz and Ruth and father of Jesse. Ruth 4:17, 21, 22; 1 Chron. 2:12. He was an ancestor of Joseph, the husband of Mary. Matt.1:5; Luke 3:32. [2] A son of Ephlal, who was a descendant of Judah. 1 Chron. 2:37, 38. [3] One of David's valiant men. 1 Chron. 11:47. [4] A porter for the Tabernacle in the time of David. 1 Chron. 26:7. [5] The father of Azariah, who was one of the captains who aided Jehoiada the priest in making Joash king of Judah. 2 Chron. 23:1.

O´bed-e´dom (*servant of Edom*). [1] A Gittite in whose house the ark of God was kept three months after the Lord slew Uzzah for putting his hand on it. 2 Sam. 6:6–10; 1 Chron. 13:13. [2] A Levite who had charge of the vessels of the sanctuary in the time of King Amaziah. 2 Chron. 25:24.

O-be´di-ence of men to God is their supreme duty. Acts 5:29. It should be from the heart. 1 John 5:2, 3. It is also due from children to parents, Exod. 20:12; from servants to their employers, Eph. 6:5; and from citizens to the government.

Rom. 13:1-5.
Also see Exod. 24:7.
Num. 27:20.
Deut. 4:30; 8:20.
2 Sam. 22:45.
Prov. 25:12.
Isa. 1:19; 42:24.
Acts 6:7.
Rom. 1:5; 5:19; 6:16; 15:18; 16:19, 26.
1 Cor. 14:34.
2 Cor. 2:9; 7:15; 10:5, 6.
Eph. 6:5.
Phil. 2:8.
Titus 2:5, 9.
Philem. :21.
Heb. 5:8.
1 Pet. 1:2, 14.

O-bei´sance, an expression of deference or respect. See SALUTE, and SALUTATION.

O´bil (*camel-driver*), the superintendent of camels in David's time. 1 Chron. 27:30.

Ob-la´tion, an offering to God. Lev. 2:4, 7. See OFFERING.

O´both (*bottles, water-skins*), a station of the Israelites in their wanderings through the desert. It was east of Edom. Num. 21:10; 33:43.

Ob-serv´ers of times, in Deut. 18:10, 14, refers to men who had a superstitious regard for days that were supposed to be lucky or unlucky, as decided by astrology. All such men were condemned. Deut. 18:9-14.

Oc´cu-pi´ers, in Ezek. 27:27, means traders.

Oc´cu-py, in Luke 19:13, means trade with, as in the Revised Version.

Oc´ran (*troubled* or *troubler*), the father of Pagiel. The latter was employed with Moses in numbering the people. Num. 1:13; 7:77.

O´ded (*erecting*). [1] The father of Azar-iah the prophet. 2 Chron. 15:1, 8. [2] A prophet in Samaria, 2 Chron. 28:9-11.

Of, in Mark 1:9, means "by;" in Acts 13:29, "concerning;" and in 1 Cor. 15:47, "out of."

Of´fend and **Of´fence** often mean that which causes one to stumble, or to sin. Thus in Matt. 5:29 the meaning is, if thy right eye "causeth thee to stumble," as in the Revised Version. In Rom. 9:33 the Saviour is referred to as a "rock of offence," because his life, teachings, and death were so totally different from what the Jews had expected as to actually prove an obstacle to their accepting him as the long-promised Messiah.

Of´fer-ing, Ob-la´tion, that which is presented to the Lord as a confession, consecration, expiation, or thanksgiving, formed a very important part of the religious worship among the Jews. The offerings were from the animal and vegetable kingdoms, and were known as *burnt-offerings, meat-offerings, heave-offerings, peace-offerings, sin-offerings, trespass-offerings,* etc., etc. Each had its own special significance, and minute directions were given for its preparation and observance. See WAVE-OFFERING.

Of´fi-cer, in Exod. 5:14, means a "scribe who keeps registers and tables," and generally has that meaning in the Old Testament. In the New Testament it is applied to bailiffs and those who collect fines. Matt. 5:25; Luke 12:58.

Oft´en. In 1 Tim. 5:23 "thine often" means "thy frequent."

Og (*long-necked?*), the king of Bashan who fought against the passage of the Israelites through his dominions. Deut. 3:1. He was of gigantic stature, Josh. 13:12, but was defeated and slain, together with his sons. Deut. 1:4; Num. 21:34.

His long "bedstead of iron" was preserved as a memorial of his stature. Deut. 3:11.

O´had (*power*), one of Simeon's sons. Gen. 46:10; Exod. 6:15.

O´hel (*tent*), a son of Zerubbabel. 1 Chron. 3:20.

Oil. Among the nations mentioned in the Bible oil was used for anointing the head and body, especially on festivals and joyous occasions. Hence the use of oil is significant of joy and gladness, Ps. 23:5, and the omission of it denoted sorrow. 2 Sam. 14:2. The oil was made from the olive-berry, and was often perfumed with spices. It was also used by the Jews in the consecration of kings and high-priests, 1 Sam. 10:1; Exod. 29:7; in their meat-offerings, Lev. 2:4-7; for illuminating purposes in lamps, Matt. 25:3; in the preparation of food, taking the place of butter and lard, 1 Kings 17:12; for medicinal purposes, Luke 10:34; and for anointing the dead. Matt. 26:12. In ancient times the methods for extracting the oil from the olive-berry was very simple: Two reservoirs, usually eight feet square and four feet deep, were arranged one above the other; the berries were placed in the upper one and were then trodden out with the feet. Another method crushed the berries under stone rollers and then subjected them to a heavy pressure. See OLIVE.

Also see Gen. 28:18; 35:14.

Exod. 25:6; 27:20; 29:2, 21, 40; 30:24, 25, 31; 31:11; 35:8, 14, 15, 28; 37:29; 39:37, 38; 40:9.

Lev. 2:1, 2, 15, 16; 5:11; 6:15, 21; 7:10, 12; 8:2, 10, 12, 30; 9:4; 10:7; 14:10, 12, 15-18, 21, 24, 26-29; 21:10, 12; 23:13; 24:2.

Num. 4:9, 16; 5:15; 6:15; 7:13, 19, 25, 31, 37, 43, 49, 55, 61, 67, 73, 79; 8:8; 11:8; 15:4, 6, 9; 18:12; 28:5, 9, 13,

20, 28; 29:3, 9, 14; 35:25.

Deut. 7:13; 8:8; 11:14; 12:17; 14:23; 18:4; 28:40, 51; 32:13; 33:24.

1 Sam. 16:1, 13.

2 Sam. 1:21.

1 Kings 1:39; 5:11; 17:14, 16.

2 Kings 4:2, 6, 7; 9:1, 3, 6; 18:32.

1 Chron. 9:29; 12:40; 27:28.

2 Chron. 2:10, 15; 11:11; 31:5; 32:28.

Ezra 3:7; 6:9; 7:22.

Neh. 5:11; 10:37, 39; 13:5, 12.

Esther 2:12.

Job 24:11; 29:6.

Pss. 45:7; 55:21; 89:20; 92:10; 104:15; 109:18; 141:5.

Prov. 5:3; 21:17, 20.

Isa. 41:19; 61:3.

Jer. 31:12; 40:10; 41:8.

Ezek. 16:9, 13, 18, 19; 23:41; 27:17; 32:14; 45:14, 24, 25; 46:5, 14, 15.

Hos. 2:5, 8, 22; 12:1.

Joel 1:10; 2:19, 24.

Mic. 6:7, 15.

Hag. 1:11; 2:12.

Zech. 4:12.

Matt. 25:4, 8.

Mark 6:13.

Luke 7:46; 16:6.

Heb. 1:9.

James 5:14.

Rev. 6:6; 18:13.

Oil tree, in Isa. 41:19, and the olive tree, in 1 Kings 6:23, 31–33, are the same words in the original, but there is some doubt whether the "oil tree" and the olive are the same. Some believe it to be oleaster, a shrub resembling the olive in leaf and general appearance, and yielding from its berries an inferior oil.

Oint´ments were used by the Hebrews more as a luxury than for medicinal purposes. They were generally made from olive oil perfumed with spices, and those used by the rich were very costly. Matt. 26:7-9. See ANOINTING.

Also see Exod. 30:25.
2 Kings 20:13.
1 Chron. 9:30.
Job. 41:31.
Ps. 133:2.
Prov. 27:9, 16.
Eccles. 7:1; 9:8; 10:1.
Song of Sol. 1:3; 4:10.
Isa. 1:6; 39:2; 57:9.
Amos 6:6.
Matt. 26:12.
Mark 14:3, 4.
Luke 7:37, 38, 46; 23:56.
John 11:2; 12:3, 5.
Rev. 18:13.

Old Age. See AGE.

Old Tes´ta-ment. See BIBLE.

Ol´ive. From the earliest times in Bible history the olive has been the most common of the fruit-trees of Palestine. In appearance it is not unlike our apple tree, and it thrives best where its roots can find their way into the crevices of a rock. The fruit is plum-shaped and when ripe is nearly black. The chief value of the olive tree is the oil which is expressed from its fruit, which is used for many purposes (see OIL), and forms an important article of commerce. From the extreme old age to which it attains, the beauty of the tree when in fruit, and the value of its products many figurative allusions are made to it in the Bible. Judg. 9:8, 9; Ps. 52:8; Hos. 14:6. The olive-branch is universally regarded as an emblem of peace. Gen. 8:11. The wood of the tree is close-grained, finely veined, and of a dark amber color.

Also see Exod. 27:20; 30:24.
Lev. 24:2.
Deut. 6:11; 8:8; 24:20; 28:40.
Judg. 15:5.

1 Kings 6:23, 31-33.
2 Kings 18:32.
1 Chron. 27:28.
Neh. 8:15.
Job 15:33.
Isa. 17:6; 24:13.
Jer. 11:16.
Amos 4:9.
Mic. 6:15.
Hab. 3:17.
Hag. 2:19.
Zech. 4:3, 11, 12.
Rom. 11:17, 24.
James 3:12.
Rev. 11:4.

Ol´ives, Mount of, or **Mount Olivet,** overlooking Jerusalem on the east, is memorable for many important and solemn events connected with the life of Christ. On its eastern slope, at Bethany, he performed his last miracle, John 11:44, and from here he made his triumphal entry into Jerusalem. Matt. 21:1-9. In a garden at its foot he was betrayed by Judas, and from it he ascended into heaven after his resurrection Acts 1:12. Olivet is a ridge about three thousand feet high, two miles long, running north and south, and so near to the walls of Jerusalem that from its summit almost every street in the city can be easily seen. It affords the finest view of the temple area and all the prominent buildings. The mount was formerly covered with olive trees (hence the name), but is now almost bare, except at the foot, in the Garden of Gethsemane (see GETHSEMANE). Titus destroyed all the trees at the siege in A. D. 70. On one of its peaks, now known as the "Mount of Offence," Solomon engaged in idolatrous worship. 1 Kings 11:5-7. See JERUSALEM.

Ol´ive-yard, in Exod. 23:11; Neh. 5:11, means a grove of olive trees.

O-lym´pas, a Christian at Rome. Rom. 16:15.

O´mar (*eloquent*), a son of Eliphaz, the son of Esau. Gen. 36:11; 1 Chron. 1:36.

Omega, o´me-gah or o-meg´ah, Rev. 1:8, the last letter of the Greek alphabet, is used in connection with ALPHA, which is the first letter of that alphabet, as a title of Christ. See ALPHA.

O´mer, a measure used by the Hebrews. It was the tenth part of an ephah, and contained nearly five pints. Exod. 16:16, 36.

Om-nip´o-tent, all-powerful. In Rev. 19:6 the "Lord God omnipotent" is mentioned.

Om-ni-pres´ence, present in all places at the same time; as the *omnipresent* Jehovah.

Omniscient, om-nish´ent, all seeing; as the *omniscient* God.

Om´ri (*servant of Jehovah*). [1] A captain of the host of Israel. He was made king instead of Zimri, who had conspired against Elah and slain him. 1 Kings 16:16-30; 2 Kings 8:26; 2 Chron. 22:2; Mic. 6:16. He founded the city of SAMARIA (which see). [2] A son of Becher, the son of Benjamin. 1 Chron. 7:8. [3] One of the descendants of Judah. 1 Chron. 9:4. [4] Prince of the tribe of Issachar in David's time. 1 Chron. 27:18.

On (*strength*), one of the sons of Peleth. He joined in a conspiracy against Moses. Num. 16:1-3.

On (*sun, light*), a famous city of Lower Egypt. It was on the east side of the river Nile, a few miles north of Memphis. Gen. 41:45, 50; 46:20. It is called BETH-SHEMESH (*house of the sun*) in Jer. 43:13, and was known to the Greeks as Heliopolis. Its site contains a few ruins, including a noted obelisk sixty-six feet

high which has been standing there about four thousand years, near the site of the temple of the sun. The obelisk (sometimes called Cleopatra's needle) now in Central Park, New York, formerly stood at On, and afterward at Alexandria in Egypt.

O´nam (*strong*). [1] A son of Shobal. Gen. 36:23; 1 Chron. 1:40. [2] One of the sons of Jerahmeel. 1 Chron. 2:26, 28.

O´nan (*strong*), the second son of Judah by the daughter of Shuah the Canaanite. He refused to obey the law concerning raising up children by the wife of his deceased elder brother. Gen. 38:4, 8, 9; 1 Chron. 2:3.

O-nes´i-mus (*useful*), a native of Colosse. He was a slave of Philemon, and probably fled from him. Philem. 15. He was converted at Rome under the preaching of Paul who wrote the Epistle to Philemon in his behalf. According to tradition, he became bishop.

On-e-siph´o-rus (*profit-bringing*), a disciple at Ephesus, who, while in Rome, sought out and befriended Paul. 2 Tim. 1:16; 4:19.

On´ion. This well known garden vegetable grew in great perfection in Egypt, where it attained a large size and exquisite flavor, differing from "the onions of our country as much as a bad turnip differs in palatableness from a good apple." The Israelites longed for them. Num. 11:5.

O´no (*strong*), a city of Benjamin. 1 Chron. 8:12; Ezra 2:33.

Onycha, on´i-ka, one of the ingredients used in making the sacred incense, Exod. 30:34, was probably prepared from a shell called *strombus* found in the Red Sea.

O´nyx, a precious stone, Exod. 25:7, consisting of different colored bands or layers, and evidently of great value from the uses made of it. Exod. 28:9-12; 39:6,

13. "Onyx stones," 1 Chron. 29:2, were used in the construction of the Temple.

Ophel, o´fel (*hill, swelling*), a part of ancient Jerusalem. It was surrounded by a wall, 2 Chron. 27:3; 33:14, but is not included in the modern city.

Ophir, o´fir (*fruitful?*), a son of Joktan, a descendant of Shem. Gen. 10:29; 1 Chron. 1:23.

Ophir, o´fir, the gold-region to which Solomon sent his fleet from a port on the Red Sea, has been variously located as being in Arabia, in eastern Africa, and in India. The Joktanite Ophir, on the coast of Arabia, is probably the place referred to, although the voyage may have been continued to India.
Gen. 10:29.
1 Kings 9:28; 10:11; 22:48.
1 Chron. 1:23; 29:4.
2 Chron. 8:18; 9:10.
Job 22:24; 28:16.
Ps. 45:9.
Isa. 13:12.

Ophni, of´ni (*mouldy*), a town of Benjamin. Josh. 18:24.

Ophrah, of´rah (*female fawn*), a son of Meonothai. 1 Chron. 4:14.

Ophrah, of´rah (*female fawn*). [1] A town of Benjamin. Josh. 18:23; 1 Sam. 13:17. [2] A town of Manasseh. It is called Ophrah of the Abi-ezrite in Judg. 6:11, 24.

Or´acle, in the Old Testament, in all cases (excepting 2 Sam. 16:23, where it means "word") refers to the Holy of Holies in the Temple, where the ark of the covenant was and where God declared his will to the Israelites. 1 Kings 6:5, 19-23; 2 Chron. 3:16. In the New Testament "oracles" is applied to the Scriptures, which contain the will of God.

Or´di-nan-ces generally mean—(1) the laws and commandments of God,

Exod. 18:20; (2) of civil rulers. 1 Pet. 2:13. It also refers to religious ceremonies, as in Heb. 9:1, 10. In 1 Cor. 11:2 the word "ordinances" is rendered "traditions" in the marginal notes and the Revised Version.

O´reb (*raven*), one of the princes of Midian whom Gideon defeated, and who was slain by the Ephraimites near the river Jordan. Judg. 7:25; 8:3; Ps. 83:11.

O´reb (*raven*), a rock named after Oreb, a prince of Midian. Judg. 7:25; Isa. 10:26.

O´ren (*pine tree*), one of the sons of Jerahmeel. 1 Chron. 2:25.

Or ever, in Ps. 90:2; Song of Sol. 6:12; Dan. 6:24; Acts 23:15, means ere or before.

Or´gan, in Gen. 4:21, was probably what the ancient Greeks called the "pipe of Pan." It consisted of a set of reeds of uneven length, closed at one end and blown into with the mouth at the other end. In skilful hands it produced moderately good music.

Orion, o-ri´un, one of the constellations. It contains about eighty stars, and is mentioned in Job 9:9; 38:31; Amos 5:8.

Or´na-ments were worn by the Hebrews and the people of the East, and the first mention of them is made in Gen. 24:22, where bracelets and earrings were presented to Rebekah by the servant of Abraham. Men wore rings and gold chains, Gen. 41:42, and the women rings for the fingers, nose and ears, bracelets, anklets, and hair ornaments. Isa. 3:18-23. In 1 Pet. 3:4 the apostle exhorts the women to wear the "*ornament* of a meek and quiet spirit" rather than gold and jewels.

Or´nan, a Jebusite by whose threshing-floor the angel of the LORD stood. 1 Chron. 21:15-25; 2 Chron. 3:1. He is called ARAUNAH (which see) in 2 Sam. 24:16–24.

Or´pah, a daughter-in-law of Elimelech and Naomi. She was a Moabitess, and appeared inclined to accompany Naomi when she returned to the land of Judah, but turned back to her own people. Ruth 1:4, 14.

Or'phans, by the Mosaic law, were to be treated with special leniency and kindness, and were accorded special privileges. Deut. 24:17, 21. In James 1:27 to visit the orphans is regarded as one of the acts of pure and undefiled religion. "Comfortless," in John 14:18, is translated "orphans" in the marginal notes.

O'see is the Greek form of the name HOSEA (which see). Rom. 9:25.

Oshea, o-she'ah or o'she-ah (*deliverance*), Num. 13:16, was the original name of JOSHUA (which see), who succeeded Moses as leader of the Jews.

Os'pray or **Os'prey** is mentioned in Lev. 11:13; Deut. 14:12 as unfit for food. It was probably a species of eagle.

Ossifrage, os'si-fraje, means in the original *bone-breaker*, and is probably the same as the bearded vulture. It receives its name from its habit of breaking bones to obtain the marrow in them. It breaks the bones by dropping them upon a rock from a great height. It was unfit for food. Lev. 11:13.

Os'trich, so well described in Job 39:13–18, is the largest of birds, often attaining the height of seven feet. It cannot fly, but it runs with an astonishing rapidity that the fleetest horse cannot equal. It is a shy bird, loving solitary and desolate places. The "owl," in Job 30:29; Isa. 13:21; Mic. 1:8, means the ostrich.

Oth'ni (*lion of Jehovah*), a son of Shemaiah. 1 Chron. 26:7. Othni was a "mighty man of valour." 1 Chron. 26:6.

Oth'ni-el, a son of Kenaz. Judg. 1:13. He became a judge of Israel after the death

of Joshua, and was instrumental in delivering the Israelites from the oppression of the king of Mesopotamia. Judg. 3:8, 9.

Ouch'es were sockets in which precious stones were set. Exod. 28:11, 14.

Out'go-ings, in Josh. 17:9, 18; Ps. 65:8, means utmost limits.

Out-land'ish, the name applied to the women who caused Solomon to sin, Neh. 13:26, means foreign.

Ov'ens served the same purpose in ancient times that they do now, though they differed from ours in construction. The most common form was an earthern vessel or large urn, open at the top, *in* which they made a fire. When its sides were sufficiently heated the dough was plastered on the *outside*, where it quickly baked and came off in thin cakes. Lev. 2:4. The cakes mentioned in Gen. 18:6; 1 Kings 17:13 were probably baked by building a fire on the sand of the earth until it was sufficiently heated, when the fire was cleared away and the dough laid in thin pieces on the hot sand. Plates of iron, flat stones, etc., were also used in baking.

O-ver-seers', in Acts 20:28, denotes one placed in charge or over a congregation, and bearing the same relation to it as a presbyter or elder, Acts 20:17, where the same persons are meant as in verse 28. In all other passages of the New Testament the corresponding Greek word is translated *bishop*. In the Revised Version the rendering is made uniform. See BISHOP.

Owl, as used in Deut. 14:16; Ps. 102:6; Isa. 34:11, 15, probably refers to some one or other of several species of owl that are found in Syria and Egypt. The word translated "owl" in Isa. 13:21; 34:13; Jer. 50:39; Mic. 1:8, etc., really means OSTRICH (which see). The sacred writers evidently used the word to allude to some bird that loved solitary and desolate places.

Ox was also applied in a general sense like "herd," and is often rendered "kine." It was clean according to the Levitical law, and its strength and patience, as well as its value for food, made it one of the highly prized possessions of the Jews. Besides answering all the uses to which we put the ox tribe, in those days they were also used for threshing (treading out) the grain, Deut. 25:4, and for sacrifices.

Ox´-goad. Judg. 3:31. See GOAD.

O´zem (*strength*). [1] The sixth son of Jesse and brother of David. 1 Chron. 2:15. [2] One of the sons of Jerahmeel. 1 Chron. 2:25.

O-zi´as, Matt. 1:8, 9, the son of Joram, is the same as UZZIAH.

Oz´ni (*attentive*), one of the sons or descendants of Gad, Num. 26:16, called EZBON in Gen. 46:16.

Oz´nites, descendants of Ozni. Num. 26:16.

P

Paarai, pa´a-ra, one of David's valiant men. 2 Sam. 23:35. He is called NAARAI in 1 Chron. 11:37.

Pa´dan (*field*) is used alone in one passage, Gen. 48:7, to denote the place elsewhere called PADAN-ARAM.

Pa´dan-a´ram (*the low highland*), the country to which Abraham sent his servant to obtain a wife for Isaac, Gen. 24:10; 25:20, and to which Isaac told Jacob to go for his wife, Gen. 28:2, is one of the Hebrew names for MESOPOTAMIA (which see). By some it is supposed to designate more particularly the plains of Mesopotamia from the mountainous dis-

tricts in the north.

Pad´dle, Deut. 23:13, a short broad blade, similar to that on an oar.

Pa´don (*deliverance*), one of the Nethinim whose descendants returned with Zerubbabel from Babylon. Ezra 2:44; Neh. 7:47.

Pa´gi-el (*God allots*), a captain of the tribe of Asher, who was appointed to aid Moses in numbering the people. Num. 1:13; 2:27.

Pa´hath-mo´ab (*governor of Moab*). [1] An Israelite some of whose descendants returned from Babylon with Zerubbabel. Ezra 2:6; Neh. 3:11. [2] A family of Jews who sealed the covenant made by Nehemiah. Neh. 10:14.

Pa´i (*bleating*), a place in Idumea, 1 Chron. 1:50, called PAU in Gen. 36:39.

Pained, in Rev. 12:2, means labored in pain or pangs.

Pain´ful, in Ps. 73:16, means hard to do.

Pain´ful-ness, in 2 Cor. 11:27, means unsparing toil.

Paint, Paint´ing. Paint was used by the Hebrews to color the walls and beams of their houses, Jer. 22:14, and the heathen used it to adorn their temples with representations of their idols. Ezek. 23:14. It was also used in Assyria and Egypt, as their ruins and monuments show. Painting the eyes was practiced to some extent among the Hebrew women, but the custom was held in contempt. Jer. 4:30.

Pal´ace, in the Old Testament, denotes either the whole group of buildings that form the royal residence, and which are enclosed by the outer wall, Dan. 1:4, or simply one of those buildings. 1 Kings 16:18. In the New Testament the word generally means the residence of a wealthy or prominent person. Matt. 26:3; Luke 11:21. The "palace," in Phil. 1:13, is rendered in the marginal notes "Cæsar's Court;" in the Revised Version, "prætorian guard" (Greek "prætorium").

Pa′lal (*judge*), a son of Uzai who aided Nehemiah in repairing the walls of Jerusalem. Neh. 3:25.

Pal-es-ti′na, Exod. 15:14, from its inhabitants, the Philistines, was the name given to the country lying along the Mediterranean coast, between Joppa and Gaza. The same country is called PHILISTIA in Pss. 60:8; 87:4; 108:9. See PALESTINE.

Pal′es-tine (*land of sojourners*), a country on the east shore of the Mediterranean Sea, is sacred not only to Christians, but to Jews and Mohammedans. Palestine is the Holy Land of the Jews, a land promised to them by God. To the Christians, it is sacred because it is the scene of so much of Jesus' life. It is sacred to the Muslims because it is the sight of Mohammad's ascent to heaven.

Names.—PALESTINE, in Joel 3:4; PALESTINA, in Exod. 15:14; Isa. 14:29, 31; and PHILISTIA, in Pss. 60:8; 87:4; 108:9, refer only to the country of the Philistines, who occupied a part of the eastern shore of the Mediterranean Sea south of Joppa. The original name of Palestine was CANAAN. Gen. 12:5; 16:3; Exod. 15:15; Judg. 3:1. It is also called the PROMISED LAND, LAND OF ISRAEL or ISRAELITES, LAND OF JUDAH or JUDEA, and the HOLY LAND. The name Palestine, including the whole land of the Hebrews on both sides of the Jordan, was first applied by Josephus and by Greek and Roman writers.

History.—Palestine had no strong government under the JUDGES (which see). During the reigns of David and Solomon it attained its highest prosperity. Visible decay began, B. C. about 975, with the secession of the ten tribes. Assyria crushed the northern kingdom of Israel B. C. about

720, and Babylon the southern kingdom of Judah B. C. about 587. Since that time Palestine has been under foreign rule. Persians, Greeks, and Romans succeeded one another in the mastery. In the time of Christ, under the Romans, there were four provinces—Galilee, Samaria, and Judea on the west side of Jordan, and Peræa on the east side. Since A. D. 637, when Palestine was conquered by the Saracens, it has, with little interruption, been under Turkish rule. The Turks seized the country in A. D. 1073, and by their barbarous treatment of Christian pilgrims provoked the Crusades. Roman rule was established in 1099, held Jerusalem till 1187, and remained in Acre till 1291. In 1517 the Ottomans came in and made Palestine part of the Turkish empire. It was suddenly taken from the sultan by Mehemet Ali, viceroy of Egypt, in 1832, but European governments intervened and in 1841 it was given back again.

By the end of World War I, the British were in control of the area. After the League of Nations approved the British mandate of Palestine in 1922, Jewish people from many lands settled there. By 1947, violence between the Jewish settlers and Arab residents had grown and the British were unable to control the problem. They turned the question of a Jewish homeland over to the United Nations who in November 1947 divided Palestine into Jewish and Arab states. In 1948 the state of Israel was recognized. Since that date, there have been several wars, and many battles and borders have often changed. But in 1993 steps toward peace were made when Israel and the representatives of the displaced Palestinians signed an accord on Palestinian self rule in Jericho and the Gaza Strip. See CANAAN; HEBREWS; ISRAEL, KINGDOM OF; JUDAH, KINGDOM OF;

JERUSALEM; SAMARIA.

Pal´lu (*distinguished*), a son of Reuben, Exod. 6:14; Num. 26:5, 8; 1 Chron. 5:3, called PHALLU in Gen. 46:9.

Pal´lu-ites, a family of Reubenites descended from Pallu. Num. 26:5.

Palm´crist, in the marginal notes, Jon. 4:6, means the GOURD (which see).

Palm´er-worm, a destructive insect, perhaps a species of locust, is mentioned in Joel 1:4; Amos 4:9 as a figurative illustration of the punishment that would befall the rebellious Jews.

Palm Tree. The date-palm abounds in Arabia, Egypt, in the whole of southern Asia, and in northern Africa, but it is now rare in Palestine, though when the scenes mentioned in the Bible occurred this tree was very common there. It is one of the most beautiful of trees, growing to a height of from sixty to one hundred feet, with no branches, strictly speaking, except the mass of graceful evergreen shoots which adorn its summit. The fruit of the palm (*dates*) is an article of food for the people, camels feed on the seed, and the leaves, fibres, and sap are all valuable. The Arabs speak of three hundred and sixty uses to which the different parts of the tree may be applied. A single tree will bear over two hundred pounds of dates. The palm tree lives more than two hundred years, and is most productive from the thirtieth until the eightieth year. The tree was held in great estimation by the Hebrews, and hence the frequent allusions to it in the Bible. Pss. 92:12,14; Jer. 10:5; John 12:13. In Rev. 7:9 it is used with special force and beauty, as the palm was an emblem of victory and was carried before the conqueror in the triumphal processions.

Also see Exod. 15:27.

Lev. 23:40.

Num. 33:9.
Deut. 34:3.
Judg. 1:16; 3:13; 4:5.
1 Kings 6:29, 32, 35; 7:36.
2 Chron. 3:5; 28:15.
Neh. 8:15.
Song of Sol. 7:7, 8.
Ezek. 40:16, 22, 26, 31; 41:18-20, 25, 26.
Joel 1:12.

Pal´sy, or paralysis, is a disease which deprives either the whole body or a portion of it of motion or sensation (feeling). In one form the muscles contract so that the limbs can be neither drawn up nor extended, and the affected part soon becomes withered. 1 Kings 13:4-6; Luke 6:6; Acts 9:33. In a violent form of this disease, in the East, the limbs became immovably fixed in the position they were in at the time of the attack. The suffering is intense, and death usually soon follows. Matt. 8:6. Palsy is one of the least curable of diseases.

Also see Matt. 4:24; 9:2, 6.
Mark 2:3-5, 9, 10.
Luke 5:18, 24.
Acts 8:7.

Pal´ti (*deliverance of Jehovah*), one of the spies sent by Moses to search the land of Canaan. Num. 13:9.

Pal´ti-el (*deliverance of God*), the chief of the tribe of Issachar. He was one of those who were appointed to divide the land west of Jordan among the tribes of Israel. Num. 34:26.

Pal´tite, The, a name applied in 2 Sam. 23:26 to one of David's mighty men. He is called the PELONITE in 1 Chron. 11:27.

Pamphylia, pam-fil´-ah (*region of every tribe*), a Roman province of Asia Minor, was bounded by Pisidia on the north, Cilicia on the east, Lycia on the west, and the Mediterranean Sea on the south. Perga was its original capital and

Attalia its chief seaport. Pamphylia was twice visited by Paul on his first missionary journey. Acts 13:13; 14:24; 15:38. Strangers from Pamphylia were at Jerusalem on the day of Pentecost. Acts 2:10.

Pan. Six different Hebrew words are thus translated in the English Bible. Some of them refer to flat metal plates much used in the East for baking cakes of meal, while others evidently were deeper vessels used for boiling purposes. Lev. 2:5; 2 Chron. 35:13.

Pan´nag, in Ezek. 27:17, is the Hebrew word for some product of Palestine, not now known, which the Jews sold to the people of Tyre. Some regard it as a kind of cake or confection, others as a kind of spice.

Pa´per, Pa´per Reeds. PAPER REEDS, Isa. 19:7, or BULRUSHES (which see), are found in the Upper Nile in Egypt, and upon the northern shores of the Sea of Galilee. PAPER, 2 John verse 12, was first made from this plant. The stalk, by means of a needle, was slit into thin layers or strips that were made as broad as possible, in some instances ten to fifteen inches wide. The strips were then laid side by side on a flat surface and immersed in water, which caused their edges to adhere to each other as though they were glued. After being dried in the sun and covered with a sort of sizing the sheets were beaten with hammers and finally polished. Writing on a paper thus made was done by means of a fine hair-pencil (brush).

Pa´phos (*boiling* or *hot*), a town on the west coast of the island of Cyprus, which is in the Mediterranean Sea. It was visited by Paul and Barnabas, and its Roman governor (proconsul) was converted. Acts 13:6-13.

Par´a-ble, a method of teaching through pictures of human life, was much employed in ancient times, and striking instances occur in the Old Testament, notably Nathan's parable of the ewe-lamb by which David was made his own judge, 2 Sam. 12:1-7; Isaiah's parable of the vineyard. Isa. 5:1-7, etc. Our Saviour used parables in his discourses to the people ("and without a parable spake he not unto them." Matt. 13:34), and, as recorded in the New Testament, they present forcibly yet briefly the most important spiritual truths concerning the kingdom of God, its growth, value, relation to the world, conflict and ultimate triumph. There is nothing equal to the parables of Christ in all literature; they are inexhaustible, simple enough for a child, and deep enough for the most advanced sage and saint. See especially Matt., chapter 13, and Luke, chapter 15. See also FABLE.

Also see Num. 23:7, 18; 24:3, 20, 21, 23.

Job 27:1; 29:1.

Pss. 49:4; 78:2.

Prov. 26:7.

Ezek. 17:2; 20:49; 24:3.

Mic. 2:4.

Hab. 2:6.

Matt. 15:15; 21:33, 45; 22:1; 24:32.

Mark 3:23; 4:2, 10, 11, 13, 33, 34; 7:17; 12:1, 12; 13:28.

Luke 5:36; 6:39; 8:4, 9-11; 12:16, 41; 13:6; 14:7; 18:1, 9; 19:11; 20:9, 19; 21:29.

John 10:6.

Par´a-clete. See ADVOCATE.

Par´a-dise is a word of Persian origin, and means a garden, orchard, or other enclosed place filled with beauty and delight. Hence it is used figuratively for any place of peculiar happiness, and particularly for the kingdom of perfect happiness which is the abode of the blessed beyond the grave. Luke 23:43; 2 Cor. 12:4; Rev. 2:7.

Pa´rah (*heifer-town*), a town of Benjamin. Josh. 18:23.

Par-a-lyt´ic. See PALSY.

Pa´ran (*place of caverns*), an extensive wilderness region on the south and southwest of Palestine, is often called the wilderness of Paran, sometimes Mount Paran, and, in Gen. 14:6, EL-PARAN. Hagar and Ishmael went into the wilderness of Paran. Gen. 21:21. It was entered by the Israelites soon after they left Sinai, Num. 10:12, and they encamped there many times during their wanderings. Num. 12:16; 13:3, 26. David fled to it from Saul, 1 Sam. 25:1, after the death of Samuel, and Hadad escaped through it to Egypt. 1 Kings 11:18.

Pa´ran, Mount of, probably in the north-east part of the wilderness of Paran is the place where the "LORD shined forth." Deut. 33:2. It is also mentioned in Hab. 3:3.

Par´bar, in 1 Chron. 26:18, evidently means some place, perhaps a building, on the west side of the Temple enclosure.

Parch´ed Corn, in Ruth 2:14, refers to the roasted heads of wheat, barley, millet or other grain, but not to the Indian corn or maize so well known in this country. See CORN.

Parch´ed Ground. Travellers on the deserts in Africa and Asia have often been deceived by the optical delusion called a "mirage," whereby the barren, sandy waste in the distance suddenly assumes the appearance of a beautiful sheet of water surrounded by luxuriant vegetation. In the above sense "parched ground" is used in Isa. 35:7.

Parch´ments, the skins of sheep or goats so dressed and prepared as to render them fit to write on. The skins of beasts were extensively used by the early writ-

ers, but they were rudely prepared. About two centuries before Christ a method was discovered for producing a very fine material. This the Latins called *pergamena*, which is translated, in 2 Tim. 4:13, "parchments."

Par´don, as used in the Bible in reference to God's grace exercised toward man, has a very different meaning from the word as used by us in our dealings with one another. There it means covering up, Ps. 85:2, blotting out, Ps. 51:9, or removing our transgressions far from us, Ps. 103:12, and no longer remembering them. Heb. 8:12.

Parmashta, par-mash´tah (*superior*), one of the sons of Haman, the enemy of the Jews in the time of Ahasuerus. Esther 9:9.

Par´me-nas (*steadfast*), one of the seven deacons of the church at Jerusalem. Acts 6:5.

Parnach, par´nak (*swift*), father of Elizaphan, prince of Zebulun. Num. 34:25.

Pa´rosh (*flea*). [1] A Jew many of whose descendants returned with Zerubbabel from Babylon. Ezra 2:3; Neh. 7:8. [2] A Jew whose son rebuilt part of the wall of Jerusalem. Neh. 3:25. [3] A family which sealed the covenant of Nehemiah. Neh. 10:14.

Parshandatha, par-shan´da-thah (*given by prayer*), one of the sons of Haman, the enemy of Jews in the time of Ahasuerus. Esther 9:7.

Parthia, par´thi-ah, originally a province of Media, was afterward united to the Persian empire, subsequently became independent, and was again conquered by Persia, A. D. 226. In the time of the apostles it included the country from India to the Tigris River and from the ocean on the south to the Kharesem desert. Seleucia was one of its chief cities.

Par´thi-ans, inhabitants of Parthia. Some of them were present at Jerusalem at the time of the Pentecost. Acts 2:9.

Par-ti´tion, Mid´dle Wall of, Eph. 2:14, is supposed to have reference to the wall in the Temple which separated the court of Israel from the court of the Gentiles, and is used here figuratively to denote whatever distinguished the Jews, as the favored people of God, from the heathen or Gentiles.

Par-tic´u-lar-ly, in Acts 21:19; Heb. 9:5, means in detail.

Par´tridge, a bird well known in Palestine, was highly prized by the peasants for its flesh and eggs. The bird seeks safety by running, and its pursuers chase it till it becomes wearied, when they kill it with a stick or stone. The allusion in 1 Sam. 26:20 may express the laborious zeal with which Saul pursued David, and in Jer. 17:11 reference is probably made to the exposure of the partridge's nest, which is built on the ground and likely to be trampled on and its eggs destroyed.

Par´u-ah (*blossoming*), the father of Jehoshaphat, who was one of Solomon's officers. 1 Kings 4:17.

Par-va´im or **Par´va-im** (*eastern regions*) is found only once in the Authorized Version, and denotes the country which produced gold used in decorating Solomon's Temple. 2 Chron. 3:6. Its location is not known.

Pasach, pa´sak (*cut off*), a son of Japhlet. 1 Chron. 7:33.

Pas-dam´mim (*boundary of blood*), mentioned in 1 Chron. 11:13, and called EPHES-DAMMIM in 1 Sam. 17:1, is the name of a place in Judah where the Philistines were encamped when David slew Goliath.

Pa-se´ah (*lame*). [1] A descendant of Judah. 1 Chron. 4:12. [2] A Jew whose descendants returned from Babylon after the captivity, Ezra 2:49, called PHASEAH in Neh. 7:51. [3] A Jew whose son repaired part of the wall of Jerusalem after the captivity. Neh. 3:6.

Pash´ur (*freedom*). [1] The founder of a family of priests. 1 Chron. 9:12; Neh. 11:12. [2] A priest who was the son of Immer. He was "chief governor in the house of the LORD" in the time of Jeremiah. Jer. 20:1. He "smote Jeremiah the prophet and put him in the stocks," but received from him a fearful sentence, and his name was changed to MAGOR-MISSABIB. Jer. 20:1-6.

Pass, in Ezek. 32:19, means surpass.

Pas´sa-ges, in Jer. 22:20, probably refers to the mountains of Abarim. See ABARIM.

Pas´sion, in Acts 1:3, denotes the last sufferings and death of Christ. "Like passions," in Acts 14:15; James 5:17, means having the same human feelings and propensities.

Pass´o-ver, a Jewish feast, commemorates the exemption or the "passing over" of the families of the Israelites when the destroying angel smote the first-born of Egypt, Exod. 12:23-29, and also their departure from the land of bondage. On the fourteenth day of the first month (Nisan), at even, the Passover was to be celebrated, and on the fifteenth day commenced the seven days' feast of unleavened bread. Lev. 23:5. Strictly speaking, the term Passover is applied only to the fourteenth day of the first month (that is, from the evening of the fourteenth to the evening of the fifteenth), but as used in sacred history the word includes the seven days' feast of unleavened bread. Luke 2:41; John 2:13, 23; 6:4; 11:55.

Patara, pat´a-rah, a city of Lycia, on the north-east coast of the Mediterranean

Sea and east of the island of Rhodes. It was visited by Paul. Acts 21:1, 2.

Path´ros (*region of the south*), a part of northern Egypt situated near the city of Thebes. It was originally independent, and is mentioned in Isa. 11:11; Jer. 44:1; Ezek. 29:14. It was probably the Said of the Arabs and the Thebaid of the Greeks. Its inhabitants were the PATHRUSIM.

Path-ru´sim, the name of a tribe which descended from Mizraim, the son of Ham, and inhabited Pathros. Gen. 10:14; 1 Chron. 1:12.

Pa´tience, as applied to God, is that manifestation of his love which causes him to bear long with sinners and to repeatedly warn them of judgments to come. Exod. 34:6; Rom. 2:4. In man it denotes a meek and trustful endurance of whatever trials God may send him, and love and forbearance with his fellow-man. Rom. 2:7; 1 Thess. 5:14.

Pat´mos, a rocky and barren island, about twenty miles in circumference, situated in the Ægean Sea, about twenty-four miles west of Asia Minor and north of the east end of the island of Crete, is memorable as the place to which the apostle John was banished. Rev. 1:9. See JOHN, No. 4.

Pa´tri-arch, one who governs his family or descendants by paternal right, is applied in the New Testament to Abraham, Heb. 7:4, to the twelve sons of Jacob, Acts 7:8, and to David. Acts 2:29. In the early history of the Jews the patriarchal form of government prevailed, the father of a family retaining authority over his descendants so long as he lived, no matter what new connections they may have formed. On the death of the father the eldest son generally succeeded to this dignity, exercising a paternal authority. From the patriarchs of the several families

that formed a tribe a prince was selected. These princes were called the "elders of Israel." Deut. 27:1.

Pat´ro-bas (*life of his father*), a Christian at Rome to whom Paul sent greeting. Rom. 16:14.

Pat´terns, in Heb. 9:23, is rendered "copies" in the Revised Version.

Pau (*bleating*), a city of Idumea, Gen. 36:39, called PAI in 1 Chron. 1:50.

Paul (*small*) or **Saul** (*asked for*), whose character, both as a man and as the great apostle to the Gentiles, stands out in the New Testament with such distinct outlines, was born in the Greek city of Tarsus, Cilicia, and with Roman citizenship, Acts 22:28, 29, but of Jewish parents belonging to the tribe of Benjamin. His original Jewish name was Saul; his Gentile name, which he uses in all his epistles, was Paul. He studied Jewish law under Gamaliel in Jerusalem, Acts 5:34, and attracted, while yet a young man, considerable attention on account of his passionate devotion to his faith. Belonging to the sect of the Pharisees, he appeared as one of the foremost among the persecutors of the Christians, Acts 7:58, but on his way from Jerusalem to Damascus he was suddenly converted by a revelation of the exalted Saviour. Acts 9:8, 9. He retired for three years, A. D. 37-40, to Arabia, in quiet preparation for the great work to which he was called at his conversion. He lived by the mechanical trade which, after the custom of Jewish rabbis, he had acquired. It was tent-making, which flourished in his native province of Cilicia. He labored a year with Barnabas at Antioch, and built up this mother-church of Gentile Christianity and center of his missionary labors. From Antioch he made five journeys to Jerusalem, A. D. 40, 44, 50, 54, 58. From Antioch he started on his three great missionary journeys, the first A. D. 45-49 (Acts 13 and 14), the second A. D. 51-53 (Acts 15:36 to 18:22), and the third A. D. 54-57 (Acts 18:23 to 21:33). On his last journey to Jerusalem he was made prisoner, sent to Cæsarea for two years, A. D. 58 to 60, appeared before Festus and King Agrippa, appealed to Cæsar, went to Rome, and was kept a prisoner there from A. D. 61 to 63, but turned his prison into a pulpit, preaching to his distant congregations in the Epistles to the Ephesians, Colossians, Philippians, and Philemon. The account breaks off with the close of his first Roman captivity (Acts 28:31). What then happened is not known with certainty. Ancient tradition is unanimous as to his martyrdom in Rome, and the reputed place on the Via Ostia where he was executed by the sword is still shown (at a place called the Three Fountains, about two miles from the Basilica of St. Paul). Some Biblical scholars place that event during the Neronian persecution, A. D. 64, while others suppose a later date, A. D. 67 or 68, after an intervening fourth missionary tour to the East, and perhaps to Spain (whither he intended to go. Rom. 15:28). In this case we must assume a second Roman imprisonment. In his last epistle he takes farewell of the world and is ready for martyrdom (2 Tim. 4:6–8). Paul is perhaps the most remarkable and influential character in history, next to his Lord and Master; he was a unique man for a unique work; he was providentially equipped by his Jewish descent, Greek education, and Roman citizenship for the apostleship of the Gentiles; he labored more in word and deed than all other apostles, and secured the victory of Christianity as the universal religion of the world. He is the model missionary, and an inspiration to all ages. His EPISTLES are a unique body of literature, full of deep and burning thoughts that can never die. They were written between A. D. 52 and 63, and touch upon all points of the Christian's faith and duty and the highest topics that can engage our attention. For his Epistles see the separate titles.

Pau´lus, Ser´gi-us. Acts 13:7. See SERGIUS PAULUS.

Pave´ment, in John 19:13, was an area in Pilate's court-room, the floor of which was paved with marble or other stones. It was the judgment-seat. In the Hebrew it is called GABBATHA (which see).

Pavilion, pa-vil´yon, a tent used by a king, prince, or general. 1 Kings 20:12, 16.

Pea´cock is mentioned among the articles which Solomon's navy brought from Tharshish. 1 Kings 10:22. "Peacocks," in Job 39:13, should be rendered "ostriches," and the word "ostrich" in the same verse should be translated, as it is elsewhere, "stork."

Pearl, found principally in the shells of the pearl-oyster, has always been highly prized as a gem, and the ancients regarded it among the most precious substances. Matt. 7:6; 1 Tim. 2:9. The pearl-oysters grow in clusters in deep water, and they are found in the Persian Gulf, on the coasts of Java, Sumatra, etc., etc. The oysters are brought up by divers who are specially trained for this arduous and dangerous work. The pearls are generally small, not as large as a cherry-stone, but some reach the size of a walnut. "Pearls," in Job 28:18, probably means "crystals."

Ped´a-hel (*whom God delivers*), chief of the tribe of Naphtali. Num. 34:28.

Pe-dah´zur or **Ped´ah-zur** (*whom the Rock—that is, God—delivers*), father of Gamaliel, the captain of the tribe of

Manasseh. Num. 1:10; 2:20.

Pedaiah, pe-da´yah (*whom Jehovah delivers*). [1] The grandfather of Josiah, king of Judah. 2 Kings 23:36. [2] A son or grandson of Jeconiah, the son of Jehoiakim, king of Judah. 1 Chron. 3:18, 19. [3] A Jew who repaired part of the wall of Jerusalem. Neh. 3:25. [4] A Levite who stood on the left of Ezra while he read the law to the people. Neh. 8:4. [5] A descendant of Benjamin. Neh. 11:7. [6] A Levite in the time of Nehemiah. Neh 13:13. [7] The father of Joel, ruler over the half tribe of Manasseh west of Jordan. 1 Chron. 27:20.

Peep, in Isa. 8:19, means to cry or chirp like a young bird, and indicates the tone in which the wizards spoke when they pretended to converse with the dead.

Pe´kah (*open-eyed*), an officer of Pekahiah, king of Israel, who conspired against his master and usurped the throne. 2 Kings 15:25-37, 2 Chron. 28:6.

Pek-a-hi´ah (*Jehovah hath opened his eyes*), son of Menahem, king of Israel, who succeeded his father as king and was murdered by Pekah. 2 Kings 15:22–26.

Pe´kod (*visitation?*). [1] A symbolical name for Babylon. Jer. 50:21. [2] Apparently a Chaldean province. Ezek. 23:23.

Pel-a-i´ah (*whom Jehovah distinguishes*). [1] One who descended from David. 1 Chron. 3:24. [2] A Levite who aided Ezra in causing the people to understand the law, Neh. 8:7, and sealed the covenant made by Nehemiah. Neh. 10:10.

Pel-a-li´ah (*whom Jehovah judges*), a priest whose grandson Adaiah dwelt in Jerusalem after the captivity. Neh. 11:12.

Pel-a-ti´ah (*whom Jehovah delivers*). [1] A son of Hananiah. 1 Chron. 3:21. [2] A captain or leader of the tribe of Simeon. 1 Chron. 4:42. [3] A Jew or a family who sealed the covenant made by Nehemiah.

Neh. 10:22. [4] One of the princes of the Jews who opposed the prophet Ezekiel, and died while the latter was prophesying concerning him and them. Ezek. 11:1-13.

Pe´leg (*division*), a son of Eber. Gen. 10:25; 1 Chron. 1:19, 25.

Pe´let (*deliverance*). [1] One of the sons of Jahdai. 1 Chron. 2:47. [2] One of the sons of Azmaveth. 1 Chron. 12:3.

Pe´leth (*swiftness*). [1] A Reubenite whose son On joined the conspiracy against Moses. Num. 16:1. [2] A descendant of Pharez, the son of Judah. 1 Chron. 2:33.

Pe´leth-ites. The title of a class of officers in David's guard. 2 Sam. 8:18.

Pel´i-can (*the vomiter*) is a voracious water-bird considered unclean by the Levitical law. Lev. 11:18. It resembles the goose, though nearly twice as large, with the exception of its peculiar bill, which is nearly fifteen inches long, and to the lower edge of which is attached a large pouch or bag. This pouch will hold two or three gallons of water and food enough for six men, and out of it the pelican feeds itself and its young. Having gorged itself with food, it seeks some desolate spot, where it will sit for hours, and even days, presenting a melancholy aspect. Ps. 102:6. "Cormorant," in Isa. 34:11 and Zeph. 2:14, is more properly called "pelican" in the marginal notes.

Pel´o-nite. [1] A name applied to Helez, one of David's valiant men. 1 Chron. 11:27; 27:10. Called PALTITE in 2 Sam. 23:26. [2] Ahijah, another of David's valiant men, is called the Pelonite in 1 Chron. 11:36.

Pen. The instruments with which the ancients formed their characters varied with the materials on which they wrote. For writing on hard substances like stone or metal plates a pointed piece of steel was used, the "iron pen" in Job 19:24. From the allusion in Jer. 17:1 it is possible that they also employed an instrument tipped or pointed with diamond, such as glaziers now use. Upon tablets of wax the stylus was used. One end of it was pointed, for tracing the characters, and the other end was broad and flat, for removing any erroneous marks by smoothing the wax. Upon paper, linen, cotton, skins, and parchments, at first hair pencils (brushes) brought to a very fine point were used, but later the reed pen was introduced. The latter was made from a reed from which the pith had been taken, and cut similar to the quill pen, only when first used the point was not split. The "penknife," in Jer. 36:23, refers to the peculiar knife used for cutting the reeds. See PAPER, and PARCHMENTS.

Pe-ni´el or **Pe-nu´el** (*face of God*). The place on the Jabbok River, east of the Jordan, where Jacob wrestled with the angel, Gen. 32:24–32, is called PENIEL in one passage, Gen. 32:30, but is elsewhere always named PENUEL. Gen. 32:31; Judg. 8:8, 9, 17; 1 Kings 12:25. A city and a tower were found there by Gideon, who slew the men of the city.

Pe-nin´nah (*coral*), one of the wives of Elkanah, the father of the prophet Samuel. 1 Sam. 1:2.

Pen´knife, Jer. 36:23, a knife used by the scribes and others for cutting the reed pen. See PEN.

Pen´ny. The word translated "penny" in Matt. 18:28; 22:19, etc. is the Roman *denarius*, and formed the bulk of the silver coins current in Palestine at that time. In those days it was the regular pay of a day-laborer. See DENARIUS, and MONEY.

Pentateuch, pen´ta-tewk (*five volumes*), is the collective name for the first five books of the Old Testament, the Five

Books of Moses, and was introduced by the Septuagint (Greek) translators, as were also the special names of the single books, each referring to the specific contents of each book: GENESIS (*origin* or *beginning*), because it gives an account of the origin of the world and the human race and the beginnings of history; EXODUS, because it narrates the departure from Egypt and the wanderings through the wilderness; LEVITICUS, because it establishes the service of the Levites and the priesthood of Aaron's descendants, and draws the fundamental lines of the theocratic (that is, as administered by the immediate direction of God) form of government; NUMBERS, because it records the two censuses taken by Moses and some legal enactments connected therewith; and DEUTERONOMY (*the second law*), because through the repetition of the Decalogue (the Ten Words) and the three addresses of Moses to the Israelites it forms, as it were, a recapitulation or final summing-up of the whole legislation. The Hebrews indicated the single books simply by the first word with each begins: *Bereshith, Shemot,* etc. The collective names with which Scripture designates all the five books taken together are: "A book of the law of the LORD given by the hand of Moses," 2 Chron. 24:14; "the book of the law of the LORD," 2 Chron. 17:9; "the book of the law," 2 Kings 22:8; "the book of the covenant," 2 Kings 23:2; "the law of Moses," Ezra 7:6; "the book of the law of Moses," Neh. 8:1; "the book of Moses," Ezra 6:18; or simply "the law," Matt. 12:5; Luke 10:26; John 8:5, 17. The composition and authorship of the Pentateuch have been and still are the subject of elaborate critical discussions which do not come within the scope of this popular summary. For the several books, see GENESIS, etc.

Pen´te-cost, from a Greek word meaning *fiftieth*, is used in the New Testament to denote the second great festival of the Jews, which was celebrated on the fiftieth day after the sixteenth of Nisan (the second day of the PASSOVER festival, which see). Lev. 23:15, 16. In the Old Testament it is called the "feast of weeks," Exod. 34:22, and the "day of the firstfruits," Num. 28:26, and was originally appointed as a simple thanksgiving for the harvest, which in Palestine was gathered between Passover and Pentecost. On the day of Pentecost the Holy Spirit was poured out on the Christian Church. Acts 2:1-41.

Pe-nu´el (*face of God*). [1] An Israelite, the father of Gedor. 1 Chron. 4:4. [2] One of the descendants of Benjamin. 1 Chron. 8:25.

Pe-nu´el. Gen. 32:31; Judg. 8:8. See PENIEL.

Peo´ple of the East, a name given in one passage, Gen. 29:1, to the dwellers in Haran.

Pe´or (*cleft*). [1] A mountain, part of the range of Abarim, in the land of Moab, east of the river Jordan. The encampment of Israel could be seen from it, and Balak brought Balaam there that the latter might curse the Israelites. Num. 23:27, 28. [2] In Num. 25:18; 31:16; Josh. 22:17 reference is made to an idol of the Moabites. Called also BAAL-PEOR in Num. 25:3.

Peræa, pe-re´ah, "beyond Jordan," a general name used in New Testament times to denote that part of Palestine which was east of the river Jordan and the Dead Sea and between the Sea of Galilee and the river Arnon.

Per´a-zim (*breaches*), a mountain in Judah or Benjamin. Isa. 28:21. It has been regarded as identical with BAAL-PERAZIM. 2 Sam. 5:20; 1 Chron. 14:11.

Pe´res, in Dan. 5:28, means "he was divided." In the original language it is the same word as "Upharsin," Dan. 5:25, but in a different case or number.

Pe´resh, one of the sons of Machir, the son of Manasseh. 1 Chron. 7:16.

Pe´rez (*a rent*). [1] An ancestor of Jashobeam. 1 Chron. 27:3. May be same as Pharez, the son of Judah. [2] A son of Judah, Neh. 11:4, 6, called PHAREZ (which see) in Gen. 38:29.

Pe´rez-uz´za (*breaking of Uzzah*), 1 Chron. 13:11, or **Pe´rez-uz´zah,** 2 Sam. 6:8, the name given by David to the place, near Jerusalem, where the LORD slew Uzzah for laying his hand on the ark of God.

Per´fect, Per-fec´tion. Complete, entire in all its parts, and without defect or blemish. While being perfect does not elevate a thing above its kind, still it gives to it the highest value it can ever reach. As used in Gen. 6:9; 1 Kings 15:14; 2 Kings 20:3; Job 1:1, the word does not necessarily imply freedom from sin, but blamelessness or uprightness. "Be ye therefore perfect," in Matt. 5:48, is rendered in the Revised Version "Ye therefore shall be perfect."

Per´fume, Prov. 27:9, was much used in the East to give an agreeable odor to the person and apparel. The word as used in Exod. 30:35 means a composition to be used only in the Temple service. The occupation of the apothecary consisted chiefly in making perfumes and ointments.

Perga, per´gah (*extremity* or *place of nuptials*), a city of Pamphylia, a province of Asia Minor. It is situated on the river Cestrus, about seven miles from the Mediterranean Sea, and had a famous temple of Diana. Paul and Barnabas visited this city. Acts 13:13, 14; 14:25.

Per´ga-mos (*place of nuptials*) was for a century before and a century after the birth of Christ a large and celebrated city situated in southern Mysia, with about 120,000 inhabitants, an impregnable fortress in which enormous public treasures were kept, one of the largest libraries in the world, etc. It was the center of the worship of Æsculapius, the place in which parchment was greatly improved, etc. It contained one of the seven churches of Asia, and is mentioned, Rev. 1:11; 2:12–17, as the city where according to the Revised Version, "Satan's throne is."

Perida, pe-ri′dah, a servant of Solomon. Neh. 7:57. See PERUDA.

Per′iz-zites (*villagers*), a nation which inhabited the hill country south of that afterward occupied by the tribe of Judah. Gen. 13:7; Exod. 3:7.
Also see Gen. 15:20; 34:30.
Exod. 3:8, 17; 23:23; 33:2; 34:11.
Deut. 7:1; 20:17.
Josh. 3:10; 9:1; 11:3; 12:8; 17:15; 24:11.
Judg. 1:4, 5; 3:5.
1 Kings 9:20.
2 Chron. 8:7.
Ezra 9:1.
Neh. 9:8.

Per′se-cute, Per-se-cu′tion. The using of force or compulsion in matters of conscience or religious belief, or the infliction of pain or punishment on account of same, is persecution. Matt. 10:23; Acts 8:1.
Also see Deut. 30:7.
Job 19:22, 28.
Pss. 7:1, 5; 10:2; 31:15; 35:3, 6; 69:26; 71:11; 83:15; 109:16; 119:84, 86, 161; 143:3.
Isa. 14:6.
Jer. 17:18; 29:18.
Lam. 3:43, 66; 5:5.
Matt. 5:10-12, 44; 13:21; 23:34.
Mark 4:17; 10:30.

Luke 11:49; 21:12.
John 5:16; 15:20.
Acts 7:52; 9:4, 5; 11:19; 13:50; 22:4, 7, 8; 26:11, 14, 15.
Rom. 8:35; 12:14.
1 Cor. 4:12; 15:9.
2 Cor. 4:9; 12:10.
Gal. 1:13, 23; 4:29; 5:11; 6:12.
Phil. 3:6.
1 Thess. 2:15.
2 Thess. 1:4.
2 Tim. 3:11, 12.
Rev. 12:13.

Per′sia, the last of the four great Asiatic empires, was founded, B. C. about 588, by Cyrus, and destroyed, B. C. 330, by Alexander the Great. Persia had a high plateau four thousand feet above the level of the sea, extending northward from the Persian Gulf, but separated from the Mesopotamian lowland by wild mountain-ranges. It was inhabited by a people entirely alien to the Chaldees, Assyrians, Babylonians, Hebrews, Phoenicians, etc., but remotely related to the Greeks and Romans. The kings of the Persian empire were generally friendly toward the Hebrews. At Babylon Cyrus became acquainted with them, and made a decree allowing them to return to Jerusalem and rebuild the Temple. A later king, Artaxerxes, cancelled Cyrus's permit, and for some time the work on the Temple ceased, but his successor, Darius Hystaspes, confirmed the decree of Cyrus, and even furthered the work. The Ahasuerus of the book of Esther was probably that Xerxes who failed so ignominiously in his attempt to conquer Greece and penetrate Europe.

Per′sians, inhabitants of Persia. Esther 1:19; Dan. 6:28.

Per′sis (*a Persian woman*), a female disciple in Rome to whom Paul sent salutation. Rom. 16:12.

Peruda, pe-ru´dah (*kernel*), one of the servants of Solomon, Ezra 2:55, called PERIDA in Neh. 7:57.

Pes´ti-lence, in Exod. 5:3; Deut. 28:21; Jer. 21:6, etc., expresses all kinds of distempers and calamities.
Also see Exod. 9:15.
Lev. 26:25.
Num. 14:12.
Deut. 28:21.
2 Sam. 24:13, 15.
1 Kings 8:37.
1 Chron. 21:12, 14.
2 Chron. 6:28; 7:13; 20:9.
Pss. 78:50; 91:3, 6.
Jer. 14:12; 21:7, 9; 24:10; 27:8, 13; 28:8; 29:17, 18; 32:24, 36; 34:17; 38:2; 42:17, 22; 44:13.
Ezek. 5:12, 17; 6:11, 12; 7:15; 12:16; 14:19, 21; 28:23; 33:27; 38:22.
Amos 4:10.
Hab. 3:5.
Matt. 24:7.
Luke 21:11.

Pes´ti-lent, in Acts 24:5, means mischievous and disposed to lead others astray.

Pe´ter (*stone* or *rock*), Syriac, CEPHAS, was a son of Jonas or John, a brother of Andrew, a native of Bethsaida, in Galilee, a fisherman by trade, and resided with his wife and mother-in-law at Capernaum. His original name was Simon or Simeon, but when he was called to the apostleship the Lord gave him the name Peter, John 1:42; Matt. 16:18, with a prophetic reference to what he should do and be for the Church. Among the apostles he stands out with singular vividness and impressiveness, one moment nearest to us, and in the next, it would seem, nearest to God. He had an impulsive temperament and was always in a hurry, the first to confess and the first to deny the Lord; but he sincerely repented and strengthened his brethren.

The earlier apostolic work of Peter is recorded in the first part of Acts, chapters 1–12 and 15. He laid the foundation of the Church among the Jews on the day of Pentecost, Acts 2, and he admitted the first Gentiles, Cornelius and his family, to baptism. Acts 10:47, 48. Of his later activity we have only a few notices. A controversy sprang up between him and Paul at Antioch concerning the treatment of Gentile converts, Gal. 2:11, but it was only temporary, and ended with perfect harmony between the two great men. 2 Pet. 3:15. From 1 Cor. 9:5 we know that at that time, A. D. about 57, Peter and his wife were engaged in missionary work, probably among the dispersed Jews in Asia Minor, to whom his two epistles are addressed. According to a tradition unanimously accepted by the whole Christian Church of antiquity, he suffered martyrdom in Rome, on the Vatican hill (where now St. Peter's church stands). probably during the Neronian persecution in A. D. 64.

Pe´ter, the First E-pis´tle of, is addressed to the Jewish churches in Asia Minor, and dated from Babylon. 1 Pet. 5:13. This may mean the old famous city of Babylon in Asia, which for centuries after its destruction continued the seat of a large Jewish colony and a center of Jewish learning. But it may also have been used in a figurative and mystic sense for heathen Rome (as in Rev. 17:5).

Pe´ter, the Sec´ond E-pis´tle of, was written shortly before his martyrdom, from the same place and to the same churches as his first epistle, but it was not mentioned or used till long after his death, and was at the time of Eusebius (about A. D. 320) numbered among the disputed books. It is, as it were, his last will and testament; a warning against dangerous errors; refers to the transfiguration; and points to the new heavens and the new earth.

Peth-a-hi´ah (*whom God sets free*). [1] The head of a course of priests in the time of David. 1 Chron. 24:16. [2] A Levite who took a foreign wife. Ezra 10:23. He was probably the one who regulated the deviations of the people. Neh. 9:5. [3] A descendant of Judah employed by the king of Persia. Neh. 11:24.

Pe´thor (*soothsayer?*) was in Mesopotamia, near the river Euphrates, and was the dwelling-place of the prophet Balaam. Num. 22:5; Deut. 23:4.

Pe-thu´el (*vision of God*) was the father of the prophet Joel. Joel 1:1.

Petra, pe´trah (*rock*), in the marginal notes, Isa. 16:1, is translated SELA (which see) in the text. Petra is the Greek name of a famous city of Edom.

Peulthai, pe-ul´thay (*wages of Jehovah*), one of the sons of Obed-edom. 1 Chron. 26:5.

Pha´lec, Luke 3:35, is the same as PELEG, the son of Eber.

Phal´lu (*distinguished*), Gen. 46:9, a son of Reuben, and called PALLU in Exod. 6:14; Num. 26:5, etc.

Phal´ti (*deliverance of Jehovah*), a Benjamite to whom King Saul gave Michal his daughter, David's wife. 1 Sam. 25:44. Same as PHALTIEL, in 2 Sam. 3:15.

Phal´ti-el, 2 Sam. 3:15, or PHALTI (which see).

Pha-nu´el (*face of God*), the father of Anna the prophetess. Luke 2:36.

Pha´ra-oh, the father of Bithiah, who became the wife of Mered, who was a descendant of Judah. 1 Chron. 4:18.

Pha´ra-oh (*sun*) was the national or official title of the Egyptian kings of the old

native dynasties. Besides PHARAOH-HOPHRA and PHARAOH-NECHO (which see) there are six kings called Pharaoh mentioned in the Bible: (1) Pharaoh in the time of Abram. Gen. 12:15, etc. (2) Pharaoh in the time of Joseph. Gen. 37:36; chapter 41. (3) Pharoah in the infancy of Moses, the "new king over Egypt, which knew not Joseph." Exod. 1:8, 11; 2:15. This is the Pharaoh of the oppression, usually identified with Rameses II. of the nineteenth dynasty, the conqueror and master builder, called Sesostris by the Greeks. (4) Pharaoh when Moses was sent to deliver the Israelites from bondage. Exod. 3:10, etc. The Pharaoh of the exodus, who perished with his army in the Red Sea (Menephtha, the son of Rameses II., whose reign was inglorious and marked the period of decline). (5) Pharaoh whose daughter Solomon married. 1 Kings 3:1; 2 Chron. 8:11; Song of Sol. 1:9. (6) Pharaoh in the time of Isaiah. Isa. 30:2, 3; 36:6. See EGYPT.

Pha´ra-oh-hoph´ra, a king of Egypt whose overthrow by Nebuchadnezzar was predicted by Jeremiah. Jer. 44:30.

Pharaoh-necho, pha´ra-oh-ne´ko, Jer. 46:2, or **Pharaoh-nechoh,** pha´ra-oh-ne´ko, 2 Kings 23:29, 33, 34, a king of Egypt who made war on Assyria in the time of Josiah, king of Judah. He is called NECHO in 2 Chron. 35:20.

Pha´res, in Matt. 1:3; Luke 3:33, is also called PHAREZ (which see).

Pha´rez (*a breach*), one of the sons of Judah by Tamar. Gen. 38:29. He was the ancestor of the Pharzites, and is called PEREZ in Neh. 11:4, 6 and PHARES in Matt. 1:3; Luke 3:33.

Phar´isees, The, formed in the time of our Lord the most powerful party among the Jews both in politics and religion. In politics they were national and opposed to the Roman rule. They were the leaders of the people in its desperate fight for its political independence, and they employed every means in their power to oppose the intrusion of Greek-Roman civilization, its paganism, and its vices. In religion they adhered strictly to the letter, but departed from the spirit, of the Old Testament. In opposition to the Sadducees they accepted and defended the doctrines of the resurrection of the body, a future reward or punishment, a divine providence, etc., but they also maintained that there existed an oral tradition descended from Moses, and to that tradition, of which they pretended to be the sole possessors, they ascribed an authority equal to the law. By this means they attempted to keep the conscience of the people in abject slavery, and troubled men's minds with questions like this: Whether it was permitted to eat an egg which was laid on a Sabbath day, etc., etc. Hence the scathing denunciations of our Lord. Matt. 23:23–33; Luke 16:14, 15. Among the Pharisees, however, were some of the noblest characters, such as Nicodemus, Joseph of Arimathea, and the wise Gamaliel (Acts 5:34), and from them came the great apostle of the Gentiles, Paul.

Pha´rosh, a Jew some of whose descendants returned from Babylon with Ezra. Ezra 8:3.

Phar´par (*swift*), one of the rivers of Damascus mentioned by Naaman. 2 Kings 5:12.

Phar´zites, a family of Israelites descended from Pharez, the son of Judah. Num. 26:20.

Pha-se´ah, Neh. 7:51, a Jew some of whose descendants returned from Babylon. See PASEAH, No. 2.

Phe´be (*shining*), a noted member and "servant of the church at Cenchrea" whom Paul commended. Rom. 16:1.

Phenice, fe-ni´see. [1] Another form of the names PHŒNICIA or PHENICIA. See the latter. [2] A town and harbor on the southwest side of the island of Crete, in the Mediterranean Sea. The captain of the ship on which Paul was a prisoner undertook to sail into it, but could not. Acts 27:12–14. Phenice, No. 2, is more properly called Phœnix.

Phenicia, fe-nish´i-ah, now called PHŒNICIA, is a narrow strip of coastland, between the Mediterranean Sea and Lebanon, which extends from the "Ladder of Tyre" to *Nahr Auly*, about thirty miles. Phœnicia was at one time one of the most flourishing places in the world. The name does not occur in the Old Testament, but is found in the New Testament in the form of "Phenice," Acts 11:19; 15:3, and "Phenicia," Acts 21:2. The Phœnicians were closely related to the Canaanites, Gen. 10:15, and to the Israelites. The relations between the two peoples were also generally very cordial. The wheat, honey, oil, balm, etc. of the Israelites were bought and exported by the Phœnicians, and Phœnician mechanics and artists went up to Jerusalem in the service of David and Saul. At the same time the Phœnician and the Hebrew fleets sailed together for Ophir. In religion the difference between the two peoples was very marked. The religion of the Phœnicians was a kind of nature-worship. The Phœnicians therefore exercised a degrading influence on the Hebrews, especially after the separation between Israel and Judah. They sided with Israel, whose people they seduced to idolatry, and made wars against Judah in which they even went so far as to sell their prisoners to the Edomites as slaves. See, for further details, SIDON and TYRE, the two great Phœnician cities.

Phichol, fi´kol, the chief captain of the host of Abimelech, king of the Philistines. Gen. 21:22; 26:26.

Phil-a-del´phi-a (*brotherly love*), a city on the borders of Lydia and Phrygia, Asia Minor, was founded in the second century B. C., and continued to flourish until the close of the fourteenth century A. D. It was the seat of one of the seven churches of Asia, and is mentioned in Rev. 1:11; 3:7-13. Its modern name is *Alah Shehr,* and it has about 10,000 inhabitants.

Phi-le´mon, a Greek to whom Paul addressed an epistle. Philem. 1:1. He had been converted to Christianity through Paul.

Phi-le´mon, the E-pis´tle to, was written by Paul from Rome, A. D. 62 or 63, and is a gem of Christian courtesy and tenderness. It consists of a singularly powerful and skilfully managed appeal to the natural benevolence and Christian sentiment of Philemon on behalf of Onesimus, his fugitive but converted slave. The epistle has always been a noble testimonial of the Christian doctrine of equal freedom to all men.

Phi-le´tus (*amiable*), a person who, together with Hymenæus, was condemned by Paul for using idle speculations in connection with the teaching of Christian doctrine. 2 Tim. 2:17.

Phil´ip (*lover of horses*). **[1]** The apostle. He was a native of Bethsaida, and is always mentioned as the fifth of the twelve. Matt. 10:3; Mark 3:18; Luke 6:14; John 1:43-46; Acts 1:13. Little is known concerning him. He is said, according to tradition, to have preached in Phrygia and died at Hierapolis.

[2] The evangelist. He was a deacon in the church at Jerusalem, Acts 6:3-5, and preached in Samaria with great success.

Acts 8:6–8. While there he was directed by "the angel of the Lord," Acts 8:26, to "go toward the south, unto the way that goeth down from Jerusalem to Gaza." He obeyed, found the Ethiopian traveller, Acts 8:27-38, preached unto him Jesus, and baptized him. Philip was probably afterward settled in Cæsarea. Acts 21:8. He was marked and had "four daughters, virgins, which did prophesy," verse 9.

[3] The tetrarch or governor of Gaulanitis, Auranitis, etc., was a son of Herod the Great by his fifth wife, Cleopatra, and reigned from his father's death to A. D. 34. He married Salome, the daughter of Herodias, and is referred to once in the New Testament. Luke 3:1. See HEROD, No. 4.

[4] The husband of Herodias. See HEROD, No. 5.

Phi-lip´pi, a city of Macedonia, was in the time of Paul a place of great celebrity, because around its walls was fought, B. C. 42, the battle between Octavius and Antony on the one and Brutus and Cassius on the other, which caused the downfall of the Roman republic and prepared the way for the establishment of the great Roman empire. In memory of his victory—Octavius afterward made it a Roman colony—that is, he settled a number of his veteran soldiers there and gave them land to cultivate. Philippi was the first place in Greece that received the gospel. The first convert was Lydia. Acts 16:14, 15. Paul visited the city twice. Acts 16:12–40; 20:6. Paul and Silas, thrown into prison there, were miraculously released, and the jailer and his family were converted. During Paul's imprisonment in Rome, A. D. 62–64, the Christians of Philippi sent Epaphroditus to him with a present of money, which became the occasion for THE EPISTLE TO

THE PHILIPPIANS (which see).

Phi-lip´pi-ans, the disciples in Philippi, Macedonia, to whom Paul addressed an epistle. Phil. 4:15.

Phi-lip´pi-ans, E-pis´tle to the, was written by Paul, then a prisoner at Rome about A. D. 62, to the Christians at Philippi, who had kindly ministered to his necessities. The second chapter contains a very important passage on the doctrine of the person of Christ, referring to his humiliation and his exaltation.

Philistia, fi-lis´ti-ah (*land of sojourners*), called also THE LAND OF THE PHILISTINES, included the coast-land of Palestine from Joppa in the north to the valley of Gerar in the south, and from the Mediterranean to the hills of Judea. (See PALESTINE.) The origin of the Philistines (the Caphtorim, Deut. 2:23; Jer. 47:4; Amos 9:7) has been much discussed, but most scholars now seem to be agreed that the Caphtorim came from the Nile delta in Egypt. At the time of the exodus the Philistines were a powerful people, far superior to the Israelites. They had fortified cities, cavalry, war-chariots, soldiers with copper helmets, etc. Consequently, although Philistia belong to the Promised Land and was assigned to Judah and Dan, no attempt was made to conquer it. But as soon as the Israelites were settled the feuds with the Philistines began, and they never really ended. There seems to have been a deadly hatred between the two people, and one of the reasons for it was certainly the peculiarly abominable idolatry of the Philistines. Their chief gods were Dagon, Judg. 16:23; 1 Sam. 5:1-5, whom they worshipped under the form of a fish, and Baalzebub, 2 Kings 1:2, 3, 6, 16, the fly-god. After "the captivity" the kingdom of Philistia ceased to exist, and after Alexander the Great nothing more is heard about the Philistines.

Phi-lis´tim, a tribe descended from a son of Mizraim. It inhabited the southwest part of Syria, on the east shore of the Mediterranean and south of the Canaanites. Gen. 10:14. The original word for Philistim is usually translated PHILISTINES.

Phi-lis´tines, the inhabitants of Philistia. Gen. 21:32; Exod. 13:17.
Also see Gen. 21:34; 25:1, 8, 14, 15, 18.
Exod. 23:31.
Josh. 13:2, 3.
Judg. 3:3, 31; 10:6, 7, 11; 13:1, 5; 14:1-4; 15:3-6, 9, 11, 12, 14, 20; 16:5, 8, 9, 13, 20, 21, 23, 27, 28, 30.
1 Sam. 4:1-3, 6, 7, 9, 10, 17; 5:1, 2, 8, 11; 6:1, 2, 4, 12, 16-18, 21; 7:3, 7, 8, 10, 11, 13, 14; 9:16; 10:5; 12:9; 13:3-5, 12, 16, 17, 19, 20, 23; 14:1, 4, 11, 19, 21, 22, 30, 31, 36, 37, 46, 47, 52; 17:1-4, 8, 10, 11, 16, 19, 21, 23, 26, 32, 33, 36, 37, 40-46, 48-55, 57; 18:6, 17, 21, 25, 27, 30; 19:5, 8; 21:9; 22:10; 23:1-5, 27, 28; 24:1; 27:1, 7, 11; 28:1, 4, 5, 15, 19; 29:1-4, 7, 9, 11; 30:16; 31:1, 2, 7-9, 11.
2 Sam. 1:20; 3:14, 18; 5:17-19, 22, 24, 25; 8:1, 12; 19:9; 21:12, 15, 17-19; 23:9-14, 16.
1 Kings 4:21; 15:27; 16:15.
2 Kings 8:2, 3; 18:8.
1 Chron. 1:12; 10:1, 2, 7-9, 11; 11:13-16, 18; 12:19; 14:8-10, 13, 15, 16; 18:1, 11; 20:4, 5.
2 Chron. 9:26; 17:11; 21:16; 26:6, 7; 28:18.
Pss. 56; 83:7.
Isa. 2:6; 9:12; 11:14.
Jer. 25:20; 47:1, 4.
Ezek. 16:27, 57; 25:15, 16.
Amos 1:8; 6:2; 9:7.
Obad. :19.

Zeph. 2:5.

Zech. 9:6.

Phi-lol´o-gus (*learned*), a disciple at Rome to whom Paul sent salutation. Rom. 16:15.

Phin´e-has (*brazen mouth*). [1] A son of Eleazar, one of the sons of Aaron. Exod. 6:25; Num. 25:7. He was high-priest for many years. [2] One of the sons of Eli the priest. He was notoriously wicked. 1 Sam. 1:3; 2:34; 4:4, 17, 19; 14:3. [3] A Levite in the time of Ezra. Ezra 8:33.

Phlegon, fle´gon (*flame*), a disciple at Rome to whom Paul sent salutation. Rom. 16:14.

Phœbe, See PHEBE.

Phœ-ni´ce. See PHENICE.

Phœ-ni-cia. See PHENICIA.

Phœ-ni´ci-ans. See PHENICIA.

Phrygia, frij´i-ah (*dry, barren*), was a district of Asia Minor, of rather undefined boundaries; at the time it included Galatia Phrygia is said to have touched every other province in Asia Minor. It contained the cities of Laodicea, Hierapolis, Colosse, and Antioch of Pisidia, and it is mentioned in Acts 2:10; 16:6; 18:23. Paul twice crossed the country, and some converts were made there. Phrygians were present at Pentecost. Acts 2:10.

Phu´rah (*bough*), a servant of Gideon who went with him to view the army of the Midianites. Judg. 7:10, 11.

Phut, fut, Gen. 10:6, or **Put,** Nah. 3:9 (*a bow?*), one of the sons of Ham; also the country which his descendants inhabited. Phut was the ancestor of an African people usually known by the same name, and it is used connection with Persia and with Lud. Ezek. 27:10.

Phu´vah (*mouth*), one of the sons of Issachar, Gen. 46:13, called PUA in Num. 26:23, and PUAH in 1 Chron. 7:1.

Phygellus, fi-jel´lus (*fugitive*), a lukewarm disciple who "turned away" from Paul after listening to him a while. 2 Tim. 1:15.

Phy-lac´ter-ies were worn by the Hebrews, and were of two kinds: The one was worn on the forehead, and was called a FRONTLET (which see); the other was worn on the arm, and consisted of two rolls of parchment containing writing and enclosed in a sort of case of black calfskin, to which was attached a strip or band of the same leather about a finger's breadth wide and two feet long. The rolls were fastened on the inner side of the left arm, opposite the elbow, and the long band to which they were attached was wound about the arm in a spiral line that ended at the top of the middle finger. The custom was founded on the literal interpretation of Exod. 13:9, 16, and is still continued. They were worn not only as a reminder of the Law, but as a charm against demons. The Pharisees made their phylacteries broad and very conspicuous, hence the rebuke of Jesus in Matt. 23:5.

Phy-si´cian. The study of medicine was followed with great zeal by the Egyptians, even in the days of Joseph. Gen. 50:2. From passages in the books of Moses it appears that in his time there were not only midwives but regular physicians among the Jews. Exod. 21:19. The priests were expected to have some knowledge of medicine, likewise the prophets, but generally it was followed as a separate profession. The ceremonial defilement caused by touching a corpse, Num. 9:6, prevented the study of anatomy, and the medical art, therefore, never reached a high degree of perfection in Palestine. Luke was a physician. Col. 4:14.

Pi-be´seth or **Pib´e-seth,** a city of Lower Egypt. It was called Bubastis by the Greeks, and was situated on the east bank of the Pelusiac branch of the river Nile. Ezek. 30:17.

Pict´ures, in the modern sense of the word as movable paintings, were unknown to the Hebrews. In Num. 33:52 idolatrous images, probably cut or engraved on stone and colored, are referred to. "Pictures of silver," in Prov. 25:11, may refer to carvings similar to those mentioned in 1 Kings 6:32, 35. In Isa. 2:16 the word is thought by some to refer to a flag. See Ezek. 27:7.

Pieces of Gold, Pieces of Silver. 2 Kings 5:5; Judg. 9:4. "Pieces," when thus used in the Old Testament, should be interpreted as "shekels." Before the captivity there was no coined money in Palestine and the shekel was the common weight for money. The "piece of silver" in Luke 15:8, 9 is the translation of "drachma," and was equivalent to about fifteen cents. As used in connection with the price paid Judas for the betrayal of our Saviour, Matt. 26:15; 27:3, 9, "piece" has the meaning of shekel, a weight, equal in our money to between fifty and sixty cents.

Pieces of Mon´ey, in Gen. 33:19; Job 42:11; Matt. 17:27, evidently meant "pieces of silver" or "shekels of silver."

Pi´e-ty is found only once in the Bible, 1 Tim. 5:4, where it means the reverence and affection children owe to their parents. For piety toward God the Scriptures use different terms, such as godliness, worship, service, holiness, etc.

Pig´eon. With the exception of Gen. 15:9, where in the original the word means a "young bird," pigeon and dove in the Old and New Testament are translated from the same words, and hence used interchangeably. They were distinct, however, from TURTLEDOVE (which see). See also DOVE.

Pi-ha-hi´roth (*mouth* or *entrance of caverns*), a place at the north end and west side of the western gulf of the Red Sea. It was the last encampment of the Israelites before they crossed that sea. Exod. 14:2, 9; Num. 33:7, 8.

Pi´late, Matt. 27:13, or **Pontius** (pon´-shi-us) **Pi´late,** Acts 4:27, was the Roman governor of Judea that delivered Jesus to the Jews to be crucified. Pilate was his surname, and the name generally used in references to him. See Matt. 27:2-65.

Pil´dash (*flame of fire*), a son of Nahor, the brother of Abraham. Gen. 22:22.

Pileha, pil´e-hah, a man or a family who sealed the covenant made by Nehemiah. Neh. 10:24.

Pil´lar, in Gen. 28:18; 35:20; 2 Sam. 18:18, means a monument. In Exod. 13:21; Judg. 20:40 it refers to the shape the fire, cloud, or smoke assumed. In architecture pillars were used both as ornaments and supports. 1 Kings 7:5; Judg. 16:26.

Pil´lar of Cloud. See CLOUD, PILLAR OF.

Pill´ed, in Gen. 30:37, 38, means peeled.

Pil´low, in Mark 4:38, is translated "cushion" in the Revised Version. Jacob used a stone for his pillow. Gen 28:18. In Ezek. 13:18, 20 pillows are referred to as appliances of luxury.

Piltai, pil´tay (*whom Jehovah delivers*), a priest at Jerusalem. Neh. 12:17.

Pine. Isa. 41:19; 60:13. It is doubtful if the pine tree is really meant in the above passages. The Hebrew word there translated "pine" denotes "curvature" or "duration," neither of which meanings suits the pine. Some authorities believe it refers to a species of elm; others suggest the oak. "Pine branches," in Neh. 8:15, is rendered "branches of wild olive" in the Revised Version.

Pin´na-cle. The word thus translated in Matt. 4:5; Luke 4:9 means not a summit, but a wing, and probably refers to an elevation over Solomon's porch which overlooked the valley of Kidron at a height of from six hundred to seven hundred feet.

Pi´non (*darkness*), a duke (prince) of Edom. Gen. 36:41; 1 Chron. 1:52.

Pins were simply pegs or stakes, and their use is evident from the passages in which the word is found. From the allusion in Ezek. 15:3 they were made of wood, but those used for the Tabernacle and the court were of brass. Exod. 27:19.

Pipe, the simplest and perhaps the oldest of musical instruments, was the principal wind-instrument among the Jews. It was made of different materials, consisted of a tube with holes, similar to the flute, and was used on all occasions. 1 Kings 1:40.

Pi´ram (*fleet as the wild ass?*), a king of the Amorites who was slain by Joshua. Josh. 10:3.

Pir´a-thon (*princely*), a town of Ephraim. It was the burial-place of Abdon, a judge of Israel. Judg. 12:15.

Pir´a-thon-ite, an inhabitant or a native of Pirathon. Judg. 12:13; 2 Sam. 23:30.

Pisgah, piz´gah (*hill* or *the height*), Deut. 3:27, was a peak in the range of mountains called Abarim, on the east of Jordan, opposite Jericho. It was the top of Mount Nebo, from which Moses beheld the land of Canaan. See NEBO.

Pisidia, pi-sid´i-ah (*pitchy*), a province of Asia Minor lying between Pamphylia on the south and Phrygia on the north. It was part of the province of Cilicia during the republic, and was twice visited by Paul. Acts 13:14; 14:24.

Pi´son (*the full-flowing* or *the free-flowing*), one of the rivers which watered the garden of Eden. Its location is unknown. Gen. 2:11.

Pis´pah (*expansion*), one of the sons of Jether. 1 Chron. 7:38.

Pit, in the Authorized Version, is the translation of several words of different meanings. The pit into which Joseph was cast, Gen. 37:24, was an empty or dry cistern or reservoir, such as are commonly built in that country to preserve the rain-water for travellers and cattle. The word is also used in reference to *Sheol*, or the under-world, Num. 16:30; Job 17:16, and in Prov. 22:14; Jer. 18:20, 22, etc. it refers to the traps or deep holes made in the ground and covered lightly with branches, in which beasts of prey were commonly caught.

Pitch. This word, as used in Gen. 6:14; Exod. 2:3, means a sort of bitumen or asphaltum which is found in pits and on the surface of the Dead Sea. In its soft or liquid state it is called SLIME, Gen. 11:3, but on exposure it becomes dry and hard like mortar. It was used for a coating on the outside of ships to make them waterproof, and in place of mortar in masonry.

Pitch´er. The custom of drawing water in pitchers still prevails in the East, an earthern vessel with two handles being used for that purpose. It was carried on the head or left shoulder. Gen. 24:16, 18, 45.

Pi´thom (*house* or *temple of Tum*, the sun-god of Heliopolis), one of the treasure-cities built in Goshen by the Israelites while in bondage. It was probably near the bitter lakes of Suez and in the vicinity of the present Suez Canal. Exod. 1:11.

Pi´thon (*harmless?*), one of the sons of Micah, the grandson of Saul's son Jonathan. 1 Chron. 8:35; 9:41.

Pit´i-ful, Lam. 4:10; James 5:11; 1 Pet. 3:8, means tender-hearted; compassionate.

Place, in 1 Sam. 15:12, is rendered "monument" in the Revised Version.

Plague, an eminently contagious and destructive disease accompanied by loathsome eruptions, prevailed in the East from the earliest ages. The word was also employed by the sacred writers to express any desolating disease, calamity, or scourge. Lev. 13:3. The judgments of God on Pharaoh are called plagues. Exod. 9:14.

Plain, referring to a tract of land, is often used alone in the Bible, and the particular plain alluded to must be inferred from the context, as in Deut. 1:1; 2:8. The word translated "plains" in Gen. 12:6; 13:18; 14:13; 18:1; Deut. 11:30; Judg. 4:11; 9:6, 37; 1 Sam. 10:3 means *places* noted for one or more oaks.

Plait'ing, 1 Pet. 3:3, means braiding. The business of dressing the hair is mentioned by Jewish writers as an art by itself, practiced by women.

Plan'ets, in 2 Kings 23:5, refer to the twelve signs or constellations which were made the objects of idolatrous worship in Judah. See STARS.

Plas'ter was used by the ancients on the walls of their houses, Lev. 14:42, 48; Dan. 5:5, and to cover the stones on which inscriptions were to be made. Deut. 27:2, 4. Plasters in the medical sense were also used. Isa. 38:21.

Pledge. That which is given as security for a loan or for the performance of a contract. The Mosaic law contained wise provisions on this subject to protect the poor from oppression. Deut. 24:6, 17.
Also see Gen. 38:17, 18, 20.
Exod. 22:26.
Deut. 24:10-13.
1 Sam. 17:18.
2 Kings 18:23.
Job 22:6; 24:3, 9.

Prov. 20:16; 27:13.
Isa. 36:8.
Ezek. 18:7, 12, 16; 33:15.
Amos 2:8.

Pleiades, ple'ya-dez. a group of seven stars in the neck of the bull in the constellation Taurus. They were associated by the ancients with the return of spring. Job. 9:9; 38:31; Amos 5:8.

Plough, a much simpler instrument than that now used, was employed from the earliest times by the Hebrews. It was sometimes made from a crotched stick or branch of a tree with the wooden share shod with a triangular or heart-shaped piece of iron. 1 Sam. 13:20. The plough was guided by a single upright held by one hand, while the other hand wielded the goad. With such an instrument the soil received no more than a mere scratching. "Earing," in Gen. 45:6; Exod. 34:21, means ploughing.

Pochereth, pok'e-reth (*snaring*), a servant of Solomon. His descendants returned from Babylon. Ezra 2:57; Neh. 7:59.

Po'e-try, Hebrew. Poetry and music were closely connected, and figured prominently in the domestic and social life of the Hebrews as narrated in the Bible. The chief subject of their poetry was religion. Exclusive of the historical books and the book of Daniel, the whole of the Old Testament is poetry in the Hebrew, and it is so distinguished in the Revised Version of the Psalms, the book of Job, and the Proverbs. There are also poetic pieces scattered through the historical books, as the Song of Moses, Exodus, chapter 15, the prophecies of Balaam, Numbers, chapter 24, the farewell and blessing of Moses, Deut. 32:1-43; 33:2-29, and the lament of David over Jonathan. 2 Sam. 1:19-27. The

Psalms belong to lyric poetry, Job and the Song of Solomon may also be classified with dramatic poetry. A characteristic feature of Hebrew poetry is the parallelism of members so called, that is, a correspondence of thought and diction, as the flapping of two wings. Poetry began, we may say, in Paradise, and pervades the first chapters of Genesis. It was cultivated by Moses, the great lawgiver, and continued till after the return from the captivity. David, the greatest of the kings of the Jews, was also the greatest of their poets. Christian psalmody takes its rise, and more or less its form, from the Psalms of David. In the New Testament, the parables of the Saviour are poetic fictions taken from real life and illustrating spiritual truths. The book of Revelation is highly poetic in its imagery and diction. The Benedictus of Zacharias, the Magnificat of the Virgin Mary, and the anthem of the heavenly host in the first and second chapters of Luke strike the keynote of Christian psalmody and hymnody.

Poll, Poll´ed. When used as a noun, as in Num. 1:2, 18, 20, 22; 3:47; 1 Chron. 23:3, 24, "poll" means a head. When used as a verb, Mic. 1:16; 2 Sam. 14:26; Ezek. 44:20, it means to cut off the hair or shave.

Pol´lux. See CASTOR.

Pomegranate, pum-gran´et, meaning "grained apple," is the name of a tree or large bush and its fruit cultivated from early times in Syria, Persia, Egypt, etc. The fruit is the size of the orange, flattened at the ends like the apple, and the rind is of a beautiful brownish-red color. The inside of the pomegranate is of a bright pink, with skinny partitions similar to the orange. It abounds with juice of a grateful flavor, and a multitude of small seeds. The tree is rarely over ten feet high, and there are both sweet and sour varieties. Num. 20:5; Deut. 8:8.

Pom´mels, 2 Chron. 4:12, 13, ball-shaped ornaments projecting from the capitals of pillars. Same as "bowls." 1 Kings 7:41.

Ponds, in Egypt, were simply sheets of water formed by the overflow of the Nile. Exod. 7:19; 8:5.

Pontius, pon´shi-us, **Pi´late,** a Roman governor of Judea. Acts 4:27. See PILATE.

Pon´tus, the north-eastern part of Asia Minor, extending along the Black Sea, was an independent kingdom until shortly before the death of Nero, during whose reign it was made a Roman province. Polemo II., who married Bernice, the great-granddaughter of Herod the Great and sister of Herod Agrippa, Acts 25:13, was its last king. There seems to have been many Jews in the country. Jews from Pontus were present in Jerusalem on the day of Pentecost, Acts 2:9; Aquila, the helper of Paul, was a native of Pontus, Acts 18:2, and Peter addressed his first epistle "to the strangers scattered throughout Pontus." 1 Pet. 1:1.

Pools were large public reservoirs for spring-or rain-water. There were numerous pools in and about Jerusalem, some being of very great dimensions. Neh. 3:15. See BETHESDA, SILOAM, SOLOMON'S POOLS.

Poor. While sometimes used in the New Testament to denote those who are humble of heart, Matt. 5:3, the word generally has the literal meaning in the Bible. The poor were specially provided for in the Mosaic law, Exod. 23:6; Lev. 19:9, 10, etc., which surrounded them with safeguards that prevented pauperism and secured for them just treatment.

Pop´lar, Gen. 30:37; Hos. 4:13. The Hebrew word means "white," but it is translated "poplar," and probably refers to the white poplar, of which four varieties are found in Palestine. Some believe the storax tree is intended, but as it is only a shrub from nine to twelve feet high it does not well answer in Hosea 4:13.

Poratha, por´a-thah (*favored by fate*), one of the sons of Haman, the enemy of the Jews. Esther 9:8.

Porch, Sol´o-mon's. John 10:23. See TEMPLE.

Porcius, por´shi-us, **Fes´tus,** the Roman governor of Judea who succeeded Felix. Acts 24:27. He is generally mentioned by his surname FESTUS alone.

Por´ters were employed to open and shut the gates of a city or house, to keep guard, etc., etc. Four thousand of them were employed in the Temple in different capacities. 1 Chron. 23:5.

Por´tion. Neh. 8:10. It was customary in ancient times, among the Greeks, Hebrews, and Egyptians, to set before each guest the portion of food intended for him. To set before a guest a greater portion than usual was to confer upon him a special honor. See the distinction shown Benjamin. Gen. 43:34. A "worthy portion," 1 Sam. 1:5, is rendered in the Revised Version "a double portion."

Posts, runners or messengers bearing special tidings, were employed in the East from very early times. See the allusion in Job 9:25. The Persians made their public announcements by means of sentinels, who, stationed at certain distances apart, cried out the news one to the other, and so passed it along. Later a system of posts was established that travelled night and day. The Romans and Persians impressed men and beasts into this public service, a work greatly disliked by the Jews. Matt. 5:41.

Pot´i-phar (*belonging to the sun*), the captain of Pharaoh's guard to whom Joseph was sold by the Midianites. Gen. 37:36; 39:1.

Poti-pherah, po-tiph´e-rah, an Egyptian priest of On who was the father of Joseph's wife Asenath. Gen. 41:45, 50; 46:20.

Pots, in the Scriptures, apply to a great variety of vessels used for domestic purposes that are more particularly distinguished in the Hebrew. "Ranges for pots," Lev. 11:35, probably means the excavations for the fire, over which the pots were placed.

Pot´sherds are broken pieces of earthenware. They are very numerous among the ruins of ancient cities, and are used in various ways by the poor. They drink water from them, and coals of fire are carried in them from one place to another. Job 2:8; Ps. 22:15; Prov. 26:23.

Pot´tage, Gen. 25:29. In the East, lentils are boiled or stewed like beans with oil and garlic, and make a dish that is eaten as pottage. Other ingredients were also used. 2 Kings 4:39.

Pot´ter. The making of earthenware was one of the first manufactures. The method employed by the Israelites seems to have been the same as that followed by the Egyptians. The clay was trodden by the feet, and when it had reached the proper consistency a lump of it was placed upon the potter's wheel, which was made to revolve rapidly while the potter worked the vessel into shape. Jer. 18:2-4. It was then glazed and baked. Such vessels were used not only for cooking, but also for preserving valuables. Jer. 32:14.

Pot´ter's Field, a burial-place. Matt. 27:7. See ACELDAMA.

Pot´tle, in the marginal notes, Luke 16:7, means an old English liquid-measure containing four pints.

Pound. In the Old Testament, 1 Kings 10:17; Ezra 2:69; Neh. 7:71, 72, the word is used as the translation of the Hebrew MANEH (which see), and means a weight. In John 12:3; 19:39 the word has the same meaning (weight) in the Greek, but in Luke 19:13, 16, 18, 20, 24, 25 it means a sum of money, about sixteen dollars.

Præ-to´ri-um, Mark 15:16, was the headquarters of the Roman governor. "Herod's judgment hall," Acts 23:35, in the Greek is *Prætorium*, and the "palace," in Phil. 1:13, is rendered in the Revised Version "prætorian guard."

Praise, as used in the Scriptures, denotes an act of worship; also thanksgiving.

Prayer is offering to God petitions for mercies desired and thanksgiving and praise for blessings received.
2 Sam. 7:27.
1 Kings 8:28, 29, 38, 45, 49, 54; 9:3.
2 Kings 19:4; 20:5.
2 Chron. 6:19, 20, 29, 35, 39, 40; 7:12, 15; 30:27; 33:18, 19.
Neh. 1:6, 11; 4:9; 11:17.
Job 15:4; 16:17; 22:27.
Pss. 4:1; 5:3; 6:9; 17:1; 35:13; 39:12; 42:8; 54:2; 55:1; 61:1; 64:1; 65:2; 66:19, 20; 69:13; 72:15, 20; 80:4; 84:8; 86:6; 88:2, 13; 90; 102:1, 17; 109:4, 7; 141:2, 5; 142; 143.
Prov. 15:8, 29; 28:9.
Isa. 1:15; 26:16; 37:4; 38:5; 56:7.
Jer. 7:16; 11:14.
Lam. 3:8, 44.
Dan. 9:3, 13, 17, 21.
Jon. 2:7.
Hab. 3:1.
Matt. 17:21; 21:13, 22; 23:14.
Mark 9:29; 11:17; 12:40.
Luke 1:13; 2:37; 5:33; 6:12; 19:46;
20:47; 22:45.
Acts 1:14; 2:42; 3:1; 6:4; 10:4, 31; 12:5; 16:13, 16.
Rom. 1:9; 10:1; 12:12; 15:30.
1 Cor. 7:5.
2 Cor. 1:11; 9:14.
Eph. 1:16; 6:18.
Phil. 1:4, 19; 4:6.
Col. 4:2, 12.
1 Thess. 1:2.
1 Tim. 2:1; 4:5; 5:5.
2 Tim. 1:3.
Philem. :4, 22.
Heb. 5:7.
James 5:15, 16.
1 Pet. 3:7, 12; 4:7.
Rev. 5:8; 8:3, 4.

Preach´ing originally meant to herald or proclaim, and in that sense it is mainly used in the Bible. In the Epistles, however, the word has nearly the same meaning it has with us now—a public discourse on the truths of religion.

Pre-des´ti-nate, Rom. 8:29, 30; Eph. 1:5, 11, foreordain or elect in Christ to everlasting life.

Prep-a-ra´tion. The word is also used with "day," and refers to Friday, as on that day meals and other matters were prepared for the Sabbath. Matt. 27:62; Mark 15:42.

Pres´by-ter-y, the assembly of elders. The name is translated "elders" in Luke 22:66; Acts 22:5, while in 1 Tim. 4:14 the Greek word "presbytery" is retained.

Pres´ent-ly, Prov. 12:16; Matt. 21:19; Phil. 2:23, means immediately.

Pres´ents. Gen. 32:13. See GIFTS.

Press, Press Fats, or **Press Vats,** Joel 3:13; Hag. 2:16, were two reservoirs or large troughs arranged one higher than the other, most generally on a hillside. In the upper vat was put the fruit, which was trodden by the bare feet of men, and the expressed juice was collected in the lower vat. Sometimes the vats were made in the ground and lined with masonry. Matt. 21:33.

Press´ed in the spir´it, in Acts 18:5, is rendered "constrained by the word" in the Revised Version.

Pre-vent´, in the Authorized Version, never means, as at present, "to hinder," but (from the latin *prævenire*) "to go before;" "to anticipate;" "to come upon," 2 Sam. 22:6. In 1 Thess. 4:15 the word is rendered "precede" in the Revised Version.

Pricks. Acts 9:5. See GOADS.

Pride, Ps. 31:20, is rendered "plottings" in the Revised Version.

Priest, a contraction of *presbyter*—"elder." Originally there seems to have been no priests—that is, special ministers of religion—among the Hebrews, though there was always a special ministration of religion, which consisted principally in the preparation and offering of the daily, weekly, and monthly sacrifices. This was simply the duty of the head of the household, and descended from the father to the firstborn son. Such was the case in the time of the patriarchs. Gen. 8:20; 12:8. But when the Hebrews developed from a household into a people, from a family into a nation, the Mosaic law instituted a special order of men for this specific service. They were inaugurated with very solemn and imposing ceremonies, minutely prescribed, Exod. 29:1-37; Lev. chapters 8 and 9, and when duly invested with the priestly office they alone had the right to offer sacrifices, to conduct the public service in the Temple, to officiate at purifications, to take care of the sacred fire and the golden lamp, etc. They were maintained at the expense of the whole people. Thirteen cities with pasture-grounds, in the lands of Judah, Simeon, and Benjamin, were set aside for them, Josh. 21:13-19, and to this general provision were added one-tenth of the tithes paid to the Levites, Num. 18:26-28; a special tithe every third year, Deut. 14:28; 26:12; the redemption-money paid for the first-born of man and beast, Num. 18:14-19, etc. As this priestly order was made up exclusively from the male descendants of Aaron, the number of its members was of course at first very small, Josh. 3:6; 6:4. but in the time of David, 1 Chron. 12:27, three thousand seven hundred priests joined him at Hebron, and under the kings the provision made for the maintenance of the order proved so utterly insufficient that many priests lived in great poverty. 1 Sam. 2:36. The number of priests who accompanied Zerubbabel from the captivity was four thousand two hundred and eighty-nine. Ezra 2:36–39. Besides their strictly priestly duties, it also belonged to the office of the Hebrew priest to sit in judgment at the trial of jealousy, to superintend the lepers, to expound the law to the people, etc.

Prince. This word, in the Authorized Version, besides its usual meaning, is used to denote local governors or magistrates, as in 1 Kings 20:14. satraps (governors of provinces), in Dan. 6:1; guardian angels, in Dan. 10:13, 21; and "a liberal man," in Prov. 19:6. The latter is so translated in the Revised Version. In Dan. 11:8 "princes" means "molten images."

Prince. [1] A title of honor applied to the Saviour. Acts 3:15; 5:31; Rev. 1:5. [2] A title given to the ruling spirit of evil. Matt. 9:34; Mark 3:22; John 12:31.

Prince of Peace, a title given to Messiah by Isaiah the prophet. Isa. 9:6.

Prince of Princes, a title given to Christ by Gabriel in explaining to Daniel the vision of the ram and the he-goat. Dan. 8:25.

Prin-ci-pal´i-ty, in Eph. 1:21, is rendered "rule and authority" in the Revised Version. "Principalities," in Jer. 13:18, is rendered "headtires" in the Revised Version, and in Titus 3:1, "rulers" and "authorities."

Print´ed, Job 19:23, is rendered "inscribed" in the Revised Version.

Prisca, pris´kah (*ancient*), 2 Tim. 4:19, or **Priscilla,** pris-sil´lah, Acts 18:2; Rom. 16:3, was a Christian and the wife of Aquila of Pontus.

Pris´on. By the Mosaic law the culprit was at once put on trial, and imprisonment was not used as a punishment. The kings of the Hebrews, however, had a prison connected with the palace. 2 Chron. 16:10. The Romans used a tower in Jerusalem and the prætorium in Cæsarea as prisons, and the religious authorities had a prison in Jerusalem. Acts 5:18-23.

Prochorus, prok´o-rus (*leader of the chorus*), was one of the seven deacons chosen by the disciples and appointed by the apostles. Acts 6:5.

Prog-nos´ti-ca-tors, in Isa. 47:13, were Chaldeans who pretended to foretell future events by changes of the moon, etc.

Prop´er, in Heb. 11:23, is rendered "goodly" in the Revised Version, and in 1 Cor. 7:7, "own."

Proph´et means, first, one who speaks or interprets; then, one who speaks or interprets a message he has received from God; and, finally, one who is sent by God to reveal something with respect to the future. It is necesary to keep in mind these three acceptations of the word prophet, in order to understand that Aaron is called the prophet of Moses, Exod. 7:1; that Abraham is called a prophet, Gen. 20:7; and

that there existed among the Hebrews, as part of their system of priesthood, a regular order of prophets, a fixed institution in which prophets were educated. It was Samuel who created this institution, and he was praised highly for his work. Jer. 15:1; Acts 3:24. Schools were founded at Ramah, 1 Sam. 19:19, Bethel, 2 Kings 2:3, Jericho, 2 Kings 2:5, Gilgal, 2 Kings 4:38, etc., and young men were there instructed in the interpretation of the law, in music, and in poetry by some older prophet, who was called their father and master. But there was of course no connection between the prophetical education and the prophetical gift. No doubt many young men went through the prophetical school without ever receiving a message from God, and Amos was called by God, though he had not gone through any school. Besides the prophetesses, the Jews reckon forty-eight prophets. Two of the greatest prophets, Elijah and Elisha, have left no writings. Among the sixteen prophets whose books are found in the Old Testament Canon, ten lived before the captivity: Jonah, Joel, Amos, Hosea, Isaiah, Micah, Nahum, Zephaniah, Jeremiah, Habakkuk; three under the captivity: Daniel, Obadiah, Ezekiel; and three after the captivity: Haggai, Zechariah, and Malachi. John the Baptist was the last prophet of the old dispensation. Matt. 11:7–9; Luke 7:28.

Proph´et-ess meant the wife of a prophet, Isa. 8:3; also a woman that had the gift of prophecy. The most noted of the prophetesses were MIRIAM, Exod. 15:20, DEBORAH, Judg. 4:4, HULDAH, 2 Kings 22:14, NOADIAH, Neh. 6:14, and ANNA. Luke 2:36. The four daughters of Philip the Evangelist prophesied. Acts 21:9.

Propitiation, pro-pish-i-a´shun, the

offering made to appease the wrath and conciliate the favor of an offended person.

Pros´e-lyte, a name given by the Jews to such as were converted from heathenism to the Jewish faith. Matt. 23:15. There were two classes: "proselytes of the gate," who adopted the Jewish monotheism and Messianic hopes, but were not circumcised, and "proselytes of righteousness," who were full Jews. To the former belonged Cornelius and Lydia and many of the earliest and best members of the apostolic churches.

Prov´erbs, The, the twentieth book of the Old Testament Canon, is a collection of keen observations, wise counsels, moral maxims, rules of conduct, etc., sometimes given in that short, forcible form which characterizes the popular adage, and sometimes in the more elaborate form of instructive poetry. The larger part of it—chapters 10 to 22:16—is by Solomon, who was celebrated as a composer of proverbs, 1 Kings 4:29-34, but the whole collection was probably not compiled until the time of Hezekiah. Prov. 25:1.

Pro-voked´, in 2 Cor. 9:2, is rendered "stirred up" in the Revised Version.

Pru´dent, in Matt. 11:25; Luke 10:21, is rendered "understanding" in the Revised Version.

Psalms, the Book of, from a Greek word which means "to strike the lyre" and "to sing," is the name introduced in the Septuagint (Greek) translation of the Old Testament for that collection of hymns in the Old Testament Canon which in Hebrew is called "Praises" or "Book of Praises." It consists of five divisions (which are marked in the Revised Version as they are in the Hebrew).

Part I. contains forty-one psalms, of which thirty-seven are ascribed to David and four are anonymous—namely 1, 2, 10, and 33.

Part II. contains thirty-one psalms, 42-72, of which seven are by the sons of Korah, one by Asaph, nineteen by David, three anonymous, and one by Solomon or for Solomon.

Part III. contains seventeen psalms, 73-89, of which eleven are by Asaph, four by the sons of Korah, one by David—namely 86—and one—namely 89—by Ethan the Ezrahite.

Part IV. contains seventeen psalms, 90-106, of which one is by Moses—namely 90—two by David—namely 101 and 103—and the rest anonymous.

Part V. contains forty-four psalms, 107-150, of which fifteen are by David, one by Solomon, and the rest anonymous, including the fifteen Songs of Degrees or Pilgrim Psalms—namely 120-134—for journeys up to the festivals in Jerusalem, and the five Hallelujah Psalms. The prophetic or Messianic Psalms are 2, 8, 16, 22, 40, 45, 68. 69, 72, 97, 110, and 118. The whole collection of Psalms is not only in point of time but also in rank the first hymn-book and prayer-book for public and private devotion, and is so used to this day by Jews, and Christians of all denominations. See POETRY.

Psal´ter-y, a musical instrument with ten strings, like a harp. Its form is not now known. It was used for sacred music. Ps. 71:22.

Ptolemæus, tol-e-me´us, or **Ptolemy,** tol´e-me, is the common name of the kings of the Greek dynasty which, after the death of Alexander the Great, B. C. 323, took possession of the Egyptian throne, and in whose wars with the Seleucidæ of Syria the Hebrews could not help being involved.

[1] PTOLEMY I., SOTER, B. C. 323–285, the founder of the dynasty, invaded Syria B. C. 320, took Jerusalem on a Sabbath day, and carried a number of the inhabitants as prisoners to Egypt, but treated them well and made them the foundation of a flourishing Jewish colony. He is probably referred to in Dan. 11:5.

[2] PTOLEMY II., PHILADELPHUS, B. C. 285–247, son of Ptolemy I., founded the great library in Alexandria, is said to have given the first impulse to the translation of the Old Testament into Greek (the Septuagint), and was active in promoting that fusion of Greek philosophy and Hebrew wisdom which afterward became of so great importance to Christianity. See GREECE.

[3] PTOLEMY III., EUERGETES, B. C. 247–222, son of Ptolemy II., conquered Syria north to Antioch and east to Babylon, offered sacrifices in the Temple at Jerusalem, and brought back to Egypt the molten images of the gods which Cambyses had carried to Babylon. Dan. 11:7–9.

[4] PTOLEMY IV., PHILOPATOR, B. C. 222–205, son of Ptolemy III., defeated the Syrian king Antiochus the Great at Raphia, near Gaza, B. C. 215, Dan. 11:10-12, offered sacrifices of thanksgiving in the Temple at Jerusalem, but was struck by paralysis when he attempted to enter the Holy of Holies.

[5] PTOLEMY V., EPIPHANES, B. C. 205–181, son of Ptolemy IV., lost Phœnicia and Judea, which were conquered by Antiochus the Great. Many Jews, however, remained faithful to the Ptolemæan dynasty, and fled to Egypt, where the high-priest Onias founded the temple at Leontopolis. With Ptolemy V.

the Egyptian power began to wane. Dan. 11:13-17.

[6] PTOLEMY VI., PHILOMETOR, B. C. 181–146, son of Ptolemy V., was an infant when his father died, and up to her death, B. C. 173, his mother, Cleopatra, reigned in his stead. In B. C. 171 he was defeated and taken prisoner by the Syrian king Antiochus Epiphanes, and though the influence of the Romans established peace between them, the Egyptian power was now wholly spent. Dan. 11:25-30. Under his reign the Jewish temple at Leontopolis was finished.

Ptolemais, tol-e-ma´is, a seaport of the Mediterranean, on the coast of Palestine, between Mount Carmel and Tyre. Acts 21:7. It is called ACCHO (which see) in Judg. 1:31.

Pua, pu´ah, one of the sons of Issachar. Num. 26:23. See PUAH, No. 1.

Pu´ah (*mouth*). [1] One of the sons of Issachar, 1 Chron. 7:1, called PUA in Num. 26:23, and PHUVAH in Gen. 46:13. [2] An Israelite of the tribe of Issachar. He was the father of Tola, who judged Israel after Abimelech. Judg. 10:1. [3] One of the midwives who was ordered by Pharaoh to kill all male children at birth. Exod. 1:15-21.

Pub´li-can, Matt. 18:17, was an under collector of the Roman tribute. The principal or chief collectors of this revenue were men of great credit and influence, but the under collectors or publicans to whom they farmed it out were noted for their rapacity and extortion, and were held in great aversion, besides being denied admittance to the Temple or synagogues. Matthew (or Levi) the Evangelist was originally a tax-gatherer near the Sea of Galilee, and was called by our Lord from the toll-booth. Luke 5:27.

Pub´li-us, the chief man of the island of Melita, in the Mediterranean Sea. He received and lodged Paul when he was shipwrecked there. Acts 28:7, 8.

Pudens, pu´denz, a Christian of Rome who, with Paul, sent salutation to Timothy. 2 Tim. 4:21.

Pu´hites, one of the families of Kirjath-jearim descended apparently from Caleb, the son of Hur. 1 Chron. 2:53.

Pul (*lord?*), a king of Assyria who invaded Israel in the time of Menahem, who bribed him by the gift of a thousand talents of silver to depart from the land. 2 Kings 15:19; 1 Chron. 5:26.

Pul, the name of a region mentioned, with Tarshish, Lud, Tubal, Javan, and "the isles afar off," in Isa. 66:19.

Pulse. While our English word pulse means peas, beans, lentiles, and the produce of similar podded plants, the word in Dan. 1:12, 16 probably means vegetable food in general, and in 2 Sam. 17:28, parched peas.

Pun´ish-ment. The general law of recompense was the supreme principle of the Mosaic law. Lev. 24:17-22. Imprisonment, while not prescribed by the law, was practiced in the times of the kings. 2 Chron. 16:10; Jer. 37:15.

Pu´nites, descendants of Pua or Phuvah, one of Issachar's sons. Num. 26:23.

Pu´non, the thirty-fifth station of the Israelites on their way from Egypt to the land of Canaan. It was north of Mount Hor and nearly east of the Dead Sea. Num. 33:42, 43.

Pu-ri-fi-ca´tions formed an important part of the religious services of the Jews, and were generally made with water. They had a spiritual meaning, and were also useful in securing health. They were carried to excess after the captivity, especially by the Pharisees. Mark 7:3, 4.

Pur, Pu´rim (*lots*), the feast or festival celebrated by the Jews to commemorate their deliverance from Haman. Esther 3:7; 9:20-32. It is called the Feast of Lots because Haman tried to fix by lot the day on which the Jews were to be slain. It was celebrated on the fourteenth and fifteenth of the Jewish month Adar (March), and is still observed by the Jews. On that occasion the book of Esther is read.

Pur´ple was obtained from a shell-fish of the Mediterranean Sea, and was the royal and noble color. The name "purple" seems to have been applied to every color in which red was mixed. Lydia was a seller of purple. Acts 16:14.

Purse. The purse, Matt. 10:9; Mark 6:8, used by the Hebrews was carried in the girdle, which confined their outside garment about the waist. See GIRDLE.

Pur´te-nance, in Exod. 12:9, is rendered "inwards" in the Revised Version.

Put, 1 Chron. 1:8; Nah. 3:9, elsewhere called PHUT (which see).

Pu-te´o-li, a seaport on the Mediterranean Sea, about six miles west of Naples. It contained hot springs, and was a favorite resort of the Romans. Paul was landed there on his way to Rome, and found Christian brethren. Acts 28:13, 14.

Pu´ti-el (*afflicted of God*) was the father-in-law of Eleazar, the son of Aaron. Exod. 6:25.

Py´garg, mentioned in Deut. 14:5, is supposed to refer to a kind of antelope. In the marginal notes, it is translated "Or, *bison*. Hebrew *dishon*."

Py´thon, mentioned in the marginal notes of Acts 16:16, was a surname of

Apollo, who was the god of divination in the mythology of the Greeks.

Q

Quails, the birds miraculously given to the Israelites while in the wilderness. Exod. 16:13; Num. 11:31. At the season when they were gathered quails pass over Arabia in immense numbers, but the vast quantities thrown into the camp of the Israelites, sufficient to furnish food for the multitude for more than a month, were certainly supernatural.

Quar´ries, Judg. 3:19, 26, is rendered in the marginal notes "graven images."

Quar´tus (*fourth*), a Christian from whom Paul sent greeting to the Romans. Rom. 16:23.

Qua-ter´ni-on, Acts 12:4, means a guard consisting of four soldiers. Two of them kept watch over the prisoner in the cell and the other two guarded the doors. They were relieved by another guard of four every three hours, or at each successive watch. The four quarternions mentioned in the text were therefore sixteen men, each of whom was on duty three hours during the day and three hours during the night.

Queen. This title was applied to the ruling monarch, if a woman, 1 Kings 10:1, to the wife of a king, Esther 7:1, and also to the mother of a king. 1 Kings 15:13. As a result of the practice of polygamy, the wife of a king did not enjoy the distinction she does now. The queen-mother, however, generally exercised great influence and power.

Queen of Heav´en, mentioned in Jer. 7:18; 44:17, 18, 19, 25, was the name given to the moon by idolatrous Hebrews. See ASHTORETH.

Quick, in Num. 16:30; Pss. 55:15; 124:3, means "alive," and is so rendered in the Revised Version. In Lev. 13:10, 24 the word means having the life of living flesh. In Heb. 4:12 it is rendered "living" in the Revised Version, and in Acts 10:42; 2 Tim. 4:1; 1 Pet. 4:5 it has the same meaning. (So also in the Apostles' Creed, "to judge the quick and the dead.")

Quick´en does not mean to hasten or accelerate, but to keep, preserve, or give life. Ps. 71:20; John 5:21, etc. The context will suggest which meaning should apply.

Quick´sands, Acts 27:17, refer to two gulfs on the northern coast of Africa, greatly dreaded by sailors on account of the variations and uncertainties of the tides on a flat coast that had many sand-bars.

Qui-rin´i-us (Revised Version), a Roman governor of Syria. Luke 2:2. See CYRENIUS.

Quit, in 1 Sam. 4:9; 1 Cor. 16:13, is used in the sense of acquit.

Quiv´er, a case or sheath for arrows. Gen. 27:3. It is often used figuratively in the Bible.

R

Ra´a-mah (*trembling*). [1] One of the sons of Cush, the son of Ham. [2] A country which appears to have been named after Raamah, the son of Cush, and to have been settled by his descendants. It was probably on the south-west shore of the Persian Gulf. Ezek. 27:22.

Ra-a-mi´ah (*whom Jehovah makes tremble*), a chief among the Jews who returned from Babylon with Zerubbabel.

Neh. 7:7. Same as REELAIAH in Ezra 2:2.

Raamses, ra-am´seez, an Egyptian city on the river Nile. Exod. 1:11. It is elsewhere called RAMESES.

Rab´bah (*greatness*). [1] Josh. 13:25. Called "Rabbath of the children of Ammon," Deut. 3:11, or "Rabbath of the Ammonites," Ezek. 21:20, or by the Greeks and Romans "Philadelphia," because it was rebuilt by Ptolemy Philadelphus. It is the modern *Amman*, a village among wonderful and extensive ruins. It was the capital of the Ammonites, and was situated twenty-two miles east of the river Jordan, and near the source of the river Jabbok. It is often mentioned in the history of David, and was one of the cities of Decapolis. [2] A town of Judah. Josh. 15:60.

Rab´bath-am´mon, called "Rabbath of the children of Ammon" in Deut. 3:11, was the capital of the Ammonites. See RABBAH, No. 1.

Rab´bath-mo´ab, the ancient capital of Moab. It was about twelve miles east of the southern part of the Dead Sea.

Rab´bi (*master* or *teacher*) was the name given by the Jews to the teachers of their law. This title was also given to Christ by his disciples and the people. John 3:2, 26.

Rab´bith (*multitude*), a town of Issachar. Josh. 19:20.

Rab-bo´ni, John 20:16, has the same meaning as RABBI, teacher, only in a higher degree, and was regarded among the Jews as the highest title of honor.

Rab´-mag (*the master of the magi?*), the name or title of a prince of Babylon. Jer. 39:3, 13.

Rab´-sa-ris (*chief eunuch*), an eminent Assyrian or Babylonian officer. 2 Kings 18:17; Jer. 39:3, 13.

Rab´sha-keh, which probably means "chief of the cup-bearers," was the name or title of one of the chief officers of Sennacherib, king of Assyria. 2 Kings 18:17; Isa. 36:2.

Ra´ca (*worthless*), Matt. 5:22, is a term of reproach and contempt, and is rendered "vain fellow" in the marginal notes. It is retained in the Revised Version with the note, "An expression of contempt."

Race. 1 Cor. 9:24. This word, in the New Testament, refers to the Grecian contests in running on foot, horseback, or in chariots. The most laborious training and preparation were made for these contests, and to win the prize was considered among the greatest of earthly honors. The contestants took off everything that would impede them, the prize was placed in full view, and the victor was crowned as soon as the result was announced.

Rachab, ra´kab, in Matt. 1:5, denotes the same person as RAHAB, mentioned in Josh. 2:1.

Rachal, ra´kal (*traffic*), a town of Judah. 1 Sam. 30:29.

Ra´chel (*a ewe*), the younger daughter of Laban. She became the wife of the patriach Jacob, and was the mother of Joseph and Benjamin. Her history is given in Genesis, chapters 29 to 36. She died soon after Benjamin's birth. Jacob erected a pillar on her grave, near the road from Jerusalem to Bethlehem. Gen. 35:19, 20. Her reputed tomb is covered by a small Mohammedan mosque (place of worship), and is about half a mile from Bethlehem.

Rad´da-i (*treading down*), the fifth son of Jesse and the brother of David. 1 Chron. 2:14.

Ra´gau, in Luke 3:35, was the same person as REU, mentioned in Gen. 11:20, 21, and was an ancestor of Joseph, the husband of Mary.

Ra-gu´el (*friend of God*), the name given in one place, Num. 10:29, to the father-in-law of Moses. He is elsewhere called REUEL and JETHRO.

Ra´hab, a Canaanitish woman of Jericho who received and concealed the two spies sent by Joshua to explore the land of Canaan. She is called RACHAB in Matt. 1:5. Her history is given in Josh. 2:1–23; 6:17–25. Her faith is mentioned in Heb. 11:31.

Ra´hab (*violence*), in Pss. 87:4; 89:10; Isa. 51:9, is generally supposed to be a symbolical name for Egypt.

Ra´ham, a grandson of Hebron. 1 Chron. 2:44.

Rain in Palestine falls abundantly during the wet season, or from November to April, but during the dry season, April to November, it rarely rains. The first rain after the drought of summer is called the "former," because it precedes the seed-time and prepares the earth for cultivation. The "latter" rain falls in April, just before the harvest, and perfects the fruits of the earth. Hos. 6:3; Joel 2:23.

Ra´kem (*flower-gardening*), a son of Sheresh, a descendant of Manasseh. 1 Chron. 7:16.

Rak´kath (*shore*), a fortified city of Naphtali. Josh. 19:35.

Rak´kon (*thinness*), a town of Dan. Josh. 19:46.

Ram (*exalted*). [1] An Israelite of the tribe of Judah, descended from Pharez through Hezron. Ruth 4:19; 1 Chron. 2:9. Called ARAM in Matt. 1:3, 4; Luke 3:33. [2] A son of Jerahmeel. 1 Chron. 2:25, 27. [3] The head of a family from which Elihu, a friend of Job, descended. Job 32:2.

Ram, Bat´ter-ing. Ezek. 4:2. See BATTERING-RAM.

Ra´ma, ra´mah, in Matt. 2:18, is the Greek form of RAMAH.

Ra´mah (*high place*). [1] A city of Benjamin. When Jerusalem was captured by Nebuchadnezzar the captives, among whom was Jeremiah, were guarded at Ramah. Jer. 40:1. Jeremiah's prophecy, Jer. 31:15, was fulfilled there. [2] A town in Mount Ephraim, also called RAMATHAIM-ZOPHIM. It was the birthplace, home, and burial-place of the prophet Samuel. 1 Sam. 1:19. [3] A town on the boundary of Asher. Josh. 19:29. [4] A fortified place in Naphtali. Josh. 19:36. [5] Another name for the city of RAMOTH-GILEAD. 2 Kings 8:28, 29. [6] A place to which some Benjamites returned after the captivity. Neh. 11:33.

Ra-math-a´im-zo´phim (*double height of the watchers*), 1 Sam. 1:1, is the full name of RAMAH, No. 2.

Ra´math-ite, a native of Ramah. 1 Chron. 27:27.

Ra´math-le´hi (*hill of Lehi*), a place in Judah were Samson cast away the jawbone of an ass, with which he slew "a thousand" Philistines. Judg. 15:17.

Ra´math-miz´peh (*height of the watch-tower*), a city of Gad. Josh. 13:26.

Ra´math of the South, a place in the southern part of Simeon. Josh. 19:8. It is called SOUTH RAMOTH in 1 Sam. 30:27.

Rameses, ra-me´seez (*son of the sun*), a city and province of Egypt, probably on the east side of the river Nile. It may have been the capital of Goshen. Gen. 47:11; Exod. 12:37. It is also called RAAMSES in Exod. 1:11.

Ra-mi´ah (*Jehovah exalted*), a Jew who took a foreign wife. Ezra 10:25.

Ra´moth (*heights*), a Jew who took a foreign wife. Ezra 10:29.

Ra´moth. [1] Deut. 4:43; Josh. 20:8; 21:38; 1 Chron. 6:20, was a city of Gad. It is admitted to be the same as Ramoth-gilead. [2] A city of Issachar. 1 Chron. 6:73. [3] A place near the desert south of Judah. 1 Sam. 30:27.

Ra´moth-gil´e-ad (*height of Gilead*), one of the principal cities of Gad. 1 Kings 4:13; 2 Kings 8:28. It was a city of refuge. It is called RAMAH in 2 Kings 8:29; 2 Chron. 22:6.

Rang´es, in 2 Kings 11:8, 15; 2 Chron. 23:14, means "ranks" (of soldiers).

Ran´som, Matt. 20:28; Mark 10:45, the price paid to purchase the freedom of a captive or slave. When the children of Israel were numbered every one was required to give an offering to the Lord as a "ransom for his soul." Exod. 30:12–16.

Rapha, ra´fah (*tall*). [1] A son of Benjamin. 1 Chron. 8:2. [2] A Benjamite of the family of Saul. 1 Chron. 8:37.

Ra´phu (*healed*), the father of one of the spies sent by Moses to search the land of Canaan. Num. 13:9.

Ra´ven, a bird of prey, was unclean according to Levitical law. Lev. 11:15. It feeds principally upon carrion, and is said to seize first upon the eyes; hence the allusion in Prov. 30:17, which implies the exposure of the corpse in the open field, than which nothing was regarded as more disgraceful.

Rav´en-ing, in Luke 11:39, means extortion; in Ps. 22:13; Ezek. 22:25, 27 it means to prey with rapacity.

Rav´in, in Gen. 49:27, means to prey with rapacity; in Nah. 2:12 it means prey; plunder.

Ra´zor. This instrument, from the custom of the Jews, who shaved their heads after completing a vow, must have been used from the earliest times. Num. 6:5; Ezek. 5:1. The word is used figuratively in Isa. 7:20. See HAIR.

Reaia, re-a-i´ah (*whom Jehovah cares for*), one of the descendants of Reuben. 1 Chron. 5:5. Another form of the name REAIAH.

Re-a-i´ah. [1] A son of Shobal, the son of Judah. 1 Chron. 4:2. [2] An Israelite whose descendants returned with Zerubbabel. Ezra 2:47; Neh. 7:50.

Reap´ing. In very ancient times the ripened grain was plucked up by the roots. Later, sickles resembling those now used were employed. Deut. 16:9; Joel 3:13. The harvest was carried to the threshing-floor, where the grain was separated from the ear. See THRESHING.

Reba, re´bah (*the fourth*), a king of the Midianites who was slain by the Israelites. Num. 31:8; Josh. 13:21.

Re-bec´ca. Rom. 9:10. See REBEKAH.

Re-bek´ah (*a cord with a noose, enchaining*), the daughter of Bethuel, the nephew of Abraham. She became the wife of Isaac and the mother of Jacob and Esau. An account of her life is contained in Gen. 24:15 to 49:31.

Rechab, re´kab (*horseman*). [1] An ancestor of Jehonadab, the founder of the Rechabites. 2 Kings 10:15, 23; 1 Chron. 2:55; Jer. 35:6-19. [2] One of Ish-bosheth's captains. 2 Sam. 4:2. [3] The father of Malchiah. Neh. 3:14.

Rechabites, re´kab-ites, the descendants of Jehonadab, who was the son of RECHAB, No. 1. They practiced circumcision and worshipped the true God, but were not included among the children of Israel. Jer. 35:2.

Rechah, re´kah (*utmost part*), a place in Judah. 1 Chron. 4:12.

Rec-on-cil-i-a´tion, Heb. 2:17, as implying the restoration of man to God's favor, denotes a change on the part of both in their relations to and with each other.

"Atonement," in Rom. 5:11, is better rendered "reconciliation," as in the Revised Version, since "atonement" now means expiation.

Rec´ord, in John 1:32, 34, etc., means "witness" or "testimony." "Take you to record," in Acts 20:26, is rendered "I testify unto you" in the Revised Version.

Re-cord´er, 2 Sam. 8:16, an officer of high rank who recorded the events as they occurred during the reign of the king, acted as his councillor, sometimes represented him, and was entrusted with important commissions. 2 Chron. 34:8.

Re-deem´er, one who frees by repaying. By the Mosaic law hereditary property that had been sold could be redeemed by the original owner or any of his descendants. In a similar sense the word is used in reference to God redeeming his people from bondage, Exod. 6:6, from sin and the law. Gal. 3:13; Titus 2:14, etc.

Red Sea, a long arm of the Indian Ocean, with which it is connected by the narrow strait of Bab-el-Mandeb, lies between Egypt and the Arabian Peninsula. It is about fourteen hundred and fifty miles long and two hundred and twenty miles wide in its broadest part. Its northern end is divided into two arms, the Gulf of Suez on the west, and the Gulf of Aqaba on the east. The Gulf of Suez was connected with the river Nile by an ancient canal. The Red Sea is famous on account of its passage by the Israelites and the destruction of the Egyptians who pursued them. Exod. chapters 14 and 15. The place at which the passage was made is not known, but it was somewhere on the Gulf of Suez, which anciently extended about fifty miles further north. The Red Sea is also called "the sea" in Exod. 14:2, 9, etc., the "Egyptian Sea," Isa. 11:15.

Reed, a plant of the grass family having a long, slender stalk. From it were made musical instruments, paper, and pens. It was also used as a measuring-rod. The sacred writers often used the word to illustrate weakness and fragility. 2 Kings 18:21. See BULRUSH, FLAG, ORGAN, PAPER, PEN, and PIPE.

Reed, a measure of length, equal to about one hundred and twenty feet. Ezek. 40:5.

Reelaiah, re-el-a´yah (*whom Jehovah makes tremble*), one of the chief Jews who returned with Zerubbabel. Ezra 2:2. Called RAAMIAH in Neh. 7:7.

Re-fin´er. In Mal. 3:3 this word is used with peculiar force from the fact that the refiner of silver sat with his eyes fixed steadily on the furnace, watching the process, which was only complete and perfect when the refiner could see his own image in the melted mass. This, during the process, had been covered with a film of the oxide of lead which grew thinner and thinner as the refining approached completion, and then suddenly disappeared, revealing the brilliant surface of the pure silver. The word is used figuratively. Isa. 48:10; Zech. 13:9.

Ref´uge, Cities of. See CITIES OF REFUGE.

Re´gem (*friend*), a son of Jahdai. 1 Chron. 2:47.

Regem-melech, re´gem-me´lek (*friend of the king*), a Jew who was sent into the Temple by the captives to "pray before the LORD" and to make inquiries. Zech. 7:2.

Re-gen-er-a´tion, the birth of a soul previously dead in sin unto a new spiritual life, through the workings of the Holy Spirit. The word is found only twice in the Bible. In Matt. 19:28 it refers to the restoration of all things at Christ's second advent; and in Titus 3:5 it denotes the new birth through the Holy Spirit. Other words in the New Testament convey the same meaning. John 3:3; 1 Pet. 1:23.

Re-ha-bi´ah (*whom Jehovah enlarges*), one of the sons of Eliezer, the son of Moses. 1 Chron. 23:17; 24:21.

Re´hob (*street, broad place*). [1] The father of Hadadezer, king of Zobah. 2 Sam. 8:3, 12. [2] One of the Levites who sealed the covenant with Nehemiah. Neh. 10:11.

Re´hob (*broad place*). [1] The extreme northern limit reached by the spies sent by Moses. Num. 13:21. It is called BETH-REHOB in 2 Sam 10:6, 8. [2] A place in Asher. Josh. 19:28. [3] Another place in Asher. Josh. 19:30; 21:31.

Re-ho-bo´am (*enlarger of the people*), the son of Solomon who succeeded him as king of Israel, but from whom the ten tribes revolted under Jeroboam. Rehoboam reigned seventeen years. 1 Kings 11:43; 14:21; 2 Chron. 12:16.

Re-ho´both (*wide places*). [1] The name which Isaac gave to a well which he dug. Gen. 26:22. [2] "Rehoboth by the river." The river referred to is supposed to be the Euphrates. Gen 36:37; 1 Chron. 1:48. [3] One of the cities founded by Asshur. Gen. 10:11. It is supposed to have been near the river Euphrates.

Re´hum (*compassionate*). [1] One of the chief men who returned with Zerubbabel, Ezra 2:2, called NEHUM in Neh. 7:7. [2] An officer of the king of Persia who opposed the rebuilding of the Temple. Ezra 4:8, 9. [3] One of the Levites who repaired part of the wall of Jerusalem. Neh. 3:17. [4] A Jew who sealed the covenant made by Nehemiah. Neh. 10:25. [5] One of the priests who returned with Zerubbabel. Neh. 12:3.

Re´i (*friendly*), an Israelite who was friendly to David when Adonijah tried to be king. 1 Kings 1:8.

Reins, in Pss. 7:9; 16:7, etc., means the kidneys or that part of the body which covers the kidneys, and refers to the inward impulses, the reins at one time being considered to be the seat of the affections and the passions.

Re´kem (*variegation, flower-garden*). [1] A king of the Midianites who was slain by the Israelites. Num. 31:8; Josh. 13:21. [2] A son of Hebron, of the tribe of Judah. 1 Chron. 2:43, 44.

Re´kem (*flowering-gardening*), one of the cities of Benjamin. Josh. 18:27.

Rem-a-li´ah (*whom Jehovah adores*), the father of Pekah. 2 Kings 15:25; 2 Chron. 28:6.

Re´meth (*height*), one of the towns of Issachar. Josh. 19:21.

Rem´mom (*pomegranate*), a town of Judah afterward given to Simeon. Josh. 19:7. See RIMMON, No. 1 (the town).

Rem´mon-meth´o-ar, a city, one of the landmarks of Zebulun. Josh. 19:13. See RIMMON, No. 2 (the town).

Rem´phan, an idol which Stephen asserts the Israelites worshipped in the wilderness. Acts 7:43.

Rend. To rend or tear the garments was from very ancient times a sign of grief or contrition. Josh. 7:6; 2 Kings 19:1. In Jer. 4:30 "rentest thy face" is rendered "enlargest thine eyes" in the Revised Version.

Re-pent´, Re-pent´ance, Matt. 3:2, 8, in its spiritual sense denotes a sense of guilt, an apprehension of God's mercy, sorrow for sin, and a turning away from it unto God. The Greek word denotes a change of mind, and is equivalent to conversion.

Re´pha-el (*whom God heals*), one of the Levite porters. 1 Chron. 26:7.

Re´phah (*riches*), one of the descendants of Ephraim. 1 Chron. 7:25.

Reph-a-i´ah (*whom Jehovah healed*). [1] The head of a family descended from David. 1 Chron. 3:21. [2] One of the captains of Simeon. 1 Chron. 4:42. [3] A son of Tola, the son of Issachar. 1 Chron. 7:2. [4] One of the descendants of Saul, 1 Chron. 9:43, called RAPHA in 1 Chron. 8:37. [5] The son of Hur. He repaired part of the wall of Jerusalem. Neh. 3:9.

Reph´a-im (*giants*), a race of giants which in the time of Abraham inhabited parts of Canaan, especially that portion east of the Jordan. Gen. 14:5; 15:20.

Reph´a-im, Val´ley of, was a landmark of Judah's territory, and was situated south or south-west of Jerusalem. 2 Sam. 5:18; 1 Chron. 11:15.

Reph´i-dim (*rest, refreshments*), the last station of the Israelites before they reached Sinai. It was at Rephidim that the people "murmured against Moses," Exod. 17:3, and that Moses smote the rock and water came out of it for them to drink. Exod. 17:6. The Amalekites were defeated there. Exod. 17:8-16.

Rep´ro-bate, Rom. 1:28; 2 Cor. 13:5-7; 2 Tim. 3:8, means not approved; unfit; abandoned.

Re-quire´, in Ezra 8:22; Prov. 30:7, means "ask," and is so rendered in the Revised Version.

Rere´ward, or as in the Revised Version, **Rear´ward,** Josh. 6:13; Isa. 52:12; 58:8, in several instances is explained in the marginal notes. In Isa. 52:12 the word has the same meaning as "rear-guard."

Re´sen (*bridle*), a city built by Asshur. It was situated in Assyria, between Nineveh and Calah. Gen. 10:12.

Re´sheph (*flame, lightning*), one of the descendants of Ephraim. 1 Chron. 7:25.

Rest, in Acts 9:31, is rendered "peace" in the Revised Version.

Res-ti-tu´tion for injury done intentionally or by accident was strictly enjoined by the Mosaic law.

Res-ur-rec´tion. A fundamental doctrine of the Christian faith is the resurrection of the dead, both of the just and the unjust. The resurrection of Christ, a fact most forcibly and clearly proved, was the crowning demonstration of the truth and divinity of his mission and character.

Re´u (*friend*), a son of Peleg, an ancestor of Abraham. Gen. 11:18-21; 1 Chron. 1:25.

Reu´ben (*behold a son!*). [1] The first-born son of Jacob and Leah. Gen. 29:32. He was one of "the twelve patriarchs." Acts 7:8, who were the ancestors of the Jewish nation. [2] The name Reuben is often applied to the tribe which descended from him. Num. 1:5; Deut. 27:13.

Reu´ben, Ter´ri-to-ry of, was on the east side of the Jordan and the Dead Sea. It was bounded on the east by the desert, on the south by the river Arnon, and on the north by the territory of the tribe of Gad. Its boundaries are described in Josh. 13:15-21.

Reu´ben-ites, the descendants of Reuben. Num. 26:7; Josh. 1:12.

Re-u´el or **Reu´el** (*friend of God*). [1] A son of Esau. Gen. 36:4; 1 Chron. 1:35. [2] The father-in-law of Moses. Exod. 2:18. He is elsewhere called JETHRO, and in Num. 10:29, RAGUEL. [3] The father of the captain of the tribe of Gad. Num. 2:14. He is called DEUEL in Num. 1:14. [4] A descendant of Benjamin. 1 Chron. 9:8.

Reu´mah (*exalted*), the concubine of Nahor. Gen. 22:24.

Rev-e-la´tion or **A-poc´a-lypse** is the only prophetic book in the New Testament, and closes the Canon of the Scriptures. It was written "in the spirit on the Lord's day" by the apostle John during his banishment to the solitary, barren, and rock island of Patmos, in the Ægean Sea, southwest of Ephesus. The time of its composition is not absolutely certain. According to Irenæus (who wrote about A. D. 170), it dates from the end of the reign of the emperor Domitian, A. D. 95, but it fits better into the period of the great tribulation after the Neronian persecution and before the destruction of Jerusalem — that is, between 64 and 70. The book contains a series of prophetic visions of the struggles and final victory of the Church over all opposition from without and all difficulties from within. It is full of mysteries which have called forth the greatest variety of expositions. No book has been more misunderstood and abused; none calls for greater modesty and reserve in its interpretation. The most important and most intelligible parts are the introduction and the close, namely, the epistles to the seven churches in Asia Minor, which represent the different conditions of the Church in all ages, with appropriate warnings and encouragements (chapters 2 and 3), and the description of the heavenly Jerusalem (chapters 20 and 21), which has inspired the choicest hymns of hope and aspiration. The Revelation is a book of hope and comfort to struggling Christians, and assures final victory and rest.

Re-venge´. While to check the crime of murder the Mosaic law permitted the family of the victim to revenge his death on the slayer, Num. 35:19, 27, the spirit of the law was opposed to revengeful feelings and actions. Lev. 19:17, 18. The teachings of the New Testament condemn the spirit of revenge. Matt. 5:39; Rom.

12:17-21; 1 Pet. 3:9.

Rev´e-nue, Ezra 4:13, is rendered in the marginal notes "strength." In other places in the Bible it means "income" or "increase." Prov. 8:19.

Re´zeph (*stone heated for baking*), a city about a day's journey west of the river Euphrates. 2 Kings 19:12; Isa. 37:12.

Rezia, re´zi-ah *(delight)*, a son of Ulla, a descendant of Asher. 1 Chron. 7:39.

Re´zin (*stable, firm*). [1] A king of Syria. 2 Kings 15:37; Isa. 7:1. [2] An Israelite some of whose descendants returned with Zerubbabel. Ezra 2:48; Neh. 7:50.

Re´zon (*prince*), a son of Eliadah. 1 Kings 11:23.

Rhegium, re´gi-um (*breach*), a seaport at the south-west extremity of Italy. Paul stopped there on his voyage to Rome. Acts 28:13. It is now called *Reggio*, and is situated in the midst of a populous district.

Rhesa, re´sah (*head*), an ancestor of Joseph, the husband of Mary. Luke 3:27.

Rhoda, ro´dah (*rose, rose tree*), a young woman in the house of Mary, the mother of John Mark. Acts 12:13.

Rhodes (*a rose*), an island of the Mediterranean, thirteen miles from the coast of Asia Minor, contains about four hundred and twenty square miles. It has a city of the same name celebrated for a brass statue, one hundred and five feet high (the so-called Colossus of Rhodes, one of the seven wonders of the world), and a beautiful temple of Apollo, built by Herod the Great. Paul visited Rhodes on his return from his third missionary journey. Acts 21:1.

Ribai, ri´bay (*for whom Jehovah pleads*), father of Ittai, one of David's valiant men. 2 Sam. 23:29; 1 Chron. 11:31.

Rib´lah (*fertility*), a city in the northeastern part of Canaan. Num. 34:11; Jer. 39:5. It has been regarded by some as the same as DIBLATH, Ezek. 6:14, but it is identified with the modern town on the river Orontes, thirty-five miles north-east of Baalbec.

Rid´dle. The solving of a riddle often requires the exercising of considerable ingenuity, and the pastime found great favor among the people in the East. Judg. 14:12-19. The Hebrew word means a "hidden saying."

Rie. Exod. 9:32; Isa. 28:25. See RYE.

Right´eous-ness. As an attribute of God, the word denotes holiness, justice, and rightness. Applied to man, righteous- ness denotes the possession of those Chris- tian virtues, faith, hope, and charity, and a conformity of life with the divine law.

Gen. 7; 15; 18; 20; 30; 38.
Exod. 9; 23.
Lev. 19.
Num. 23.
Deut. 4; 6; 9; 16; 24; 25; 33.
Judg. 5.
1 Sam. 12; 24; 26.
2 Sam. 4; 22.
1 Kings 2; 3; 8.
2 Kings 10.
2 Chron. 6; 12.
Ezra 9.
Neh. 9.
Job 4; 6; 8–10; 15; 17; 22; 23; 27; 29; 32–36; 40.
Pss. 1; 4; 5; 7; 9; 11; 14; 15; 17–19; 22–24; 31–37; 40; 45; 48; 50–52; 55; 58; 64; 65; 69; 71; 72; 75; 85; 88; 89; 92; 94; 96–99; 103; 106; 107; 111; 112; 116; 118; 119; 125; 129; 132; 140–143; 145; 146.
Prov. 2; 3; 8; 10–16; 18; 21; 23–25; 28; 29.
Eccles. 3; 7–9.
Isa. 1; 3; 5; 10; 11; 16; 24; 26; 28; 32; 33; 41; 42; 45; 46; 48; 51; 53; 54; 56–64.
Jer. 4; 9; 12; 20; 22; 23; 33; 51.
Lam. 1.
Ezek. 3; 13; 14; 16; 18; 21; 23; 33.
Dan. 4; 9; 12.
Hos. 2; 10.
Amos 2; 5; 6.
Mic. 6; 7.
Hab. 1.
Zeph. 2.
Zech. 8.
Mal. 3; 4.
Matt. 3; 5; 6; 9; 10; 13; 21; 23; 25.
Mark 2.
Luke 1; 5; 18; 23.
John 7; 16; 17.
Acts 10; 13; 17; 24.
Rom. 1–6; 8–10; 14.
1 Cor. 1; 15.
2 Cor. 3; 5; 6; 9; 11.
Gal. 2; 3; 5.
Eph. 4–6.
Phil. 1; 3.
2 Thess. 1.
1 Tim. 1; 6.
2 Tim. 2–4.
Titus 3.
Heb. 1; 5; 7; 11; 12.
James 1–3; 5.
1 Pet. 2–4.
2 Pet. 1–3.
1 John 2; 3.
Rev. 16; 19; 22.

Right Hand. In ancient times, as now, the right hand was the symbol of power and strength. Exod. 15:6; Ps. 77:10. It is said the Jews swore by their right hand, and that this is implied in Isa. 62:8. To give the right hand was a mark of friend- ship. Gal. 2:9. To be seated on the right hand of one higher in position or authority was a token of great honor, 1 Kings 2:19; and as applied to Christ standing on the right hand of God, Acts 7:55, it implies his unequalled dignity and exaltation. Instead of the right hand denoting the *east*, as is common with us, among the Jews it usually denoted the *south*. See HAND.

Rim´mon (*pomegranate*). [1] An idol of the Syrians. 2 Kings 5:18. [2] A Benjamite whose sons were captains in the army of Ish-bosheth. 2 Sam. 4:2, 5, 9.

Rim´mon (*pomegranate*). [1] A town of Judah afterward given to Simeon. Josh. 15:32; 1 Chron. 4:32; Zech. 14:10. It is also called REMMON in Josh. 19:7. [2] A city of Zebulun. 1 Chron. 6:77. It is called REMMON-METHOAR in Josh. 19:13. It is now the village of *Rummaneh*, near Nazareth. [3] A rocky region near Gibeah in Benjamin, called "the rock Rimmon," to which the surviving Benjamites retreated after the slaughter of most of their tribe. Judg. 20:45, 47; 21:13.

Rim´mon-pa´rez (*pomegranate of the breach*), one of the encampments of the Israelites in the wilderness. Num. 33:19, 20.

Rings. The wearing of rings was a very ancient custom. Besides being used as ornaments, Luke 15:22, and seals, Esther 8:8, they were employed as tokens of authority, and the giving of a ring was the sign of imparting authority. Gen. 41:42; Esther 3:10. As ornaments rings were worn on the fingers, in the ears and nose, and around the wrists and ankles. Isa 3:20, 21.

Ring´straked, in Gen. 30:35, means having circular lines or streaks on the body.

Rin´nah (*shout*), one of the descendants of Judah. 1 Chron. 4:20.

Ri´ot, Ri´ot-ing, Ri´ot-ous, Rom. 13:13; Luke 15:13, etc., means extrava-

gant; squandering; revelling.

Riphath, ri´fath (*a crusher*), one of the sons of Gomer, the son of Japheth. Gen. 10:3; 1 Chron. 1:6.

Ris´sah (*a ruin, a worm*), an encampment of the Israelites in the wilderness. Num. 33:21, 22.

Rith´mah (*broom*), one of the encampments of the Israelites in the wilderness. Num. 33:18, 19.

Riv´er of E´gypt, in Num. 34:5; Josh. 15:4, 47; 1 Kings 8:65; 2 Kings 24:7, refers to a river which flows into the Mediterranean Sea, and was the old boundary between Palestine and Egypt. It must not be confounded with the Nile, which is the proper river of Egypt. The Revised Version renders the word more correctly "the brook of Egypt." It is usually dry, or nearly so, in the summer, and is now called *Wâddy el-Arish*.

Riz´pah, one of King Saul's concubines. 2 Sam. 3:7; 21:10, 11.

Road, in 1 Sam. 27:10, means "raid." What we now call a road is rendered in the Bible "path" or "way."

Rob´bers. Among the wandering tribes of the East, from the earliest times until even now, might has been right, and in consequence robbery has been their chief pursuit. Job suffered from the raids of the Sabeans and Chaldeans, Job 1:14-17, and the allusions in Luke 10:30; 2 Cor. 11:26 show that life and property were alike insecure in Palestine. "Robbery," in Phil. 2:6, means "prize" or "a thing to be grasped."

Rob´o-am, in Matt 1:7, is the Greek form for REHOBOAM, a son of Solomon.

Rock is used figuratively to designate the LORD, who is the Rock of safety and strength to his people. Deut. 32:4; 1 Sam. 2:2; 2 Sam. 22:2; Pss. 18:31, 46; 28:1; also in many other Psalms, and Isa. 17:10.

In Isa. 44:8 "there is no God," in the Authorized Version, is rendered "there is no Rock" in the Revised Version; and in Hab. 1:12 "O mighty God" is rendered "O Rock." In Deut. 32:31, 37 the word "rock" means the object of false confidence of nations.

Rod. In the sense of a branch or shoot of a tree this word is applied figuratively to Christ, Isa. 11:1, and to the tribes of Israel as springing from one root. Ps. 74:2; Jer. 10:16. The word is also used in the sense of a staff, Ps. 23:4; as a symbol of power and authority, Rev. 2:27; and to convey other meanings which are made plain by the context. "Passing under the rod," in Ezek. 20:37, may refer to the custom of having the sheep pass under a rod that had been dipped in red ochre and with which every tenth sheep was touched, and so became "holy unto the LORD." Lev. 27:32.

Roe, Roe´buck, an animal clean by the Mosaic law and highly prized as food, was noted for its graceful form and its fleetness, and is generally believed to be the same as the gazelle, a species of antelope that abounds in Syria, Arabia, and the adjacent countries. Deut. 12:15; Isa. 13:14. The FALLOW DEER, mentioned in Deut. 14:5; 1 Kings 4:23, has been identified by some as closely allied to the European roebuck.

Ro´gel (*a fuller*) is found in the marginal notes, 1 Kings 1:9, and is translated ENROGEL in the text of that verse.

Ro-ge´lim, one of the towns of Gilead. 2 Sam. 17:27; 19:31.

Roh´gah (*outcry*), one of the sons of Shamer, a descendant of Asher. 1 Chron. 7:34.

Roll. Jer. 36:2. See BOOKS.

Rol´ler, in Ezek. 30:21, means a bandage.

Rolls, House of. See HOUSE OF THE ROLLS.

Ro-mam´ti-e´zer, one of the sons of Heman. He was engaged in the service of song in the sanctuary. 1 Chron. 25:4, 31.

Ro´man Cit´i-zen-ship. See CITIZENSHIP.

Ro´mans, the people named from their chief city, Rome. John 11:48; Acts 16:21.

Ro´mans, the E-pis´tle to the, was written by Paul from Corinth, A. D. 58, shortly before he left that city for Jerusalem. Rom. 15:25; Acts 20:2.

There was at that time a large and flourishing Christian congregation in Rome, whose origin is involved in obscurity. Paul had not yet been there; on the contrary, this epistle was written preparatory to his going to Rome. Jews from Rome were present at the Pentecostal miracle in Jerusalem, Acts 2:10, and they may have been the founders of the congregation. As to Peter, we only know that, according to the general tradition of the ancient Church, he suffered martyrdom in Rome, A. D. 64 or later.

This epistle is the most elaborate and the most systematic exposition, in the New Testament, of the great central truth of Christianity, that the gospel is a power of salvation to all on the sole condition of faith in Christ (1:16, 17). It shows (1) that all men, Gentiles and Jews, need salvation (1:18-32); (2) that salvation is provided for all by Jesus Christ, and is applied to the believer, in the successive acts of justification, sanctification, and glorification (3:21 to 8:39); (3) that salvation was offered first to the Jews, then to the Gentiles, and that after the conversion of the Gentiles salvation will return to the Jews (chapters 9–11); (4) that we should show our gratitude for this great salvation by a life of consecration to the service of God, which is perfect freedom (chapters 12–15). It closes with salutations (chapter 16). The Epistles to the Romans and to the Galatians furnished the leading impulse in the reformatory movement of the sixteenth century, and they are the Magna Charta of evangelical Protestantism.

Rome, at the time of Christ, was, from her size, splendor, wealth, and power, and from her position as capital of the Roman empire, the heart of the civilized world. From Rome radiated the influences that controlled that mighty empire, which then stretched from the Atlantic on the west to the Euphrates on the east, and from the Rhine, the Danube, and the Black Sea on the north to the African Desert and the Nile Cataract on the south. Hence the city offered the most favorable condition for spreading the Christian religion, and so it happened that though Christianity was born at Jerusalem and grew up in the Greek language, it was Rome that gave it to the world. Many Jews dwelt at Rome, Acts 28:17, and thither went Paul and Peter. At the time of Christ the republic and the frightful civil wars had given place to a monarchy, and peace reigned at Rome and throughout the empire, and the people were prosperous and susceptible to new influences. Before the first century had closed Christian churches were busy spreading the gospel in all the great cities of the empire, and, first and foremost, in Rome. The relations between the Romans and the Jews were very singular. The Romans were exceedingly liberal toward other religions, not from religious indifference, but from policy. When, however, a religion aspired to become a regulator in state matters, the Romans at once became intolerant beyond description. The fury

and stubbornness with which the Jews opposed them time after time finally created a hatred among the Romans that resulted in the complete dissolution and dispersion of the Hebrew race. At first the Romans considered the Christians merely a Jewish sect, and protected or persecuted them together with the Jews. Then the Jews themselves considered the Christians a mere sect, and stirred up the Roman authorities to persecute them. Finally, when the Romans discovered that the Christians represented a new religion very different from Judaism both in spirit and in practice, and that Christianity was destroying the Roman social organization, frightful persecutions followed until the time of Constantine the Great, when Christianity gradually became the religion of the Roman empire.

Rome is situated in Italy, on the river Tiber, about fifteen miles from its entrance into the Mediterranean Sea, and when Paul was a prisoner there it contained about 20,000 Jews and was at the height of its power. In the gardens of Nero, A. D. 64, Christians were put to death in the most cruel manner; some were crucified, others were covered with pitch and burned to death as torches (as we learn from Tacitus, the heathen historian).

The Coliseum or *Colosseum* in Rome was an immense theatre built by Vespasian for 100,000 spectators, and was used for various games and for conflicts between gladiators. Christians were obliged to fight wild beasts there, and many suffered martyrdom in that place. The ruins of the Coliseum are very imposing.

The Catacombs of Rome are underground excavations extending for many miles. They were used as places for burial by the early Christians during the first three centuries, and contain many devotional symbols and a very large number of inscriptions.

Rome is said to have had a population of about 1,200,000 in New Testament times.

Roof. See HOUSE.

Room, in Ps. 31:8; Luke 14:8, 9, 10; 20:46; 1 Cor. 14:16, is rendered in the Revised Version "seats" and "places."

Ropes. 1 Kings 20:31, 32. The putting of ropes on the head or neck was significant of great distress and earnestness, and may also denote submission, as ropes or cords were used for binding prisoners. Judges 15:13.

Rose. The flower known to us as the rose is not the one referred to in the Song of Sol. 2:1; Isa. 35:1. The Hebrew word translated "rose" probably refers to the *polyanthus narcissus*, a beautiful and fragrant flower that grows in the plain of Sharon. True wild roses are seldom found except in the extreme north of Palestine.

Rosh (*head, chief*), one of the sons of Benjamin. Gen. 46:21.

Roy´al Cit´y, the name given by Joab to Rabbah of the children of Ammon, or part of it. 2 Sam. 12:26. It was apparently same as CITY OF WATERS.

Ru´bies. A precious stone of a rose-red color, and next to the diamond in hardness, beauty, and value. The Hebrew word translated "rubies" in Job 28:18; Prov. 3:15; 8:11; etc. means "red coral" or "pearls."

Rud´der Bands. In ancient times ships were steered by means of two large paddles near the stern of the vessel. When at anchor these steering-paddles were lashed to the side of the vessel by ropes called "rudder bands." Acts 27:40.

Rude, in 2 Cor. 11:6, means "unpolished."

Ru´di-ments. "Elements," Gal. 4:3, 9;

2 Pet. 3:10, 12, and "rudiments," Col. 2:8, 20, are translated from the same Greek word, and mean the first and simplest principles of a science or literature.

Rue, Luke 11:42, an herb that grows wild in Palestine, and is also cultivated as a medicine and disinfectant. It has a strong odor and a bitter taste. The hypocritical Pharisees tithed rue and left more important things undone.

Ru´fus (*red*), a disciple who lived at Rome. Paul sent salutation to him. Rom. 16:13. He was probably the same person as Rufus, the son of Simon the Cyrenian, mentioned in Mark 15:21.

Ru´ha-mah (*compassionated*), a symbolical name which the ransomed of the LORD are directed to use. Hos. 2:1.

Ru´mah, a town which was the home of Pedaiah. 2 Kings 23:36. Its location is not known.

Rump, in Exod. 29:22; Lev. 3:9; 7:3; 8:25; 9:19, means "fat tail," as in the Revised Version, and refers to the tail of a broad-tailed variety of sheep, which sometimes weighs about ten or fifteen pounds. See SHEEP.

Rush. The expression "branch and rush," in Isa. 9:14; 19:15, is used in the sense of "top and bottom" or "utterly." In Job 8:11, etc. it refers to a reed or plant evidently the same as the BULRUSH, or PAPER REEDS (which see).

Ruth (*a friend?* or *a beauty?*), a Moabitess, one of the daughters-in-law of Elimelech and Naomi, who accompanied Naomi on her return to Bethlehem. She became the wife of Boaz and an ancestor of Joseph, the husband of Mary. Ruth 1:4; Matt. 1:5. The history of her life is found in the book of Ruth.

Ruth, the Book of, named from Ruth the Moabitess, the chief person mentioned in it, is a simple but charming narrative of domestic life, with its virtues and happiness in the thirteenth century before Christ, and receives a special significance from the fact that Ruth was the great-grandmother of King David, who was an ancestor of Joseph, the husband of Mary. The author of the book is unknown.

Rye, or "rie" in the Authorized Version, Exod 9:32; Isa. 28:25, is rendered more correctly "spelt" in the text of the Revised Version. The latter grain resembles closely wheat, but it yields an inferior flour. "Spelt" was extensively cultivated in the East. "Fitches," in Ezek. 4:9, means "spelt." It is translated from the same Hebrew word, and is so rendered in the Revised Version.

S

Sa-bac-tha´ ni (*thou hast forsaken me*), a word spoken by Christ on the cross. Matt. 27:46; Mark 15:34. It is part of an exclamation expressive of the acuteness of his sufferings and his horror at the hiding of his Father's countenance.

Sab´a-oth or Sa-ba´oth, in Rom. 9:29; James 5:4, does not mean Sabbath or rest, as many suppose. The word in the Greek means *hosts*, and it is applied to God as Ruler over all in the same sense that the expression "LORD of hosts" is used in Isa. 1:9.

Sab´bath was instituted by God in paradise for the benefit of man as a weekly day of rest for the body and for the spirit. It is found, in some form or other, also among pagans. The Jewish Sabbath was placed at the end of the week in commemoration of the creation. The word

means "rest," but the fourth commandment gives that rest a definite religious character, and subsequent legislation made the Jewish Sabbath a day of religious rites and practices. The Christian Sabbath takes the place of the Jewish, with the difference that it is placed at the beginning of the week in commemoration of the resurrection of Christ. It is therefore called "the Lord's Day." Rev. 1:10. The word Sunday means "the day of the sun," and is of heathen origin, but is now used to denote the Christian Sabbath.

Also see Exod. 16:23, 25, 26, 29; 20:8, 10, 11; 31:13-16; 35:2, 3.

Lev. 16:31; 19:3, 30; 23:3, 11, 15, 16, 24, 32, 38, 39; 24:8; 25:2, 4, 6, 8; 26:2, 34, 35, 43.

Num. 15:32; 28:9, 10.

Deut. 5:12, 14, 15.

2 Kings 4:23; 11:5, 7, 9; 16:18.

1 Chron. 9:32; 23:31.

2 Chron. 2:4; 8:13; 23:4, 8; 31:3; 36:21.

Neh. 9:14; 10:31, 33; 13:15-19, 21, 22.

Ps. 92.

Isa. 1:13; 56:2, 4; 58:13; 66:23.

Jer. 17:21, 22, 24, 27.

Lam. 1:7; 2:6.

Ezek. 20:12, 13, 16, 20, 21, 24; 22:8, 26; 23:38; 44:24; 45:17; 46:1, 3, 4, 12.

Hos. 2:11.

Amos 8:5.

Matt. 12:1, 2, 5, 8, 10-12; 24:20; 28:1.

Mark 1:21; 2:23, 24, 27, 28; 3:2, 4; 6:2; 15:42; 16:1.

Luke 4:16, 31; 5:1, 2, 5-7, 9; 13:10, 14-16; 14:1, 3, 5; 23:54, 56.

John 5:9, 10, 16, 18; 7:22, 23; 9:14, 16; 19:31.

Acts 1:12; 13:14, 27, 42, 44; 15:21; 16:13; 17:2; 18:4.

Col. 2:16.

Sab´bath Day's Jour´ney, Acts 1:12, was nearly a mile. It was lawful to walk thus far on the Sabbath.

Sab-bat´i-cal Year was appointed by God, Lev. 25:3-7, who commanded that every seventh year should be set aside as a year of rest and for "a sabbath for the LORD." The land was not to be tilled, and whatever the ground might bring forth during that year was to be left to the poor and the beasts of the field. Exod. 23:11. Every seventh year the poor Jew was to be released from his debts. Deut. 15:1, 2. See JUBILEE.

Sa-be´ans. [1] A tribe that descended from Seba, the son of Cush. Isa. 45:14. [2] A tribe that descended from Sheba, son of Joktan. Joel 3:8. [3] There may be a third tribe mentioned in Job 1:15. "Sabeans," in Ezek. 23:42, should be "drunkards," as in the Revised Version.

Sabta, sab´tah, 1 Chron. 1:9, or **Sab´-tah,** Gen. 10:7, one of the sons of Cush.

Sabtecha, sab´te-kah, 1 Chron. 1:9, or **Sabtechah,** sab´te-kah, Gen. 10:7, one of the sons of Cush.

Sacar, sa´kar (*hire*). [1] The father of Ahiham, one of David's valiant men, 1 Chron. 11:35, called SHARAR in 2 Sam. 23:33. [2] A Levite porter for the Tabernacle in David's time. 1 Chron. 26:4.

Sack´but. This musical instrument, mentioned in Dan. 3:5, 7, 10, 15, was not a wind instrument (its present meaning), but a stringed instrument played with the fingers, like the harp. It was triangular in form and had a very penetrating sound.

Sack´cloth was a coarse dark fabric made of goats' hair and other materials, and was worn as a sign of mourning or repentance. Gen. 37:34; Jer. 4:8; Matt. 11:21.

Sac´ri-fice. Gen. 31:34. Among all nations of the world, and from the earliest

times, it has been the custom of the people to endeavor to appease by sacrifices the anger of the objects they worship. This natural inclination of mankind was gratified and properly directed by the Mosaic law. Also see OFFERING.

Sac´ri-lege is the crime of violating or profaning sacred things. "Commit sacrilege," in Rom. 2:22, is rendered "rob temples" in the Revised Version, and probably refers to the guilt of the Jews in withholding the tithes and offerings which God required of them. Mal. 3:8–10.

Sad´dle. Lev. 15:9. In early Bible times the saddle was simply a mat or rude cushion.

Sadducees, sad´du-seez, Acts 5:17, formed in the time of our Lord a small but influential sect among the Jews. They were wealthy and in high position, but their interest in religion was hardly anything more than a superficial ritualism. In doctrine they were strongly opposed to the PHARISEES (which see). They denied the divinity of the oral Law, accepted only the teachings of Moses, and did not believe in the resurrection, Matt. 22:23, nor in angels or spirits. Acts 23:8. Though they are not spoken of in the New Testament so severely as the Pharisees, they were determined adversaries of our Lord. Annas and Caiaphas were Sadducees.

Also see Matt. 3:7; 16:1, 6, 11, 12; 22:34.

Mark 12:18.

Luke 20:27.

Acts 4:1; 23:6, 7.

Sa´doc (*just*), an ancestor of Joseph, the husband of Mary. Matt. 1:14.

Saf´fron, Song of Sol. 4:14, is a plant that abounds in Palestine. It is mentioned among spices owing to its value as a perfume. It is used as a dye, as a medicine, and for flavoring food and drink.

Saint is one set apart or separated for the service of God. Paul uses the word as applying to all Christians. Rom. 1:7; 15:26; Phil. 1:1, etc. The special application of the word to apostles, evangelists, and prominent Christians dates from the fourth century.

Sala, sa'lah, in Luke 3:35, and **Sa'lah** (*sprout*), Gen. 10:24; 11:12, one of the descendants of Shem. He was an ancestor of Joseph, the husband of Mary, and is called SHELAH in 1 Chron. 1:18, 24.

Sal'a-mis, a city and seaport on the south-east coast of the island of Cyprus, which is in the Mediterranean Sea. It was visited by Paul and Barnabas. Acts 13:5. It was once the capital of Cyprus. Its ruins are called *Old Famagusta.*

Sa-la'thi-el (*I have asked God*), a descendant of Jeconiah, the son of King Jehoiakim. 1 Chron. 3:17; Matt. 1:12; Luke 3:27. He is usually called SHEALTIEL.

Salcah, sal'kah, in Josh. 12:5; 1 Chron. 5:11, and **Salchah,** sal'kah, Deut. 3:10, a chief city of the kingdom of Og in Bashan.

Sa'lem (*peace*), the place of which Melchizedek was king. Gen. 14:18; Ps. 76:2; Heb. 7:1, 2. It was an ancient name of Jerusalem.

Sa'lim (*peace* or *fountains?*), a place not far from Jerusalem. John 3:23. It is mentioned to indicate the location of Ænon on the Jordan, where John the Baptist baptized.

Sal'la-i (*basket-maker*). **[1]** The head of a family of Benjamites. Neh. 11:8. **[2]** One of the priests that returned with Zerubbabel, Neh. 12:20, called SALLU in Neh. 12:7.

Sal'lu (*weighed*). **[1]** A Benjamite, the grandson of Joel. 1 Chron. 9:7; Neh. 11:7.

[2] One of the priests that returned with Zerubbabel. Neh. 12:7.

Salma, sal'mah (*clothed, a garment*), one of the sons of Caleb, the son of Hur. 1 Chron. 2:51, 54.

Salma, sal'mah, 1 Chron. 2:11, or **Sal'mon** (*clothed, a garment*), Ruth 4:20, 21; Matt. 1:4, 5; Luke 3:32, the father of Boaz, the husband of Ruth. He is supposed to be the same as SALMA, the son of Caleb. 1 Chron. 2:51, 54.

Sal'mon (*shady*), Ps. 68:14, a high hill near Shechem, in Samaria. Probably same as ZALMON (which see).

Sal-mo'ne (*clothed*), a promontory at the east end of the island of Crete, in the Mediterranean Sea. It is mentioned in the account of Paul's voyage to Rome. Acts 27:7.

Sa-lo'me. [1] A woman who followed Jesus from Galilee and witnessed his crucifixion "afar off." Mark 15:40; 16:1. She was the wife of Zebedee and the mother of the apostles James and John. **[2]** "The daughter of Herodias." She danced before Herod, and asked for the head of John the Baptist. Matt. 14:6-8; Mark 6:22-25. She is not named in the New Testament, but is mentioned by Josephus, an ancient Jewish historian.

Salt was not only important among the Jews as a seasoning and a preservative, but from its use in the sacrifices that were offered to God. Lev. 2:13. New-born children were rubbed with salt. Ezek. 16:4. A "covenant of salt," Num. 18:19; 2 Chron. 13:5, indicated a most sacred obligation and a perpetual covenant. With the Arab the eating of salt with any one is a pledge of mutual friendship, and among the Persians and East Indians to "eat the salt" of a person is to be in his employ. Salt abounds in Palestine, and excellent table-salt is obtained from the waters of the Dead Sea.

Salt, City of, a city in the south-east part of Judah, near the Dead Sea. Josh 15:62.

Salt Sea. Deut. 3:17; Josh. 3:16; 12:3. See DEAD SEA.

Salt, Valley of, is at the south-west extremity of the Dead Sea. The soil is wholly covered with salt. 2 Sam. 8:13; 1 Chron. 18:12.

Salu (*weighed*), an Israelite of the tribe of Simeon. Num. 25:14.

Sa-lute'. Matt. 10:12. Salutations among the Jews and people of the East were usually attended with much ceremony. They addressed one another with an exclamation, as "The Lord be with thee," or "Peace be with thee." There was also repeated bowing, kissing of the beard, etc., Gen. 33:3, 4, which often occupied considerable time. This will account for the advice given in Luke 10:4.

Sal-va'tion, Exod. 14:13, or deliverance, supposes evil or danger. In its ordinary use, in the New Testament especially, the word is used to denote the deliverance from sin and death through faith in Christ.

Sa-ma'ri-a. In the Old Testament the kingdom of Samaria and the kingdom of Israel were essentially the same. In the time of our Lord Samaria was the name of the middle province of Palestine, situated between Galilee and Judea. When the "king of Assyria" (2 Kings 17:6) took the city of Samaria, B. C. 722, and carried the ten tribes of Israel away as prisoners, the land was repeopled by Assyrian colonists, and from them descended the Samaritans of the New Testament. Probably the colonists were not of purely foreign blood. At all events, they obtained a Jewish priest to teach them "the manner of the God of the land." 2 Kings 17:25-41. But when the Jews returned from the captivity they would have nothing to do with the Samaritans. An offer to help the Jews in the rebuilding of the Temple at Jerusalem was rejected, and the Samaritans set up a rival temple on Mount Gerizim. It stood for two hundred years, but was destroyed by the Jews under John Hyrcanus. In the time of our Lord the hatred between the Jews and the Samaritans was still so bitter that the Galileans when going up to Jerusalem avoided passing through Samaria. See the parable of the good Samaritan, the healing of the ten lepers, and the account of Christ's conversation with the woman of Samaria at Jacob's well. Luke 10:30-37; 17:11-19; and John 4:1-42. The gospel was preached successfully among the Samaritans. Act 1:8; 8:5-26. There yet remains a small community of them, living at *Nabulus*, the old SHECHEM (which see), and possessing the Pentateuch in the old Hebrew or Samaritan writing.

Sa-ma'ri-a (*watch-post*), **the City of,** was founded by Omri, B. C. 925, 1 Kings 16:23, 24, and by him made the capital of the kingdom of Israel. Even during the period of the captivity it did not cease to be a place of some importance. But it was completely destroyed by the Jews under John Hyrcanus, B. C. 109. Herod the Great, however, rebuilt it with great splendor, and called it *Sebaste*. Philip preached the gospel there. Acts 8:5, 9.

Sa-mar'i-tans, inhabitants of Samaria. In the New Testament the name Samaritans was given to the people whom the Assyrian king placed in the cities of Israel when he had carried away the ten tribes captive. 2 Kings 17:29; Matt. 10:5; Luke 9:52; John 4:9. See SAMARIA.

Sam´gar-ne´bo (*sword of Nebo*), one of the princes of Babylon. Jer. 39:3.

Sam´lah (*garment*), one of the ancient kings of Edom. Gen. 36:36, 37; 1 Chron. 1:47, 48.

Sa´mos (*a height*), an island of the Ægean Sea, has an area of one hundred and sixty-five square miles, is situated forty-two miles south-west of Smyrna, and was visited by Paul on his third missionary journey. Acts 20:15.

Samothracia, sam-o-thra´shi-ah (*Thracian Samos*), an island about eight miles long and six miles wide, in the Ægean Sea. It is about ten miles south of Thrace, and was visited by Paul. Acts 16:11.

Sam´son (*sun-like*), the son of Manoah, was an Israelite of the tribe of Dan. He was for twenty years one of the judges of Israel, had wonderful strength, and partially delivered his people from the power of the Philistines, but was finally captured by them, and killed himself and a very large number of his enemies by pulling down upon them the building in which they were assembled. A full account of his life is found in Judg. 13:24 to 16:31. He is mentioned in Heb. 11:32 among the heroes of the faithful.

Sam´u-el (*heard of God*), a noted prophet, and one of the noblest men of Old Testament times, was the last of the judges among the Hebrews. He was the son of Elkanah and Hannah, and resided at Ramah, but made each year a circuit through the country, administering justice among the people, until he became very old. For account of his life see 1 Sam., beginning with 1:20. His sons having proved unworthy to succeed him, he, under divine direction, anointed Saul king, and when Saul proved unworthy on account of disobedience, Samuel anointed David king, and shortly after that died. 1 Sam. 25:1. Samuel is called SHEMUEL in 1 Chron. 6:33.

Sam´u-el, First and Sec´ond Books of, formed originally one book in the Old Testament, and are also called the First and Second Books of the Kings. They bear the name of Samuel probably because he is the hero of the first part of the history, though it is also probable that he may have written that part of the First Book that narrates the occurrences during his lifetime.

The books of Samuel constitute a history of the Jews for about one hundred and twenty years, or from B. C. 1135 to B. C. 1016, beginning with the birth of Samuel, in the time of the judgeship of Eli, including the establishment of the Hebrew monarchy, and ending with the story of the numbering of the people by David, and his punishment. The narrative may be divided as follows: In the First Book of Samuel: (1) Chap. 1–4. The history of the judgeship of Eli. (2) Chap. 5–12. The history of the judgeship of Samuel. (3) Chap. 13–31. The history of the inauguration and reign of Saul. In the Second Book of Samuel: (4) Chap. 1–10. The history of the internal proceedings which resulted in placing David upon the throne, and of his victories over the surrounding nations. (5) Chap. 11–20. The story of David's sins and of the domestic and national troubles which were the consequence, down to the death of Absalom, David's return to Jerusalem, and the insurrection of Sheba. (6) Chap. 21–24. The history of the remainder of David's reign.

The books of Samuel are among the most interesting of the whole Old Testament, as containing the romantic story of David, the shepherd, soldier, poet, and king.

San-bal´lat (*a hero?*), an officer of the king of Persia. He greatly hindered the efforts of the Jews to rebuild the walls of Jerusalem after the captivity. Neh. 2:10; 4:1; 13:28.

Sanc´ti-fy is to prepare or set apart a person or thing to a holy use. Exod. 13:2. When applied to men, sanctification denotes the effect of God's spirit upon the soul which is manifested in the exercise of faith, love, and humility toward God and man. Rom. 15:16; 1 Cor. 1:2; 6:11.

Sanc´tu-a-ry, a holy or sanctified place. Ps. 20:2. The name given to the Temple or Tabernacle, Josh. 24:26; to the apartment that contained the golden candlestick, the altar of incense, etc., 2 Chron. 26:18; and the furniture of the Tabernacle. Num. 10:21. It was more particularly applied to the most secret part of the Temple, in which was the "ark of the covenant" (which see). There no one could enter except the high-priest, and he only once a year, on the day of solemn expiation. Lev. 4:6.

Sand. In Palestine sand is found along the sea-shore, and rarely anywhere else. The desert wastes consist mainly of parched soil, and gravel. It abounds, however, in Egypt, and some parts of the Nile valley are constantly menaced by the shifting sands of the great desert on the west. The word is often used figuratively in the Bible. Gen. 32:12; Job 6:3; Matt. 7:26; etc.

San´dals. Mark 6:9; Acts 12:8. The common sandal consists of a sole made from the hide of the camel, and two straps (called "latchet," Gen. 14:23) to fasten it to the foot. One strap passed between the great and the second toe, and the other passed from the heel over the instep. Some sandals had the sole-piece made from wood. They were easily removed, and were never worn in the house. With such simple footgear the necessity of washing the feet after a journey is very evident, and to offer water for this purpose was one of the first tokens of hospitality. Gen. 24:32; Luke 7:44.

To take off the shoes, Josh. 5:15, was an act of reverence; it also denoted humiliation and subjection. 2 Sam. 15:30; Isa. 20:2-4. To cast a shoe over a country denoted its subjection, Ps. 60:8, and to pluck off one's shoe and give it to another signified the surrendering of a privilege. Ruth 4:7.

San´he-drin (*council*), incorrectly called **San´he-drim,** was the supreme privy council among the Jews, at once a court of final appeal and last resort and an executive and legislative assembly. It consisted of seventy-one members, and met in a room adjoining the Temple where the seats were arranged in a semi-circle. Its origin is obscure. The Jews trace it back to the time of Moses. It was probably the result of a long development, but did not become conspicuous in Jewish history until after the Babylonian captivity. After the destruction of Jerusalem, A. D. 70, it was moved to Tiberias, where it continued till A. D. 425, when it became extinct. Christ was condemned by it for blasphemy. Matt. 26:65, 66. Besides the *Great Sanhedrin*, the name generally given to the council described above, almost every town had its own provincial Sanhedrin, the number of whose members varied according to the population of the place.

San-san´nah (*palm-branch*), a town in the south of Palestine. Josh. 15:31.

Saph (*tall*), a giant and champion of the Philistines, 2 Sam. 21:18, called SIPPAI in 1 Chron. 20:4.

Saph´ir (*fair*), a town supposed to have

been in Judah. Mic. 1:11.

Sapphira, saf-fi´rah (*beautiful*), the wife of Ananias, who joined with her husband in endeavoring to deceive the apostles, and fell dead. Acts 5:1-10.

Sapphire, saf´fire, a gem noted for its beauty, hardness, and lustre. It was of a blue color, Exod. 24:10; Ezek. 1:26, and formed one of the stones in the high-priest's breastplate. Exod. 28:18. See HIGH-PRIEST.

Sara, sa´rah. Heb. 11:11; 1 Pet. 3:6. Same as SARAH.

Sa´rah (*princess*). [1] The name which God gave to Sarai, the wife of Abram, when his name was changed to Abraham. Gen. 17:15. She was the mother of Isaac (who was born when his parents were very old), and died at the age of one hundred and twenty-seven. Gen. 23:1. She was a subject of special promises, Gen. 17:16, and her faith is commended in Heb. 11:11; 1 Pet. 3:6. The account of her life is found in Gen. 11:29 to 49:31. [2] A daughter of Asher, Num. 26:46, called SERAH in Gen. 46:17; 1 Chron. 7:30.

Sarai, sa´ray (*my princess*), the original name of the wife of Abraham. Gen. 11:29. See SARAH.

Sa´raph (*burning*), one of the descendants of Shelah, the son of Judah. 1 Chron. 4:22.

Sar´dine, Rev. 4:3, or **Sar´di-us,** Exod. 28:17, a stone in the high-priest's breastplate, was of a blood-red or flesh color, susceptible of a high polish, and well suited for engraving. It received its name from Sardis in Asia Minor, where it was first found. It is similar to our Cornelian, or, more properly, Carnelian.

Sar´dis, the capital of Lydia, Asia Minor, famous as the residence of Crœsus and the place in which the art of dyeing

wool was discovered, was the seat of one of the seven churches of Asia. Rev. 3:1-5; see also Rev. 1:11.

Sar´dites, descendants of Sered, a son of Zebulun. Num. 26:26.

Sar´di-us. Exod. 28:17. See SARDINE.

Sar´do-nyx, Rev. 21:20, is a precious stone combining the qualities of the SARDIUS and ONYX, whence its name. It is found in Judea.

Sarepta, sa-rep´tah (*smelting-house*), a town of Phœnicia on the Mediterranean Sea, between Tyre and Sidon. Luke 4:26. Called ZAREPHATH in 1 Kings 17:9, 10; Obad., verse 20. See ZAREPHATH.

Sar´gon, a king of Assyria who invaded Palestine in the time of Hezekiah. Isa. 20:1.

Sa´rid (*a survivor*), a place on the border of Zebulun and Issachar. Josh. 19:10, 12.

Sa´ron, Acts 9:35, a plain of Palestine. See SHARON.

Sarsechim, sar-se´kim, one of the princes of Babylon when Nebuchadnezzar took Jerusalem. Jer. 39:3.

Saruch, sa´ruk, Luke 3:35, a patriarch. See SERUG.

Sa´tan (*adversary*) is the name given to the devil, the adversary of goodness and the author of evil. He is also called "the prince of this world," "the wicked one," "the tempter," "the old serpent," etc.

Sa´tyr, in Isa. 13:21; 34:14, means "he-goat," and is so rendered in the marginal notes in the Revised Version.

Saul (*desired*). [1] One of the kings of Edom. Gen. 36:37, 38. He is called SHAUL in 1 Chron. 1:48, 49. [2] The first king of Israel. He was the son of Kish (Cis), of the tribe of Benjamin. Saul was anointed king by the prophet Samuel. 1 Sam 10:1. He began well, but ended badly. He persecuted David, his successor. He reigned forty years, Acts 13:21, and fought a great battle with the Philistines, but was defeated with terrible slaughter and his three sons were killed. Saul took his own life on the field of battle. 1 Sam. chapter 31. His history is found in 1 Sam. 9:2-27, and in the remaining chapters of that book.

Saul of Tar´sus. See PAUL.

Save, in 1 Kings 3:18; Matt. 11:27, means except.

Sav´iour. Luke 2:11. See CHRIST.

Sa´vour-est, in Matt. 16:23; Mark 8:33, means "mindest."

Saw. The tool by this name used by the Hebrews was probably similar to that of the Egyptians. The workman drew his saw toward him to make the cut, and hence the teeth were inclined toward the handle instead of away from it. They had saws for wood and for stone. Isa. 10:15; 1 Kings 7:9. Saws were also used as instruments of torture. 1 Chron. 20:3. Tradition asserts that the prophet Isaiah was thus killed.

Scall, Lev. 13:30, a scurf or scabby disease, especially of the scalp.

Scape´goat. Lev. 16:10. See GOAT.

Scar´let. Gen. 38:28. See COLORS.

Scep´tre, an ornamental rod or staff borne by a king or ruler as a token of his authority. Gen. 49:10; Amos 1:5, 8. It may have had its origin in the shepherd's staff, as the patriarchal chiefs were shepherds as well as princes.

Sce´va (*fitted*), a Jewish priest at Ephesus, whose seven sons attempted to expel an evil spirit from a man in the name of Jesus. Acts 19:14–16.

Schism, in 1 Cor. 12:25, is supposed to denote any lack of sympathy or any contention that disturbs the harmony and union that should exist between

Christians, without an outward break or separation.

School, Acts 19:9, **Schol´ar,** 1 Chron. 25:8, **School´mas-ter** (*tutor* in the Revised Version). Gal. 3:24. Schools existed among the Jews from a very early period. They were established under the prophets to fit young men for priestly and prophetical offices. 1 Sam. 19:20; 2 Kings 2:3, 5, 7. While parental instruction was relied upon to a great extent, the higher schools provided instruction in the law and traditions. The schoolmaster also exercised a careful supervision over his scholars, forming their manners, etc. Every synagogue was a school of religious and moral instruction, and hence Jewish servant-girls, as Josephus says, knew more about religion than heathen priests.

Schools of the Proph´ets. 1 Sam. 10:5. See PROPHET.

Scor´pi-on, a venomous insect allied to the spider. In appearance it resembles the lobster, and its usual length is from one to two inches, though in tropical countries it is sometimes found from six to eight inches long. Its sting, which causes excruciating pain, is inflicted by a curved claw at the end of the tail. 1 Kings 12:11, 14; Rev. 9:3, 5, 10.

Scourge, skurj, Matt. 27:26, a whip or instrument of punishment used by the Romans and also by the Jews, though probably by the latter only after the Babylonish captivity. It consisted of three lashes made of leather or small cords, to the ends of which sharp pieces of metal or bone were sometimes attached to increase the sufferings of the victim. A citizen of Rome could not be thus punished, though the Romans scourged slaves and foreigners. Acts 22:25, 26. In earlier times a rod was used, and under the law no more than forty stripes could be given. Deut. 25:1-3.

Screech Owl, Isa. 34:14, may refer to a member of the owl family that utters a disagreeable cry at night. See OWL. It is rendered "night-monster" in the marginal notes and in the Revised Version.

Scribe, in Old Testament times, was a person that was employed in correspondence and in keeping accounts. Sheva, the scribe of King David, is mentioned in 2 Sam. 20:25. His duty was to record proclamations, etc. In New Testament times the scribe was a copyist of the law, and one who prided himself on his knowledge of it and of the traditions of the elders. Matt. 2:4; Mark 1:22.

Scrip, in 1 Sam. 17:40; Matt. 10:10; etc., means a small bag, generally suspended from the shoulder, and for carrying food.

Scrip´ture. See BIBLE.

Scroll, Isa. 34:4; Rev. 6:14; refers to the roll, or ancient form of book. See BOOKS.

Scur´vy, as known to us, is caused by long confinement in cold and damp climates, without fresh provisions. The skin becomes dry and scaly, with livid spots. It may be this appearance of the skin that is referred to in Lev. 21:20; 22:22.

Scythians, sith´i-ans, natives of Scythia, a region not easily defined. It was on the north of the Black and Caspian Seas. Col. 3:11.

Sea. In Gen. 1:10 "seas" refers to the ocean. The term sea is also applied to a great collection of water caused by the overflowing of the river Nile or of the river Euphrates.

The following names are also applied to the different seas. "The sea" occurs frequently, and the particular sea it refers to is generally made clear by the context:

East Sea, Ezek. 47:18; Joel 2:20, means Dead Sea.

Egyptian Sea, Isa. 11:15, means Red Sea.

Former Sea, Zech. 14:8, means Dead Sea.

Great Sea, Num. 34:6; Josh. 15:47, means Mediterranean Sea.

Hinder Sea, Zech. 14:8, means Mediterranean Sea.

Salt Sea, Gen. 14:3; Num. 34:12; Josh. 18:19 means Dead Sea.

Sea of Cilicia and Pamphylia, Acts 27:5, means the sea "off Cilicia and Pamphylia."

Sea of Joppa, Ezra 3:7, means Mediterranean Sea

Sea of the Philistines, Exod. 23:31, means Mediterranean Sea.

The Sea, Ezek. 47:8, means the Dead Sea; in Isa. 9:1; Matt. 4:13, 15; 17:27, the Sea of Galilee; in Josh. 15:46; 16:3; Acts 10:6, the Mediterranean Sea; in Exod. 14:2, 9; Josh. 24:6, 7, the Red Sea.

Utmost Sea, Joel 2:20; Deut. 34:2, means Mediterranean Sea.

Uttermost Sea, Deut. 11:24, means Mediterranean Sea.

Sea of Chinnereth, kin´ne-reth, Num. 34:11, or **Chinneroth,** kin´ne-roth. Josh. 12:3. See GALILEE, SEA OF.

Sea of Gal´i-lee. Matt. 15:29. See GALILEE, SEA OF.

Sea of Ja´zer. Jer. 48:32. See JAZER, SEA OF.

Sea of the Plain. Deut. 4:49. See DEAD SEA.

Sea of Ti-be´ri-as. John 21:1. See

GALILEE, SEA OF.

Sea, The Dead. See DEAD SEA.

Sea, The Med-i-ter-ra´ne-an. See GREAT SEA.

Sea, The Mol´ten or **Bra´zen.** See BRAZEN or MOLTEN SEA.

Sea, The Red. Exod. 10:19. See RED SEA.

Sea, The Salt. Gen. 14:3. See DEAD SEA.

Seal. This was used in ancient times for much the same purposes as now—to authenticate public and private papers, and also to so secure any receptacle that any access to its contents can be easily discovered. Frequently a ring with an inscription on it was used as a seal. 1 Kings 21:8; Jer. 32:14.

Sea´sons. Gen. 1:14. In Palestine the year is very nearly divided (as in California) into two seasons, the wet and the dry, each subdivided into three periods of about two months each.

The *grain harvest* is from April to June. The sky is clear and the weather warm, like early summer with us. During the next two months, the *vernal summer* of the Arabs, the heat increases and people are compelled to sleep in the open air. Then comes the *season of fruits*, August to October. The heat is now intense but toward the end of this season the nights begin to grow cool. During these three periods of the dry season the earth is moistened by the dew. Rain does not fall, with the exception of a few days in October.

This "former rain" prepares the earth for *seed-time*, October to December. The days are still hot, but grow cooler as the season advances. *Winter*, December to February, brings snow on the highlands and rain-, hail-, and thunder-storms in the lower lands. Toward the end of January the fields become green, and in early February the trees begin to blossom. *Spring* follows, and lasts till about the middle of April. The weather grows warm, and toward the close of this period the rains cease. The last rain, called the "latter rain," gives strength to the filling grain, which will soon be ready for the harvest. See MONTH, PALESTINE, RAIN.

Seats. Mark 11:15. Among the Jews and other nations of the East "seats" were mats, and sometimes, among the wealthier classes, cushions and broad, low divans. On these they either reclined at full length or sat in a half-kneeling posture, with their legs bent or crossed under them. See EATING.

Seba, se´bah (*man?*). [1] One of the sons of Cush, the son of Ham. Gen. 10:7; 1 Chron. 1:9. [2] The country occupied by his descendants. It is supposed to have been the southern part of Upper Egypt. Ps. 72:10; Isa. 43:3.

Se´bat, Zech. 1:7, or, more properly, **She´bat,** is the eleventh month of the Hebrew sacred year and the fifth month of the civil year. See MONTH.

Sec´a-cah (*enclosure*), a city in the wilderness of Judah. Josh. 15:61.

Sechu, se´ku (*the hill or eminence*), a place near Ramah, apparently in Benjamin. 1 Sam. 19:22.

Sect. This word signifies, primarily, "choice," "party," and means the religious parties among the Jews, Acts 5:17, Christians, 1 Cor. 11:19, etc. There were five sects among the Jews, who, though of one communion and united as a nation, held distinct opinions and practiced them. They were known as the PHARISEES, the SADDUCEES, the ESSENES, the HERODIANS, and the ZEALOTS (each of which see). The first three were religious, the last two were political parties. The Pharisees and Sadducees are frequently mentioned in the Gospels; the Essenes (a mystical and ascetic sect) lived retired on the shores of the Dead Sea, and are not mentioned in the New Testament. The early Christians were regarded as a new sect of Judaism, and were called "the sect of the Nazarenes." Acts 24:5. See HERESY.

Se-cun´dus (*second* or *fortunate*), a disciple of Thessalonica. Acts 20:4.

Se-di´tions, Gal. 5:20, means "divisions."

Seed. Matt. 22:24. In this and many other passages in the Bible the word means progeny; descendants; offspring.

Seed Time. Gen. 8:22. See SEASONS.

Seer, 1 Sam. 9:9, one who foresees events. See PROPHET.

Seethe, Exod. 16:23, means to boil.

Se´gub (*elevated*). [1] The youngest son of Hiel the Bethelite. 1 Kings 16:34. [2] One of the sons of Hezron, the grandson of Judah. 1 Chron. 2:21, 22.

Se´ir (*hairy*), the grandfather of Hori. Gen. 36:20. His name was probably given to the mountainous district in which he lived.

Se´ir (*hairy*). [1] A mountainous district extending from the Dead Sea to the eastern gulf of the Red Sea. It was occupied by the Horites, and afterward by the descendants of Esau. Gen. 14:6; 36:8. Seir sometimes means Edom. [2] Mount Seir, a landmark of Judah. Josh. 15:10.

Se´i-rath (*she-goat*), a place near Gilgal, to which Ehud fled after he had murdered Eglon, king of Moab. Judg. 3:26.

Sela, se´lah, Isa. 16:1, and **Se´lah** (*rock*), 2 Kings 14:7, a famous city of Edom. Its Greek name is PETRA, and it is so called in the marginal notes, Isa. 16:1. It was captured by Amariah, who called it JOKTHEEL. 2 Kings 14:7.

Se´lah. Nothing definite is known about this word. It occurs seventy-one times in thirty-nine Psalms, and three times in the book of Habakkuk. It is most probably a direction for the orchestra to fall in with or accompany the other music. It occurs where very warm emotions have been expressed. Ps. 32:7.

Se´la-ham-mah-le´koth (*rock of divisions*), a place in the wilderness south-east of Hebron, where David escaped from Saul. 1 Sam. 23:28.

Se´led (*exultation*), a descendant of Jerahmeel, the grandson of Pharez, the son of Judah. 1 Chron. 2:30.

Seleucia, se-leu´shi-ah, a city of Syria situated on the Mediterranean Sea, about five miles north of the river Orontes and fifteen miles west of Antioch, of which it is the seaport. Paul and Barnabas embarked from Seleucia on their first missionary journey. Acts 13:4.

Sem, Luke 3:36, is the Greek form for SHEM (which see).

Semachiah, sem-a-ki´ah (*Jehovah sustains him*), one of the sons of Shemaiah. He was a Levite porter in the Tabernacle. 1 Chron. 26:7.

Sem´e-i (*renowned*), an ancestor of Joseph, the husband of Mary. Luke 3:26.

Se-na´ah or **Sen´a-ah** (*thorny*), a town of Judah some of whose inhabitants returned with Zerubbabel. Ezra 2:35; Neh. 7:38.

Sen´ate, Acts 5:21, refers to the "elders of Israel," who formed one of the three classes that made up the Sanhedrin. The scribes and priests formed the other two classes. See PATRIARCH, and SANHEDRIN.

Se´neh (*bush* or *thorn-rock*), a rock near which the Philistines had a garrison, at the pass of Michmash, near Gibeah in Benjamin. 1 Sam. 14:4.

Se´nir (*coat-of-mail* or *cataract*), 1 Chron. 5:23; Ezek. 27:5, another name for Mount Hermon. See HERMON.

Sennacherib, sen-nak´e-rib or sen-na-ke´rib, the son of Sargon, was king of Assyria, to which at that time the kingdom of Judah was tributary. But Hezekiah, the king of Judah, refused to pay the tribute, and Sennacherib invaded Judea and forced him to submit. Hezekiah revolted a second time, but the army Sennacherib sent against him was smitten by a plague and 185,000 are said to have died in one night. 2 Kings 19:35. Sennacherib reigned for many years, but was killed by his sons and succeeded by Esarhaddon. 2 Kings 19:37.

Se-nu´ah (*bristling*), one of the Benjamites. Neh. 11:9.

Se-o´rim (*barley*), the head of a course of priests. 1 Chron. 24:8.

Se´phar is mentioned as the extreme limit of the settlement of the Joktanites. Gen. 10:30.

Seph´a-rad (*separation*), a place where some of the inhabitants of Jerusalem were settled during the captivity. Obad. verse 20.

Seph-ar-va´im (*the two Sipparas*), a place in Assyria from which colonists were settled in Samaria. 2 Kings 17:24; Isa. 36:19.

Se´phar-vites, the people of Sephar-vaim. 2 Kings 17:31.

Septuagint, sep´tu-a-jint (*Seventy*), the Greek version of the Old Testament, was made by seventy or seventy-two interpreters, at Alexandria, Egypt, in the third century before Christ, for the Jews of the dispersion (called *Hellenists*). It is of unequal merit, and often differs from our (Massoretic) Hebrew text. It was used in the synagogues at the time of Christ, and is usually quoted from in the Greek Testament. The oldest manuscripts of the Sep-tuagint are in the Vatican and Sinaitic codices, both of the fourth century; while our oldest Hebrew manuscripts date from the ninth century; hence the Septuagint may in part represent an older Hebrew text. See BIBLE.

Sep´ul-chre, a place or house for the dead. Mark 15:46. Among the Jews it was not unusual for a single family to have near their dwelling-house a small building of stone or other durable material, without window or door, in which they deposited their dead. Some of the sepulchres were very expensively built, and were whitened, Matt. 23:27, frequently to make them conspicuous and easy to be avoided, as contact with them rendered one ceremonially unclean. Num. 19:16.

Se´rah (*princess*), one of the daughters of Asher, Gen. 46:17; 1 Chron. 7:30, called Sarah in Num. 26:46.

Ser-a-i´ah (*warrior of Jehovah*). [1] David's scribe or secretary. 2 Sam. 8:17. He is called SHEVA in 2 Sam. 20:25, SHISHA in 1 Kings 4:3, and SHAVSHA in 1 Chron. 18:16. [2] The chief priest in the reign of Zedekiah. 2 Kings 25:18; 1 Chron. 6:14. [3] An Israelite of Nopha. 2 Kings 25:23; Jer. 40:8. [4] A son of Kenaz. 1 Chron. 4:13, 14. [5] A descendant of Simeon. 1 Chron. 4:35. [6] A priest who returned with Zerubbabel. Ezra 2:2; Neh. 10:2. [7] An ancestor of Ezra. Ezra 7:1; Neh. 11:11. [8] A chief man under Jehoiakim. Jer 36:26. [9] One of the princes of Jerusalem who accompanied King Zedekiah to Babylon. Jer. 51:59, 61.

Ser´a-phim (*princes*), an order of angelic beings mentioned in Isa. 6:2, 6.

Se´red (*fear*), a son of Zebulun. Gen. 46:14; Num. 26:26.

Ser´gi-us Pau´lus, the Roman deputy or governor (proconsul) of the island of

Cyprus, in the Mediterranean Sea. He was converted under the ministry of Paul. A statue with his name has been discovered recently by Cesnola. Acts 13:7, 12.

Ser´jeants or **Ser´geants,** Acts 16:35, 38, were Roman lictors or officers who attended the chief magistrates when they appeared in public, and inflicted the punishment that had been pronounced.

Ser´pent, Gen. 3:1, or snake is a creature noted for its subtilty, its wisdom in avoiding danger, and for the dread it instinctively inspires in man and beast. Serpents abound in Syria, and many of them are poisonous. They were worshipped by the Egyptians and other nations in the East. Frequent allusions are made by the sacred writers to the serpent as an emblem of wickedness, Matt. 23:33, cruelty, Prov. 23:32, treachery. Gen 49:17. The devil is called "the old serpent," Rev. 12:9, with reference to our first parents. 2 Cor. 11:3. The FIERY SERPENTS mentioned in Num. 21:6; Deut. 8:15 were probably so called from the burning sensation that followed their deadly bite. The FIERY FLYING SERPENTS, Isa. 14:29; 30:6, probably refers to the quick darting movements of the serpents in Eastern deserts.

Ser´pent, Bra´zen. Num. 21:6-9. See BRAZEN SERPENT.

Se´rug (*branch*), a grandson of Peleg, Gen. 11:20; 1 Chron. 1:26, called SARUCH in Luke 3:35.

Serv´ant. Gen. 49:15. This word, as used in the Bible, does not necessarily imply a domestic or slave, for it was applied to any one under the authority of another. Thus, in Matt. 26:58; Mark 14:54, 65; John 18:36 it means "officers."

Serv´i-tor, 2 Kings 4:43, one who ministers to, or serves. See SERVANT.

Seth (*substitution*), a son of Adam and Eve. He was nine hundred and twelve

years old when he died. Gen. 4:25; 5:8. Called also SHETH in 1 Chron. 1:1.

Se´thur (*hidden*), one of the spies whom Moses sent to search the land of Canaan. Num. 13:13.

Set´tle, Ezek. 43:14, 17, 20, means "ledge."

Sev´en. From the beginning this was the number of days in the week, and hence it has a special emphasis attached to it, and is used in Scripture as a round number, or, as some would say, a *perfect* number, and in much the same way we use "ten" or "a dozen." Gen. 7:2; Matt. 12:45. In like manner, "seven times" or "sevenfold" means "often," "abundantly," while "seventy times seven" denotes a still higher degree. Gen. 4:15; Matt. 18:21, 22.

Also see Gen. 4; 5; 7; 8; 11; 21; 23; 25; 29; 31; 33; 41; 46; 47; 50.

Exod. 2; 6; 7; 12; 13; 22; 23; 25; 29; 34; 37; 38.

Lev. 4; 8; 12–16; 22; 23; 25; 26.

Num. 1–4; 8; 12; 13; 16; 19; 23; 26; 28; 29; 31.

Deut. 7; 15; 16; 28; 31.

Josh. 6; 18.

Judg. 6; 8; 12; 14; 16. 20.

Ruth 4.

1 Sam. 2; 6; 10; 11; 13; 16; 31.

2 Sam. 2; 5; 8; 10; 21; 23; 24.

1 Kings 2; 6–8; 11; 16; 18–20.

2 Kings 3–5; 8; 11; 24; 25.

1 Chron. 3; 5; 7; 9; 10; 12; 15; 18; 19; 26; 29.

2 Chron. 7; 13; 15; 17; 24; 26; 29; 30; 35.

Ezra 2; 6–8.

Neh. 7; 8.

Esther 1; 2; 8; 9

Job 1; 2; 5; 42.

Pss. 12; 79; 119.

Prov. 6; 9; 24; 25.

Eccles. 11.
Isa. 4; 11; 30.
Jer. 15; 34; 52.
Ezek. 3; 29; 39–41; 43–45.
Dan. 3; 4; 9.
Amos 5.
Mic. 5.
Zech. 3; 4.
Matt. 12; 15; 16; 18; 22.
Mark 8; 12; 16.
Luke 2; 8; 11; 17; 20.
Acts 6; 13; 19–21; 28.
Rom. 11.
Heb. 11.
Rev. 1–5; 8; 10–13; 15–17; 21.

Sev´en Stars, The, Amos 5:8, refers to the PLEIADES (which see).

Sev´er-al, 2 Kings 15:5; Matt. 25:15, means separate; individual.

Sha-al-ab´bin (*city of jackals*), a border town of Dan, Josh. 19:42, called also SHAALBIM in Judg. 1:35; 1 Kings 4:9.

Sha-al´bim, Judg. 1:35. See SHAAL-ABBIN.

Sha-al´bo-nite, a native of Shaalbon, whose location is unknown. 2 Sam. 23:32; 1 Chron. 11:33.

Sha´aph (*division*). [1] A son of Jahdai. 1 Chron. 2:47. [2] A son of Caleb, the son of Hezron. 1 Chron. 2:49.

Sha-a-ra´im (*two gates*). [1] A city in the north of Judah, 1 Sam. 17:52, called SHARAIM in Josh. 15:36, and SHILHIM, in Josh. 15:32. [2] One of the towns of Simeon, 1 Chron. 4:31, called also SHARUHEN.

Sha-ash´gaz (*beauty's lustre*), one of the chamberlains of Ahasuerus. Esther 2:14.

Shab-beth´a-i (*sabbath-born*), a Levite who assisted Ezra in taking account of those who had taken foreign wives and in expounding the law. Ezra 10:15; Neh. 8:7; 11:16.

Shachia, shak´i-ah (*Jehovah protects*), a son of Shaharaim, a Benjamite. 1 Chron. 8:10.

Shadrach, sha´drak (*royal?*), the name given to HANANIAH by the chief of Nebuchadnezzar's eunuchs. He was thrown into a fiery furnace with Meshach and Abednego and was unhurt. Dan. 1:7; 3:20-27.

Sha´ge (*erring*), the father of one of David's mighty men. 1 Chron. 11:34.

Sha-ha-ra´im (*the two dawns*), a descendant of Benjamin. 1 Chron. 8:8.

Sha-haz´i-mah (*heights*), a town of Issachar. Josh. 19:22.

Shak´ing, Ezek. 37:7, means "earthquake."

Sha´lem (*peaceful*), a town or city near Shechem. Gen. 33:18.

Sha´lim, the Land of, a region of uncertain location through which Saul passed. 1 Sam. 9:4.

Shalisha, shal´i-shah, **Land of** (*triangular*), a district near Mount Ephraim. 1 Sam. 9:4.

Shallecheth, shal´le-keth (*a casting down*), one of the gates of the Temple. 1 Chron. 26:16.

Shal´lum (*retribution*). [1] An Israelite who slew Zachariah, king of Israel, and "reigned in his stead." 2 Kings 15:10-15. He was killed by Menahem after reigning one month. [2] The husband of Huldah the prophetess. 2 Kings 22:14; 2 Chron. 34:22. [3] A descendant of Jerahmeel. 1 Chron 2:40, 41. [4] A son of Josiah, king of Judah. He was king three months. 1 Chron. 3:15; Jer. 22:11. Called JEHOAHAZ in 2 Kings 23:31-34; 2 Chron. 36:1-4. [5] A grandson of Simeon, the son of Jacob. 1 Chron. 4:25. [6] A priest whose son Hilkiah found the book of the law in the Temple. 1 Chron. 6:12, 13;

Ezra 7:2. [7] One of the sons of Naphtali. 1 Chron. 7:13. See SHILLEM. [8] Head of a family of Levite porters in the Tabernacle. 1 Chron. 9:17; Ezra 2:42. [9] A Levite porter in the Tabernacle. 1 Chron. 9:19, 31. [10] One of the chief Ephraimites. 2 Chron. 28:12. [11] A Levite porter who had taken a foreign wife. Ezra 10:24. [12] A Jew who had taken a foreign wife. Ezra 10:42. [13] A Jew who repaired part of the wall of Jerusalem. Neh. 3:12. [14] A Benjamite, uncle of Jeremiah the prophet. Jer. 32:7. [15] One of the Temple door-keepers. Jer. 35:4.

Shal´lun (*retribution*), a Jew who repaired a gate of Jerusalem. Neh. 3:15.

Shal´ma-i (*my thanks*), one of the Nethinim whose descendants returned with Zerubbabel. Ezra 2:46; Neh. 7:48.

Shal´man, an Assyrian king before Pul. Hos. 10:14.

Shalmaneser, shal-ma-ne´zer (*Salman is gracious*), an Assyrian king who invaded Israel, 2 Kings 17:3; 18:9, made Hoshea tributary to him, and prosecuted a vigorous siege against Samaria which led to its capture and the carrying away of the ten tribes into captivity.

Shama, sha´mah (*obedient*), one of David's warriors. 1 Chron. 11:44.

Sham-a-ri´ah (*whom Jehovah keeps*), one of the sons of Rehoboam, 2 Chron. 11:19, called SHEMARIAH in the Revised Version.

Sham´bles. 1 Cor. 10:25. A place where butcher's meat is sold.

Sha´med (*a destroyer*), a son of Elpaal, a Benjamite. 1 Chron. 8:12.

Sha´mer (*a keeper*). [1] The son of Mahli, the grandson of Merari. 1 Chron. 6:46. [2] A descendant of Asher, the son of Jacob. 1 Chron. 7:34. Called SHOMER in 1 Chron. 7:32.

Sham´gar (*cup-bearer?*), one of the judges of Israel. He slew six hundred Philistines with an ox-goad, and "delivered Israel." Judg. 3:31; 5:6.

Sham´huth (*desolation*). 1 Chron. 27:8. See SHAMMAH, No. 4.

Sha´mir (*a thorn*), a descendant of Uzziel, the grandson of Levi. 1 Chron. 24:24.

Sha´mir (*a sharp point*). [1] A city of Judah. Josh. 15:48. [2] A place in Mount Ephraim. Judg. 10:1, 2.

Shamma, sham´mah (*desolation*), one of the Asherite chiefs. 1 Chron. 7:37.

Sham´mah (*desolation*). [1] One of the sons of Reuel, the son of Esau. Gen. 36:13, 17; 1 Chron. 1:37. [2] A son of Jesse. 1 Sam. 16:9, 17:13, called also SHIMEAH and SHIMMA. [3] One of the chief among David's valiant men. 2 Sam. 23:11, 33. [4] One of David's valiant men, 2 Sam. 23:25, called also SHAMMOTH the Harorite in 1 Chron. 11:27, and SHAMHUTH the Izrahite in 1 Chron. 27:8.

Sham´ma-i (*desolated*), three descendants of Judah. 1 Chron. 2:28, 32, 44, 45; 4:17.

Sham´moth. 1 Chron. 11:27. See SHAMMOH, No. 4.

Shammua, sham´mu-ah. [1] One of the spies sent by Moses to search the land of Canaan. Num. 13:4. [2] One of the Levites. Neh. 11:17. [3] A priest of the family of Bilgah. Neh. 12:18. [4] A son of David, 1 Chron. 14:4, called also SHAMMUAH.

Sham´mu-ah, a son of David. 2 Sam. 5:14, called SHIMEA in 1 Chron. 3:5, and SHAMMUA in 1 Chron. 14:4.

Sham-she-ra´i (*heroic*), a son of Jeroham, a Benjamite. 1 Chron. 8:26.

Shapham, sha´fam (*bald*), head of a family in Gad. 1 Chron. 5:12.

Sha´phan (*coney*). [1] King Josiah's scribe or secretary. 2 Kings 22:3-14; 2 Chron. 34:8. [2] A Jew whose son was seen in a vision by Ezekiel. Ezek. 8:11.

Sha´phat (*judge*). [1] One of the spies sent by Moses to search the land of Canaan. Num. 13:5. [2] The father of the prophet Elisha. 1 Kings 19:16; 2 Kings 3:11. [3] A member of the royal line of Judah. 1 Chron. 3:22. [4] A Gadite chief. 1 Chron. 5:12. [5] A chief herdsman of David. 1 Chron. 27:29.

Sha´pher (*brightness*), a mountain on or near which was one of the encampments of the Israelites in their wanderings. Num. 33:23, 24.

Shar´a-i (*Jehovah frees him*), a Jew who took a foreign wife. Ezra 10:40.

Shar´a-im (*two gates*), a city of Judah, Josh. 15:36, called SHAARAIM in 1 Sam 17:52. See SHILHIM.

Sha´rar (*cord*), father of one of David's valiant men. 2 Sam. 23:33. Called SACAR in 1 Chron. 11:35.

Sha-re´zer (*prince of fire*), one of the sons of Sennacherib, king of Assyria. 2 Kings 19:37.

Shar´on (*the plain*), a plain of Palestine on the Mediterranean Sea, between Joppa and Cæsarea. It is about twenty-five miles long and from eight to fifteen miles wide, and is called SARON in Acts 9:35. In Isa. 35:2; 65:10 it is praised for its fertility.

Shar´on-ite, a dweller in Sharon. 1 Chron. 27:29.

Sha-ru´hen (*pleasant dwelling*), one of the cities of Simeon, Josh. 19:6, called SHAARAIM in 1 Chron. 4:31.

Shash´a-i (*whitish* or *noble*), a Jew who took a foreign wife. Ezra 10:40.

Sha´shak (*eagerness*), a son of Elpaal, a descendant of Benjamin. 1 Chron. 8:14, 25.

Sha´ul (*desired*), [1] A son of Simeon. Gen. 46:10; Exod. 6:15. [2] An ancient king of Edom, 1 Chron. 1:48, 49, called SAUL in Gen. 36:37, 38. [3] A descendant of Kohath, the son of Levi. 1 Chron. 6:24.

Sha´ul-ites, descendants of Shaul, the son of Simeon. Num. 26:13.

Sha´veh (*a plain*), a valley on the east side of Jerusalem, Gen. 14:17, called also the KING'S DALE.

Sha´veh Kir-i-a-tha´im (*plain of Kirjathaim*), a plain or valley near Kirjathaim in Moab. Gen. 14:5.

Shavsha, shav´shah (*warrior of Jehovah*), David's scribe or secretary, 1 Chron. 18:16, called also SERAIAH and SHISHA.

She´al (*asking*), a Jew who took a foreign wife. Ezra 10:29.

She-al´ti-el (*I have asked him of God*), Zerubbabel's father, Ezra 3:2, 8; Neh. 12:1, called also SALATHIEL.

She-a-ri´ah (*whom Jehovah estimates*), one of the descendants of Saul. 1 Chron. 8:38; 9:44.

Shear´ing House, a place between Samaria and Jezreel, where Jehu slew forty-two of the royal family of Judah. 2 Kings 10:12, 14.

She´ar-ja´shub (*a remnant returns*), a symbolical name given by Isaiah to one of his sons. Isa. 7:3.

Sheba, she´bah (*an oath*). [1] A man of Benjamin who raised a rebellion against David. 2 Sam. 20:1-22. [2] One of the chiefs of Gad. 1 Chron. 5:13.

Sheba, she´bah (*man?*). [1] A descendant of Ham. Gen. 10:7; 1 Chron. 1:9. [2] A descendant of Shem. Gen. 10:28; 1 Chron. 1:22. [3] A descendant of Abraham by Keturah. Gen. 25:3; 1 Chron. 1:32.

Sheba, she´bah (*seven,* or *an oath*). [1] A very fertile country in Arabia, adjoining the Red Sea. The queen of Sheba visited Solomon and brought him many presents. 1 Kings 10:1-13; 2 Chron. 9:1-12. [2] A town of Simeon. Josh. 19:2.

She´bah (*seven,* or *an oath*), a well at Beer-sheba which Isaac's servants dug. Gen. 26:15-33.

She´bam (*coolness*), a town or city of Reuben east of the Jordan. Num. 32:3. It is also called SHIBMAH and SIBMAH.

Sheb-a-ni´ah (*whom Jehovah has made grow up*). [1] A priest who assisted in bringing up the ark of God. 1 Chron. 15:24. [2] One of the Levites who assisted Ezra. Neh. 9:4, 5; 10:10. [3] One of the priests who sealed the covenant. Neh. 10:4; 12:14. [4] A Levite who sealed the covenant. Neh. 10:12.

Sheb´a-rim (*ruins*), a place near Ai. Josh. 7:5.

She´bat or **Se´bat,** the eleventh month of the Hebrew sacred year and the fifth month of the civil year, is called "Sebat" in Zech. 1:7, and "Shebat" in the Revised Version. See MONTH.

She´ber (*breaking*), one of the sons of Caleb. 1 Chron. 2:48.

Shebna, sheb´nah (*youth*). [1] A treasurer in the time of Hezekiah. Isa. 22:15. [2] The scribe or secretary of Hezekiah. 2 Kings 18:18; 19:2.

Sheb´u-el (*captive of God*). [1] A son of Gershom, the son of Moses, 1 Chron. 23:16; 26:24, called SHUBAEL in 1 Chron. 24:20. [2] A Levite singer, 1 Chron. 25:4, called SHUBAEL in 1 Chron. 25:20.

Shec-a-ni´ah (*familiar with Jehovah*). [1] A priest in the time of David. 1 Chron. 24:11. [2] A Levite in the time of Hezekiah. 2 Chron. 31:15.

Shechaniah, shek-a-ni´ah (*familiar with Jehovah*). [1] A descendant of the royal line. 1 Chron. 3:21, 22. [2, 3] Israel-ites whose descendants returned with Ezra. Ezra 8:3, 5 [4] A Jew who took a foreign wife. Ezra 10:2. [5] The father of Shemaiah. Neh. 3:29. [6] A Jew whose daughter married Tobiah the Ammonite. Neh. 6:18. [7] A priest who returned with Zerubbabel. Neh. 12:3.

Shechem, she´kem (*the shoulder-blade*). [1] The son of Hamor. Gen. 33:19; 34:2-26. [2] A son of Gilead, the son of Manasseh. Num. 26:31; Josh. 17:2. [3] An Israelite, the son of Shemidah. 1 Chron. 7:19.

Shechem, she´kem (*shoulder*), a city of Samaria, thirty-four miles north of Jerusalem. It is beautifully situated between Mounts Ebal and Gerizim, at an elevation of over nineteen hundred feet above the Mediterranean. Shechem is also called SICHEM, Gen. 12:6, SYCHEM, Acts 7:16, and is generally supposed to be the same as SYCHAR. John 4:5. It is about four thousand years old, and was a Hivite city when Jacob came from Mesopotamia. Joseph was buried there. Josh. 24:32. It was fortified by Jeroboam, and became the first capital of the ten tribes that revolted. 1 Kings 12:1-19.

Shechemites, she´kem-ites, descendants of Shechem, the son of Gilead. Num. 26:31.

Shed´e-ur (*darting of fire*), the father of Elizur. Num. 1:5; 2:10.

Sheep. This animal was probably the first that was domesticated by the Hebrews, Gen. 4:4, and it often constituted the chief wealth of a family in patriarchal times. It was especially an animal of sacrifice, and there were very few offerings in which it was not permitted. The ancient Israelites probably kept the broad-tailed variety, the tail or "rump" of which is a mass of delicate fat weighing from ten to fifteen pounds, and considered the choicest part of the animal. Exod. 29:22. The *shepherd* held a position of trust and responsibility. He tended the flock constantly, day and night, Luke 2:8, and was responsible for any that were missing. Luke 15:4-6. The care he exercised over the sheep gave him great control over them. They recognized his voice and promptly obeyed his call. John 10:3-5. The sheep were kept in an enclosure called a *sheepfold* or *sheepcote*. John 10:1; 2 Sam. 7:8. In a figurative sense, believers are called sheep on account of their obedience and gentleness. Matt. 25:33; John 10:16. Christ himself is called "the lamb of God. " John 1:29.

Sheep Gate, a gate of Jerusalem. Neh. 3:1; 12:39.

Sheep Market, John 5:2, should read SHEEP GATE (which see).

Sheets, Judg. 14:12, means "linen garments," and is so rendered in the Revised Version.

She-ha-ri´ah (*Jehovah seeks him*), a son of Jeroham. 1 Chron. 8:26.

Shek´el denotes a weight, and refers to a certain weight of uncoined metal. Lev. 5:15. See WEIGHTS.

She´lah (*petition*), the youngest son of Judah by the daughter of Shua. Gen. 38:5; Num 26:20.

She´lah (*sprout*), the son of Arphaxad. 1 Chron. 1:18, 24. He is called SALAH in Gen. 10:24; 11:12.

She´lan-ites, descendants of Shelah, the son of Judah. Num. 26:20.

Shel-e-mi´ah (*whom Jehovah repays*). [1] A Levite porter for the Tabernacle, 1 Chron. 26:14, called also MESHELE-MIAH. [2, 3] Jews who took foreign wives. Ezra 10:39, 41. [4] Father of Hananiah. Neh. 3:30. [5] A priest who became a trea-

surer. Neh. 13:13. [6] Grandfather of Jehudi. Jer. 36:14, 26. [7] The father of Jehucal. Jer. 37:3; 38:1. [8] Father of Irijah. Jer. 37:13.

Sheleph, she´lef (*drawn out*), one of the sons of Joktan. Gen. 10:26; 1 Chron. 1:20.

She´lesh (*tried*), one of the chiefs of Asher. 1 Chron. 7:35.

Shel´o-mi (*pacific*), father of Ahihud, prince of Asher. Num. 34:27.

Shelo-mith (*pacific*). [1] A woman of the tribe of Dan. Lev. 24:11. [2] One of the daughters of Zerubbabel. 1 Chron. 3:19. [3] A descendant of Gershon, the son of Levi. 1 Chron. 23:9. [4] One of the Kohathite Levites. 1 Chron. 23:18. Called SHELOMOTH. [5] One who had charge of dedicated things. 1 Chron. 26:25, 26. [6] One of the sons of Rehoboam. 2 Chron. 11:20. [7] A Jew whose sons returned with Ezra. Ezra 8:10.

Shel´o-moth. 1 Chron. 24:22. See SHELOMITH, No. 4.

She-lu´mi-el (*friend of God*), prince of the tribe of Simeon. Num. 1:6; 10:19.

Shem (*name*), a son of Noah. Gen. 5:32; 9:20–27. The Jews descended from him; also the Aramæans, Persians, Arabians, and Assyrians. The various languages of the descendants of Shem are called Shemitic languages.

Shema, she´mah (*rumor*). [1] One of the descendants of Judah. 1 Chron. 2:43, 44. [2] A descendant of Reuben. 1 Chron. 5:8. [3] A descendant of Benjamin. 1 Chron. 8:13. [4] One who stood with Ezra when he read the law to the people. Neh. 8:4.

Shema, she´mah (*rumor*), a town of Judah. Josh. 15:26.

She´ma-ah or **Shem´a-ah** (*rumor*), one whose sons joined David at Ziklag. 1 Chron. 12:3.

Shem-a-i´ah (*Jehovah hears*). [1] A prophet sent by the LORD to stop Rehoboam from making war against Israel. 1 Kings 12:22; 2 Chron. 11:2. [2] One of the descendants of Zerubbabel. 1 Chron. 3:22. [3] A descendant of Simeon. 1 Chron. 4:37. [4] A descendant of Reuben. 1 Chron. 5:4. [5, 6, 7, 8, 9, 10, 11] Levites. 1 Chron. 9:14; Neh. 11:15; 1 Chron. 9:16; 15:8, 11; 24:6; 2 Chron. 17:8; 29:14; 31:15; 35:9. [12] A son of Obed-edom. 1 Chron. 26:4, 6, 7. [13] A son of Adonikam who returned with Ezra. Ezra 8:13, 16. [14, 15] A priest and another person who took foreign wives. Ezra 10:21, 31. [16] A Jew who tried to make Nehemiah distrust God. Neh. 6:10. [17] One of the priests who sealed the covenant. Neh. 10:8; 12:6. [18] A prince of Judah. Neh. 12:34. [19] A member of the choir at the dedication of the wall. Neh. 12:36. [20] One of the priests. Neh. 12:42. [21] The father of Urijah. Jer. 26:20. [22] A false prophet. Jer. 29:24, 31, 32. [23] The father of a prince of the Jews. Jer. 36:12.

Shem-a-ri´ah (*whom Jehovah keeps*). [1] A soldier of David at Ziklag. 1 Chron. 12:5. [2, 3] Two Jews who took foreign wives. Ezra 10:32, 41.

Shem´e-ber (*lofty flight*), a king of Zeboiim. Gen. 14:2.

She´mer (*lees of wine*), the owner of the hill on which King Omri, after buying it, built the city of Samaria. 1 Kings 16:24.

Shemida, she-mi´dah, Num. 26:32; Josh. 17:2, **She-mi´dah,** 1 Chron. 7:19 (*fame of wisdom*), a descendant of Manasseh.

She-mi´da-ites, descendants of Shemida. Num. 26:32.

Shem´i-nith (*the eighth*), found in 1 Chron. 15:21, and in the titles of Pss. 6 and 12, is a musical term whose meaning is doubtful.

She-mir´a-moth (*name most high*). [1] A Levite engaged in the choral service of the Tabernacle. 1 Chron. 15:18, 20; 16:5. [2] A Levite in the time of Jehoshaphat. 2 Chron. 17:8.

She-mu´el (*heard of God*). [1] A chief of Simeon. Num. 34:20. [2] The prophet Samuel. 1 Chron. 6:33. See SAMUEL. [3] One of the chieftains of Issachar. 1 Chron. 7:2.

Shen (*the tooth*), a place in Benjamin, west of Jerusalem and east of Kirjathjearim. 1 Sam. 7:12.

She-na´zar (*fiery tooth*), one of the descendants of David. 1 Chron. 3:18.

She´nir, a name given to Mount Hermon. Deut. 3:9; Song of Sol. 4:8. See HERMON.

She´pham (*bear-region*), a place in the east border and near the north end of Canaan. Num. 34:10, 11.

Shephathiah, shef-a-thi´ah (*Jehovah judges*), a descendant of Benjamin. 1 Chron. 9:8.

Sheph-a-ti´ah (*Jehovah judges*). [1] David's fifth son. 2 Sam. 3:4; 1 Chron. 3:3. [2] A Benjamite who joined David at Ziklag. 1 Chron. 12:5. [3] Prince of Simeon. 1 Chron. 27:16. [4] One of the sons of Jehoshaphat. 2 Chron. 21:2. [5, 6] Two Jews whose descendants returned with Zerubbabel. Ezra 2:4, 57; Neh. 7:9, 59. [7] A descendant of Judah. Neh. 11:4. [8] A prince of Judah in the time of Zedekiah. Jer. 38:1-4.

She´phi (*a naked hill*), one of the descendants of Seir, 1 Chron. 1:40, called also SHEPHO.

She´pho (*smoothness*), a descendant of Seir, Gen. 36:23, called also SHEPHI.

Shephuphan, she-fu´fan (*serpent*), a son of Bela, the son of Benjamin, 1 Chron. 8:5, called also SHUPHAM, SHUPPIM, and MUPPIM.

She´rah (*blood-kindred*), a daughter of Ephraim. 1 Chron. 7:24.

Sherd, Isa. 30:14; Ezek. 23:34, means fragment.

Sher-e-bi´ah (*heat of Jehovah*), a chief Levite and helper of Ezra. He sealed the covenant. Ezra 8:18, 24; Neh. 8:7; 9:4; 10:12.

She´resh (*root*), a son of Machir, the son of Manasseh. 1 Chron. 7:16.

She-re´zer (*Asur protect the king!*), a Jew mentioned in Zech. 7:2.

Sher´iffs, Dan. 3:2, 3, were officers among the Babylonians, probably similar to the muftis, or head doctors of the Mohammedan law, in the Turkish empire.

Sheshach, she´shak, a symbolical name applied to Babylon. Jer. 25:26; 51:41.

Sheshai, she´shay (*whitish*), a son of Anak. Num. 13:22; Josh. 15:14.

She´shan (*lily*), one of the descendants of Judah. 1 Chron. 2:31, 34, 35.

Shesh-baz´zar (*fire-worshipper*), the name borne by Zerubbabel at the Persian court. Ezra 1:8, 11; 5:14, 16.

Sheth (*tumult*). [1] Sheth, the patriarch. 1 Chron. 1:1. Same as SETH (which see). [2] Sheth, in Num. 24:17, is translated "tumult," or "Sheth" in the Revised Version.

She´thar (*a star*), a Persian prince. Esther 1:14.

She´thar-boz´na-i (*star of splendor*), the name or title of a Persian officer in Syria. Ezra 5:3, 6; 6:6, 13.

Sheva, she´vah (*Jehovah contends*). [1] A son of Maachah, the concubine of Caleb, the son of Jephunneh. 1 Chron. 2:49. [2] David's scribe or secretary. 2 Sam. 20:25. Same as SERAIAH, No. 1.

Shew Bread, Exod. 25:30, was unleavened bread prepared anew every Sabbath and offered on the golden table in twelve loaves (according to the number of the tribes of Israel), and arranged in two rows or piles of six loaves each. It was called "shew bread" or "bread of the face," because it stood continually before the Lord. Only the priests could lawfully eat it.

Shib´bo-leth (*an ear of corn,* or *a stream, a flood*), a word which was made the test in separating the Ephraimites from the Gileadites in a battle between them. The Ephraimites were unable to pronounce "Shibboleth" properly—called it *Sibboleth*—and forty-two thousand of them were slain by the Gileadites. See the account in Judg. 12:1-6.

Shib´mah (*fragrance*), a town of Reuben, east of the Jordan. Num. 32:38. It is also called SIBMAH and SHEBAM.

Shi´cron (*drunkenness*), a town in the west of Judah. Josh. 15:11.

Shield, a piece of defensive armor, usually round or oval, borne on the left arm near the elbow, and used to protect the bearer from the missiles and weapons of the enemy. Shields were made of a light wooden framework covered with tough hides, and of metal. 2 Sam. 1:21; 1 Chron. 18:7. A long shield that protected the whole body was called a *target*. 1 Kings 10:16.

Shiggaion, shig-ga´yon, in the title of Ps. 7, probably means "wild and mournful."

Shi-gi´o-noth, Hab. 3:1, is the plural of SHIGGAION (which see).

Shi´hon (*destruction*), a city of Issachar. Josh. 19:19.

Shi´hor, 1 Chron. 13:5, a name of the river Nile. See NILE.

Shi´hor-lib´nath (*black-white*), a river which was part of the boundary of Asher. Josh. 19:26.

Shil´hi (*armed*), father of Azubah, the mother of Jehoshaphat. 1 Kings 22:42; 2 Chron. 20:31.

Shil´him (*armed men*), a town in the south of Judah, Josh. 15:32, called also SHAARAIM and SHARAIM.

Shil´lem (*requital*), one of the sons of Naphtali, Gen. 46:24; Num. 26:49, called SHALLUM in 1 Chron. 7:13.

Shil´lem-ites, descendants of Shillem. Num. 26:49.

Shi-lo´ah (*sending forth*), Isa. 8:6, a fountain near the foot of Mount Zion, the water of which was carried in an aqueduct to a pool or reservoir called Ophel, near Jerusalem. See SILOAH.

Shi´loh, in Gen. 49:10, is applied to the MESSIAH (which see).

Shi´loh (*place of rest*), a city, Judg. 21:19, seventeen miles north of Jerusalem; it was the site selected by Joshua for the Tabernacle, Josh. 18:1, where it remained over three hundred years. Near *Seilun*, the modern name of the city, is an open level court, four hundred and twelve feet by seventy-seven feet, partly hewn out from the rock, which probably was the spot on which the Tabernacle stood. Also see Gen. 49:10.
Josh. 18:8-10; 19:51; 21:2; 22:9, 12.
Judg. 18:31; 21:12, 21.
1 Sam. 1:3, 9, 24; 2:14; 3:21; 4:3, 4, 12; 14:3.
1 Kings 2:27; 14:2, 4.
Ps. 78:60.
Jer. 7:12, 14; 26:6, 9; 41:5.

Shi-lo´ni, a descendant of Shelah. Neh. 11:5.

Shi´lo-nite or **Shi-lo´nite,** an inhabitant of SHILOH. 1 Kings 11:29.

Shi´lo-nites or **Shi-lo´nites, The,** 1 Chron. 9:5, descendants of Shelah.

Shil´shah (*the third son*), a descendant

of Asher. 1 Chron. 7:37.

Shimea, shim´e-ah, and **Shim´e-ah** (*the hearing—that is, answering—prayer*). **[1]** A brother of David, 2 Sam. 21:21, called also SHAMMAH and SHIMMA. **[2]** A descendant of David and Bathsheba, 1 Chron. 3:5, also called SHAMMUA and SHAMMUAH. **[3]** A descendant of Merari, the son of Levi. 1 Chron. 6:30. **[4]** A son of Gershon, the son of Levi. 1 Chron. 6:39. **[5]** A man of Benjamin. 1 Chron. 8:32.

Shim´e-am (*the hearing—that is, answering—prayer*). 1 Chron. 9:38. Same as SHIMEAH, No. 5.

Shim´e-ath (*the hearing*), an Ammonitess, the mother of Jozachar. 2 Kings 12:21; 2 Chron. 24:26.

Shim´e-ath-ites, a family of scribes. 1 Chron. 2:55.

Shim´e-i (*renowned*). **[1]** A son of Gershon, the son of Levi, Num. 3:18; 1 Chron. 6:17, called also SHIMI. **[2]** A Benjamite, of the family of Saul, who cursed David when he fled from Absalom. 2 Sam. 16:5-13; 19:23. **[3]** An officer of David who remained faithful when Adonijah rebelled. 1 Kings 1:8. **[4]** One of the provision-officers of Solomon. 1 Kings 4:18. **[5]** A grandson of Jeconiah. 1 Chron. 3:19. **[6]** A descendant of Simeon. 1 Chron. 4:26, 27. **[7]** A descendant of Reuben. 1 Chron. 5:4. **[8]** A descendant of Merari, the son of Levi. 1 Chron. 6:29, 42. **[9]** The head of the tenth course in the service of song. 1 Chron. 25:17. **[10]** An overseer of David's vineyards. 1 Chron. 27:27. **[11]** A descendant of Heman. 2 Chron. 29:14. **[12]** A Levite in charge of offerings. 2 Chron. 31:12, 13. **[13]** A Levite who took a foreign wife. Ezra 10:23. **[14, 15]** Two Jews who took foreign wives. Ezra 10:33, 38. **[16]** An ancestor of

Mordecai. Esther 2:5.

Shim´e-on (*a hearing*), one of the family of Harim that had taken a foreign wife. Ezra 10:31.

Shim´hi (*renowned*), one of the heads of families of the tribe of Benjamin. 1 Chron. 8:21.

Shi´mi. Exod. 6:17. See SHIMEI, No. 1.

Shim´ites, Num. 3:21, the descendants of Shimei, the son of Gershon.

Shimma, shim´mah (*the hearing*), a son of Jesse and brother of David. 1 Chron. 2:13. See SHIMEA, No. 1.

Shi´mon (*desert*), a descendant of Judah. 1 Chron. 4:20.

Shim´rath (*watch*), a son of Shimhi, a descendant of Benjamin. 1 Chron. 8:21.

Shim´ri (*watchful*). [1] Head of a family of Simeonites. 1 Chron. 4:37. [2] Father of one of David's valiant men. 1 Chron. 11:45. [3] A Levite in the time of Hezekiah. 2 Chron. 29:13.

Shim´rith (*watchful*), a Moabitess whose son Jehozabad was one of the conspirators against King Joash. 2 Chron. 24:26. She is called SHOMER in 2 Kings 12:21.

Shim´rom, 1 Chron. 7:1, should be **Shim´ron** (*watch*), as in Gen. 46:13; Num. 26:24. He was one of the sons of Issachar.

Shim´ron (*watch-post*), one of the ancient cities of Canaan, Josh. 11:1; 19:15, is probably the same as SHIMRON-MERON in Josh. 12:20.

Shim´ron-ites, descendants of Shimron, the son of Issachar. Num. 26:24.

Shim´ron-me´ron. Josh. 12:20. See SHIMRON.

Shimshai, shim´shay (*sunny*), Rehum's scribe or secretary. Ezra 4:8, 9.

Shi´nab (*cooling*), a king of Admah. Gen. 14:2.

Shi´nar, the Land of (*casting out? country of two rivers*), was probably the plain of Mesopotamia on the Euphrates and Tigris Rivers. Gen. 10:10; 11:2.

Ship. This word, when applied to vessels on the Sea of Galilee, means a fishing-boat impelled by oars, and sometimes having a mast and sail. Mark 6:48; Luke 8:23. The Jews were not sailors, and the shipping trade on the Mediterranean and Red Seas was held by their heathen neighbors, who had ships of considerable size. These ships were steered by two large paddles, and though they usually had a mast with a huge sail, they were also propelled by oars in the hands of rowers. When one of these vessels was subjected to any great strain likely to make it leak, chains or ropes called "helps" were passed around (underneath) the vessel to tighten the planks. Acts 27:17. Their anchors were like ours, only they had no flukes. The account of Paul's voyage and shipwreck in the twenty-seventh chapter of Acts gives us more information about ancient navigation than all ancient classics.

Shi´phi (*abundant*), a chief among the descendants of Simeon. 1 Chron. 4:37.

Shiphmite, shif´mite, 1 Chron. 27:27, a native of SHEPHAM.

Shiph´rah (*beauty*), a chief midwife among the Hebrews in Egypt. Exod. 1:15.

Shiph´tan (*judicial*), father of Kemuel. Num. 34:24.

Shisha, shi´shah (*Jehovah contends*), the father of the two scribes of Solomon. 1 Kings 4:3. See SERAIAH, No. 1.

Shi´shak, a king of Egypt to whom Jeroboam fled when Solomon sought to kill him. 1 Kings 11:40; 2 Chron. 12:2.

Shit´ra-i (*scribe*), a chief herdsman of David. 1 Chron. 27:29.

Shit´tah Tree. Isa. 41:19. See SHITTIM WOOD.

Shit´tim (*acacias*) was the last encampment of the Israelites before they entered Canaan. It was in the plains of Moab and near Mount Peor. Num. 25:1; 33:49; Josh. 2:1; 3:1. It is also called ABEL-SHITTIM.

Shit´tim, Val´ley of, mentioned in Joel 3:18, may be same as SHITTIM.

Shit´tim Wood was used extensively in the construction and furnishing of the Tabernacle. Exod. 25:10-16. It was the wood of the shittah tree, Isa. 41:19, probably a species of the acacia tree, once abundant and still found in the peninsula of Sinai. The wood is well adapted for cabinet-work, having a close grain. It is hard, tough, and of a brownish color.

Shiza, shi´zah (*loving*), father of Abina, one of David's valiant men. 1 Chron. 11:42.

Shoa, sho´ah (*opulent*), Ezek. 23:23, may be the name of a place, or only a title. Its meaning is unknown.

Sho´bab (*apostate*). [1] A son of David and Bathsheba. 2 Sam. 5:14; 1 Chron. 3:5. [2] A son of Caleb, the son of Hezron. 1 Chron. 2:18.

Shobach, sho´bak (*pouring*), the captain of the host of Hadarezer. 2 Sam. 10:16, 18. He is called SHOPHACH in 1 Chron. 19:16.

Sho´ba-i (*taking captive*), a Tabernacle porter whose descendants returned with Zerubbabel. Ezra 2:42; Neh. 7:45.

Sho´bal (*flowing*). [1] A son of Seir. Gen. 36:20; 1 Chron. 1:38. [2] A son of Caleb, the son of Hur. 1 Chron. 2:50, 52. [3] Shobal, in 1 Chron. 4:1, 2, is probably the same as SHOBAL, No. 2.

Sho´bek (*forsaking*), one who sealed the covenant made by Nehemiah. Neh. 10:24.

Sho´bi (*taking captive*), a chief of the Ammonites. He provisioned David when he fled from Absalom. 2 Sam. 17:27.

Shocho, sho´ko, 2 Chron. 28:18, **Shochoh,** sho´ko, 1 Sam. 17:1, and **Sho´co,** 2 Chron. 11:7 a city of Judah. See SOCOH, No. 1.

Shoes, Exod. 3:5. **Shoe Latch´et,** Mark 1:7. See SANDALS.

Sho´ham (*onyx*), a Levite of the family of Merari. 1 Chron. 24:27.

Sho´mer (*a keeper*). [1] A great-grandson of Asher. 1 Chron. 7:32. He is called SHAMER in 1 Chron. 7:34. [2] Shomer. 2 Kings 12:21. See SHIMRITH.

Shophach, sho´fak (*pouring*). 1 Chron. 19:16, 18. See SHOBACH.

Sho´phan, a city of Gad. Num. 32:35. It is part of the preceding name, "Atroth," and is so rendered, "Atroth-shophan," in the Revised Version.

Sho-shan´nim (*lily*), in titles of Psalms 45 and 69, and **Sho-shan´nim-E´duth** (*lily, a testimony*), in title of Ps. 80, probably denote the melody that was used for those Psalms.

Shoul´der. To "bow the shoulder," Gen. 49:15, indicates servitude, and to "withdraw" it, Neh. 9:29, denoted rebellion. To "put upon" one's shoulder, Isa. 9:6; 22:22, means to entrust to his keeping or charge.

Shov´el, in Isa. 30:24, means a winnowing-fork or fan. See FAN, WINNOWING.

Show Bread. See SHEW BREAD.

Shrines, mentioned in Acts 19:24, refer to small models of the temple of Diana, containing a little image of the goddess. Pilgrims to Ephesus bought them to set up in their homes as objects of worship. See DIANA.

Shroud, Ezek. 31:3, means cover, shelter.

Shua, shu´ah (*riches*). [1] 1 Chron. 2:3, father-in-law of Judah, called SHUAH in

Gen. 38:2, 12. [2] Daughter of Heber. 1 Chron. 7:32.

Shu´ah (*a pit*). [1] A son of Abraham and Keturah. Gen. 25:2; 1 Chron. 1:32. [2] A descendant of Judah. 1 Chron. 4:11.

Shu´al (*a fox*), an Israelite of Asher. 1 Chron. 7:36.

Shu´al, the Land of, was probably near Bethel. 1 Sam. 13:17.

Shu´ba-el (*captive of God*). [1] A name in 1 Chron. 24:20. See SHEBUEL, No. 1. [2] A name in 1 Chron. 25:20. See SHEBUEL, No. 2.

Shu´ham (*pit-digger?*), a son of Dan, Num. 26:42, called HUSHIM in Gen. 46:23.

Shu´ham-ites, descendants of Shuham. Num. 26:42, 43.

Shu´hite, a name applied to members of a tribe supposed to have descended from Shuah, a son of Abraham by Keturah. Job 2:11; 8:1.

Shu´lam-ite, Song of Sol. 6:13, a woman from Shulem, probably same as SHUNEM.

Shu´math-ites, inhabitants of Shumah, a village whose location is not known. 1 Chron. 2:53.

Shu´nam-mite, a female inhabitant of Shunem. 1 Kings 1:3, 15; 2:17.

Shu´nem (*two resting-places*), one of the cities of Issachar. Josh. 19:18; 1 Sam. 28:4. It was the residence of the Shunammite woman by whom Elisha was entertained. 2 Kings 4:8.

Shu´ni (*quiet*), one of the sons of Gad. Gen. 46:16; Num. 26:15.

Shu´nites, descendants of SHUNI. Num. 26:15.

Shu´pham, Num. 26:39, **Shup´pim,** 1 Chron. 7:12, 15 (*serpents*). [1] A descendant of Benjamin. [2] SHUPPIM, one of the Levite porters for the Tabernacle.

1 Chron. 26:16.

Shu´pham-ites, descendants of Shupam. Num. 26:39.

Shur (*fort-wall*), a place situated in the wilderness on the south-west of Palestine. Gen. 16:7; Exod. 15:22.

Shu´shan (*a lily*), a chief city of Susiana in Persia. It was the winter palace of the kings, and was known to the Greeks as *Susa*. Neh. 1:1; Esther 1:2; Dan. 8:2.

Shu´shan-e´duth is found in the title of Ps. 60, and is the same as SHOSHANNIM (which see).

Shu´thal-hites, descendants of Shuthelah. Num. 26:35.

Shu´the-lah (*noise of breaking*). [1] One of the sons of Ephraim. Num. 26:35, 36; 1 Chron. 7:20. [2] A descendant of Ephraim. 1 Chron. 7:21.

Sia, siah, Neh. 7:47, **Siaha,** si´a-hah, Ezra 2:44 (*congregation*), a Jew whose descendants returned with Zerubbabel.

Sibbecai, sib´be-kay, 1 Chron. 11:29; 27:11, **Sibbechai,** sib´be-kay, 2 Sam. 21:18; 1 Chron. 20:4 (*thicket of Jehovah*), a descendant of Judah. He slew a champion of the Philistines. He is called MEBUNNAI in 2 Sam. 23:27.

Sib´bo-leth, Judg. 12:6. See SHIBBOLETH.

Sib´mah (*coolness* or *fragrance*), a town east of the Jordan, Josh. 13:19; Isa. 16:8, called also SHEBAM and SHIBMAH.

Sib´ra-im (*twofold hope*), a city of Syria, between Damascus and Hamath. Ezek. 47:16.

Sichem, si´kem. Gen. 12:6. See SHECHEM.

Sick´le. Joel 3:13. From representations on Egyptian monuments the ancient sickle was very much like our implement. The scythe was unknown in Bible times.

Sid´dim, Vale of, Gen. 14:3, is supposed to have been the site of Sodom and Gomorrah. Its exact location is not established. See SODOM. It was the scene of the battle between Chedorlaomer and his allies and the kings of Sodom, Gomorrah, etc.

Si´don or **Zi´don,** one of the oldest cities of the world, named after the "first-born" of Canaan, the grandson of Noah, Gen. 10:15; 1 Chron. 1:13, stands on the Mediterranean shore, twenty-five miles south of the modern *Beirut* and one hundred and twenty-three miles north of Jerusalem, and was in ancient times the principal city of Phœnicia until her own colony, Tyre, situated twenty miles to the south, became the more important. Sidon was celebrated both among the Jews and the Greeks for its ship-building industry, its purple-dyed fabrics, its silver-ware, etc., and though it was often rebuked by the prophets on account of its idolatry and moral laxity, it was generally spoken of with less severity than Tyre. Isa. 23:2, 4, 12; Jer. 25:22; 27:3; 47:4; Ezek. 27:8; 28:21; etc. It was once visited by Jesus, Matt. 15:21; Mark 7:24; Luke 4:26, and some of its people went to hear his preaching. Mark 3:8; Luke 6:17.

Si-do´ni-ans, Deut. 3:9, inhabitants of Sidon.

Sieve. Isa. 30:28; Amos 9:9. This necessary article for separating the fine meal from the coarse was in very early times made of rushes or papyrus. Sieves were of different degrees of fineness, as ancient writers mention four kinds of meal.

Sig´net, Gen. 38:18; Dan. 6:17, a seal. See SEAL.

Si´hon (*sweeping away*), a king of the Amorites who refused to let the children of Israel pass through his country. His army was routed in a battle that ensued, Sihon was killed, and his dominions divided between Reuben and Gad. Num. 21:21–30; Josh. 13:15–28.

Si´hor, Josh. 13:3; Isa. 23:3; Jer. 2:18, refers to the river NILE (which see).

Si´las, one of the chiefs of the brethren of the early Church, was probably a native of Antioch. Acts 15:37-41. He accompanied Paul on several of his missionary tours, and was imprisoned with him at Philippi. Acts 16:19-40. He is called a prophet, Acts 15:32, and is supposed to be the SILVANUS mentioned in 2 Cor. 1:19.

Silk. In Prov. 31:22, Revised Version, the word is rendered "fine linen," and it may be that it has the same meaning in Ezek. 16:10, 13, as it is a question whether the Hebrews knew anything about silk at that time. It was used, however, in New Testament times. Rev. 18:12.

Sil´la (*a twig*), a place near which King Joash was killed. 2 Kings 12:20.

Si-lo´ah or **Sil´o-ah,** Neh. 3:15, the name of a pool near Jerusalem, called SHILOAH in Isa. 8:6, and SILOAM in the New Testament. See SILOAM, No. 2.

Si-lo´am or **Sil´o-am.** [1] A tower in Siloam, on Olivet, near Jerusalem. This tower fell and killed eighteen men. See Luke 13:4, 5. [2] SILOAM, SHILOAH, or SILOAH, a pool near Jerusalem. It is referred to in Isa. 8:6 as "the waters of Shiloah that go softly," in Neh. 3:15 as "the pool of Siloah by the king's garden," and as "the pool of Siloam" in John 9:7, 11. It is doubtless the same as a pool now at the mouth of the Tyropœan valley at Jerusalem.

Sil-va´nus (*woody*). [1] A disciple who accompanied Paul in several of his journeys. 2 Cor. 1:19; 1 Thess. 1:1; 2 Thess. 1:1. Supposed to be same as SILAS (which see). [2] A disciple by whom Peter sent his first epistle, addressed to the churches in Asia. 1 Pet. 5:12. He may be same as SILVANUS, No. 1.

Sil´ver. This precious metal was known very early in human history, Gen. 13:2, formed a common medium of trade, and was then not coined, but used by weight. Gen. 23:16. It was used in the construction of the Tabernacle, Exod. 26:19, for the furniture of the Temple, 1 Chron. 28:14-17, for musical instruments, Num. 10:2, and for adorning idols. Isa. 40:19. In the Hebrew the word was used to apply to money in general. Silver was abundant in Palestine in the time of Solomon, 1 Kings 10:27, who had it brought from Tharshish (probably Spain), 1 Kings 10:22, and from other places. 2 Chron. 9:14. For the beauty and force of the allusion in Mal. 3:3 see REFINER.

Sil´ver-ling, Isa. 7:23, probably refers to a shekel of silver. See SHEKEL.

Sim´e-on (*a hearing*). [1] The second son of Jacob and Leah. Gen. 29:33; Exod. 1:2. He was one of "the twelve patriarchs," and was the ancestor of the tribe of Simeon. [2] A just and devout man of Jerusalem, who waited for the consolation of Israel and was permitted to see the infant Saviour. Luke 2:25, 34. [3] A disciple and prophet who was at Antioch when Barnabas and Saul returned from Jerusalem. Acts 13:1. [4] Simeon, in Acts 15:14, is applied to the apostle Peter, who was more frequently called SIMON. [5] An ancestor of Joseph, the husband of Mary. Luke 3:30.

Sim´e-on. One of the tribes of Israel is often so called. Num. 1:6; Deut. 27:12; Ezek. 48:24.

Sim´e-on, Ter´ri-tory of, was in the south-west part of Canaan, and within the inheritance of Judah. Josh. 19:1-9.

Sim´e-on-ites, descendants of Simeon. Num. 25:14; 26:14; 1 Chron. 27:16.

Si´mon (*a hearing*). [1] A sorceror who practiced his arts and deceived the people of Samaria. Acts 8:9, 13, 18, 24. [2] A name often applied to the apostle Peter. Matt. 4:18; Mark 1:16; Luke 4:38; John 1:40; Acts 10:5; 2 Pet. 1:1, and elsewhere. [3] Simon the Canaanite, Matt. 10:4; Mark 3:18; Luke 6:15, called Simon Zelotes in Acts 1:13, one of the twelve apostles. [4] One of the brethren of our Lord. Matt. 13:55; Mark 6:3. [5] A Pharisee in whose house Jesus' feet were washed with tears and anointed with ointment. Luke 7:36-40. [6] A leper in Bethany. Matt. 26:6; Mark 14:3. [7] The father of Judas Iscariot. John 6:71; 12:4. [8] Simon the Cyrenian, who was compelled to bear the cross of Jesus on the way to Golgotha. Matt. 27:32; Mark 15:21; Luke 23:26. [9] Simon the tanner at Joppa, with whom Peter lodged. Acts 9:43; 10:6.

Sim´ri (*watchful*), one of the Merarite Levites. 1 Chron. 26:10.

Sin is the transgression of the law of God, 1 John 3:4, and "all unrighteousness is sin." 1 John 5:17. The word is sometimes used for a *sin-offering*, as in Hos. 4:8; Rom. 8:3; 2 Cor. 5:21.

Sin (*mire*), a city of northern Egypt, Ezek. 30:15, 16, called by the Greeks *Pelusium.* It was near the eastern mouth of the Nile.

Sin, Wil´der-ness of, is on the east shore of the Gulf of Suez and between Elim and Sinai. Exod. 16:1; Num. 33:11.

Sina, si´nah, in Acts 7:30, 38, is the Greek form of SINAI (which see).

Sinai, pronounced si´nay, si´ny or si´na-i (*burning bush?*). [1] The peninsula of Sinai is a triangular-shaped district lying between the two arms (gulfs) of the Red Sea. Its westerly boundary-line, along the Gulf of Suez, is about one hundred and ninety miles long, its easterly boundary, along the Gulf of Akabah, is about one hundred and thirty miles long, and its northern boundary-line, which stretches from the head of the Gulf of Akabah, is one hundred and fifty miles long. The peninsula contains about 11,500 square miles. The narrow strips of low coast-land along the two gulfs are backed by mountain-masses of granite with summits rising to the height of over 8500 feet. These mountains, shaply cleft by deep valley, enclose on the south, east, and west the wedge-shaped plateau known as the "Wilderness of Wandering." The ancient Egyptians called this peninsula the "land of the gods," and its solitary grandeur impresses all travellers alike.

[2] Mount Sinai, from which the Law was given to the Israelites, is in the southern part of the peninsula of the same name. In the Old Testament the name is used interchangeably with Mount HOREB (which see). It is difficult to locate exactly the Mount Sinai of the Bible, but most scholars now agree that it must have been one of the peaks of *Jebel Musa*, a gigantic mass two miles long, one mile broad, and running north-east and south-west. *Ras Sufsâfeh*, the northern peak of *Jebel Musa*, over 7300 feet high, and overlooking a plain that could have easily afforded standing-room for over two million Israelites, meets all the requirements of the text, Exod. 19:11-20; 20:18, and is regarded as the place from which the Law was given. The impression made upon the traveller by standing on the peak can never be effaced. It is the most appropriate pulpit for the proclamation of Jehovah to his people for all generations. The

sound of it could be heard in every spot of the surrounding valley *Er Râhah*, which is two miles and half a mile wide, and embraces four hundred acres of available standing-ground. All the surroundings are terribly sublime.

Sin´gle, Matt. 6:22; Luke 11:34, means clear, unclouded or presenting a clear, single image.

Sin´gu-lar, Lev. 27:2, means "special."

Si´nim is found in the Bible only in Isa. 49:12, and probably refers to China.

Sin´ite, descendant of Canaan, the son of Ham. Gen. 10:17; 1 Chron. 1:15.

Sin´-Mon´ey. Money sent by persons at a distance, with which to buy the required offerings. 2 Kings 12:16. As there was usually some surplus, it was the perquisite of the priest, and was called sin-money or sin-offering money. Num. 18:9.

Sin-Of´fer-ing. Lev. 4:21. See OFFERING.

Si´on (*lofty*). [1] One of the names of Mount Hermon. Deut. 4:48. See HERMON. [2] The Greek form of ZION. Matt. 21:5; John 12:15. See ZION.

Siph´moth (*fruitful places*), a place in Judah which was often visited by David when an outlaw. 1 Sam. 30:28.

Sippai, sip´pay (*threshold*), a giant. 1 Chron. 20:4. He was a Philistine, and is also called SAPH.

Si´rah, the Well of. 2 Sam. 3:26, near Hebron.

Sir´i-on (*breastplate?*), a Sidonian name for Mount Hermon. Deut. 3:9; Ps. 29:6.

Si-sam´a-i, (*distinguished?*), one of the descendants of Judah. 1 Chron. 2:40.

Sisera, sis´e-rah (*battle-array*). [1] The commander of the army of Jabin, king of Canaan. Judg. 4:2–22; 5:20. [2] A Jew whose descendants returned with

Zerubbabel. Ezra 2:53; Neh. 7:55.

Sis´ter. In Scripture this word has a wide application, being applied not only to a full sister, but to a step-sister, or half-sister, 2 Sam. 13:2, and to any near female relative. Matt. 13:56. It also denotes one of the same spiritual family. Rom. 16:1. "Sister's son," Col. 4:10, means "cousin."

Sith, Ezek. 35:6, means since; forasmuch as.

Sit´nah (*hatred*), the name given to a well dug by Isaac's servants, and for which they strove with the herdsmen of Gerar. Gen. 26:19-21.

Si´van, Esther 8:9, the ninth month of the Jewish civil year, and the third month of the sacred year. It corresponds nearly with our June. See MONTH.

Skill, 1 Kings 5:6; 2 Chron. 2:7, 8; 34:12, means to understand; to know how.

Skins of animals were used for clothing, Gen. 3:21, for a covering for the Tabernacle, Exod. 26:14, for BOTTLES (which see), and other domestic purposes. Num. 31:20. They were also used as coverings for shields.

Slav´er-y. Among the Jews there were Hebrew and Non-Hebrew slaves, and both were carefully protected by the law. The former became such through poverty or debt, through theft and inability to repay, or, in the case of females, because they had been sold by their parents as maid-servants. Theirs was the mildest form of bond-service. The Non-Hebrew slaves were captives taken in war or purchased, and they constituted a majority of the slaves among the Hebrews. At the time of Christ slavery was established throughout the world and interwoven with domestic and social life. It was regarded even by the wisest men as a normal state of society. But Christianity, by teaching the common creation and redemption of men, the fatherhood of God and the brotherhood of men, and enjoining the law of kindness and love to all, first moderated the evils of slavery, then encouraged emancipation, and the ultimate extinction of the whole institution.

Slime. Gen. 11:3. See PITCH.

Sling, 1 Sam. 17:40; Judg. 20:16, an early weapon of war, with which stones were thrown with great force and accuracy of aim. The slingers formed a regular branch of the army, ranking next to the archers in efficiency.

Slow Bel´lies, Titus 1:12, is rendered in the Revised Version "idle gluttons."

Smyrna, smir´nah (*myrrh*), a city of Asia Minor, on the Ægean Sea, forty miles north of Ephesus and opposite the island of Mytilene, is mentioned in Rev. 1:11 and 2:8-11 as one of the seven churches of Asia. It seems to have been founded by Greek colonists B. C. about 1500, and became an important commercial place in the days of Alexander the Great, B. C. 323. Polycarp, a pupil of the apostle John, was martyred there about A. D. 155. It is still a flourishing city with about 180,000 inhabitants.

Snail. In Lev. 11:30 a kind of lizard is probably meant, perhaps the sand-lizard, which is found in the desert of Sinai and in Palestine. The Arabs eat it, but the Jews regard it as unclean. In Ps. 58:8 the common snail is evidently meant. In moving it leaves a trial of thick slime. It may be to this peculiarity of the creature, or to the effect of the summer heat, which shrivels it up, that the Psalmist alludes in the expression, "As a snail which melteth."

Snow. Isa. 55:10. The fall of snow in Palestine varies with the face of the countries. It sometimes falls to the depth of a foot in Jerusalem, but soon disappears. In the ravines of the highest ridges of Hermon and on the peaks of Mount Lebanon snow is found during the whole year. See SEASONS.

Snuff´dish-es, Snuffers, Exod. 25:38; 37:23, were articles of furniture belonging to the GOLDEN CANDLESTICK (which see). The snuffers were tongs for removing the snuff from the wicks of the lamps, and the snuffdishes received the snuff thus removed.

So, a king of Egypt with whom Hoshea, the last king of Israel, made an alliance. 2 Kings 17:4.

Soap was made from oil or other fatty substances and potash obtained from the ashes of alkaline shrubs that grew along the Dead Sea and the Mediterranean. It was a soft soap that was thus made, and it was used from very early times not only for washing purposes, but in the refining of metals. Jer. 2:22; Mal. 3:2.

Socho, so´ko, 1 Chron. 4:18, and **Sochoh,** 1 Kings 4:10 (*branches*). See SOCOH.

So´coh (*branches*). **[1]** A city in the plains of Judah. Josh. 15:35. It is also called SHOCO, SHOCHO, and SHOCHOH. **[2]** A town in the mountains of Judah. Josh. 15:48.

Sod, Sod´den, Gen. 25:29; Exod. 12:9, means boiled.

So´di (*a confidant*), Num. 13:10, the father of Gaddiel, one of the twelve spies sent by Moses to view the land.

Sod´om (*burning?*), one of the cities in the vale of Siddim which were destroyed on account of the wickedness of their inhabitants. Gen. 10:19; 13:3, 10-13; 19:1-29; Matt. 10:15; 11:23, 24. Its exact location is not known. Some place it at the southern, others at the northern end of the Dead Sea.

Sodoma, sod´o-mah, the Greek name

for SODOM (which see). Rom. 9:29.

Sod´om-ite. Deut. 23:17. The word does not imply an inhabitant of Sodom, but rather one guilty of the crime to which the inhabitants of that city were addicted.

Sod´om, Vine of, Deut. 32:32, may refer to one of several plants, growing near the Dead Sea, which bear a beautiful fruit that is not fit to eat.

Sol´o-mon (*peaceful*), the son of David and Bathsheba, succeeded his father as king of Israel, and reigned forty years. He was noted for his wisdom, and was the chief author of the Proverbs. See PROVERBS. The principal event in his reign was the building of the TEMPLE (which see) in Jerusalem. Solomon was also famous for his riches. 1 Kings, chapter 10. His character in early life was noted for its excellence, but in his latter days he was led into idolatry and other sins by his numerous foreign wives and concubines. 1 Kings, chapter 11. ECCLESIASTES (which see) contains the lesson of his life.

Sol´o-mon's Pools are three large reservoirs, in a narrow valley south-west of Bethlehem, which supplied Jerusalem with water. They are built on different levels, one slightly above the other, and connected by underground passages, so that the water collected in the highest pool can be emptied in the lower pools. Eccles. 2:6.

Sol´o-mon's Porch, a cloister or colonnade on the east side of the Temple. A double row of white marble Corinthian columns supported the ceiling, which was finished with cedar and forty feet above the floor. John 10:23; Acts 3:11; 5:12.

Sol´o-mon, Prov´erbs of. Prov. 1:1. See PROVERBS.

Sol´o-mon's Song. See SONG OF SOLOMON.

Some´times, Eph. 2:13; 1 Pet. 3:20,

means "once;" "aforetime."

Son. This word is used in the Scriptures to imply almost any kind of descent or relationship. In Gen. 29:5 it is used for grandson; in Matt. 22:42 for a remoter descendant; in 1 Pet. 5:13 for disciple. "Sons of God" or "children of God" are those that are born of God or regenerated by the Holy Spirit. Adam is called "the son of God," as his creature made in his image. Luke 3:38. In one passage the term is applied to an inanimate object, the threshed-out grain, which is called in Hebrew the "son" of the threshing floor—Isa. 21:10, marginal notes.

Song of Sol′o-mon, The, SOLOMON'S SONG, or the SONG OF SONGS, or, after the Latin, CANTICLES, is a poem in dramatic form with dialogues and monologues. It is interpreted *literally* as a picture of pure bridal love, and *allegorically* as a typical representation of the relation between the Lord and Israel, or Christ and the Church. Each of these interpretations has its charm, and there is no reason why both should not be true. It has always formed part of the Canon.

Sooth′say-er. Dan. 2:27, etc. One who pretended to foretell future events.

Sop means morsel. Among the Hebrews and other nations of the East our modern table utensils were unknown or little used. Food was conveyed to the mouth by the finger, and in eating liquid food a small piece of bread was dipped into it. John 13:26, 27, 30.

Sop′a-ter (*father saved*), a disciple from Berea who accompanied Paul from Macedonia. Acts 20:4. Perhaps same as SOSIPATER.

Sope. Mal. 3:2, etc. See SOAP.

Soph′e-reth (*scribe*), a servant of Solomon whose descendants returned with Zerubbabel. Ezra 2:55; Neh. 7:57.

Sor′cer-y was one of the arts of the magicians, by which they pretended to foretell events with the supposed assistance of evil spirits. Exod. 7:11; Acts 8:9.

Sore, in Gen. 43:1; Deut. 6:22, etc., means grievous.

So′rek, Val′ley of (*a choice vine*), was a little east of Gaza, and was the home of Delilah, whom Samson loved. Judg. 16:4.

So-sip′a-ter (*preservation of a father*), a kinsman of Paul, Rom. 16:21, perhaps same as SOPATER.

Sosthenes, sos′the-neez (*safe in strength*). [1] The ruler of the synagogue at Corinth. Acts 18:17. [2] A disciple at Rome, 1 Cor. 1:1, perhaps same as SOSTHENES, No. 1.

So′ta-i (*a deviator*), a servant of Solomon. His descendants returned with Zerubbabel. Ezra 2:55; Neh. 7:57.

Soul. The Scriptures evidently distinguish between the spirit and the soul. 1 Thess. 5:23; Heb. 4:12. The word we call soul is used to denote mere animal life—the seat of feeling, appetite, and passion. The spirit is the higher portion of our nature—the seat of intellect and the loftier affections; "the holy of holies in that temple which God has constructed for himself within us." But the word soul is often used in the Bible and in all languages in a wider sense for the internal, spiritual side of the constitute of man, as consisting of a mortal body and an immortal soul. Gen. 2:7; Matt. 10:28. In many passages it means person. Rom. 13:1.

South Ra′moth, a place bordering on the desert south of Judah. 1 Sam. 30:27.

Spain, the extreme south-west part of Europe, in ancient times included Portugal, and was known to the Hebrews. Paul desired to preach the gospel there. Rom. 15:24-28. Many scholars identify

TARSHISH with the southern part of Spain and with *Tartessus*.

Span, a measure of length, equal to about nine inches. Exod. 28:16; 1 Sam. 17:4. "Spanned," in Isa. 48:13, means spread out.

Spar´rows, Matt. 10:29, 31; Luke 12:6, 7, were little birds of the sparrow-like species that were very plentiful in Palestine. They were sold for food at a very low price and generally in pairs.

Spear. This weapon of warfare was a long wooden staff with a heavy metal point on one end. 1 Sam. 13:19, 22. The *dart* and *javelin* were similar to the spear, only lighter, and were probably used to be thrown with the hand. 2 Chron. 32:5; Num. 25:7.

Speck´led Bird, in Jer. 12:9, probably refers to the HYÆNA (which see).

Spelt, in marginal notes, Isa. 28:25. See RYE.

Spi´cer-y, Spi´ces. The former word, in Gen. 37:25, and "spices," in Gen. 43:11, are translated from the same Hebrew word, which is rendered "gum tragacanth" in the marginal notes of the Revised Version. This gum had a medicinal value. "Spices," as used elsewhere in the Scriptures, denotes not only fragrant gums, roots, and barks, but also the odors of flowers and various perfumes. Song of Sol. 4:14, 16.
Also see Exod. 25:6; 30:23, 34; 35:8, 28; 37:29.
1 Kings 10:2, 10, 15, 25.
2 Kings 20:13.
1 Chron. 9:29, 30.
2 Chron. 9:1, 9, 24; 16:14; 32:27.
Song of Sol. 4:10; 5:1, 13; 6:2; 8:14.
Isa. 39:2.
Ezek. 24:10; 27:22.
Mark 16:1.
Luke 23:56; 24:1.
John 19:40.

Spi´der. This well-known insect of very singular structure and habits was abundant in Palestine. The hopes and schemes of wicked men are compared with the frailty of the spider's web. Job 8:14; Isa. 59:5.

Spike´nard. Mark 14:3; John 12:3. See NARD.

Spin, Spin´dle. Among the nations of antiquity spinning was distinctively a woman's occupation. Woollen and linen cloth were made from wool and flax, and camels' and goats' hair were spun for sackcloth. Wheel-spinning was apparently unknown. The fibers were drawn from the distaff and twisted into thread by means of the spindle. Exod. 35:25, 26. Prov. 31:19.

Spir´it is a word used to denote— (1) the Spirit of God, Gen. 6:3; Num. 11:17; Neh. 9:20; Ps. 51:11; Prov. 1:23; Isa. 32:15; Zech. 4:6, etc., or the HOLY GHOST. Matt. 3:11; Mark 1:8; Luke 1:15; John 1:33; etc. (2) An evil, lying, or unclean spirit. 1 Sam. 16:14, 15; 18:10; 2 Chron. 18:21; Zech. 13:2; etc (3) A familar spirit. Lev. 19:31; 1 Sam. 28:3, 7; Isa. 8:19, etc. (4) The actuating spirit or power in man, 2 Cor. 7:1; Eph. 4:23; James 4:5, as contrasted with the SOUL (which see). The same word in Hebrew and Greek which means *spirit*, means also *wind*; hence the comparison in John 3:8.

Spoil means plunder taken in war. Num. 31:9; Nah. 2:9. It also means to plunder, Gen. 34:27; to recover property taken away by violence, Exod. 3:22; to make a captive. Col. 2:8.

Spring sometimes means commencement. 2 Sam. 9:26. "Springs of Pisgah," Deut. 4:49, means "slopes of Pisgah."

Sprink´ling, Blood of, Heb. 12:24, refers to the custom of the high-priest, who once a year entered the holy of holies and sprinkled blood on the mercy-seat, to "make an atonement for the holy *place* because of the uncleanness of the children of Israel." Lev. 16:15, 16.

Stachys, sta´kis (*an ear of corn*), a disciple in Rome to whom Paul sent salutation. Rom. 16:9.

Stacte, stak´te (*a drop*), Exod. 30:34, was one of the ingredients of the sacred incense. It was either a substance that flowed from the balsamodendron or a gum from the storax tree. Modern styrax is an entirely different substance.

Star´-gaz-ers, in Isa. 47:13, implies raving or dreaming about the stars.

Stand´ard. Num. 1:52. See BANNER.

Star of the Wise Men. Matt. 2:1–21. Concerning the appearance of this star there are two theories: (1) A miraculous star, seen only by the wise men, and serving as their guide until it led them to "where the young child was." Matt. 2:9. (2) A remarkable conjunction of Jupiter, Saturn, Mars, and a star of extraordinary brilliancy, which took place about the time of Christ's birth (according to astronomical calculations), and which would naturally attract the Magi, with their ideas of astrology and their expectations of the coming Messiah.

Stars. The Hebrews included under the names of stars, the planets and all other heavenly bodies except the sun and moon. The stars are often mentioned in the Bible, and are very frequently referred to figuratively, as in Ps. 147:4; Gen. 15:5; 22:17; 26:4; Exod. 32:13; Ps. 8:3, 4. In Rev. 22:16 Christ is called the "morning star," because the light of the gospel day was introduced by him. See ASTRONOMY.

Steads, 1 Chron. 5:22, means "places."

Steel. This word, in the Authorized Version, 2 Sam. 22:35; Job 20:24; Ps. 18:34; Jer. 15:12, is translated from a Hebrew word meaning brass or copper, and in the Revised Version is always rendered "brass." It is very doubtful whether steel was known to the ancient Jews.

Stephanas, stef´a-nas (*crown*), a Corinthian disciple whose household Paul baptized. 1 Cor. 1:16; 16:15, 17.

Stephen, ste´vn (*crown*), one of the seven disciples who were appointed to superintend the distributions to the poor. He was "full of faith and of the Holy Ghost," Acts 6:5, and "did great wonders and miracles among the people." Acts 6:8. He was stoned to death, Acts 7:59, and is usually called the first martyr. Saul (Paul) was present, "consenting unto his death." Acts 8:1.

Stew´ard, one to whose care is committed the management of the household, Gen. 43:19; Luke 16:1, etc., and so naturally applied to ministers, 1 Cor. 4:1, and Christians. 1 Pet. 4:10. "Steward," in Gen. 15:2, has a different meaning, and is rendered in the Revised Version "he that shall be possessor."

Stocks, Acts 16:24; Jer. 20:2, 3, were instruments for securing the feet of prisoners. They were made of two pieces containing grooves, which, when closed, fitted closely around the leg just above the ankle, and held both limbs firmly in one position. They were also made to confine the arms and the neck.

Sto´ics, a sect of Greek philosophers, among whom contempt of external circumstances and an absolute self-constraint were considered to be chief virtues. Acts 17:18.

Stone, Gen. 49:24, is a name applied to God by Jacob.

Stone is abundant in Palestine, and besides being used for building purposes stones were used as we do knives, Exod. 4:25; as weapons of warfare, being discharged from slings, 1 Sam. 17:40, and from catapults, 2 Chron. 26:14, 15; for millstones, 2 Sam. 11:21; etc. They were set up as boundary marks, Josh. 15:6; to commemorate remarkable events, Josh. 4:4–7; and also served as weights (see marginal notes, Lev. 19:36). Idols were sometimes made of stone. Lev. 26:1; Hab. 2:19.

Stones, Pre´cious. Though about twenty names of precious stones are mentioned in the Bible, it is impossible to identify them positively with the gems we now know by the same names. The same term was often used for different substances that possessed common properties. For example, "crystal" (*kerach*) denotes either ice or rock crystal (transparent quartz). Gems, however, were highly prized by the ancients. They were used in the high-priest's breast-plate, Exod. 28:15–21, and were mentioned by the sacred writers to denote value, beauty, and durability. Isa. 54:11, 12; Rev. 4:3; 21:11, 18–20. For the different precious stones see the separate titles.

Ston´ing was the most general way of inflicting capital punishment. Lev. 20:2, 27; 24:14, 16, 23.

Stork. Jer. 8:7. A bird like the crane, only much larger. It feeds on insects and frogs, and seeks its food in marshes and watery places. It was classed among unclean birds. Lev. 11:19. In flying it presents a noble sight, with its long red legs extending far beyond its tail. It is fond of the society of men, and in the East it is superstitiously protected. It is noted for its tenderness to its young. Ps. 104:17; Zech. 5:9.

Strain at, Matt. 23:24, means "strain out."

Strait, Matt. 7:13, is rendered "narrow" in the Revised Version.

Strait´ly, Gen. 43:7; Mark 1:43, means strictly or sternly.

Strake, Gen. 30:37, means streak. "Strake sail," Acts 27:17, is rendered in the Revised Edition "lowered the gear."

Strange is sometimes used to denote foreign. Exod. 21:8; Neh. 13:27. Its other meanings are clearly indicated by the context

Strang´er. The Jews applied this name to any person of foreign birth or who was not a Jew, even though that person lived among them. Exod. 20:10; 2 Chron. 2:17; Isa. 14:1. It was also applied to one not a priest, Num. 3:10, or of a different family. Mat. 17:25.

Strange Gods, a name often applied in the Bible to the false gods of the various nations. Deut. 32:12; Ps. 81:9.

Straw of wheat and barley was used as fodder. Gen. 24:25, 32. It was also very necessary for making brick. Exod. 5:7-18. As a verb, "straw" means to spread or scatter, Matt. 21:8; 25:24.

Street. 2 Sam. 22:43. In the East the streets are generally made very narrow, in order to secure shade from the hot sun. Mats are sometimes stretched across the streets from roof to roof for the same purpose. Streets were not lighted at night, and the houses rarely having any windows on the street side, travellers were obliged carry a lantern. Men used to spread their rugs and sit at prominent places on the street, Job 29:7, and they also performed their devotions there. Matt. 6:5. To "make streets," 1 Kings 20:34, probably means to obtain commercial advantages.

Strength of Is´rael, 1 Sam. 15:29 is a descriptive title of the God of Israel.

Su´ah (*sweepings*), a chieftain of Asher. 1 Chron. 7:36.

Suc´coth (*booths*). [1] The place to

which Jacob went after leaving Esau, "and built him a house and made booths for his cattle." Gen. 33:17. It was given to Gad. Josh. 13:27. [2] The Israelites' first encampment in the desert after leaving Egypt. Exod. 12:37; Num. 33:5.

Suc´coth-be´noth (*tents of daughters*), an idol of the Babylonians for which they built a temple in Samaria when they settled there. 2 Kings 17:30.

Suchathites, su´kath-ites, a family of scribes which dwelt at Jabez. 1 Chron. 2:55.

Suk-ki´ims, a name of part of the allies of the Egyptian king Shishak who invaded Judea. 2 Chron. 12:3.

Sum´mer. Gen. 8:22. See SEASONS.

Sun. This center of the planetary system and the great source of light and heat was the object of idolatrous worship from the earliest times. Sun-worship existed among all the nations around Palestine, and the Jews themselves burned incense to the sun. 2 Kings 23:5, 11; Ezek. 8:16.

Sun of Right´eous-ness, a title of the Messiah. Mal. 4:2.

Sun´day. See SABBATH.

Superstitious, su-per-stish´us, in Acts 17:22, is more correctly rendered in the Revised Edition "somewhat superstitious" in the text, and "religious" in the marginal notes. The American Revisers prefer "very religious" in the text, which best corresponds to the Greek. Paul was too courteous and prudent to insult and alienate his Athenian hearers by charging them with superstition; he meant rather to compliment them for their overreligiousness that led them to build an altar even to the "unknown God," whom they "unknowingly" (not "ignorantly") worshiped, and whom he came to preach to them.

Sur, one of the gates of the Temple at Jerusalem. 2 Kings 11:6.

Sure´ty, one who is bound with and for another. The danger of this situation is plainly shown in Prov. 6:1; 11:15. To strike or join hands with another, Job 17:3, was a sign of suretyship.

Susa, su´sah, the Greek name for the city called SHUSHAN (which see) in Esther 2:3; 9:11, 18.

Susanchites, su´san-kites, inhabitants of the city of Susa (Shushan). Ezra 4:9.

Susanna, su-zan´nah (*lily*), a woman who "ministered unto" Jesus. Luke 8:3.

Su´si (*horseman*), the father of Gaddi, the spy from Manasseh. Num. 13:11.

Swal´lows still make their nests in the buildings on the site of Solomon's Temple. Ps. 84:3; Prov. 26:2.

Swan is mentioned in the Bible only in Lev. 11:18; Deut. 14:16, where it is said to be unclean. It is very rare in Palestine and neighboring countries.

Swear. Gen. 21:24. **Swear´ing.** Hos. 4:2. See OATH.

Swine or **Hog,** an unclean animal according to the law, Deut. 14:8, is despised both by the Jews and the Mohammedans, and rarely found in Palestine. The occupation of the prodigal son, Luke 15:15, was extremely degrading. Eating swine's flesh is mentioned among sinful practices in Isa. 65:4; 66:17. The herd of swine miraculously destroyed, Matt. 8:32, if it belonged to Jews, was kept contrary to their law.

Sword. The sword in ancient times was short, two-edged, and resembled a dagger. It was carried in a scabbard and suspended from the belt or girdle. Gen. 27:40; Jer. 47:6; Judg. 3:16.

Syc´a-mine, Luke 17:6, is the common black mulberry tree, still called *sycamenea* by the Greeks. It belongs to the same order as the sycamore and the fig.

Syc´a-more (*fig-mulberry*), SYCOMORE in the Authorized Version, a large tree is the common in Egypt and once very abundant in the Jordan valley, but not often found now in Palestine, except near the coast. It closely resembles the common fig tree in it fruit, but has an aromatic leaf shaped like that of the mulberry tree. It bears fruit during over half the year, and its wood is exceedingly durable. Mummycases were made from it. It is entirely different from trees of the same name in the United States and in England. 1 Kings 10:27; 2 Chron 1:15; 9:27; Luke 19:4.

Sychar, si´kar (*drunken*), John 4:5, is commonly supposed to be a name for the city of SHECHEM (which see).

Sychem, si´kem, Acts 7:16, is the Greek form of the name SHECHEM, applied to persons and to a city. See SHECHEM.

Sy-e´ne (*opening* or *key*), a city in the south of Egypt, on the Nile and bordering on Ethiopia. Ezek. 29:10. It was named from the stone called syenite which is quarried there.

Syl´va-nus. See SILAS.

Synagogue, sin´a-gog (*an assemblage*), a meeting of the Jews for prayer and instruction in the law on the Sabbath and at other appointed times. Such meetings were probably not held before the Babylonish captivity, and took place at first in the open air or in private houses. The *buildings* subsequently erected for these meetings were also called synagogues. In Rev. 2:9; 3:9 assemblies of those who profess to be God's people while their hearts were not right with Him are called "synagogues of Satan." The GREAT SYNAGOGUE was a council composed of one hundred and twenty men, who, according to Hebrew tradition, formed the He-brew Canon and established worship in synagogues.

Syntyche, sin´ti-ke (*event*), one of the female members of the church at Philippi. Phil. 4:2.

Syr´a-cuse, a famous ancient city in the eastern part of Sicily, the largest island of the Mediterranean Sea, was settled by the Corinthians B. C. 758 and conquered by the Romans B. C. 212. It has a fine harbor, and was visited by Paul on his voyage to Rome. Acts 28:12.

Syria, seer´i-ah, the Greek name for the country which the Hebrews called ARAM, or "the region of Tyre" (see LEBANON). It was inhabited by the Hittites and other Hamitic tribes. Joshua conquered the country near Hermon and Lebanon, Josh. 11:2-18, and David conquered the Syrians of Damascus. 2 Sam. chapter' 8; 10:6-19. Under David and Solomon Syria was held by the Israelites, but after Solomon's time an independent Syrian kingdom was founded at Damascus, which frequently carried on war with the kingdom of Israel. After the death of Alexander the Great, B. C. 323, a new Syrian kingdom was established under the dynasty of Seleucicæ, to which Judea finally became subject. The valley between the Lebanon and Anti-Lebanon ranges of mountains if called Cœle-Syria, which means *hollow Syria*. Syria became a Roman province B. C. 64. Among its principal cities are Damascus, Antioch, and *Berytus* or *Beirut*.

Syr´i-ack, Dan. 2:4, means the Syrian language.

Syria-maachah, syr´i-ah-ma´a-kah, a region on the north-east border of Palestine. 1 Chron. 19:6.

Syr´i-an, a native of Syria. Gen. 25:20; Luke 4:27.

Syrophenician, si´ro-fe-nish´i-an, a native of that part of Syria which was near Tyre and Sidon. Mark 7:26.

T

Taanach, ta´a-nak, Josh. 12:21, and **Tanach,** ta´nak, Josh. 21:25 (*sandy soil*), a royal city of the Canaanites, was west of the Jordan, and was taken by Joshua. It was in Issachar, but was assigned to Manasseh and became a Levitical city.

Ta´a-nath-shi´loh (*approach to Shiloh*), a landmark on the border between Benjamin and Ephraim. Josh. 16:6.

Tab´ba-oth (*rings*), one of the Nethinim whose descendants returned with Zerubbabel. Ezra 2:43; Neh. 7:16.

Tab´bath (*celebrated*), a place in Issachar or in Ephraim, mentioned in the account of the flight of the host of the Midianites. Judg. 7:22.

Ta´be-al (*God is good*), a Jew whose son the Syrians and Ephraimites intended to make king of Judah. Isa. 7:6.

Ta´be-el (*God is good*), a Persian officer in Samaria. Ezra 4:7.

Tab´e-rah (*a burning*), a place situated in the wilderness of Paran, Num. 11:3; Deut. 9:22, called also KIBROTH-HAT-TAAVAH.

Ta´ber-ing, Nah. 2:7, means to beat as upon the TABRET (which see).

Tab´er-na-cle meant originally simply a tent, Num. 24:5; Job 11:14, etc., but received later a specific meaning as the name of that tent which Moses constructed under divine direction for the worship of the Jews. It is described in Exod. 26, and 36:8-38.

The Tabernacle stood in a court or enclo-sure, one hundred and fifty feet by seventy-five feet, made of canvas screens hung by hooks and fillets of silver from brazen pillars eight feet apart. This enclosure was broken only on the eastern side, where there was an entrance thirty feet wide hung with curtains of fine twined linen embroidered with figures of cherubim. At the upper end of the enclosure, and facing the entrance, stood the Tabernacle. The latter was forty-five feet long, fifteen feet wide, and fifteen feet high. Its two sides and rear were enclosed with boards, each of which had at its lower end two tenons which fitted into silver sockets placed on the ground, and at the top were fastened by bars of acacia wood run through rings of gold. The entrance was hung with costly curtains. The top of the Tabernacle was covered with fine linen embroidered with colored figures of cherubim; over this was goats'-hair cloth, above which was a covering of rams' skins dyed red, and outside of all was another covering which was composed of "badgers' skins." The Tabernacle was divided into two apartments by a veil or richly-wrought curtain extending entirely across it and from top to bottom. This veil is called the "second veil" in Heb. 9:3, because the outside entrance was also curtained. The outer apartment was called the "sanctuary" or "holy place," also the "first tabernacle," and the inner was the "second tabernacle," or the "most holy place," or the "Holiest of all." Heb. 9:2, 3.

Within the court, and opposite the entrance, stood the ALTAR OF BURNT-OFFER-ING (see ALTAR), and between that altar and the Tabernacle was the BRAZEN LAVER, Exod. 30:18, in the form of an urn, and containing water for washing the hands and the feet of the priests before they entered the sanctuary.

In the sanctuary, at the left of a person entering it, stood the golden candlestick, opposite to which, on the right, was the table of shew bread. Beyond the golden candlestick and the table of shew bread, and in front of the ark of the covenant, but separated from it by the "second veil," was the altar of incense. See ALTAR; ARK, No. 3; CANDLESTICK, GOLDEN; and SHEW BREAD.

About nine months' labor was required to complete the Tabernacle, which, with its furniture, was so constructed that it could be conveniently taken down and set up again. It was consecrated to the service of Jehovah with solemn ceremonies, Exod. 30:23-33; 40:9-11; Heb. 9:21, and "a cloud covered the tent of the congregation, and the glory of the LORD filled the tabernacle." Exod. 40:34.

This Tabernacle was built by the Israelites near the close of their encampment at the foot of Mount Sinai, and carried with them in their wanderings in the wilderness, in which they were directed by a cloud. Exod. 40:36-38. The Tabernacle was always placed in the middle of the camp, surrounded by the tents of the priests and the Levites in appointed order, at some distance from which were the tents of the other tribes, in four large divisions. On the arrival at Canaan the Tabernacle was first placed at Gilgal, Josh. 4:19; then at Shiloh, 1 Sam. 1:3; then at Nob, 1 Sam. 21:1-9; and finally, in the reign of David, at Gibeon, 1 Chron. 21:29, where it was when the reign of Solomon began. 2 Chron. 1:1-13.

Two Tabernacles are mentioned in the Old Testament. One was made in the wilderness, and in the other the ark was put by David, where it remained till the Temple was completed. 2 Sam. 6:17; 1 Kings 8:1; 1 Chron. 16:1. The old Tabernacle was meanwhile at Gibeon. Also see Exod. 25-31; 33; 35; 36; 38-40. Lev. 1; 3; 4; 6; 8-10; 12; 14-17; 19; 23; 24; 26. Num. 1-12; 14; 16-20; 24; 25; 27; 31. Deut. 16; 31. Josh. 18; 19; 22. 1 Sam. 2. 2 Sam. 6; 7. 1 Kings 1; 2; 8. 1 Chron. 6; 9; 16; 17; 21; 23. 2 Chron. 1; 5; 8; 24. Ezra 3. Job 5; 11; 12; 15; 18-20; 22; 29; 31; 36. Pss 15; 19; 27; 43; 46; 61; 76; 78; 83; 84; 118; 132. Prov. 14. Isa. 4; 16; 33. Jer. 10. Lam. 2. Ezek. 37; 41. Dan. 11. Hos. 9; 12. Amos 5; 9. Zech. 14. Mal. 2. Matt. 17. Mark 9. Luke 9. John 7. Acts 7; 15. 2 Cor. 5. Heb. 8; 9; 11; 13. 2 Pet. 1. Rev. 13; 15; 21.

Tab'er-na-cles, Feast of, lasting eight days, Num. 29:12-40, was one of the three great feasts of the Jews, and commemorated the long tent-life of the Israelites while journeying through the wilderness. During its celebration the people all lived in booths. Neh. 8:14-18. The feast was held at Jerusalem, and began on the fifteenth day of the seventh month (Ethanim), about the time when the fruits were gathered, and hence it was also called the *feast of ingathering*. Exod. 23:16.

Tabitha, tab´i-thah (*gazelle*). Acts 9:36–40. See DORCAS.

Ta´ble. This, in ancient times, was simply a piece of skin or leather spread on the floor, and served both as a table and a cloth. Later a very low table, not much more than a span high, was used, and in the time of Christ the Jews had adopted the Persian custom of reclining at meals. See EATING, SEATS. "Table," in Exod. 24:12; Prov. 3:3; Luke 1:63; etc., means a tablet for writing. See TABLET.

Tab´let, a flat piece of stone or metal on which to write or engrave. Stones were sometimes covered with plaster, on which, while soft, the characters were traced. Deut. 27:2-4. A framework covered with wax was also employed, on which writing was traced with a pointed instrument called a stylus. Luke 1:63. See WRITING.

TABLETS, Isa. 3:20, means "perfume boxes," and in Exod. 35:22; Num. 31:50, "armlets" or "necklaces."

Ta´bor (*mound, height*). [1] A famous mountain on the north-east edge of the great plain of Esdraelon, and on the border between Zebulun and Issachar, is six miles south-east of Nazareth. Josh. 19:22; Ps. 89:12. Barak gathered his army there to overthrow Sisera. Judg. 4:6-14. Its summit is about two thousand feet above the Mediterranean Sea. It rises from the plain as an isolated mass in the shape of a dome. Tradition makes it the Mount of Transfiguration, but many place that event on Mount Hermon, since it occurred only a few days after Christ's arrival in that region. [2] A city of Zebulun. 1 Chron. 6:77.

Ta´bor, Plain of, 1 Sam. 10:3, in Benjamin, is translated "oak of Tabor" in the Revised Version. See OAK.

Tab´ret, Tim´brel, Gen. 31:27; Judg. 11:34, were musical instruments resembling very nearly, it is supposed, the tambourine. A piece of skin was stretched over a rim like the end of a drum, and on this skin the player beat with one hand while shaking the timbrel with the other. Small bells were also attached to the rim.

Tab´ri-mon (*Rimmon is kind*), the father of Benhadad, king of Syria. 1 Kings 15:18.

Tach´es, Exod. 26:6, fastenings made of gold and of brass, used in connecting the curtains of the Tabernacle.

Tachmonite, tak´mo-nite, 2 Sam. 23:8, the name given to the first of David's valiant men. HACHMONITE, in 1 Chron. 11:11, refers to the same family.

Tack´ling, in Isa. 33:23, refers to the ropes attached to the mast, but in Acts 27:19 it has a wider meaning, and includes the furniture of the ship—in fact, everything except what was necessary for the preservation of the vessel.

Tad´mor (*palms*), a city in the wilderness, built by Solomon, is mentioned twice in the Bible, 1 Kings 9:18; 2 Chron. 8:4, but has never been identified, though it is usually considered to be the ancient *Palmyra*, which lies one hundred and twenty miles north-east of Damascus (a five days' journey on camels), and of which imposing ruins of temples, palaces, colonnades, and tombs remain to this day.

Ta´han (*station*), Num. 26:35; 1 Chron. 7:25, a descendant of Ephraim.

Ta´han-ites, Num. 26:35, the descendants of Tahan.

Ta-hap´a-nes. Jer. 2:16. See TAHPANHES.

Ta´hath (*place*), one of the camping-stations in the wilderness. Num. 33:26, 27.

Ta´hath (*station*). [1] A descendant of Kohath, the son of Levi. 1 Chron. 6:24, 37. [2, 3] Two Ephraimites. 1 Chron. 7:20.

Tah´pan-hes, a city in lower Egypt, on a branch of the Nile. After the capture of Jerusalem by Nebuchadnezzar many Jews fled there, carrying with them Jeremiah and Baruch. Jer. 43:7, 8, 9; 44:1; 46:14. It is called TAHAPANES, Jer. 2:16, and TEHAPHNEHES. Ezek. 30:18.

Tah´pe-nes (*head of the world?*), a queen of Egypt whose sister became the wife of Hadad. 1 Kings 11:19, 20.

Tah´re-a (*cunning*), a son of Micha and a descendant of Saul. 1 Chron. 9:41. He is called TAREA in 1 Chron. 8:35.

Tah´tim-hod´shi, The Land of, a name given to a district lying to the northward of Gilead. 2 Sam. 24:6.

Tale, Exod. 5:8, 18, means count, in distinction from weight or measure.

Tal´ent, a weight, is said to contain three thousand shekels. 1 Chron. 20:2; Matt. 18:24.

Tal´i-tha cu´mi, a Syro-Chaldaic expression, is interpreted in Mark 5:41.

Talmai, tal´may (*brotherly*). [1] A son of Anak. Num. 13:22; Josh. 15:14. [2] A king of Geshur whose daughter was a wife of David. 2 Sam. 3:3; 1 Chron. 3:2.

Tal´mon (*oppressed*), a Levite whose descendants returned with Zerubbabel. 1 Chron. 9:17; Ezra 2:42.

Ta´mah (*laughter*), a Nethinim whose descendants returned with Zerubbabel, Neh. 7:55, called THAMAH in Ezra 2:53.

Ta´mar (*palm tree*). [1] The wife of Er, the son of Judah, and afterward of his brother Onan. Gen 38:6–30. [2] A daughter of David. 2 Sam. chapter 13; 1 Chron.

3:9. [3] One of the daughters of Absalom. 2 Sam. 14:27.

Ta´mar (*palm tree*`), a place on the southeast of Palestine. Ezek. 47:19; 48:28.

Tam´muz (*sprout of life*), Ezek. 8:14, a Syrian idol, corresponding to the Adonis of the Greeks.

Ta´nach, ta´nak. Josh. 21:25. See TAANACH.

Tan´hu-meth (*comfort*), the father of one of Gedaliah's captains. 2 Kings 25:23; Jer. 40:8.

Ta´nis, in the marginal notes, Ezek. 30:14. See ZOAN.

Tan´ner. Among the ancient Jews ceremonial uncleanness was attached to the occupation of the tanner, and hence he was obliged to pursue his calling outside of the town. Acts 9:43; 10:6, 32.

Taphath, ta´fath (*drop*), a daughter of Solomon. 1 Kings 4:11.

Tap´pu-ah (*apple tree*), a son of Hebron, a descendant of Judah. 1 Chron. 2:43.

Tap´pu-ah (*apple-region*). [1] A royal city of the Canaanites which was taken by Joshua, and was in Judah. Josh. 12:17; 15:34. [2] A city of Ephraim, on the border of Ephraim and Manasseh. Josh. 16:8; 17:8.

Ta´rah (*station*), the twenty-third station of the Israelites in their wanderings through the wilderness. Num. 33:27, 28.

Tar´a-lah (*a reeling*), one of the cities of Benjamin. Josh. 18:27.

Ta´re-a, 1 Chron. 8:35. See TAHREA.

Tares, Matt. 13:25, etc., a grass very common in Eastern countries. It is difficult to distinguish it from wheat until the head appears. The grain of tares is poisonous, and even when a small quantity of it is mixed with wheat and made into bread it produces dizziness. The grain, however, is so much smaller than that of wheat that the two can be easily separated.

Tar´get. 1 Kings 10:16; 2 Chron. 9:15. See SHIELD. In 1 Sam. 17:6 the word means "javelin," and is so rendered in the Revised Version.

Tar´pel-ites, an Assyrian tribe some of whom were sent to colonize Samaria after the removal of the Israelites. Ezra 4:9.

Tar´shish, 2 Chron. 9:21, or **Thar´-shish,** 1 Kings 10:22 (*rocky ground?*), is often mentioned in the Old Testament, and always as a distant place and situated on the sea-coast, but it has never been identified. Some considered it the same as Tarsus in Cilicia, and other as *Tartessus* in southern Spain.

Tar´shish. [1] One of the sons of Javan, the grandson of Noah. Gen. 10:4; 1 Chron. 1:7. [2] One of the seven princes of Persia who "saw the king's face." Esther 1:13, 14.

Tar´sus, the birthplace of Paul, Acts 9:11, 20; 11:25; 21:39; 22:3, was the capital of the province of Cilicia in Asia Minor, and stood on both banks of the river Cydnus, in a fertile plain twelve miles north of the Mediterranean Sea. Its schools were celebrated, and ranked next to those of Alexandria and Athens, so that rich people liked to have a pupil from Tarsus for tutor to their sons. There Paul learned the Greek language and acquired some knowledge of Greek literature, although he got his theological (rabbinical) education at Jerusalem under Gamaliel.

Tar´tak (*prince of darkness*), an idol worshipped by the Avites who were removed to Samaria. 2 Kings 17:31.

Tar´tan, 2 Kings 18:17; Isa. 20:1, is the title of the commander of an army.

Tatnai, tat´nay or tat´na-i (*gift*), a governor, under the king of Persia, of the province west of the river Euphrates. Ezra 5:3, 6; 6:6, 13.

Tav´erns, The Three, Acts 28:15, a place thirty-three miles south-east of Rome. Paul met some of "the brethren" there.

Tax´es. Before the time of the kings the taxes of the Hebrews were light and were applied to the support of the priests and Levites, and were called first-fruits, tithes, etc. See FIRST-FRUITS, and TITHES. With the kings came heavier taxes. 2 Kings 23:35. They were levied for almost every conceivable purpose, until finally the ten tribes of Israel rebelled against Rehoboam. 1 Kings 12:4, 18. The foreign nations that became conquerors of the Hebrews burdened them so heavily with taxes that the people were in great distress. See Neh. chapter 5; 9:37. Under the Romans and in the time of Christ the taxes were farmed out, and this led to great extortion and oppression.

Tax´ing, as mentioned in Luke 2:1-3, 5; Acts 5:37, means a writing off, registering, or, as the Revised Version renders it, "enrolment." It was the taking of a census of the people, and its object was taxation. It was held by the order of the Roman emperor, but, according to Jewish custom, the registration was made according to the tribes or families. Luke 2:4.

Tears. The expression "put thou my tears into thy bottle," Ps. 56:8, refers to an ancient custom in which the falling tears of the mourners at funerals were collected and put into an urn or bottle, and preserved as a memorial of the grief of the survivors.

Jesus shed tears of friendship at the grave of Lazarus, and tears of sorrow over the unbelief of Jerusalem.

Te´bah (*slaughter*), one of the sons of Nahor, the brother of Abraham. Gen. 22:24.

Teb-a-li´ah (*Jehovah purifies*), a son of

Hosah, a descendant of Merari. 1 Chron. 26:11.

Te´beth, the tenth month of the Hebrew sacred year and the fourth month of the civil year. Esther 2:16. See MONTH.

Teeth. Figurative references are frequently made to the teeth. Cleanness of teeth, Amos 4:6, denoted a famine. Gnashing the teeth, Matt. 8:12, indicated terror; rage; despair. The Jewish law of retaliation required a tooth for a tooth. Exod. 21:24.

Tehaphnehes, te-haf´ne-heez. Ezek. 30:18. See TAHPANHES.

Te-hin´nah (*cry for mercy*), one of the sons of Eshton, a descendant of Judah. 1 Chron. 4:12.

Teil Tree, in Isa. 6:13, is translated from the same Hebrew word that in Hos. 4:13 is rendered "elm," and in many other passages "oak." See OAK. In all these cases probably the terebinth, a noble looking tree resembling somewhat the oak, is meant. This tree was abundant in Palestine. It furnished a pure quality of turpentine, and was noted for its long life.

Te´kel. Dan. 5:25. See MENE.

Tekoa, te-ko´ah, 2 Chron. 11:6; 20:20; Jer. 6:1; Amos 1:1, and **Te-ko´ah,** 2 Sam. 14:2, 4, 9 (*pitching of tents*), a city of Judah about five miles south of Bethlehem. It was the birthplace and residence of Amos the prophet.

Te-ko´a, the title of a family descended from Hezron, the grandson of Judah. 1 Chron. 2:24; 4:5.

Te-ko´ite, an inhabitant of Tekoa. 2 Sam. 23:26; 1 Chron. 11:28.

Tel´-a-bib (*corn-hill*), a city of Chaldea. It was the residence of Ezekiel. Ezek. 3:15.

Te´lah (*breach*), a descendant of Ephraim. 1 Chron. 7:25.

Tel´a-im (*young lambs*), the place where Saul gathered the forces of Israel when about to attack the Amalekites. 2 Sam. 15:4.

Te-las´sar, Isa. 37:12, and **The-la´sar,** 2 Kings 19:12, a region whose inhabitants were destroyed by kings of Assyria. It may have been in Mesopotamia.

Te´lem (*oppression*), one of the porters of the sanctuary who took a foreign wife. Ezra 10:24.

Te´lem (*oppression*), a city of Judah. Josh. 15:24.

Tel-haresha, tel-ha-re´shah, Neh. 7:61, and **Tel-harsa,** tel-har´sah, Ezra 2:59, a place in Babylonia, some of whose inhabitants returned after the captivity.

Tell, as in Gen. 15:5; 2 Kings 12:10, means to count or number.

Tel-melah, tel-me´lah, (*salt-hill*), a place in Babylonia from which some of the inhabitants returned with Zerubbabel. Ezra 2:59; Neh. 7:61.

Tema, te´mah (*south desert*). [1] One of the sons of Ishmael. Gen. 25:15; 1 Chron. 1:30. [2] An Ishmaelite tribe in northern Arabia descended from Tema, son of Ishmael. The name Tema is also applied to the country occupied by that tribe. Job 6:19; Isa. 21:44; Jer. 25:23.

Te´man (*south desert*). [1] One of the sons of Eliphaz, the son of Esau. Gen. 36:11, 15; 1 Chron. 1:36. [2] An Edomite chief, apparently of a later period. Gen. 36:42; 1 Chron. 1:53. [3] A district east of Edom. Jer. 49:7, 20; Amos 1:12.

Tem´a-ni, Gen. 36:34, and **Te´manite,** Job 2:11; 4:1, the inhabitants of TEMAN, No. 3.

Tem´e-ni, one of the sons of Asher. 1 Chron. 4:6.

Tem´per-ance, Tem´per-ate, Acts 24:25; Gal. 5:23; etc., mean self-restraint, moderation, self-control in all things, eating as well as drinking. In Titus 2:2 "temperate" means prudent or discreet.

Tem´ple, The, stood on Mount Moriah, Jerusalem (See JERUSALEM), and resembled in its general form the Tabernacle. There were three successive temples, built respectively by Solomon, Zerubbabel, and Herod the Great. The last mentioned was the Temple of the time of Christ.

Also see Judg. 4:21, 22; 5:26.

1 Sam. 1:9; 3:3.

2 Sam. 22:7.

1 Kings 6:3, 5, 17, 33; 7:21, 50.

2 Kings 11:10, 11, 13; 18:16; 23:4; 24:13.

1 Chron. 6:10; 10:10.

2 Chron. 3:17; 4:7, 8, 22; 23:10; 26:16; 27:2; 29:16; 35:20; 36:7.

Ezra 3:6, 10; 4:1; 5:14, 15; 6:5.

Neh. 6:10, 11.

Pss. 5:7; 11:4; 18:6; 27:4; 29:9; 48:9; 65:44; 68:29; 79:1; 138:2.

Song of Sol. 4:3; 6:7.

Isa. 6:1; 44:28; 66:6.

Jer. 7:4; 24:1; 50:28; 51:11.

Ezek. 8:16; 41:1, 4, 15, 20, 21, 23, 25; 42:8.

Dan. 5:2, 3.

Hos. 8:14.

Joel 3:5.

Amos 8:3.

Jon. 2:4, 7.

Mic. 1:2.

Hab. 2:20.

Hag. 2:15, 18.

Zech. 6:12-15; 8:9.

Matt. 4:5; 12:5, 6; 21:12, 14, 15, 23; 23:16, 17, 21, 35; 24:1; 26:55, 61; 27:5, 40, 51.

Mark 11:11, 15, 16, 27; 12:35; 13:1, 3; 14:49, 58; 15:29, 38.

Luke 1:9, 21, 22; 2:27, 37, 46; 4:9; 11:51; 18:10; 19:45, 47; 20:1; 21:5, 37, 38; 22:52, 53; 23:45; 24:53.

John 2:14, 15, 19-21; 5:14; 7:14, 28; 8:2, 20, 59; 10:23; 11:56; 18:20.

Acts 2:46; 3:1-3, 8, 10; 4:1; 5:20, 21, 24, 25, 42; 7:48; 17:24; 19:27; 21:26-30; 22:17; 24:6, 12, 18; 25:8; 26:21.

1 Cor. 3:16, 17; 6:19; 8:10; 9:13.

2 Cor. 6:16.

Eph. 2:21.

2 Thess. 2:4.

Rev. 3:12; 7:15; 11:1, 2, 19; 14:15, 17; 15:5, 6, 8; 16:1, 17; 21:22.

I. SOL´O-MON'S TEM´PLE, B. C. 1005–588.—The design, plan, and location of this building were furnished by David, under divine direction. 1 Chron. chaps. 21; 22; 28:11-19. He collected an immense amount of gold, silver, and brass (bronze or copper) for its erection, besides great quantities of iron, stone, timber, etc., although he was forbidden by God from beginning the work. 2 Sam. 7:5-13. The building was commenced by Solomon in the fourth year of his reign. For seven and a half years 183,600 men were working on the Temple—namely, 30,000 Jews in three divisions, 10,000 in each, and 153,600 Canaanites, of whom 70,000 were bearers of burdens, 80,000 were hewers of wood and stone, and 3600 overseers. Its parts were all prepared at a distance from it, and when brought together the Temple was built; nor was the sound of "hammer, nor axe, nor any tool of iron, heard in the house while it was in building." 1 Kings 6:7. The front of the Temple was toward the east, and the dimensions of the Temple proper were ninety feet long, thirty feet wide, and thirty feet high—exactly double those of the Tabernacle, after the fashion of which it was made. There were additions to the building for the priests, etc. The Temple was completed B. C. 1005. The brazen laver, which in the Tabernacle was a simple urn, was represented in the Temple by a great basin resting on twelve brazen bulls. The Holy of Holies was a small square dark chamber. There the ark stood on a rough protuberance of the natural rock on which the Temple was built. On each side stood a golden cherub, and the wings of these figures met above the ark. The connection between this chamber and the sanctuary was through folding-doors of olive-wood hung with costly embroidered linen fabrics.

This Temple was destroyed by Nebuchadnezzar, B. C. 588, after having stood more than four hundred years, but it had been plundered during the reign of Rehoboam, 1 Kings 14:25, 26, by the Egyptian king Shishak, and often afterward. For fifty years after their destruction Jerusalem and Solomon's Temple laid in ruins.

II. ZE-RUB´BA-BEL'S TEM´PLE, B. C. 515–64.—In B. C. 536 permission was given by Cyrus, the Persian conqueror of Babylon, for the captive Jews to return to Jerusalem. Many of them did return with Zerubbabel, governor of Judea, and Joshua (Jeshua), the high-priest. In the second year after their return the foundation of the Temple was laid. Ezra 3:8. The work of rebuilding was superintended by Zerubbabel and Joshua (Jeshua), but was not finished until twenty years later, B. C. 515, on account of the intrigues of the Samaritans and other parties, as recorded by Ezra. It was in nearly all its dimensions one-third larger than Solomon's Temple, but not so magnificent, Ezra 3:12, 13, and, besides, it had no ark of the covenant and no sacred fire. The principal differences between this and the old building, with respect to construction, were the arrangements of the court of worshippers, which was divided into two parts, an outer court for the Gentiles and an inner court and an

inner court for Israel, and the fortress-tower at the north-western corner, which was the residence of the Persian, and afterward of the Roman, governor. This Temple was the scene of more glorious illustrations of the divine attributes than were ever seen in Solomon's Temple, Hag. 2:6–9; Mal. 3:1 and it stood for nearly five hundred years, when it was rebuilt by Herod the Great.

II. HER´OD'S TEM´PLE, B. C. 20–A. D. 70. This is the Temple in which Christ worshipped and the apostles until they were expelled, and the destruction of which was predicted by our Lord. It was not strictly a new building, but rather the second Temple completely repaired. The work was done by Herod the Great to secure the favor of the Jews and to make a great name for himself. It was begun B. C. 20, and the main building was completed in one year and a half, but the whole work was not ended till A. D. 64, under Herod Agrippa II. Solomon's Porch was on the east side. The Temple enclosure had five gates, the gate Shushan being opposite the Temple proper, which was surrounded by several courts of different elevations. The outer court was the court of the Gentiles; next, the court of the women; then the court of Israel; then the court of the priests, next to the Temple itself. Between the court of the Gentiles and the court of the women was the "middle wall of partition" (Eph. 2:14), which had thirteen openings. The Temple was two stories high. Its front was gilded. Before the entrance to the Holy of Holies hung two veils a cubit apart, and consequently no glimpse of what was behind the veil could be obtained by any one but the high-priest. Among the adjoining buildings was the assembly-hall of the

Sanhedrin. This Temple was destroyed by Titus A. D. 70, in literal fulfilment of the prophecy of Christ. Matt. 24:2.

Tempt, Temp-ta´tion. Matt. 22:18; Luke 4:13. These words ordinarily imply enticement or sin. They also denote a trial or a proving. Thus "temptation" in the Lord's prayer, Matt. 6:13, means a trial of our moral nature; for God, being holy, does not tempt men to sin. James 1:13.

Ten Com-mand´ments, Exod. 20:3-17, called by the Jews "The Ten Words," was the name applied to the writing on the two tablets of stone given on Mount Sinai. Five of the commandments enjoin the duties to God, and five the duties to our neighbor. Taken together they form a complete and comprehensive summary of the moral law. Christ summed them up in the two great commandments, "Thou shalt love the Lord thy God with all thy heart, and with all thy soul, and with all thy mind;" and "Thou shalt love thy neighbour as thyself." Matt. 22:37-40.

Tents, Gen. 13:5, were among the earliest dwellings of man, and they were used by the Hebrews until they entered the Promised Land. The ease with which they could be carried from one place to another specially adapted them to the needs of the people of the East, who had to move frequently to find fresh pasturage for their flocks. Tent-making was the trade of Paul by which he supported himself while preaching the gospel.

Tenth Deal, Exod. 29:40; Lev. 14:10; 23:17, means the tenth part, and probably referred to the tenth part of an ephah.

Te´rah (*loiterer*), the father of Abraham, whom he accompanied to Haran, where Terah died. Gen. 11:31, 32.

Ter´a-phim, Judg. 17:5; 18:14, were probably small images resembling the human figure and regarded as household gods. The word is rendered "images," Gen. 31:19, 34, 35; "idolatry," 1 Sam. 15:23; "idols," Zech. 10:2.

Te´resh (*severe*), one of the chamberlains of Ahasuerus, king of Persia. Esther 2:21; 6:2.

Tertius, ter´shi-us (*the third*), a disciple at Corinth, who was Paul's amanuensis when he dictated the Epistle to the Romans. Rom. 16:22.

Ter-tul´lus, an orator (lawyer) who accompanied the high-priest and the elders to Cæsarea to plead before Felix against Paul. Acts 24:1-9.

Tes´ta-ment, Heb. 9:15, etc., when applied to the Scriptures, is used in the same sense as COVENANT (which see). The old covenant (which was a type of the new) is spoken of in Exod. 24:8, and was ratified by the blood of sacrifices. The new covenant, mentioned in Matt. 26:28, was ratified by the blood of Christ. In the Revised Version the word is always rendered "covenant," except in Heb. 9:16, 17, where it evidently refers to the legal instrument called a "will."

Tes´ta-ment, Old, New. See BIBLE.

Tes´ti-mo-ny, a solemn affirmation made for the purpose of establishing or proving a fact. John 8:17. The word is also used to denote the whole revelation of God's will, Ps. 119:88; the two tables of stone on which the Law was written, Exod. 25:16; the ark of the covenant in which those stones were deposited, Exod. 25:22; and the Gospel. 1 Cor. 1:6.

Tetrarch, te´trark, Matt. 14:1, a ruler of the fourth part of a kingdom or province. In the Scriptures it is applied to any one who governed a Roman province. His authority was similar to that of a king, and that title was often given to him. Matt. 14:9.

Thad´dæ-us or **Thad-de´us,** Matt. 10:3; Mark 3:18, one of the twelve apostles. See JUDE.

Tha´hash (*a badger* or *seal*), one of the sons of Nahor. Gen. 22:24.

Tha´mah. Ezra 2:53. See TAMAH.

Tha´mar, Matt. 1:3, the Greek form of TAMAR. See TAMAR, No. 1.

Thank-of´fer-ing, Thanks´giv-ing, 2 Chron. 29:31; Lev. 22:29, the expression of gratitude to God for his mercies and favors. The Hebrews offered thank-offerings on stated and special occasions. Lev. 7:12, 15; Neh. 12:31, 43. See OFFERING.

Thara, tha´rah. Luke 3:34. See TERAH.

Thar´shish (*fortress*), a son of Bilhan, the grandson of Benjamin. 1 Chron. 7:10.

Thar´shish, 1 Kings 10:22; 22:48, a better form of TARSHISH, the city (which see).

The´a-tre. Acts 19:29, 31. The theatre at Ephesus was a building of great grandeur in full view of the temple of Diana. Ruins of its wall still remain.

Thebes, a city of Egypt. See NO-AMON.

The´bez (*brightness*), a town of Ephraim, eleven miles north-east of Shechem. Judg. 9:50; 2 Sam. 11:21.

Theft. Under the Mosaic law this crime was severely punished. Restitution was to be made, and if the thief could not restore he was sold into temporary bondage. Exod. 22:1-4.

The-la´sar. 2 Kings 19:12. See TELASSAR.

The-oph´i-lus (*lover of God*), a noted Christian disciple and friend of Luke, to whom the latter addressed his Gospel and the book of Acts. Luke 1:3; Acts 1:1.

Thes-sa-lo´ni-ans, inhabitants of Thessalonica. Acts 20:4; 1 Thess. 1:1; 2 Thess. 1:1.

Thes-sa-lo´ni-ans, E-pis´tles to. The FIRST EPISTLE was written by Paul from Corinth, A. D. 52, 53, principally for the purpose of correcting certain mistakes which prevailed in Thessalonica with respect to what the apostle had taught there concerning the second advent. As this epistle did not succeed in setting the matter right immediately, it was soon followed by The SECOND EPISTLE, from the same place. These two epistles are the earliest among the Pauline writings, and form the oldest portion of the New Testament Canon.

Thes-sa-lo-ni´ca was the most populous city of Macedonia, a great commercial center, and the seat of a large colony of Jews, who had their synagogue outside the city. Paul visited it, Acts 17:1-14, on his second missionary journey, A. D. 51, coming from Philippi, but after a short stay was compelled to leave the place by the fanaticism of the Jews. The young church, which had been founded, was left in charge of Timothy, and it was his report of the state of affairs, not unfavorable it would seem, which called forth from Paul two epistles to the Thessalonians. An arch at Thessalonica, considerably older than the first century of our era, has an inscription containing the names of seven of the Thessalonian magistrates whom it calls "politarchs," thus confirming the accuracy of the writer of Acts in using this rare word (*in the original*) to describe the "rulers," 17:6, 8, of this city.

Theu´das (*God-given*), a man who persuaded several men to join him in rebellion, but was slain and his followers scattered. Acts 5:36.

Thigh. Putting the hand under the thigh, Gen. 24:2, probably denoted obedience or subjection. The inscription on the thigh mentioned in Rev. 19:16 refers to the custom of conquerors bearing on their weapons and garments their names and deeds. The angel smote Jacob's thigh to show that he had yielded in mercy, and not from force. Gen. 32:25.

Thim´na-thah, a town. Josh. 19:43. See TIMNATH, No. 2.

This´tles and **Thorns.** Gen. 3:18. These plants are abundant in Palestine, and prove very troublesome to the husbandman. Thorns were much used for fuel, Ps. 58:9, and formed durable and impenetrable hedges. Hos. 2:6.

Thom´as (*twin*), one of the twelve apostles. He was also called "Didymus," which means "the twin." Little is known of his history. He would not believe in the resurrection of Christ until he had positive evidence of it, when he exclaimed, "My Lord and my God." He died a martyr. Matt. 10:3; Mark 3:18; Luke 6:15; John 11:16; 14:5; 20:20–29; Acts 1:13.

Thorns. Gen. 3:18. See THISTLES.

Thought. "Take no thought," in Matt. 6:25, 34; Luke 12:11, is rendered in the Revised Version "Be not anxious."

Thou´sand Years. Rev. 20:1-7. See MILLENNIUM.

Three Tav´erns. Acts 28:15. See TAVERNS, THE THREE.

Thresh, Thresh´ing-floor. Threshing in the East was performed by means of the flail, Ruth 2:17, by oxen who trod out the grain, Deut. 25:4, and with a threshing-machine or sledge. Isa. 28:27, 28. The latter was a rude affair, having a heavy frame in which were fitted three or four rollers. The machine was drawn by oxen, and the rollers passing over the grain crushed it out. Another form of threshing-machine consisted of several planks fastened together, through the under side of which projected pieces of flint or sharpened iron. Isa. 41:15. These served as teeth, and tore the husk of the grain in pieces as they passed over it. When the grain had been well loosened it was winnowed (see WINNOWING), and for this purpose the threshing-floors were situated on a hilltop open on all sides to the wind. The threshing-floor was simply a piece of ground that had been levelled and beaten down hard. 1 Chron. 21:15-28. Often a whole village would have but one threshing-floor, each husbandman, in a fixed order, taking his turn in using it.

Throne, Esther 5:1, the seat of a king on state occasions, was an emblem of royalty. Solomon's throne was noted for its magnificence. It is described in 1 Kings 10:18-20.

Through´ly, Matt. 3:12, means thoroughly.

Thum´mim. Exod. 28:30. See **Urim.**

Thun´der is very rare in Palestine from April to September (see SEASONS). It was regarded as Jehovah's voice, Job 37:2; Isa. 30:30, 31, and as a symbol of divine power. 1 Sam. 2:10; Isa. 29:6. "Hot thunder-bolts," Ps. 78:48, is rendered "lightnings" in the marginal notes.

Thy-a-ti´ra, a city of Lydia, Asia Minor, noted for its purple-dyeing industry, is mentioned in Acts 16:14 and Rev. 2:18–29; in the latter place as one of the seven churches of Asia.

Thy´ine-wood, Rev. 18:12, as the highly-prized wood of a small tree that resembled our cedar or arbor-vitæ, and grew in northern Africa. Close-grained, fragrant, and of a beautiful brown color, often variegated by knots, it was peculiarly adapted for fine cabinet-work.

Ti-be´ri-as, a city of Palestine, on the western shore of the Sea of Galilee, was founded by Herod Antipas, A. D. 16-22, and named in honor of the emperor Tiberias. It was for many years after the destruction of Jerusalem the seat of the Jewish Sanhedrin and of Jewish learning. The older Talmud (called the Jewish Talmud) was prepared there. It is mentioned only once in the Bible. John 6:23.

Ti-be´ri-as, Sea of. John 6:1; 21:1. See GALILEE, SEA OF.

Ti-be´ri-us Cæ´sar (TIBERIUS CLAUD-IUS NERO), the step-son of Augustus, Luke 2:1, whom he succeeded as second emperor of Rome. Luke 3:1. He was a cruel despot, reigned twenty-three years, commencing A. D. 14, and was murdered.

Tib´hath (*butchery*), 1 Chron. 18:8, a city of Hadadezer (Hadarezer), called BETAH in 2 Sam. 8:8.

Tib´ni (*building of Jehovah*), an Israelite whom part of the people wished to make king of Israel on the death of Zimri. 1 Kings 16:21, 22.

Ti´dal (*great son*), a "king of nations" who joined Chedorlaomer. Gen. 14:1-9.

Tig´lath-pi-le´ser (*my help is the son of Esarra's,* that is, *Adar*), an Assyrian king who invaded "Galilee, all the land Naphtali," etc., and carried away many captives to Assyria. 2 Kings 15:29. He met Ahaz (who became his dependent) at Damascus, 2 Kings 16:10. He reigned B. C. 747–730. See TILGATH-PILNESER.

Ti´gris, not found in the Authorized Version, is mentioned in the marginal notes, Gen. 2:14, of the Revised Version, where it is said to be the same as HID-DEKEL (which see).

Tik´vah, 2 Kings 22:14, **Tik´vath,** 2 Chron. 34:22 (*expectation*). [1] The father of Shallum, the husband of Huldah the prophetess. [2] The father of Jahaziah. Ezra 10:15.

Til´gath-pil-ne´ser, 1 Chron. 5:6, 26; 2 Chron. 28:20, is a corruption of TIGLATH-PILESER (which see).

Til´ling, Luke 5:19, a thin piece of baked clay, used for covering the roofs of houses. See HOUSES.

Ti´lon (*lofty*), a son of Shimon, a descendant of Judah. 1 Chron. 4:20.

Timæus, ti-me´us (*polluted?*), the father of Bartimæus, a blind man of Jericho, whose sight was restored by Jesus. Mark 10:46.

Tim´brel. Exod. 15:20. See TABRET.

Time. See DAY, HOUR, MONTH, WATCHERS OF THE NIGHT, and YEAR.

Timna, tim´nah, and **Tim´nah** (*restrained*). [1] The concubine of Eliphaz, the son of Esau. Gen. 36:12, 22; 1 Chron. 1:39. [2] One of the chiefs of Edom descended from Esau. Gen. 36:40; 1 Chron. 1:51. [3] A son of Eliphaz, the son of Esau. 1 Chron. 1:36.

Tim´nah (*portion assigned*). [1] A town in the north border of Judah. Josh. 15:10; 2 Chron. 28:18. It is probably the same place as TIMNATH, No. 1. [2] A town in the mountains of Judah. Josh. 15:57.

Tim´nath (*portion assigned*). [1] The place mentioned in Gen. 38:13. It is perhaps the same as TIMNAH, No. 1 (the town). [2] A city of the Philistines and the home of Samson's wife. Judg. 14:1, 2, 5. Probably same as THIMNATHAH.

Tim´nath-he´res (*portion of the sun*), Judg. 2:9, and **Tim´nath-se´rah** (*portion of abundance*), Josh. 19:50; 24:30, a city in Mount Ephraim, given to Joshua by the Israelites. It was his residence and burial-place.

Tim´nite, The, a name applied to Samson's father-in-law. Judg. 15:6.

Ti´mon (*honoring*), one of the seven disciples ordained as deacons by the apostles. Acts 6:5.

Ti-mo´the-us (*honoring God*), Acts 16:1; Rom. 16:21, and elsewhere, the name generally applied to TIMOTHY (which see).

Tim´o-thy (*honoring God*), a favorite

disciple of Paul, was born either at Derbe or at Lystra, both in Lycaonia, Asia Minor. His father was a Greek and a heathen, but both his mother and grandmother were Jewesses, and by them he was instructed in the Old Testament Scriptures. 2 Tim. 3:15. He was converted by Paul, and afterward became his companion. While still a young man he took charge of the church at Ephesus. 1 Tim. 4:12. Tradition makes him bishop of Ephesus. Two of the epistles of Paul are addressed to him. He is also called TIMOTHEUS in the Authorized, but not in the Revised Version, which introduces uniform spelling of proper names.

Tim´o-thy, the First E-pis´tle to, was written by Paul about A. D. 64 (between the first and second Roman captivity). The epistles of Paul to Titus and Timothy are called the "Pastoral Epistles" on account of their contents—instructions concerning pastoral care and church government.

Tim´o-thy, the Sec´ond E-pis´tle to, is the last letter of Paul, written when he was confidently expecting martyrdom, 2 Tim. 4:6-8, and contains his dying counsel to his spiritual son.

Tin was very early known to the Hebrews, Num. 31:22, and was one of the articles brought by the ships of Tyre from Tarshish. Ezek. 27:12. Tin-ore has recently been found in the land of Midian. "Tin," in Isa. 1:25, is rendered "alloy" in the marginal notes of the Revised Version.

Tiphsah, tif´sah (*ford*). [1] A city on the river Euphrates which was the northeastern frontier of the kingdom of Solomon. 1 Kings 4:24. [2] Tiphsah is mentioned in 2 Kings 15:16, and is supposed by some to be the same as Tiphsah, No. 1. Others consider it to be in Palestine, near the city of TIRZAH (which see).

Ti´ras (*desire?*), a son of Japheth. Gen.

10:2; 1 Chron. 1:5.

Ti´rath-ites, a family of scribes which dwelt at Jabez. 1 Chron. 2:55.

Tire, 2 Kings 9:30, to dress or adorn.

Tires, Isa. 3:18; Ezek. 24:23, were ornaments used in dressing the hair, and possibly as necklaces.

Tir´ha-kah (*exalted?*), a king of Ethiopia. 2 Kings 19:9; Isa. 37:9.

Tir´ha-nah (*favor*), one of the sons of Caleb, the son of Hezron. 1 Chron. 2:48.

Tiria, tir´i-ah (*godly fear*), one of the descendants of Judah. 1 Chron. 4:16.

Tirshatha, tir´sha-thah, **The** (*lord of the province*), a title of the governors of Judea, appointed by the king of Persia. Ezra 2:63; Neh. 7:65.

Tir´zah (*charm*), a daughter of Zelophehad. Num. 26:33; Josh. 17:3.

Tir´zah (*delight*), a city of the Canaanites taken by Joshua. Josh. 12:24. It was the capital of the northern kingdom of Israel from the time of Jeroboam till the reign of Omri. 1 Kings 14:17; 15:21, 33; 16:6-17.

Tish´bite, a name applied to the prophet Elijah in 1 Kings 17:1; 21:17, 28; 2 Kings 1:3, 8; 9:36. He is called the Tishbite from his birthplace, probably *Tishbeh*, according to the marginal notes of 1 King 17:1 in the Revised Version. *Tishbeh* is twenty-two miles south of the Sea of Galilee and ten miles east of the Jordan, but is not mentioned in the Authorized Version.

Tis´ri or **Tish´ri,** a month in the Jewish year. See ETHANIM.

Tithes means *tenths*, and refers to a form of taxation, which under Levitical law required the Hebrews to render a certain proportion (one-tenth) of the produce of the earth, herds, etc. to the service of God. Lev. 27:30. This one-tenth went to the Levites, who had no part in the soil and were dependent on their brethren for means of subsistence. The Levites, in turn, gave one-tenth of what they received to the priests. Num. 18:26-28.

Ti´tle, 2 Kings 23:17, means "monument," and is so rendered in the Revised Version.

Tit´tle, Matt. 5:18; Luke 16:17, means a very small particle, and refers to the fine stroke or minute turn which often distinguishes one letter of the Hebrew alphabet from another.

Ti´tus was of Gentile descent and converted under the preaching of Paul. Titus 1:4. He then became the companion of the apostle, and had charge of the church in Crete when Paul wrote his epistle to him.

Ti´tus, the E-pis´tle to, is one of the pastoral epistles of Paul, and was probably written from Asia Minor in A. D. 64. This and the two epistles to Timothy are called the "Pastoral Epistles" on account of their contents—instructions concerning pastoral care and church government.

Ti´zite, The, a name applied to one of David's valiant men. 1 Chron. 11:45.

To´ah (*inclined*), one of the Kohathite Levites, 1 Chron. 6:34, called TOHU in 1 Sam. 1:1.

Tob (*good*), the district beyond Jordan to which Jephthah fled. Judg. 11:3, 5. It is called ISH-TOB in 2 Sam. 10:6, 8.

Tob-ad-o-ni´jah (*good is my Lord Jehovah*), one of the Levites sent by Jehoshaphat to teach the people of Judah the law. 2 Chron. 17:8.

To-bi´ah (*goodness of Jehovah*). [1] A person whose posterity were unable to show their descent. Ezra 2:60; Neh. 7:62. [2] An Ammonite who was a leader in the opposition to Nehemiah. Neh. 2:10, 19; 6:1.

To-bi´jah (*goodness of Jehovah*). [1] One of the Levites sent out by Jeh-

oshaphat through Judah to teach the law. 2 Chron. 17:8. [2] A chief man of the Jews whose descendants returned from Babylon. Zech. 6 10, 14.

Tochen, to´ken (*a measure*), a town of Simeon. 1 Chron. 4:32.

To-gar´mah, descendants of Gomer, the son of Japheth, supposed to have settled in the northern part of Armenia. Gen. 10:3; 1 Chron. 1:6; Ezek. 27:14.

To´hu. 1 Sam. 1:1. See TOAH.

To´i (*wandering*), king of Hamath in the time of David, 2 Sam. 8:9, 10, is also called TOU in 1 Chron. 18:9.

Tola, to´lah (*worm*). [1] A son of Issachar. Gen. 46:13; Num. 26:23. [2] One of the judges of Israel. Judg. 10:1, 2.

To´lad (*birth*), a town of Judah, and afterward of Simeon. 1 Chron. 4:29. It is called ELTOLAD in Josh. 15:30; 19:4.

To´la-ites, descendants of Tola, a son of Issachar. Num. 26:23.

Toll, Ezra 4:13, 30; 7:24, appears as one of the three branches of the king's revenue, and was probably a payment required from those crossing bridges or fords or travelling on the public roads.

Tomb. Matt. 27:60. See BURIAL, SEPULCHRE.

Tongues, Acts 10:46, means languages, especially those foreign to, or unknown by, the speaker.

Tooth. See TEETH.

Top, Judg. 15:8, 11; Isa. 2:21, means "cleft."

To´paz, a precious stone in the highpriest's breastplate, is regarded by many to be the modern chrysolite, a rather soft stone of a greenish tinge. Exod. 28:17; Job 28:19; Rev. 21:20.

Tophel, to´fel (*lime*), Deut. 1:1, a place a little south-east of the Dead Sea.

To´phet, Jer. 7:31; 19:12, and elsewhere, and **To´pheth,** 2 Kings 23:10, a place in the valley of Hinnom where human sacrifices were offered to Molech (Moloch). See HINNOM, VALLEY OF.

Torch´es were pieces of resinous wood or bunches of flax twisted together and covered with an inflammable substance. Zech. 12:6; John 18:3.

Tor-ment´ors, Matt. 18:34, were probably keepers of the prison who endeavored, by torturing the prisoner, to find out if he had any money hidden away.

Tortoise, tor´tis, Lev. 11:29, is rendered "great lizard" in the Revised Version, and probably refers to the *dhabb,* or Arabian lizard, a slow-moving reptile sometimes found two feet long. The Arabs eat it, but according to the Mosaic law it was unclean.

To´u. 1 Chron. 18:9. See TOI.

Touch´ing, Lev. 5:13; Ps. 45:1; Matt. 18:19, means concerning.

Tow, Judg. 16:9; Isa. 1:31, the coarse and broken part of flax. In Isa. 43:17 it means "flax," and the Revised Version renders it "a wick" in the marginal notes.

Tow´er, a high building erected in vineyards, which served as a shelter and refuge for the watchmen and afforded an extensive view of the surrounding country. Isa. 5:2; Matt. 21:33. Shepherds erected towers for similar purposes. Towers were also built on forts, and near the gates of a city for refuge and defense in the time of war. Judg. 9:51.

Tow´er of Ba´bel. See BABEL, THE TOWER OF.

Tow´er of Shechem, she´kem, a castle or fort in the town of Shechem, to which the people fled when Abimelech besieged the town. Judg. 9:46-49.

Tow´er of Si-lo´am. See SILOAM, No. 1.

Town-clerk. Acts 19:35. This official

held a position of great importance in Ephesus. He kept the public records, presided over public gatherings, and performed the duties of the chief magistrate when the latter was away.

Trachonitis, trak-o-ni´tis (*a rugged region*), a Roman province, in New Testament times, north-east of the river Jordan. Luke 3:1.

Tra-di´tions, Matt. 15:2; Gal. 1:14, certain rules which the Jews claimed were given by God to Moses, and which, though not contained in the written law, were handed down by word of mouth from generation to generation.

Trans-fig-u-ra´tion, The, was a supernatural manifestation of the Saviour's inherent glory in which his divinity and mission were most solemnly attested. It took place, most probably, on Mount Hermon. The events connected with the transfiguraton are particularly described in Matt. 17:1-9; Mark 9:2-10; Luke 9:28-36.

Trans-late´, 2 Sam. 3:10; Heb. 11:5, to remove from one place to another; to transfer.

Trav´ail, Job 15:20; Isa. 53:11, means labor; pain; trouble generally.

Treas´ure Cit´ies and **Hous´es,** Exod. 1:11; Ezra 5:17, were fortified cities and well-guarded houses in which the king stored his treasures for safe-keeping. 1 Chron. 27:25.

Treas´ur-y or **Treas´ur-ies,** as in John 8:20; 1 Chron. 9:26, refers to the place in the Temple where gifts were received.

Trench. Besides meaning a ditch, as in 1 Kings 18:32, 35, 38, trench was a name applied to a bulwark or rampart formed by arranging the vehicles and baggage of a camp in a circle. See 1 Sam. 26:5, 7; 2 Sam. 20:15.

Tres´pass-of´fer-ing, Lev. 5:6, an individual sacrifice made for some specific sin or offence. Restitution was first to be made, and then this offering presented to God for an atonement. See OFFERING, and RESTITUTION.

Tri´al. See PRISON, and PUNISHMENT.

Tribe. The descendants of each tribe of the twelve sons of Jacob formed a tribe. Num. 1:4. On his death-bed the patriach Jacob adopted the two sons of Joseph (Ephraim and Manasseh), Gen. 48:5, thus making two tribes of one. In dividing the Promised Land, however, only twelve shares were made, the LEVITES (which see) not receiving any of the land, as they were to minister in the Temple and were to be supported by their brethren. See TITHES. The tribes of the sons of Jacob lived together as one people until after the death of Solomon, when ten of them revolted, forming the kingdom of Israel under Jeroboam. The tribes of Benjamin and Judah remained faithful to Rehoboam, the successor of Solomon, and were known as the kingdom of Judah. For each of the tribes see separate titles. Also see HEBREWS; ISRAEL, KINGDOM OF; JUDAH, KINGDOM OF.

Trib´ute. The tax paid for the support of the government, or levied on a people by their conquerors. Every Hebrew over twenty years of age was obliged to pay a tribute of a half-shekel (about twenty-five cents) for the maintenance of the Temple-service. Exod. 30:13, 14. See TAX, and TITHES.

Tro´as, a city of Mysia, Asia Minor, on the sea-coast, six miles south of the entrance to the Hellespont, was founded by Alexander the Great, but is now only a heap of ruins. It was visited twice by Paul. Acts 16:8-11; 20:5-10.

Tro-gyl´li-um, a seaport of Caria, the south-west province of Asia Minor and nearly opposite the island of Samos, was visited by Paul on his third missionary journey. Acts 20:15.

Trophimus, trof´i-mus (*foster-child*), an Ephesian disciple who accompanied Paul on his return from Greece to Jerusalem. Acts 20:4; 21:29; 2 Tim. 4:20.

Trow, Luke 17:9, means think; believe.

Trum´pet. The difference between this instrument and the HORN (which see), as they were used by the ancient Hebrews, is not known. Silver trumpets were used by the priests alone, to announce the approach of festivals, give signals of war, etc. Num. 10:2-10.

Trum´pets, Feast of. was celebrated on the first day or new moon of the seventh month (Tishri) of the sacred year, which was the New Year's Day of the Jewish civil year. The feast was begun with the sound of trumpets, and, besides the usual sacrifices that took place on the first of each month (see MOON), there was a total cessation from labor and a special burnt-offering into the Lord of a young bullock, a ram, and seven lambs. Num. 29:1-6.

Tryphena, tri-fe´nah a female disciple at Rome to whom Paul sent salutation. Rom. 16:12.

Try-pho´sa, a Roman female disciple to whom Paul sent salutation. Rom. 16:12.

Tu´bal, one of the sons of Japheth. Gen. 10:2; 1 Chron. 1:5 The name Tubal is also applied to his descendants, who apparently settled on the south side of the Black Sea. Ezek. 27:13; 38:2.

Tu´bal-cain (*hammer-blows of the smith?*), a son of Lamech (of the family of Cain) by his wife Zillah, Gen. 4:22, was an instructor of every artificer in brass (copper) and iron.

Tur´tle, Song of Sol. 2:12; Jer. 8:7, and elsewhere, *always* means TURTLE-DOVE (which see).

Tur´tle-dove, Ps. 74:19, a species of

dove found in great numbers in Palestine. It is smaller than the pigeon, differently marked, and has a soft, plaintive note. The Jewish law permitted the poor, who could not afford a more costly sacrifice, to offer two pigeons or turtle-doves, Lev. 12:8, and their use by Joseph and Mary, Luke 2:24, is an evidence of the outward circumstances of Christ's parents. "Turtle" is often used in the Scriptures for turtledove, which it always refers to.

Tu´tors, Gal. 4:2, means "guardians."

Twain, Isa. 6:2, means two.

Tychicus, tik´i-kus, a disciple who accompanied Paul when he left Greece on his way to Jerusalem. Acts 20:4; Eph. 6:21.

Ty-ran´nus (*tyrant*), a man of Ephesus in whose school Paul preached when the Jews had compelled him to stop visiting the synagogue. Acts 19:9.

Tyre or **Ty´rus** (*rock*), an ancient and wealthy city of Phœnicia, was on the Mediterranean coast, twenty miles south of Sidon, from which it was founded as a colony about two thousand years before Christ. In Josh. 19:29 it is spoken of as a strong city, and the relations between its king, Hiram, and David and Solomon were very friendly. Afterward Tyre became very hostile to the Israelites, and partly on that account and partly because of its idolatry it is spoken of by the prophets with great severity. Isa. 23:1, 5, 8, 15-17; Jer. 25:22; 27:3; etc. These prophecies were wonderfully fulfilled. It was besieged, but not taken, by Shalmaneser, B. C. 721, and by Nebuchadnezzar, B. C. 592. After a siege of seven months Alexander the Great took the city, B. C. 332, pillaged and burnt it, and sold the inhabitants into slavery. Nevertheless, it was again a flourishing place in New

Testament times; Paul visited it and spent seven days there. Acts 21:3, 4.

U

U´cal (*I am strong*) is found only in Prov. 30:1. Nothing is known of him except that he was one of those to whom Agur spake. See Prov. 30:1.

U´el (*will of God*), a Jew of the family of Bani, who took a foreign wife. Ezra 10:34.

Uk´naz, the name given in the marginal notes, 1 Chron. 4:15, is the same as KENAZ with a prefix.

U´la-i (*strong water*), a river near Susa (Shushan), flowing from the east into the Euphrates below its junction with the Tigris. Dan. 8:2, 16.

U´lam (*vestibule*). [1] One of the descendants of Manasseh. 1 Chron. 7:16, 17. [2] One of the descendants of the family of Saul. 1 Chron. 8:39, 40.

Ulla, ul´lah (*yoke*), a descendant of Asher. 1 Chron. 7:39.

Um´mah (*community*), one of the cities of Asher. Josh. 19:30.

Un-cir-cum-cis´ion, as in Rom. 4:9, refers to the Gentiles, in contrast with the Jews, who were circumcised. The word was also used to denote impurity or wickedness. Ezek. 44:7.

Un-clean´. Lev. 5:2. See CLEAN.

Un-cov´er. To uncover the head was a sign of grief or mourning, and also a token of captivity. Lev. 10:6; Isa. 47:2.

Unction, unk´shun, 1 John 2:20, means "anointing," and is so rendered in the Revised Version. See ANOINTING.

Un-der-gird´ing the ship, Acts 27:17, was to strengthen the vessel by means of ropes or cables called "helps." See HELPS; SHIPS.

Un-der-set´ters, 1 Kings 7:30, 34, were projections on the bases of the brazen laver. They may have served as supports or ornaments.

U´ni-corn, Num. 23:22; Job 39:9; Ps. 22:21, and elsewhere, does not mean the fabulous animal known to us by that name, but the "wild ox," and it is thus rendered in the Revised Version.

Un-leav´ened Bread, Exod. 12:15, 17, was made very thin and from unfermented dough, and was broken, not cut. For the PASSOVER (which see) unleavened bread was prescribed, and hence that festival was often called the "Feast of the Unleavened Bread." Luke 22:1.

Un´ni (*depressed*). [1] One of the Levites appointed for the choral service of the Tabernacle. 1 Chron. 15:18, 20. [2] A Levite who returned from Babylon. Neh. 12:9.

Un-to´ward, Acts 2:40, means perverse; crooked.

Un-wit´ting-ly, Lev. 22:14; Josh. 20:3, 5, means unintentionally.

Upharsin, u-far´sin. Dan. 5:25. See MENE; PERES.

U´phaz, Jer. 10:9; Dan. 10:5, a region where gold was found, is probably same as OPHIR (which see).

Up´per Coasts, Acts 19:1, means the countries of Galatia and Phrygia, in Asia Minor, where Paul passed through on his third missionary journey.

Up´per-most Rooms, Mark 12:39, is rendered in the Revised Version "chief places."

Ur (*light*), the father of Eliphal, one of David's valiant men, 1 Chron. 11:35, called AHASBAI in 2 Sam. 23:34.

Ur of the Chaldees, kal´dees (*light?*), the place where Abram lived before he

was called to go into Canaan. Gen. 11:28, 31; 15:7. Stephen spoke of it, Acts 7:2, as being in Mesopotamia It was probably in the extreme north of that country, near the source of the river Tigris.

Ur´bane (*polite*), a disciple at Rome to whom Paul sent salutation. Rom. 16:9.

U´ri (*fiery*). [1] The father of Bezaleel. Exod 31:2; 35:30; 38:22; 1 Chron. 2:20; 2 Chron. 1:5. [2] The father of Geber. 1 Kings 4:19. [3] A porter who took a foreign wife. Ezra 10:24.

U-ri´ah. [1] 2 Sam 11:3, 6 and elsewhere. A Hittite, one of David's valiant men, who was the husband of Bathsheba. He is also called URIAS. David caused his death, that his own guilt concerning Bathsheba might be concealed and that she might become his wife. 2 Sam. 11:14-17. [2] A priest whom Isaiah took as a witness. Isa. 8:2. See URIJAH, No. 1.

U-ri´as. Matt. 1:6. See URIAH, No. 1.

U-ri-el (*fire of God*). [1] One of the Levites, of the family of Kohath. 1 Chron. 6:24 [2] Chief of the Kohathites. 1 Chron. 15:5, 11. [3] The father of Michaiah. 2 Chron. 13:2.

U-ri´jah (*flame of Jehovah*). [1] A priest in Jerusalem in the time of King Ahaz. 2 Kings 16 10, 11. See URIAH, No. 2. [2] The son of Shemaiah. Jer. 26:20–23. [3] A priest, the father of Meremoth. Neh. 3:4, 21. May be the same person mentioned in Neh. 8:4.

U´rim and Thum´mim (*light and perfection*). The Scriptures do not describe Urim and Thummim, nor does Jewish tradition give any information. It was placed in the high-priest's breastplate in order to be upon his heart when he went in before the Lord, and was the medium through which the divine will was sought and made known. Exod. 28:30; 1 Sam. 28:6.

U´su-ry, in the Scriptures, means simply interest, and has not the significance that is now attached to the word. Exod. 22:25; Lev. 25:36. The Mosaic law forbade the Jews receiving any interest from each other for the loan of money or anything else, though they might require interest of strangers.

U´tha-i (*Jehovah succors*). [1] One of the descendants of Pharez, the son of Judah. 1 Chron. 9:4. [2] A chief man of the Jews who returned from Babylon with Ezra. Ezra 8:14.

Ut´ter, Ezek. 42:1, 3, etc., means outer.

Ut´most Sea, Joel 2:20; Deut. 34:2, means Mediterranean Sea.

Utter-most Sea, Deut. 11:24, means Mediterranean Sea.

Uz (*fruitful in trees*). [1] One of the sons of Aram, the son of Shem. Gen. 10:23; 1 Chron. 1:17. [2] One of the sons of Dishan, of the family of Seir. Gen. 36:28; 1 Chron. 1:42.

Uz, The Land of (*fertile land*), the country of Job, was probably that part of Arabia which is east of Edom and south of Trachonitis. Job 1:1; Jer. 25:20; Lam. 4:21.

U´za-i (*strong*), a Jew whose son Palal repaired part of the wall of Jerusalem. Neh. 3:25.

U´zal, one of the sons of Joktan. His descendants settled in south-western Arabia (Yemen) and founded the city of *Uzal*, afterward Sanaa, capital of Yemen. Gen. 10:27; 1 Chron. 1:21.

Uzza, uz´zah (*strength*). [1] One of the inhabitants of Jerusalem, who owned the garden in which Manasseh, king of Judah, and his son Amon were buried. 2 Kings 21:18, 26. [2] An Israelite of the tribe of Benjamin. 1 Chron. 8:7. [3] The founder of a family of Nethinim that returned with Zerubbabel. Ezra 2:49; Neh. 7:51.

[4] A descendant of Merari, the son of Levi. 1 Chron. 6:29. [5] A son of Abinadab. 1 Chron. 13:7-11. See UZZAH.

Uz´za, Gar´den of. 2 Kings 21:26. See UZZA, No. 1.

Uz´zah (*strength*), one of the sons of Abinadab. He was miraculously killed for touching the ark of God (see Num. 4:15) while it was being carried back from the country of the Philistines. 2 Sam. 6:3-8. Called UZZA. 1 Chron. 13:7-11. See UZZA, No. 5.

Uz´zen-She´rah (*ear of Sherah*), one of the cities of Sherah. 1 Chron. 7:24.

Uz´zi (*might of Jehovah*). [1] A descendant of Aaron through Phinehas. 1 Chron. 6:5; Ezra 7:4. [2] A grandson of Issachar. 1 Chron. 7:2, 3. [3] A son of Bela, the son of Benjamin. 1 Chron. 7:7. [4] A Benjamite whose descendants dwelt in Jerusalem after the captivity. 1 Chron. 9:8. [5] An overseer of the Levites in Jerusalem after the return from Babylon. Neh. 11:22. [6] A priest of the family of Jedaiah. Neh. 12:19. [7] A priest who assisted Ezra in dedicating the walls of Jerusalem. Neh. 12:42. Perhaps same as No. 6.

Uzzia, uz-zi´ah (*strength of Jehovah*), one of David's valiant men. 1 Chron. 11:44.

Uz-zi´ah (*might of Jehovah*). [1] A son and successor of Amaziah, king of Judah, 2 Kings 15:13; 2 Chron. 26:1, 3, and elsewhere, is also called AZARIAH. He reigned fifty-two years, but was smitten with leprosy by the LORD. 2 Kings 15:2-5. See AZARIAH, No. 3. [2] A descendant of Kohath the son of Levi. 1 Chron. 6:24. [3] The father of Jehonathan, one of David's officers. 1 Chron. 27:25. [4] A priest who took a foreign wife. Ezra 10:21. [5] A man of Judah whose son lived in Jerusalem after the captivity. Neh. 11:4.

Uz-zi´el or **Uz´zi-el** (*might of Jehovah*). [1] A son of Kohath, the son of Levi, Exod. 6:18; Lev. 10:4, was the ancestor of the UZZIELITES. [2] A captain of the Simeonites who destroyed the remnants of the Amalekites. 1 Chron. 4:42, 43. [3] A son of Bela, the son of Benjamin. 1 Chron. 7:7. [4] One of the sons of Heman. He was a Levite musician, 1 Chron. 25:4; is called AZAREEL in 1 Chron. 25:18. [5] One of the Levites who cleansed the house of the LORD in the time of Hezekiah. 2 Chron. 29:14-19. [6] A Jew who aided in repairing the walls of Jerusalem. Neh. 3:8.

Uz-zi´el-ites, Num. 3:27; 1 Chron. 26:23, were the descendants of UZZIEL, No. 1.

V

Vag´a-bond means simply a wanderer, fugitive, and in Acts 19:13 the Revised Version renders it "strolling."

Vajezatha, va-jez´a-thah (*strong as the wind*), a son of Haman, the enemy of the Jews. Esther 9:9.

Vail or **Veil**, in early times, was worn only on special occasions, Gen. 24:65; 38:14; the Hebrew women generally appearing in public without veils. Gen. 12:14; 1 Sam. 1:12. The veil is now, however, an indispensable portion of a woman's dress in the East (especially among the Mohammedans), where custom forbids her face being seen by any man except her husband. See GARMENTS.

Veil of the Tab´er-na-cle or **Tem´ple.** See TABERNACLE and TEMPLE.

Val´ley gate, one of the gates of Jerusalem. 2 Chron. 26:9.

Va-ni´ah (*weak*), a Jew of the family of Bani. He took a foreign wife. Ezra 10:36.

Van´i-ty, Job 7:3; Eccles. 1:2, means emptiness; giving no satisfaction.

Vash´ni means "second," and by a curious error is applied in 1 Chron. 6:28 to JOEL, the oldest son of the prophet Samuel. It refers to ABIAH, his *second* son.

Vash´ti (*a beautiful woman*), the queen whom Ahasuerus, king of Persia, repudiated, and who was succeeded by Esther. Esther 1:9.

Vat. See PRESS, PRESS FATS, etc.

Ve-a´der. See MONTH.

Ven´geance does not necessarily imply a revengeful state of mind. The word rather denotes retribution or punishment inflicted as an act of justice. Gen. 4:15; Deut. 32:35; Rom. 12:19, and elsewhere.

Ven´i-son, Gen. 25:28, means the flesh of beasts taken in hunting.

Ver-mil´ion, a bright red coloring substance much prized in the East for ornamenting dwellings and painting images. Jer. 22:14; Ezek. 23:14

Vi´al, 2 Sam. 10:1, probably was a vessel similiar to the CENSER (which see).

Vile, Jer. 15:19; James 2:2, means beggarly; valueless; worthless.

Vine, Vineyard, vin´yerd. The vine was among the first plants cultivated, and a vineyard is mentioned among the possessions of Noah. Gen. 9:20. Vines were usually planted in rows, generally on the southern slope of a hill, and were supported by strong stakes, by trellises or arbors, and sometimes by heaps of stones over which the vines crept, and which offered a dry and warm exposure for ripening the fruit. The vineyards were enclosed with a hedge or wall to protect the vines from the ravages of wild beasts. Ps. 80:8–13, and towers were erected in them for the watchmen. Matt. 21:33. See WINE.

Vin´e-gar was the name applied to a kind of sour wine used as a beverage. Num. 6:3; Matt. 27:48; etc. In Prov. 10:26; 25:20 it probably refers to the common sharp vinegar.

Vine of Sod´om. Deut. 32:32. See SODOM, VINE OF.

Vi´ol, Isa. 5:12; Amos 6:5, a stringed instrument of music, supposed to be similar to the PSALTERY (which see).

Vi´per, Job 20:16, is used in the Old Testament probably to designate a *certain* hissing and venomous serpent. In the New Testament it is used in reference to *any* poisonous snake. Acts 28:3.

Vis´ion, Dan. 2:19; 7:2, was the means God often employed in early times to reveal himself and his will to men.

Vophsi, vof´si (*my increase*), father of Nahbi, the spy from Naphtali. Num. 13:14.

Vow, Gen. 28:20-22, a solemn promise or covenant with God, binding one to do certain things by his help.
Also see Gen. 31:13.
Lev. 7:16; 22:18, 21, 23; 23:38; 27:2, 8.
Num. 6:2, 5, 21; 15:3, 8; 21:2; 29:39; 30:2-14.
Deut. 12:6, 11, 17, 26; 23:18, 21-23.
Judg. 11:30, 39.
1 Sam. 1:11, 21.
2 Sam. 15:7, 8.
Job 22:27.
Pss. 22:25; 50:14; 56:12; 61:5, 8; 65:1; 66:13; 76:11; 132:2.
Prov. 7:14; 20:25; 31:2.
Eccles. 5:4, 5.
Isa. 19:21.
Jer. 44:25.
Jon. 1:16; 2:9.
Nah. 1:15.
Mal. 1:14.
Acts 18:18; 21:23.

Vul´gate, the Latin Version of the Bible made by Jerome in about A. D. 400. It is "the Authorized Version" in the Church of Rome. See BIBLE.

Vul´ture, a greedy and filthy bird, unclean under the ceremonial law. Deut. 14:13. Vultures flocked to battle-fields to feed upon the unburied dead. Isa. 34:15. Its sight is very acute. Job 28:7. The Egyptian vulture (Pharaoh's hen) is common in Egypt.

W

Wa´fer, a thin cake made of fine flour and used in various offerings, anointed with oil. Exod. 29:2; Num. 6:15, 19.

Wa´ges. The law required that wages should be paid daily, Lev. 19:13; Deut. 24:14, 15, and failure to pay for services received is denounced. Jer. 22:13; Mal. 3:5. In the time of Christ a laborer received "a penny" (in Greek a *denarius*, that is, a silver coin worth about fifteen cents) a day for his work. Matt. 20:2-13. In very early times wages were paid in produce or in kind. Gen. 29:15-18; 30:28.

Wag´on. The Egyptian wagon was a very simple affair resembling our cart, and the wagons mentioned in Num. 7:3, 8 for carrying the Tabernacle were no doubt similarly constructed. Two solid wooden wheels were connected by an axle on which rested the body. Vehicles of any kind are but little used in the East, where travellers and merchandise are carried on the backs of mules, horses, and camels.

Wall of Par-ti´tion. Eph. 2:14. See PARTITION, MIDDLE WALL OF.

Walls. Num. 13:28. As a means of defence Eastern cities were generally surrounded with walls, on which houses and towers were often erected. Josh. 2:15. The walls were made of clay, earth, or sun-dried brick, and though built very thick to insure strength and permanency, they were constantly liable to serious damage from heavy rains or from some defect in their construction. Ps. 62:3; Isa. 30:13.

War. Gen. 14:2. Among the ancients every citizen was a soldier. Their wars were virtually hand to hand combats, carried on with great vigor and ferocity. Mercy was seldom shown the vanquished, unless to make him a slave, and the number of the slain was often appalling. The sword, bat-tle-axe, dart, spear, javelin, bow and arrow, and the sling were the weapons in the hands of the combatants, while shields and targets were used to protect their bodies. Machines for hurling heavy stones in a measure took the place of artillery, and the BATTERING-RAM (which see) was employed to make breaches in the walls of a city through which the besiegers could enter. The CHARIOT (which see), however, was the most dreaded of all the equipments of war. The army was divided into companies, each having its commander or captain. Among the Hebrews these divisions had some ref-erence to the several families or tribes, and the heads of families were their officers. The armies were led by their kings or com-manders-in-chief who were attended by ARMOR-BEARERS (which see). The end of wars is prophesied. Isa. 2:4; Mic. 4:3.

Ward means a room in a prison, a guard room, and also applied to the guards or to persons set aside for any certain duty. The context generally makes clear the par-ticular application of the word. Gen. 40:3; 1 Chron. 9:23; Neh. 12:25, 45; Ezek. 19:9.

Ware. Acts 14:6. "Were ware" is translat-ed "became aware" in the Revised Version.

Wash, Wash´ing. Mark 7:3, 4. The Jews laid great stress on frequent ablu-tions. The water was not first poured into a basin as is common with us, but the ser-vant poured the water from a pitcher on his master's hands, and the basin was used simply to receive the falling water. 2 Kings 3:11. See FOOT, HAND.

Watch´es of the Night. Originally the Hebrews divided the night (from sunset to sunrise) into three watches: "the beginning of the watches," "the middle watch," and "the morning watch," but after the captivi-ty they adopted the custom of the Romans and Greeks and divided the night (twelve hours from 6 P. M. to 6 A. M.) into four watches of three hours each, called re-spectively "even," "midnight," "cock-crow-ing," and "morning." Judg. 7:19; 1 Sam. 11:11; Matt. 14:25; Luke 12:38.

Watch´man. Besides protecting the city and its inhabitants from violence the watchmen were required to call out, as they patrolled the streets, the hours of the night. Watchmen were also stationed at the gates of the city and in the towers on its walls. 2 Sam. 18:24-27; Song of Sol. 5:7; Isa. 21:11, 12.

Wa´ter. During the long seasons of drouth, which periodically occurred in Palestine and other countries of the East, man and beast were likely to suffer great distress, to guard against which great care was taken to collect the rain- and spring-water in cisterns or reservoirs. See CISTERN, PIT, and POOLS. Eccles. 2:6; Isa. 22:9-11. When used figuratively, water is the symbol of purification and regeneration, as in the case of baptism. John 1:26; 3:5; etc.

WELLS were also provided, especially where the flocks were pastured, and as they were generally very deep and required great labor to dig and maintain them, they were regarded as very valuable and their possession was often coveted. Gen. 21:25; 26:14-21. The water was usually drawn from wells by means of a pitcher fastened to a rope. See BEER-SHEBA, and JACOB'S WELL.

Wa'ter of Jeal'ous-y was a mixture prescribed as a test in cases where a woman was accused by her husband of adultery. See Num. 5:11-31.

Wa'ter of Pu-ri-fi-ca'tion or **Sep-a-ra'tion,** Num. 19:2-10, 17-22, was sprinkled upon a person defiled by contact with the dead.

Wa'ter-pots, John 2:6, were vessels for holding water which was used by the family and guests for washing the hands and feet. See WASHING.

Wa'ters of Me'rom, a lake or marsh situated near the foot of Mount Lebanon, and through which the river Jordan flows. Josh. 11:5, 7.

Wa'ters of Strife, the name given by the prophet Ezekiel to a place in the wilderness through which the Israelites wandered. Ezek. 47:19; 48:28. See MERIBAH.

Wave-of'fer-ing, Exod. 29:24–28, was a peculiar feature in the service of the peace-offering. The right shoulder of the animal sacrificed was "heaved" upward, and the breast "waved," from side to side, before the Lord. Lev. 10:14, 15.

Wax, Pss. 22:14; 68:2; 97:5; Mic. 1:4, refers to the well-known substance made from the combs of bees. The word elsewhere in the Scriptures is used as a verb, and means to grow or become. Luke 2:40.

Weap'ons. Deut. 1:41. See separate titles; also ARMS, ARMOR, and WAR.

Wea'sel, Lev. 11:29, was classed among unclean animals. The name probably includes the polecat and ichneumon, very common in Palestine.

Weav'er. Exod. 35:35. The art of weaving was probably learned by the Hebrews during their sojourn in Egypt, for mention is made of curtains of goats' hair, woollen garments, etc. having been produced after their departure from that country and during their wanderings. Exod. 26:1, 7; 28:4, 39; Lev. 13:47. No mention of the loom is made in the Scriptures, though the shuttle, beam, and pin are referred to. Judg. 16:14; 1 Sam. 17:7; Job 7:6. See SPIN, SPINDLE.

Wed'ding Gar'ment. Matt. 22:11. The host provided the wedding garments and required all those who attended the feast to wear them.

Week. Besides the week of seven days, from one Sabbath to another, the Jews also observed a week of years, or seven years, and a week of seven times seven years. See SABBATICAL YEAR, and JUBILEE, THE YEAR OF. They had no special names for the days of the week, designating them simply as the first day, second day, etc. Matt. 28:1. See SABBATH.

Weeks, Feast of. Exod. 34:22. See PENTECOST.

Weights. The subject of Hebrew weights is very obscure. The principal weight was the shekel, which varied with the value of the metal weighed by it. See SHEKEL in the following list.

The weights mentioned in the Bible are as follows:

A gerah was the twentieth part of the shekel of the sanctuary, which was of silver.
A bekah was equal to half a shekel of the sanctuary.
A shekel of gold weighed 132 grains; a shekel of silver, 220 grains; a shekel of copper, 528 grains.
A maneh was equal to one hundred

shekels, about three pounds.

A talent was about 3000 shekels.

A mina, in marginal notes, Luke 19:13, is translated pound in the text, and was twelve ounces and a half.

Pound, in the Old Testament, is used as the translation of the Hebrew Manah (which see). It has the same meaning in John 12:3; 19:39.

Wells. Gen. 26:15. See WATER, JACOB'S WELL, and BEER-SHEBA.

Wench, 2 Sam. 17:17, is translated "maidservant" in the Revised Version.

Whales, Gen. 1:21, evidently refers to great sea-monsters, without designating any particular species. The white shark in the Mediterranean Sea reaches an enormous size, and is very likely the "great fish" (correct translation) mentioned in Jonah 1:17; Matt. 12:40. See JONAH, BOOK OF.

Wheat, Matt. 13:25, was the most important of all grains cultivated in Palestine, and vast quantities of it were produced. It was sown late in the fall and harvested in May. The many-eared variety, or mummy-wheat, was cultivated in Egypt, and is the kind referred to in Pharaoh's dream. Gen. 41:22. In the Authorized Version wheat is mentioned under the general name CORN (which see). The "meat-offerings" rendered in the Revised Version "meal-offerings," were all made of wheat flour. Lev. 2:1. See MILL, THRESHING, etc.

Whis´per-er, Prov. 16:28; Rom. 1:29; 2 Cor. 12:20, means a secret informer; a slanderer.

Whit´ed Sep´ul-chres. Matt. 23:27. See SEPULCHRE.

Wid´ow. The Mosaic law carefully guarded the rights of widows and orphans, and the Scriptures show their claims for care and protection.

Wife. Though the Mosaic law discouraged polygamy, it prevailed among the Hebrews up to the time of the captivity. A distinction, however, was always made between the chief wife and the secondary wives, and to that extent, at least, the principle of monogamy was observed. The New Testament goes back to the primitive monogamy; for God gave to Adam only one wife. Hence polygamy is forbidden in all Christian countries. See MARRIAGE, and DIVORCE.

Wil´der-ness, Exod. 14:3, sometimes means an extensive uncultivated region affording excellent pasturage. The wildernesses of Beer-sheba, Beth-aven, En-gedi, etc. were of this kind. Wilderness is also called DESERT.

THE WILDERNESS in which the Israelites wandered forty years on their way from Egypt to Canaan is included in the peninsula of SINAI (which see). Deut. 1:1; 8:2; Josh. 5:6.

Wil´der-ness-es. The following are the principal ones mentioned in the Bible:

Be´er-she´ba, south of the city of Beer-sheba and in Simeon. Gen. 21:14.

Beth-a´ven, in the north of Benjamin and a little east of Bethel. Josh. 18:12.

Da-mas´cus, near the city of Damascus, Syria. 1 Kings 19:15.

E´dom, south and east of the Dead Sea. 2 Kings 3:8.

En-ge´di, on the west side of the Dead Sea, in Judah. 1 Sam. 24:1.

E´tham, Num. 33:8, on the east side of the western gulf (Suez) of the Red Sea.

Gib´e-on, apparently on the west of Gibeon, and in Benjamin. 2 Sam. 2:24.

Jer´u-el. 2 Chron. 20:16. See JERUEL, WILDERNESS OF.

Ju´dah, in the south of Judah. Judg. 1:16; Ps. 63, title.

Ka´desh, near Kadesh-barnea. Ps. 29:8.
Ked´e-moth, east side of the Dead Sea and north of the river Arnon. Deut. 2:26.
Ma´on, west side of the Dead Sea toward its south end. 1 Sam. 23:24, 25.
Mo´ab, part of the land of Moab nearly east of the Dead Sea. Deut. 2:8.
Pa´ran. Gen. 21:21; Num. 10:12; 12:16; 13:3, 26; 1 Sam. 25:1. See PARAN.
Red Sea, Exod. 13:18, same as ETHAM.
Shur, near western gulf (Suez) of Red Sea, on its east side. Exod. 15:22.
Sin. Exod. 16:1; 17:1; Num. 33:11, 12. See SIN, WILDERNESS OF.
Sinai, si´nay, si´ny or si´na-i, in vicinity of Mount Sinai, apparently mostly on north side. Exod. 19:1; Num. 1:1, 19; etc. See SINAI.
Zin. Num. 13:21; Deut. 32:51; etc. See ZIN, WILDERNESS OF.
Ziph, zif. 1 Sam. 23:14, 15; 26:2. See ZIPH, WILDERNESS OF.

Wil´low. This tree flourished in marshy places and along the banks of rivers, and before their captivity the Jews regarded it as an emblem of joy, and bore its branches before the Lord in token of rejoicing during the FEAST OF TABERNACLES (which see). The weeping willow, also called the Babylonian willow, is probably alluded to in Ps. 137:2. After the captivity the willow became an emblem of mourning.

Wil´lows, Brook of the, Isa. 15:7, on southern boundary of Moab, flows into the south-east extremity of the Dead Sea.

Wim´ples, Isa. 3:22, is rendered "shawls" in the Revised Version.

Win´dows in houses in the East were simply openings in the wall for light and air, and were protected, at times, by lattice-work, glazed windows being unknown. The windows usually opened on the inner court,

but there sometimes was one in the front of the house, opening on a sort of porch or balcony, and used only on special occasions. 1 Sam. 19:12; Prov. 7:6. See HOUSES.

Winds. Palestine is bounded on the south and east by a great desert, and hence the winds from those directions are hot and dry, the east wind in particular being very injurious to vegetation. Winds from the south-west and north bring fair weather, while the west wind, coming from the Mediterranean Sea, brings rain. Prov. 25:23; Luke 12:54, 55.

Wine was a common beverage of the ancient Hebrews, as well as Greeks and Romans and other nations. It was kept in every household and offered on occassions of hospitality and festivity. Gen. 14:18. Its misuse, however, is strongly condemned in the Scriptures. Prov. 20:1; 23:29–32; Isa. 28:1–7. Mixed wine, Ps. 75:8; Prov. 23:30, was wine made stronger by adding spices, herbs, and drugs. In the article GRAPES and VINE (which see) mention is made of the cultivation of the fruit from which wine was principally made, and the method commonly adopted for expressing the juice is treated in the article PRESS, PRESS-FATS (which see). The new wine was preserved in large earthen vessels or jars, and also in bottles made from goats' skins that were fresh and pliable, the better to withstand the strain caused by fermentation. See BOTTLES.

Wine´bib-ber, Matt. 11:19, means an immoderate drinker of wine.

Wine-fat, Wine-press. Isa. 63:2, 3. See PRESS.

Win´now-ing. The threshing-floors of the Hebrews were situated on a hill-top exposed on all sides to the wind, and they winnowed their grain by throwing it up in the air by means of a shovel, and letting the wind carry off the chaff and straw. Sometimes the operation was aided by means of the fan. Ruth 3:2; Isa. 30:24; 41:15, 16.

Win´ter. Gen. 8:22. See SEASONS.

Wise. "Shalt in any wise rebuke," Lev. 19:17, is translated "shalt surely rebuke" in the Revised Version.

Wise Men. Matt. 2:1. See MAGI.

Wist, Exod. 16:15; 34:29; Mark 14:40, means knew.

Wit, to: "do you to wit of," 2 Cor. 8:1, is "make known to you" in the Revised Version.

Witch. Exod. 22:18. See WITCHCRAFT.

Witch´craft, 2 Chron. 33:6, was the pretended communication with demons and the spirits of the dead, by means of which the pretender professed to reveal future events, cure diseases, drive away evil spirits, etc. Wizard was a name given to the man, and witch to the woman, who practiced witchcraft. Witchcraft is most severely denounced in the Scriptures. Lev. 20:6; Deut. 18:10-12; Gal. 5:19-21.

With-out´, 2 Cor. 10:13, 15, is translated "beyond" in the Revised Version.

Withs, or **Withes,** in the Revised Version, were bands made by twisting together pliable twigs, and were used in place of ropes. Judg. 16:7-9.

Wit´ness. By the Mosaic law the evidence of at least two witnesses was required to convict the prisoner, Deut. 17:6, and if the latter was condemned to be stoned, the witnesses were obliged to cast the first stones. Deut. 17:7. A false witness was to receive the punishment which he had endeavoured to bring upon the prisoner by his testimony. Deut. 19:19.

Wit´ting-ly, Gen. 48:14, means intentionally; knowingly.

Wit´ty, Prov. 8:12, means wise.

Wiz´ard. Lev. 20:6. See WITCHCRAFT.

Woe is often used as an exclamation to

denote sympathy, compassion, or lamentation. Num. 21:29; 1 Sam. 4:7; Matt. 24:19. It is also used as threatening coming punishment. Hab. 2:6, 9, 15; Zech. 11:17.

Wolf. This animal is still found in Palestine, and is of a pale fawn color. It is a terrible enemy of the sheep and the dread of the shepherds. Isa. 65:25; Matt. 7:15; etc.

Wo´man. The social position of the Hebrew woman in ancient times contrasted very favorably with that enjoyed at the present day by woman in the East among the Mohammedans. The book of Proverbs, 31:10-31, gives a beautiful account of the model Hebrew woman in her domestic and social relations. She had the care of the household, did the spinning, and made the clothes. She mingled freely in social festivities, and even held public positions.

The term "woman," when used in addressing one, implied no disrespect, but rather tenderness and courtesy. Compare John 2:4 with John 19:26, 27; 20:13-15.

Won´der-ful, a title of the Messiah. Isa. 9:6.

Wont, Matt. 27:15, means accustomed.

Wool was the chief material used in the manufacture of clothing, and was highly prized by the Hebrews. Lev. 13:47; Job 31:20; Prov. 31:13, etc. From the allusion in Ezek. 27:18 the wool of Damascus was greatly esteemed in the markets of Tyre.

Word (in Greek *Logos*, which means both *reason* and *word*) is used by John five times as a name or title of the eternal Son of God. John 1:1, 14.

Word of God, a name for the gospel generally. Mark 7:13; Luke 5:1; John 10:35; Acts 4:31, and elsewhere in the New Testament. See BIBLE.

Word of Life, a name applied to the gospel generally. 1 John 1:1. See BIBLE.

Word of the Lord, applied to the gospel

in general. Acts 8:25; 1 Thess. 1:8, and else-where in the New Testament. See BIBLE.

World. This word is used by the sacred writers in a number of senses, each of which can generally be distinguished by its connection. Thus, in Ps. 33:8 it means the habitable earth; in Isa. 45:17 it refers to time; in Luke 2:1 it means the nations subject to Rome at that time; in John 3:16 it means all mankind. In the widest sense it means the universe or all things visible and invisible, which is expressed in the Bible by the term "heaven and earth," Gen. 1:1, or "all things." John 1:3.

Worms. This term was evidently used to designate the caterpillar of the clothes-moth, the maggot, and possibly the earth-worm. Job 7:5; Isa. 51:8.

Worm'wood, a plant found in Palestine, noted for its extreme bitterness. The word is often used in the same sense as "gall," to denote whatever is offensive and destructive. Jer. 23:15; Lam. 3:15, 19.

Wor'ship. This word is often employed in the Bible to denote simply an act of respect, without implying any religious emotion. Josh. 5:14; Matt. 9:18; Acts 10:25.

Worship, as the act of religious reverence and homage paid to God, is commanded in the Scriptures.

Wot, Wot'teth, Gen. 39:8; Acts 3:17, are other forms of the old verb "to wit," which means "to know."

Wreath'en, Exod. 28:14, means twisting; twined.

Writ'ing. From the mention made in Exod. 17:14, writing was evidently well known to, and practiced by, the ancient Hebrews. The materials employed by them in writing differed widely according to the time and circumstances. Thus, they wrote on tablets of stone, metal, plaster, on frames covered with wax, on paper made from paper-reeds or bulrushes, on skins, and, later, on fine parchment. See PAPER, PARCHMENTS, and TABLET. Pointed pieces of iron, the hair-pencil (brush), and the reed-pen were used to form or trace the characters. See PEN.

The INK used was much thicker than ours, but was not permanent and could be easily washed off with water. It was made of pow-ered charcoal, lamp-black, or ivory-black, mixed with water and some kind of gum.

The INK-HORN was a long tube for hold-ing the reed-pens, with a small vessel on its side, in which the ink was carried.

Wrought means "worked," Gen. 34:7; Exod. 36:1; Matt. 20:12, and "did," 1 Kings 16:25; 2 Chron. 21:6; the context generally showing which meaning is intended.

Y

Yarn. "Linen yarn," 1 Kings 10:28; 2 Chron. 1:16, is rendered in the Revised Version "droves" (referring to horses).

Year. The Jews observed a religious or sacred year and a civil year. The sacred year began with the month of Abib, or Nisan, that is, with the first new moon after the ver-nal equinox, and the civil year commenced six months later with the month of Ethanim, or Tishri. See MONTH, and SEASONS.

Year of Ju'bi-lee. Lev. 25:8-12. See JUBILEE, YEAR OF.

Year, Sab-bat'i-cal. Lev. 25:2-7. See SABBATICAL YEAR.

Yes'ter-day, Heb. 13:8, time past.

Yes'ter-night, Gen. 31:29, 42, means last night.

Yoke. This, in its essential features, did not differ much from the yokes now used. It probably was lighter, and made so that the cattle stood farther apart. Two straight sticks, fastened in the beam at the top and joined at the bottom by thongs, supplied the place of our wooden bow. The word is often used in the Scriptures to denote servitude or oppression. 1 Kings 12:4-14. Figuratively it means burden. Matt. 11:29; Acts 15:10.

Yoke´fel-low, Phil. 4:3, means comrade; fellow-laborer.

Z

Za-a-na´im (*removals*), **the Plain of,** a place near Kedesh in Naphtali. Heber the Kenite pitched his tent there. Judg. 4:11. In the Revised Version ZAANANNIM, as in Josh. 19:33.

Za´a-nan (*place of flocks*), a town of Judah or Benjamin. Mic. 1:11. See ZENAN.

Za-a-nan´nim (*removals*), a place on the borders of Naphtali. Josh. 19:33. Same as ZAANAIM.

Za´a-van (*disquieted*), a son of Ezer, the son of Seir. Gen. 36:27. Same as ZAVAN.

Za´bad (*gift*). [1] One of David's mighty men. 1 Chron. 2:36, 37; 11:41. [2] A descendant of Ephraim. 1 Chron. 7:21. [3] One of the conspirators who slew Joash, king of Judah. 2 Chron. 24:26. Called JOZACHAR in 2 Kings 12:21. [4, 5, 6] Three Jews who took foreign wives. Ezra 10:27, 33, 43.

Zabbai, zab´bay (*pure*). [1] A Jew who took a foreign wife. Ezra 10:28. [2] Father of Baruch. Neh. 3:20.

Zab´bud (*given*), a Jew who returned with Ezra. Ezra 8:14.

Zab´di (*gift of Jehovah*). [1] Grandfather of Achan. Josh. 7:1, 17, 18. [2] A son of Shimhi, a Benjamite. 1 Chron. 8:19. [3] One who had a charge of David's wine cellars. 1 Chron. 27:27. [4] One of the Levites. Neh. 11:17.

Zab´di-el (*gift of God*). [1] Father of a captain of David's army. 1 Chron. 27:2. [2] A priest who was overseer of part of the priest in Jerusalem. Neh. 11:14.

Za´bud (*given*), a son of Nathan, also a "friend" of Solomon. 1 Kings 4:5.

Zab´u-lon, Matt. 4:13, 15; Rev. 7:8, is the Greek form of ZEBULUN (which see).

Zaccai, zak´ka-i (*pure*), ancestor of many who returned from Babylon with Zerubbabel. Ezra 2:9; Neh. 7:14.

Zacchæus, zak-ke´us (*pure*), a rich man among the publicans, whom Jesus called while passing through Jericho. The account of his conversation is given in Luke 19:2–10.

Zac-che´us. See ZACCHÆUS.

Zacchur, zak´kur (*mindful*), a descendant of Simeon. 1 Chron. 4:26.

Zac´cur (*mindful*). [1] The father of the spy from Reuben. Num. 13:4. [2] One of the Merarite Levites. 1 Chron. 24:27. [3] One of the sons of Asaph, and the head of a course of singers. 1 Chron. 25:2, 10; Neh. 12:35. [4] One who rebuilt part of the wall of Jerusalem. Neh. 3:2. [5] One of the Levites who sealed the covenant. Neh. 10:12. [6] Father of one whom Nehemiah made treasurer. Neh. 13:13.

Zachariah, zak-a-ri´ah (*remembered by Jehovah*), is the same name, in Hebrew, as ZECHARIAH (which see). [1] The son and successor of King Jeroboam II. 2 Kings 14:29; 15:8-11. [2] Father of Abi or Abijah, the mother of King Hezekiah, 2 Kings 18:2, called ZECHARIAH in 2 Chron. 29:1.

Zacharias, zak-a-ri´as, properly **Zach-a-ri´ah** (*remembered by Jehovah*). [1] A son of Barachias. Matt. 23:35; Luke

11:51. [2] The father of John the Baptist. Luke 1:5-40, 67; 3:2.

Zacher, za´ker (*memorial*), a man of the tribe of Benjamin. 1 Chron. 8:31, called ZECHARIAH in 1 Chron. 9:37.

Za´dok (*just*). [1] One of the two high-priests in David's time. He joined David at Hebron. 1 Chron. 12:28; 2 Sam. 20:25. He anointed Solomon king, 1 Kings 1:39, and was afterward made sole high-priest. [2] A priest in King Ahaziah's time. 1 Chron. 6:12. [3] Father of Jerusha, King Uzziah's wife. 2 Kings 15:33; 2 Chron. 27:1. [4] One of the Jews who repaired the wall of Jerusalem. Neh. 3:4. [5] A priest. Neh. 3:29. [6] A Jew who sealed the covenant. Neh. 10:21. [7] A scribe in charge of the treasuries. Neh. 13:13.

Za´ham (*loathing*), one of the sons of Rehoboam. 2 Chron. 11:19.

Za´ir (*small*), a place probably on the south-west side of the Dead Sea, where Joram, king of Judah, defeated the Edomites. 2 Kings 8:21.

Zalaph, za´laf (*bruise*), a Jew whose son repaired part of the wall of Jerusalem. Neh. 3:30.

Zal´mon (*shady*), one of David's valiant men, 2 Sam. 23:28, called ILAI in 1 Chron. 11:29.

Zal´mon (*shady*), **Mount,** a high hill near Shechem, Judg. 9:48, probably same as SALMON. Ps. 68:14.

Zal´mo´nah (*shady*), the thirty-fourth encampment of the Israelites after they left Egypt. Num. 33:41, 42.

Zalmunna, zal-mun´nah (*shelter denied to one?*), one of the kings of Midian defeated and slain by Gideon. Judg. 8:5–21; Ps. 83:11.

Zam-zum´mims. Deut. 2:20. A race of giants, probably the same as ZUZIMS (which see).

Za-no´ah. In 1 Chron. 4:18 Jekuthiel is called "the father of Zanoah," that is, he was the founder of the village of that name. See ZANOAH, No. 2, below.

Za-no´ah (*marsh*). [1] A town in the lowlands of Judah. Josh. 15:34; Neh. 3:13; 11:30. [2] A town in the hill country of Judah. Josh. 15:56.

Zaph´nath-pa-a-ne´ah, the name or title which Pharaoh gave to Joseph. Gen. 41:45.

Zaphon, za´fon (*the north*), one of the cities of Gad. Josh. 13:27.

Zara, za´rah. Matt. 1:3. See ZARAH.

Za´rah (*rising of light*), a son of Judah and Tamar, Gen. 38:30; 46:12, called ZERAH, Num. 26:20; Josh 7:1, 18, etc., and ZARA in Matt. 1:3.

Za´re-ah. Neh. 11:29. See ZORAH.

Za´re-ath-ites, inhabitants of Zareah or Zorah. 1 Chron. 2:53.

Za´red (*exuberant growth*). Num. 21:12. See ZERED, VALLEY or BROOK OF.

Zarephath, zar´e-fath (*smelting-house*), a town of Phœnicia, on the Mediterranean Sea between Tyre and Sidon. The prophet Elijah found shelter there. 1 Kings 17:8-24; Obad., verse 20. It is called SAREPTA in Luke 4:26.

Zar´e-tan (*cooling?*). Josh. 3:16. Probably same as ZARTHAN (which see).

Za´reth-sha´har (*splendour of the dawn*), one of the cities of Reuben. Josh. 13:19.

Zar´hites, descendants of Zarah, son of Judah. Num. 26:13, 20; Josh. 7:17; 1 Chron. 27:11, 13.

Zar´ta-nah (*cooling*). 1 Kings 4:12. Probably same as ZARTHAN (which see).

Zar´than (*cooling*), one of the towns in the Jordan valley. 1 Kings 7:46. It may be same as ZARETAN, ZARTANAH, and ZEREDA.

Zat´thu (*sprout*), a Jew who sealed the covenant. Neh. 10:14.

Zat´tu (*sprout*), an Israelite whose descendants returned with Zerubbabel. Some of them took foreign wives. Ezra 2:8; 10:27; Neh. 7:13.

Za´van (*disquieted*), a son of Ezer, the son of Seir. 1 Chron. 1:42. Same as ZAAVAN.

Zaza, za´zah (*plenty*), a son of Jonathan. 1 Chron. 2:33.

Zeal´ots, the name of a party among the Jews who, under the leadership of Judas of Galilee (see JUDAS, No. 5), claimed that God was the only king of Israel, refused to pay tribute to, and at length openly rebelled against. the Romans. They were soon routed, but for some time afterward kept up a sort of guerilla warfare. See Acts 5:37.

Zeb-a-di´ah (*gift of Jehovah*). [1, 2, 3] Descendants of Benjamin. 1 Chron. 8:15, 17; 12:7. [4] One of the sons of Meshelemiah. 1 Chron. 26:2. [5] One of the Levites sent by Jehoshaphat to teach the law. 2 Chron. 17:8. [6] A son of Asahel. 1 Chron. 27:7. [7] Son of Ishmael. 2 Chron. 19:11. [8] A Jew who returned with Ezra. Ezra 8:8. [9] A priest who took a foreign wife. Ezra 10:20.

Ze´bah (*sacrifice*), a king of Midian who was defeated and slain by Gideon. Judg. 8:5–21; Ps. 83:11.

Ze-ba´im (*the gazelles*), Ezra 2:57; Neh. 7:59, is translated "hazzebaim" in the Revised Version, and as part of the name of Pochereth, one of Solomon's servants. Thus, "Pochereth-hazzebaim."

Zeb´e-dee (*Jehovah's gift*), a fisherman in or near Bethsaida, who was the husband of Salome, and the father of James (the elder) and John, two of the apostles of Christ. Matt. 4:21; Mark 1:19.

Zebina, ze-bi´nah (*bought*), one of the sons of Nebo. He took a foreign wife. Ezra 10:43.

Ze-boi´im, Gen. 14:2, 8, and **Ze-bo´im** (*roes*), Gen. 10:19; Deut. 29:23; Hos. 11:8. [1] One of the "cities of the plain" near the Dead Sea, destroyed at the same time with Sodom. [2] A town of Benjamin. Neh. 11:34.

Ze-bo´im (*valley of hyænas*), **Val´ley of,** a ravine apparently east of Michmash in Benjamin. 1 Sam. 13:18.

Ze-bu´dah (*bestowed*), the wife of Josiah and mother of Jehoiakim. 2 Kings 23:36.

Ze´bul (*habitation*), an officer of Abimelech, and a governor of Shechem. Judg. 9:28–41.

Zeb´u-lon-ite, Judg. 12:11, 12, or **Zeb´u-lun-ites,** Num. 26:27, the descendants of Zebulun.

Zeb´u-lun (*habitation*), a son of Jacob and Leah, and the founder of the tribe of Zebulun. Gen. 30:20; Exod. 1:3.

Zeb´u-lun, the name of the tribe descended from Zebulun, a son of Jacob. Num. 1:9; Deut. 27:13.

Zeb´u-lun, a place mentioned in Josh. 19:27 in describing the southern boundary of Asher.

Zeb´u-lun, Ter´ri-to-ry of, was in the north of Canaan, and between Issachar, Asher, and Naphtali.

Zechariah, zek-a-ri´ah (*Jehovah remembers*). Besides the prophet Zechariah (see ZECHARIAH, No. 28), the following persons of the same name are mentioned in the Bible.

Seven Levites. [1] 1 Chron. 9:21; 26:2, 14. [2] 1 Chron. 15:18, 20; 16:5. [3] 1 Chron. 24:25. [4] 1 Chron. 26:11. [5] 2 Chron. 20:14. [6] 2 Chron. 29:13. [7] 2 Chron. 34:12.

Four priests. [8] 2 Chron. 35:8. [9] Neh. 11:12. [10] Neh. 12:16. [11] Neh. 12:35, 41.

[12] The son of Jehoiada the high-priest. He was stoned to death at the command of King Joash. 2 Chron. 24:20, 21. [13, 14] Two chief men who returned from Babylon with Ezra. Ezra 8:3; 8:11, 16. [15] The father of Iddo. 1 Chron. 27:21. [16] The son of Jeberechiah. Isa. 8:2. [17] A chief of Reuben. 1 Chron. 5:7. [18] A Benjamite. 1 Chron. 9:37, called ZACHER in 1 Chron. 8:31. [19] A priest. 1 Chron. 15:24. [20] A prince of Judah. 2 Chron. 17:7. [21] A son of Jehoshaphat. 2 Chron. 21:2. [22] A man who lived in the time of Uzziah. 2 Chron. 26:5. [23] One who took a foreign wife. Ezra 10:26. [24] A prince who stood beside Ezra while he read the law. Neh. 8:4. [25, 26] Two descendants of Pharez. Neh. 11:4; 11:5. [27] Father of Abi. See ZACHARIAH, No. 2.

[28] ZECHARIAH, the eleventh of the twelve minor prophets and a priest, was born in Babylon of priestly descent, and returned to Jerusalem with Zerubbabel and the high-priest Joshua. Ezra 5:1; 6:14; Zech. 1:1, 7; 7:1, 8. He prophesied B. C. 520–518.

Zech-a-ri′ah, the Book of. Of all the prophetic writings this is the most difficult to understand, owing to its concise form of expression and the figurative language employed. The book contains several specific references to the Messiah, 3:8; 6:12; 9:9; 11:12; 12:10; 13:7, in which he is represented as a lowly servant, the priest that should build the Temple of the Lord, the king that should come riding upon an ass, the shepherd betrayed for thirty pieces of silver and crucified, and having his sheep scattered.

Ze′dad (*mountain-side*), a city on the north boundary of the Promised Land. Num. 34:8; Ezek. 47:15.

Zed-e-ki′ah (*justice of Jehovah*). [1] The last king of Judah. His proper name was Mattaniah, but it was changed by Nebuchadnezzar to Zedekiah when he made him king. He reigned eleven years. 2 Chron. 36:11. At the capture of Jerusalem his eyes were put out and he was carried to Babylon. 2 Kings 25:1-7. [2] A false prophet who encouraged Ahab to attack the Syrians. 1 Kings 22:11, 24; 2 Chron. 18:10, 23. [3] A false prophet. Jer. 29:21, 22. [4] A prince of Judah. Jer. 36:12. [5] A grandson of Jehoiakim. 1 Chron. 3:16.

Ze′eb or **Zeeb** (*wolf*), a Midianite prince, who was slain by Gideon near one of the fords of the Jordan. Judg. 7:25; 8:3; Ps. 83:11.

Ze′lah (*a rib*), a city in Benjamin where Saul and his sons were buried. Josh. 18:28; 2 Sam. 21:14. See also ZELZAH.

Ze′lek (*fissure*), an Ammonite, one of David's valiant men. 2 Sam. 23:37; 1 Chron. 11:39.

Zelophehad, ze-lo′fe-had (*first-born*), a descendant of Manasseh, died in the wilderness, leaving five daughters but no sons. A law was then established that under such circumstances females should succeed to the inheritance, but they must not marry out of their tribe. Num. 26:33; 27:1, 7; 36:2–11; Josh. 17:3; 1 Chron. 7:15.

Ze-lo′tes, Luke 6:15; Acts 1:13. See SIMON, No. 3.

Zel′zah (*shade from the sun*), a town on the border of Benjamin. 1 Sam. 10:2.

Zem-a-ra′im (*double mount*). [1] A town of Benjamin. Josh 18:22. [2] Mount Zemaraim in Ephraim. 2 Chron. 13:4.

Zem′a-rites, a tribe descended from

Canaan, the son of Ham. Gen. 10:18; 1 Chron. 1:16.

Zemira, ze-mi´rah (*a song*), a son of Becher and a descendant of Benjamin. 1 Chron. 7:8.

Ze´nan (*place of flocks*), a city of Judah. Josh. 15:37. It may be same as ZAANAN. Mic. 1:11.

Ze´nas, a believer who was skilled in the law of Moses, and whom Paul wished Titus to bring along with him. Titus 3:13.

Zeph-a-ni´ah (*Jehovah hides*). [1] The priest whom the captain of the king of Babylon took to Riblah. 2 Kings 25:18; Jer. 21:1. [2] An ancestor of the prophet Samuel. 1 Chron. 6:36. [3] A priest, the father of Josiah and Hen. Zech. 6:10, 14.

[4] ZEPHANIAH, the ninth of the minor prophets, lived in the days of Josiah, a contemporary of Jeremiah, and uttered his prophecies between B. C. 620 and 609.

Zeph-a-ni´ah, the Book of, contains, 1:14, 15, that description of the final judgment from which Thomas da Celano, in the middle of the thirteenth century, took the key-note for his judgment-hymn, *Dies iræ, dies illa,* the most sublime hymn of the middle ages.

Zephath, ze´fath (*watch-tower*), a royal city of the Canaanites, near Kadesh. Judg. 1:17. It was afterward called HORMAH (which see).

Zephathah, zef´a-thah (*watch-tower*), **Valley of,** was in the western part of Judah, near the city of Marashah. 2 Chron. 14:10.

Ze´phi (*watch-tower*), 1 Chron. 1:36 or **Ze´pho,** Gen. 36:11, 15, a son of Eliphaz, the son of Esau.

Ze´phon (*a looking out*), a descendant of Gad. Num. 26:15. He is called ZIPHION in Gen. 46:16.

Zephonites, zef´o-nites, Num. 26:15,

descendants of Zephon.

Zer (*flint*), a city in Naphtali near the Lake of Gennesaret. Josh. 19:35.

Ze´rah (*a rising* of light). [1] A king of Ethiopia who made war against Asa, king of Judah. 2 Chron. 14:9. [2] One of the sons of Reuel, the son of Esau. Gen. 36:13, 17; 1 Chron 1:37. [3] One of the sons of Simeon. Num. 26:13; 1 Chron. 4:24, called ZOHAR in Gen. 46:10. [4] A Levite of the family of Gershom (Gershon). 1 Chron. 6:21, 41. [5] A son of Judah and Tamar. Num. 26:20; Josh. 7:1, 18, etc. He is called ZARAH in Gen. 38:30; 46:12. [6] The father of Jobab, king of Edom. Gen. 36:33; 1 Chron. 1:44.

Zer-a-hi´ah (*whom Jehovah caused to be born*). [1] A descendant of Phinehas, the grandson of Aaron. 1 Chron. 6:6, 51; Ezra 7:4. [2] One whose descendants returned from Babylon with Ezra. Ezra 8:4.

Ze´red (*exuberant growth* of trees), **Valley** or **Brook of,** was between Edom and Moab. Deut. 2:13, 14. It is called ZARED in Num. 21:12.

Zereda, zer´e-dah (*cooling?*), a place in the plain of the river Jordan. 1 Kings 11:26. See ZARTHAN.

Ze-red´a-thah, a town of Manasseh. 2 Chron. 4:17.

Zer´e-rath, a district near Abel-meholah. Judg. 7:22.

Ze´resh, the wife of Haman, the enemy of the Jews. Esther 5:10, 14; 6:13.

Ze´reth (*splendor*), a descendant of Judah. 1 Chron. 4:7.

Ze´ri (*built*), a son of Jeduthun. 1 Chron. 25:3.

Ze´ror (*a bundle*), an ancestor of Saul, the first king of Israel. 1 Sam. 9:1.

Ze-ru´ah (*leprous*), the mother of JEROBOAM, No. 1 (which see). 1 Kings 11:26.

Ze-rub´ba-bel (*begotten in Babylon*) was a descendant of David and Jehoiakim, and the leader of the first band of Jews that returned from the captivity in Babylon. He superintended the building of the second Temple (see TEMPLE, II.), and was chiefly instrumental in restoring the religious rites of the nation. 1 Chron. 3:19; Ezra 3:2; Zech. 4:6–10. He is called ZOROBABEL in Matt. 1:12, 13; Luke 3:27, but uniformly ZERUBBABEL in the Revised Version.

Also see Ezra 2:2; 3:8; 4:2, 3; 5:2. Neh. 7:7; 12:1, 47.

Hag. 1:1, 12, 14; 2:2, 4, 21, 23.

Ze-ru-i´ah (*cleft, wounded*), a daughter of Jesse, the father of David. Her three sons, Joab, Abishai, and Asahel, were officers in David's army. 2 Sam. 2:18; 3:39; 1 Chron. 2:16.

Ze´tham (*olive tree*), a descendant of Gershon, one of the sons of Levi. 1 Chron. 23:8; 26:22.

Ze´than (*olive tree*), a descendant of Benjamin. 1 Chron. 7:10.

Ze´thar (*star?*), a chamberlain of Ahasuerus. Esther 1:10.

Zia, zi´ah (*motion*), a Gadite. 1 Chron. 5:13.

Ziba, zi´bah (*statue*), a servant of Saul, who afterward served Mephibosheth treacherously. 2 Sam. 9:2-12; 16:1-4; 19:17, 29.

Zib´e-on (*dyed*). A chief of the Hivites. Gen. 36:2, 14, 20; 1 Chron. 1:38, 40.

Zibia, zib´i-ah (*a roe*), a Benjamite. 1 Chron. 8:9.

Zib´i-ah, the mother of Joash, a king of Judah. 2 Kings 12:1; 2 Chron. 24:1.

Zichri, zik´ri (*remembered, renowned*). [1] A son of Izhar, a Levite. Exod. 6:21. [2, 3, 4] Three chief men of Benjamin. 1 Chron. 8:19; 8:23; 8:27. [5] A Levite, a

son of Asaph, 1 Chron. 9:15, called ZABDI in Neh. 11:17. [6] A descendant of Eliezer, the son of Moses. 1 Chron. 26:25. [7] A descendant of Reuben. 1 Chron. 27:16. [8] Father of one of the captains of Jehoshaphat. 2 Chron. 17:16. [9] Father of a captain who aided in making Joash king. 2 Chron. 23:1. [10] A man of Ephraim. He slew the son of Ahaz, king of Judah. 2 Chron. 28:7. [11] An overseer of Benjamites in Jerusalem. Neh. 11:9. [12] A priest of the family of Abijah. Neh. 12:17.

Zid´dim (*the sides*), a town of Naphtali. Josh. 19:35.

Zid-ki´jah (*justice of Jehovah*), a chief prince of the Jews. He sealed the covenant made by Nehemiah, Neh. 10:1, and is called ZEDEKIAH in the Revised Version.

Zi´don. Josh. 11:8; 1 Chron. 1:13. See SIDON.

Zi-do´ni-ans, Judg. 10:12, inhabitants of Zidon or Sidon.

Zif, the second month of the Hebrew sacred year, and the eighth month of the civil year. 2 Kings 6:1, 37. See MONTH.

Ziha, zi´hah (*dry*). [1] A Nethinim whose descendants returned from Babylon. Ezra 2:43; Neh. 7:46. [2] A ruler of the Nethinim. Neh. 11:21.

Zik´lag (*outpouring of a fountain?*), a city of Judah, Josh. 15:31, afterward of Simeon. Josh. 19:5. It is interesting for its connection with David. 1 Sam. 27:6; 30:1, 14, 26; 2 Sam. 1:1; 4:10; 1 Chron. 4:30; 12:1-20.

Zil´lah (*shade*), a wife of Lamech. Gen. 4:19, 22, 23.

Zil´pah (*dropping*), the handmaid of Leah. Gen. 29:24; 35:26.

Zilthai, zil´thay (*shade*). [1] A son of Shimhi, a Benjamite. 1 Chron. 8:20. [2] A captain of Manasseh. 1 Chron. 12:20.

Zim´mah (*mischief*), a descendant

of Gershom (Gershon), the son of Levi. 1 Chron. 29:12.

Zim´ran (*celebrated*), one of the sons of Abraham and Keturah. Gen. 25:2; 1 Chron. 1:32.

Zim´ri (*snug*). [1] Son of a chief among the Simeonites. Num. 25:14. [2] A captain who conspired against Elah, king of Israel. 1 Kings 16:9-20. [3] A son of Zerah, the son of Judah, 1 Chron. 2:6, called ZABDI in Josh. 7:1, 17, 18. [4] One of the descendants of Saul. 1 Chron. 8:36; 9:42. [5] A name applied to a tribe and supposed to refer to people in Eastern Arabia. Jer. 25:25.

Zin (*a low palm tree*), **Wil´der-ness of,** formed part of the Arabian desert south of Palestine. It joined the territory of Judah on the south, Josh. 15:1, 3, and was west of Idumea. Num. 20:1; 27:14; 33:36.

Zina, zi´nah. 1 Chron. 23:10. See ZIZAH.

Zi´on (*sunny mount*), 2 Sam. 5:7; 2 Kings 19:31; etc., sometimes denotes the whole of JERUSALEM (which see), but literally means its south-western hill, which was two thousand five hundred and fifty feet above the level of the sea. It was surrounded on all sides except the north by deep valleys, and is called SION in Matt. 21:5; John 12:15; Rom. 9:33; 11:26; Heb. 12:22; 1 Pet. 2:6; Rev. 14:1.

Zi´or (*smallness*), a place situated in the mountains of Judah and near Hebron. Josh. 15:54.

Ziph, zif (*a flowing*). [1] One of the descendants of Judah. 1 Chron. 4:16. [2] A name applied to a grandson of Caleb, the son of Hezron. 1 Chron. 2:42.

Ziph (*a flowing*). [1] A city of Judah. Josh. 15:24. [2] A town in the hill country of Judah. Josh. 15:55; 2 Chron. 11:8.

Ziph, Wil´der-ness of, was between Hebron and the Dead Sea. 1 Sam. 23:14, 15; 26:2.

Ziphah, zi´fah, a descendant of Judah. 1 Chron. 4:16.

Ziphims, zif´ims, Ps. 54, title, the inhabitants of Ziph.

Ziph´i-on. Gen. 46 16. See ZEPHON.

Ziph´ites, the name given to the inhabitants of Ziph. 1 Sam. 23:19; 26:1.

Zi´phron (*sweet odor*), a city in the north of Palestine. Num. 34:9.

Zip´por (*a little bird*), the father of Balak, king of Moab. Num. 22:2, 4, 10, 16; 23:18; Josh. 24:9; Judg. 11:25.

Zip-po´rah, the wife of Moses and daughter of the Midianite priest Jethro. Exod. 2:21; 4:25; 18:2.

Zith´ri (*protection of Jehovah*), a descendant of Levi. Exod. 6:22.

Ziz, The Cliff of, was in the south-east part of Judah. 2 Chron. 20:16. Ziz was a place in its neighborhood.

Ziza, zi´zah (*abundance*). [1] A descendant of Simeon. 1 Chron. 4:37. [2] A son of Rehoboam. 2 Chron. 11:20.

Zi´zah (*abundance*), a son of Shemei, a descendant of Gershon, the son of Levi. 2 Chron. 23:11.

Zo´an (*place of departure?* or *low region?*), a city in Lower (northern) Egypt, called by the Greeks *Tanis*, built seven years after Hebron, Num. 13:22, and at one time a city of considerable importance, Isa. 19:11, 13; 30:4; is called TANIS in the marginal notes. Ezek. 30:14. In the "field of Zoan" God wrought wonders, Pss. 78:12, 43; and tradition makes it the place where God, through Moses, performed those miracles that induced Pharaoh to let the Israelites depart. Several colossal statues of kings of various dynasties, obelisks, sphinxes, and temple ruins have been brought to light by excavations of Brugsch-Bey and others. The sacred enclosure of the Temple adorned by Rameses II was fifteen hundred feet long by twelve hundred and fifty feet wide.

Zo´ar (*smallness*), one of the cities of the plain, originally called BELA, to which Lot and his two daughters fled for refuge when Sodom and Gomorrah were about to be destroyed. Gen. 13:10; 14:2, 8; 19:22–30; Jer. 48:34.

Zoba, zo´bah, **Zo´bah** (*station*), a district or kingdom of Syria, north-east of Palestine. In the time of the first Hebrew monarchs it was a powerful nation, and its kings made frequent wars on Israel during the reigns of Saul, David, and Solomon. 1 Sam. 14:47; 2 Sam. 8:3–5; 1 Kings 11:23.

Zo-be´bah (*slow-moving*), a daughter of Coz and a descendant of Judah. 1 Chron. 4:8.

Zo´har (*whiteness*). **[1]** The father of Ephron, from whom Abraham purchased the cave of Machpelah. Gen. 23:8; 25:9. **[2]** A son of Simeon. Gen. 46:10; Exod. 6:15. See ZERAH, No. 3.

Zo´he-leth (*serpent*), the name given to a stone that was near the fountain of Enrogel. 1 Kings 1:9.

Zo´heth, a son of Ishi, a descendant of Judah. 1 Chron. 4:20.

Zophah, zo´fah (*a cruse*), a descendant of Asher. 1 Chron. 7:35, 36.

Zophai, zo´fay (*honeycomb*), one of the sons of Elkanah, who was an ancestor of the prophet Samuel. 1 Chron. 6:26.

Zo´phar, a native of Naamah and a friend of Job. Job 2:11; 11:1; 20:1; 42:9.

Zo´phim (*watchers*), a place on "the top of Pisgah," from where Balaam could see the camp of Israel. Num. 23:14.

Zo´rah (*hornets' town*), a town in the west part of Judah. It was afterward pos-sessed by Dan, Josh. 19:41, and was the birthplace and burialplace of Samson. Judg. 13:2, 25; 16:31. It was fortified by Rehoboam, 2 Chron. 11:10, and is called ZOREAH in Josh. 15:33, and ZAREAH in Neh. 11:29.

Zo´rath-ites, a family of the tribe of Judah. 1 Chron. 4:2.

Zo´re-ah. Josh. 15:33. See ZORAH.

Zo´rites, a family of Judah of the posterity of Salma. 1 Chron. 2:54.

Zo-rob´a-bel, Matt. 1:12, 13; Luke 3:27, the Greek form of ZERUBBABEL (which see).

Zu´ar (*smallness*), the father of Nethaneel. Num. 1:8; 2:5; 7:18, 23; 10:15.

Zuph, zuf (*honeycomb*). **[1]** A Levite of the family of Kohath, who was an ancestor of Samuel the prophet. 1 Sam. 1:1; 1 Chron. 6:35.

Zuph, the Land of, a district not far from Jerusalem on the north and west. 1 Sam. 9:5.

Zur (*rock*). **[1]** A prince of Midian who was slain by Phinehas. Num. 25:15; 31:8; Josh. 13:21. **[2]** A Benjamite and an ancestor of Saul. 1 Chron. 8:30; 9:36.

Zu´ri-el (*my rock is God*), a Levite and a chief of the families of Merari. Num. 3:35.

Zu-ri-shad´da-i (*my rock is the Almighty*), the father of Shelumiel, who aided Moses in numbering the people. Num. 1:6; 2:12; 7:36, 42; 10:19.

Zu´zims, the name of a tribe of great stature and strength, that inhabited the country east of the Jordan in the time of Abraham. Gen. 14:5.

Notes

Notes

Notes

Notes